Child Welfare

CURRENT DILEMMAS · FUTURE DIRECTIONS

BRENDA G. McGOWAN · **WILLIAM MEEZAN**

Columbia University   University of Illinois at Chicago

Quotations from pages 29, 225, 316, 324, and 411 all reprinted with permission of Macmillan Publishing Co., Inc. from *Child Welfare Services, Third Edition* by Alfred Kadushin. Copyright ©1980 by Alfred Kadushin.

The following quotations were reprinted with the permission of the Child Welfare League of American, Inc.

Page 180. From "The Case Advocacy Function in Child Welfare Practice" by Brenda G. McGowan, Vol. 57, May 1978, pgs. 281, 283.

Pages 238, 239. From "Effective Practice with Families in Protective and Preventive Services: What Works?" by Mary Ann Jones, Stephen Magura, and Ann W. Shyne, Vol. 55, Feb. 1981, pp.71-72 and 72-75.

Page 330. From "Dividing Case Management in Foster Family Cases" by Theodore J. Stein, Eileen D. Gambrill, and Kermit T. Wiltse, Vol. 56, May 1977, pp. 326-327; 330.

Page 334. From "CWLA's Statement on Foster Care Services" by CWLA, Vol. 58, Jan. 1979, p. 50.

Page 436. From "Subsidized Adoption: A Crucial Investment" by Kenneth W. Watson, Vol. 51, April 1972, p. 224.

Photos courtesy of:

Page 142. Photo 1-Rohn Engh, Star Prairie, Wis.; Photo 2-R. Meyer, Osceola, Wis.; Photo 3-Bernard J. Reilly.

Page 170. Vera Wolf, Sunrise Photos, Osceola, Wis.

Page 210. Beth Dacey and Marie Gesuela Wilson.

Page 478. Columbia University School of Social Work (Photographer, Ann Johnson) and Lenox Hill Neighborhood Association (Photographer, Stacy Pennebaker)

The photographs in this book are for illustrative purposes only; there is no relationship between the particular children or adults pictured and the text.

Child Welfare

CURRENT DILEMMAS
FUTURE DIRECTIONS

F. E. Peacock Publishers, Inc.
115 North Prospect
Itasca, Illinois 60143

TO OUR PARENTS
who, through example, taught us the meaning
of commitment to children

and

TO MICHAEL BRITTENBACK AND ELAINE WALSH
for their support, encouragement, and patience

CONTENTS

CONTRIBUTORS

MaryLee Allen, M.S.W., Director, Child Welfare, Children's Defense Fund, Washington, D.C.

Karen Blumenthal, M.S., Program Specialist, North American Center on Adoption, Child Welfare League of America, New York, N.Y.

Jon Conte, Ph.D., Assistant Professor, School of Social Service Administration, University of Chicago, Chicago, Illinois.

Sister Mary Paul Janchill, D.S.W., Director of Clinical Services, Center for Family Life in Sunset Park, Brooklyn, N.Y., and Lecturer, Columbia University School of Social Work, New York, N.Y.

Alfred J. Kahn, D.S.W., Professor, Columbia University, School of Social Work, New York, N.Y.

Sheila B. Kamerman, D.S.W., Professor, School of Social Work, Columbia University, New York, N.Y.

Jane Knitzer, Ed.D., Director, Institute for Child and Youth Policy Studies, Rochester, New York.

Carmine J. Magazino, M.S.W., Assistant Administrator, St. Joseph's Children's Services, Brooklyn, N.Y., and Adjunct Assistant Professor, Fordham University School of Social Service, New York, N.Y.

Brenda G. McGowan, D.S.W., Associate Professor, Columbia University, School of Social Work, New York, N.Y.

William Meezan, D.S.W., Associate Professor, Jane Addams College of Social Work, University of Illinois at Chicago, Chicago, Illinois.

Carol H. Meyer, D.S.W., Professor, Columbia University, School of Social Work, New York, N.Y.

Tina L. Rzepnicki, Ph.D., Project Director, Jane Addams College of Social Work, University of Illinois at Chicago, Chicago, Illinois.

Joan F. Shireman, Ph.D., Associate Professor, Jane Addams College of Social Work, University of Illinois at Chicago, Chicago, Illinois.

Theodore J. Stein, D.S.W., Associate Professor, Jane Addams College of Social Work, University of Illinois at Chicago, Chicago, Illinois.

PREFACE

This book represents over three years of work on the part of the editors and is the outcome of more than a dozen years of friendship and informal collaboration. We are most grateful to those who have made it possible to see this project through to completion.

We have each been fortunate over the years to have mentors and colleagues who supported our interest in child welfare, challenged our thinking, and encouraged us to persist in our efforts to grapple with the complex issue in this field of practice. A number of these friends' names appear as contributors to the book, but in addition Brenda McGowan must acknowledge her real debt to Margaret Sullivan and Hon. Justine Wise Polier; and Bill Meezan to David Fanshel, Ann Shyne, Mary Ann Jones, and Trudy Festinger.

We each owe a special debt to our colleagues and students and to Deans George Brager and Donald Brieland at Columbia University and at the University of Illinois at Chicago. They have served as sources of ideas, support, and goodwill.

Our families and friends have somehow managed to tolerate our frustrations and mood swings during heavy work stages. For their endurance and support, as well as their love, we are indebted to Martha Beuerle, Mike Brittenback, Prue Brown, Andrew Charles, Roslyn Chenesky, Anthony De Blaise, Jay Hamlin, Sheila Kamerman, Wynne Korr, Linda Mansdorf, Carol Meyer, Pat Newman, Karen Peterlin, Don Riseborough, Kevin Ryan, Joan Shireman, Drew Stannard, Ted Stein, Richard Steinman and Jane Stewart. Dorothy Sumner and Dorothy McGowan provided especially helpful comments on early drafts of some of the chapters. And Elaine Walsh not only contributed her ideas and criticism, but she shared her home in Westhampton, New York, with us while we completed our major editing tasks, tolerating with good humor our efforts to turn her favorite retreat into a mad work place.

Special thanks go to our contributors, all of whom are friends as well. Their obvious hard work is evidenced in their respective chapters. They wrote with conviction, shared their ideas freely, accepted our criticism and prodding graciously, and even managed to meet most of our sometimes demanding deadlines without complaint!

Finally, the staff of F. E. Peacock Publishers, Inc., have been most supportive in this endeavor. We are indebted to Ted Peacock, Thomas LaMarre, Joyce Usher and Linda Pierce for their support.

The ordering of our names on the cover is an accident of alphabet and not a reflection of seniority. As we have shared over the years, so we have worked as co-equals throughout this venture, and Bill Meezan, in fact, assumed the responsibility for negotiations and meetings with our publisher and preparing the final manuscript in the fall before we went to press.

INTRODUCTION

In recent years the child welfare system in the United States has been under attack. Research studies conducted within the field and program audits, class-action lawsuits and legislative reviews initiated outside the field have all served to focus attention on the perceived failures of this system. Service providers and consumers alike have begun to recognize the problems within this service delivery system and the damaging effects they may have on its client population.

Although various commentators have chosen to emphasize different aspects of the "crisis" in child welfare, the central theme in all critiques is that child welfare agencies and their workers expend most of their energy and resources providing care of questionable quality to children outside their own homes. Charges are made that little is done to prevent children from entering substitute care, that placement resources are limited and often inappropriate to the needs of children and their families, and that efforts to restore children to stable living situations after a period in substitute care are often lacking. In sum, critics of the system believe that too many children enter substitute care and "drift" for long periods of time.

Why should this be when social workers have long recognized that the separation of children from their families is often painful and potentially damaging and when mission statements of child welfare agencies have long proclaimed the importance of the parent-child relationship? We believe that a major explanation is that the current expectations of the child welfare system are unrealistic. Early child welfare agencies were established to care for children without parents—a function they were able to perform fairly well. However, demographic changes coupled with rising social expectations as to the quality of home life to which children are entitled have led to a new set of demands, which child welfare agencies are now expected to address. In addition to providing appropriate care for children who cannot live with their parents, child welfare agencies are now asked to provide services designed to:

—support family life and prevent family dysfunction in all families

—enhance the functioning of troubled families without the use of placement resources

—help increasing numbers of children with special developmental, remedial, and treatment needs including many formerly served by other, more specialized service systems

—protect children from parental abuse and neglect while preventing placement whenever practicable

—make appropriate determinations regarding the necessity of placement

—treat child and family problems during the period of substitute care

—ensure that children are discharged speedily from substitute care to nurturing home environments

—find alternative permanent families for children who cannot return to their biological homes

—reduce strain and enhance the quality of parent-child interaction in reunited biological families and/or newly created adoptive families

—protect the sometimes conflicting legal rights of all of the parties involved in the delivery of child welfare services

In order to meet these new demands, many child welfare professionals, including the editors of this volume, have strenuously advocated for the expansion of the boundaries of the child welfare system. However, we now question whether this system is, or can ever be, properly equipped to meet all of these expectations. While it is admirable for this field to want to promote the welfare of *all* children, the reality is that in the United States child welfare has served, and will continue to serve, a residual population of parents and children unable to fulfill their normal role expectations. In our view, recent attempts to reach a wider range of families and children, without a concurrent expansion of resources and/ or any redefinition of the field's primary mission, has led to a demand overload, which has caused system entropy and disorganization. Consequently, the child welfare system is now not only failing to meet new expectations but is having increasing difficulty carrying out its original goal of providing care to children whose basic needs cannot be met by their families and/or by the community support services available to all children.

Rather than continuing to berate child welfare agencies for their failure to perform the impossible, we would suggest that the demands on this system be reduced, that realistic expectations for child welfare agencies be carefully delineated, and that mechanisms be developed to ensure that agencies fulfill their primary, if residual, functions. This would require that child welfare agencies refocus their energies on basic child welfare tasks including (1) provision of support services to families in crisis in order to prevent the placement of children outside their homes, (2) development and use of standards for the removal of children from their biological parents, (3) development of appropriate, differential placement resources for children who require substitute care, (4) provision of ongoing services to families while children are in care in order to alleviate the problems that necessitated placement, (5) development of appropriate treatment resources and strategies for children and families with special needs, (6) maintenance of family ties while children are in placement in order to promote timely discharges from foster care, (7) refinement and use of realistic standards for termination of parental rights and experimentation with alternative joint custody arrangements for children who cannot return home, (8) recruitment of appropriate adoptive families for children who have experienced substitute care and may have special needs, and (9) data gathering and knowledge building, so that the field can respond appropriately to the changing needs of its clients.

This is not to suggest that attention should be diverted from developing needed institutional supports for all families. It is futile to think that the welfare of children in this country can be enhanced without further efforts to (1) provide an adequate minimum income to all families, (2) provide an acceptable level of housing and health care for families with children, (3) develop universally available, comprehensive, neighborhood-based family social services, and (4) expand community resources for children with special needs. However, asking the child welfare system to provide these needed family supports is like asking the tail to wag the dog. Child welfare services can function appropriately only when they form a subsystem of a larger personal social service network that is closely tied to adequate systems of income maintenance, housing, and health care. Neither the provision of emergency services to families in crisis nor the provision of out-of-home care for children can substitute for needed, institutionalized social supports and appropriate developmental services to families.

In recent years, experts from such diverse disciplines as law, business, public administration, and government have focused attention on the problems in the child welfare system and have proposed remedies for change. But child welfare is primarily the domain of social workers; and

ultimately social work is the only profession that has both the responsibility and the expertise to address these dilemmas. Therefore, this book
attempts to analyze the factors that created and perpetuate the current
crisis in child welfare and to propose future directions for the field. Its
intent is to heighten the awareness of social work students, practitioners,
administrators, and planners about the problems that exist in the field
and possible alternative approaches for meeting the needs of clients.
Our goal is neither to provide a comprehensive description of services
that currently exist nor to provide a "how to" guide for child welfare
practitioners. Rather our goal is to focus attention on the service delivery
issues with which the field must grapple in order to improve policy,
service provision, and practice effectiveness. In this way we hope to
serve as catalysts so that those in the field can discover opportunities for
change.

The book is divided into three sections. The first is an overview of the
current problems in the child welfare field and the antecedent conditions that contributed to their development. The second section discussed the policy and programmatic framework needed to enhance the
functioning of families within the community. The final section examines programmatic aspects of the child welfare system and suggests alternate strategies for meeting the needs of the children and families who
appropriately enter this system of services.

THE CURRENT PROBLEMS AND THEIR ANTECEDENTS

The three chapters in Part I describe the problems that have been identified in the field of child welfare as well as the service delivery and policy choices and mandates that have contributed to their development. This material is presented in order to give a clear understanding of the current concerns within the field and the factors that led to their development. This section sets the stage for the remainder of the book, which is an exploration of the possible directions that can be taken to remedy the identified problems.

Chapter 1 first defines the scope of child welfare services and describes the children and families currently served by this service delivery system. Then, through the framework of *permanency planning,* the author develops a set of principles against which the child welfare system can be judged. Each of these principles is then discussed, and the evidence that has been used to criticize service delivery within child welfare is presented within this framework.

Chapter 2 presents a broad overview of the historical evolution of the child welfare system and examines the major trends and shifts in service provision for dependent, neglected, and troubled children. It demonstrates that the group of children for whom child welfare services are deemed appropriate has been expanded and that various programmatic and administrative approaches have been taken to care for these children. It notes the shifts in governmental responsibility for these children and the fact that there have been historical inequities in the services provided to certain groups of children. These factors influence the current service delivery patterns within the field. The chapter suggests that child welfare services are shaped by social forces and trends in the larger society and concludes by noting that the dilemmas confronting the field today reflect the solutions devised to address the problems of the past.

Chapter 3 examines the policy framework for child welfare services that has guided the field since the Great Depression. It describes the myriad of forces that have shaped this field of service. Through an examination of state and federal law, court decisions, administrative directives, and funding levels and priorities this chapter demonstrates that many of the current problems in child welfare are the direct result of the piecemeal development of social policy, contradictory policy mandates, inadequate funding for specific programs, and a lack of program monitoring. The chapter then goes on to describe recent efforts to redefine the child welfare policy framework through comprehensive federal legislation. It concludes by noting the difficulties inherent in implementing children's policy in general as well as in specific legislation.

CHILDREN IN FOSTER CARE

Children Without Homes

*Beyond the
Best Interests of
the Child*

All Our Children

The American Family
under Pressure

CHILDREN
IN NEED OF
PARENTS

Children of the Storm

Black Children and American Child Welfare

CHAPTER 1

CHILD WELFARE: AN OVERVIEW OF THE ISSUES

William Meezan

"For numbers alone, if for no other reasons, these voteless fellow citizens who hold the national future in their bodies and minds are necessarily a first interest of the nation."
—*1940 White House Conference on Children*

Statements such as this have been made repeatedly for many decades. How often have we heard that the "future rests with the young," that we are a "child-centered society," or that children are our "most precious resource"? Few situations evoke more public sympathy and outrage than a homeless or battered or neglected child.

Yet despite our public posture, the programs designed to help children in need are seen by many as inadequate and, at times, counterproductive. For a number of years, the child welfare service system in this country has been under attack by service providers, service consumers, and other concerned groups. As one expert in the field has noted:

> For more than several decades now the literature repetitiously and persistently has identified these shortcomings, each study uncovering again what had been uncovered before. Reading the more recent studies, one gets a strong sense of *déjà vu*.
> With disheartening repetitiveness the charge is made that access to service is difficult and discouraging; that service is fragmented, poorly coordinated vertically and horizontally, and discontinuous; that there is an overuse of substitute care services and an underuse of supportive services, that the service offered is not appropriate to the problem presented nor to the clients presenting the problem; that the approach to clients is unnecessarily authoritarian and coercive and the workers' decisions are often arbitrary and made without regard to a systematic diagnostic assessment of the situation; that children get lost in the system, temporary care becomes permanent care, systematic periodic review of case planning is often neglected and there is studied indifference to parental needs once the child has been removed; that the system operates against the achievement of permanence for many children; that large groups of children particularly the nonwhite and poor are not adequately served by the system; that the system is unresponsible and inequitable; that it tends to be reactive rather

than proactive, responding lethargically only to crisis situations; that there is no well-developed systematic program of worker and agency accountability. The available evidence suggests that much of this is true.[1]

The purpose of this chapter is to introduce the reader to the current service delivery issues in the field of child welfare. Presenting these issues as the first chapter sets the stage for the remainder of the book, which explains the reasons why these problems exist and offers current thinking about possible solutions.

CHILD WELFARE SERVICES

Child welfare, as a field of social work practice, has traditionally been concerned with the service needs of children and their families when parental functioning is impaired or when the child, because of developmental, emotional, or behavioral problems, may not be able to function within a family setting. Thus, the field has had a relatively narrow focus. Child welfare services have been directed at only a residual group of children whose basic needs cannot be met either through the family or through existing social institutions.

While some would define child welfare more broadly to include "whatever is considered essential for [the child] to develop fully and to function effectively in society,"[2] the current system of social services provided through child welfare agencies is comprehensive neither in coverage nor in scope. To fulfill this broader definition, child welfare agencies would have to provide a range of developmental services to families as well as other social supports such as income maintenance, housing, health and mental health services, food and nutrition, job training, and employment. While each of these may be essential to the optimal development of children, they are provided primarily by other service systems; the child welfare system "has neither the social policy know-how, the community sanction, nor the political muscle to effect changes . . ."[3] within these other service sectors nor the resources to provide these services directly.

Services within the current scope of child welfare have traditionally been divided between those services provided to children in their own homes and those provided to children removed from their parents' care and placed in substitute living arrangements. Services that can be provided while the child remains at home include:[4]

Day care: a family or group service operating on less than a twenty-four-hour basis for the care of children away from their own homes during some part of the day. It includes the provision of food and shelter, adult supervision, and educational and developmental experiences

Homemaker services: services that provide a qualified person to assist families with children in home maintenance and management in order to strengthen, support, and/or restore parental capacity to care for the children and prevent their unnecessary removal from home

Protective services: services designed to identify, diagnose, treat, and care for children suspected or identified as being neglected, abused, or exploited

Day treatment: services operating on a less than twenty-four-hour basis providing clinically oriented and supportive services for children with emotional, social, developmental, or behavioral problems

Counseling: clinically oriented and/or supportive services provided while the child remains at home, designed to enhance family functioning, resolve crises, and/or prevent placement

In addition to these traditional in-home services, some agencies have begun to provide "preventive" or "developmental" services to families and their children in order to maintain family functioning and prevent out-of-home placement. The parameters of these services within the child welfare field have not yet been clearly defined, so that agencies offer a variety of programs and utilize a range of interventive techniques under these rubrics. In addition to utilizing the traditional in-home services, some agencies are now providing family life education, advocacy, case management services, respite services, and self-help groups as part of their preventive or developmental programs.

Services provided by child welfare agencies to children living outside of their own homes include diagnostic services, foster, group and institutional care, and adoption services. These services take a variety of forms and can include:

Emergency care: a temporary placement for children, expected to last up to thirty days, in a group shelter or a family setting

Diagnostic center: a residential group facility that performs clinically oriented evaluations and recommends appropriate treatment interventions and/or other services

Foster family care: a twenty-four-hour service providing substitute care for up to six children in a family environment

Agency boarding home: a neighborhood-based, twenty-four-hour service providing substitute family care for up to six children supervised by adults employed by the agency

Group home: a neighborhood-based, twenty-four-hour facility providing care for six to twelve children in a group setting supervised by adults employed by the agency

Group residence: a neighborhood-based, twenty-four-hour facility providing care for twelve to twenty-five children in a group setting supervised by adults employed by the agency

Institution: a residential facility providing twenty-four-hour care in a group setting for more than twenty-five children

Residential treatment center: a twenty-four-hour residential facility providing care, treatment, and related services to emotionally disturbed or developmentally disabled children through an institution with appropriate therapeutic services and environment

Adoption services: services designed to create a family by law rather than by procreation, and the concomitant services related to the formation of such a family

While it is convenient to classify child welfare services as either in-home or out-of-home, it should be noted that these categories need not be mutually exclusive. Counseling and other personal social service often continue after a child has been placed in a foster home. Similarly, a child in group care may continue in day treatment after placement, or day care may be provided after a child has been placed in a foster family. The availability of the proper "mix" of services is essential to the effective functioning of the child welfare system.

The history of services to children, examined in the following chapter, provides insights as to why child welfare services in the United States have retained their relatively narrow focus. Traditionally, there has been a reluctance to intervene in family life. Child rearing has been viewed as a private matter; governmental responsibility has been limited. Intervention on behalf of children traditionally occurred only when there was no family to care for the child or when parents flagrantly violated the accepted norm of the time. As these norms changed and the needs of children were articulated more fully, the circumstances under which intervention could take place were broadened. However, the family always had to be seen as deficient for intervention to occur. As a recent commission noted:

> If a family proves less than independent, if it is visibly needy, if its members ask for help, then it is by definition not an "adequate" family. Adequate families, the assumption runs, are self-sufficient and insulated from outside pressure.[5]

Policy in this country has never acknowledged that in a complex, mobile, industrial society all families may need help in maintaining their equilibrium. Access to services has traditionally been granted only after it has been determined that a problem exists. This view of social services has meant that programs established for children and their families have not been developed in a planned, comprehensive way, but rather as a response to changing definitions of needs and problems.

Because services were developed only as specific needs were recognized, it is not surprising that the first services developed in child welfare were those that substituted for the family. Orphaned, abandoned, and homeless children had obvious needs, and those whose parents had no visible means of support posed a threat to the social order. Thus, indenture, institutions, and eventually foster care were developed to care for homeless and poor children.

As norms changed and society recognized that children might not be adequately cared for by their parents, the out-of-home services initially developed for homeless children were extended to other groups. There was little attempt to help families maintain their child-rearing functions even when doing so might have been possible. As one commentator noted about the early Societies for the Prevention of Cruelty to Children:

> . . . their single-minded and vigorous approach to the enforcement of laws to protect children and prosecute parents substantially increased the numbers of children becoming wards of public or private charity. Because the societies saw their overriding purpose to be the *rescue* of children, they displayed little or no interest in helping parents to reestablish a home for the return of the children. . . .[6]

Only relatively recently have programs to help maintain families begun to develop, and this effort has been frustrated by a lack of resources. Legislated budget constraints, including constant ceilings on available funding during periods of high inflation and the nonallocation of appropriated monies, have limited the resources available for programs with this goal. The fact that substitute care programs are already in place and funded has also hampered the development of alternative services. Thus, the boundaries of the child welfare system have remained modest. As one commentator has noted:

During the late 1960's and early 1970's . . . child welfare agencies widened their concern to refocus on the needs of all children. Despite the belief that the new focus was equitable and desirable, such an orientation was clearly beyond the resource capabilities of most agencies. More recently, child welfare services have regrouped around the traditional services, but not without some sense of guilt.[7]

The current policy framework for child welfare services is presented in Chapter 3.

THE CHILDREN SERVED

Until quite recently it was virtually impossible to describe the group of children receiving child welfare services either through voluntary agencies, through the public sector, or through public monies used to purchase services from voluntary agencies. A recent study analyzing the problems in child welfare concluded:

The absence of useful national information about children out of their homes and about the impact of relevant federal programs prevents meaningful planning, monitoring and evaluation efforts.[8]

While this situation was remedied in part by a survey conducted in 1978,[9] this problem is likely to reoccur, since statistical information becomes obsolete quickly. Based on a probability sample of almost 10,-000 cases, the findings of this study indicate that there were 1.8 million children receiving social services through the child welfare system. The children were about equally divided between males (52 percent) and females (48 percent), and all age groups were about equally represented in the service population. The data also reveal that children of minority background are overrepresented among children receiving child welfare services. While 15 percent of all children in the population were black at the time of the study, black children comprised 28 percent of the children receiving services. Similarly, while 2 percent of the population were classified as neither white nor black in 1978 (for example, Hispanic, Asian Pacific, Native American), 11 percent of the children receiving child welfare services were classified in this way.

Most children (68 percent) received service while living with at least one parent, usually their mothers. Only 15 percent of the children lived with both of their parents. However, almost one-third of the children received services outside their home—22 percent in foster families, 2 percent in group homes, 4 percent in institutions, and 2 percent in other facilities. This represents *more than 500,000 children separated from their families* and a threefold increase in the number of children living outside their homes and under the jurisdiction of a child welfare agency since the last national survey was conducted in 1961. Younger children were more likely to be receiving service in their own home than older children, although children of all ages were present in the substitute care system. Two-thirds of the children under seven in the current survey were living with parent(s) compared to only one-half of the children over the age of eleven.

For the most part the families of the children receiving services conform to a profile often associated with families in poverty. Only one child in five had parents who lived together. About 60 percent of the children were from families where public assistance or other cash transfer programs were the primary source of income. These families presented a wide range of problems which led to the need for service. Many had multiple problems. Precipitating reasons for the need for service to the families included child neglect, emotional problems of the parent(s), financial needs, conflicts in the parent-child relationship, inadequate housing, child abuse, unwillingness to care for the child, alcoholism, abandonment of the child, and physical illness of the parent.

Similarly, some of the children have multiple problems which led to the need for services. Included here are emotional problems of the child, behavior problems at home and school, problems in the community including court action and problems of delinquency, and developmental disabilities.

ISSUES IN THE DELIVERY OF CHILD WELFARE SERVICES

In order to understand the criticisms leveled against the child welfare system and the issues involved in the delivery of these services, it is necessary to articulate standards against which the current system can be judged. These principles are embodied in the concept of *permanency planning,* which will provide the framework for analyzing the current child welfare service delivery system. The concept of permanency planning in the child welfare field is relatively recent. Its acceptance has been influenced by a number of factors including influential theoretical works,[10] research demonstrating problems in the current service system,[11] concerns about the costs of the existing system,[12] legal challenges to the service delivery system,[13] and exposés in the media. Permanency planning takes as its major premise the idea that the child's "well-being" must be paramount in any service delivery plan. In order to insure this, children must have a home in which they feel a *sense of belonging* and *permanent membership.*[14] This guarantees the continuity of relationships necessary for the development of a positive self-image, the establishment of healthy relationships with others, and the ability to function effectively in society.[15]

Permanency planning thus suggests that the biological family is primary to the care and upbringing of a child. Here an initial sense of belonging is developed, and here family membership initially lies. Disrupting this tie is a major decision—one that must be based on evidence that serious harm will come to the child if left at home.

If the situation is serious enough to warrant the child's removal from home, it is incumbent upon the agency to provide an alternative for the child in which these needs can be met. Placement should be in the least detrimental alternative—one that fosters continuity of relationships with people and the environment. Restorative work with the biological family must be ongoing, so that the child can be returned home to an improved situation as quickly as possible. If restorative work is not successful and the biological family cannot resume the care of the child, a home "intended to last indefinitely"[16] must be found. This can be accomplished either through the termination of parental rights and the placement of the child in an adoptive home or through *planned* long-term foster care in a single home, which allows the child to develop substitute parental ties.

Thus, in the context of permanency planning, child welfare services can be conceptualized as services provided around a set of decisions.[17] (See Chapter 6 for a full discussion of decision making.) On a full continuum these decisions include whether to:

—accept a case for service. It should be noted that in some cases the agency has little control over this decision, since the process of child welfare services can be mandated by law (as in cases of child abuse or neglect) or by the courts when they order the removal of a child from the home.

—provide services to the family in the home in order to prevent placement. Included here is a planned determination of which services are appropriate and how best to secure them for the client.

—remove a child from home and provide an alternative living situation.

—restore children to their biological families after the specific causes of placement have been alleviated.

—terminate parental rights and/or insure a permanent living situation in which new ties can be fostered and developed.

If permanency planning is to fulfill its promise of maintaining biological families for children, restoring children in care to their biological homes in a timely fashion, or finding permanent homes for children who cannot return home—all of which are currently believed to represent the best practice in child welfare—a number of principles must be adhered to. These include:[18]

1. There must be early identification of cases in which family dysfunction can lead to the placement of the child.
2. There must, whenever possible, be work with parents and children in their own homes to prevent entry into the placement system.
3. Removal of a child from home must be based on specific guidelines and should occur only after it has been determined that the parents, with agency supports, cannot remediate the situation with the child in the home.
4. Prior to or shortly after the removal of the child from home, there must be an examination of the various placement alternatives, and the child must be placed in the least detrimental alternative available.
5. There must be established for children and their families a time-limited casework plan designed to achieve, as soon as possible, an appropriate permanent placement. Appropriate services must be provided to establish and carry out this plan.
6. There must be established a consistent set of guidelines regarding the termination of parental rights, which can be implemented if children cannot return to their biological home.
7. There must be sufficient resources available for the child who cannot return home to insure that a permanent substitute home can be arranged.

Before presenting evidence of the current child welfare system's adherence to these principles, one caveat is in order. While the child welfare system is currently judged against this set of principles it must be remembered that these were *not* the original goals of the child welfare system. Only relatively recently has substitute care come to be seen as a temporary situation and work with parents to enable the child to remain at home or to return from foster care become a goal of the child welfare system. Likewise, formal adoption of children who have been in foster care is also a relatively new concept. Thus, the child welfare system is in transition and should be viewed as such.

Principle 1: *There must be early identification of cases in which family dysfunction can lead to the placement of the child*

The early identification of such cases presupposes a service delivery system that is broader than the current child welfare system and that can identify instances in which placement may become necessary and refer such cases to appropriate agencies. This assumes that the child welfare system will continue to operate as a residual system within a larger service system, and as such should come into play only when family functioning is disrupted. It should not attempt to become this broader service delivery system or to extend beyond its current boundaries. This broader service system has been referred to as a "personal social service system."[19]

Such a social service "system" does not exist currently in this country, although variations of such systems do exist in other nations.[20] What does exist in this country is a series of parallel structures that provide social services to limited, nonuniversal populations. Each of these structures provides social services related to the specific, categorical problems the clients present. Clients with multiple problems often have to relate to a number of these structures simultaneously and often have to find their way from one structure to another by themselves.

This nonsystem has been described in the literature alternately as "fragmented," "duplicative," "uncoordinated," and "noninclusive." The services provided differ on a large number of dimensions dependent upon their legislative base, organizational context, available resources, and organizational structure. The programs differ one from another in terms of target populations, program components, size, staffing patterns, and coverage. As Kamerman and Kahn have noted, "there is no national integrated social service system and no nationally instituted, locally-based structure for providing general (personal) social services."[21] These authors list the following five reasons for this situation:

> First, and most important, the whole history of social service development in the United States is a story of state—not federal—priority in general social services and of categorical programs established in response to discrete problems. . . .
> Second, the one existing structure which might have developed into such a system—the service arm of the public welfare system . . . almost collapsed when services and income maintenance programs were separated early in the 1970s and service staff were either switched to eligibility tasks or were left with limited support and no clear sense of role or function. . . .
> Third . . . [recent] U.S. policy has stressed implementation of an income strategy as the means for helping people in need. . . . the explicit preference for this strategy resulted for some time in a relative lack of interest in

program developments which might be perceived as more relevant to a service strategy. . . .

Fourth, growing federal stress during the late sixties and early seventies on decentralization of policy and programming through general and special revenue sharing, block grants, and administrative measures decreased the likelihood of any "standard" approach. . . .

Fifth, the voluntary sector, sectarian and nonsectarian, has always been significant and autonomous in several U.S. regions in the social services field. . . . [Because of purchased care] the fact of public funding has not been converted into an opportunity to construct a coherent system.[22]

A number of other reasons that currently deter the development of a comprehensive personal social service system can also be cited. Foremost is the fact that until the passage of Title XX of the Social Security Act there was little demand for systematic planning for social services within the individual states. While Title XX has begun to provide a framework for planning social services aimed at specific goals, there have been a number of problems within the planning process, which keep it from being carried out effectively. First, while formal needs assessment and community participation in the planning process have been mandated by law, needs have more often been assessed through open meetings rather than formal needs assessment procedures. This has allowed vocal constituent groups to dominate discussion and skew perceptions. Such a process has created an advocacy atmosphere, which often pits categorical service providers and consumers against each other in a scramble for limited funds. This situation is further complicated by the fact that "hard services" such as day care have been more easily understood by legislators and planners than counseling services and therefore have been more likely to receive priority.[23]

There are a number of obstacles to more systematic needs assessment, including limited fiscal flexibility for planning or reordering current programs under federal spending ceilings; lack of state planning staff and resources to undertake needs assessment; hostility on the part of program managers, providers, and advocacy groups toward overall needs assessment; lack of certainty as to the eventual utility of such processes; the difficulty of quantifying needs and problems; and lack of federal leadership in providing states with technical assistance in the development of comprehensive needs assessment methodologies.[24] What this has meant is that few needs assessment procedures go beyond the examination of past data and that those needs assessments that are completed are pursued in connection with specific programs rather than the overall service needs of a community.

Even if systematic and reliable needs assessments were carried out, it must be remembered that funding decisions are political and subject to influence. Thus, even if new needs were identified, the implementation of new service programs would have to compete for scarce resources with already existing programs. Existing programs are more likely to be continued, since they are likely to have political constituencies and backing.

Another obstacle to the development of comprehensive personal social services is a lack of knowledge about which services work. Without such knowledge the decisions regarding service structuring and delivery are difficult to make and are often based on "beliefs" rather than on facts. Often the result is that no changes in the service structures are made. While evaluations of service programs and service systems may be difficult to plan, implement, and conduct and such evaluations are often met with resistance by service delivery staff, it seems clear that they must be undertaken if rationality is to guide the service delivery pattern. Yet, reports indicate that fewer than one-half of the states have any service evaluation programs and the development of evaluation systems is not seen as a priority within the states.[25]

With the current fragmentation in the social service sector and a categorical approach to the problems of individuals and families, it is not surprising that the "average middle-size city has between 400 and 500 human service providers. . . . chances are one in five that a client referred from one service to another will ever get there. . . ."[26] Consequently, families generally do not reach child welfare agencies until they are in crisis and are requesting placement for their children. In one study "66% of the natural parents interviewed reported that a specific crisis precipitated the foster plan and they were unable to get assistance for their problem until placement was the impending plan."[27]

The alternative to the current system of service delivery is a better coordinated, more comprehensive social service network. This has been called for on numerous occasions,[28] and Chapters 4 and 5 of this volume deal with service delivery mandates, that must be filled if such a system is to be established.

Principle 2: *There must, whenever possible, be work with parents and children in their own homes to prevent entry into the placement system*

If one accepts the premise that the family is the primary child-rearing institution and that disruption of this pattern should be viewed as a drastic measure, this principle becomes self-evident. Yet, there is evidence that a proportion of children currently in the foster care system should never have been removed from their own homes and that services to the family could have prevented the child's removal. One study found "in every community we visited we found policies and/or practices that overtly or covertly discouraged parents from keeping their children at home. . . ."[29] The exact number of children for whom placement can be avoided through provision of in-home services is difficult to determine. Often *ex post facto* judgments by researchers are used to make estimates of the number, but the reliability of these judgments may be questioned. Using this method, the figure in one city was placed at 8 percent of the foster care population[30] by one study and at 17 percent[31] by another. Other methods, such as reports by parents as to the need for placement, place this figure at a much higher level—often as much as 30 percent.[32] If the lower figures were to hold true nationally, it can be estimated that between 40,000 and 85,000 children in foster care should never have entered this system. The higher figure suggests an even more alarming rate of children who should never have entered care. A commission in New York State concluded:

> Wherever the fault may lie, it is self-evident . . . that the hour is at hand for careful but massive redirection of the child care industry toward preventive services for children and their families. Foster care and other forms of away-from-home residential treatment will never cease to be used as a last resort for many children. But they must cease . . . to enjoy their present status as an almost knee-jerk reaction to threatening family crisis.[33]

This concern is echoed in another report that synthesizes studies conducted in five other states. It concludes:

> The studies indicate that workers had little alternative to placement, in many cases, once family problems reached the crisis state. There were, nevertheless, several indications from the studies that many children were placed in foster care because a simpler, less traumatic alternative had not been provided.
> The studies give little evidence of concerted efforts to work with natural families to strengthen their ability to cope with life's problems or prevent separation of families.[34]

There is evidence that services can deter some placements. Formal evaluations of demonstration projects as well as program reports indicate that intensive efforts of the staffs to deter placement can accomplish this goal.[35] The question is why is this not done more frequently?

Two reasons for the lack of preventive services have previously been mentioned—the historical roots of the child welfare system as a placement system and the fragmentation of community services, which hinders efforts on the part of families to obtain needed services on their own before crisis. Additionally, many child welfare agencies, especially in the voluntary sector, function primarily as placement services. It has been argued that workers in such agencies have more negative attitudes toward biological parents and less confidence in the biological parents' ability to use such services, and they may be more "placement prone" than workers in agencies in which the commitment is to providing services to children in their own homes.[36] Thus, families who come to such agencies may not be offered the array of services necessary to prevent placement, either because the agency does not provide such services or because the worker believes they will not be effective.

Federal policy has also encouraged the provision of placement rather than in-home services. (For a full discussion see Chapter 3.) While federal reimbursement to the states for out-of-home care has, in the past, been open-ended, monies that could be used for in-home services have been appropriated at levels significantly below those authorized by Congress. Furthermore, many of the appropriated funds that could be used for in-home services have been used for out-of-home care. Until very recently, there has been no federal program in operation that encourages states to develop services to children in their homes.[37] If the newly passed Adoption Assistance and Child Welfare Act of 1980 is fully implemented, such programs may develop in the states in the near future.

These fiscal incentives for out-of-home care are also played out on a local level. It has been argued that purchase-of-service arrangements between public and voluntary agencies encourage the placement of children. Voluntary agencies are often reimbursed at a per diem rate for each child *under care,*[38] but not for services provided to children in their own homes; and the agencies are often unable to provide these services without reimbursement.

In addition to fiscal disincentives that have deterred the development of in-home services, social attitudes have also mitigated against keeping children at home. Institutional racism, negative attitudes toward the poor, and a fear of life-styles different from those of mainstream America have all allowed society to condemn the parents and remove the child rather than provide the supports necessary to maintain family integrity.

If in-home services are to be effective, programs must be imaginatively developed, innovative in their approaches to service delivery, and executed with conviction by their staffs. Recent research has shown that a number of program elements must be present including: (1) an appropriate array of services, both concrete and counseling, (2) a willingness on the part of agencies to facilitate transportation for clients to the agency, (3) advocacy on the part of workers to obtain needed services for their clients from a number of agencies, (4) workers with case management skills to assure that the various services needed are provided by the multiple service providers involved, and (5) an availability and ability to provide services to multiple family members simultaneously.[39] While some programs are able to provide this,[40] such services are expensive *in the short run* and require staff trained for this type of service delivery. Fiscal constraints thus hamper the provision of such comprehensive in-home services, as do large case loads and untrained personnel.[41]

Numerous reports echo the staffing problems common to many child welfare agencies. One states:[42]

> In state and local foster care offices throughout the country:
> 1. Staff with insufficient background or training are recruited and expected to deal with complex family, social and financial issues.
> 2. Little on-the-job training or meaningful supervision of staff takes place.
> 3. Caseloads are crushing. Seventy to ninety cases per worker are common. . . .
> 4. The workload and lack of professional preparation make meaningful involvement with parents, children, foster parents, courts, and potential adoptive parents almost impossible. Staff personnel respond to daily crises. Face-to-face contact by workers with parents, other relatives, children, foster parents over the course of a year is measured in hours.

With such work pressure, it is not surprising that worker turnover is reported to be as high as 50 to 100 percent[43] or that workers are "prone to changing their jobs after relatively short periods of involvement with their clients."[44] What is even more disheartening is that workers who leave child welfare positions are those that the system appears to need most. For example, a study of child welfare workers with bachelor's degrees found that workers who leave their agencies and go on to graduate education tend to reject authority, have a higher tolerance of ambiguity, see a greater need for change, be more client-oriented, and not find the client-worker relationship frustrating more often than their counterparts who stay.[45] Although making a career commitment to social work, these workers are unlikely to return to child welfare positions.

The services needed to prevent children from unnecessarily entering the foster care placement system and the organization of such services are discussed in Chapter 6 of this book. Personnel matters and the child welfare workers' predicament are discussed in the book's final chapter.

Principle 3:   *Removal of a child from home must be based on specific guide-lines and should occur only after it has been determined that the parents, with agency supports, cannot remediate the situation with the child in the home*

The decision to separate a child from his or her family is one of the most important decisions child welfare workers and juvenile court judges can make. The lives of the children and their parents are altered in significant ways. Despite this knowledge, research within child welfare has suggested that such decisions are often made on a nonsystematic basis and that the biases, values, and assumptions of the decision maker are often the primary rationale for the separation. Shinn has stated, ". . . research about decision-making in child welfare suggests that the making of a decision pertaining to various aspects of foster care is still at a stage where it involves more art and intuition than science."[46] This idea was also advanced by Fanshel when he stated, ". . . by and large child welfare workers are often guilty of a kind of rank empiricism in the way they work with children and much of their effort is guided by a kind of 'seat of the pants' intuitiveness."[47]

The lack of standards for the removal of children means that they may enter care when they are not in jeopardy in their homes. Placement decisions can reflect the bias of a worker, a worker's misunderstanding of the culture from which the client comes,[48] or the amount of information that the worker has about the client. Reviewing a series of studies, Shyne and associates commented that questions have to be raised as to "whether own home and placement cases were as different as they seemed or whether some of the differences reflected merely fuller information on the placement cases."[49]

There are other factors that also may influence the placement decision. The availability of community resources has been suggested as one factor that influences whether children remain at home and what type of placement they enter if they do come into care.[50] It has also been suggested that the orientation of the responding personnel may influence whether a child enters care. For example, one study[51] found that suspected victims of child abuse and neglect were more likely to be removed from their homes and placed in foster care if police rather than social workers respond to the complaint, even when the severity of the case was controlled.

Furthermore, there is evidence that agency goals influence decision making in child welfare. Billingsley, in a classic study of child protective workers, notes that a worker must respond to the expectations of the agency, the profession, the clients, and the community. Such expectations are often in conflict. Decisions, he concludes, are based more on the expectations of the agency than on the needs of the client or the expectation of the community. He states "both caseworkers and supervisors are relatively more oriented to carrying out agency policies and procedures than toward carrying out their professional commitments when these are in conflict."[52] Along these same lines Blau has concluded that "internalized bureaucratic constraints tended to govern the decisions and actions of caseworkers, their protestations against bureaucracy notwithstanding."[53]

These findings should not suggest that placement decisions are completely void of clinical grounding. There is some limited evidence that the amount of family pathology is important to this decision and that maternal and paternal behavior bear on it.[54] But it is not the only factor involved and may not be the most important at this time.

The lack of clear standards for decision making for social workers and the effects of these deficits on clients are further compounded by similar problems in the courts. In most jurisdictions children may be removed from their homes and placed in the custody of the state when it is deemed to be in the "best interest of the child." This legal standard has come under attack by numerous authors as being broad and vague, leaving an inordinate amount of discretion in the hands of judges. Among the identified problems with this standard are:[55]

1. It ignores completely the interest of the parents in raising the child.

2. It allows the ad hoc creation of standards by individual judges (based on their own value systems) to determine what constitutes the child's "best interest" because the statutes do not specify what factors the court should take into account in making this determination.

3. It allows variation in the application of these standards from case to case, between groups of children, and among judges. People in similar situations may be treated differently by different judges leading to the possibility of cultural and racial biasing.

4. It assumes that judges have had training relevant to making such decisions and that they are aware of and can adequately assess the risks to the children ordered removed from home. Since judges are often unaware of the consequences of their decisions, such determinations may favor the removal of a child.

5. It assumes that judges can predict what will happen to children

who are removed from their homes and judge this against what will happen if the child remains at home. Even with the best clinical information such predictions are almost impossible.

Because of these arguments many critics have called for a change in the legal standard for removal of children from their homes. They argue that the discretion of the judge and the social worker should be limited and that the standard of *demonstrable, specific harm* to the child should replace the current standard. While the authors vary to some extent on what constitutes specific harm, there is general agreement that prior to removal from the home the state must demonstrate that there is an "immediate and substantial danger" to children and that there are no means short of removal to protect the children.[56] It is believed that such a standard would decrease the discretion available to judges and help to guarantee that children are treated equally in the system and do not enter foster care unnecessarily. The current state of decision making and possible alternatives are discussed in Chapter 6 of this book.

Principle 4: *Prior to or shortly after the removal of the child from home, there must be an examination of the various placement alternatives, and the child must be placed in the least detrimental alternative available*

If it is determined that children must be placed in a substitute care arrangement, it is incumbent upon the agency to provide an alternative living arrangement consistent with their needs. A number of authors have written about the kinds of facilities that would best serve the individual child entering care. Generally, these formulations follow the premise that the most appropriate placement is the least restrictive, most family-like setting appropriate to the child's needs.

Consistent with this approach would be placing children within their extended families and providing agency supports to relatives. This alternative provides the child with a substitute living arrangement with known people and perhaps in a known environment. However, there are indications that workers often leave this alternative unexplored, and there is some indication that policy mitigates against this possibility. It appears that when a nuclear family is perceived as inadequate, so too is the extended family. In addressing this issue, one report noted:

> We have seen relatives making valiant efforts to care for children who cannot remain with their natural parents. And we have seen these efforts defeated by administrative regulations, by state laws, and sometimes by arbitrary decisions. . . . The failure . . . of the child welfare system to turn

to interested and willing relatives at the point of placement, or to enable relatives who have been informally caring for children to continue to do so, violates every principle of good child development.[57]

When a child cannot be placed with relatives, another appropriate resource must be found. The type of facility for a given child is determined by the child's age; emotional, physical, or developmental impairment; need for clinical help; ability to establish relationships with substitute parents; ability to use community resources properly; and need for specialized programming.[58] Based on these considerations, the following classification of appropriate facilities has been posited:[59]

A *foster home* is appropriate when:

—the child is of any age (although essential if the child is under age six).

—the child can profit from open access to schools, friends, recreational resources, and extracurricular enrichments in the neighborhood.

—the child is normal or has certain limited personality, physical, or developmental handicaps with which the foster parents feel comfortable.

—child can accept and needs close relationships with substitute parents.

An *agency boarding home* is appropriate when:

—the child is of any age.

—the child can profit from open access to schools, friends, recreational resources, and extracurricular enrichments in the neighborhood.

—the child has limited personality, physical, or developmental handicaps.

—child cannot cope with the more intensive emotional involvement of a foster home.

A *group home* is appropriate when:

—the child is six or over.

—the child can profit from open access to schools, friends, recreational resources, and extracurricular enrichments in the neighborhood.

—the child cannot tolerate close emotional ties to a foster family.

—the child has a special emotional, physical, or developmental problem which needs more frequent professional help than is available in a foster home.

A *group residence* is appropriate when:

—the child is over age six.

—the child can be sustained in a regular or alternative community school.

—the child has behavior and/or emotional problems that require on-site therapy.

—the child needs professionally-toned relationships with adult child-caring personnel.

—the child has sufficient impulse control to maintain curfews and generally assure safety in an open setting.

—the child can profit from positive peer pressure.

—the child needs more specialized programming (recreation, learning enrichment) than is possible in smaller settings.

A *residential treatment center for acting-out children* is appropriate when:

—the child is over age six.

—the child is moderately disturbed.

—the child is severely acting out.

—the child manifests deviant acting-out behaviors including antisocial behavior and drug or alcohol abuse.

—the child needs a high level of structure and a wide range of supportive services as well as individualized programming within a more closed facility.

A *residential treatment center for seriously disturbed children* is appropriate when:

—the child is over age six.

—the child is so emotionally disturbed that he needs twenty-four-hour supervision.

—the child is self- or other-destructive.

—the child has thought or affect disorders.

—the child is severely withdrawn.

—the child is a firesetter.

—the child engages in bizarre sexual behavior.

—the child has a severe form of anorexia.

The reader will note that among these facilities and their respective criteria there is no mention of the large congregate institution for the dependent or neglected child who is not manifesting emotional problems.

This is because there is an emerging consensus that such facilities are never appropriate for a normal or near normal child, since this child can function in the community. It is also not appropriate for the disturbed child because necessary intensive, on-site professional help is not available in such institutions. As one report recently stated:

> The legitimacy of the dependency institution is dubious, and the profession of child welfare as a whole has frowned upon such institutions. As a result, their status today is untenable. They exist in a professional no-man's-land. The dependency institution has been proclaimed by professionals as undesirable for normal children as well as inadequate for disturbed children.[60]

Using these criteria, it has become apparent that children entering the foster care system are often not placed in the appropriate type of facility. Two studies, one done in New York City[61] and one in the upstate counties of New York State,[62] found an alarmingly high number of children inappropriately placed by these criteria. Findings indicated that 58 percent and 34 percent of the children respectively in the two studies were inappropriately placed initially, and 45 percent and 53 percent were inappropriately placed at the time the studies were done. The problem of inappropriate placements was found to be even more profound for children of minority backgrounds.[63]

These findings seem to indicate that children are placed on the basis of available facilities and not according to their individual needs for a number of interrelated reasons. First, it appears that children are currently entering foster care at older ages than has been true in the past. Thus, there is a greater demand for group facilities and residential treatment centers (older children are more likely to enter care due to their own disturbed behavior). The supply of group and residential facilities has simply not kept up, and thus older children are more likely to be inappropriately placed than younger children. To illustrate, the New York studies previously mentioned found significant deficits in the numbers of group homes, group residences, and both types of residential treatment facilities, and they projected, based on population trends, that such deficits would continue in the future.[64]

Despite the known need for such community-based facilities, there are obstacles to their development. As one report noted:

> Attempts to develop community based facilities have been beset by legal and fiscal difficulties. Very often communities try to block efforts to establish group homes through legal tactics, political action, and harassment, primarily because they do not want "troublemakers" around. Zoning

regulations are often restrictive. Courts have generally upheld the group home efforts, but at times the cost is high in terms of ultimate community acceptance. Further, start-up monies—either for building renovations or staffing—are often not available either from the local community, the state, or the federal government. Nor are reimbursement formulas structured to encourage development of community based alternatives.[65]

A further obstacle to the development of appropriate facilities is current purchase-of-service agreements between state and voluntary agencies. Such arrangements for out-of-home services are particularly prevalent; nationally, 56 percent of foster care services are purchased.[66] One possible result of this heavy reliance on purchased service is that the voluntary agencies become selective in their admission criteria. Children with behavior problems may be denied appropriate placements based on inconsequential—potentially discriminatory—admission requirements and may be forced into settings that are less likely to meet their needs. When this does occur, "the responsible public agency is faced . . . with choosing the politically difficult route of challenging the private facilities, developing sanctions for inappropriate refusals to serve children, and setting up [their own] alternatives, or continuing to make inappropriate placements."[67] There are few alternatives to the inappropriate placements, since many states do not have the resources to develop the alternatives on their own at this time.

Principle 5: *There must be established for children and their families a time-limited casework plan designed to achieve, as soon as possible, an appropriate permanent placement. Appropriate services must be provided to establish and carry out this plan*

If one is to develop case plans for children to insure permanent homes for them, it is essential that parents are helped either to remove the factors that lead to the placement and/or to recognize that they are either unwilling or unable to raise their child. Yet, studies note that the child welfare system is deficient in providing services to families after the child has entered care. A Children's Defense Fund study concluded:

A few indices of agency efforts to strengthen the family and alleviate problems which precipitated the child's removal from the home are the number of contacts between the agency and the parent and the amount and quality of services offered the natural parent. Locating missing parents, involving parents in planning activities for the child, and involving parents in participating in activities with their child are also crucial to effective

service. Data on the foregoing aspects of family services indicate that services provided natural families are not adequate to achieve the goals of the
foster care system.[68]

Regarding contact between social workers and families during placement, studies have shown that it is not uncommon for parents of children in foster care to have infrequent and sporadic agency contacts.
Sixty-five percent of the biological mothers in an Iowa study and almost
60 percent of these mothers in a Massachusetts study had not seen an
agency worker for at least six months.[69] Few families of children in foster
care appear to have contact with social agencies more than once a
month.

If children are to be discharged from the foster care system, greater
contact between worker and parent is needed. Successful projects have
demonstrated the relationship between parental contact and discharge
from care. They have also noted that many social workers are spending
their time in endeavors that do not enhance the child's probability of
return home—concentrating their efforts on the child–foster parent relationship rather than the child–biological parent relationship.[70]

In addition, regulations often do not mandate caseworker-parent contact, and most child welfare statutes do not require provision of services
to restore families.[71] There is often little follow-up to insure that biological parents are receiving services when referred for them, and one study
has concluded that those families in greatest need are the least likely to
use services for which they are referred.[72]

The effects of this lack of contact between the placement agency and
the family are compounded by a lack of contact between the parent and
the child once the child is in placement. There is evidence that, for most
children in care, parental visiting is strongly related not only to the discharge of the child back to the biological home, but also to the child's
well-being while in care.[73] Yet a recent survey indicates that one-third of
the children currently in care, and for whom a parent (or other child-
caring person) is available for visiting, did not have a service plan that
provided for contact between the child and the parent.[74] Vasaly's summary of studies done in five states concludes that "only about one-third
of the children [in foster care] had meaningful, regular contacts with a
parent."[75] In the same vein, Fanshel has found that almost one-half of
the children in foster care in New York City had no parental visiting for
six months or more.[76]

Reports further indicate that many agencies fail to articulate visiting
policies and explain them to parents. When policies about parental visit-

ing do exist, they are often restrictive and require a worker to be present during the contact and/or they specify when and where the contact is to take place—often in agency offices on specific days.[77] Such policies may hinder the natural interaction necessary to maintain a meaningful parent-child relationship and lead to the perception that visiting between child and parent is either discouraged or prohibited.[78]

The consequences of the lack of meaningful work with biological parents and contact between parent and child are reflected in statistics regarding discharge of children to their biological home from the foster care system. Research results from a number of studies throughout the country indicate that for a large minority of children separated from their families foster care is not the temporary service it is supposed to be. Many children who enter care spend long periods of time in a home in which they have no permanent status, and some live out their childhood in such arrangements. Cross-sectional studies have shown the average length of time a child spends in foster care to be four years or more and indicate that 10 to 15 percent of the children in care have been there ten years or more.[79] A national survey indicates that almost one-fourth of the children have been in care more than six years at the time the study was completed.[80] Vasaly's data from four states found that between 35 percent and 68 percent of the children had been in care more than two years.[81] In another report, twelve of twenty-two states reporting indicated that their average length of time in foster care was at least thirty months.[82] Fanshel and Shinn, in a longitudinal study in New York City, found that 36 percent of the children in the study were still in care after five years.[83]

While the most comprehensive study of children in foster care "did not show that children who remained in care fared less well with respect to intellectual abilities, school performance and personal and social adjustment compared to those who returned to their own homes,"[84] there is a relationship between the length of time a child remains in foster care and the number of times the child is moved from placement to placement within the foster care system. This movement is generally considered harmful to children. As one psychoanalyst has noted:

> If a child is separated from his biological parents but is able to develop a permanent relationship with another mother and father, there may be no long-term damage done. If, instead, the child is moved from one foster home to another, a variety of harmful consequences may occur.[85]

Studies indicate that a substantial minority of children in the foster care system are moved an inordinate number of times during their tenure in foster care. Most studies have shown that about 25 percent of the sample (be it cross-sectional or longitudinal) experience three or more placements during their time in foster care.[86] One report noted that of twenty-seven states reporting, sixteen estimated an average of more than two moves per child for their children in care, and one state reported an average of 5.5 moves per child.[87]

The above discussion leads one to conclude that, for a large minority of children currently in foster care, permanent plans are never achieved. The authors of one study note that this is due to a "lack of systematic case management and accountability mechanisms rather than through design."[88] It appears that the foster care system is beginning to address this problem:

> Agency inefficiency in monitoring the "drift" of children in foster care is addressed in a set of proposed solutions. In general these involve: (1) more explicit intra-agency efforts to monitor plans for the child and to implement more intensive effort to achieve permanency, and (2) arrangements for extra-agency monitoring, by courts and citizens' review boards, of agency efforts toward permanence. . . . In general, what is suggested is more explicit planning, monitoring and review of worker activity in response to the central problem of deficiencies in care management.[89]

While such monitoring efforts will enhance permanency planning and have been demonstrated effective in helping reduce foster care drift,[90] they will not, in and of themselves, solve the problem. Concentrated, effective work with parents and children is needed if permanent plans are to be achieved. These services are discussed in Chapters 9 and 10 of this book.

Principle 6: *There must be established a consistent set of guidelines regarding the termination of parental rights if children cannot return to their biological home*

While much of the previous discussion has focused on the need to protect the children's ties to their biological parents, it must be recognized that even with the best help available, many placements in the foster care system are unavoidable, and some children who enter the system will never return to their biological home. Some children are abandoned and need placement in the child welfare system, and others are abandoned by their parents (both physically and psychologically) after they enter care. Some families are so disorganized and troubled that no amount of effort will help ameliorate the conditions that led to the child's placement. While more can be done to enhance family functioning, it is evident that some children will never return home.

The deficiencies in the current service system add to the number of children abandoned to foster care. The lack of meaningful contact with biological parents and policies that discourage parental visiting mean that children who under good circumstances might return home continue to drift in the system. Many of these children currently remain in foster care until they reach majority, after experiencing multiple placements and unstable living situations. For these children permanence in living arrangements is often not achieved.

One alternative to this drift for children who cannot return home is the severing of ties to biological parents and creating new families through adoption. Yet there is "a widespread unwillingness to initiate termination proceedings or to actually terminate the rights of biologic parents."[91] There is no question that terminating parental rights is a serious step that should not be entered lightly. However, for some children, avoiding this procedure means that permanency is not achieved.

It has been noted that both social workers and judges are reluctant to move toward the termination of parental rights. There appear to be numerous reasons for this hesitancy. First, there is often no consistent mechanism to identify the children for whom termination would be appropriate. Mandatory periodic review of all children in foster care, either by the court or by an administrative structure outside the agency structure, is still lacking in many states.[92] Furthermore, information systems capable of identifying children in jeopardy of spending large parts of their childhood in the foster care system have not been developed or utilized in many states despite the fact that many of the variables that are related to the length of time a child spends in care are known.[93]

Added to the inability to identify children for whom this service would be appropriate is the reluctance of caseworkers and other agency personnel to pursue this course. Some are reluctant to move in this direction because the child has "settled in" to a foster home and appears to be adjusting well, causing no disruption or work pressure for the worker. Others do not pursue this course because they have failed, during the child's placement, to work actively with the biological parents. As a Children's Defense Fund report commented:

> Case documentation that efforts to work with parents have been tried and have failed is crucial to the success of a termination effort. Often . . . such efforts do not take place, or if they do, they are poorly documented. Caseworkers feel that if they bring a petition, natural parents or their lawyers can correctly argue that they were not given a chance. As a compensation for past agency failures, the parent is protected at the expense of the child and his current situation.[94]

Still other workers do not pursue termination of parental rights because they believe that the parent might be able to resume care at some point in the future, despite the fact that the child has already been in care for a number of years. For example, a parent may have episodic mental hospitalizations. At points, the parent appears to be making progress, but this is not sustained over time. The worker may hold to the idea that "some day" the child will be able to return home and thus not move in the direction of termination of rights. Such reluctance is compounded by the fact that we often do not know and cannot predict whether a parent will, at some point in the future, be able to care for the child.

Agencies may also be reluctant to terminate parental rights because these procedures are often complex and agency funds (or reimbursements from the states in the case of voluntary agencies) for such proceedings, which may last many months, are not available. Moreover, under a Supreme Court decision[95] agencies are required to give notice not only to the child's legal parents, but to the putative father. Locating such absent parents can be time-consuming and costly and may deter agencies from proceeding in this direction. Furthermore, preparing cases and testifying in court hearings (which are often delayed) are skills many workers do not have, and thus they are reluctant to undertake these tasks. Finally, workers may feel that such preparation is too time-consuming, given that the child may be doing well in foster care, and that time is better spent on more immediate problems within their case load.

Compounding the agencies' reluctance to move for termination of parental rights are problems in the termination statutes of the various states. Criticisms of the current statutes are, in part, similar to those mentioned for statutes governing the removal of children from their home and include:[96]

1. Definitions of what constitutes grounds for termination are vague, leaving the decision to the individual interpretations and predilections of the judge hearing the case.
2. Statutory grounds for termination often focus on the idea of "parental fault." Thus, even if the child cannot be returned home, parental rights may not be terminated if the parents are not found blameworthy for the condition. The condition of the child and his or her experience in foster care may not be considered in such proceedings at all.
3. Some states cannot consider termination of parental rights until an adoption hearing. If the child cannot be freed until this

point, the possibility of finding an adoptive home is diminished, since adoptive parents may not be willing to assume the legal risks involved in such cases.

Some critics have noted that without specific grounds for making such serious and irrevocable decisions, judges often rule not to terminate parental rights in order to avoid taking responsibility for this decision. One report states that the faintest "flicker of interest [on the part of biological parents] often deters judges from severing the rights of persons who have demonstrated for years unfitness, disinterest or inability to be responsible parents."[97] Thus, what is meant by "meaningful contact" between the parent and the child is left to the determination of judges, who may not be aware of the potential consequences for the child if the rights of the parents are not terminated.

There appears to be consensus that the termination of parental rights statutes should be revised, so that parental rights do not take precedence over the rights of the child to a permanent, stable home. Wald states that court action in this area should be based on two grounds: (1) the length of time the child has been in the foster care system, and (2) whether termination of parental rights will harm the child.[98] Parental rights should be terminated in cases of children drifting in foster care (no matter who is to blame) and in which there is little possibility of the child ever returning home—determined by the current strength of the biological parent–child relationship, the child's current response to the parent if such contact exists, and (depending on age) the child's wishes.[99] This position is controversial, as it risks the possibility of the violation of parental autonomy, but without such statutes some children will continue to drift in foster care and be subjected to the most damaging aspects of the foster care system. This issue of terminating parental rights in order to insure permanence for children who cannot return home is further discussed in Chapters 10 and 11.

Principle 7: *There must be sufficient resources available for children who cannot return home to insure that a permanent substitute home can be arranged*

Simply terminating the parental rights of families whose children have spent a number of years in the foster care system does not ensure that a permanent home will be found for the child. Large numbers of children remain in foster care after termination has taken place.[100] Efforts to find adoptive homes for these children are limited by current agency attitudes and practices.

For many years adoption was a service provided primarily to middle- and upper-class couples wishing to complete their family through the adoption of a normal, healthy, white infant (see Chapter 2). Children who did not fit this pattern were considered "unadoptable" or "hard to place," and little effort was made to find homes for them. While this definition is beginning to change and the field is recognizing that no child is, by definition or labeling, unadoptable, much still needs to be done if we are to find permanent homes for the large and growing numbers of waiting children who have spent time in the foster care system. Many of these freed children are older, belong to minority groups, or have developmental, emotional, or physical problems. Others are members of sibling groups who need to be placed together. Yet, if permanence is to be achieved, agencies must address the needs of these "children who wait."

Successfully increasing the pool of adoptive parents available for this group of children means that agencies need to recruit adoptive parents actively and aggressively, remove agency requirements for adoptive parents that screen out rather than screen in applicants, consider groups of people who have traditionally been excluded from consideration as potential adoptive parents, and develop support mechanisms for parents who have chosen to adopt the special needs child.

In the past, most adoption agencies have not needed to recruit adoptive parents actively. These agencies, concerned primarily with the adoption of healthy, white infants, have had many more applicants than children available. Waiting lists for such children are typically over two years.[101] Consequently, traditional agencies often have not seen the need to recruit potential adoptive families.

Even with the increased recognition of the need for adoptive homes for special needs children, agencies often do not actively recruit families for these children. Compounding the fiscal problems that hamper recruitment efforts is a lack of knowledge in many agencies about how to recruit adoptive parents and a lack of commitment to such efforts. A recent monograph concluded:

> Although most agencies are aware of adoptive parent recruitment techniques, few agencies engage in them effectively. While the knowledge is present, it is present only in piecemeal fashion. Knowledge regarding effective methods has not been effectively disseminated or taught to agency staff.[102]

Because some agencies do not perceive themselves as part of a total child care system, they may be reluctant to expand their resources for children technically in the care of other agencies. Thus, provincialism also hampers recruitment efforts. If agencies do not serve waiting children, they may not recognize the need to recruit homes for children available through other agencies.

Just as agencies traditionally limited the children who were acceptable for adoption, so also did they limit the type of families they would consider as potential adoptive parents. A number of socioeconomic and demographic criteria have been used to determine eligibility. These include age, income, family composition, infertility, length of marriage, working status of the adoptive mother, sexual orientation, housing, and religion. Requirements in these areas are viewed as protections for the child.

However, these requirements have an additional effect. When enforced, numerous prospective adoptive parents become ineligible to adopt through the agency. Agencies are thus able to screen out prospective couples and maintain manageable intake case loads. But these criteria have come under attack as the field has focused on special needs children because of (1) a growing realization that the criteria were not predictive of parenting ability, (2) a greater acceptance of differing life-styles in society and a recognition that different life-styles were not necessarily harmful to children, and (3) a growing need for adoptive homes for children with special needs.

Unfortunately many agencies, for whatever reasons (including concern for the child), continue to hold to such requirements. One study surveyed ninety-two agencies[103] and found a majority continue to have requirements about the length of the current marriage, age, the presence of other children in the home, and infertility in the couples. A minority had minimum income and minimum space requirements.

In addition, agencies have often barred entire groups of people from becoming prospective adoptive parents. For many years foster parents were not considered suitable adoptive parents and were barred from applying by agency policy[104] and court decision.[105] Single parents have also been barred from consideration by some agencies.

It seems clear that the lack of recruitment, agency requirements, and the barring of certain groups from the adoption process all decrease the number of homes available to children who are waiting for adoption. A further deterrent to the adoption of waiting children is the lack of services the agency can provide during the adoption process and after its completion. When one considers the added difficulties and stresses that the adoption of a special needs child can place on a family, it is not surprising that the general view in the field is that there may be a continued need for service from the agency if the adoption is to succeed.

The greater the stress placed on the family, the greater the possible need for such services. While some of the problems faced by adoptive families may be transient, others are complex and may require long-term services if they are to be resolved.[106] Yet child welfare agencies often do not have the resources necessary to provide such post-adoptive services. Some, working in the traditional model of adoption services, do not see this as a need.

In addition to the need for services, many families will need financial assistance if they are going to adopt a special needs child. In response to this need almost all of the states have passed adoption subsidy legislation. Subsidies help with the cost of special medical care and/or living expenses. In addition they facilitate the adoption of special needs children in homes that could otherwise not afford to rear the child.

There are, however, a number of problems with the current subsidy legislation.[107] Perhaps paramount in these concerns is the fact that subsidy is currently provided through local and state funding (this will change if newly passed legislation is fully funded and implemented) and that such programs can be terminated if monies for them are not appropriated annually. Some potential adoptive parents who need subsidies fear they may be placed in hazardous financial situations because of this situation.

While adoption is appropriate for any child who can benefit from being part of a family, there are some children in the foster care system who cannot return home and for whom adoption is not an appropriate plan. Such children may have strong ties to a foster family who are unable to adopt. Others may not be able to be freed for adoption. Still others cannot tolerate close family ties.

For these children, *planned* long-term foster care may be appropriate. This means that the child's placement in the foster family is expected to last indefinitely. It may also mean that the agency has transferred guardianship to the foster parents, enabling them to make decisions about the children in their care without the approval of the agency.

There are a number of advantages to planned, long-term, foster care as compared to the current unplanned, long-term care so prevalent in agencies today. Stability in placement is most likely to be achieved if foster parents make a long-term commitment to the child. The likelihood of multiple placements is diminished. Since decision making may be transferred from the agency to the family, agency involvement in the family is diminished, thus enhancing the child's sense of belonging to a family. Finally, because the need for agency supervision of the child and family is reduced in these situations, some of the administrative costs of foster care are reduced.

CONCLUSIONS

Having read this chapter, one could be left with the impression that the attacks on the child welfare system are totally justified and that few children are served well by this system of services. This is not the case. For most children, the current system of child welfare services performs its tasks adequately—and for some, admirably. Most children who can be served at home are. For most children, foster care is the temporary arrangement it is supposed to be. When reunited, many families function more effectively because their children were able to enter foster care temporarily. Many children are adopted successfully after a period of time in care when it has been determined that they cannot return home. It is this record of achievement that gives us confidence that current deficiencies can be corrected.

This chapter and the others in this book focus attention on the children who are not well served and who can be damaged by the service system provided to help them. They constitute *a minority* of the children who come into contact with child welfare agencies. But overall success rates mean little to the lives of individual children. Perhaps more than any other service system, child welfare must be concerned with individual outcomes. By focusing attention on the problems of the system, the reasons that these problems exist, and potential solutions to these problems, it is hoped that changes will occur to insure that even fewer children have negative experiences.

NOTES

1. Alfred Kadushin, "Child Welfare Strategy in the Coming Years: An Overview," *Child Welfare Strategy in the Coming Years* (Washington, D.C.: U.S. Department of Health, Education and Welfare, 1978), pp. 41–42.

2. *A National Program for Child Welfare Services* (New York: Child Welfare League of America, 1971), p. 2.

3. Kadushin, "Child Welfare Strategy," p. 18.

4. Some of these definitions are taken from "The Provision of Social Services to Children and Their Families: The Child Questionnaire " (Rockville, Md.: Westat, Inc., 1977), pp. 3–5.

5. Kenneth Keniston and the Carnegie Council on Children, *All Our Children: The American Family Under Pressure* (New York: Harcourt Brace Jovanovich, 1977), p. 9.

6. Lela Costin, *Child Welfare: Policies and Practices,* 2nd ed. (New York: McGraw-Hill, 1979), pp. 189–90.

7. Kadushin, "Child Welfare Strategy," p. 12.

8. Jane Knitzer, Mary Lee Allen, and Brenda McGowan, *Children Without Homes* (Washington, D.C.: Children's Defense Fund, 1978), pp. 137–38.

9. Ann Shyne and Anita Schroeder, *National Study of Social Services to Children and Their Families* (Washington, D.C.: Department of Health, Education and Welfare, 1978). All statistics, unless otherwise noted, are taken from this work.

10. See, for example, Joseph Goldstein, Anna Freud, and Albert Solnit, *Beyond the Best Interests of the Child* (New York: The Free Press, 1973); Joseph Goldstein, Anna Freud, and Albert Solnit, *Before the Best Interests of the Child* (New York: The Free Press, 1979).

11. See, for example, Blanche Bernstein, Donald Snider, and William Meezan, *Foster Care Needs and Alternatives to Placement* (Albany, N.Y.: New York State Board of Social Welfare, 1975); David Fanshel and Eugene Shinn, *Children in Foster Care: A Longitudinal Investigation* (New York: Columbia University Press, 1978); Alan Gruber, *Children in Foster Care: Destitute, Neglected, Betrayed* (New York: Human Sciences Press, 1978); Shirley Jenkins and Elaine Norman, *Beyond Placement: Mothers View Foster Care* (New York: Columbia University Press, 1975); Knitzer, Allen, and McGowan, *Children Without Homes;* Henry Maas and Richard Engler, *Children in Need of Parents* (New York: Columbia University Press, 1959); Shirley Vasaly, *Foster Care in Five States* (Washington, D.C.: U.S. Department of Health, Education and Welfare, 1976).

12. See, for example, Bernstein, Snider, and Meezan, *Foster Care Needs,* pp. 41–54; David Fanshel and Eugene Shinn, *Dollars and Sense in Foster Care* (New York: Child Welfare League of America, 1972); Mary Ann Jones, Renee Neuman, and Ann Shyne, *A Second Chance for Families* (New York: Child Welfare League of America, 1976), pp. 97–101; Vivian Hargrave, Joan Shireman, and Peter Connor, *Where Love and Need Are One* (Chicago: Department of Children and Family Services, 1975), pp. 76–79.

13. For example, *Wilder* v. *Sugarman,* 73 Civ. 2644 (SDNY); *Parker* v. *Bernstein,* 78 Civ. 957 (SDNY).

14. Arthur Emlen et al., *Overcoming Barriers to Planning for Children in Foster Care* (Portland, Ore.: Regional Research Institute for Human Services, Portland State University, 1977), pp. 10–11.

15. Goldstein, Freud, and Solnit, *Beyond the Best Interests,* pp. 9–28.

16. Emlen et al., *Overcoming Barriers*, pp. 9–11.

17. Theodore Stein, Eileen Gambrill, and Kermit Wiltse, *Children in Foster Homes: Achieving Continuity of Care* (New York: Praeger Publishers, 1978), pp. 8–34; Kermit Wiltse, "Current Issues and New Directions in Foster Care," in *Child Welfare Strategies in the Coming Years* (Washington, D.C.: U.S. Department of Health, Education and Welfare, 1978), pp. 67–84.

18. Some of these points are taken from Anthony Maluccio et al., "Beyond Permanency Planning," *Child Welfare* 59 (November 1980): 503–19.

19. Sheila Kamerman and Alfred Kahn, *Social Services in the United States* (Philadelphia: Temple University Press, 1976), pp. 503–19.

20. Alfred Kahn and Sheila Kamerman, *Not for the Poor Alone: European Social Services* (Philadelphia: Temple University Press, 1975); Sheila Kamerman and Alfred Kahn, eds., *Family Policy: Government and Families in Fourteen Countries* (New York: Columbia University Press, 1978).

21. Kamerman and Kahn, *Social Services*, p. 439.

22. Ibid., pp. 439–40.

23. *Child Welfare in 25 States—An Overview* (Washington, D.C.: U.S. Department of Health, Education and Welfare, 1976), pp. 11, 35–37.

24. Peter O'Donnell, *Social Services: Three Years After Title XX* (Washington, D.C.: National Governors Association, 1978), pp. 39–40.

25. *Child Welfare in 25 States*, p. 126.

26. Elliot Richardson, *Responsibility and Responsiveness* (Washington, D.C.: U.S. Department of Health, Education and Welfare, January 18, 1973), p. 19, quoted in Kamerman and Kahn, *Social Services*, p. 441.

27. Alan Gruber, *Foster Home Care in Massachusetts* (Boston: Governor's Commission on Adoption and Foster Care, 1973), pp. 46, 54, as cited in Vasaly, *Five States*, p. 27.

28. See, for example, *A Dream Deferred* (New York: Citizens' Committee for Children, 1971).

29. Knitzer, Allen, and McGowan, *Children Without Homes*, p. 15.

30. Bernstein, Snider, and Meezan, *Foster Care Needs*, p. 25.

31. Mignon Sauber, "Preplacement Situations of Families: Data for Planning Services," *Child Welfare* 46 (October 1967), p. 449.

32. Gruber, *Children in Foster Care,* p. 140; Shirley Jenkins and Elaine Norman, *Filial Deprivation and Foster Care* (New York: Columbia University Press, 1972).

33. Temporary State Commission on Child Welfare, *The Child and the State: A Time for Change in Child Welfare* (Albany, N.Y.: Temporary State Commission on Child Welfare, 1975), p. 24.

34. Vasaly, *Five States,* pp. 29–30.

35. Jones, Neuman, and Shyne, *Second Chance for Families.*

36. William Meezan, "Program Orientation as a Factor in Workers' Attitudes and Perceptions of the Need for Placement in Child Welfare" (D.S.W. dissertation, Columbia University, 1978).

37. Knitzer, Allen, and McGowan, *Children Without Homes,* pp. 123–24.

38. George Strauss, *The Children Are Waiting: The Failure to Achieve Permanent Homes for Foster Children in New York City* (New York: New York City Comptroller's Office, 1977), p. 39.

39. Mary Ann Jones, Stephen Magura, and Ann Shyne, "Effective Practice with Families in Protective and Preventive Services: What Works?", *Child Welfare* 60 (February 1981): 73.

40. Ibid.; Rod Tomlinson and Peg Peters, "An Alternative to Placing Children: Intensive and Extensive Therapy with the 'Disengaged,'" *Child Welfare* 60 (February 1981): 98–103.

41. *Child Welfare in 25 States,* p. 55; Knitzer, Allen, and McGowan, *Children Without Homes,* pp. 123–28; Joseph Persico, *Who Knows? Who Cares?: Forgotten Children in Foster Care* (New York: National Commission on Children in Need of Foster Parents, 1979), p. 11.

42. Persico, *Who Knows? Who Cares?,* p. 15.

43. Ibid., p. 6.

44. Deborah Shapiro, *Agencies and Foster Children* (New York: Columbia University Press, 1976), p. 121.

45. Ibid., pp. 154–56.

46. Eugene Shinn, "Is Placement Necessary?: An Experimental Study of Agreement Among Caseworkers in Making Foster Care Decisions" (D.S.W. dissertation, Columbia University, 1968), p. 1.

47. David Fanshel, "Research in Child Welfare: A Critical Analysis," *Child Welfare* 41 (December 1962): 488.

48. Bernice Boehm, "An Assessment of Family Adequacy in Protective Cases," *Child Welfare* 41 (January 1962): 12.

49. Ann Shyne, Edward Sherman, and Michael Phillips, "Filling the Gap in Child Welfare Research: Services to Children in Their Own Home," *Child Welfare* 51 (November 1972): 564.

50. Stein, Gambrill, and Wiltze, *Children in Foster Homes,* pp. 11–12.

51. Joan Shireman, Baila Miller, and H. Frederick Brown, "Child Welfare Workers, Policy and Child Placement," *Child Welfare* 60 (June 1981): 417–20.

52. Andrew Billingsley, "Bureaucratic and Professional Orientation Patterns in Social Casework," *Social Service Review* 38 (December 1964): 400.

53. Peter Blau, "Orientation Toward Clients in a Public Welfare Agency," *Administrative Science Quarterly* 5 (December 1960): 345.

54. Stein, Gambrill, and Wiltze, *Children in Foster Homes,* pp. 9–10.

55. These points are based on Goldstein, Freud, and Solnit, *Beyond the Best Interests,* pp. 17, 49–52; Robert Mnookin, "Foster Care: In Whose Best Interest?", *Harvard Educational Review—The Rights of Children,* Reprint Series No. 9, 1974, pp. 173–80; Michael Wald, "State Intervention on Behalf of Neglected Children: Standards for Removal of Children from Their Homes, Monitoring the Status of Children in Foster Care and Termination of Parental Rights," *Stanford Law Review* 28 (April 1976): 628–39.

56. Mnookin, "Foster Care," p. 185; Wald, "State Intervention," pp. 649–53.

57. Knitzer, Allen, and McGowan, *Children Without Homes,* pp. 20–21.

58. Sr. Mary Paul Janchill, *Criteria for Foster Placement and Alternatives to Foster Care* (Albany, N.Y.: New York State Board of Social Welfare, 1975).

59. Ibid., pp. 29–58.

60. Morris Fritz Mayer et al., *Group Care of Children* (New York: Child Welfare League of America, 1977), p. 71.

61. Bernstein, Snider, and Meezan, *Foster Care Needs,* pp. 20–36.

62. Virginia Sibbison and John McGowan, *New York State Children in Foster Care* (Albany, N.Y.: Welfare Research, Inc., 1977), pp. 90–101.

63. Setsuko Nishi, *Discrimination in Foster Care for New York City*

Children (New York: Metropolitan Applied Research Center, 1974).

64. Bernstein, Snider, and Meezan, *Foster Care Needs,* p. 34.
65. Knitzer, Allen, and McGowan, *Children Without Homes,* p. 46.
66. Ibid., p. 47.
67. Ibid., p. 49.
68. Vasaly, *Five States,* p. 36.
69. Ibid.
70. Stein, Gambrill, and Wiltse, *Children in Foster Homes,* p. 106.
71. Knitzer, Allen, and McGowan, *Children Without Homes,* pp. 24, 80.
72. Jenkins and Norman, *Beyond Placement,* p. 93.
73. Fanshel and Shinn, *Children in Foster Care,* pp. 85–111, 486–87.
74. Shyne and Shroeder, *National Study of Social Services,* p. 121.
75. Vasaly, *Five States,* p. 52.
76. David Fanshel, "Parental Visiting of Foster Children: A Computer-ized Study," *Social Work Research and Abstracts* 13 (Fall 1977): 2–10.
77. Knitzer, Allen, and McGowan, *Children Without Homes,* p. 22.
78. Gruber, *Children in Foster Care,* pp. 142–46.
79. Alfred Kadushin, "Children in Foster Families and Institutions," in Henry Maas, ed., *Social Service Research: Reviews of Studies* (Washington, D.C.: National Association of Social Workers, 1978), p. 98.
80. Shyne and Shroeder, *National Study of Social Services,* p. 118.
81. Vasaly, *Five States,* p. 54.
82. Persico, *Who Knows? Who Cares?,* p. 32.
83. Fanshel and Shinn, *Children in Foster Care,* p. 115.
84. Ibid., p. 479.
85. Ner Littner, "Testimony Before the National Commission on Children in Need of Parents," as quoted in Persico, *Who Knows? Who Cares?,* p. 5.
86. Fanshel and Shinn, *Children in Foster Homes,* p. 139; Kadushin, "Children in Foster Families," p. 101; Strauss, *The Children Are Waiting,* p. 10; Vasaly, *Five States,* p. 56.
87. Persico, *Who Knows? Who Cares?,* p. 32.
88. Fanshel and Shinn, *Children in Foster Care,* p. 481.

89. Reprinted with permission of MacMillan Publishing Co., Inc. From *Child Welfare Services*, 3rd ed. by Alfred Kadushin, Copyright © 1980 by Alfred Kadushin. Excerpt taken from p. 384.

90. Martha Jones, "Stopping Foster Care Drift: A Review of Legislation and Special Programs," *Child Welfare* 57 (November 1978): 571–79.

91. Knitzer, Allen, and McGowan, *Children Without Homes*, p. 91.

92. Ibid., pp. 229–49.

93. Fanshel and Shinn, *Children in Foster Care*, pp. 112–65.

94. Knitzer, Allen, and McGowan, *Children Without Homes*, p. 28.

95. *Stanley* v. *Illinois*, 405 US 645, 31 L ED 2nd 551, 92 Sup Ct 1208 (1972); *Rothman* v. *Lutheran Social Services of Wisconsin and Upper Michigan*, 47 Wisc 2d 220, 173 NW 2nd 56, vacated 4/17/72, 40 USWI 3198.

96. Wald, "State Intervention," pp. 688–90.

97. Persico, *Who Knows? Who Cares?*, p. 6.

98. Wald, "State Intervention," pp. 691–99.

99. Ibid.

100. Shyne and Schroeder, *National Study of Social Services*, pp. 124–34.

101. William Meezan, Sanford Katz, and Eva Russo, *Adoptions Without Agencies* (New York: Child Welfare League of America, 1978), pp. 35–36.

102. William Meezan, *Adoption Services in the States* (Washington, D.C.: U.S. Department of Health and Human Services, 1980), p. 12.

103. Meezan, Katz, and Russo, *Adoptions Without Agencies*, pp. 37–39.

104. Trudy Festinger, "Placement Agreements with Boarding Homes: A Survey," *Child Welfare* 53 (December 1974): 647.

105. For a review of these cases, see Kathleen Proch, "Adoption by Foster Parents" (D.S.W. dissertation, University of Illinois-Urbana, 1980), pp. 9–12.

106. Christopher Unger et al., *Chaos, Madness and Unpredictability* (Chelsea, Mich.: Spaulding for Children, 1977), p. 153.

107. Rita Simon and Howard Alstein, *Transracial Adoption* (New York: John Wiley and Sons, 1977), p. 166.

Hull House Sewing Classes. From the Jane Addams Memorial Collection, The Library, University of Illinois at Chicago. Photographer: Allen, Gordon, Schroeppel and Redlich, Inc.

CHAPTER 2

HISTORICAL EVOLUTION OF CHILD WELFARE SERVICES: AN EXAMINATION OF THE SOURCES OF CURRENT PROBLEMS AND DILEMMAS

Brenda G. McGowan

The major forces shaping the provision of child welfare services in this country—the size and composition of the population at large and the child population at risk; social, economic, and technological demands on families; prevailing ideologies regarding the proper relationship of children, parents, church, and state; dominant views about the causes of poverty, illness, and crime; and the political influence of different interest groups—have all shifted significantly since early colonial days. Yet many of the issues that plague the child welfare field today reflect the unresolved tensions and debates of the past. These tensions include:

—parents' rights versus children's needs

—child saving versus family support

—federal versus state versus local responsibility

—public versus voluntary financing and service provision

—developmental versus protective services

—in-home versus foster family versus institutional care

—appropriate boundaries between the child welfare, family service, juvenile justice, mental health, and mental retardation systems

—individualized, pluralistic modes of interventions versus uniform standards and treatment

—specialized professional services versus informal, natural helping networks

—social costs versus benefits of providing varying levels of care

All of these issues appear and reappear in the major historical documents on the American child welfare system.

The one theme that never disappears is the search for a panacea, a solution to the problems of children whose parents are unable to provide adequate care. The proposed solution of today is the concept of permanency planning, but a careful reading of history suggests that the implementation of this concept is no more likely to eliminate the need for extensive, ongoing public provision for children who are poor, neglected, unwanted, socially deficient, or disabled than the infanticide, warehousing, banishment, and foster home programs of the past. The earliest biblical accounts of Moses, Abraham, Isaac, and Jesus all refer in different ways to the problems of dependent and maltreated children. Therefore, although the concept of permanency planning seems to offer the most promising route for service provision in the next decade, it would be naive to assume that movements in this direction will meet all the needs of the child welfare population without creating or drawing attention to still other problems.

This chapter will present a broad overview of the historical evolution of the child welfare system via examination of the major trends and shifts in service provision for dependent, neglected, and troubled children. It is hoped that this historical overview will give readers a clearer understanding of the sources of some of the current dilemmas and strains in the child welfare field, thereby providing an analytical base for addressing problematic issues that are likely to arise in the future.

Social trends seldom fit into neat lines of demarcation. Unlike historical events, the beginnings of social movements can rarely be traced to a single action or a specific date. They are the result of numerous forces that come together at an approximate time. While century boundaries are used as the organizing framework for this chapter, these dates cannot be taken too rigidly. To do so poses the risk of historical distortion, for social movements and social changes often span more than one century.

SEVENTEENTH AND EIGHTEENTH CENTURIES

The early American settlers were preoccupied with issues of freedom and survival for themselves and their new country. The demands of exploring, settling, and cultivating vast expanses of land were enormous, and because of the small size of the population, contributing members of society were at a premium. The family was the basic economic unit, and all members were expected to contribute to the work of the household.

The concept of childhood, as it is currently understood, was unknown except for very young children. Although there was a high birthrate, approximately two-thirds of all children died before the age of four. Those who lived past this age were expected to start contributing labor as soon as possible by helping with household and farming chores, caring for younger siblings, and so forth. Hence, children moved quickly from infant status to serving essential economic functions for their families. Children were perceived as a scarce and valued resource for the nation, but little attention was paid to individual differences or needs, and the concept of children's rights was nonexistent. As Rodham has commented:

> In eighteenth century English common law, the term children's rights would have been a *non sequitur*. Children were regarded as chattels of the family and wards of the state, with no recognized political character or power and few legal rights.[1]

Although there was no child welfare system as such in those early days, two groups of children were presumed to require attention from the public authorities: orphans and children of paupers. Because of the high maternal mortality rates and high adult male death rates caused by the vicissitudes of life in the new world, large numbers of children were orphaned at a relatively young age and required special provisions for their care. Children of paupers were also assumed to require special care because of the high value placed on work and self-sufficiency and the concomitant fear that these children would acquire the "bad habits" of their parents if they were not taught a skill and good working habits at an early age. Parents who could not provide adequately for their children were deprived of the right to plan for their children and were socially condemned. To illustrate, a record of the selectmen's meeting in Watertown, Massachusetts, on March 3, 1671, describes the following incident:

> There coming a complaint to us the Selectmen concerning the poverty of Edward Sanderson's family: that they had not wherewith to maintain themselves and children either with supply of provision or employment to earn any, and considering that it would be the charge of the town to provide for the whole family which will be hard to do this year, and not knowing how to supply them with provisions, we considering if we should supply them and could do it, yet it would not tend to the good of the children for their good education and bringing up so they may be useful in the commonwealth or themselves to live comfortably and usefully in time to come; we have, therefore, agreed to put out two of his children into some honest families where they may be educated and brought up in the knowledge of God and some honest calling or labor . . .[2]

Social provisions for dependent children during this early period derived from the English Poor Law tradition. Children and dependent adults were treated alike and were generally handled in one of four ways:

—Outdoor relief, a public assistance program for poor families and children consisting of a meager dole paid by the local community to maintain families in their own homes

—Farming-out, a system whereby individuals or groups of paupers were auctioned off to citizens who agreed to maintain the paupers in their homes for a contracted fee

—Almshouses or poorhouses established and administered by public authorities in large urban areas for the care of destitute children and adults

—Indenture, a plan for apprenticing children to households where they would be cared for and taught a trade, in return for which they owed loyalty, obedience, and labor until the costs of their rearing had been worked off.

In addition to these provisions under the public authorities, dependent children were cared for by a range of informal provisions arranged through relatives, neighbors, or church officials. A few private institutions for orphans were also established during this early colonial period. The first such orphanage in the United States was the Ursuline Convent, founded in New Orleans in 1727 under the auspices of Louis XV of France.[3] However, prior to 1800 most dependent children were cared for in almshouses and/or by indenture, the most common pattern being that very young children were placed in public almshouses until the age of eight or nine, and then they were indentured until they reached majority.

Thus, the social provisions for dependent children during the first two centuries of American history can be characterized as meager arrangements made on a reluctant, begrudging basis to guarantee a minimal level of subsistence. The arrangements were designed to insure that children were taught the values of industriousness and hard work and received a strict religious upbringing. Provisions were made at the lowest cost possible for the local community, in part because of the widespread concern that indolence and depravity not be rewarded. Parents who were unable to provide for their children were thought to have abrogated their parental rights, and children were perceived primarily as property that could be disposed of according to the will of their owners—parents, masters, and/or public authorities who assumed the costs of their care. The goal was to make provisions for dependent children that would best serve the interests of the community, not the individual child.

NINETEENTH CENTURY

Massive social changes occurred in the United States during the nineteenth century, all of which influenced the nature of provisions for dependent children. The importation of large numbers of slaves and the eventual abolition of slavery first reduced the number of requests for indentured white children and later created opposition to a form of care for white children that was no longer permitted for blacks. The emergence of a bourgeois class of families in which the labor of children and wives was not required at home permitted upper-income citizens to turn their attention to the educational and developmental needs of their own children as well as the orphaned, poor, and delinquent. The large-scale economic growth of the country after the Civil War helped to expand the tax base and to free funds for the development of private philanthropies aimed at improving the lives of the poor. The massive wave of immigrants from countries other than England created a large pool of needy children, primarily Catholic and Jewish, from diverse cultural backgrounds. Finally, the Industrial Revolution changed the entire economic and social fabric of the nation. New industry required different, more dangerous types of labor from parents and youth and created a new set of environmental hazards and problems for low-income families.

The Rise of the Institution

Perhaps the most significant change in the pattern of care for dependent children during the early nineteenth century was the dramatic increase in the number of orphanages, especially during the 1830s. These facilities were established under public, voluntary, and sectarian auspices and were designed to care for children whose parents were unable to provide adequately for them, as well as for true orphans. Two reports issued in the 1820s contributed heavily to the decline of the earlier system of indenture and outdoor relief and to the expansion of congregate care facilities. The 1821 Report of the Massachusettes Committee on Pauper Laws concluded that "outdoor relief was the worst and almshouse care the most economical and best method of relief, especially when it provided opportunities for work."[4] The other report, known as the Yates Report of 1824, was issued by the secretary of state for New

York following a year's study of poor laws. This report took an even stronger position against outdoor relief and indenture and advocated the care of dependent children and adults in county-administered alms-houses. Mr. Yates concluded:

1. Removal of human beings like felons for no other fault than poverty seems inconsistent with the spirit of a system profess-ing to be founded on principles of pure benevolence and humanity.
2. The poor, when farmed out, or sold, are frequently treated with barbarity and neglect by their keepers . . .
3. The education and morals of the children of paupers (*except* in almshouses) are almost wholly neglected. They grow up in filth, illness, ignorance and disease, and many become early candidates for the prison or the grave . . . [5]

A major expansion in almshouse care occurred in the years succeed-ing the publication of these reports. But what was not foreseen by the early advocates of the use of almshouses were the physical and social risks to children posed by housing them with all classes of dependent adults. Although facilities in some of the larger cities established sepa-rate quarters for children, most were "mixed" almshouses caring for young children, "derelicts," the insane, the sick, the blind, the deaf, the retarded, the delinquent, and the poor alike.

By mid-century, investigations of the living conditions of children in poorhouses had started, creating strong pressure for the development of alternative methods of care. For example, a Select Committee of the New York State Senate reported on a study conducted in 1856, just thirty-two years after the publication of the Yates Report:

> The evidence taken by the committee exhibits such a record of filth, nakedness, licentiousness, general bad morals, and disregard of religion and the most common religious observances, as well as of gross neglect of the most ordinary comforts and decencies of life, as if published in detail would disgrace the State and shock humanity . . . They are for the young, notwithstanding the legal provision for their education, the worst possible nurseries; contributing an annual accession to our population of three hundred infants, whose present destiny is to pass their most impressible years in the midst of such vicious associations as will stamp them for a life of future infamy and crime . . . [6]

State after state issued similar reports, characterizing almshouses as symbols of human wretchedness and political corruption and calling for special provisions for the care of young children in orphanages under public or private auspices. But reform came slowly, in part because public funds had been invested in the poorhouses and in part because there were no readily available alternatives for the large number of children housed in these facilities. Therefore, laws prohibiting the care of children in mixed almshouses were not passed until the latter part of the century.[7]

Black dependent children who were not sold as slaves were cared for primarily in the local almshouses. They were explicitly excluded from most of the private orphanages established prior to the Civil War. Consequently, several separate facilities for black children were founded during this period, the first of which was the Philadelphia Association for the Care of Colored Children established by the Society of Friends in 1822. To insure the survival of these facilities, their founders attempted to separate the orphanages from the abolitionist movement, with which they were identified. However, the shelter in Philadelphia was burned by a white mob in 1838 and the Colored Orphan Asylum in New York was set on fire during the Draft Riot of 1863.[8]

The Beginnings of "Foster" Care

With the recognition of the condition of children cared for in mixed almshouses, the stage was set for a number of reform efforts. One such effort began in 1853 with the founding of the Children's Aid Society in New York by Charles Loring Brace. By the end of the century, Children's Aid Societies had been established in most of the other major eastern cities.

Brace was strongly committed to the idea that the best way to save poor children from the evils of urban life was to place them in Christian homes in the country, where they would receive a solid moral training and learn good work habits. Consequently, he recruited large numbers of free foster homes in the Midwest and upper New York State and sent trainloads of children to these localities. By 1879 the Children's Aid Society in New York City had sent 40,000 homeless or destitute children to homes in the country.[9]

A somewhat parallel development was the establishment of the Children's Home Society movement. These societies were statewide child-placing agencies under Protestant auspices, also designed to provide free foster homes for dependent children. The first such society was established by Martin Van Buren Van Arsdale in Illinois in 1883. His idea spread rapidly, and by 1916 there were thirty-six Children's Home Societies located primarily in midwestern and southern states.[10]

The free foster home movement was not without its critics for several reasons. First, although Brace and Van Arsdale viewed their programs as conceptually quite different from the indenture system of the past, in practice it was difficult to make such a distinction. Their arrangements involved essentially the same three-part contract between the family, the child, and the agency officially responsible for the child. Children were expected to pay for their bread and board through their labor. Investigations of the receiving families were minimal, and many reports were received of children who received poor treatment and were exposed to bad influences during their placement.

A second concern voiced was that foster families, almost by definition, did not have the structure and specialized resources necessary to ensure that children received a formal education and thorough training in the tenets of their own religion. Finally—and perhaps most significantly—a number of Roman Catholic leaders opposed this movement on the grounds that children were placed primarily in Protestant homes and were likely to lose their religious faith if they were not given the opportunity to be raised in Catholic settings.

The Care of Delinquent Youth

Parallel to the recognition that children are different from adults and need different forms of care came the realization that not all children should be cared for in the same way. While it had long been recognized that there were differences between dependent children who needed care because their parents could not provide for them and children who needed to be "punished" because they had committed criminal acts, early nineteenth-century America often cared for both groups in the same way—the almshouse. This had not been the case in colonial America; hence, reformers during this later period sought to reestablish differences in the care of these two groups of children.

Under English Common Law children over the age of seven who committed criminal offenses were treated the same as adults and subjected to harsh, cruel punishments such as whipping, mutilation, banishment, and even death. The early American colonies adopted very similar procedures and continued to use various forms of corporal punishment for children until the concept of confinement was introduced in the eighteenth century. The predominant mode of punishment shifted to various types of confinement, and by the beginning of the nineteenth century, many of the public almshouses and workhouses held a mixed population of juvenile and adult offenders as well as the dependent children and paupers for whom they were originally intended. This created pressure to establish special facilities for child offenders, and in 1824 the Society for the Reformation of Juvenile Delinquents established the New York City House of Refuge, an asylum for vagrant youth and juvenile offenders designed to provide work training and some formal education.[11]

Other cities quickly followed the New York example, and Lyman School, the first state reform school in the United States, opened in Massachusetts in 1848. Numerous other states established separate institutions for delinquent children in the years preceding and following the Civil War, all of which emphasized rigid discipline and hard work. Although many of these facilities were designed as experimental efforts in the reformation of troubled youth, they were forced to derive much of their income from the contracted labor of the juvenile inmates. This inevitably resulted in institutional corruption, exploitation, and brutal treatment of the youths. For example, one of the leading juvenile authorities of the day, William Letchworth, commented:

> While flogging has long been abolished in the Navy and the use of the "cat" in the state prisons, it is still thought necessary in order to realize a fair pecuniary return from the children's labor, for the contractor to inflict severe corporal punishment for deficiency in imposed tasks. One institution in the state, in order to meet the expectation of contractors, was forced in a single year to inflict on the boys employed . . . corporal punishment *two-thousand-two hundred-and-sixty-three times.*[12]

During the latter part of the century there were a number of investigations and exposés of institutional abuse in reform schools, and many public officials and concerned citizens made valiant attempts to improve the quality of life for youngsters in these facilities. But these reform efforts had little impact. Attention gradually turned to developing voluntary institutions for juvenile offenders and finding alternative, community-based means of caring for these youth. Massachusetts and Michigan passed laws permitting the appointment of state probation officers for delinquents, and several other states authorized voluntary aid societies to represent youth in court and supervise their probation. The passage of the first juvenile court law in 1899 represented what Bremner termed "the culmination of various efforts to reform children without committing them to reform schools."[13]

The development of the juvenile court has long been viewed by authorities in the child welfare field as a landmark event in the history of services to dependent and delinquent children. As suggested above, it did not represent a major shift in orientation; the reform efforts of the nineteenth century had been moving in the direction of an approach that emphasized the concept of treatment rather than punishment for youth who had committed delinquent offenses and of separate, individualized services for different groups of children. On the other hand, the passage of this law did signal a significant change in the degree to which courts would sanction state intervention in the lives of children.

The first juvenile court law in Illinois resulted from the efforts of a coalition of middle-class reform groups representing a range of civic, feminist, and children's interests. Two of the best-known leaders of this coalition were Julia Lathrop and Jane Addams. Frustrated by their inability to effect any basic reforms in the institutions caring for delinquent youth, they decided that more fundamental changes were necessary to insure that younsters could be removed from corrupting influences. But they needed to find a constitutionally acceptable basis for intervening in the lives of children considered at risk. After much effort a bill was worked out with a committee from the Chicago Bar Association giving the Illinois courts of equity jurisdiction over juvenile offenders. These noncriminal courts of equity derive from the English chancery courts that exercise the privilege of the state as *parens patriae* and do not require the application of rigid rules of law to permit state intervention designed to protect the interest of children.[14]

> It was believed that if children were separated from adult offenders and the judge dealt with the problems of "erring children" as a "wise and kind father"—as the statute creating the juvenile courts sometimes directed— wayward tendencies would be checked and delinquency and crime prevented or reduced. Under these laws the child offender was regarded not as a criminal but as a delinquent, "as misdirected and misguided and needing aid, encouragement, help, and assistance." The challenging and seminal idea which was back of the juvenile court was that its function was to cure, rather than to punish, delinquency—a very much more difficult task.[15]

The concept of the juvenile court took hold quickly, spreading rapidly throughout the United States and to various European countries during the early twentieth century. It has had a major impact on the development of children's services in the twentieth century. In fact, the debates engendered by the actions of the juvenile court regarding punishment versus treatment of juvenile offenders, and children's rights versus children's needs, persist to this day.

The Expansion of Services

Until the last quarter of the nineteenth century state intervention in a child's life occurred, for the most part, only when the child threatened the social order. Dominant members of society feared that dependent children would grow up without the moral guidance and education necessary to enable them to become productive members of society. Children violating the law posed not only an immediate threat but also the fear that, without intervention, they would grow up to be adult criminals.

During the latter part of the last century the focus of concern began to change. Voluntary organizations founded during this period recognized that families had an obligation to provide for their children's basic needs. If they did not, it was argued, society had the right and obligation to intervene. Thus, the concept of minimal social standards for child rearing was introduced.

The founding of the New York Society for the Prevention of Cruelty to Children in 1874 signaled the beginning of this broader concept of societal intervention on the child's behalf. Similar societies were quickly established in other areas of the country, and by 1900 there were more than 250 such agencies.[16] The New York society was established in the wake of the notorious case of "little Mary Ellen." A woman visiting in the child's neighborhood was horrified by the abusive treatment the child had received from her caretaker and sought help from several child welfare institutions to no avail. Finally she turned to Henry Bergh, president of the Society for the Prevention of Cruelty to Animals, who promptly brought the case to court, requesting that the child be removed from her caretaker immediately. "The apprehension and subsequent conviction of the persecutors of little Mary Ellen . . . suggested to Mr. Elbridge T. Gerry, the counsel engaged in the prosecution of the case, the necessity for the existence of an organized society for the prevention of similar acts of atrocity."[17]

Newspaper accounts of the early meetings of the society indicate that the founders saw their primary function as prosecuting parents, not providing direct services to parents or children; in fact, the society was denied tax-exempt status by the State of New York in 1900 because its primary purpose was defined as law enforcement, not the administration of charity.[18] However, this agency as well as the other early child protection societies quickly turned their interests to all forms of child neglect and exploitation, not confining their activities merely to the prevention of physical abuse of children in their own homes.

The establishment of the Charity Organization Society movement, starting in 1877, also contributed to the expansion of services to children. Founded as a response to unorganized outdoor relief and indiscriminant giving, these societies set out to rationalize charity. Initially their leaders perceived poverty as the fault and responsibility of the individual, and their programs were designed to help the individual correct the situation. They were opposed to monetary giving and to any public sector involvement in the relief of destitution; government was not to be trusted nor to provide a "dole," which would encourage laziness and moral decay.

In order to accomplish this mission, the societies enlisted the aid of "friendly visitors"—the forerunner of the modern social worker—whose responsibilities were to seek out the poor, investigate their need, and certify them as worthy for private help. They were to provide a role model, advice, and moral instruction to the poor in order that they could rid themselves of poverty. These ideas had a profound influence on the orientation of the early social workers in the family service field.

However, what the friendly visitors discovered was that much poverty was the result of societal forces far beyond the individual's control. Many children were destitute not because their parents were lazy or immoral, but because jobs were not available, breadwinners were incapacitated by industrial accidents, or parents had died. While the friendly visitors continued to minister to the poor on a case-by-case basis, their recognition of the social roots of poverty converged with the philosophy underlying the establishment of the first settlement houses at the end of the nineteenth century.

The settlement house movement was a middle-class movement designed to humanize the cities. It emphasized total life involvement, decentralization, experimental modes of intervention, and learning by doing. Although the early leaders shared the Charity Organization Societies' suspicion of public institutions, they were influenced by the concepts of philosophical idealism and pragmatism that shaped the Progressive Era. Consequently, they had a more communal orientation, were concerned about environmental as well as individual change, and placed a strong priority on empirical investigation of social conditions. Their programs included "developmental" services such as language classes, day-care centers, playgrounds, family life education, and so forth. Convinced of the worth of the individuals and immigrant groups they served and the importance of cultural pluralism in America, they saw the causes of many social problems in the environment and sought regulations to improve them.

Thus, by the end of the nineteenth century, services were expanded to protect children and provide for some of their developmental needs within their own homes and communities. Such services were further developed and expanded in the twentieth century.

The Administration of Services

By the last quarter of the nineteenth century two distinct systems of out-of-home care for children had evolved to replace the care of children in mixed almshouses: free foster homes and children's institutions. Four different models were eventually adopted to administer these systems, each typified by the respective provisions of the laws enacted in Massachusetts, New York, Michigan, and Ohio.[19]

In Massachusetts, almshouse care for children was abolished in 1879, and legislation was passed in 1887 requiring that city overseers place dependent children in private homes. If cities failed to comply, the State Board of Charities was authorized to place them at the expense of the local communities. Although some private institutions had been established in the state earlier in the century, there was little public subsidy for these facilities. Hence, the Massachusetts solution was primarily a system of state and locally funded foster home care for dependent children.[20]

A very different approach was followed in New York State after the care of children in almshouses was prohibited in 1875. Local communities were given the responsibility of planning for these children and had the option of providing either subsidies to private agencies or developing a county-based system of public care. However, an earlier law required that children be placed in facilities under the auspice of the same religious faith as their parents, and sectarian agencies were pressing hard for subsidy. Consequently, a system developed whereby local communities paid a per capita subsidy to voluntary, primarily sectarian, agencies for the care of dependent children.[21]

Michigan adopted still another approach after almshouse care for children was prohibited in 1881. A state school for dependent children had been established in 1871, which included a program to investigate and supervise foster homes for children placed by the school. This facility became the major resource for dependent children, although local counties were permitted to provide their own care and a few elected to do so.[22]

Finally, instead of developing a state program of care as Michigan did, the Ohio legislature authorized the establishment of children's homes or orphanages in each local county.[23]

Each of the remaining states adopted a slightly different model of care following the abolition of almshouse care for children. However, these tended to cluster around the example of one of the four state plans described above, and remnants of these patterns of service provision can be seen in the ways child welfare services are organized in different states today. The major distinctions are related to the allocation of responsibility between state, county, and local governmental units; the relative emphasis given to foster home versus institutional care; and the degree of public reliance on and subsidy of voluntary agency services.

Related to the development of state systems of child care was the introduction of state policies and procedures for licensing and regulating child care facilities. As Grace Abbott noted in her classic documentary history, *The Child and the State:*

> Most of the states drifted into the policy of aiding private institutions because they were unwilling to accept responsibility for the care of the dependent, and because it seemed to be cheaper to grant some aid to private institutions than for the state to provide public care. . . . Private agencies increased and expanded when public funds became available, and as the money was easily obtained, they accepted children without sufficient investigation of the family needs and resources and kept them permanently or long after they could have been released to their families. This was costly to the taxpayer, but even more important, large numbers of children were deprived of normal home life by this reckless policy.[24]

Later she goes on to say:

> The responsibility of the state to know how all its dependent children are cared for was not recognized and was little discussed until the end of the nineteenth century. . . .
> At the meetings of the National Conference of Charities and Correction, discussion of the need and the results that might be expected from state supervision of child caring agencies began during the nineties. The case for state responsibility was well put at that time although the administrators' problems were not fully appreciated. . . . It was pointed out that the state should know where its dependent children are, its agents should visit and inspect institutions and agencies at regular intervals—including local public as well as all private agencies—and both should be required to make full reports to the State. Usually welcomed and even demanded by the best private agencies, state supervision was opposed by the poorer agencies and by many individuals who thought a private charity sponsored by a church or one which included the names of leading citizens on the list of board members was, of course, well-administered.[25]

What is important about these comments from a historical perspective is that by the turn of the century, leaders in the child welfare field had begun to recognize (1) the state's responsibility for all dependent children, (2) the potential conflict between agencies' needs for ongoing funding and support and children's need for permanency planning, and (3) the importance of instituting strong regulatory systems including licensing, service monitoring, and case accountability to protect the interests of children in the child care system.

Thus, by the end of the nineteenth century the roots had been laid for a complex system of child care. Dependent children were cared for by one group of agencies providing institutional and foster care services. Child offenders were being cared for in a different system. Still a third set of agencies, characterized by the Charity Organization Societies and the settlement houses, had started to care for children in their "own homes" in organized ways.

THE TWENTIETH CENTURY

The developments at the end of the last century set the stage for what were to become the hallmarks of the child welfare field during the twentieth century: bureaucratization, professionalization, and expanded state intervention in the lives of families and children. The social status of children was elevated, but this came at the price of some loss of individual freedom and some diminution of voluntary involvement and community control. Bremner notes:

> As the state intervened more frequently and effectively in the relations between parent and child in order to protect children against parental mismanagement, the state also forced children to conform to public norms of behavior and obligation. Thus the child did not escape control; rather he experienced a partial exchange of masters in which the ignorance, neglect, and exploitation of some parents were replaced by presumably fair and uniform treatment at the hands of public authorities and agencies. The transfer of responsibilities required an elaboration of administration and judicial techniques of investigation, decision, and supervision.[26]

Some of the very factors contributing to the current dilemmas in child welfare are directly related to these shifts in responsibility.

The Children's Bureau

The first major event affecting the development of child welfare services in this century was the establishment of the U.S. Children's Bureau in 1912, three years after the first White House Conference on Children. The movement to create a federal agency representing children's interests was led by Jane Addams and Lillian Wald and included a coalition of leaders from the state boards of charities and corrections, voluntary social service agencies, settlement houses, labor and women's groups, and the National Child Labor Committee. Although the initial funding for the Children's Bureau was very small, restricting the number and range of activities it could undertake, it was given a very broad mandate to:

> Investigate and report . . . upon all matters pertaining to the welfare of children and child life among all classes of our people, and . . . investigate the questions of infant mortality, the birth rate, orphanage, juvenile courts, desertion, dangerous occupations, accidents and diseases of children, employment, legislation affecting children in the several states and territories.[27]

What was most significant about the passage of this law was that it represented the first Congressional recognition that the federal government has a responsibility for the welfare of children. It also introduced the concept of public responsibility for *all* children, not just the groups of poor, neglected, disturbed, and delinquent children served by public and private agencies. Julia Lathrop was appointed the first chief of the Children's Bureau, and under her skilled leadership, the office gained widespread public support and multiplied its annual budget rapidly, enabling its staff to undertake a wide range of investigatory, reporting, and educational activities. The Sheppard-Towner Act of 1921 gave the Bureau responsibility for administering grants-in-aid to the states for maternal and child health programs, thereby expanding its influence even further and introducing the concept of federal payment for direct service provision.

The entry of the federal government into the children's field did not occur without conflict. The initial bill authorizing the establishment of the bureau was opposed by some of the leaders in the voluntary social welfare sector who feared governmental monitoring and scrutiny and by others who viewed the creation of such a federal agency as an unnecessary intrusion on states' rights. The debate on the Sheppard-Towner Act was more vitriolic, perhaps because of the early successes of the Children's Bureau, and perhaps because by 1921 the country had again entered a more conservative social era. For example, a senator from Kansas commented:

> Fundamentally the scheme of the bill amounts to this: We are asked to select from all the millions of women of the United States four or five spinsters, whose unofficial advice would probably not be sought by a single mother in the land . . .; we are asked to confer upon these inexperienced ladies a title and salary, whereupon it is assumed they will immediately become endowed with wisdom and be qualified to instruct the mother, who has been with her baby before it was born and after it was born, how to take care of that baby. Also it is assumed that this band of lady officials can perform that function in the homes of a hundred and ten million people. . . .

> To what purpose do we make this revolutionary change? Why do we create this new army of government employees? . . .
> If it is claimed that the Children's Bureau is to devote its attention chiefly to the poor, my answer is that the poor are entitled to the best as well as the rich. . . . But this is not the purpose of the bill. I repeat that its basic idea is that the American people do not know how to take care of themselves; and that the state must force its official nose into the private homes of the people; that a system of espionage must be established over every woman about to give birth to a child and over the child, at least until it arrives at school age. . . .[28]

Despite periodic attacks such as these, the Children's Bureau continued to serve as the primary governmental agency representing the interests of children for many years. The activities of the Children's Bureau changed considerably over the years as the leadership shifted from those concerned with broad economic and social issues affecting the welfare of children to those who focused more narrowly on issues and problems in the child welfare field. But despite differing emphases and varying levels of influence, it has continued to carry out its primary functions of investigation, advocacy, standard setting, public education, research, and demonstration.

Early Developments in the Organization and Provision of Services

During the first three decades of this century, many of the trends in child welfare initiated during the late nineteenth century continued. In part because of the leadership of the Children's Bureau, notable progress was made during the early part of the century in improving the administration of child welfare services. An increased number of public child welfare agencies were established; separate children's bureaus or divisions within the department of public welfare were created in some of the more progressive states; many states moved to county-based rather than local systems of service provision; and state departments of welfare assumed increased responsibility for setting standards, licensing, and regulation of public and voluntary child care facilities.

Before 1935 the states had little leverage for influencing service provision at the local or county level. But Alabama assumed the lead in developing a coordinated system of state and county child welfare services, in part via the use of state grants-in-aid to counties for administration of the state truancy law. As additional numbers of state grants-in-aid were made available, other states followed this model.

Significant progress was also made in establishing civil service standards for the hiring and promotion of personnel in child welfare positions, insuring that more qualified persons were available to carry out what were increasingly being recognized as professional tasks.[29]

Two major national voluntary organizations concerned with standard setting, coordination, agency accreditation, research, and knowledge dissemination in the field of family and children's services were established during this period: the American Association for Organizing Family Social Work (later the Family Service Association of America) in 1919 and the Child Welfare League of America in 1920. Both of these organizations have had a long and continuing record of influence on the nature of family and child welfare services especially in relation to the role of the social work profession in this service arena.

Also during this era the long, rather notable history of child welfare research was initiated with the publication in 1924 of Sophie Van Theis's outcome study of 910 children placed in foster care by the New York State Charities Aid Association.[30] Although it is never certain what combination of facts, values, and external social circumstances contribute to the shaping of public policy in a specific service domain, it is clear that the extensive research on child welfare services conducted since this first study has contributed heavily to the various ongoing debates regarding goals and models of service provision.

The scope and level of juvenile court activities also increased considerably during this period in spite of the concerns expressed by some immigrant and minority groups about excessive state intervention in their children's lives. By 1919 all but three states had passed juvenile court legislation, and the jurisdiction of the court had been extended in many locations.[31] Also related to increased court intervention in family life were the expansion of court services, the assignment of the work of the courts to specialists trained in social investigation, the establishment of the first court clinic in Chicago in 1909 by psychologist William Healy, and the initiation of the child guidance movement a few years later with the founding of the Judge Baker Clinic in Boston. These developments both reflected and contributed to a different understanding of the causes and solutions for juvenile delinquency, leading to a greater emphasis on individual treatment of children in the community and a blurring of the distinctions between delinquent, disturbed, and dependent youth.

Protective services for children were also expanded during this period, especially after 1912 when public agencies began to be charged with responsibility for this population.[32] These agencies gradually moved away from their earlier emphasis on law enforcement, focusing on providing casework services to parents to permit children to remain in their own homes.

At the same time foster boarding homes and child care institutions for dependent children continued to expand. And the debate regarding the relative merits of foster homes versus institutions, a debate that traditionally had strong religious overtones because of the lack of sufficient foster homes for Roman Catholic and Jewish children, continued well into the 1920s.[33]

Another significant development of the 1920s was the establishment of adoption as a child welfare service. Informal adoptions had, of course, occurred since early colonial days, and laws providing for public record of the legal transfer of parental rights from biological parents to adoptive parents were passed in the mid-nineteenth century in a number of states. But public recognition of the need to protect the interests of children in these transactions did not develop until the early twentieth century. Minnesota was the first state to pass a law in 1917 requiring that judges refer nonrelative adoption cases to a voluntary or public welfare agency for investigation prior to approval of the petition to adopt; by 1938 twenty-four states had passed similar legislation.[34]

It is important to note that although these investigations were designed to insure that the biological family ties had been appropriately terminated and that the adopting parents could provide adequate care and would accept full parental responsibilities, adoption at the time was viewed primarily as a service for couples unable to have children of their own, not as a service for dependent children in need of care. Adoption was provided only for young, healthy, white children, most of whom were born out of wedlock to middle-class women. This service was seldom planned for children of the poor. Moreover, although public agencies carried out many of the court-ordered investigations of adoptive parents, separate adoption services were established only under voluntary auspices. Adoption was not considered a right or even a need of dependent children in care of public agencies.[35]

Expansion of In-Home Services

In reviewing various developments in the organization and provision of children's services during the early twentieth century, special emphasis must be given to Bremner's comment: "The great discovery of the era was that the best place for normal children was in their own homes. This idea conflicted with the widespread dislike of public relief but coincided with the philanthropic desire to preserve the integrity of the family."[36] Delegates to the first White House Conference on Children in 1909 went on record as supporting the following principles:

1. Home life is the highest and finest product of civilization. . . . Children should not be deprived of it except for urgent and compelling reasons. Children of parents of working character, suffering from temporary misfortune, and children of reasonably efficient and deserving mothers who are without the support of the normal breadwinners, should as a rule be kept with their parents, such aid being given as may be necessary to maintain suitable homes for the rearing of the children. . . .
2. The most important and valuable philanthropic work is not the curative, but the preventive; to check dependency by a thorough study of its causes and by effectively remedying or eradicating them should be the constant aim of society. . . .[37]

Progress was made in the succeeding years toward the goal of maintaining children in their own homes by the institution of mothers' pensions or public aid to dependent children in their own homes. Illinois provided leadership in this direction by passing a Funds to Parents Act in 1911, and twenty other states passed similar legislation within the next two years. By 1935 all but two states had passed some type of mothers' aid laws.[38] These funds were provided on a very restricted, limited, and somewhat arbitrary basis. But even this small improvement in public assistance provisions for children in their own homes did not take place without controversy. For example, in 1912 Mary Richmond, author of the first basic text on social casework, is quoted as saying:

So far from being a forward step, "funds to parents" is a backward one—public funds not to widows only, mark you, but to private families, funds to the families of those who have deserted and are going to desert.[39]

Edward Devine, director of the New York School of Social Work, took a similar position, challenging the proposal for mothers' pensions:

. . . as having no claim to the name of pension and no place in a rational scheme or social legislation; as embodying no element of prevention or radical cure for any recognized social evil; as an insidious attack upon the family, inimical to the welfare of children and injurious to the character of parents. . . .[40]

However, other leading social reformers and social workers of the time vigorously supported the concept of maintaining children in their own families, and by 1923 "the number of dependent children being maintained in their own homes was approaching the number of those in institutions and far in excess of those in foster homes."[41] A statement from the annual report of the New York Children's Aid Society for 1923 conveys the consensus that was gradually emerging among professional child welfare workers:

> There is a well-established conviction on the part of social workers that no child should be taken from his natural parents until everything possible has been done to build up the home into what an American home should be. Even after a child has been removed, every effort should be continued to rehabilitate the home and when success crowns one's efforts, the child should be returned. In other words, every social agency should be a "home builder" and not a "home breaker."[42]

The nature of services provided to dependent children was modified still further during the 1920s by the growing preoccupation of leading social work educators with psychoanalytic theory and individual treatment. In conjunction with an expanded professional knowledge base about the developmental needs of children and adolescents, this trend led to widespread adoption of the goal of providing individualized services to dependent children and attending to their emotional needs as well as to their needs for economic security. For example, in 1930 Henry Thurston commented:

> What religion and theology have told us of the further needs of children to whom bread alone has been given, we have often failed to understand; but we are slowly learning to understand it as it is being restated for us in terms of the new psychology of the emotions and of behaviors. Dr. Herman Adler, of the Juvenile Psychopathic Institute of Chicago . . . says that to answer the question fully as to what a child needs, we must understand "a total personality in a total situation."[43]

This expanded understanding of children's emotional needs contributed greatly to the development of improved child welfare services, but it had two unfortunate consequences. First, it led to increased emphasis on individual psychopathology rather than social conditions as the source of family and child dysfunctioning and hence to the expansion of psychological rather than environmental services in the voluntary child care sector. Second, it contributed to the increased separation of voluntary family service and child welfare agencies, as the former were more likely to be staffed by professional workers interested in providing pure "casework," that is, counseling, whereas workers in the latter were required to provide a broader range of services.

These early twentieth-century developments in the field of family and children's services had a major impact on the nature and scope of programs designed to help American families cope with the economic and social problems experienced in the aftermath of the depression that began in 1929. The trends that had special significance for subsequent policy and program development were:

—expansion of public sector involvement in the lives of families and children.

—intensification of the traditional separation between the public and voluntary service sectors especially in the eastern and midwestern states where the voluntary agencies were firmly entrenched.

—increasing preoccupation with psychological modes of treatment, especially among professional workers in the voluntary sector as they relinquished responsibility for traditional forms of alms giving and concrete service provision.

—the crystallizing of boundaries between voluntary child welfare and family service fields due to increasing emphasis on specialization in out-of-home versus in-home treatment.

Special Arrangements for the Care of Black Children

The history of child welfare services prior to the passage of the Social Security Law in 1935 is essentially a history of services for white children. Standard texts on the history of child welfare provide little information on services for black children; in fact, because of the middle-class white bias that has pervaded most studies of American history, relatively little was known about services for black families and children until the publication in 1971 of a text by Billingsley and Giovannoni on black children and American child welfare.[44]

Because black children were systematically excluded from the child welfare services that developed for white children in the late nineteenth and early twentieth centuries—sometimes by explicit exclusionary clauses, sometimes by more subtle forms of discrimination—the black community developed what was essentially a separate system of care for their dependent children. During the period after the Civil War black children were cared for through a variety of informal helping arrangements and through a range of orphanages, old folks and children's homes, day nurseries, and homes for working girls.[45]

This picture remained relatively constant until the 1920s when several converging factors led to changes in the child welfare system's response to black children. One was the establishment in 1910 of the National Urban League, an organization that took a vocal, active role in pressing for more equitable distribution of child welfare services as part of its broader mission to achieve freedom and equality for all blacks. Another major impetus for change was the large-scale migration of blacks to urban areas during and after World War I, a development that forced increased recognition of the needs of black children. Finally, the changes taking place in the child welfare system itself created greater openness to black children: the number of public facilities increased; many of the voluntary agencies changed their exclusionary intake policies; and the shift from institution to foster home as the predominate form of care permitted agencies to recruit black foster homes for black children, thereby avoiding potential racial tensions.[46]

Thus by 1930 there was a general expectation, strongly supported by the participants at the White House Conference on Children, that black children were entitled to the same standards of care as white children and that they should generally be served through the existing child welfare system. This changed perception of the needs of black children had obvious benefits in relation to the goal of racial integration. But it also had several unfortunate consequences, as it halted the growth of the black child care system, limited the possibility of blacks assuming leadership roles in agencies caring for black children, and served to hide some of the subtler but ongoing forms of discriminatory treatment of black children in the child welfare system.[47]

Passage of the Social Security Act

It has often been suggested that the legislation introduced in the first one hundred days of the Roosevelt administration in 1933 changed the entire social fabric of the country by redefining the role of the federal government in addressing social welfare problems and moving the United States reluctantly, but inexorably, toward becoming a welfare state.[48] Certainly the Social Security Act, passed in 1935, had a major impact on the structure and financing of child welfare services; in fact, some of the deficiencies in the current service system can be traced directly to the provisions of this law (see Chapter 3). Yet the roots of many of the current policy dilemmas and service delivery problems were present before the passage of this law.

To summarize briefly, the emerging issues in the child welfare field prior to 1935 can be characterized as follows:

1. The goals of child welfare services had begun to shift, *in principle,* from rescuing the children of poor families and providing them a minimal level of substance, moral guidance,

and work training via the provision of substitute care to providing the supports necessary to enable parents to care adequately for children in their own homes, arranging substitute care only on the basis of individualized assessment of case need.

2. The concept of state intervention in family life to protect the interests of children was gaining increased acceptance, and efforts had been made to expand societal provisions and protections for all children via the establishment of free compulsory education, child labor protections, the development of limited homemaker services, day nurseries, maternal and child health programs, mothers' pensions, and child guidance clinics.

3. As a consequence of the establishment of the juvenile court, juvenile offenders were receiving more individualized treatment, a larger number of youth were coming under the purview of the legal system, and the boundaries between the child welfare and criminal justice systems were becoming increasingly blurred.

4. The increasing bureaucratization and professionalization of the child welfare field, while improving standards for service and highlighting the goal of providing equal treatment to all, also functioned to increase the social distance between service providers and consumers and to deepen the gap between the goals and realities of service provision.

5. Large numbers of children continued to be placed in substitute care arrangements with little individualized case planning.

6. Black children continued to receive inferior, more punitive treatment than whites; and poor families and children served through the public sector were less likely to receive the intensive individualized treatment available to those served by some of the voluntary, primarily sectarian, agencies.

7. Adoption was viewed as a service designed primarily for adoptive parents, and white, healthy infants of middle-class unmarried mothers were the only children likely to be placed in adoptive homes.

Two components of the Social Security Act of 1935, both stemming in large measure from the recommendation of the Children's Bureau, had a significant impact on the subsequent development of child welfare services. Title IV, Grants to States for Aid to Dependent Children, sought to extend the concept of mothers' pensions by providing federal matching funds for grants to fatherless families, requiring a single state agency to administer the program, and mandating coverage of all political subdivisions in each state. It was designed as a federal grant-in-aid program and permitted state autonomy in setting eligibility standards, determining payment levels, and developing administrative and operational procedures. The program, later named Aid to Families of Dependent Children (AFDC), was eventually extended to families with a permanently and totally disabled parent, and, at state option, to families with an unemployed parent. Although the AFDC program has become increasingly expensive and controversial, it has undoubtedly contributed more than any other social program to the goal of enabling children at risk of placement to remain with their own families.

The other major component of the Social Security Act affecting the provision of child welfare services was Title V, Part 3, Child Welfare Services. This program was designed not only to help children in their own families, but also to benefit those in substitute care by "... enabling the United States, through the Children's Bureau, to cooperate with State public welfare agencies in establishing, extending, and strengthening, especially in predominantly rural areas, public welfare services ... for the protection and care of homeless, dependent, and neglected children, and children in danger of becoming delinquent ...."[49] Although the funding for this program was quite modest, states quickly took advantage of this relatively permissive legislation to obtain federal funding for child welfare services. To illustrate, prior to the passage of the Social Security law, the organization of child welfare services at the state and county was in relative disarray in most jurisdictions. However, by 1938, all but one state had submitted a plan for the coordinated delivery of child welfare services.[50] This component of the Social Security Act, later subsumed under Title IV-B, has had continuing influence on the development of child welfare services (see Chapter 3).

1940–1960

The period from the late 1930s to the late 1950s was a time of relative quiet, consolidation, and gain for the child welfare field. The total number and rate of children placed in foster home and institutional care declined substantially after 1933,[51] while the proportion of children receiving services in their own homes, the total public expenditures for child welfare, and the total number of professional staff in public child welfare increased significantly during this period.[52] Major strides were made by the Children's Bureau and the Child Welfare League of America in formulating and monitoring standards for service provision. Every state made significant progress in developing public comprehensive, coordinated child welfare services, insuring equal access to children of different social, economic, and ethnic backgrounds, and expanding professional educational opportunities for child welfare staff.[53] And because of the growing emphasis in the social work profession on the development of clinical knowledge and skills, the quality of individual services provided to families and children was greatly enhanced during this period.

The only significant shifts in service provision during these years took place in the voluntary sector, partly as a consequence of the public sector's assumption of many of the functions formerly assumed by private agencies, and partly as the result of demographic changes. The Child Welfare League of America published its first standards for adoption practice in 1938, and many agencies initiated and expanded adoption services in the years after World War II. More elaborate procedures were instituted for studying potential adoptive couples, "matching" children and families, and monitoring the adoptive families during the period preceding legal adoption. Adoption studies were frequently assigned to the most experienced staff, and adoption workers began to acquire special status in the child welfare field. Although the emphasis shifted from viewing adoption primarily as a service for parents to seeing the child as the primary client, in most settings healthy white infants continued to be considered the only real candidates for adoption. However, as the number of adoptive applicants increased, a few agencies began to experiment with intercountry and interracial adoptions. Also, the National Urban League sponsored a major project on foster care and adoption of black children from 1953 to 1958, and a five-year interagency demonstration adoption project was established by thirteen adoption agencies in the New York City area in 1955 to develop and implement methods of recruiting adoptive families for black and Puerto Rican children.[54]

During the 1940s and 1950s increased emphasis was also given to services for unmarried mothers. Although illegitimacy is a centuries-old social problem and special programs for unwed mothers were developed in this country early in the century, the historical concern was the protection of the child and the punishment of the mother. It was not until the late 1930s that social workers started to focus attention on the needs of the unmarried mother. During the next two decades there was a great upsurge in social work publications on the psychodynamic causes of unwed motherhood, the meaning and potential benefits of surrendering a child for adoption, the role of the caseworker in working with unmarried mothers and so forth.[55] As the illegitimate birthrate began to increase following World War II, many voluntary child welfare agencies established special services for unwed parents incorporating these new theoretical insights.[56]

During this same period there was also a marked shift in the types of institutional care provided to dependent youth as many of the traditional child care facilities began to be converted into various types of residential treatment centers. For example, in 1950, 45 percent of the white children in residential care were in institutions for dependent children, and 25 percent were in institutions for the mentally disabled. By 1960 only 29 percent were in child care institutions, and 36 percent were in facilities for the mentally disabled. Although the distribution of nonwhite children showed a similar trend, in 1960 over half of the nonwhite children (54 percent) were confined in correctional facilities compared to only 25 percent of the white children,[57] suggesting that the trend toward individualized treatment planning was not strong enough to counter patterns of racially discriminatory treatment.

The relatively slow pace of change in the child welfare field during the 1940s and 1950s can be explained in part by the fact that social workers were forced to deal with other, more pressing problems—the aftermath of the depression and World War II. They then needed time to implement, refine, and expand existing services before turning their attention to new service needs. Much professional energy during this period was also devoted to exploring psychological problems, improving casework methods, and enhancing professional status by providing service to clients above the poverty line. Most child welfare workers during this period tended to view the provision of individual casework services as the most prestigious and critical of their professional tasks. Having been relieved of their earlier public assistance functions, social workers were endeavoring to provide high-quality therapeutic services to the clients who happened to request help from their agencies. They raised few questions about what was happening to the families and children not referred for casework services or to those who were unable to benefit from the types of service offered in the established family service and child welfare agencies.

While the problems of the poor were brought to the attention of the profession again in the 1950s with the publication of several studies discussing efforts to work with "multiproblem," "disorganized," and "hard-to-reach" families,[58] these developments served primarily to stimulate workers to seek more effective ways of providing existing modes of casework service to this population. Although it was clear that this subgroup of poor families was demanding a disproportionate amount of attention from public assistance, family service, child welfare, and public health agencies, direct service providers gave relatively little thought to their inability to work effectively with this population. Questions that should have been raised about the organization of services and the effectiveness of prevailing interventive strategies were rarely discussed.

The 1960s

Early in the 1960s child welfare agencies began to be severely criticized for their failure to attend to the changing needs of the child welfare population. The first major challenge to the field was the publication of Maas and Engler's study, *Children in Need of Parents,* in 1959.[59] This study of children in foster care in nine communities posed many of the questions raised repeatedly since that time about children in "limbo," children who had drifted into foster care, had no permanent family ties, and were not being prepared for adoptive placement. The field has been attacked repeatedly in succeeding years—both from within and without —for its failure to insure permanency planning, its inability to prevent placement, its failure to place children in need of protection, its inherent racism and classism, its anti-family bias, its violation of parents' and children's rights, its arbitrary decision-making procedures, the incompetency and inefficiency of its staff, its costs, and its mismanagement.[60]

The juvenile court has also come under attack. Several recent histories of American child welfare have challenged the traditional view of the juvenile court as protecting the interests of children and representing a radical change in their treatment. For example, in their analysis of the impact of the American child welfare system on black children, Billingsley and Giovannoni suggest that the labeling process by which black youth were described a "delinquent" in order to remove them from what were considered the less acceptable nineteenth-century forms of child care forced them to accept a more socially deviant label and to enter a less desirable system of care than that available to white youth.[61] And Anthony Platt concludes his study of the movement to create the juvenile court in the late nineteenth century as follows:

> The child savers should in no sense be considered libertarians or humanists . . . The child-saving movement was not so much a break with the past as an affirmation of faith in certain aspects of the past. Parental authority, home education, domesticity, and rural values were emphasized because they were in decline as institutions at this time. . . . In a rapidly changing and increasingly complex urban society, the child-saving philosophy represented a defense against "foreign" ideologies and a preservation of cherished values.[62]

These attacks have done much to refocus attention on the problems in the field and to set a number of internal reform processes in motion. But the more significant determinant of changes in the child welfare field during the past two decades has been the external environment: the demographic shifts, political events, changing economic and social conditions, shifting interest groups, and belief systems that shape the context in which child welfare services operate.

The inauguration of the Kennedy administration in 1961 ushered in an era of tremendous social ferment and change. The major issues and themes of these past two decades are probably well known to the reader, at least in broad strokes. But to recap briefly, in the 1960s we witnessed the rediscovery of poverty as a public issue; the ill-fated War on Poverty under the Johnson administration; the expansion of the civil rights movement, leading to the passage of the 1964 Civil Rights Act and the subsequent shocking realization that the guarantee of civil rights alone could not insure justice; the emergence of the concept of black power and the racial conflicts of the late 1960s; the development of the welfare rights movement and the establishment of other related types of clients' rights groups; the burgeoning of a youth culture that symbolized many challenges to traditional American values and mores; and the perpetuation of an unpopular war that contributed to the growing distrust and alienation of large segments of the population from governmental institutions.

The forces for change began to shift slightly in the 1970s. The women's liberation movement exploded on the American scene; blacks and other minority groups organized to develop political and economic power; the call for affirmative action and equal treatment replaced the push for civil rights and equal opportunities; self-help and advocacy groups representing a wide range of interests such as children, prisoners, homosexuals, mental patients, physically disabled and retarded citizens, and single parents began to recognize the sources of their own oppression and to organize more effectively to secure their rights. Quite inevitably, "middle America" began to react. Concern was growing about the national economy, rampant inflation, and unemployment; the United States seemed to be losing its status as a world power and leader of the forces for good; fear of crime was becoming universal; the role of the churches was declining; the problems of divorce, delinquency, illegitimacy, and drug abuse could no longer be viewed solely as the province of the poor; historical allocations of power and resources were changing; and traditional values, beliefs, and modes of behavior no longer seemed to bring promised results.

In some ways all of these pressures seem very far removed from recent developments in the child welfare field, but unfortunately they are intimately related. The children served by this system—poor, often minority, neglected, dependent, abused, delinquent, and disturbed—constitute the very populations that should have benefited most from the broad social reform efforts of the past two decades. Yet these youngsters and their families continue to be troublesome to the larger community, and their very visibility and vulnerability make them convenient scapegoats for the inadequacies and failures of these recent reform efforts and for the discomfort and alienation experienced by so many families today.

The child welfare field of the early 1960s was a relatively small, self-contained service system with limited staff and resources. It maintained rather rigid system boundaries, making it difficult for many children and families to gain access to services and equally difficult for other clients to be discharged from care. Quality and coverage were very uneven; while some agencies, primarily in the voluntary sector, were providing intensive, highly specialized, professional services to a small number of select clients, other public and voluntary agencies struggled to provide minimum care and protection to large numbers of needy youngsters. Services were geared almost entirely toward placement, and individual casework was the primary interventive modality. Concepts of a community control and clients' rights were essentially nonexistent.[63]

Although the Children's Bureau attempted to provide leadership and direction via the promulgation of standards and the administration of small research and demonstration grants, until the late 1960s overall federal participation in the child welfare field was minimal. Organizational and funding arrangements varied from state to state, but some combination of state and local responsibility for service provision was utilized in most areas. The participation of the public sector in the financing and direct provision of child care services had increased steadily since the turn of the century, but control of program planning and development, service priorities and policies, and program monitoring and evaluation remained primarily in the voluntary sector under the auspices of local coordinating councils and welfare planning bodies.[64] Consequently, there were minimal efforts to insure case integration or program coordination within the child welfare system; boundaries and linkages between child welfare and other social service systems were frequently haphazard, often dysfunctional; and agency accountability mechanisms were minimal.

The findings of a study by Ryan and Morris of the child welfare networks in metropolitan Boston in 1964 illustrate quite graphically the nature of the child welfare services in this era. Although there were obviously some idiosyncratic factors in the way services were organized in Boston, the consequences for families and children seeking help within the existing service network were not atypical of the experiences of similar clients in other areas of the country at the time. The study consisted of an examination for five weeks in 1964 of the total intake (N = 683) of thirteen public, voluntary, and sectarian agencies constituting the basic child welfare network for the metropolitan area and an intensive case reading analysis of the 265 cases ultimately accepted for service.[65]

The study revealed that the child welfare network consisted of two relatively independent systems, one serving the suburban, white-collar, unmarried mother–adoptive family population; and the other, the urban-poor "child-in-family-in-trouble" population. Approximately 29 percent of the service inquiries could be categorized as unmarried mothers, 21 percent as child problems, and 50 percent as parenting problems. The agencies responded very differently to the requests for help, accepting about 65 percent of the unmarried mother cases, 34 percent of the child problem cases, and 29 percent of the parental problem situations. Moreover, the data suggest that intake decisions were made on a very stereotypical basis, largely unrelated to individual case need.[66]

The agency network dealing with the unmarried mother population seemed to provide relatively efficient and effective services, helping women to plan for the birth of their children and arranging a significant number of adoptions. However, this population represented only about one-third of the total number of illegitimate births in the metropolitan area that year; little was known about the much larger number of unmarried mothers who did not approach the child welfare network for help and/or were not accepted for service if they did request assistance.[67]

The other child welfare network attempted to serve a very different population of parents and children, many of whom were low-income urban residents, had long-standing familial difficulties, and presented a range of environmental, parent-child relationship, and mental health problems. For these clients, the child welfare system was clearly viewed as the end of the line. They were usually referred by the community after other attempts at service provision had failed and placement was seen as the only solution. Yet only about one-third of these cases were actually accepted for services. Little is known about what happened to the other potential clients, all of whom were apparently in need of intensive child welfare services.[68]

Based on their findings, the authors concluded that the concept of a comprehensive child welfare service network in metropolitan Boston was essentially a myth. The lack of flexibility in intake policies and decision-making processes, combined with the lack of resources necessary to deal with the magnitude of the problem, made it impossible for the participating agencies to accept and serve many of the clients appropriately referred for services. Ryan and Morris's recommendations reflected the thinking of many other leaders in the field at the time: the development of a comprehensive, public family and children's service system; joint planning between the public and voluntary child welfare sectors; development of rational policies on specialization by voluntary agencies; expanded resources, financing, and staff; development of joint planning, coordinating, and accountability mechanisms for subsystems within the child welfare network; decentralization of program operations; closer coordination at the local level with other major public service systems; and expansion of preventive service and social action efforts.[69]

The study has been described in some detail because it conveys clearly the nature of concern about family and children's services in the early 1960s that precipitated and accompanied many of the subsequent changes in the organization and delivery of social services. Forces for reform were in ascendancy again during these years, and several advisory committees and task forces composed of leading social welfare experts and key policymakers in the Kennedy administration were formed to study public welfare policy and consider needed changes in public assistance and social service programs. The 1962 and 1967 amendments to the Social Security Act reflected the recommendations of these advisory bodies, particularly in relation to the expansion of provisions for public social services, and set a policy framework for subsequent developments in this sphere.[70]

The specific legislative changes in the Social Security Act are discussed in Chapter 3; therefore, they will not be described here. What is important from a historical perspective is that the clear intention of the social welfare leaders involved in these deliberations was to develop a comprehensive public service system that would meet the service needs of low-income families, diminish the dysfunctional separation between child welfare and family service programs, and insure children in families receiving AFDC the services and benefits available to children in foster care. In other words, it was hoped that the development of comprehensive public social services for families and children would help to alleviate many service delivery problems and inequities of the type described in the Ryan and Morris study.

Unfortunately, this goal was essentially doomed from the start because of the unrealistic expectations, conflicting objectives, hopes, and fears that quickly developed among advocates and skeptics alike around the concept of expanded public social services. Social welfare leaders, envisioning a grand new scheme of service provision, failed to antici-pate the degree to which legislative intent and rational social planning could be undermined by restrictive federal and state administrative regu-lations; political, bureaucratic, and staffing constraints within the public sector; and the intransigence of established interest groups in the family and children's service field. Political and civic leaders, concerned about the escalating costs of public assistance, supported the concept of ex-panded social services on the assumption that they would help to reduce welfare rolls. They were then sorely disillusioned when welfare costs continued to multiply as a consequence of changing demographic pat-terns, relaxed eligibility requirements, and increased "take-up" among potential AFDC recipients. Direct service providers and consumers were led to believe that the expansion of public funding would enhance the quality and quantity of service provision, and they were frequently frus-trated, often enraged, when these expectations were not fulfilled. Civil rights and consumer groups, concerned about the potential for social control and invasion of privacy inherent in any effort to tie public assis-tance to service provision, became increasingly wary of efforts to ex-pand state intervention in family life, no matter how well intentioned the motivation. And welfare rights activists and leaders of the War on Pov-erty, committed to the concept of maximum feasible participation of the poor, disparaged the so-called service strategy as a naive attempt to solve the problems of poverty via the provision of casework services; instead they argued that organizing efforts should be directed toward placing more resources in the hands of the poor, deprofessionalizing services, and challenging the policies and practices of established agen-cies.[71]

Despite this tremendous ambivalence about the potential costs and benefits of an expanded role for the public sector in the provision of services to families and children, federal and state investments in social services escalated rapidly during the 1960s, especially after the 1967 amendments to the Social Security law, which permitted the purchase of service from voluntary agencies. Community and professional expecta-tions regarding the social good and social reform that might be achieved through these investments expanded equally rapidly.

Many established child welfare agencies responded readily to the de-mands and opportunities posed by this changing perception of public responsibility for service provision. They expanded their range of service provision, increased efforts to ensure better coordination of services, initiated demonstration projects aimed at reaching newly defined popu-lations at risk, developed more specialized foster home and group care facilities, and invested heavily in efforts to enhance the general level of staff training and program administration. But during the very period that the field was attempting to improve the quantity and quality of its service provision, it was also being exposed to new challenges and expectations.

Foster parent and adoptive parent groups began to organize, demanding more equitable treatment for themselves and the development of new types of adoption and foster care programs for children with "special needs" within the existing child welfare population. The movement toward de-institutionalization of youngsters confined in correctional facilities, mental hospitals, and schools for the retarded yielded whole new populations of children and youth that child welfare agencies were expected to serve. The emergence of the child advocacy movement in the late 1960s created pressure for child welfare workers to engage in social action efforts aimed at improving the quality of services provided by schools, hospitals, mental health facilities, and other community agencies impinging on the lives of children. Legal reformers concerned about parents' and children's rights began to challenge established agency policies and procedures regarding the movement of children in and out of care, as well as the quality, accessibility, and appropriateness of substitute care provisions. And renewed concern about the problems of child abuse and neglect led to the passage of state mandatory reporting laws, a dramatic increase in the number of cases of alleged child abuse and neglect that agencies were required to investigate, and expanded requests for assistance from police and hospital personnel attempting to provide protective services to children who were being defined as a new population at risk.

As a consequence of these various forces emerging in the late 1960s and early 1970s, the child welfare field was pressured to expand its boundaries in three basic directions: (1) to enhance and expand in-home services for families and children, especially for those of low-income, minority backgrounds, (2) to establish more specialized substitute care resources for children formerly channeled to other service systems, and (3) to develop opportunities for adoptive placement of the formerly "unadoptable" special needs children in long-term foster care.

Yet, these demands were exploding at a time when established child welfare agencies were losing their preeminence in the social welfare field; social work, long the dominant profession in the welfare field, was under attack for its failure to solve the problems of poverty; the medical and legal professions were redefining critical policy and service delivery issues in the children's field; community groups were demanding increased consumer participation in agency decision making; agencies were being expected to develop new funding sources and new patterns of service coordination; the distribution of power among voluntary, state, and local service planners was shifting; the Child Welfare League of America, the primary research, standard-setting, and accrediting body in the voluntary sector, was being challenged for defining its organization's priority as membership services, not social action;[72] and the Children's Bureau, the only federal agency with an established record of commitment to improving the delivery of child welfare services, was decimated by the reorganization of the Department of Health, Education and Welfare in 1969. In other words, the child welfare field was attempting to respond to new demands and expectations by expanding its service boundaries and resources at the same time that the very underpinnings of the field were under attack. The result was an inevitable system overload.

Developments of the Past Decade

Emerging directions in social service provision during the past decade have begun to create still different expectations for child welfare services. As Wickenden has suggested, "It is difficult to fix an exact year or month when the goal of a 'comprehensive public welfare system' . . . began to be replaced by its opposite, the ideal of separation of services and money payments."[73] Nor is it possible to determine precisely when the basic concepts underlying the structure of service provision in this country began to be reformulated. But early in the 1970s it was clear that the winds of change had again arrived. Congress imposed a 2.5 billion dollar ceiling on funding for social services in 1972, and Title XX of the Social Security Act was passed in 1975, redefining historical concepts regarding the appropriate decision-making responsibility, objectives, interventive strategies, and organizational and funding patterns for social services in this country.

The specific provisions of Title XX are discussed in Chapter 3, and other commentators have provided thoughtful analyses of the ways in which this act is shaping future directions in social service provision.[74] However, the trends embodied in the enactment and the implementation of this legislation are very relevant to the current crises in child welfare, as they run directly counter to many of the traditions that characterize the history of this field.

The basic shifts in the policies and patterns of service provisions reflected in this legislation can be summarized briefly as follows:

—greater state responsibility for social service planning and program development

—public participation in service needs assessment and review

—sharp reduction in the range and extent of federal regulations governing service provision

—development of comprehensive, integrated service plans

—complex and varied funding packages between the various levels of government and public and private provider agencies

—diversification in the range of service provision

—diminished provisions for categorical programs aimed at special populations at risk

—expansion of joint public-voluntary programs

—increased emphasis on the objectives versus the process of service delivery

—diminished role for social workers in the administration and delivery of services

—expanded opportunities for provision of services to families above the poverty line

—democratization and decentralization of funding decisions and allocations

—increased emphasis on fiscal and program accountability

Recent criticisms of the child welfare field, like recent changes in service delivery patterns, reflect these shifting perceptions of the appropriate role of government in social service provision. As Austin has suggested, "the financing, regulation and management of human service programs has become a major domestic policy issue in the United States."[75] And therein lies the source of the newest forces impinging on the child welfare field, for this development has placed on the public agenda the issue of appropriate responsibility and care for dependent, neglected, troubled, and troublesome children. It has transferred the awesome responsibility for shaping the lives of children—a responsibility formerly entrusted only to parents and/or persons with professional expertise in child welfare—to contending forces in the political arena, and it has created increased emphasis on rationality, efficiency, and control in the exercise of that trust.

Child welfare agencies, for example, are now being attacked for their failure to keep children out of placement, minimize costs while maintaining appropriate resources for children who must be placed in temporary substitute care, and move children back into their own families or into permanent adoptive homes as quickly as possible.[76] The tenor of these critiques contrasts markedly with the concerns raised by earlier commentators regarding the need to broaden the base of service delivery, reach underserved populations, and expand economic and social supports for all families.[77] In essence, earlier visions of using public funding to stimulate the development of child welfare services designed to enhance the development of all children at risk have been replaced by the expectation that the child welfare field should serve only those children for whom state intervention is essential to ensure a minimal level of care and protection and that these children should be cared for in as rational, time-limited, and cost-efficient a manner as possible.

This redefinition of the expectations and potentials of the child welfare system has significantly diminished the priority given to children's services within the human service sector and has led to some marked changes in the way child welfare services are organized and delivered. To illustrate, a recent study of child welfare in twenty-five states provides some interesting insights regarding changing patterns of service provisions.[78] The researchers observed that the development of child welfare service delivery systems in various states was very uneven, that the structures and organization of these delivery systems were constantly changing, and that although child welfare services were doing relatively well in the competition with other service systems for resources, this picture was likely to change as the constituencies of other service systems gain increased political influence and control.[79]

The relative importance attached to child welfare services in different areas "was found to be associated with the leadership within state agencies of persons with child welfare experience."[80] But as a consequence of widespread reorganization of state human service departments and frequent redefinitions of the client groups and services falling within the province of "child welfare," the authors observed that child welfare services seemed to be losing their organizational visibility and coherence. For example, among the twenty-five states surveyed, three had separate child welfare divisions, thirteen administered child welfare services through their welfare departments, and nine incorporated child welfare services in umbrella human service agencies. This suggests that opportunities for individuals with significant experience and interest in child welfare to provide leadership in state social service agencies may decrease as persons with other professional commitments gain ascendency in the human service arena.[81] And as the role of child welfare advocates within state government diminishes, the priority and resources allocated to children's services are likely to decrease proportionally.

Another concern raised by this study and echoed in the findings of a related study focused on the clients seeking services from public social service agencies is the competency of staff now providing child welfare services.[82] No matter how far diminished the organizational role of child welfare services or how devalued the status of those providing these services, the families and children seeking help from public social service agencies continue to present serious, complex, multiple problems that require the skilled intervention of highly experienced and knowledgeable practitioners. However, the merger of public welfare and child welfare staff in many states, combined with the general trend toward lower educational and experience requirements for social service personnel and reduced opportunities for workers to receive advanced training and specialized consultation, has resulted in a gradual de-professionalization of child welfare services. This raises serious question about the capacity of current staff to provide the quality and range of services required by the families and children now entering the child welfare system and the tremendous personal burdens that may be placed on workers struggling to help despite the lack of needed resources.

Recent efforts to reform the delivery of child welfare services have been directed primarily toward revising the statutory base governing state intervention in family life and increasing the requirements for public accountability of service providers. For example, by 1977 twenty states plus the District of Columbia had instituted some type of formal judicial, court-administered, or citizen review.[83] Other states have undoubtedly initiated similar external review procedures since that time, and the trend toward developing increasingly complex and sophisticated systems for internal case monitoring and program review is virtually universal.

The accountability concerns embodied in these reform efforts were translated into explicit public policy with passage of P.L. 96-272, the Adoption Assistance and Child Welfare Reform Act of 1980 (see Chapter 3 for a full discussion of this law). This act, if adequately funded and properly implemented, has the potential for greatly enhancing the quality of traditional child welfare services. It essentially reverses the recent trend toward a diminished role for the federal government in the funding and structuring of social service provision, and it addresses directly many of the most frequently documented problems in the child welfare system. However, it sharply underlines the current thrust toward viewing the child welfare system itself, rather than the children and families this field was developed to serve, as the primary object of concern—the essential target for social reform.

What explains this redefinition of the problems and potentials of child welfare? How can a field with such a long and proud tradition of service, a field that has had the leadership of some of the most eminent social reformers in American history, now be subject to so much criticism? History has taught us the futility of attempting to rescue, reform, and rehabilitate these children without parental involvement. And there is an evolving social consensus that the nation cannot or will not create the social conditions necessary to enable all families to function happily and effectively. Consequently, in an era in which it is assumed that there is a rational explanation and solution for every social problem, it was somewhat inevitable that the burden of responsibility and blame for needs of children would be shifted to the child welfare system itself. We now seem to be in a period in which the most universal desire is to turn back the clock, to return to the fantasized comfort and certitude of earlier periods in American history, and to rediscover ways of hiding or rationalizing the social problems and forces that threaten to disturb the general peace.

We are writing in the midst of a rapidly changing social climate. It would be foolhardy, if not impossible, to predict the ultimate impact of current political forces on reform efforts in the child welfare system. But the history of American child welfare suggests that many of the dilemmas confronting the field today reflect the solutions devised to address the problems of the past, and we can anticipate that although current proposals for change will resolve some issues, they will create still others. Henry Thurston, writing fifty years ago about the history of child welfare, quoted Lowell's couplet:[84]

> New occasions teach new duties;
> Time makes ancient good uncouth.

Certainly this is equally applicable today. Only a few relatively self-evident lessons seem clear from the child welfare history reviewed in this chapter:

—Child welfare services are shaped primarily by social forces and trends in the larger society.

—Individuals and groups engaged in the design and provision of child welfare service can contribute—modestly and imperfectly, but consistently—to improving the quality of life for children.

—The inherent tensions between the interest of children, parents, and the community-at-large can never be perfectly resolved.

—American society's willingness to invest in programs designed to enhance the welfare of families and children is meager and begrudging at best.

—The nature and definition of children's needs may shift over time, but social responsibility for the provision of supports and services responsive to these needs remains constant.

NOTES

1. Hillary Rodham, "Children Under the Law," *Harvard Educational Review* 43 (November 1973): 489.

2. *Watertown Records, I,* 105, cited in Robert H. Bremner, ed., *Children and Youth in America: A Documentary History,* 3 vols. (Cambridge, Mass.: Harvard University Press, 1970–1974), I: 68.

3. Homer Folks, *The Care of Destitute, Neglected and Delinquent Children,* Classic Edition (New York: National Association of Social Workers, 1978), p. 9.

4. Grace Abbott, *The Child and the State,* 2 vols. (Chicago: University of Chicago Press, 1938), 11: 5.

5. *Annual Report of the State Board of Charities of New York, 1900,* which reprinted the report from the *New York State Assembly Journal* (February 9, 1824), p. 946. Cited in Henry W. Thurston, *The Dependent Child* (New York: Columbia University Press, 1930), p. 24.

6. New York State Senate, "Report of Select Committee Appointed to Visit Charitable Institutions Supported by the State," *Documents,* 1857 Doc. 8 (Albany, N.Y.: New York State Senate, 1857), I: 2–10, cited in Bremner, *Children and Youth in America,* I: 648–49.

7. Abbott, *The Child and the State,* II: 7.

8. Andrew Billingsley and Jeanne M. Giovannoni, *Children of the Storm: Black Children and American Child Welfare* (New York: Harcourt Brace Jovanovich, 1972), pp. 29–30.

9. Bremner, *Children and Youth in America,* II: 291.

10. Thurston, *The Dependent Child,* p. 150.

11. Abbott, *The Child and the State,* II: 324–25.

12. William Pryor Letchworth, *Labor of Children in Reform Schools* (New York, 1882), cited in Bremner, *Children and Youth in America,* II: 470.

13. Bremner, *Children and Youth in America,* II: 440.

14. For fuller discussion of this concept see ibid., pp. 440–41; and Abbott, *The Child and the State.* II: 330–32.

15. Abbott, *The Child and the State,* II: 331–32.

16. Bremner, *Children and Youth in America,* II: 117.

17. *New York Times,* December 17, 1874, cited in ibid., II: 190.

18. Bremner, *Children and Youth in America,* II: 189–201.

19. Abbott, *The Child and the State,* II: 8–9.

20. Ibid., pp. 9–10.

21. Ibid., pp. 10–12.

22. Ibid., pp. 12–13.

23. Ibid., p. 14.

24. Ibid., p. 15.

25. Ibid., pp. 17–18.

26. Bremner, *Children and Youth in America,* II: 117.

27. *U.S. Statutes at Large,* 37, pt. I (1912), 79–80, cited in Jacqueline K. Parker and Edward M. Carpenter, "Julia Lathrop and the Children's Bureau: The Emergence of an Institution," *Social Service Review* 55 (March 1981): 62.

28. *Congressional Record,* 67 Cong., 1 Sess. (1921), 61, pt. 9, pp. 8759–60, 8764–65, 8767, cited in Bremner, *Children and Youth in America,* II: 1017–18.

29. Abbott, *The Child and the State,* II: 614–20.

30. Sophie Van Theis, *How Foster Children Turn Out* (New York: Charities Aid Association, 1924).

31. Abbott, *The Child and the State,* II: 333–34.

32. Bremner, *Children and Youth in America,* II: 118.

33. Ibid., p. 247.

34. Abbott, *The Child and the State,* II: 164–66.

35. Billingsley and Giovannoni, *Children of the Storm,* p. 71.

36. Bremner, *Children and Youth in America,* II: 247–48.

37. "Letter to the President of the United States Embodying the Conclusions of the Conference on the Care of Dependent Children," *Proceedings of the Conference on the Care of Dependent Children, 1909* (Washington, D.C.: 1909), pp. 192–97, cited in ibid., II: 365.

38. Abbott, *The Child and the State,* II: 229.

39. Quoted by Frederic Almy, "Public Pensions to Widows: Experiences and Observations Which Lead Me to Oppose Such Law," *Proceedings of the National Conference of Social Work* (Cleveland, Ohio: 1912), p. 492, cited in ibid., p. 232.

40. Edward T. Devine, "Pensions for Mothers," *American Labor Legis-*

lation Review (1913), p. 193, cited in Abbott, *The Child and the State,* II: 232.

41. Bremner, *Children and Youth in America,* II: 248.
42. New York Children's Aid Society, *Annual Report* (New York: Children's Aid Society, 1923), p. 14, cited in Thurston, *The Dependent Child,* p. 138.
43. Thurston, *The Dependent Child,* p. 199.
44. Billingsley and Giovannoni, *The Children of the Storm.*
45. Ibid., p. 51.
46. Ibid., pp. 74–77.
47. Ibid., pp. 74–76.
48. The merits of specific proposals aside, much of the consternation expressed by social welfare leaders about the proposals of the current administration reflects the concern that the goal is to eliminate or diminish the social guarantees instituted during the New Deal and to dismantle the machinery created to insure adequate delivery of these social provisions.
49. Title V, Part 3, Social Security Act, 1935–Ch. 531, *U.S. Statutes at Large* 49, Pt. I, p. 633, cited in Bremner, *Children and Youth in America,* III: 615.
50. Mary Irene Atkinson, "Child Welfare Services," *The Annals of the American Academy of Political and Social Sciences* (1939), p. 82, cited in Bremner, *Children and Youth in America,* III: 617.
51. Seth Low, "Foster Care of Children: Major National Trends and Prospects," *Welfare in Review* (October 1966): 12–13, cited in Bremner, *Children and Youth in America,* III: 643–44.
52. Willard C. Richan, "Personnel Issues in Child Welfare Services," *Child Welfare Strategy in the Coming Years* (Washington, D.C.: U.S. Department of Health, Education and Welfare, 1978), pp. 246–49.
53. Mildred Arnold, "The Growth of Public Child Welfare Services," *Children,* 7 (1960): 131–35, cited in Bremner, *Children and Youth in America,* III: 622–23.
54. Billingsley and Giovannoni, *The Children of the Storm,* pp. 141–73.
55. See, for example, Leontine Young, *Out of Wedlock* (New York: McGraw Hill, 1954); Clark Vincent, *Unmarried Mothers* (New York: Free Press, 1961); Margaret W. Miller, "Casework Service for the Unmarried Mother," *Casework Papers, 1955* (New York: Family Service Association of America, 1955), pp. 91–101; Rose

Bernstein, "Are We Still Stereotyping the Unmarried Mother?" *Social Work* 5 (July 1960): 22–28.

56. Lela Costin, *Child Welfare: Policies and Practices,* 2nd ed. (New York: McGraw Hill, 1969), pp. 366–68.

57. Seth Low, *America's Children and Youth in Institutions: 1950–1960–1964; a Demographic Analysis* (Washington, D.C.: U.S. Department of Health, Education and Welfare, 1965), p. 38, as cited in Billingsley and Giovannoni, *The Children of the Storm,* p. 89.

58. See, for example, Bradley Buell et al., *Community Planning for Human Services* (New York: Columbia University Press, 1952); L. L. Geisman and Beverly Ayers, *Families in Trouble* (St. Paul, Minn.: Family Centered Project, Greater St. Paul Community Chests and Councils, 1958); *Reaching the Unreached Family,* Youth Board Monograph No. 5 (New York: New York City Youth Board, 1958).

59. Henry Maas and Richard Engler, *Children in Need of Parents* (New York: Columbia University Press, 1959).

60. See, for example, Blanche Bernstein, Donald Snider, and William Meezan, *Foster Care Needs and Alternatives to Placement* (Albany, N.Y.: New York State Board of Social Welfare, 1975); Alan Gruber, *Children in Foster Care: Destitute, Neglected, Betrayed* (New York: Human Sciences Press, 1978); Jane Knitzer, Mary Lee Allen, and Brenda McGowan, *Children Without Homes* (Washington, D.C.: Children's Defense Fund, 1978); Joseph Persico, *Who Knows? Who Cares?: Forgotten Children in Foster Care* (New York: National Commission on Children in Need of Parents, 1979); George Strauss, *The Children Are Waiting: The Failure to Achieve Permanent Homes for Foster Children in New York City* (New York: New York City Comptroller's Office, 1977); Temporary State Commission on Child Welfare, *The Children and the State: A Time for Change in Child Welfare* (Albany, N.Y.: Temporary State Commission on Child Welfare, 1975); Shirley Vasaly, *Foster Care in Five States* (Washington, D.C.: U.S. Department of Health, Education and Welfare, 1976); *Child Welfare in 25 States: An Overview* (Washington, D.C.: U.S. Department of Health, Education and Welfare, 1976).

61. Billingsley and Giovannoni, *The Children of the Storm,* pp. 31–33.

62. Anthony Platt, *The Child Savers: The Invention of Delinquency* (Chicago: University of Chicago Press, 1969), pp. 176–77.

63. For further discussion of the organization of family and child welfare services in this period, see Alfred J. Kahn, *Studies in Social*

Policy and Planning (New York: Russell Sage Foundation, 1969), Chapter 7.

64. David M. Austin, "Title XX and the Future of Social Services," *The Urban and Social Change Review* 13 (Summer 1980): 19.

65. William Ryan and Laura Morris, *Child Welfare: Problems and Potentials* (Boston: Massachusetts Committee on Children and Youth, 1967).

66. Ibid., Chapter 3.

67. Ibid., Chapter 6.

68. Ibid.

69. Ibid., Chapters 6 and 7.

70. Elizabeth Wickenden, "A Perspective on Social Services: An Essay Review," *Social Service Review* 50 (December 1976): 574–88.

71. Ibid., pp. 577–81.

72. Gilbert Steiner, *The Children's Cause* (Washington, D.C.: The Brookings Institution, 1976), p. 146.

73. Wickenden, "A Perspective on Social Services," p. 581.

74. See, for example, Neil Gilbert, "The Transformation of Social Services," *Social Service Review* 51 (December 1977): 624–41; "Special Issue on Public Social Services: From Title IV A to Title XX," *The Urban and Social Change Review* 13 (Summer 1980): entire issue; Sanford Schram, "Politics, Professionalism and the Changing Federalism," *Social Service Review* 55 (March 1981): 78–92; Dorothy Miller, "Children's Services and Title XX from a National Perspective," *Child Welfare* 57 (February 1978): 134–39.

75. Austin, "Title XX," p. 19.

76. See, for example, Knitzer, Allen, and McGowan, *Children Without Homes;* Persico, *Who Knows? Who Cares?;* Strauss, *The Children Are Waiting.*

77. See, for example, Billingsley and Giovannoni, *The Children of the Storm; A Dream Deferred* (New York: Citizens' Committee for Children, 1970); *A Dream Still Deferred* (New York: Citizens' Committee for Children, 1975); Kenneth Kenniston, *All Our Children* (New York: Harcourt Brace Jovanovich, 1977); Alvin Schoor, ed., *Children and Decent People* (New York: Basic Books, 1974).

78. *Child Welfare in 25 States.*

79. Ibid., pp. vii–viii.

80. Ibid., pp. viii.

81. Ibid., pp. viii–x.

82. Shirley Jenkins et al., *Beyond Intake: The First Ninety Days* (Washington, D.C.: U.S. Department of Health and Human Services, 1981).

83. Barbara Chappell and Barbara Hevener, "Periodic Review of Children in Foster Care: Mechanisms for Reviews," paper prepared for the Child Service Association, Newark, N.J., March 1977 (mimeographed), p. 3.

84. Thurston, *The Dependent Child*, p. ix.

ADDITIONAL REFERENCES

Axinn, June, and Levin, Herman. *Social Welfare: A History of the American Response to Need.* New York: Harper and Row, 1975.

Bane, Mary Jo. *Here To Stay: American Families in the Twentieth Century.* New York: Basic Books, 1976.

Beck, Rochelle. "White House Conferences on Children: An Historical Perspective." *Harvard Educational Review* 43 (November 1973): 653–68.

Bremner, Robert. *From the Depths: The Discovery of Poverty in the United States.* New York: New York University Press, 1956.

Breul, Frank, and Diner, Steven, eds. *Compassion and Responsibility: Readings in the History of Social Welfare Policy in the United States.* Chicago: University of Chicago Press, 1980.

Coll, Blanche. *Perspectives in Public Welfare: A History.* Washington, D.C.: U.S. Department of Health, Education and Welfare, 1969.

Chambers, Clarke A. *Seedtime of Reform: American Social Service and Social Action, 1918–1933.* Minneapolis, Minn.: University of Minnesota Press, 1963.

Davis, Allen F. *Spearheads for Reform: The Social Settlements and the Progressive Movement, 1890–1914.* New York: Oxford University Press, 1967.

Grotberg, Edith H., ed. *Two Hundred Years of Children.* Washington, D.C.: U.S. Department of Health, Education and Welfare, Office of Child Development, 1976.

Hofstadter, Richard. *The Age of Reform.* New York: Random House, 1955.

Jenkins, Shirley. "Child Welfare as a Class System," *Children and Decent People,* edited by Alvin Schoor. New York: Basic Books, 1974, pp. 3–23.

Kahn, Alfred J. "Child Welfare." *Encyclopedia of Social Work,* 17th ed., vol. I. Washington, D.C.: National Association of Social Workers, 1978, pp. 100–114.

Kahn, Alfred J.; Kamerman, Sheila B.; and McGowan, Brenda G. *Child Advocacy: Report of a National Baseline Study.* Washington, D.C.: U.S. Government Printing Office, 1973.

Kamerman, Sheila B., and Kahn, Alfred J. *Social Services in the United States: Policies and Programs.* Philadelphia: Temple University Press, 1976.

Leiby, James. *A History of Social Welfare and Social Work in the United States.* New York: Columbia University Press, 1978.

Listening to America's Families: Action for the 80's. Report of the White House Conference on Families, October 1980.

Lubov, Roy. *The Professional Altruist.* Cambridge, Mass.: Harvard University Press, 1965.

Maluccio, Anthony, et al. "Beyond Permanency Planning." *Child Welfare* 59 (November 1980): 515–30.

Maroney, Robert M. *Families, Social Services and Social Policy: The Issue of Shared Responsibility.* Washington, D.C.: U.S. Department of Health and Human Services, 1980.

Pumphrey, Ralph E., and Pumphrey, Muriel W., eds. *The Heritage of American Social Work: Readings in Its Philosophical and Institutional Development.* New York: Columbia University Press, 1961.

Rein, Martin; Nutt, Thomas E.; and Weiss, Heather. "Foster Family Care: Myth and Reality," in *Children and Decent People,* edited by Alvin Schoor. New York: Basic Books, 1974, pp. 24–52.

Rothman, David. *The Discovery of the Asylum.* Boston: Little Brown and Co., 1971.

Scull, Anthony T. *Decarceration.* Englewood Cliffs, N.J.: Prentice-Hall, 1977.

Trattner, Walter I. *From Poor Law to Welfare State: A History of Social Welfare in America,* 2nd ed. New York: Free Press, 1979.

Wolins, Martin, and Piliavin, Irving. *Institution or Foster Family: A Century of Debate.* New York: Child Welfare League of America, 1964.

Public Law 96 – 272
96th Congress

An Act

June 17, 1980

|H.R. 3434|

Adoption
Assistance and
Child Welfare
Act of 1980

42 USC 1305
note.

To establish a program of adoption assistance, to strengthen the program of foster care assistance for needy and dependent children, to improve the child welfare, social services, and aid to families with dependent children programs, and for other purposes.

Be it enacted by the Senate and House of Representatives of the United States of America in Congress assembled,

SHORT TITLE

SECTION 1. This Act, with the following table of contents, may be cited as the "Adoption Assistance and Child Welfare Act of 1980".

TABLE OF CONTENTS

CHAPTER 3
CHILD WELFARE: EXAMINING THE POLICY FRAMEWORK

d Jane Knitzer

eefold: to examine the components of
e delivery of child welfare services, to
framework (including the passage in
ation, P.L. 96-272) and highlight their
child welfare services, and finally to
nvolved in implementing child welfare
policies.

Policy refers to federal and state statutes, administrative regulations, and fiscal patterns that together with their implementation determine the shape of public response to a particular set of issues. More specifically, for child welfare, there are five central policy determinants.

First, child welfare policy is shaped by federal laws. Such laws both directly affect the functioning of child welfare services and have a significant impact upon children involved in the child welfare system.

Second, child welfare policy is shaped by state laws, particularly family law statutes. These include laws pertaining to child abuse and neglect, dependency, status offenders, termination of parental rights, and adoption. Such statutes articulate the grounds for state intervention into family life. They also define the scope of the rights of affected parents and children as well as the obligations of the state to provide services. Increasingly they also define sanctions for states' failure to meet mandated obligations.

Third, child welfare policy is influenced by court decisions involving both individual children and classes of children. These decisions provide a basis for interpreting statutory and constitutional intent and can have a significant impact upon how complex legal and service issues are resolved.

Fourth, child welfare policy is shaped by administrative directives that elaborate upon and often clarify statutory mandates. These include regulations, which often have the force of law; administrative guidelines, such as those describing permanency planning procedures; policy manuals designed for caseworkers and supervisors; and standards for licensing and other program inspections.

Fifth, child welfare policy is shaped by the program funds available and the purposes for which such funds are allocated, for example, whether they can be used for in-home services or only out-of-home care. Policy is also shaped by the ways funds are distributed—on a formula basis or as grants. Funding levels and utilization directives are greatly influenced by the political realities of the budgetary process, including competing demands from other systems as well as the statutory and administrative framework.

Finally, child welfare policy is affected by the ways each of these components interact in practice. For example, what happens in instances of potential conflict between state and federal law, or in situations in which lack of funds means statutory mandates cannot be carried out? In this first section, we discuss each of these aspects of child welfare policy in greater detail.

FEDERAL LEGISLATION: BEFORE P.L. 96-272*

Federal child welfare policy has been shaped by two major pieces of legislation: the Child Welfare Services provisions of the Social Security Act, originally enacted in 1935; and the AFDC-Foster Care provision of the Social Security Act, originally enacted in 1961. These two pieces of legislation, taken together, have shaped the federal response to children at risk of placement or in out-of-home care and have had a significant impact on state response as well.

Child Welfare Services Program

The Child Welfare Services Program,** since 1967 authorized under Title IV-B of the Social Security Act,[1] essentially provides funds for a broad range of services for children. Over the years, the emphasis in the

---

*P.L. 96-272, the Adoption Assistance and Child Welfare Act of 1980, was enacted on June 17, 1980. It amended both the Title IV-B Child Welfare Services Program and the AFDC-Foster Care Program.
**Originally the program was authorized under Part 3 of Title V of the Social Security Act and administered by the U.S. Department of Labor.

program changed slightly. Originally, the major aim was to stimulate the development of child welfare services in rural areas on behalf of homeless, dependent, and neglected children, and children in danger of becoming delinquent.[2] In 1958 the emphasis on rural areas was eliminated, enabling states to provide services wherever they were needed. In addition, for the first time, states were required to match federal funds.[3] In 1962 the scope of the program was broadened; funds were made available for any social services necessary to promote the well-being of all children, not just for services for homeless, dependent, and neglected children and children in danger of becoming delinquent. Furthermore, states were required to coordinate child welfare services with welfare and other social services programs and to provide child welfare services on a statewide basis by 1975.[4]

Training grants and research and demonstration grants were also authorized under Title IV-B of the Social Security Act.[5] Research and demonstration projects have been directed at improving the quality of child welfare programs and demonstrating new service approaches. Training funds have been used primarily for teaching and traineeship grants to colleges and universities, although limited funds have been available for short-term in-service training grants.

Despite the broad scope of the IV-B legislation, its promise was never fulfilled because funding levels were never sufficient to carry out the statutory intent. From the program's inception (with an authorized funding level of $1.5 million) it has been plagued by insufficient funds. In recognition of this, the authorization levels for the program were repeatedly increased, from $50 million in Fiscal Year 1967 to $100 million in 1969 and $266 million in 1977. But appropriations have never matched the authorization levels. Until Fiscal Year 1980 no more than $56.5 million was ever actually appropriated for the IV-B program. As a result, despite the rhetorical recognition in federal policy that children at risk of or in out-of-home placement could benefit from child welfare services, federal dollars distributed on a formula basis provided no incentives to create such services. Furthermore, most of the federal money available was absorbed by the costs of out-of-home placement. The limited funds available for research, demonstration, and training, however, have had a positive effect on the stimulation of state activities in these areas.

AFDC-Foster Care Program

The second major piece of federal child welfare legislation was not enacted until twenty-six years after the Child Welfare Services Program;

yet, it rapidly became a more significant determinant of outcomes for children at risk of placement than the earlier legislation. Unlike the Child Welfare Services Program mandate, the AFDC-Foster Care Program[6] was created solely for the purpose of providing funds for the out-of-home care of children, a purpose that until 1961 was viewed entirely as a state responsibility.

The impetus for the legislation came from a dramatic episode in Louisiana in which 22,000 poor black children were suddenly cut from the welfare roles because the homes in which they were living were deemed unsuitable and their mothers were ruled ineligible for AFDC. The federal government responded to the Louisiana action by ruling that states could not deny the children support in such situations.[7] In order to provide for these children, Congress amended the AFDC program to permit the use of the funds to pay for suitable foster homes.

To protect against the possibility of capricious removals of the children, Congress required that the AFDC-Foster Care funds be used only for the care of children removed from their homes as a result of a judicial determination that remaining in the home would be contrary to the welfare of the child.[8]

The AFDC-Foster Care Program was initially to be a temporary one, but in 1962 Congress made it permanent and permitted children to be placed in private, nonprofit child care institutions as well as in foster family homes.[9] In 1967 Congress increased the level of federal participation for foster care payments and mandated all states to have AFDC-Foster Care programs in place by 1969.[10]

In contrast to the Title IV-B Child Welfare Services Program, the AFDC-Foster Care Program has always been part of the AFDC Program and therefore has been an open-ended entitlement program.[11] Thus, states can claim federal reimbursement for the care of as many children as are eligible for the program. Not surprisingly, therefore, expenditures under the program increased rapidly (up to $270 million in 1979), and support for out-of-home care quickly became the major thrust of federal policy. Particularly troubling was the fact that this legislation provided no checks on the extent to which the federal funds were being used appropriately—whether children in placement did in fact need placement or whether anyone was attempting to secure permanent homes for them.[12] Although only approximately one-fifth of the children in foster care in 1979 were claimed as eligible for AFDC-Foster Care,* the federal program greatly influenced state practice.

---

*Only AFDC-eligible children who were removed from their homes pursuant to a judicial determination and placed in foster family homes or private, nonprofit child care institutions were eligible for reimbursement under the program.

Other Relevant Federal Legislation

Although the Title IV-B Child Welfare Services Program and the AFDC-Foster Care Program have traditionally been recognized as the core of the federal government's child welfare program, there are numerous other pieces of federal legislation that have impacted significantly on the children and families served by the child welfare system.* They, too, contribute to the formulation of child welfare policy.

Seven of the most critical of these programs will be discussed briefly in this section. The first, the Title XX Social Services Program authorized under Title XX of the Social Security Act, is the major federal social services program. It addresses the needs of both adults and children. Four others focus on specific groups of children at risk of placement or in care—the Child Abuse Prevention and Treatment and Adoption Opportunities Act, the Juvenile Justice and Delinquency Prevention Act, the Developmentally Disabled Assistance and Bill of Rights Act, and the Indian Child Welfare Act. The other two programs focus on the health and special education needs of the child welfare population—the Early and Periodic Screening, Diagnosis and Treatment Program (EPSDT) authorized under Medicaid (Title XIX of the Social Security Act) and the Education For All Handicapped Children Act of 1975 (P.L. 94-142).

In 1975 Congress enacted the Title XX Social Services Program,[13] providing funds to the states for a broad range of social services. In 1981 the act was substantially amended.[14] Under the act's original mandate, each state was required to provide at least one service directed toward meeting each of five goals: self-support; self-sufficiency; preventing abuse and neglect and preserving and reuniting families; preventing inappropriate institutional care; and securing appropriate institutional care and services. Although Congress provided only minimal direction to the states as to how the funds were to be used, it provided clear instructions on funding levels, incorporating the $2.5 billion ceiling on the program that had been imposed on the predecessor social services program three years earlier.** Generally the legislation also required states to provide a 25 percent match for federal dollars received. Although one-half of the funds had to be targeted to low-income persons and eligibility for most

---

*In 1978 the Children's Defense Fund identified thirty-four federal programs that potentially have either a direct or an indirect impact on children at risk of placement or in out-of-home care and their families. At that time they were administered from seventeen offices in six federal agencies. Their differing eligibility requirements, funding patterns, and administrative provisions comprised an unwieldy, haphazard, and often contradictory set of policies. Jane Knitzer, MaryLee Allen and Brenda McGowan, *Children Without Homes* (Washington, D.C.: Children's Defense Fund, 1978), pp. 106–123.
**The Title XX program replaced the social services programs previously authorized under Titles IV-A and VI of the Social Security Act.

services was income-related, some services such as protective services for children, could be provided to anyone regardless of income.

Federal Title XX funds were also available, at a 75 percent matching rate, for training costs related to the delivery of social services.[15] While originally available on an open-ended basis, federal matching for training expenditures was limited in both Fiscal Year 1980 and Fiscal Year 1981 to $75 million.

Although several of the goals of the Title XX legislation clearly pertain to child welfare, it is difficult to assess the extent to which Title XX funds have actually been used for child welfare services or child welfare–related training. Available national data suggest that approximately 25 percent of federal Title XX service funds were used for day care (primarily for children of working parents, not for children at risk of placement); about 12 percent for homemakers and preventive services (although not necessarily for children); and only 2 percent for adoption-related services (excluding subsidies, which are not reimbursable under Title XX).[16] Some funds have also been used for residential treatment services for children.

Overall, this picture suggests that Title XX has had only a limited impact on increasing services for the population at risk of or in out-of-home placement. This is due, in part, to the fact that the allocation of funds within each state is largely determined by the strength of constituencies seeking the funds. Systematic advocacy for a range of services that are crisis-oriented and specifically directed toward families who abuse or neglect their children is limited. Furthermore, the fiscal ceiling imposed on the program since its inception has sharply limited the capacity of states to expand services, even in the face of need. In fact, the majority of the states were spending their total federal Title XX allotments in 1976, and new dollars available after that time were used to absorb inflationary costs rather than for new or expanded services.

In 1981 the Title XX Social Services Program was turned into a social services block grant.[17] States are no longer required to target services toward stated goals or to provide free services to public assistance recipients. The program's ceiling was also cut back to $2.4 billion—an amount below its Fiscal Year 1975 funding level and 20 percent below the Fiscal Year 1981 funding level. Furthermore, both the state matching requirement and the requirement that states maintain their 1973 or 1974 level of spending for services were eliminated. These actions are likely to result in an overall reduction of state investment in social services.

The laissez-faire block grant approach to Title XX adopted in 1981 further jeopardizes the likelihood that new services under this program will be made available to children at risk of placement or in care. The tight fiscal constraints will likely focus all efforts on maintaining current programs with reduced funding levels. The competition among constituency groups will also probably intensify, with the result that the most vulnerable children and their families are likely to lose out. Yet, the reduction in available supportive services for children and families generally is also likely to increase the demand for specialized child welfare services.*

The Child Abuse Prevention and Treatment Act,[18] first authorized in 1974, has provided a small amount of money for grants to states and research and demonstration projects dealing with the prevention and treatment of child abuse and neglect. In order for a state to qualify for a grant under this program, the state's child abuse and neglect law must: (1) provide for representation by a guardian ad litem** for each child involved in judicial abuse and neglect proceedings, (2) require that there be mandated reporting of known and suspected cases of child abuse and neglect, (3) provide immunity for those reporting, and (4) specify a procedure for ensuring the confidentiality of records. Additional provisions require states to provide for the dissemination of information to the public regarding abuse and neglect and support parental organizations combating child abuse and neglect. States must also have a system to track and investigate reports of abuse and neglect.

Although funding for the Child Abuse Prevention and Treatment Act has always been limited (never more than $22 million), the legislation has served to focus attention on the problems of one group of children involved in the child welfare system at both the federal and state levels.

It is also noteworthy that the Child Abuse Prevention and Treatment Act became the vehicle for the first federal effort designed specifically to encourage the adoption of special needs children. When reauthorized in 1978, a new Title II was added to the act, the Adoption Opportunities Act of 1978.[19] Authorized at $5 million, the new title provided for the establishment of a panel to develop a Model Adoption Act and Procedures† and for the development of a national adoption information

---

*The 1981 modifications in Title XX represent but one of a series of extensive changes in the structure and funding levels for a range of income support, food, health, and social welfare programs. These revisions were all included in the Omnibus Reconciliation Act of 1981 (P.L. 97-35).
**A guardian ad litem is a person, who may or may not be an attorney, appointed by a court to represent the best interests of a minor or an incompetent adult in a judicial proceeding.
†The panel's draft Model State Adoption Act and Procedures were published for comment in the *Federal Register* on February 15, 1980. The Model Act for Adoption of Children with Special Needs was published in the *Federal Register* in final form by the Secretary of Health and Human Services on October 8, 1981.

exchange system. It also established regional adoption resource centers in each of the ten federal Department of Health and Human Services regions and provided limited funding for small grants to parent groups advocating on behalf of special needs children in each of the regions.

The Juvenile Justice and Delinquency Prevention Act,[20] originally enacted in 1974, reflects another effort to use federal dollars to improve the systems that serve youth at risk of or in placement—delinquent youth, status offenders, and to a lesser extent, dependent and neglected children. The act authorizes funds to improve the quality of juvenile justice, divert youth from the traditional juvenile justice system, and provide critically needed alternatives to institutionalization. As a condition of funding, each state must assure in its state plan that it will try to improve the juvenile justice system. For example, the law requires that status offenders and dependent and neglected children not be placed in juvenile detention or correctional facilities, and that delinquent youth, status offenders, and dependent and neglected children be separated from adults in jails and prison facilities. Funds for grants for special projects and for research, training, and demonstration functions are also authorized under the act.

Through the Juvenile Justice and Delinquency Prevention Act Congress also turned its attention to the special and widespread problems of runaway youth. Under Title III of the act, it authorized the Runaway Youth Program,[21] providing funds for the development of temporary care programs for runaway and other homeless youth.

The Developmentally Disabled Assistance and Bill of Rights Act,[22] among other things, requires each state to establish a Protection and Advocacy System to protect the rights of developmentally disabled persons, including children. It also specifies the obligation of the state and federal governments to enforce specific protections for developmentally disabled persons, including their right to appropriate treatment, services, and habilitation in the least restrictive setting, habilitation plans, and periodic reviews.

Although funds under the act have been limited, in many states developmentally disabled children comprise a relatively large portion of the children in the child welfare system. The act potentially offers these children and their families significant procedural protections.

The Indian Child Welfare Act,[23] like the Developmental Disabilities Act, was an attempt by the Congress to focus specifically on the needs of a high-risk population. The Indian Child Welfare Act was enacted to prevent the unwarranted breakup of Indian families, a problem that has been amply documented for the Congress.[24] The law establishes minimum federal standards affecting the removal of Indian children from their families and their placement in out-of-home care. It also defines the rights of Indian tribal governments to intervene in custody proceedings and to assume jurisdiction over the placement of Indian children, both those living on the reservation and those living off it. It also clarifies state and tribal roles in the delivery of child welfare services to Indian families.

The primary purpose of the act is not to fund special child welfare programs focused on Indian children and their families, although the act authorizes the Secretary of Interior to make grants for Indian child and family programs. Rather, it attempts to establish by law certain priorities that reflect the importance of Indian culture to Indian children. It requires, for example, that preference be given to the placement of an Indian child in the home of an extended family member, a tribal member, or another Indian home or institution rather than a non-Indian home or institution. The law also requires that efforts to prevent removal must be made prior to placement and that any child accepted for foster care must be placed in "the least restrictive setting which most approximates a family and in which his special needs, if any, may be met" and "within reasonable proximity to his or her own home."[25]

The Medicaid Program, funded under Title XIX of the Social Security Act, and the Early and Periodic Screening, Diagnosis and Treatment Program (EPSDT), which is part of Medicaid,[26] offer hope of improved health care to many of the children in out-of-home care. Under the Medicaid program, which is basically for low-income families, over one-half of the states provide coverage to all children in foster homes and private institutions for whom public agencies are providing some financial responsibility. Many states also extend Medicaid coverage to children in hospitals, intermediate care facilities, and in-patient psychiatric facilities. The coverage of children in these latter categories has had both positive and negative effects. Although important to some children, the coverage of such care also serves as a disincentive to move them into less restrictive (and non-Medicaid-reimbursed) facilities.

The EPSDT Program, too, has had both positive and negative results. Under this program all Medicaid-eligible children under twenty-one, including children in out-of-home care, have a right to periodic medical screening, diagnosis, and treatment. However, in spite of its potential value in eliminating serious health problems by early identification, the EPSDT Program is extremely underutilized. Although it began in 1967, ten years later only 25 percent of needed screenings were being provided, and many children did not receive the indicated follow-up care.[27] States have been particularly slow to recognize the crucial role that EPSDT can play for children in foster care who have been shown to have multiple health problems.[28]

The Education for All Handicapped Children Act (P.L. 94-142) also has far-reaching implications for children at risk of placement and in foster care.[29] P.L. 94-142 affords the right to a free, appropriate, public education to handicapped children, including children in out-of-home care. Among other things, the act explicitly defines a handicapped child's right to an individual evaluation and education plan and periodic reviews of progress. It also establishes the parent's right to participate in all decisions concerning a child's evaluation and placement.

P.L. 94-142 and similar state laws have resulted in the stimulation of improved educational services for many handicapped children. Special education often comprises a major supportive service for handicapped children who are at risk of entering foster care or already in placement. The availability of a good daily special education program for children may enable their families to care for them at home or enable children to be cared for by foster parents rather than in a more restrictive residential setting.

A provision in P.L. 94-142 of specific importance for children in the child welfare system is the requirement that surrogate parents be appointed to advocate on behalf of handicapped children in need of special education services who are wards of the state or whose parents are unknown or unavailable. Their task is to ensure that these children have appropriate evaluations and plans, are educated in the least restrictive environment possible, and to the extent possible, are placed with children who are not handicapped. The surrogate parents may participate in all decisions concerning the children's placements and have the right to challenge placements. The foster parents of a child may serve as surrogate parents, but employees of the agency caring for the child may not. The provision for a surrogate parent to oversee the education of handicapped children whose own parents cannot represents a potentially vital link in ensuring the well-being of children in foster care. Unfortunately the concept has not been widely implemented.

The Overall Impact of Federal Programs

On paper it appears that there are federal programs targeted to meet the needs of many vulnerable children and families. In reality, however, these programs do not live up to their promise to enrich the lives of children at risk of or in out-of-home placement.

The categorical nature of the programs has made it difficult for service systems to respond to children whose needs cut across the categories established by legislation. Furthermore, strict categorical programs have in some instances encouraged the labeling of children to make them eligible for certain federally reimbursed services, and set the stage for time-consuming interagency disputes about which sources of federal funding should be used.

In addition, some of the federal programs provide incentives for needlessly restrictive care. Other programs define rights for the children but do not provide mechanisms to insure they are enforced. Still others fail to require regular monitoring of the programs' impact on children. For example, the two major federal child welfare programs prior to 1980 provided no mandates to prevent unnecessary placements, to keep placements as short as possible, or to ensure the reunification of children with their families or their adoption when return home was not possible. As a result, the federal legislative framework itself has been a force exacerbating the many problems facing children and child welfare services all over the country.

STATE STATUTES

State statutes significantly affect the development and implementation of child welfare policies in two major ways. First, they articulate the grounds for state intervention into family life and define the substantive rights and due process protections accorded to children and families. Second, state statutes also specify the obligations of the state to the children in its care. State statutes govern dependency, neglect, and abuse proceedings as well as termination of parental rights and adoption proceedings. In addition, in some states, statutes define the types of reviews required for children in out-of-home placement.

Statutes pertinent to various aspects of the placement process have developed in a piecemeal fashion. Until recently there has been little recognition that what happens at one proceeding affects another. As a result, protections and criteria are often inconsistent. Thus, in one state children and parents involved in an abuse matter may have the right to appointed counsel at the time of adjudication but be denied this right in termination proceedings. Below we highlight the general characteristics of statutes governing the different types of child welfare proceedings.

Neglect and Abuse

The current doctrine of *parens patriae,** under which states intervene in families through the courts to protect children from physical and emotional neglect and abuse and from situations of dependency, developed slowly. Coverage of emotional neglect was the last to emerge. Areen's careful analysis of the history of neglect intervention from Tudor times through the nineteenth century documents that even in the early nineteenth century, neglect proceedings continued to be primarily part of the Elizabethan Poor Law goal of providing work and training for poor children at minimal cost.[30] The application of neglect laws without a direct connection to poverty came much later.[31]

All states and the District of Columbia now have statutes addressing child neglect, defined broadly for purposes of this discussion to include abuse and dependency. But there is great variation from state to state in definitions and grounds for neglect; the statutory criteria for the court's removal of a child from the home where there is a finding of neglect; and the rights afforded to various parties at a neglect hearing. Generally, however, these statutes provide specific dispositions that may be ordered by a court after a hearing and finding of neglect—either a child remains in the home under protective supervision of the court or a designated agency, or the child is removed from his or her family and legal custody for the child transferred temporarily to a public agency, institution, or department, which then has responsibility for placing the child in a living arrangement outside the home.

Current advances in child welfare policy have resulted in the development of more specific standards for removal in neglect proceedings, requirements for periodic review of children once removed, and procedural protections for children in the neglect system. Before discussing these developments, however, it is important to examine the emergence of termination of parental rights and adoption statutes in the states.

Termination of Parental Rights

Although an initial finding of neglect may result in a temporary transfer of custody for a child from a parent to an agency, a permanent transfer of custody usually necessitates an additional legal proceeding

---

*The concept of *parens patriae* has emerged over several centuries. In essence it reflects the power of the state, often a court or public agency, to intervene on behalf of a child or another dependent party to ensure their protection. In such instances the state assumes the role of parent.

specifically for the purpose of terminating a parent's rights to his or her child.*

For many years a permanent change in custody of a child could occur only through adoption and only if the child's biological parents consented to the permanent transfer and adoption. A child whose parent was unknown or unavailable or unwilling to give voluntary consent was thus sentenced to foster care for the duration of childhood.

The procedure for the involuntary permanent transfer of parental custody was first enacted in statutory form in New York State in 1959. Since then most states have enacted separate statutes for termination of parental rights or made termination of parental rights a disposition in a neglect proceeding. About five states still provide for termination only in the context of an adoption proceeding. In those states termination can only occur in response to an adoption petition for a particular child. Many states also provide for voluntary termination of parental rights before a court, and for parents to relinquish their rights voluntarily to an agency.

In states where termination is a separate proceeding it usually may occur before potential adoptive parents are identified for a particular child. This may facilitate the likelihood that an adoptive family can be found. Some termination statutes also provide for subsequent periodic reviews by the court to insure that a permanent adoptive family is, in fact, being sought. Termination in and of itself is of little value except as it makes possible a more permanent familial arrangement for a child.

As in neglect, state statutes vary significantly in the grounds for termination and the rights accorded to the parents and the child in the termination proceeding. Many states amended their statutes in the middle to late 1970s and are continuing to do so, making grounds more specific and clarifying due process protections for both the child and parents.

Adoption

No provision was made for legal adoption of children in the United States until the mid-nineteenth century, and early adoption laws merely required documentation of the legal transfer of a child from one set of parents to another.[32] Not until the late 1930s did a large number of states revise their adoption statutes to require agency investigations before approval of an adoption.[33] This development paralleled the recognition of

---

*Termination of parental rights refers to a legal action whereby a parent's rights to his or her child, including the rights to visitation and to consent to adoption, are permanently and irrevocably severed.

the need for protection of children in other areas as well. About this same time, for example, a number of states passed laws requiring the licensing of child placing agencies.[34]

State statutes providing for subsidies to assist with the financial responsibilities involved in the adoption of certain children with special needs did not emerge until later. New York and California were the first states to enact subsidized adoption legislation in 1968 and 1969, respectively. The emergence of adoption subsidy legislation accompanied some of the early termination or parental rights legislation previously described and was in part responsive to a growing awareness that many children who should be adopted were remaining in foster care. By August 1981 the District of Columbia and all states except Hawaii had passed some form of adoption subsidy legislation.

New Directions in State Statutes

The various types of state statutes just described have been challenged in a number of states during the last decade for failing to protect adequately the interests of the children and families they were intended to serve.[35] Furthermore, increased recognition that children have a fundamental interest in the continuity and permanence of family relationships has also stimulated significant revisions in state neglect and termination of parental rights statutes.[36] Generally these revisions have involved strengthening procedural protections, mandating periodic reviews of the children in care, and to a lesser extent, enacting broad-based comprehensive reform legislation or systematically amending the statutes to make them more consistent.

Statutes in a number of states now provide for the right to counsel for parents and children in neglect and termination of parental rights proceedings.[37] More than thirty states have gone beyond the establishment of this right and now have statutory provisions that require the appointment of counsel for parents in termination proceedings when they are unable to pay.

Fewer states have required that separate counsel be appointed for both the parent and the child in neglect and termination proceedings. To some extent the federal Child Abuse Prevention and Treatment Act described earlier in this chapter has stimulated representation for children in neglect proceedings. The act requires that a guardian ad litem, who does not necessarily have to be an attorney, be appointed to represent the best interests of a child in any judicial proceeding in an abuse or neglect case.[38] As of 1980 most states had complied, at least on paper, with the act's requirement.

Many of the state statutes now provide other procedural protections for the parents as well. These include the right to receive advance written notice of a hearing in a proceeding, to participate in the hearing, to cross-examine witnesses, to receive written findings, and to appeal. The provision of similar protections to the child has progressed more slowly.

In addition to seeking to insure that children and families have access to counsel, state statutory reforms have also addressed the state's obligation to provide quality care for the children for whom it is responsible and to prevent the long-term placement of the children. By mid-1981 either as a result of litigation or advocacy efforts and/or documentation of the cost effectiveness to the state and the benefit to the children of such reviews, more than thirty states had enacted periodic review legislation.[39]

These statutes vary widely. In some states reviews are conducted periodically by the courts; in others, by boards comprised of citizens; and in still others, by some combination of the two. Some review statutes provide extensive due process protections to the participants. Other include only minimal requirements. The more detailed statutes also require a decision as to whether the child being reviewed should be returned home, continued in care for a specified period of time, or referred for termination of parental rights and adoption, as well as a justification for the decision. Some even specify a mechanism to insure that the decisions are carried out.

Beyond these particular reforms, a small number of states have undertaken more comprehensive revisions of their child welfare codes in order to strengthen key aspects of their statutory framework. The state of Washington, for example, in addition to including a provision for counsel and for periodic judicial review in its juvenile court act, also included in its 1978 statutory revision a requirement that efforts be made to prevent removal before a child can be placed in care except when a manifest danger to the child exists.[40] The statute further requires that when removal is recommended, the predisposition report to the court must include a full description of the reasons why the child cannot be protected adequately in the home, including a description of efforts to work with the parents and child, in-home treatment programs that have been considered and rejected, and the likely harms the child will suffer as a result of removal.[41] The amendment also included funds for service programs to prevent unnecessary placements.

Since 1977 California has had in place comprehensive child welfare legislation addressing the prevention of placement, the appropriateness of placements, periodic review, reunification, termination, and adoption.[42] However, this legislation has been applied only on an experimental basis in two demonstration counties. Legislation to mandate the reforms statewide is now pending before the California legislature.[43]

New York State has also enacted legislation that places increased emphasis on the prevention of placement in its statutory framework. This legislation, the Child Welfare Reform Act of 1979,[44] marks the first state attempt to eliminate the fiscal incentives that in the past have encouraged foster care to the detriment of both prevention and adoption. The law has three major components: (1) it reverses the customary funding pattern in child welfare by providing open-ended state support for services that prevent or shorten placements, while limiting state aid for foster care; (2) it defines a careful planning process for child welfare services, which includes the development of district-wide plans as well as individual child and family assessments; and (3) it requires that the state monitor the counties' performance in moving children through foster care and apply sanctions to counties that fail to provide required protections and services to individual children and families.

The New York legislation is particularly interesting because it reflects the necessity for statutes to address actual performance standards. It suggests that the protections already provided for children in New York State through periodic judicial review, termination, and adoption statutes were not sufficient to meet the system's goals of prevention and permanence.

Although Ohio had lagged far behind both New York and Washington in its statutory framework in the early 1970s, it has seen significant advances due in large part to the efforts of state child advocacy organizations, foster and adoptive parent organizations, and some of the state's juvenile judges. Legislation mandating annual review of children in the care and custody of the state was passed in 1976.[45] This legislation was then closely followed by three additional statutes that build upon this move toward permanency. These included Ohio's first real termination of parental rights statute;[46] a strengthened adoption subsidy law,[47] and amendments to the neglect statute, which strengthen public agencies' case planning responsibilities and require documented efforts to promote reunification.[48]

Approaches to the reform of state statutory schemes have varied significantly across the country in the last decade. Yet, there seems to be a clear pattern to the statutory elements being addressed. Efforts are underway in many states to strengthen the statutory framework governing entry and exit from the placement system, as well as statutory provisions for protecting children while in the system.

COURT DECISIONS

Court suits and decisions in the area of child welfare have had a significant impact on the evolution of child welfare policy in at least two important ways. First, they have been the major forum through which difficult questions about the boundaries of the rights of children and parents involved in the child welfare system have been addressed. Second, they have been a vehicle through which advocates have sought to challenge and correct quality-of-care issues, often by raising claims that children were being deprived of basic constitutional rights. A brief discussion of various types of legal advocacy follows.

Court decisions have defined the rights of parents and children in neglect, termination of parental rights, and adoption proceedings. By doing so they have exerted pressure on individual courts and public agencies to acknowledge these rights.

For example, the issue of the right of parents to counsel in termination proceedings has been litigated in both state and federal courts.[49] In some states children as well as parents have a right to counsel in such proceedings. Pressure for this has arisen, in large part from decisions in cases in state courts involving individual children. The law is less clear as to the constitutional right of parents to counsel in such proceedings. A 1981 U.S. Supreme Court decision in *Lassiter* v. *Department of Social Services of Durham County, North Carolina,* 452 U.S. 18 (1981), declared that there was no constitutional right to appointed counsel for all indigent parents but that the decision had to be made on a case-by-case basis. The language of the Court's opinion, however, does suggest that counsel would be disallowed only in exceptional circumstances.

The only Supreme Court attention to the rights of children to counsel has been directed toward delinquent youth. In a landmark case, *In re Gault,* 387 U.S. 1 (1967), the Court ruled that juveniles charged with delinquent acts had a constitutional right to certain procedural protections, including the right to counsel. The question of the constitutionality of the right to counsel for children in child welfare proceedings has not yet reached the Supreme Court.

The courts have also examined at least two special questions regarding the rights of putative fathers and the rights of foster parents in child welfare proceedings.

In 1972 a U.S. Supreme Court decision in *Stanley* v. *Illinois,* 405 U.S. 645 (1972), said that a father who had raised his illegitimate children had a right to notice and a hearing on the issue of his fitness as a parent in a termination proceeding. This case has had a significant impact on service delivery issues, because, although other cases have distinguished the putative father in *Stanley* from fathers who have never had custody of their children or taken responsibility for them,[50] the *Stanley* case has been interpreted by some states as requiring extensive efforts to track down putative fathers prior to termination. These states argue that *Stanley* applies even when paternity has not been established and the father has not expressed any interest in caring for the child. Since finding absent fathers is often a time-consuming, difficult process, such an interpretation clearly conflicts with policy mandates that encourage ensuring permanent families for children on a timely basis.

A series of cases has also addressed the rights of foster parents with regard to children in their care. The U.S. Supreme Court in *Smith* v. *Organization of Foster Families for Equality and Reform (OFFER)*, 431 U.S. 816 (1977), examined the procedural protections afforded foster parents when a state agency seeks to return foster children who have been in their home to their biological parents. The Court in *Offer* recognized the warmth of ties that may form between a child and foster parents and emphasized the need to balance carefully the interests of the child, the foster parent, and the biological parent when evaluating the effect of state decisions on children and families. However, the Court avoided confronting the issue of whether foster parents have constitutionally protected interests in their relationships with their foster children. Decisions by lower courts have answered this question both in the negative and in the affirmative.[51]

All of this activity about what standing and basic due process protections should be afforded to parents, children, and foster parents has cumulatively had an impact on definitions of good child welfare policy and practice. They have resulted in increased demands on child welfare agencies to recognize the rights of the clients receiving child welfare services. Agencies, for example, are increasingly including biological parents in the development of case plans for their children. Individual foster parents and foster parent organizations have also been able to use the visibility accorded this issue to argue for increased involvement in decisions about the children they are charged to care for.

Litigation challenging the failure of public agencies to plan appropriately for children, to provide services to children in their care, and to review case plans and progress has also put pressure on some state child welfare systems to reexamine their policies and procedures. For the most part this litigation has focused on the later stages of state intervention. Several suits have challenged the failure of state agencies to review children periodically,[52] to provide reunification services,[53] or to provide permanence in other ways.[54] There have also been challenges to the inappropriate placement of children in out-of-state institutions,[55] in overly restrictive settings,[56] and in inadequate, harmful settings.[57] Such challenges, when coupled with other pressures for reform, have resulted in the initiation of case planning and case review procedures in many states.

Litigation has even been used to pressure some state and local agencies to redirect their fiscal priorities and fund services or mechanisms necessary to protect the rights of individual children or classes of children. For example, in *Gary W.* v. *State of Louisiana,* 437 F. Supp. 1209 (E.D. La. 1976), the attorneys for the plaintiffs argued that the children in state custody had a right to care that is appropriate to their needs in the least restrictive setting possible. The court in its final order not only declared that all Louisiana children placed in Texas had a right to care, education, and treatment suited to their needs, but directed the state to spend at least as much per capita for alternative care as it was currently spending on Louisiana children in Texas facilities.

The increased focus in child welfare policy on the public system's responsibility for children in its care has also been stimulated by damage actions directed toward individual child welfare caseworkers and their supervisors. These cases have asked for fiscal compensation to the parents and children for the damages inflicted on the children by workers charged with caring for them.[58] Such litigation has undoubtedly been an impetus for shared responsibility in decision making on behalf of individual children. Unfortunately, while some of these suits have cited the lack of training for workers charged with making decisions about individual children, they have not resulted in increased funds for training.

Court decisions in the child welfare area have by no means charted a clear course for the development of child welfare policy. Yet the presence of litigation in crucial areas such as the rights of parents and children and the statutory obligations of agencies in meeting their responsibilities to individual children has been an important factor in making child welfare policy more responsive to children's needs.

ADMINISTRATIVE DIRECTIVES

The fourth component of a child welfare policy framework is in many ways the most diffuse. It is marked by a range of federal, state, and local administrative directives, that either interpret specific statutes or reflect other types of practice standards and guidelines to be followed in the provision of services and enforced by the respective levels of government. The universe of such directives is vast. There is no way to catalogue the myriad and sometimes conflicting policy directives that those working directly with children and families must assimilate. Nor, however, can their impact be denied.

Regulations are the rules that are usually developed by an agency responsible for administering a particular law. They explain how the agency will interpret the letter and spirit of the law. On the one hand, regulations, which often carry the force of law, can be useful in expanding on principles and terms in a specific statute and detailing activities necessary for compliance. On the other hand, regulations can also be used to defeat or at least subvert the intent of good legislation, particularly if many of the essential concepts of the law are not defined by statute.

Regulations are often an important link in the effect a statute will have on policy and practice implementation. For example, regulations developed for New York State's Child Welfare Reform Act of 1979[59] will have a significant impact on the extent to which children and families benefit from the act's provisions. The act theoretically provides unlimited funds for preventive services for children at risk of imminent placement. However, the New York legislature in drafting the statute left to the administering agency, in this instance the New York Department of Social Services, the task of defining precisely what the terms "at risk of imminent placement" and "preventive services" mean. The state agency, in turn, had the option of either defining the group of at-risk children and covered services so narrowly as to restrict sharply the eligibility for the program; making the coverage so broad as to diffuse totally the potential impact of the legislation; or finding a way to strike a balance that would realize the law's intent.*

Regulations can also be issued on subjects not addressed by statutes. In the state of Pennsylvania, for example, the Philadelphia Department of Public Welfare developed administrative regulations pursuant to a court case, *Emory* v. *Sosnowski* (C.A. No. 79-99, E.D. Pa., filed January 1979), which are designed to strengthen the state's obligation to ensure permanence for children. The regulations specifically include requirements for individual case plans; periodic reviews by the agency, an administrative hearing officer, and the court; involvement of the parents and child in case planning; and specification of visiting arrangements. Meanwhile, legislation mandating similar reviews had been proposed but not yet enacted in the state. The danger in using regulations alone as a basis for a policy framework is that their implementation is dependent upon a supportive administration, and they may sometimes be withdrawn without public comment.

Practice guidelines and agency manuals are also often important components of child welfare policy. Although unlike regulations, they seldom carry the force of law, they stress for line workers the values incorporated in policies and suggest ways to translate them into prac-

---

*Official regulations of the New York State Department of Social Services, Sections 430.8–430.13 as amended, effective April 1, 1982, narrowly restrict eligibility for mandated preventive services to families in which the risk of child placement is imminent, that is, likely to occur within sixty days if services are not provided.

tice. For example, a statutory requirement that efforts be made to provide services prior to placement is more likely to be implemented if the manual of the agency with responsibility for serving children instructs workers concerning the range of services available to them in supporting families, the criteria to be used in determining the appropriateness of removal, and the documentation of efforts to prevent placement that is required when removal proves necessary. Similarly, mandates for reunification services can be strengthened by clear directives to workers about the importance of parental visiting. For example, the New York City Office of Special Services for Children issued an extensive policy statement in 1978 on parental visiting, which not only described why visiting was important and the problems around visiting but also included specific guidelines for the development of better visiting practices (see Chapter 9).[60] In other states, workers are instructed to develop parent/agency agreements that include, among other things, specific visiting timetables and transportation arrangements.

FISCAL PATTERNS

The amount and nature of funds available to implement federal and state statutes and regulations have a significant impact on the implementation of child welfare policies. For example, although there has been much emphasis in the Social Security Act on the importance of preserving families, until 1980 unlimited federal reimbursement was available to the states for the out-of-home care of children under the AFDC-Foster Care Program, but only limited funds for services to prevent the need for placement and to reunify families. Similarly, although Congress authorized $266 million for the Title IV-B Child Welfare Services Program, which could have been used for a range of such services, the administration never requested and Congress never appropriated more than $56 million for the program until 1980. And many states chose to spend even that limited amount for foster care rather than for alternative services.

The availability of federal funds for the medical care of children in foster care has also served as a disincentive to the placement of these children with permanent adoptive families. As mentioned earlier, most children in publicly supported foster care are eligible for Medicaid, entitling them to a range of general and specialized medical services for which the state only has to provide at most one-half of the cost; the federal government provides the remainder. Children's eligibility for Medicaid often ceased when they are adopted, and the cost of any necessary medical services becomes totally the responsibility of the adoptive parents or the state. The incentive for the states, then, has been to leave children with special medical needs requiring expensive treatment in foster care where a federal contribution to the cost of services is provided, in spite of policy directives urging their placement with permanent families. (See discussion below regarding changes mandated by P.L. 96-272.)

Lack of funding for services specified in a statute can certainly undermine its intent. For example, although most states had passed adoption subsidy legislation by 1979, a much smaller number of states were actually operating such programs because funds were not available. In some states funding for subsidies was the responsibility of individual counties. These counties had little motivation for moving children into adoptive families with a county-financed subsidy when the state was paying a portion of the foster care costs for these children. One state, Ohio, addressed this problem by amending its adoption subsidy statute to require county participation in the program as a condition of eligibility for foster care reimbursement.[61] Other states, like Minnesota, attempted to encourage the use of subsidies by counties by providing 100 percent state reimbursement for them.[62]

Implementation of foster care review laws has also been thwarted in some states by the lack of a specific appropriation for management of the review systems. The legislation establishing citizen review boards in Arizona and South Carolina included specific funding allocations for the operation of the review systems.[63] However, many of the judicial review statutes have no specific funding provisions.

There is an additional way in which fiscal policies can affect outcomes for children. Increasingly, fiscal agencies are being granted authority to review the impact of regulations and administrative directives prior to their promulgation, always with an eye to containing costs. This predictably creates tensions within a state system between those who oversee services and those who oversee dollars. For example, if regulations were written mandating medical coverage for special needs children in foster care, including foster family homes and residential treatment centers, but the budget office excluded coverage of children in residential treatment centers because of the significant costs involved, the intent of the regulations would be significantly undermined and their positive impact on children diminished.

REDEFINING THE POLICY FRAMEWORK: P.L. 96-272

This review of the components of the child welfare policy framework and the identification of some recent policy modifications indicates there has been considerable activity in the development of child welfare policies in recent years. In June 1980 this activity culminated in the most comprehensive change of all, the enactment of Public Law 96-272, the Adoption Assistance and Child Welfare Act of 1980 (hereafter referred to as P.L. 96-272). This law, which amends the AFDC-Foster Care Program and the Title IV-B Child Welfare Services Program, fundamentally restructures the federal role in child welfare and requires a similar restructuring in all states.

As a context for assessing the strength and limits of P.L. 96-272, it is first necessary to summarize the child welfare problems it purports to address, many of which have been alluded to earlier, and to describe briefly some of the forces that led to its enactment.

Old Problems

In 1959 Maas and Engler conducted a now classic study entitled *Children in Need of Parents* on the problems of children in placement.[64] They documented the fact that children often enter care unnecessarily and once in the system are likely to remain there until reaching majority. Subsequent studies over the intervening decades conducted in individual states such as Arkansas,[65] California,[66] New York,[67] North Carolina,[68] Massachusetts,[69] and New Mexico,[70] and nationally[71] have documented similar problems. In fact, in some respects the situation has not only failed to improve but has worsened.

In summary, six problems affecting children at risk of placement and in out-of-home care have been repeatedly documented. These problems are to a great extent the outgrowth of the malfunctions of the components of child welfare policy just described.

First, all over the country, children continue to be placed in out-of-home care inappropriately, often by default, because funds to create alternatives to placement are scarce.[72] As discussed earlier in this chapter, policies shaped by federal funding patterns have clearly emphasized placement rather than alternative services. Reports from individual states document that many more dollars are spent on out-of-home care for children than for preventive services.[73] This problem is intensified by the fact that judges only infrequently even explore alternatives before ordering a child removed from his or her home.[74]

Second, once children are removed from their homes, whether correctly or not, they are at great risk of being placed in settings that are inappropriate to meet their individual needs.[75] These settings may be, for example, too restrictive or too far from their home communities, making it difficult if not impossible for the children to remain in meaningful contact with their families or for the state to monitor their care adequately.[76] Again, the roots of this problem lie in part in federal policies. The major source of federal funds for the out-of-home care of children in the child welfare system included* no requirements that children be placed close to home or in the most family-like setting possible.[77] Furthermore, regulations for the AFDC-FC Program specifically stated that children placed in out-of-state institutions were eligible for reimbursement under the program.[78] Other federal programs have added to this problem. For example, the availability of full Medicaid funding for children in hospitals sometimes keeps children in hospital wards after their need for in-patient medical care ceases.[79]

A third major problem is the fact that public policies and practices often cut off children who are placed in care from contact with their biological families. As suggested earlier in this chapter, this severing of family ties is in part a function of federal and state statutory schemes that fail to require attention to the child's family throughout the placement process. Too frequently, even when case plans and case reviews are mandated, parental involvement is not required. Although the purpose clauses of many state neglect statutes, and the statute authorizing the federal AFDC-Foster Care Program itself, recognize reunification as an essential goal of the child welfare system, none of the state or federal statutes, until recently, mandated that visiting plans be specified for a child in care. Yet the importance of visiting in predicting the likelihood of reunification has been well documented.[80] Local administrative policies also ignore the importance of parental visiting. For example, a survey of visiting policies of local child welfare agencies found that more than one-half of the reporting agencies had no policies, and those that did tended to restrict the opportunities for visiting. Furthermore, funds were not available to assist with visiting costs.[81]

The fourth problem is that public officials have failed to monitor the quality of care that a child receives while in placement, to review the child's progress, and to decide on the most appropriate permanent placement for the child in a timely fashion. In spite of the fact that the 1959 study *Children in Need of Parents* reported that children who remained in care for eighteen months or more were likely to grow up in the foster care system,[82] only fairly recently have states passed legislation mandating the periodic review of children in foster care to determine whether appropriate and timely dispositional plans are being made for them. Moreover, although both the Title IV-B and AFDC-Foster Care

---

*The past tense is often used in this section in discussions of programs subsequently amended by P.L. 96-272.

programs required case plans and periodic case reviews in the past, there was ample evidence that these vague requirements were not enforced. In fact federal audits revealed that the availability of federal dollars for foster care resulted in AFDC-Foster Care children lingering in "temporary" care even longer than children for whom the state was paying the whole bill.[83] Children placed out-of-state were particularly vulnerable to getting lost without any reviews of their status.[84] Yet, even the Interstate Compact on the Placement of Children, which most states have incorporated in their statutes, includes no provision to ensure continued monitoring of children's progress while in care.[85]

A fifth problem is the failure of public systems to hold themselves accountable for the care they provide for children for whom they are responsible. The public neglect of children in out-of-home care is compounded by the absence of effective licensing and regulatory mechanisms.[86] Licensing requirements often refer only to physical standards for care. Although several of the federal statutes allow reimbursement only for children placed in licensed facilities, even that minimal requirement has been ignored.[87] State licensing laws that mandate annual reviews of facilities and mandatory renewals of licenses have also been ignored, and licensing reviews are not uncommonly two or three years late. Until recently, none of the federal programs providing board payments have addressed either licensing standards or the adequacy of payments for foster family homes. Although the Child Abuse Prevention and Treatment Act of 1974 prohibited the abuse of children in institutions and other out-of-home settings,[88] the federal government established no mechanism for monitoring such abuses. Similarly there was no federal mechanism for monitoring the Juvenile Justice and Delinquency Prevention Act requirement that neglected children not be housed in institutions.[89]

The sixth major problem repeatedly highlighted in the various reports is the absence of accurate aggregate data at all levels of government about children facing or in placement.[90] The lack of even basic data impedes efforts to know how many children are in care, where they are and how long they have been there, or whether their needs are being met. The inability to track the progress of children in care also limits efforts to develop resources to meet their needs and plan meaningfully for specific groups of children.

New Expectations

The problems just described have drawn increasing attention from a broad range of professionals, including social workers and lawyers, other advocates including parents, and child welfare officials themselves. A consensus has emerged about the nature of the problems facing children and families served by the child welfare system and the reforms necessary to begin to remedy them. This consensus has been fostered by activities over the past two decades. Several of these are discussed briefly below.

First, during the past two decades increasing attention has been focused on the rights of disenfranchised groups including children and on the need to empower parents and children in the face of ever-present and complex human services bureaucracies.[91] This has led in turn to considerable legal scrutiny of child welfare policies[92] as well as both case and class action litigation challenging harmful practices affecting children and allegedly unconstitutional statutes.[93]

There has also been increased criticism of the child welfare system from a psychological perspective. The negative consequences of the system's fairly typical pattern of frequent placements and replacements and of the severing of family ties have been well documented.[94] And anti-family practices in the system have been given new significance by the findings from a careful empirical study showing that the more frequently children and parents are in contact, the more likely the children are to return home.[95] There has also been further exploration into what constitutes a child's best interest. For example, the notion that biological parents should automatically be considered a child's psychological parents has been severely criticized and the notion of the importance of permanence for children highlighted.[96] There have also been challenges on psychological grounds to inappropriate state intervention in family life.[97]

Finally, there have been successful programmatic attempts, primarily on a demonstration basis, both to prevent placement[98] and to ensure permanence for children in placement either through reunification or through adoption.[99] Evaluations of such programmatic efforts have not only documented their positive consequences for children, but have also documented significant cost savings, based on the elimination or reduction of stays in foster care.[100]

As indicated earlier, in part in response to new intolerances for old problems, piecemeal efforts to modify state and local policies have been appearing throughout the last decade. But these efforts have been limited by the fundamental inadequacy of the federal policy framework. Thus, a state seeking to expand preventive services or to strengthen adoption programs by increasing the availability of subsidies for hard-to-place children could go only so far. To illustrate, a state could only rely on state funds for meeting these goals; it could not reallocate any federal AFDC-Foster Care funds for these purposes, and federal funds for IV-B child welfare services were so limited as to be virtually meaningless. As the significance of the federal framework in aggravating problems in the child welfare system became clear, it became obvious that without major federal reforms, efforts to improve the quality of care and ensure permanence for the over one-half million children in foster care and those at risk of placement would be sharply circumscribed.

Toward Federal Reform

The process of restructuring the federal role, as is often true of legislative change, did not begin as a comprehensive reform effort. Instead it focused on a small but familiar piece of the child welfare continuum— adoption. Interest in Congress arose first not in the committees with jurisdiction over the majority of federal dollars affecting children in the child welfare system, but in subcommittees long concerned about numerous related needs of children in this country.

The Subcommittee on Children and Youth of the Senate Committee on Labor and Public Welfare held hearings in April 1975 on baby selling[101]—an issue that had received considerable media attention and had been the subject of some public outrage. These were followed in July 1975 by hearings on the adoption of special needs children.[102] In these hearings testimony frequently addressed the barriers in the broader child welfare system that left many of these children lingering in foster care. The Senate subcommittee then commissioned a policy analysis of foster care and adoption issues[103] and in December 1975 held joint hearings with the Subcommittee on Select Education of the House Education and Labor Committee[104] which again looked at the issue in September 1976.[105] The specialized attention given to foster care issues and the commitment to reform by members of Congress involved in these early efforts proved invaluable in the later enactment of the Adoption Opportunities Act[106] and the eventual enactment of the major child welfare reforms in P.L. 96-272, the Adoption Assistance and Child Welfare Act of 1980.

Testimony at the hearings in 1975 and 1976 emphasized the role that federal policies and dollars played in exacerbating the problems in the child welfare system. But in fact the committees first giving visibility to these issues did not have any authority over the relevant federal programs, the Title IV-B Child Welfare Services Program and the AFDC-Foster Care Program. Morover, the committees that did, the House Ways and Means and Senate Finance committees, although responsible for the purse strings for these programs, lacked both knowledge of the issues and a commitment to children's concerns. Thus the task was both to educate and to convince these committees that the questions raised about the inadequacies of the federal role in child welfare not only reflected concerns about children but concerns about fiscal accountability as well.

As a way of stimulating the process, Representative George Miller introduced a comprehensive child welfare reform bill in the House of Representatives in March 1977. The bill, which became H.R. 7200, was given extensive attention by the House Ways and Means Subcommittee on Public Assistance and Unemployment Compensation and later by the Senate Finance Committee. Although H.R. 7200 passed both the House and the Senate, the 95th Congress ended before differences between the two bills could be resolved. Similar legislation (H.R. 3434) moved forward early in the 96th Congress and set the stage for the ultimate passage of P.L. 96-272.

The New Mandate: P.L. 96-272

P.L. 96-272, the Adoption Assistance and Child Welfare Act of 1980,[107] was enacted on June 17, 1980, with the overwhelming support of both houses of Congress and a commitment to its philosophy and approach coming from a broad range of federal, state, and local officials; interested professionals; foster parents; adoptive parents; and children's advocates. The law is comprehensive. It reflects the belief that a piecemeal approach to child welfare reform, addressing, for example, how children get out of the system but not how they get in, will not work. P.L. 96-272, through a system of fiscal incentives and procedural reforms, is explicitly designed to address the problems in the child welfare system discussed earlier in this section.

Structurally P.L. 96-272 uses a carrot-and-stick approach to redirect funds away from inappropriate, often costly, out-of-home care and toward alternatives to placement. It also encourages states to develop and implement important protections for children including case plans, periodic reviews, and information systems. The act amends the Title IV-B Child Welfare Services Program and the AFDC-Foster Care Program. It creates a new Foster Care and Adoption Assistance Program under Title IV-E of the Social Security Act, effective October 1, 1982, replacing the AFDC-Foster Care Program.

P.L. 96-672 redirects federal fiscal incentives toward the development of preventive and reunification services and adoption subsidies. It requires that any increased funds for the Title IV-B program (over the $56.5 million appropriated in Fiscal Year 1979) be targeted for the development of these alternative services.[108] It prohibits the use of these funds for such services as foster care board payments or employment-related day care.[109]

P.L. 96-272 also encourages the development of these services by requiring that to be eligible for increased Title IV-B funds (over their share of $141 million) states must implement a service program to reunify children with their families or otherwise provide permanence.[110] It also requires other protections to ensure that children enter care only when necessary, are placed appropriately, and are moved on to permanent families in a timely fashion.[111]

In addition, the law incorporates a fiscal penalty for states that do not have both preventive and reunification service programs and the protections in place by the time appropriations for the IV-B Program reach $266 million (the authorized level) for two consecutive years.[112] If a state is not in compliance with the mandates by that time, it will have to forfeit its allotment of Title IV-B monies beyond its share of the Fiscal Year 1979 appropriation level of $56.5 million.[113]

States are also required to make reasonable efforts to provide preventive and reunification services as a condition of funding under the Title IV-E Program.[114] Furthermore, a state's federal reimbursement for foster care or adoption assistance for eligible children* is contingent, after October 1, 1983, upon a judicial determination that efforts to prevent placement and to encourage reunification were made.[115]

P.L. 96-272 also creates fiscal incentives to facilitate the adoption of children with special needs. In the past, federal reimbursement had been available to the states for foster care but not for adoption subsidies. Thus, there was a fiscal benefit to the states to keep children, particularly those with special needs, in foster care rather than to place them in adoptive homes with subsidies that were financed totally with state or local funds. P.L. 96-272 for the first time provides for federal reimbursement on a matching basis to the states for adoption assistance payments on behalf of as many eligible children** as are claimed by the states.[116]

P.L. 96-272 also makes children receiving federally reimbursed subsidies automatically eligible† for Medicaid.[117] This will eliminate the

---

*States that have all of the protections and the preventive and reunification services programs in place are also eligible to claim federal reimbursement under the IV-E program until October 1, 1983, for otherwise eligible children voluntarily placed in foster care. Otherwise, eligibility is limited to children placed pursuant to court order.
**Eligible children include AFDC, AFDC-FC, and SSI eligible children in out-of-home care who have special needs. A special needs child is defined as one who cannot be returned home and cannot be placed for adoption without assistance, in spite of reasonable efforts to do so, because of a specific factor such as ethnicity, age, membership in a minority or sibling group, medical condition or physical, mental, or emotional handicaps.
†The act also made these children eligible for Title XX social services, but when the Title XX program was block granted in 1981, the targeting provisions were eliminated.

incentive to leave children with special needs in foster care to maintain their eligibility for publicly supported medical assistance. As discussed earlier, most states currently give Medicaid cards to all children in publicly supported foster care, but permit adoptive families to keep the card only if they meet the income eligibility requirements for the Medicaid program. The high costs of medical care for special needs children, coupled with the fact that many potential adoptive families cannot get insurance coverage for these children, has made the failure to continue Medicaid eligibility a serious problem, even for non-low-income families.

The act also includes a fiscal incentive to encourage the development of small, community-based facilities for children in the federal foster care program. For the first time, eligible children are allowed to be placed in public group care facilities, but only if the facilities accommodate no more than twenty-five residents.[118]

Although Congress recognized the need for a redirection of funds, it also recognized that increased targeted funds alone would not correct all the problems. P.L. 96-272 therefore mandates implementation of a series of protections designed to ensure that children enter care only when necessary, are placed appropriately, and are provided permanent families (their own or adoptive ones) in a timely fashion. As described above, the availability of both IV-B and IV-E funds is made contingent upon both the state's capacity to monitor and gather information on the child welfare system and its ability to ensure adequate safeguards for individual children at risk of placement or in care.[119] For example, to correct for the absence of aggregate information about children in care, states are required to establish statewide information systems from which the status, demographic characteristics, location, and goals for placement of children currently in care and those in care within the preceding twelve months can be identified.[120] States are also required to conduct a one-time inventory of all children in foster care for more than six months and to determine the appropriateness of the current placement and best disposition for each child.[121]

To address the widespread absence of monitoring of individual children, the inadequate attention to the appropriateness of placements, and the failure to ensure permanence, states are required to establish a case review system. This system must be designed so that children in care have written plans, have their status reviewed at least every six months by a court or a panel of persons (at least one of whom is not responsible for the case management or delivery of services to the child or family), and within eighteen months of placement and periodically thereafter, they must have a dispositional hearing before a court or court-appointed or approved body to determine the most appropriate disposition.[122] These requirements, taken together, constitute a basis for insuring that a child receives continuing review and that specific plans for the child's future are implemented. By mandating both internal and external reviews, Congress sought to provide a failsafe system of checks and balances.

The law further provides that the case plan for an individual child be designed to achieve placement in the least restrictive, most family-like setting available located in close proximity to the parents' home, consistent with the best interests and special needs of the child.[123] Legislative history for the act suggests that Congress was trying to balance its concerns about inappropriately restrictive and distant placements of children with an awareness that needs of individual children and the availability of resources do vary and that many factors must be weighed in choosing the most appropriate placement for an individual child.

The protections in P.L. 96-272 also recognize that parents frequently are neglected by the public systems once children are removed from their care. Thus, the law specifies that parents may participate in the semi-annual reviews.[124] It also requires that the eighteen-month dispositional hearing be a court hearing[125] in which basic due process protections are extended to parents including the right to counsel, to written advance notice about the hearing, and to participation in the hearing. There is also a provision that requires safeguards for the parents when children are removed from the home and when changes in placements and visitation arrangements are made.[126] Those denied benefits or services under the act must also have the opportunity for an administrative fair hearing.[127]

Beyond the Letter of the Law

P.L. 96-272 is likely to play a significant role in the development of child welfare policy that goes well beyond its specific mandates for services and protections.

First, it represents a national commitment to the principles of permanency planning. It acknowledges new ways of thinking about vulnerable children at risk of placement and their families as well as innovative state reform efforts and the best models for service delivery. It reflects awareness that permanency planning is a process that requires attention to preventive services, case plans and reviews, appropriate placements, and adoption. It establishes, in policy, the scope of public responsibility to children throughout the placement process. It is not enough for a state to protect children from grave risk in their own families; the state also has specific affirmative and legally enforceable obligations to children and their families once responsibility for their care is assumed.

Second, the law provides a stimulus to states to begin to make the administrative and legislative changes necessary to achieve meaningful child welfare reforms. For states that have not previously examined their systems, the promise of new monies serves as an incentive to do so; for states where legislative and administrative changes were already underway, it reinforces those efforts.

At the same time, although P.L. 96-272 offers a real challenge for child welfare reform, it has its limitations as well. It is focused narrowly on one group of children and families. It has the capacity to reach adjudicated delinquents and youths diagnosed as developmentally disabled and/or emotionally disturbed, but only if they are the responsibility of the agency administering the IV-B and IV-E programs.

Furthermore, the law does not attempt to address the problems of fragmentation or duplication among federal programs with similar foci such as those authorized under the Education for All Handicapped Children Act, the Child Abuse Prevention and Treatment Act, or the Juvenile Justice and Delinquency Prevention Act. Nor does it set forth any mechanisms by which states can do the kind of planning necessary to put systems of services in place to enable an appropriate response to each individual child.

The enactment of P.L. 96-272, however, does establish the federal legislative framework for meaningful reforms on behalf of the over one-half million children and their families affected by the child welfare system.

IMPLEMENTING CHILD WELFARE POLICIES

Thus far we have focused on the parameters of child welfare policy as it is written in statutes, regulations, and guidelines and on the problems and forces that have led to formal policy changes over the past few years. But no discussion of policy issues would be complete without attention to the complex issues involved in implementing formal policy mandates.

Some of the issues are general and are relevant to the implementation of any policy. Others flow directly from the specifics of a particular policy mandate. Consider first the generic issues.

Fundamental to effective implementation of any child welfare policy are the attitudes, training, and skills of those charged with implementation responsibility. For example, P.L. 96-272 is essentially a pro-family law; it requires that prior to placement of a child some serious effort be made to work with the family to avoid its disruption. If the worker, supervisor, or agency director charged with making this effort still fundamentally believes that poor families are bad families whose children are better off in foster care, it is unlikely that the new law can be meaningfully implemented. At the other end of the process, permanency will never become a reality for all children, in spite of the adoption-related provisions of P.L. 96-272, if agency staff responsible for implementing the subsidy provisions believe that successful adoptions of black teenagers or other "special needs" children are impossible. Attitudes toward the underlying philosophies of legislative reform are a potent but often invisible force facilitating or inhibiting policy implementation.

The issue of the adequacy of training is also key to policy implementation. The lack of adequate training for administrators, supervisory staff, and caseworkers, as well as judges and other court staff, inhibits the implementation of policies. It has been argued, for example, that one of the reasons children are so frequently removed from their homes inappropriately is that workers do not know how to cope with the real and psychological needs of multiproblem, crisis-ridden families, and that they receive little pre- or in-service training to give them the necessary knowledge and tools.[128]

Despite the recognition that training is essential to the implementation of reforms, such training is still frequently seen as a luxury for which no funds exist. P.L. 96-272, for example, makes no mention of training or educational requirements of staff. And, at the same time that Congress was considering P.L. 96-272, funds for the previously open-ended Title XX training program were substantially cut back. Similarly, the progressive New York State Child Welfare Reform Act, described earlier, requires training be provided to caseworkers in a number of specific skill areas related to preventing placements, reunifying families, and getting children adopted[129] but provides no funds for conducting such training.

Training designed to familiarize and sensitize participants in the system about the intent of new reforms is also often nonexistent or inadequate. As a result, instead of seeing new opportunities that can benefit children, staff often only feel resentful of any additional burdens (particularly paperwork burdens) imposed by the reforms. Training is thus a crucial policy implementation issue that remains basically unaddressed.

Civil service requirements exacerbate the problems of inadequate training. Such requirements often allow persons who have little or no interest, much less experience, in working with children and families to fill child-oriented service jobs. Civil service requirements for child-sensitive jobs rarely include criteria relevant to working with children and families. And notwithstanding the fact that the inappropriateness of civil service exams for recruiting staff who work with children has been cited as a problem at both the local and national levels,[130] the problem has rarely been actively addressed. This, therefore, is another crucial issue that remains on the agenda for further policy change. In the meantime, it creates sometimes insurmountable barriers to a sensitive response to children and families from public agencies.

The third generic issue that is relevant to policy implementation has to do with fiscal resources. Inadequate funds even in the face of the most progressive policy make a charade out of that policy and simply create expectations that cannot be fulfilled. Moreover, since budgetary decision making both in public agencies that administer child welfare programs and in legislatures that enact laws is typically carried out by those not familiar with intricacies of child welfare issues, the risk of creating unimplementable policies looms large. For instance, in the early stages of developing comprehensive federal child welfare legislation, a proposal was made to permit the use of federal funds for adoption subsidies to a special needs child for as many years as the child had been in foster care. In other words, if a special needs child was eight years old and had been in care three years, the adoptive family would receive a subsidy but only until the child was eleven. Congressional intent was to avoid any incentives for parents to adopt children just for the money. Members of Congress did not understand that the limited subsidy approach would neither ensure children permanence nor save money; many special needs children would simply remain in foster care.

It is also true that money problems can too easily become a convenient excuse for not acting upon, or for resisting, changes. In many instances the problems in child welfare have not really been the low level of available funding, but rather the absence of creativity and flexibility in the use of those funds.

While attitudes, training, and funding are probably the most central determinants of how effectively a policy can be carried out, there are also at least three other relevant generic issues. First, there is the ongoing need to ensure that mechanisms to monitor the adequacy of policy implementation are in place. Without monitoring and subsequent enforcement of sanctions for noncompliance, the force of legislative mandates, regulations, guidelines, and even court decrees can too easily become diluted.

Secondly, those who implement policies must often find ways to deal with changing priorities and sometimes conflicting legislative and legal mandates. For example, some states were forced to respond to the mandate of the federal child abuse law for improved reporting procedures, although officials in those states recognized that without additional funds for services, the law's promises could not be delivered. Similarly, legislation to decriminalize status offenders may merely add more pressures to the child welfare system without providing any additional help in addressing the needs of adolescents. Juggling different mandates becomes a difficult task, one that can sometimes, in the end, be harmful rather than helpful to the children and families affected, despite the seeming correctness of the individual mandates.

Finally, it is important to note that policy mandates often have implications for the way service delivery units are organized within agencies, the way courts and social services departments interrelate, and the way voluntary providers relate to public agencies. Policies will not be effectively implemented if necessary structural changes and coordination issues are not addressed. For example, if P.L. 96-272 is to be well implemented, close linkages among traditionally distinct components of the child welfare delivery system must be developed. Workers in the foster care system must be aware of efforts made by protective service staff to try to prevent placements. Similarly the adoption of special needs children requires close links between foster care and adoption units, so that when reunification appears unlikely, steps toward termination of parental rights can be pursued and adoption planning begun.

The link with the courts is also essential to effective implementation of reforms such as those in P.L. 96-272. For example, implementation of permanency efforts, when appropriate, may be hampered in a judicial system where the court that initially removes a child from his or her family and periodically reviews the case is not the same court that can terminate parental rights. Even within courts, rotation of judges is a problem. Similarly, if judges believe that they cannot review cases after parental rights have been terminated, they will not keep pressure on an agency to ensure efforts are made to place children in adoptive homes.

Beyond these generic issues, there are also a series of potential implementation barriers that may stem directly from a particular policy that is being carried out. Consider three that have special relevance for the mandates of P.L. 96-272.

In the first place, there is the danger of oversimplification of the philosophical intent of the new reforms. For example, while the underlying goals of P.L. 96-272 emphasize alternatives to placement, this does not mean that the designers of or advocates for the legislation thought that these services would work for every child, or that foster care per se was a bad thing to be avoided at all costs. Implementation of the new law will be severely undermined if persons charged with implementing it attempt to use the law's mandates to rationalize a decision to leave an abused child in a home without sufficient supports, or to return a child home prematurely.

Similarly, overzealous interpretations of the law's mandates for permanent families for children can also result in harm to children, contrary to the law's intent. For example, the law's emphasis on ensuring that children be adopted would not justify a worker's efforts to remove a fifteen-year-old adolescent from the foster home in which the youth had lived since the age of three because the foster parents wanted the youth to remain with their family but could not adopt.

A second potential barrier is the danger of interpreting the procedural protections required under P.L. 96-272 in a mechanical, *pro forma* way without capitalizing on the opportunity to use them to do thoughtful, individualized case planning and careful reviews of each child. This danger, of course, is always present in creating a system of checks and balances. At the same time, even if much of the implementation is mechanical, the fact that the safeguards are included as statutory requirements makes possible challenges by advocates when abuses are gross. Indeed, the detail included in P.L. 96-272 for the case plans and periodic reviews gives those interested in monitoring implementation of the law criteria upon which to challenge noncompliance. If such detail were not included and regulations for the law were not issued, there would be no basis upon which to argue that a certain minimum level of performance was required.

Third, but closely related to the danger of carrying out safeguards in a *pro forma* way, is the danger of creating paper accountability systems that do not feed back in a meaningful way into future administrative and policy decisions. For example, unless state information systems that are developed pursuant to P.L. 96-272 make aggregate data readily available to state officials and advocates in useful ways, the state may be technically in compliance with the law but losing an opportunity to create an active management tool. Similarly the information system should be set up in a way that will assist in updating case plans and case reviews while protecting the privacy rights of individual clients.

It is obvious from this discussion that the principles reflected in new child welfare policies will only benefit real children and families if they are meaningfully carried out. The issues involved in implementing formal policy mandates are complex, but the challenge is clear. If that challenge is to be met, social workers and other child welfare professionals, public and voluntary service providers, foster parents, adoptive parents, other child advocates, lawyers, judges, and legislators will have to strengthen their efforts to make sure the policies work for individual children and that the system is reformed so that it better meets the needs of all the children and families it intends to serve.

CONCLUSION

In this chapter we have examined the basic policy framework for child welfare as reflected in federal and state statutes, administrative directives, and fiscal policies, and as it has been modified over time by court decisions. We have highlighted implications of the most recent and major shift in child welfare policy, the enactment of P.L. 96-272, the Adoption Assistance and Child Welfare Act of 1980, and we have described the challenges involved in implementing formal policy mandates.

In concluding, it is appropriate to emphasize three points. First, the changes in child welfare policy over the past decade reflect an effort to strengthen the states' capacity to carry out their responsibilities to children needing child welfare services. More specifically, the thrust of these changes has been to see that mechanisms and services are in place to prevent the inappropriate use of foster care, to insure permanence for children in the system, and to strengthen procedural protections afforded to children and parents being served by the system.

Second, while the rhetoric of prevention and permanence may sometimes seem simplistic and overstated, the actual modifications in existing systems that are necessary to make the concepts of prevention and permanence work for individual children and families are extremely complex. They require balancing many different issues and dealing with predictable but not easily solved dilemmas. So, for example, caseworkers must weigh the risks of keeping a child in the home; service planners must balance the need to create preventive and reunification services with the recognition that some children will always need to be in out-of-home care; and proponents of new policies must seek data to evaluate the impact of these changes. This last element is particularly crucial because some critics have charged that the pendulum has swung too far toward families, that we lack the knowledge to predict accurately which children are truly endangered by remaining with their families, and that the skills and strategies necessary to keep many of the troubled families who come to the attention of child welfare agencies together have still not been adequately developed.

Third, although many recent policy reforms have been justified appropriately on grounds that they are cost-effective as well as child- and family-effective, it must be acknowledged that such arguments can be overstated. There is no doubt that long-range cost savings will be realized once a continuum of preventive and reunification services programs is in place and is coupled with case planning and review mechanisms to insure that children are cared for appropriately and moved on to permanent families as quickly as possible. However, costs will be incurred in the development and operation of these services and safeguards.

As a cautionary note in closing, it must also be said that as this chapter is being written, a new set of political and ideological forces has emerged that poses a substantial threat to the recent child welfare policy gains and their continued implementation. The threat is clearest in the emerging support for block grant programs as opposed to categorical grant programs, both at state and federal levels. Categorical grant programs, such as federal child welfare and foster care programs and the federal education programs for handicapped children, can be targeted to respond to specific needs and problems. Block grant programs, in contrast, provide funds to the states with minimal or no direction as to their use. Furthermore, they provide for no continued federal oversight of states' performance on behalf of vulnerable populations with special needs. No conditions are imposed on the state for receipt of the funds.

In the first session of the 97th Congress legislation was introduced to abolish P.L. 96-272 and merge the federal child welfare, foster care, and adoption programs in a general social services block grant. This, of course, would have eliminated the carefully crafted pattern of fiscal incentives and protections built into the law. Any successful move of this nature can be expected to have three very serious consequences for efforts to improve child welfare services. First, it would mark the elimination of any national recognition of the problems in child welfare services across the country. Any federal role on behalf of the vulnerable children and families served by this service would be lost. Second, it would undermine the growing movement within the states, particularly those that have made little or no effort on behalf of children at risk of or in placement, to improve child welfare policies and practices as a result of the reforms in P.L. 96-272. And third, since the effort to repeal P.L. 96-272 is but one piece of a larger effort to repeal all federal support for services to poor and handicapped persons, any weakening of the child welfare system at this time will make it less capable of meeting the increased demands on it caused by other cutbacks in basic support programs. This increased demand on the system will also result in great pressure to maintain the status quo which, as has been learned over the last couple of decades, holds grave risks for children.

NOTES

1. 42 U.S.C. §§620–625.

2. Robert H. Bremner, ed., *Children and Youth in America: A Documentary History, Vol. 3: 1933–1973* (Cambridge, Mass.: Harvard University Press, 1974), p. 615.

3. Bremner, *Children and Youth in America*, p. 623.

4. Bremner, *Children and Youth in America*, pp. 629–30.

5. 42 U.S.C. §626.

6. 42 U.S.C. §608.

7. See Winifred Bell, *Aid to Dependent Children* (New York: New York University Press, 1965), and Bremner, *Children and Youth in America*, p. 593.

8. Winford Oliphant, *AFDC Foster Care: Problems and Recommendations* (New York: Child Welfare League of America, 1974), p. 2.

9. Bremner, *Children and Youth in America*, p. 593.

10. Oliphant, *AFDC Foster Care*, pp. 6–7.

11. An "entitlement program" is one in which the legislative authority requires the payment of benefits to any person meeting the requirements established by law. General Accounting Office, *Budgetary Definitions* (Washington, D.C.: GAO, November 1975), p. 11.

12. See Jane Knitzer, MaryLee Allen, and Brenda McGowan, *Children Without Homes: An Examination of Public Responsibility to Children in Out-of-Home Care* (Washington, D.C.: Children's Defense Fund, 1978), pp. 123–26, 129–31, 133–34.

13. 42 U.S.C. §1397 et seq. For a useful analysis of the Title XX Program from 1975 to 1980, see Candice P. Mueller, "Five Years Later—A Look at Title XX: The Federal Billion Dollar Social Services Fund," *The Grantsmanship Center News* (November/December 1980), pp. 26–68.

14. Title XXIII, Omnibus Reconciliation Act of 1981, P.L. 97-35, August 13, 1981.

15. 42 U.S.C. §§1397 a(a)(2) and (18).

16. See, for example, Eileen Wolff, *Technical Notes—Summaries and Characteristics of States' Title XX Social Services Plan for Fiscal Year 1979* (Washington, D.C.: Department of Health, Education and Welfare, 1980).

17. Title XXIII, Omnibus Reconciliation Act of 1981, P.L. 97-35, August 13, 1981.

18. 42 U.S.C. §5101 et seq.

19. 42 U.S.C. §5111 et seq.

20. 42 U.S.C. §5601 et seq.

21. 42 U.S.C. §5701 et seq.

22. 42 U.S.C. §6001 et seq.

23. 25 U.S.C. §1901 et seq.

24. See, for example, Task Force on Federal, State and Tribal Jurisdiction, *Report on Federal, State and Tribal Jurisdiction—Final Report to the American Indian Policy Review Commission* (Washington, D.C.: U.S. Government Printing Office, 1976).

25. 25 U.S.C. §1915.

26. 42 U.S.C. §1396 et seq.

27. See Children's Defense Fund, *EPSDT: Does It Spell Health Care for Poor Children?* (Washington, D.C.: Children's Defense Fund, 1977).

28. See, for example, the Report of the Select Panel for the Promotion of Child Health to the U.S. Congress and the Secretary of Health and Human Services, *Better Health for Our Children: A National Strategy, Vol. I* (Washington, D.C.: U.S. Department of Health and Human Services, PHS No. 79-55071, 1981), pp. 308–12; and Margaret R. Swire and Florence Kavaler, "The Health Status of Foster Children," *Child Welfare* 56 (December 1977): 635–53.

29. 20 U.S.C. §1401 et seq.

30. Judith Areen, "Intervention Between Parent and Child: A Reappraisal of the State's Role in Child Abuse and Neglect Cases," *The Georgetown Law Journal* 63 (1975): 887–937.

31. Areen, "Intervention Between Parent and Child," pp. 903–10.

32. Grace Abbott, *The Child and the State,* 2 vols. (Chicago: University of Chicago Press, 1938), 2: 164–65.

33. Ibid., p. 166.

34. Ibid., p. 20.

35. See, for example, Robert H. Mnookin, "Foster Care—In Whose Best Interest," *Harvard Educational Review* 43 (November 1973): 599–638; Michael S. Wald, "State Intervention on Behalf of 'Neglected' Children: A Search for Realistic Standards," *Stanford Law Review* 27 (April 1975): 985–1040; and Michael S. Wald, "State Intervention on Behalf of 'Neglected' Children: Standards for Re-

moval of Children from Their Homes, Monitoring the Status of Children in Foster Care, and Termination of Parental Rights," *Stanford Law Review* 28 (April 1976): 623–706.

36. See, for example, Joseph Goldstein, Anna Freud, and Alfred Solnit, *Beyond the Best Interests of the Child* (New York: Free Press, 1973), and *Before the Best Interests of the Child* (New York: Free Press, 1979).

37. Knitzer, Allen, and McGowan, *Children Without Homes*, pp. 195–209.

38. 42 U.S.C. §5103 (b)(2).

39. See Children's Defense Fund, "Statutory Provisions for Periodic Foster Care Review," (Washington, D.C.: Children's Defense Fund, in Press) for a brief description of these review systems. For a further description of several of the models of review, see National Institute for Advanced Studies, *Overview of Five Foster Care Review Systems* (Washington, D.C.: Department of Health and Human Services, OHDS 80-30263, 1980). And for evaluations of two of the models in place in individual states, see Center for Analysis of Public Issues, *In Search of the Paper Children: An Analysis of New Jersey's Foster Care Review Board System* (Princeton, N.J.: Center for Analysis of Public Issues, 1982); and Trudy Festinger, "The New York Court Review of Children in Foster Care," *Child Welfare* 54 (April 1975): 211–45; Trudy Festinger, "The Impact of the New York Court Review of Children in Foster Care: A Follow-up Report," *Child Welfare* 55 (September–October 1976): 525–44.

40. Wash. Rev. Code Ann. §13.34.130.

41. Wash. Rev. Code Ann. §13.34.120.

42. Family Protection Act, S.B. 30, 1976.

43. S.B. 14, Proposed August 18, 1980.

44. Chapters 610 and 611, Laws of 1979, State of New York.

45. Ohio Rev. Code Ann. §5103.151 (Baldwin).

46. Ohio Rev. Code Ann. §§2151.413–2151.414 (Baldwin).

47. Ohio Rev. Code Ann. §§5103.152, 5153.16(N) (Baldwin).

48. Ohio Rev. Code Ann. §2151.412 (Baldwin).

49. Courts have also addressed other due process safeguards to be afforded parties to termination proceedings. For example, the U.S. Supreme Court ruled in March 1982 that before a state may terminate the rights of a parent, due process requires that the state support its allegations by at least clear and convincing evidence.

See *Santosky* v. *Kramer, Commissioner, Ulster County Department of Social Services,* ___ U.S. ___ (1982), No. 80-5889, decided March 24, 1982. See also *Sims* v. *State Department of Public Welfare,* 438 F. Supp. 1179 (S.D. Tex. 1977), *sub nom. Moore* v. *Sims,* 442 U.S. 415 (1979), and *Alsager* v. *District Court of Polk County,* 406 F. Supp. 10 (S.D. Iowa, 1975), 545 F. 2d 1137 (8th Cir. 1976).

50. See, for example, *Quilloin* v. *Walcott,* 434 U.S. 246 (1978) [father of illegitimate child who has never had custody of nor taken responsibility for child is not entitled to "veto" adoption by mother's husband].

51. Courts faced with foster parents who have wished to adopt have denied the existence of any constitutionally protected interest in the foster parent–child relationship. See, for example, *Kyees* v. *County Department of Public Welfare,* 600 F. 2d 693 (7th Cir. 1979), and *Drummond* v. *Fulton County Department of Families,* 563 F. 2d 1200 (5th Cir. en banc 1977). Some state courts have recognized a constitutionally protected interest entitling foster parents to a hearing before removal of children from their homes. See *Goldstein* v. *Lavine,* 418 N.Y.S. 2d 845 (Sup. Ct. 1979). Other state courts have also recognized the child's interest in the preservation of a relationship with a foster parent even when the natural parent is not unfit. See *Bennett* v. *Jeffreys,* 40 N.Y. 2d 543, 387 N.Y.S. 2d 821 (1976).

52. See, for example, *Emory* v. *Sosnowski,* C.A. No. 79-99 (E.D. Pa., filed Jan. 1979).

53. See, for example, *Callis* v. *Railey,* No. NA 79-132-cm (S.D. Ind., filed Sept. 21, 1979); *Lynch* v. *Dukakis,* No. 78-2152-G (D. Mass., filed Aug. 22, 1979); *Cameron* v. *Montgomery County Child Welfare Service,* No. 78-3677 (E.D. Pa., filed May 22, 1979); *Lisa F.* v. *Snider,* No. S79-0103 (N.D. Ind., filed Apr. 19, 1979); and *O'Dell* v. *O'Bannon,* No. 79-744 (E.D. Pa., filed Mar. 2, 1979).

54. See, for example, *In Re: P.* v. *Kentucky Department of Human Resources,* 88 *Family Law Reporter* 2008, Nov. 3, 1981; *Joseph and Josephine A.* v. *New Mexico Department of Human Services,* No. 80-623-J (D.N.M., filed July 25, 1980); *Smith* v. *Alameda County Social Services Agency,* 153 Cal. Rptr. 711 (Cal. App. 1979); and *Child* v. *Beame,* 412 F. Supp. 593 (S.D. N.Y., 1976).

55. See, for example, *Sinhogar* v. *Parry,* No. 14138/77 (N.Y. Supreme Ct., filed July 26, 1977); and *Gary W.* v. *Cherry, sub nom. Gary W.* v. *Louisiana,* 437 F. Supp. 1209 (E.D. La. 1976).

56. See, for example, *Bobby D.* v. *Barry,* No. Misc. 16-77 (D.C. Superior Ct., filed Nov. 21, 1977), and *Player* v. *Alabama,* 400 F. Supp. 249 (M.D. Ala. 1975). See also cases raising concerns about the treatment of developmentally and mentally disabled persons, *Halderman* v. *Pennhurst State School and Hospital,* 446 F. Supp. 1295 (E.D. Pa., 1978), modified 612 F. 2d 84 (3rd Cir. 1979), remanded 101 S. Ct. 1531 (1981), reinstated No. 78-1490 (3rd Cir. Feb. 26, 1982); and *Evans* v. *Washington,* 459 F. Supp. 483 (D.D.C., 1978).

57. See, for example, *Terry D.* v. *Rader,* No. CIV-78-004-T (W.D. Okla., filed Sept. 25, 1979) and *G. L.* v. *Missouri Division of Family Services,* No. 77-0242-CV-W-3 (W.D. Mo., filed May 2, 1979). See also *Inmates of Boys Training School* v. *Affeck,* 346 F. Supp. 1354 (D.R.I., 1972), and *Marterella* v. *Kelley,* 349 F. Supp. 575 (S.D. N.Y., 1972).

58. See, for example, *Bradford* v. *Davis,* No. A7810-16902 (Ore. Cir. Ct., Multnomah Co., filed Feb. 22, 1979), and *Smith* v. *Alameda County Social Services Agency,* No. 488366-5 (Alameda Co., Calif., Super. Ct., filed Nov. 15, 1976).

59. Chapters 610 and 611, Laws of 1979, State of New York.

60. A copy of the Policy Statement on Parental Visiting is set forth in Knitzer, Allen, and McGowan, *Children Without Homes,* pp. 192–94.

61. Ohio Rev. Code Ann. §5153.16(N) (Baldwin).

62. Minn. Stat. Ann. §259.40 Subd. 7.

63. See Ariz. Rev. Stat. §§8-515, 516, and S.C. Code Ann. §§43-13-10-43-13-70.

64. Henry Maas and Richard Engler, *Children in Need of Parents* (New York: Columbia University Press, 1959).

65. Caren Masem, *Child Welfare in Arkansas* (Little Rock, Ark.: Human Services Providers Association of Arkansas, 1979).

66. See, for example, State Social Welfare Board, *Children Waiting: Report on Foster Care* (Sacramento, Calif.: California Health and Welfare Agency, 1972); and Delmer J. Pascoe, *Review, Synthesis and Recommendations of Seven Foster Care Studies in California* (Sacramento, Calif.: Children's Research Institute of California, 1974).

67. There have been numerous studies of foster care in New York State and New York City. They include Blanche Bernstein, Donald Snider, and William Meezan, *Foster Care Needs and Alternatives to Placement: A Projection for 1975–1985* (Albany, N.Y.:

New York State Board of Social Welfare, 1975); David Fanshel and Eugene B. Shinn, *Children in Foster Care: A Longitudinal Investigation* (New York: Columbia University Press, 1978); Mayor's Task Force on Foster Care Services, *Redirecting Foster Care: A Report to the Mayor of the City of New York* (New York: Mayor's Task Force on Foster Care Services, 1980); and New York City Comptroller's Office, *The Children Are Waiting* (New York: Institute of Public Affairs, 1977).

68. Governor's Advocacy Council for Children and Youth, *"Why Can't I Have a Home?" A Report on Foster Care and Adoption in North Carolina* (Raleigh, N.C.: Governor's Advocacy Council for Children and Youth, 1978).

69. Alan Gruber, *Children in Foster Care: Destitute, Neglected, Betrayed* (New York: Human Services Press, 1978).

70. New Mexico Department of Human Services, *In Limbo: A Study of New Mexico's Foster Care Children* (Santa Fe, N.M.: New Mexico Department of Human Services, 1978).

71. See, for example, Knitzer, Allen, and McGowan, *Children Without Homes;* Joseph Persico, *Who Knows? Who Cares? Forgotten Children in Foster Care* (New York: National Commission on Children in Need of Parents, 1979); and Ann Shyne and Anita Schroeder, *National Study of Social Services to Children and Their Families* (Washington, D.C.: Administration for Children, Youth and Families, HEW, 1978).

72. See, for example, Knitzer, Allen, and McGowan, *Children Without Homes*, pp. 15–20; Persico, *Who Knows? Who Cares?*, p. 28. Data from individual states also indicate that families are seldom offered services prior to placement. Shirley Vasaly, *Foster Care in Five States: A Synthesis and Analysis of Studies from Arizona, California, Iowa, Massachusetts, and Vermont* (Washington, D.C.: Office of Human Development Services, HEW, 1976), pp. 24–27.

73. See, for example, *The State of Children in Need* (Chicago, Ill.: Better Government Association, 1979), p. 11; and Office of the Governor, State of New York, *State of New York Children's Budget, 1980–81* (Albany, N.Y.: 1980), pp. 60, 80, and 82.

74. See, for example, Robert Mnookin, "Child Custody Adjudication: Judicial Functions in the Face of Indeterminacy," *Law and Contemporary Problems* 39 (Summer 1975): 226–93; and Wald, "State Intervention on Behalf of 'Neglected' Children: A Search for Realistic Standards."

75. See, for example, Bernstein, Snider, and Meezan, *Foster Care Needs and Alternatives to Placement*, pp. 20–25; and Knitzer, Allen, and McGowan, *Children Without Homes*, pp. 37–40. The harm of inappropriate placements is intensified by the frequent movement of children from one placement to another. See New York City Comptroller's Office, *The Children Are Waiting*, pp. 10–11; and Vasaly, *Foster Care in Five States*, pp. 55–57.

76. For a detailed discussion of issues related to the out-of-state placement of children, see the series of articles in J. C. Hall et al., eds., *Major Issues in Juvenile Justice Information and Training: Readings in Public Policy*, Section I: *The Interstate Placement of Children* (Columbus, Ohio: Academy for Contemporary Problems, 1981) pp. 3–165.

77. 42 U.S.C. §608 (1980).

78. 45 C.F.R. §233.110(a)(5).

79. Whereas a state can claim federal reimbursement for room and board as well as medical care for a Medicaid-eligible child in a hospital, it can only claim federal reimbursement for medical care for a Medicaid-eligible child in a foster family home. Susan Jacoby in "The $73,000 Abandoned Babies," *New York Times Magazine*, March 6, 1977, reported on the nearly 300 children growing up in New York City hospitals.

80. See, for example, Fanshel and Shinn, *Children in Foster Care*, pp. 85–111.

81. Knitzer, Allen, and McGowan, *Children Without Homes*, pp. 22–23.

82. Numerous studies have reported children remaining in care for over eighteen months. Shyne and Schroeder in *National Study of Social Services to Children* estimate that the average length of stay in foster care is 2.5 years, with one-fourth of the children in care for over six years (pp. 120–21). Other studies suggest that five years is the average length of time in care. See David Fanshel and John Grundy, *Computerized Data for Children in Foster Care: First Analyses From a Management Information System in New York City* (New York: Child Welfare Information Services, Inc., 1975), p. 7; and Vasaly, *Foster Care in Five States*, p. 21. There are also some significant variations by race. See Masem, *Child Welfare in Arkansas*, p. 12.

83. See General Accounting Office, *Children in Foster Care Institutions: Steps Government Can Take to Improve Their Care* (Washington, D.C.: General Accounting Office, 1977); and reports by

the HEW Audit Agency of reviews of the AFDC-Foster Care Programs in Kansas (Kansas City Regional Office, Audit Control No. 07-60251, June 16, 1976), Maryland (Philadelphia Regional Office, Audit Control No. 03-70256, February 11, 1977), and North Carolina (Atlanta Regional Office, Audit Control No. 04-60255, December 17, 1976).

84. See Knitzer, Allen, and McGowan, *Children Without Homes*, p. 69; and *Where Are the Children?* (New York: New York State Council of Voluntary Child Care Agencies, 1978), pp. 14–15.

85. Several studies have reported that participation in the compact has little impact on the knowledge of state officials about children placed out-of-state. Knitzer, Allen, and McGowan, *Children Without Homes*, pp. 70–73; *Where Are the Children?*, p. 7. But for further information about the compact and its potential, see Bruce Gross and Mitchell Wendell, "Interstate Services for Children and Interstate Compacts: An Analysis of Approaches for Effecting Change," and Jane C. McMonigle, "Strengthening the Compacts: Administrative and Bureaucratic Approaches," in Hall et al., *Major Issues in Juvenile Justice Information and Training.*

86. Knitzer, Allen, and McGowan, *Children Without Homes*, p. 66.

87. General Accounting Office, *Children in Foster Care Institutions*, pp. 23–26.

88. 42 U.S.C. §5102.

89. 42 U.S.C. §5633 (a)(12)(A).

90. See, for example, both national studies: Knitzer, Allen, and McGowan, *Children Without Homes*, pp. 97–99, 137–140, 185–191; and Persico, *Who Knows? Who Cares?*, pp. 30–39; and state studies: Governor's Advocacy Council on Children and Youth, *Why Can't I Have a Home?*, pp. 8–9; Masem, *Child Welfare in Arkansas*, pp. 23–24; and New Mexico Department of Human Services, *In Limbo*, pp. 65–66.

91. See Brenda G. McGowan, "The Case Advocacy Function in Child Welfare Practice," *Child Welfare* 52 (May 1978): 275–84; and Brenda G. McGowan, "Strategies in Bureaucracies," in *Working for Children*, ed. Judith S. Mearig (San Francisco: Jossey-Bass, 1978); and Report of the Joint Commission on Mental Health of Children, *Crisis in Child Mental Health: Challenge for the 1970s* (New York: Harper and Row, 1970).

92. See, for example, Sanford Katz, *When Parents Fail: The Law's Response to Family Breakdown* (Boston: Beacon Press, 1971); Jo-

seph Goldstein, "Finding the Least Detrimental Alternative: The Problem for the Law of Child Placement," *The Psychoanalytic Study of the Child, 1972* (New York: Quadrangle Books, 1973); Mnookin, "Foster Care—In Whose Best Interest?"and "Child Custody Adjudication: Judicial Function in the Face of Indeterminacy;" and Wald, "State Intervention on Behalf of 'Neglected' Children: A Search for Realistic Standards," and "State Intervention on Behalf of 'Neglected' Children: Standards for Removal of Children From Their Homes."

93. See earlier discussion on Court Decisions.

94. See, for example, Knitzer, Allen, and McGowan, *Children Without Homes*, pp. 22–25, 40–42.

95. Fanshel and Shinn, *Children in Foster Care*, pp. 85–111.

96. See, for example, Goldstein et al., *Beyond the Best Interests of the Child.*

97. See, for example, Goldstein et al., *Before the Best Interests of the Child.* Contrast with Michael S. Wald, "Thinking About Public Policy Toward Abuse and Neglect of Children: A Review of *Before the Best Interests of the Child,*" *Michigan Law Review* 78 (March 1980): 645–93.

98. For descriptions of a variety of preventive service efforts, see Bertram Beck, *The Lower East Side Family Union: A Social Invention* (New York: Foundation for Child Development, 1979); Marvin Bryce and June C. Lloyd, eds., *Treating Families in the Home: An Alternative to Placement* (Springfield, Ill.: Charles C Thomas, 1981); Marvin R. Burt and Ralph R. Balyeat, *A Comprehensive Emergency Services System for Neglected and Abused Children* (New York: Vantage Press, 1977); Esther Callard and Patricia Morin, *PACT (Parents and Children Together): An Alternative to Foster Care* (Detroit, Mich.: Department of Family and Consumer Resources, Wayne State University, 1979); Sheila Maybanks and Marvin Bryce, eds., *Home-Based Services for Children and Families* (Springfield, Ill.: Charles C Thomas, 1979); and Elsa ten Broeck, "The Extended Family Center: A Home Away from Home for Abused Children and Their Parents," *Children Today* 3 (March–April 1974): 2–6.

99. For descriptions of a variety of permanency efforts, see Sallie Churchill, Bonnie Carlson, and Lynn Nybell, *No Child Is Unadoptable: A Reader on Adoption of Children with Special Needs* (Beverly Hills, Calif.: Sage Publications, 1979); Martha L. Jones, "Stopping Foster Care Drift: A Review of Legislation and Special

Programs, *Child Welfare* 57 (November 1978): 571–80; Anthony N. Maluccio and Paula A. Sinanoglu, eds., *The Challenge of Partnership: Working with Parents of Children in Foster Care* (New York: Child Welfare League of America, 1981); Victor Pike, "Permanent Planning for Foster Children: The Oregon Project," *Children Today* 5 (November–December 1976): 22–25, 41; *Foster Care Reform in the 70's: Final Report of the Permanency Planning Dissemination Project* (Portland Ore.: Regional Research Institute, Portland State University, 1981).

100. See, for example, Arthur Emlen et al., *Overcoming Barriers to Planning for Children in Foster Care* (Portland Ore.: Regional Research Institute, Portland State University, 1978); David Fanshel and Eugene Shinn, *Dollars and Sense in Foster Care of Children: A Look at Cost Factors* (New York: Child Welfare League of America, 1972); Mary Ann Jones, Renee Neuman, and Ann W. Shyne, *A Second Chance for Families* (New York: Child Welfare League of America, 1976); and "Cost-effectiveness: Home Based Family Centered Service Programs" (Oakland, Iowa: National Clearinghouse for Home-Based Services to Children and Their Families, 1980), pp. 3–5.

101. See Hearings before the Subcommittee on Children and Youth of the Senate Committee on Labor and Public Welfare, *Adoption and Foster Care, 1975*, 94th Cong., 1st Sess., 1975.

102. Ibid.

103. Paul Mott, *Foster Care and Adoption: Some Key Policy Issues*, A Report of the U.S. Senate Committee on Labor and Public Welfare, Subcommittee on Children and Youth (Washington, D.C.: U.S. Government Printing Office, 1975).

104. See Joint Hearing before the Subcommittee on Children and Youth of the Senate Committee on Labor and Public Welfare and the Subcommittee on Select Education of the House Committee on Education and Labor, *Foster Care: Problems and Issues, Part 1*, 94th Cong., 1st Sess., 1975.

105. See Hearing before the Subcommittee on Select Education of the House Committee on Education and Labor, *Foster Care: Problems and Issues, Part 2*, 94th Cong., 2nd Sess., 1976.

106. 42 U.S.C. §5111 et seq.

107. 42 U.S.C. §§620 et seq. and 670 et seq.

108. 42 U.S.C. §623 (c).

109. 42 U.S.C. §623 (c)(1).

110. 42 U.S.C. §627 (a)(2)(C).
111. 42 U.S.C. §627 (a)(1) and (2)(B), (C).
112. 42 U.S.C. §627 (b).
113. 42 U.S.C. §627 (b).
114. 42 U.S.C. §671 (a)(15).
115. 42 U.S.C. §672 (a)(1).
116. 42 U.S.C. §673.
117. 42 U.S.C. §673 (b).
118. 42 U.S.C. §672 (b) and (c).
119. 42 U.S.C. §§627, 671, and 672.
120. 42 U.S.C. §627 (a)(2)(A).
121. 42 U.S.C. §627 (a)(1).
122. 42 U.S.C. §§627 (a)(2)(B), 671 (a)(16), and 675 (1)(5), and (6).
123. 42 U.S.C. §675 (5)(A).
124. 42 U.S.C. §675 (6).
125. 42 U.S.C. §675 (5)(C).
126. 42 U.S.C. §675 (5)(C).
127. 42 U.S.C. §671 (a)(12).
128. For example, a recent national study reported that three out of four children being served by public social service departments were assigned to staff who were dependent on in-service training to acquire whatever knowledge and skill they had about families and children. Shyne and Schroeder, *National Study of Social Services to Children,* pp. 147–48.
129. See N.Y. Soc. Serv. Law §409-g.
130. See, for example, *Report of Special Grand Jury Regarding the Handling of Child Abuse and Maltreatment in Monroe County, N.Y., 1973–1978* (Empaneled on February 14, 1978) and "Validation Studies Regarding Declassification Trend," *NASW News,* November 1977, p. 8.

PART II
ENHANCING FAMILY FUNCTIONING

The three chapters in Part II attempt to specify a foundation for child welfare services by describing policy and program initiatives designed to enhance the functioning of all families within our society and the special service needs of families and children at risk of separation. The purpose of these chapters is to highlight the fact that all families in a modern, industrial nation face developmental tasks and stresses that may require a societal response and that families at risk demand a special response. We believe that without improvements in social provisions for families, the child welfare system will continue to be overburdened and reforms within this residual field of service will have only a limited impact on service recipients.

Chapter 4 presents a policy framework for the provision of social supports to all families. It argues that a general reform agenda is too broad to impact significantly on the needs of families with children and that there is a need for policy initiatives that are immediately relevant to families. According to the authors, such a "family policy" would be comprised of a "benefit-service package," which would include cash and in-kind benefits as well as social services. Such a package would include changes and additions to the current income maintenance, housing, and health care systems; programs to address the need for maternity benefits and child care; and the further development of the personal social service system.

Chapter 5 describes new directions for service delivery that will enhance family functioning. It argues that many families in society, not just "problem" families, may need service, and that a broader perspective on service delivery is called for. In this regard, the chapter advocates for an expansion of the interventive repertoires of individual workers as well as changes in the current service delivery system. The need for a coordinated approach to service delivery and the delivery of services within the families' environment are highlighted.

Chapter 6 focuses on the importance of services to families and children at risk of separation from each other. It looks at services such as day care and homemaker service in light of the roles they can play in preventing family dissolution. It examines planned emergency placement as a way of insuring that placements are brief and appropriate. Using available research findings as a springboard, the chapter then looks at the need to expand the preventive/protective service repertoire of agencies. It concludes with an example of a neighborhood-based agency that provides a comprehensive array of services to families in order to reduce family stress and limit the entrance of children into substitute care.

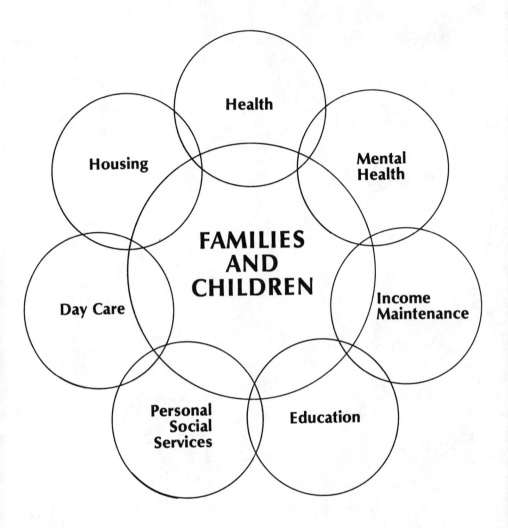

CHAPTER 4

"CHILD WELFARE" AND THE WELFARE OF FAMILIES WITH CHILDREN: A CHILD AND FAMILY POLICY AGENDA

Sheila B. Kamerman and Alfred J. Kahn

Those most concerned with reform of the traditional child welfare "system" in the U.S. have focused on such goals as de-institutionalization, permanency planning, subsidized adoption, case review, normalization, administrative and management changes, and additional and more reliable funding. These generally accepted orientations are reflected in organizational resolutions, legislative advocacy, articles in professional journals, training programs, and technical assistance activities by federal and state government agencies. Some child welfare reformers also advocate basic changes in social policy. As summarized by Billingsley and Giovannoni, these include: a full employment economy, a guaranteed minimum income, comprehensive child development services, meaningful education, a restructured health care system, and decent housing.[1]

Our contention is that not only are the proposed child welfare reforms too scattered and unfocused, but the proposed social policy agenda is too diffuse and overarching, lacking any specific targeting on children or families with children. Suggestions for specific child welfare reforms are addressed elsewhere in this volume. Our focus in this chapter is on the policy and program context in which child welfare services are embedded and on the need for a new perspective and a new direction in the policy agenda.

THE CURRENT SITUATION

A review of recent activities in the child welfare field reveals that the locus of legislative and executive branch attention and organizational initiative on the part of all parties has shifted from improving child welfare practice by direct service practitioners to improving administration and control of the child welfare service system or "nonsystem." Generalist administrators, lawyers, and advocates have taken the lead. Considerable power and initiative have been wrested from professional child welfare workers. Though the latter have not disputed the goals of the administrative reforms, they have not adequately and successfully protected the staffing and practice requirements necessary to carry out their own ends. This conclusion is suggested by an outside perspective, supported by an examination of developments that goes beyond statements of intent, and is documented elsewhere in this volume.

In attempting to assess what this means and what should be expected if current directions continue to be followed and current proposals for reform implemented, several observations must be summarized.

First, a variety of developments on the national scene have led to a *downplaying of educational and training requirements for front-line child welfare staff.* The data available are not fully satisfactory, but there is evidence of a substantial decline in "average" preparation for this difficult work and in average practice competence. This decline has come at a time when greater demands are being made upon personnel in the ways in which they deal with specific cases, in the types of cases presented to them, and in the ways in which they participate in tighter administrative control procedures.[2]

Second, there has been a *major increase in the number of cases being fed into the system.* This is explained, in part, by federally funded initiatives in child abuse and neglect and by federal funding under AFDC-Foster Care, which permits transfer of some costs previously borne by states to the federal government but requires court approval of placement decisions. The large increase in the number of children entering the system resulted from an earlier wave of initiatives and "reforms" in the mid-1960s and is sometimes used to "prove" child welfare system failures.

Third, as the administrative and control requirements have increased, *there clearly has been a major decline in time and opportunity for staff to do direct work with families and children,* who are the clients of the system. Presumably, helping families and children cope with the major transitions in their lives related to substitute and supplementary care and understanding their preferences and their responses makes a major difference in the meaning of the service to them and the success of the intervention. While not deliberately, these services appear to have been traded off for administrative reform.

Fourth, there has been an *ever larger fragmentation of federal funding support* through ad hoc purchase of service and care for children and families through voluntary and public agencies. The system reforms being promoted call for coherence, integration, "system." Mandating or encouraging special outlets for abuse and neglect, home finding, adoption planning, staff training, and strengthening information and management—while at the same time subsidizing the purchase of care through multiple providers in most of the states—complicates the task of developing and implementing a cohesive policy and achieving professional goals or national goals endorsed by Congress.

Fifth, *voluntary child welfare agencies,* once the field's "cutting edge," *have lost their clarity as to identity and mission.* Each agency now "is" what its grants dictate and its funders have contracted for; each jurisdiction has developed its own special pattern. In prior years, each year brought new changes as federal funding opportunities changed and as community-based services or institutions attempted to meet their budgets.

Sixth, *the Adoption Assistance and Child Welfare Reform Act of 1980,* which provided for subsidized adoption and increased funding for "preventive" child welfare services also *sets a cap on foster care funding under AFDC.* The effects of this legislation cannot be assessed now, but there are significant possibilities for unanticipated negative consequences as well as for the projected benefits.

Finally, exacerbating all these trends are the *as yet unknown consequences of Reagan administration policies,* which include major funding cuts and some possible clustering of selected categorical programs into broader social services block grants.

At the same time, over the past decade the country has witnessed a shift in the poverty problem from the aged and large families with low-paid workers to single mothers, many of whom are not working but are at home rearing children. This development has increased still further the demands upon the child welfare service system. Other developments of recent years which have resulted in increased service demand include: the disproportionately high minority—especially black—poverty and unemployment rates; the continued failures of schools and labor markets to deal effectively with large percentages of black and other minority youth, and the apparent relationship of the resulting deviant career patterns to a variety of social problems, including teenage childbirth; and the continued evidence of family structural difficulties and personal problems, which generate problems for children in all strata of our society. Clearly, the feeder system for children's programs affecting those in trouble is not changing significantly for the better.

Given these developments, we would suggest skepticism that either the administrative and control reforms or the practice upgrading—espoused by all parties, however different their emphases—will respond adequately to the child welfare service problem or the current interest in prevention. The practice initiatives and the administrative-control initiatives are both required, and they must be coordinated and balanced. Yet, together, they remain limited, even if the demands on the system are reduced, realistic expectations carefully delineated, and mechanisms developed for ensuring that agencies fulfill their primary, if traditional, functions.

Moreover, even assuming some improvement in child welfare services narrowly defined, no one would suggest that attention should be diverted from developing better social policies. Nor would we—or others—suggest that adequate child welfare services can in any way substitute for basic social provision any more than good social policy can completely eliminate the need for child welfare services. Indeed, our contention is that, ultimately, effective reform of children's services is contingent on a foundation of basic social provision. Where such provision does not exist, child welfare services will be overburdened and inevitably prove inadequate. The question, therefore, is what are the components of such a social policy agenda? And how can such an agenda be achieved at a time when resources are limited and there is apparently much disaffection with the involvement of the federal government in social programs?

We do not quarrel with general statements about the need for labor market reform, adequate income, health services, decent housing, and so forth. These goals are shared by people of many backgrounds and reflect needs that are not limited to families who enter the child welfare system. It does seem reasonable to hope that the flow of children into substitute care and the break-up of families would to some degree be decreased by adequate attention to a social reform agenda of the kind often proposed. A further attack on discrimination should also show significant results.

However, it is also our view that within such broad reform agenda there is need for *specific* attention to the needs, problems, and circumstances that especially affect families with young children. There is need for a social reform agenda focused on the typical needs and problems of such families on the premise that a more adequate social minimum for families with children and a more satisfactory pattern for supplementing family capacities would have some relationship to the difficulties experienced by parents as individuals and the problems within families that constantly feed the child welfare system its large numbers of cases.

Our argument, therefore, is that although existing policy recommendations have addressed important societal reform issues, they have failed to specify adequately a variety of targeted and feasible policy initiatives directly and immediately relevant to the problems of families with children. Furthermore, the service reforms that have been proposed or initiated have failed to seek the placement of child welfare services within a family support system, thus continuing an emphasis on substitute care and missing preventive and basic family support initiatives.

The remainder of this chapter is devoted to some hypotheses in these two domains.

POLICY AND PROGRAM INITIATIVES

We begin with a statement of our perspective. Where others suggest broad social policy goals, we start from a perspective that is directly focused on children and families, namely the subcategory of social policy called "family policy." We use the concept of "family policy" to suggest a particular concern for the quality of family life and the well-being of families with children generally.[3]

Employing family and child well-being as a criterion for developing a social policy agenda suggests:

—a view of the family as a central institution in the society

—a definition of "family" that is sufficiently broad to encompass a variety of types, structures, roles, and relationships while maintaining some discriminatory power

—a definition of "policy" that assumes a diversity and multiplicity of policies rather than a uniform, monolithic, comprehensive legislative act

—a definition of "family policy"—in other words, famil*ies* polic*ies* —that goes beyond the concept of a policy field (specific laws, regulations, activities explicitly designed to affect families, such as Aid to Families with Dependent Children [AFDC], maternal and child health programs, child care services) and/or a policy instrument (labor market or population policies, social control policies) to include all governmental and, as relevant, nongovernmental policies which seek to affect primary group relationships and structures.

We would stress that our focus is on child and family well-being broadly defined. We do not mean to minimize the needs of the aged or of the handicapped or of isolated individuals. However needy, worthy, and vulnerable these groups are, they are not our policy targets here, although they clearly are among those addressed by social policy generally. Furthermore, our concern is with all children and all families with children, not just those who are particularly vulnerable or at special risk (whatever that may mean). Our thesis is that only on such a base can we build adequate special services for those children who need them.

Applying a family policy perspective, we note at the onset the need to develop an agenda that includes cash and in-kind benefits, as well as services—what we have termed elsewhere a child and family policy "benefit-service package."[4] Historically, the provision of a cash or of an in-kind benefit was viewed as a choice between two alternative strategies for achieving the same goal, usually income support. The conventional distinction between the functions of the two has usually focused on the question of which values are to be maximized in relation to an objective. Where freedom of choice is most important, the policy has been to provide cash; where the goal is to guarantee access to a particular good (food, housing) or to a particular service (health care, education) or to constrain a recipient's use of a grant, an in-kind benefit has been preferred. We do not ignore other motives, such as insuring sales of farm produce, constraining choice of people believed to be unreliable, exerting control over those viewed as deviant, and so forth. In recent years, an equally useful further distinction has been made in relation to in-kind benefits between an entitlement to use a service and the offer of financial supports, fee payments, or a voucher with which to purchase the service. The enormous expansion of Medicare, Medicaid, and food stamps in the United States during the 1970s highlighted this latter approach.

Our family policy agenda, therefore, takes the form of a benefit-service package, which includes cash benefits, in-kind benefits, and direct provision of services. We emphasize that this is an agenda, not a detailed proposal; where we offer detail, it is for illustrative purposes only.

THE COMPONENTS OF A CHILD AND FAMILY BENEFIT-SERVICE PACKAGE

Income Maintenance

Earned income continues to be the primary source of income for the overwhelming majority of individuals and families in the U.S., primarily because more people are working today than ever before. Thirty years ago less than 70 percent of people eighteen and over received income; today 92 percent of the adult population has income. Although this change partly reflects the higher incidence of transfer payments, an overwhelming rise in employment has significantly increased the number of people with wages and salaries, or earnings from paid work. Of a total civilian noninstitutional population aged sixteen and over of about 166 million, 108 million or 65 percent were in the labor force in 1981 (and 60 percent were employed).[5] Close to 90 percent of the families in the U.S. receive earned income.[6]

Yet despite the growth in the proportion of families receiving earned income, 9 percent of the families, including 13 percent of the families with children (with 16 percent of the children) had incomes under the poverty level in 1979, and 60 percent of these poor families were headed by females.[7] (The poverty threshold for a nonfarm family of four was $7400 in 1979 and $8400 in 1981.) Most of these women were not working or were working in low-paying jobs. Only those single mothers who worked full time all year managed to have family income above the poverty level, and only the availability of food stamps brought some more of these women up to or above the poverty threshold. We are not even mentioning here the large numbers of families with children whose incomes are above the poverty level but below the Bureau of Labor Statistics "modest but adequate" minimum standard.

Clearly, a policy that views labor market issues in a family as well as a social policy context must address the need for what is most fundamental here—the availability of jobs. In addition, however, one must look at the important role played by government transfer payments in maintaining family income, particularly social insurance benefits (old age, survivors, and disability benefits [OASDI], unemployment insurance, veterans benefits) received primarily by the aged but also by children as "survivors" and dependents, and public assistance benefits (AFDC, SSI, home relief), most of which are received by female-headed families with children. Almost one-half of all families received some form of government transfer payments in 1979. About 3 million children benefited under OASDI, a small additional number under unemployment insurance and SSI, and 7.5 million under AFDC.[8] The primary functions of these programs are: (1) to replace the earnings of those forced out of employment temporarily by unemployment (or in many countries by sickness) or permanently by age or disability, and thus to protect their standard of living, and (2) to substitute for earnings for those viewed as unemployable (sole mothers with children).

If a major cause of poverty is the absence or loss of employment income, the major secondary cause is the poor "fit" between employment income and family needs. Current U.S. policies are largely directed toward solving the problems of absent or lost employment income.

Even here, however, coverage is not complete as we indicate below. Perhaps more important is that except in a very modest fashion through the earned income tax credit and food stamps, no policies exist to address the gap between wages and family needs.

Stated somewhat differently, the major functions of a country's income maintenance policies are:

(1) to replace earnings lost temporarily or permanently as a consequence of certain socially defined risks (for example, OASDI)

(2) to substitute for earnings for those viewed as unable to work and in financial need (for example, AFDC)

(3) to supplement the income of those whose earnings may be inadequate to meet the needs of their families (for example, family allowances or child benefits)

This last function has increasingly been expanded in other countries to include both a universal income supplement for all families with children (to compensate for the economic costs of rearing children) and some form of income-tested benefit (to supplement the income of families with low earned income). Though these latter benefits are income-tested, eligibility criteria are such that half or more of the families with children may be beneficiaries, thus substantially reducing, if not eliminating, the likelihood of stigma.

Currently, two of these functions are inadequately addressed by U.S. policies, and families with children suffer undue economic penalties as a consequence. Further, our income maintenance system is skewed, leading to an overemphasis on means testing and a concomitant discouragement of work by low-skilled women.

More specifically, although U.S. policies have been relatively generous in replacing earnings lost for the most frequently defined social risks (through OASDI), we have no provision in the case of one short-term risk—the loss of earned income that may occur when a child is born or at the time of maternity. Moreover, those benefits that substitute for earnings (such as AFDC) under no circumstances provide a full substitute. As in other countries, public assistance benefits alone never fully meet the economic needs of a family with children; yet they represent a far larger proportion of government transfer payments in the U.S. than they do in most comparable industrialized Western countries. Finally, in contrast to sixty-seven other countries, including all industrialized nations, the United States does little in the way of supplementing income, despite the role such benefits can play in offsetting some of the costs of rearing children and in providing work incentives to beneficiaries for whom these may represent valuable additions to wages.

It is in this context that we would urge as the foundation of any child and family policy agenda two basic income maintenance benefits. *First, there should be a universal child or family benefit provided as an income supplement to all parents to help with the costs of rearing children.* Raising children adds a burden to the family budget that is not considered in salary scales. Moreover, well-reared children provide benefits to the society that go beyond the personal rewards and satisfactions provided their parents.

One such income supplement are family allowances, which typically provide supplements to family income equal to from about 5 to 10 percent of average wages for one child to as much as 35 to 45 percent of average wages to a family with four children (in West Germany and France, respectively.)[9] An income supplement in the form of direct cash benefit such as a family or child allowance is a very widely used device throughout the industrialized world and even in some of the developing countries. An alternative strategy is to provide this benefit indirectly through the tax system as a child tax credit benefiting all those with children equally when it is refundable (as in Canada) instead of as a child or dependent's tax allowance (as we have in the U.S.), which benefits only those who pay income taxes and benefits most those who earn most, rather than those with low incomes.* If enacted in a proper relationship to the tax system, the benefit can be recouped from those who do not need it, while giving support to families who suffer deprivation and stress as they perform the important societal task of bearing, rearing, and nurturing our next generation.

The United States has a device in place that could be expanded to fill this function on a large scale: the earned income tax credit. This tax credit is available to low-income workers who maintain a household for one or more of their dependent children who are either under nineteen, students, or disabled. The credit is described as a partial offset to Social Security taxes on low-income workers and an incentive for such workers to obtain employment and thus reduce the demand for AFDC. However, the maximum credit of 10 percent is available only on the first $5000 of earned income. Credits for income above this amount are smaller, and it becomes zero at $10,000. The credit is subtracted from tax liability if

---

*A tax allowance represents a deduction from income before taxes; therefore, the net benefit to the tax payer is a reflection of the taxpayer's own marginal tax rate. A tax credit constitutes a deduction from the taxpayer's tax liability and therefore has the same net value to all taxpayers. When refundable, that same benefit is provided the taxpayer who has no (or very low) tax liability in the form of a direct cash payment.

any exists. When the credit exceeds tax liability, the difference is paid in cash to the eligible workers.

About 1.2 million families benefited from this tax credit in 1979. Making this credit available for each child or for each child up to a specified maximum such as three (rather than for each household) and phasing it out at a higher income level could provide a significant income supplement to low- and middle-income working families with children.

Fundamental to support for such a policy is the recognition that supplemental income is a critical component of family policy and income maintenance. Family income supplements exist in all major industrialized countries. Yet, in the United States, the gap between wages and family needs is either denied or ignored, and the function of government transfers supplementing income is rejected as too expensive and fostering dependency. Children are not viewed as providing an economic benefit to the society, nor, apparently, is the effectiveness of these benefits as work incentives appreciated.

The second cash benefit we would recommend is the statutory provision of *maternity or parental benefits and leaves for working parents in two-earner families, or for a sole parent who is in the labor force.* Such provision is necessary to ensure that all parents and children have a period of growing together before parents must return to the work force. The U.S. is the only major country in the world without such a statutory provision. Three months is now a minimum in Europe, Canada, Israel, and several other countries; nine months, the maximum, is provided as a parental insurance benefit in Sweden. Six months is becoming the norm.[10]

More than 80 percent of the working women in the U.S. are in the prime childbearing years, ages fifteen through forty-four. An astonishing 65 percent of these women were in the labor force in 1980, including 54 percent of the mothers in this age group. Women aged twenty-five to thirty-four, at the peak of their childbearing years, accounted for nearly half the increase in the number of female workers during the 1970s. Almost all of those not-yet-mothers are likely to become pregnant at some point in their work lives. Most of these, when they become mothers, will remain at work. Well over one-half of the mothers of children aged three to five and close to one-half of those with children under age three are now in the labor force. Of the 2.5 million married women aged eighteen to thirty-four who gave birth within one year before a 1978 survey, over one-third were in the labor force. (Although the figures are not available for the nonmarried, they are likely to be significantly higher.) In the more than one-quarter of all families in which women work full time all year round, they contribute on average 40 percent of family income. In the age group twenty-five to thirty-five, more than one-half of the women work full time all year. Of children under age six 43 percent (and 40 percent of those under age three) had working mothers in 1980[11] as contrasted with 29 percent in 1970 (and 32 percent of those under age three in 1976, the first year for which such data are available.)[12] Thus, women are increasingly likely to be in the labor force at the time of pregnancy and childbirth. Women are increasingly likely to be in the labor force within one year after childbirth. Women in the peak childbearing years are increasingly likely to be making a significant contribution to family income, if married, or to be the sole source of family support, if not.

Medical and psychological research as well as morbidity and mortality statistics argue strongly for an investment in ensuring a secure first year of life for a child.[13] A significant element in this is ensuring the opportunity for adequate parental care of—and involvement with—the child at this time. While the research results are not always definitive, it would appear that the ability of a parent to devote himself or herself to the child, without excessive diversion or external pressure, can have important consequences for a good physical start including less mortality in the first year; cognitive enrichment; and emotional bonding, with its long-range implications for personality development.

The critical issue appears to be whether the parents must immediately surrender the child to external care or can share intensively the early weeks and months of their child's life and thus respond sensitively to growth, change, and their child's individualized needs. The consensus seems to be that when individual resources or social policy can make it possible, it is a good investment to ensure a joint child-parent start for a period of time ranging from three to twelve months, even though parental circumstances might require labor force participation of both parents, or a single parent, and alternative child care arrangements subsequently. Any concern for maternal and child health, child development, marital and family solidarity, and family income (as well as for equality for women in employment) requires some attention to provision for maternity leaves and protection against loss of earnings.

Unlike seventy-five other countries, including all other advanced industrialized societies, the United States has no statutory provision that guarantees a woman the right to a leave from employment for a specified period, protects her job while she is on leave, and provides a cash benefit equal to all or a significant portion of her wage while she is not working because of pregnancy and childbirth. Such benefits cover most employed women in these other countries and play an essential role in maternal and child health care as well as in protecting family income at a critical time in the family life cycle.

Five states (California, Hawaii, New Jersey, New York, and Rhode Island, as well as Puerto Rico) provide for such benefits in a very limited fashion to some workers. But the numbers covered are relatively small, benefit levels are low, and all are of very short duration. Some civil servants (for example, federal, state employees, some public school teachers) have benefits, too.

The major source of maternity benefits in the U.S. is through the private industrial or "corporate" welfare system—as an employee benefit. The 1977 Quality of Employment Survey highlights the inadequacy of such coverage: only 29 percent of the working women surveyed (a nationally representative sample) stated that they were entitled to a paid maternity leave.[14] A 1981 survey of U.S. business firms confirms that this benefit is still available only to a minority of employed women.[15] Less than one-half of the companies responding to the survey (and very small local business establishments were not included) indicated that they provided such a benefit.

If we are concerned with assuring children a good start in life, then it is essential that we make it possible for women—and ultimately for men, too—to be involved with their new babies for at least some time after childbirth. Whether or not such a benefit should be provided as a national statutory benefit, as a federally mandated employee benefit, or as some combination, can be explored separately. First there must be some recognition of the importance of such a benefit to assure good child development. After that there must be a commitment to establish the benefit on such a scale that all working women would be covered at the time of childbirth. Then the policy instrument to carry out this objective can be chosen.

Personal Social Services

It is our position that the child welfare service reforms are currently placed in too constricted a framework and that those who are trying to improve child welfare services still tend to conceive of the field in its traditional sense—focused on foster homes, group residences, children's institutions, and adoption services. They seek to improve such services, to direct them in accord with the new philosophical orientations, to upgrade staff so as to permit implementing of the services effectively, and to institute the administrative controls necessary to avoid losing children in the system. Essentially, however, this remains a child placement service system with occasional access to such supportive services as day care and homemakers. The "work with children in their own homes" remains limited and related to the child welfare task narrowly conceived. (See Chapter 6 for further discussion.)

At the same time there exists in the U.S. a "family service agency" network, much of it voluntary if partially publicly supported, as a thing apart. The family service agencies offer family counseling—marital therapy, advocacy, and family life education. (See Chapter 5 for further description of these services.) In a good number of places family and children's agencies in the voluntary sector have been combined, but each unit tends to offer the traditional categorical programs and has its separate client group.

Given the complexities of the problems that create temporary or permanent child placement, the personal social services system, of which child welfare services and family service agencies are component parts, should be offering more.

We digress here, briefly, to explain what we mean by "personal social services."[16] We use this term to describe those publicly subsidized and publicly and/or privately delivered "personal" services designed to meet the ordinary as well as special needs of individuals and families concerning:

—life cycle development and socialization

—therapy, counseling, and rehabilitation

—practical help and care

—self-help and mutual aid

—information, referral, advice

Beginning initially as individualized responses to poor orphans, widows, and the severely handicapped and focused largely on providing only the most basic necessities, these services have gradually changed in range, in function, and in the population served. In more recent years, differential social provisions for distinctive types of human needs (income, health care, education, housing, employment) has led to the emergence of an important, separate component in the overall societal effort at maintaining an adequate standard of living for its citizenry. This component is now increasingly described as the "personal" social services. Over time, these services have been transformed from discrete categorical services, responding to the most extreme problems requiring control, protection, or help, to a broad cluster of services, addressing aspects of development, socialization, and enrichment as well as self-help, therapeutic aid, practical assistance, and liaison with other services, benefits, and resources. Though not necessarily delivered through any one system (public or private, for-profit or nonprofit, religious or secular, integrated or categorical), these services have begun to be recognized as sharing common functions regardless of the setting in which they are provided (residential facility, community mental health center, work place, school, family and children's service agency), the age group served (child, youth, adult, aged), or the presenting problem (alcoholism, parent/child or marital conflict, social isolation).

It should be stressed that as important as these services are in assuring an adequate quality of life, they can fulfill their primary function only when all other forms of basic social provision are in place: income transfers or maintenance programs; health and medical care; education; housing and employment. The personal social services are important supplements to the other "human" or "social" service programs, not alternatives to them. Certainly one would not expect personal social services to be offered to—or if offered be very useful to—people without adequate food, shelter, clothing, schools, or medical care. But it is also true that the solution of problems of economic need, housing and employment does not wipe out the requirements of people for personal social services. Indeed, such services grow and expand (whether in laissez-faire, capitalist societies; welfare states; socialist countries; or the developing world) as countries can afford them and can train qualified personnel. This is understandable, given the essential place of such services in daily living and their relevance to all people, not to the poor alone.

To illustrate the importance of these services, one need only think of society's concern with child abuse and neglect, alienation, marital problems, new roles in the family as more mothers work outside the home, alcoholism and drugs and their impact on family life, and the changing relationships of adolescents to their parents. Because issues such as these are experienced in all social classes and economic groups, there is a trend toward greater universalism in all social services (not for the poor alone, not only means-tested programs) as there has been in the past a trend toward universalism in public education, public health, and housing initiatives and income transfer programs.

Marketplace expenditures for services in general are very large; private expenditures for personal services in the marketplace, which are similar to personal *social* services, are also substantial, for example, for counseling, advice, child care, vacations, school, camp, adoption, housekeeping services. We are unable to suggest a total price.

The personal social services are modest in their claims on public expenditures as contrasted with social insurance, public assistance, education, and health. While there are no precise data, since boundaries are uncertain and the services are located in several "systems," we are here discussing a domain claiming in its public and nonprofit sectors somewhere between 1 and 2 percent of the Gross National Product (GNP), perhaps $10 to 15 billion annually, most of it public funds (calculated in 1976–1977 before the most recent explosion of inflation).[17] The contrasting figures are over 11 percent of GNP for income maintenance, almost 7 percent for education, and over 8 percent for health.

With this as backdrop we now turn specifically to family and child personal social services and how these services provide the context for the more specialized kinds of help needed by children and families in trouble.

Families in the United States today experience unprecedented pressures and needs as they learn to live in a world involving major changes in parental and child roles and responsibilities. We have two-earner families (constituting more than one-half of all two-parent families) trying to manage complicated daily routines of work, commutation, household care, child care, leisure, and community participation. They need all the support they can get from friends, neighbors, relatives, and informal and formal networks. There are large numbers of one-parent families with children—17 percent of all families with children today, now raising almost one out of every five children—who must manage all of the same responsibilities with much less income, time, or other resources. Some of these families are receiving public assistance and not working; this presents other kinds of problems. There are families with handicapped children and families where one or both parents may have physical or emotional problems or handicaps. And there also are, crosscutting these categories, the minority families, the immigrant families, the refugee families. Each of these faces additional hazards and needs.

It does not seem too much to suggest that the personal social services field should offer more than child welfare services in their constricted sense. The personal social services addressed to families and children should encompass (a) developmental and socialization services, what are often called "prevention," (b) helping and therapeutic services, operated in a family context to protect the family from disintegration, and (c) access services, which can assure family members whatever benefits they are entitled to and provide linkage with whatever other kinds of help they might need.

This is not the place for specific models. Current legislative and funding pressures may now provide the stimuli to seek out new approaches to service delivery. The challenge is to create a broader framework and context than traditional child welfare services. The task is to develop family support services within a personal social services system, to include both services of the developmental-socialization type and those that will offer help to individuals in the early stages of difficulties, when family integrity is more readily preserved.

Despite the ideological commitment to prevention, the support for such initiatives and the dissemination of the results of these efforts have been quite limited. In general, government, as well as those private foundations that have sponsored research and demonstration programs in the children's services field, have tended to follow traditional categorical separations between family service work and child welfare work. This emphasis on categorical services could have serious limitations and hamper the development of a broader personal social services system. It is as yet unclear what the future patterns will be.[18]

Moreover, those concerned with children do not always seem clear as to where the best interests of children lie in the debates about federal funding and service delivery. Many child advocates rallied against block grants in mid-1981 when it was proposed that child welfare services should be grouped with many categorical programs in other personal social service fields. The fear was that if this occurred, the specifics of the Adoption Assistance and Child Welfare Reform Act of 1980 would be lost. We would urge that the need to fight against poorly formulated block grants and the severe budget cutbacks that accompanied these proposals not be construed as an argument for categorical programming, which fragments child welfare services into many components or separates child from family services.

Sufficient interesting initiatives, small exemplars on which to build a personal social service system, already exist. A good system would involve establishing formal family support services on a foundation of mutual aid and voluntary activity. The formal systems could be used to support the informal with specific tasks assigned to trained professionals and bureaucratized services only as their effectiveness is validated and when the proper balance and integration between the formal and the informal is fully understood and emphasized.

It must be stressed that the need is great. Personal services are very important, and the experience of society with education, health, religion, and recreation suggests that everything required will not be accomplished by informality, goodwill, happenstance, or the marketplace. There will also need to be a formal system and personnel qualified for difficult tasks.

Those who plan such undertakings and experiment with them obviously should give attention to content, not merely to administrative structure and delivery systems. Clearly, a high priority must be assigned to the teenage parent and to the alienated adolescent. The latter needs practical and social-emotional supports oriented toward full social participation. The former must be assured access to school and to the work world, with whatever help is needed with child rearing at the same time, so that the episode of teenage parenthood and the overwhelming responsibility associated with it does not lead inexorably to a life of poverty, dependence, passivity, and social exclusion.

Somewhere in the community there is need for a respite service, too, preferably on a mutual aid basis, but perhaps with support from private or public agencies. Parents who experience intra-familial crises, whether between parents and children or parent and parent, need a period of sustenance and relief to help the crisis pass.

For families which are not "in trouble" but who are experiencing the normal life milestones and the challenges that they involve and who may have to do so without the support of intimate family and friends and without relevant experience, there is need for a variety of educational, advice, and counseling services. We refer to the periods right before and right after childbirth, the entry of children into child care programs or elementary school, the death of loved ones, the breaking up of families through separation and divorce, and the reconstitution of families—the joining of children of different parents, the development of new parenting responsibilities by stepparents, and so forth. Mention might also be made of the crisis for child and/or parent of major illness or accident for either. Again, we stress, most of this kind of need is cared for, absorbed by, and more than adequately helped by relatives, friends, neighbors, and the kinship network. However, there is also need for a societal response that buttresses these, reinforces them, and offers more formal provision because there also is need for technical expertise, continuity, and the deployment of resources—the strengthening of the informal by the formal. Approaches to assuring access to such services and the nature of the delivery system require experimentation.

The system must also give major attention to the daily life experiences of working parents with children. Certainly there is need for a broader view of child care programs. Recognizing that elementary schools are our major child care resource serving almost all from age five, the adequate provision for care after school hours, whether for nursery-school-aged children, the kindergarteners, or elementary-aged children, must be addressed. Such programming is less expensive than many other types of day care (but of course both types are needed) and would have large pay-off in protecting children and reassuring parents. Major expansion is required to meet the underserved three-to-five age group with child care. An even greater effort is needed to provide care for infants and toddlers, the "under three" age group whose mothers have experienced the largest growth in labor force participation during the past decade. Over 42 percent of the children of this age now (1982) have working mothers (two working parents or a sole working parent). Given the continuing growth in the proportions of women working among those with children of this age, a large-scale policy response is essential. Yet, social provision is less adequate for children of this age than it is for all others (that is not to say it is adequate for any). Moreover, the need for child care for these children is closely tied to the length of maternity leave. Where no such benefit exists, or the leave is brief, the need for infant and toddler care services becomes even more urgent.

Not only is the need great for child care services but an effective demand for such care had already emerged, as can be seen from the growth in the numbers of proprietary (for-profit) child care services for infants, toddlers, preschoolers, and even before- and after-school programs for pre- and primary-school-age children. Similarly, there has been an enormous increase in the amount of discussion about employer-sponsored child care activities. Vouchers subsidizing a specified number of "slots" in community programs, co-sponsorship of centers, as well as work-site-based care are now being discussed. However, very few employer-sponsored day-care programs currently exist.

We are not taking a position here on any one approach to providing child care. Publicly operated child care services (under education or social service auspices); publicly subsidized and privately operated (nonprofit) programs; employer-sponsored programs publicly subsidized through tax policy and privately operated (for-profit or nonprofit); publicly subsidized programs allowing consumer choice (through the child care tax credit which can be applied to informal as well as formal care and for-profit as well as nonprofit care) are all possible options which can meet a diversity of preferences. Our goal would be to assure access to good quality, reasonably priced care, located near the child's place of residence. Firm criteria for choosing among these different options do not yet exist, since neither their costs nor their effects are now established in a comparative sense.

Other In-Kind Benefits

Two other in-kind benefits are essential for any family policy agenda: a health insurance and/or a health delivery system for children and housing allowances to supplement the income of families with children. These are areas of basic need where costs have risen sharply in recent years. Space does not permit more than a brief mention of these here.

There are specific proposals in the field of health care on the national agenda. It has been suggested that policymakers could act immediately on an expanded program of health care for children, while the society debates the larger health insurance issues and awaits an economic recovery, which will make a larger and more expensive general initiative possible. The need for such provision is truly urgent. No major industrialized country other than the United States is without a free, locally based, publicly funded, maternal and child or family and child health delivery system. Such a system can play an essential role in preventive social, physical, and psychological health and can provide a mechanism for early case finding.

Of lesser importance, yet providing a significant additional supplement to the income of low- and middle-income families while protecting the quality of their living environment, are housing allowances. The United States provides something akin to such a benefit for home owners by permitting interest payments on mortgages to be tax deductible. There are also various types of rent and mortgage supports to low-income families, but they are not entitlement programs and their coverage is limited. Given the increasingly high costs of housing, it is time something comparable to the European housing allowances were done for all low- and moderate-income families, either as an "energy" allowance, a refundable tax credit, or another alternative.

THE CHALLENGE BEFORE US

Our agenda is only illustrative; family policy is clearly an arena for imagination and innovation. The challenge is before us and, indeed, may be even greater over the next few years.

While not possible here, serious and specific attention needs to be given to the ways in which public funds are expended in this area. We should not replace voluntary and spontaneous primary groups' responses to problems. At the same time, we must promote coherence, integration, and accountability within the formal public and private service system.

Attention must also be given to the growing interrelationship of public and private sectors, as public monies are spent in direct support of private service organizations (through grants or purchase-of-services contracts) or indirectly (through tax policies benefiting providers or consumers or both). Clearly the conventional distinction between public and private sectors (for-profit as well as nonprofit, with regard to benefits and services) can no longer be maintained. What the consequences of this may be for access, accountability, quantity, and quality of services is not clear, nor are the consequences for benefit receipt and allocation, nor for costs and who bears the burden.

For those who are concerned about the well-being of children and families, we have suggested a broad yet focused perspective. This, we believe, is needed to assure better care for those who are experiencing difficulties. Reforms are also needed to reduce the numbers of those entering the child welfare system and to protect the vulnerable. Our focus in this chapter has been to suggest policy initiatives and interventions that may decrease the number of cases fed into the substitute care system. We have suggested what we believe are the critical components of such a social policy agenda. There is need for imagination and for political courage, for responsible action of an expert type, and for willingness to consider new patterns and new departures.

NOTES

1. Andrew Billingsley and Jeanne M. Giovannoni, *Children of the Storm* (New York: Harcourt Brace Jovanovich, 1972).

2. *Child Welfare in 25 States—An Overview* (Washington, D.C.: U.S. Department of Health, Education and Welfare, 1976).

3. For a more extensive discussion of this concept, its meaning, and its application, see Sheila B. Kamerman and Alfred J. Kahn, eds., *Family Policy: Government and Families in Fourteen Countries* (New York: Columbia University Press, 1978).

4. For some discussion of the concept of a benefit-service package, see Sheila B. Kamerman and Alfred J. Kahn, *Child Care, Family Benefits and Working Parents* (New York: Columbia University Press, 1981).

5. Employment data, *Monthly Labor Review*, June 1981. The increased unemployment rate in 1982 led to a slight decrease in labor force size and in percentage employed; a decrease in the unemployment rate is likely to lead to return to the earlier pattern.

6. U.S. Department of Commerce, Bureau of the Census, *Current Population Reports*, Series P-60, No. 123, "Money Income of Persons in the United States: 1978" (Washington, D.C.: Government Printing Office, 1980).

7. U.S. Department of Commerce, Bureau of the Census, *Current Population Reports*, Series P-60, No. 124, "Characteristics of the

Population Below the Poverty Level: 1978" (Washington, D.C.: Government Printing Office, 1980).

8. *Social Security Bulletin: Annual Statistical Supplement, 1980.*

9. For a description and analysis of the role of different income transfers in the incomes of families with children in different countries, see Alfred J. Kahn and Sheila B. Kamerman, *Income Transfers from a Family Policy Perspective: A Comparative Study* (forthcoming).

10. For a discussion of this issue and the relevant benefits in the U.S. and elsewhere, see Sheila B. Kamerman, *Maternity and Parental Benefits and Leaves: An International Review* (New York: Columbia University Center for the Social Sciences, 1980).

11. Unpublished data obtained from the Bureau of Labor Statistics, 1976.

12. Allyson Sherman Grossman, "More Than Half of All Children Have Working Mothers," *Monthly Labor Review* 105 (February 1982): 41–43.

13. For some selected studies of the significance of the first year of a child's life and the importance of the mother-child relationship, see Bettye M. Caldwell, "The Effects of Infant Care" and Leon J. Yarow, "Separation from Parents During Early Childhood," in *Review of Child Development Research, I,* ed. Martin L. and Lois W. Hoffman (New York: Russell Sage Foundation, 1964); Mary D. S. Ainsworth, "The Development of Infant-Mother Attachment," in *Review of Child Development Research, II,* ed. Bettye M. Caldwell and Henry N. Ricciuti (Chicago: University of Chicago Press, 1966); Burton L. White, *The First Three Years of Life* (Englewood Cliffs, N.J.: Prentice-Hall, 1975); Alison Clarke-Stewart, *Child Care in the Family* (New York: Academic Press, 1977).

14. These data are presented in a chapter by Sheila B. Kamerman and Paul W. Kingston, "Employer Responses to the Family Responsibilities of the Employees," in *Families that Work: Children in a Changing World of Work, Family and Community,* ed. Sheila B. Kamerman and Cheryl A. Hayes (Washington, D.C.: National Research Council/National Academy of Science, 1982).

15. A study of maternity policies in the United States, including a report of this survey, will be published in 1982 in a volume by Sheila B. Kamerman, Alfred J. Kahn, and Paul W. Kingston.

16. For more extensive discussion of the concept of "personal social services" and its application, see Alfred J. Kahn and Sheila B. Kamerman, "The Personal Social Services and the Future of Social

Work," in *Perspectives for the Future: Social Work Practice in the 80s,* ed. Kay Dea (Washington, D.C.: NASW, 1980). See also Alfred J. Kahn, *Social Policy and Social Services,* 2nd ed. (New York: Random House, 1979).

17. Alfred J. Kahn, *Social Policy and Social Services.*

18. Advisory Committee on Child Development, National Research Council, *Toward a National Policy for Children and Families* (Washington, D.C.: National Academy of Sciences, 1976), pp. 3–4. Is it possible to think of family support services which also protect child welfare's "categorical" expertise? Jenkins found in a large-sample study that access to child welfare services is now "almost evenly divided between integrated and specialized intake points." Each has some advantages, and each loses something. She comments as follows: "A prototype which might resolve this dilemma would be a system where families and children could come to a single access point; where skilled diagnostic workers would evaluate needs and plan services. The clients would then be referred to specialized units. . . ." Shirley Jenkins, *Intake: The Discriminant Function* (Washington, D.C.: Children's Bureau/Administration for Children, Youth and Families, DHEW, 1980).

CHAPTER 5
SERVICE PROVISION TO ENHANCE FAMILY FUNCTIONING

Jon Conte

The purpose of this chapter is to describe new directions for service delivery that will enhance family functioning, a difficult task to address at the present time. Although the policy directions of the current administration seem relatively clear, their effects on the social services have just begun to crystallize. And it is not yet clear what the form or effect will be of the social work profession's response to this all-out assault on social services and social service clientele. Although the immediate future is uncertain, this chapter is written on the assumption that social work efforts on behalf of families will be needed in the future as never before.

The task of writing about new directions in family services is further complicated by a lack of research in this area. First, there exist no comprehensive national data concerning public and private service delivery to families. Consequently, trends described in this chapter must be based on descriptions of specific services and programs appearing in the literature and not on empirical evidence. Second, as it has become increasingly popular to speak of services to enhance family life, a larger number of agencies have begun to describe their focus as "family-oriented." However, there is no evidence available to determine whether the services actually provided by these agencies are more "family-focused" than in the past or have changed in any way from the traditional services provided by agencies in this field. Finally, in the almost total absence of research documentation on the effects of services on family functioning, statements about whether or not services improve family functioning are more likely to reflect the writer's perspective and values than factual data.

With these caveats in mind, this chapter will attempt to take stock of where the profession has been in terms of its efforts on behalf of families and suggest areas for future work. Specifically, it will summarize statistics describing changes in the American family, review major frames of reference for family practice, identify possible directions for family services in the future, and discuss issues in the delivery of social services to families.

DEMOGRAPHIC TRENDS

If most people in this country were asked to describe the "typical American family," their response would probably include a breadwinning father and a homemaker mother, married in their early twenties, who raise two or three children and remain together until one dies. But demographic data[1] show that this pattern is more "myth" than reality for many families in the United States, and many families are experiencing significant changes.

—The average size of the American family is decreasing. The average number of persons living in a family in 1960 was 3.33; in 1978 it was 2.81. This decrease was due primarily to a declining birthrate.

—One-parent families are increasing, representing 7 percent of all households in 1978, an increase from 4 percent in 1960.

—Female-headed households are increasing—family households maintained by women living without husbands accounted for 11 percent of all households in 1978, an increase of 46 percent since 1970.

—Divorce rates are high. There are about 90 divorced persons for every 1000 married, an increase of 91 percent since 1970 and 157 percent since 1960. Estimates indicate that one out of every three marriages will end in divorce.

—The proportion of one-parent families headed by never-married mothers increased from 7 percent to 15 percent between 1960 and 1978. Many of these never married mothers are teenagers.

—About 50 percent of all women are in the labor force. The rate of working mothers with children under six rose from 19 percent in 1969 to 42 percent in 1978.

In addition to these specific demographic trends recent economic conditions have placed stress on the family and its structural underpinnings. Despite high annual inflation rates in the past decade, the median family income in 1978 ($17,640) was only 6 percent higher than the 1970 level. Current unemployment rates are very troubling. And families with a female head and no husband present are concentrated at the lowest end of the income scale.

We are also currently more aware that the family may not provide a nurturing environment for some of its members. For example, 1 million children may be abused or neglected and 1.6 million wives beaten each year.[2] Although estimates vary, one out of ten boys and one out of five girls may be sexually exploited by the time they reach adulthood,[3] many by members of their own families.[4]

From these demographic trends it appears that families are smaller and have fewer children than in the past, although most Americans continue to live in families. There are more single-parent families, and many of these families experience major financial problems. The divorce rate is high, and many children are exposed to the effects of divorce at least once in their childhood. Many family members, especially women and children, are abused, neglected, or sexually exploited. Hence, it is not surprising then that 75 percent of Americans believe that family life has gotten worse over the last fifteen years.[5]

It is difficult to interpret these trends. Any or all may be offered as indicators of a decline in the American family.[6] However, these trends may only represent changes in the structure of the family, not its role or function; the family may be strong and "here to stay."[7] Whether one sees a particular trend or all trends taken together as negative or positive depends, in large part, upon one's values. For example, divorce may reflect a dissatisfaction with marriage as an institution, or it may be a search for a more satisfying marriage and hence an expression of a positive belief in marriage.

What does seem clear is that individuals and the families in which they live can experience change throughout their life histories. These changes may or may not be problematic for the family as a whole or the individuals within families. However, from a family welfare point of view it is important to recognize that some people affected by such changes may require services to cope with them satisfactorily. For example, parents who divorce may need a range of services including counseling to deal with the emotional effects of the divorce for themselves and their children, economic supports, day care for their children, and peer support and comfort. Similarly, the sexually abused child may require a full range of services including protection, assessment of the danger for reabuse, emergency medical and crisis intervention, counseling for the child and the nonoffending parent, specialized treatment for the sex offender, and family counseling.

If one begins to think of the needs of families, both developmental and restorative, illustrated in these examples and compares them with the services available through many agencies, a number of issues arise. First, some of the needed services may not be available in a given community. Second, if they are available, many families may not be eligible to receive them. Finally, the families may have to seek a number of different service providers to attain the total service package desired.

This situation exists because social services in the United States developed with a residual or "problem orientation." Most social services for children are provided to supplement or substitute for parents who fail or are unable to carry out their parenting responsibilities. Because of the prevailing minimalist attitude toward service provision (see Chapter 6) services are seldom available to help families with normal developmental difficulties and are often limited to families meeting specific eligibility requirements. Even with the loosening of eligibility requirements that resulted from Title XX's extension of services to those who are not welfare recipients, services are usually provided only after problems have come to the attention of social welfare professionals. These problem-identified families are a small proportion of the families who might actually be experiencing difficulties. And the actual services provided do not appear to reflect the range of services described in the literature as of potential help to such families.

This range of needed services has been described by a number of authors. For example, the National Commission on Families and Public Policy of the National Conference on Social Welfare[8] has identified the following as essential service supports for families: income and employment, physical and mental health, child-rearing services (for example, day care and parental support), and personal social services. The personal social services identified by the commission include information; advice; referral; case advocacy related to all social problems; protective programs; substitute care arrangements; concrete support services (such as delivered or congregate meals, homemaker, home health, and escort services); advice services related to child rearing, budgeting, family planning, abortion, and so on; mutual aid programs for families with common problems; counseling and concrete help related to environmental, interpersonal, or intrapsychic difficulties.

Another result of this "problem orientation" to service delivery is that services have not developed in a cohesive way. Most social service programs have been instituted only after a specific need has been identified. This "band-aid" approach to service has meant that service systems and agencies often fail to plan together; instead they tend to develop dysfunctional service boundaries, frequently making access and referral from one to another difficult. As several chapters in this text indicate, American social services constitute a "nonsystem" characterized by fragmentation, duplication, discontinuities in service and care, inequities, inadequacies, and unresponsiveness.[9]

Within the social work practice community there is disagreement concerning the proper organization of services, the appropriate mix of services, the proper allocation of services, and the right way to establish priorities. In part, this disagreement reflects the on-going tension within the social work profession about frames of reference for family services.

FRAMES OF REFERENCE FOR FAMILY SERVICES

The history of social work seems in part to be a history of shifting self-definition. As Hartman has noted, the answer to "what is casework?" depends very much on which social worker you ask.[10] Two major orientations to intervention currently exist: the mini-system perspective and the mega-system perspective.[11]

Mini-System Perspective

The mini-system perspective of intervention directs attention to specific individuals or families and their problems. Although there is some variation in how these problems are conceptualized (for example, behavioral versus psychoanalytic views), each of the mini-system theories tends to view the source of problems within either the individual or the family. In fact, the generic term used to refer to these theories, "clinical," suggests a disease or illness orientation.* For example, the major "clinical" models of family therapy describe and identify the disease as being located in different areas of human functioning. The psychoanalytic model views family dysfunction in terms of interlocking pathologies in which symptoms are a function of the pathological relationships among family members, originating within an individual family member's psychopathology. The communications model

---

*The NASW Task Force on Clinical Social Work Practice recently proposed a new definition of clinical practice that involves social as well as personal intervention. See Jerome Cohen, "Nature of Clinical Social Work," in *Toward a Definition of Clinical Social Work,* ed. Patricia L. Ewalt (Washington, D.C.: National Association of Social Workers, 1980), pp. 23–32. In this chapter the term "clinical" is being used in its more traditional sense.

emphasizes dysfunctional relationships as seen in patterns of communication among family members, resulting from unexpressed needs or expectations. The structural model emphasizes the activities of various subsystems and alliances among specific family members. The behavioral model stresses specific behavior patterns resulting from exchanges of reinforcement and punishment among family members. While there are obvious differences in these models, they share a common emphasis on locating and treating the problem within the mini-systems of either the individual or the family.

There are a number of reasons why this view can be detrimental to the goal of shifting toward a family welfare orientation. First, although it is somewhat less true of the behavioral model, these interventive models are largely unvalidated theories.[12] Many of the concepts, their interrelationships, and the meaning attached to them are more statements of perspective than of empirical realities. Yet, while many of the basic assumptions of the various models are unvalidated, practitioners tend to employ them to define client problems and to plan services as if the models were validated.

A second problem resulting from this orientation has to do with the goals established for service. Recognizing the importance of the family to the child's growth and development, these various models of intervention all tend to locate problems within the individual or family system and to describe goals for intervention in terms of something that is to happen to the individual or family unit in order to strengthen family functioning. Such models underplay the importance of the environment and the stress that it can place on the family. They locate the problem within a narrow system, which becomes the target for intervention.

This is not to say that this perspective is inappropriate to a family welfare perspective. Rather, these points are made to call attention to the dual nature of social interventions on behalf of families. This dual nature, as both Hartman[13] and Hollis[14] have pointed out, considers both "people changing or . . . situation changing or a combination of both."[15] This view does not reject the mini-system perspective but calls attention to a mega-system perspective as well.

Mega-System Perspective

A mega-system perspective for practice extends the worker's view beyond the individual case to the case-in-situation and has long been part of the social work profession. Most recently this view has been expressed within an ecological perspective. One of the most consistent voices describing an ecological view of practice has been Carel Germain,[16] who indicates that it is not a new form of intervention bu broader definition of it.*[17]

The ecological view directs professional attention to the person-in-environment. It suggests that organisms and environments can be thought of in terms of an adaptive balance or "goodness of fit."[18] Human problems develop as the outcome of transactions between environments and people. To the extent that the "fit" violates physical, psychological, or social needs, people experience stress or disjunction between themselves and "environmental nutriments." Three general goals for intervention are possible: (1) to relieve, develop, and strengthen people's innate capacity for growth and creative adaptation, (2) to remove environmental blocks and obstacles to growth and development, and (3) to increase the nutritive properties of the environment.[19]

In addition to focusing attention on "clinical" needs, this perspective serves to direct practice in three ways. First, it restates the importance of understanding the effects of physical, social, and cultural environments on the lives of individuals and families. Second, it encourages the development of service delivery arrangements in environments where people live, work, go to school, and recreate. Third, it calls attention to change efforts designed to modify environments that produce stress for people.

The utility of this perspective for professional efforts to enhance family functioning can be illustrated in a number of problem areas. For example, James Garbarino and colleagues[20] have found significant relationships between child abuse and specific environmental stresses: social isolation, socioeconomic stress, inadequate social support systems, and living in high-risk neighborhoods characterized by low socioeconomic status, families headed by females, and a high percentage of women in the work force with children under six years of age. Similarly, Conte and Berliner[21] describe an approach to social work services for sexually abused children and their families that includes both mini- and mega-system perspectives. The multiple-service interventions should be designed to protect the child from additional abuse or intimidation by the offender, assure the child and family that the child is physically and emotionally all right, insure that the response of institutions (such as hospitals, police, and social agencies) will be supportive and not contribute to further traumatization, and assist the child and family to resolve emotional reactions to the abuse and to make decisions about their lives in the future. Specific services may include crisis counseling, the

---

*Other recent social work practice theorists who have also emphasized the importance of this mega-system perspective: include Carol Meyer, Harriett Bartlett, William Gordon, Max Siporin, Allen Pincus and Anne Minahan, and others. And Gordon Hamilton first highlighted the concept of "person-in-situation" in the early 1940s.

f concrete services, home visits, case advocacy, and individ-
nily therapy.

ption of a mega-system perspective means that workers must
e than narrowly defined "clinical" skills to perform their job
y and that agencies have to develop new service delivery patterns and ways of working with each other if service goals are to be met.
It is in these areas that some of the new directions for family services lie.

EXPANDING WORKERS' INTERVENTIVE REPERTOIRE

If the mega-system perspective is more widely employed, there are a
number of interventive approaches that may be particularly useful for
workers attempting to enhance family functioning. This section will
briefly review three of these: advocacy, family life education, and the
use of social networks.

Advocacy

The advocacy role of the social worker, although long a part of the
social work tradition, is a source of some tension among clinical social
workers. The Family Service Association of America has defined advocacy as follows:

> Family advocacy is a professional service designed to improve life condi-
> tions for people by harnessing direct and expert knowledge of family
> needs with the commitment to action and the application of skills to pro-
> duce the necessary community change. The purpose of family advocacy
> service is to insure that the system and institutions with direct bearing on
> families work for those families, rather than against them. Family advoca-
> cy goals include not only improvement of existing public and voluntary
> services and their delivery, but also development of new or changed forms
> of social services.[22]

Two approaches to advocacy have been identified: the casework advocate and the community advocate,[23] or the client advocate and the
political advocate.[24] The casework advocate acts on behalf of an individual case and attempts to affect the relationship between the client and
social agencies and institutions. The community advocate works on behalf of an entire group or class of clients suffering with a common problem caused, aggravated, or ignored by institutions or agencies in the
community. In spite of discussions suggesting the importance of advocacy efforts in the context of treatment[25] and as a vital function of voluntary
agencies,[26] the place of advocacy efforts within social work continues to
be debated.

There are a number of obstacles to greater use of advocacy efforts within social work practice, including a preference and preoccupation with (narrowly defined) clinical practice, a combination of timidity and naiveté in exercising influence on policy, increased use of government funds to purchase service from voluntary agencies thereby compromising social workers' capacity to serve as advocates with their potential funding sources,[27] professional values that support consensus over conflict,[28] and lack of technical expertise in advocacy skills.[29] Furthermore, the different processes involved in advocacy efforts versus other kinds of clinical practice may make it difficult for one person to perform both roles effectively. For example, advocacy may require extensive meetings, at "odd" times, with people in authority. Direct practice, on the other hand, requires that regular times be allotted to appointments with clients, and purchase-of-service contracts often provide reimbursement only for hours spent in direct client contact, not for time spent attempting to effect environmental change on the client's behalf. Agencies may also fear publicity or "earning the wrath" of the powerful as their caseworkers try to change conditions affecting some groups of clients.

And yet, much of what causes families' problems are environmental conditions or events. Both the tradition of social work and the ecological perspective for practice call attention to the importance of moving into the client's environment to change problematic situations. For example, the problems faced by abused women, while they may originate in the actions of individual men, also take place within a societal context. Thus, it is important that law enforcement responses be supportive and that restrictions preventing abused women from receiving aid if their family's income is above a certain level be lifted. Additionally, medical, housing, job training, and counseling services should be available.

Although practitioners' capacity to engage in both case and class advocacy may be debated, case advocacy is an essential part of the social worker's role in any family and children's service agency. McGowan[30] has described the process workers should follow in case advocacy on behalf of clients and notes that these processes may be initiated by either the client or the worker. Together, these two individuals define the problem. Much of the advocacy process stems from this problem definition, for it determines:

—The *target system* (who the advocacy will be directed at)—the worker's agency (internal) or another social institution (external)

—The *objective* (what is to be accomplished)—to obtain a right for a client, to enhance existing services for the client, or to develop a new resource

—The *sanction* (the legitimitizing reason for the action)—existing laws or regulations, the stated goals or policies of the target system, professional values, or client needs

The selection of a particular advocacy strategy is dependent on these factors as well as the resources available to the advocate and the anticipated receptivity of the target system to the advocate's action.

Three advocacy strategies have been identified: (1) collaborative, in which the advocate attempts to elicit the interest and support of the target system, (2) mediatory, in which the worker acknowledges differences with the target system and attempts to negotiate an acceptable agreement or compromise, and (3) adversarial, in which the advocate uses actual or implied power to effect needed change.

In addition to choosing one of these strategies, the advocate must also determine the appropriate level at which to intervene within the target system. It has been noted that:

> Generally the successful advocate uses a blend of interventions, starting with intercession or persuasion at the lowest level with the most readily accessible members of the target system. If it seems necessary, (s)he may decide to negotiate or intervene with different segments of the target system. If these approaches fail and (s)he has a strong enough case . . . the advocate may move into an adversarial stance, intervening at top-levels and using pressure or coercion if necessary.[31]
>
> [Effective case advocacy] . . . demands sensitivity, flexibility and imagination, qualities that reflect the skill and style of the individual worker.[32]

Family Life Education

Educational approaches to prevention and treatment appear to be an increasingly popular form of service in social work agencies. Since 1976 the national board of the Family Service Association of America (FSAA) has recognized family life education as being of coequal importance with family counseling and family advocacy. In a 1977 survey of member agencies, FSAA found that 78 percent of the membership offered some form of family life education.[33]

One tension that runs through discussions about family life education activities has to do with whether it is a therapeutic strategy. For example, Cantoni describes family life education as a form of treatment and then distinguishes it from group counseling on the basis that participants come to family life courses without professional diagnosis as a prerequisite.[34] This ambiguity runs through many discussions of family life education.

What may be a more important issue is the relative emphasis placed on skill building versus understanding in family life education. Ambrosino has recently given voice to a major orientation in family life education that stresses understanding, sensitivity, or awareness when he says:

> Family life education programs provide a unique opportunity for groups to learn, to listen, to express concerns, clarify confusions, give and receive support, and to review options for improving relationships.[35]

Fine, in defining parent education, gives voice to both understanding and skill development when he indicates:

> Parent education . . . refers to systematic and conceptually based programs, intended to impart information, awareness, or skills to the participants. . . . The format usually includes the presentation of specific ideas, some group discussion, sharing or processing of ideas and experiences, and some skill-building activities.[36]

The emphasis on understanding, awareness, or sensitivity seems to be a function of the humanistic perspective of many family life educators and their assumption that these qualities will lead to change. Research on family life education is so lacking that it is impossible to support or reject these assumptions and the relative merits of emphasizing understanding or awareness versus skill development.

Whether it is viewed as a preventive or therapeutic service and whatever the mix of skill-building versus understanding experiences, family life education has the following characteristics:

—It is goal-directed and topic specific.

—It is nonthreatening and encourages participants to examine issues they might normally avoid.

—The group format allows for both professional and peer feedback.

—The group format is an economical use of professional time.

—The format can encourage problem solving, and other group members can help clarify issues.

—Family life education reduces the stigma associated with asking for and receiving help.

—The educational format can help set limits in topics and intensity of participation, which creates a sense of psychological safety among group members.[37]

Most family life education groups use a combination of methods including short lectures and reading assignments, group discussions, films or role plays, and some kind of homework. Groups or classes are offered on a wide range of topics. For example, Simon describes a program that included classes on parenting skills—focusing on improving communication and family relationships; couples' issues—focusing on individual identity, communication skills, and intimacy; women's issues—focusing on a range of concerns including a support and awareness group for women with mastectomies; university students' concerns—including a group for black students dealing with race as a factor in their lives; and family enrichment—a series for families focusing on awareness and growth of the family unit.[38] Similarly, Levin describes course offerings on such topics as marriage, single parenthood, divorce, changing roles and values, and problems encountered in the developmental cycle including problems faced by adolescents, women over forty, and senior citizens.[39] The Family Service Association of America has developed a series of modules for family life education, including parent-child communication[40] and separation and divorce.[41]

Use of Social Networks

There have been several approaches developing out of the ecological perspective for practice that attempt to connect or reconnect hurting individuals and families with social networks.[42] One approach has been to use the natural helping networks that already exist in communities or can be stimulated around a central figure, a person who has the personal characteristics to be a helper and is in a position to help.[43] A professional may serve as a consultant to the natural helper, providing information on human behavior and community resources, helping to solve problems and teach problem-solving skills, and/or providing support.

Another approach to networking has been to create support networks in the form of self-help groups or to encourage a family to use such groups. It has been estimated that there are currently one-half million self-help groups in the United States[44] and that some 5 million people participate in them.[45] These groups are characterized by

> . . . the intense personal involvement of members with others who share common experiences and needs in an ongoing process of mutual support, help and advocacy. Members relate on an equal status basis, defining their problems and needs in normal, nonstigmatized ways, and strong emphasis is placed on cognitive and behavioral, rather than emotional change. Strength is found in the power of the group and reinforcement for

desired attitudes and behaviors is sought through associations with others who share similar experiences and views. There is a strong emphasis on activity as a means of developing a sense of competency and personal responsibility and learning new behaviors. Members are expected to help other members and contribute to the work of the group as a whole, both to help themselves and to share in the attainment of common goals.[46]

Six types of self-help groups for persons experiencing family difficulties have been identified. These include groups for family members with special needs and problems such as Alcoholics Anonymous and Parents Anonymous; groups for the relatives of these people such as Al Anon; groups for parents of children with special needs such as the National Association of Retarded Children; groups for families with special concerns such as the Committee on Adoptable Children and Foster Parent Associations; groups for families in transitional crises such as Parents Without Partners; and finally, professionally initiated helping networks for families with normal needs or transitional crises, such as family network intervention (described later).[47]

Such groups, in addition to providing ongoing emotional support for their members, can also act as advocates. These advocacy efforts can be on an individual case basis as well as on a "class" or group basis. By engaging in this activity, the group can encourage existing social systems to be more responsive to the members' needs, and they can teach members to intervene more effectively on their own behalf.

Leadership in self-help groups is achieved by group members demonstrating desired leadership behaviors. It is not ascribed by professional status. Thus, the role of the professional in self-help groups is not one of service provider. Rather, the professional can act as a facilitator for these groups and can encourage their efforts by helping to organize new groups, providing consultation and technical assistance, referring individuals who might benefit from the service to the self-help group, and learning from the successful efforts of such groups.[48] While most self-help groups encourage professional involvement, they rightfully protect the control of the organization and reserve it for the membership.

These groups can provide an important resource for families in that they provide services that are different from those usually provided by a social agency. They may reach people who would otherwise not come into contact with social agencies or who have not been helped by traditional service programs. Thus, they can serve a useful function in supporting family life.[49]

However, it should be remembered that while such groups provide an important service, the help they offer is different from that provided by agencies. Thus, they do not and should not be expected to replace professional interventions. Self-help groups can be complementary to, but should not substitute for, agency activities.

A third approach to social support is frequently referred to as *networking*. According to Rueveni,

> Family network intervention is an attempt to mobilize the social network support system in a collaborative effort to solve an emotional crisis. It is a time-limited, goal-directed approach that will help family members in crisis to assemble and mobilize their own social network of relatives, friends, and neighbors; this network will become collectively involved in developing new options and solutions for dealing with a difficult crisis.[50]

Social networks are made up of links between people. They can be described in terms of *density*—the relation of actual links to potential links; *range*—the number of individuals involved in the network; and *pathways*—the indirect links between two individuals through at least one intermediary.[51] Hartman describes the use of an *eco-map* to depict family members' relationships with systems in their environment, and a *genogram*, which locates a family's place in the generational history of the extended family.[52] Both devices may easily be used to depict graphically the individual's and/or family's social network.

According to Rueveni, the goals of networking are to:

—Facilitate rapid connections, familiarity, and readiness to participate, which increases the level of involvement and energy (of the assembled network)

—Develop and encourage the sharing of problems and concerns by members of the immediate family, which allows for increased involvement and exchange of a variety of viewpoints by network members

—Facilitate communications between the family and the extended network system, which emphasizes the need for network activities

—Provide direct intervention and a deeper exploration of the nature of the difficulty during impasse periods, which leads to crisis resolution

—Assist in the development and formulation of temporary support groups, which serve as resource consultants.[53]

In network intervention the therapist convenes the family's social network and acts as a facilitator in the beginning stages as the network forms an interacting support group. Once this is accomplished, the assembled network progresses through a series of stages, which have been called *retribalization, polarization, mobilization, depression, breakthrough,* and *exhaustion-elation.*[54] As the network progresses through these phases, the convenor becomes less involved in directing the process but may continue to act as a consultant to various subnetworks, which form support groups to various members of the family. These support groups essentially help the family resolve problems by developing alternatives and supporting individual family members as they undertake new courses of action.

Although it is not completely clear from the descriptions of actual networking cases,[55] this intervention appears to have two major elements. First, using techniques of traditional family therapy, the network convenor works with the family to pinpoint the problem and the variables associated with it. The presence of the family's social network may serve to intensify the impact of the convenor's activities with the family. Second, individuals in the family's social network gradually become more intensely involved or "reconnected" with the family. These individuals frequently form support groups around individual family members and assist the family in moving toward problem resolution. Often, this resolution involves new resources developed or provided by the network.

In the absence of research data describing the effects of networking efforts, it is impossible to regard it as more than a promising service strategy. However, on an impressionistic basis, several aspects of family networking do seem noteworthy. First, if descriptions are accurate, networking families in crisis can serve to facilitate change. These changes can be produced within an intensive but relatively short period of professional involvement. Second, the formulation of an activated network with a history of helping a particular family may serve as a means of insuring generalization and maintenance of treatment effects across time. Third, many types of people who seek service from social work agencies appear to be socially isolated. Whether this is a function of a real lack of a social network or a consequence of the problems they experience varies among cases. However, if it is the family's reaction to or perception of a problem that serves to isolate them, networking may have a positive effect. For example, Kozloff has described the isolating effects of a "problem behavior" child on a family.[56] These effects include an increased amount of work, a negative perception of self, a real or imagined social stigma, and an increased social vulnerability. Such families would seem good candidates for networking intervention.

On the negative side, several issues regarding family networking require attention. First, part of the language of networking interventions (for example, "retribalization") seems to serve no useful communication purpose; more traditional small group concepts can accomplish the same goals more easily. More importantly, such terminology may impede the dissemination of networking ideas. Second, evaluative research describing the process and especially the effects of networking interventions is nonexistent. Without such studies, networking should be approached cautiously. Third, networking describes an approach to intervention in which a family's social network is used to help the family resolve problems. Some descriptions of networking almost seem to suggest a magical and unspecified event or condition that produces change. In fact, it appears that change comes about as the result of specific solutions developed by and often implemented by subgroups within the activated social network.

SERVICE DELIVERY

In the preceding pages an argument was made for the need to provide a range of services for families. We said that the mega-system perspective suggests expansion of practitioners' interventive repertoires and provision of services in the family's environment. It was further noted that, because of the problem-oriented focus of many services, the current delivery system may be dysfunctional in meeting the multiple needs of some families. In pursuit of these concerns three topics will be addressed in this final section: the provision of service in the client's environment, the management and coordination of services on the client's behalf, and the role of the voluntary sector in the delivery of social services to families.

The Provision of Services in the Client's Environment

Discussion about providing services in the "neighborhoods" developed in the 1960s, in part out of a desire to reach low-income, ethnic, inner-city families more effectively. This concern was expressed within mental health, health, legal, child welfare, and other social service circles. To accomplish this goal, "neighborhood service centers" or "multiservice centers" were created. Often, a number of agencies established offices within these multiservice centers.

Although the number of multiservice and neighborhood service centers has declined rapidly during the past decade as a result of diminished funding, service delivery in the remaining facilities is usually characterized by services designated for the population of a defined geographical area; a heavy use of personnel, especially paraprofessionals, indigenous to the neighborhood; commitment to both direct service and social action; and universal eligibility.[57] Two major types of services are usually provided: *access services*, including information, advice, and referral; community and group education; escort; case advocacy; institutional and individual linkage; and social brokerage; and *direct services*, including provision of housing; employment training; day care; legal aid; and individual or family counseling.

Ayres describes an agency on the West Side of Chicago, which began during the late 1960s to provide a full range of services in the neighborhood.[58] Using community aides, the project was an attempt by the parent agency to make services more available and "relevant" to the minority community. The aides, recruited from the local community, fulfilled a variety of roles, including interpreting agency services to clients; learning the nature of the clients' concerns; reaching out to the family; observing the family in its home; obtaining collateral information; exploring community resources; assisting clients in obtaining other agency services; accompanying clients on recreational, cultural, and educational trips designed to enhance and enrich their lives; and obtaining concrete services (for example, housing, work, financial assistance). Also included were social action tasks. Such efforts included creating a day-care center, increasing the positive relationships between students and their local school, and creating a community-controlled credit union. Counseling, including family and group therapies, was also offered.

Kahn's review of neighborhood service centers found "a striking imbalance between access and direct social services of all kinds"[59] within these agencies. He found that most centers provided good access services and the core service of the sponsoring agency plus one or two additional ones. However, most centers did not offer a full range of social services, and clients with special needs had to become involved with other service systems. While this can create difficulties for the client, this potential problem can be circumvented if the multiservice center worker coordinates the use of other services and acts as a client advocate within them.

Part of the problem one faces in determining the accomplishments of neighborhood service centers is that these agencies have been assigned a range of broad goals. Neighborhood service delivery has been seen as a means of providing services, changing the nature of the neighborhood itself, and using the resources of the revitalized neighborhood to produce large social change. For example, writing from a mental health perspective, Riessman describes the goals of a neighborhood service center as:

1. Expediting and providing services relevant to mental health. This includes bringing new clients into the system of services, making service systems more responsive to clients, and providing additional new services.
2. Increasing social cohesion within the concentration area. An effort is made to produce community impact, particularly with regard to the development of community action. Thus, the effort is to provide a sociotherapeutic approach oriented toward reducing powerlessness, building community ties, and group involvement.
3. Initiating various types of institutional change, particularly with regard to better *coordination of services* for the people in the community (emphasis added).[60]

With the change of social service agendas in the last few years (see Chapter 2) there has been relatively less talk of neighborhood service centers and their goal of changing environments. However, concern for providing service in neighborhoods is still definitely present. The most recent expression of this idea focuses on providing services "in the home."

The last few years have witnessed considerable development of home-based service delivery arrangements. Home-based programs exist in every region of the country and the federally funded National Clearinghouse for Home-Based Services at the School of Social Work, University of Iowa, has done much to publicize these arrangements.[61] Although these programs differ on a number of variables, such as services provided, staff employed, and type of client served, the programs tend to have a number of similarities:

1. Services are as complete, comprehensive, and intensive as necessary to relieve the crisis and to strengthen the family's ability to function in the future. Staff are often available twenty-four hours a day, 365 days a year.
2. The service is most often provided *in the family's home* or within the ecological system in which the family lives, works, goes to school, and recreates.
3. The focus of the service is the family unit, and the family is recognized as the primary care giver, educator, health center, and source of emotional support.
4. While services may be under social, health, or educational auspices, all needed service components are made available to the family.

5. To the extent feasible, resources within the family, extended family, and community are utilized.[62]

While the National Clearinghouse for Home-Based Services to Children and Their Families has suggested that home-based services are "not merely services to children who live at home," services delivered to children and families in their own homes and environments are an important characteristic of many of the programs.[63] In addition, many programs appear to be characterized by intensity of service, consistent availability of staff to family, and a wide range of services.

Several examples of programs which are categorized as "home-based" will illustrate the variety of programs that this concept can include. Levine and McDoud describe a family-based service designed to transfer the skills and resources of child care and social work staff through the use of counseling and education in the homes of needy families.[64] Families who were served by the program were in crisis and characterized by histories of abuse and neglect. These families were isolated from positive social relationships, experienced severe environmental stress, and were unable to break the cycle of poverty and deprivation. A staff of one social worker with a master's degree and four family care workers (working with two families each) provided a range of services. The family care workers helped and taught parents various household and child-caring tasks, assisted families in using outside and community resources, and provided material goods as needed by the family. The professional social worker provided case management, planned and implemented the casework plan, and served as a linkage between the agency and the family care workers.

A different program, Homebuilders, is described by Kinney and associates[65] and Haapala and Kinney.[66] To be eligible for the program, at least one member of a family must be on the "verge of out-of-home placement." Homebuilder therapists work with families in crisis on an "as-needed" basis for as long as necessary to resolve the immediate crisis and to teach new skills, which the family may use to prevent future crises. Each worker sees two cases a month and provides a range of services. The general service approach includes (1) helping the family learn more effective communication skills by modeling positive communication, reinforcing clients for successful communication, and providing advocacy for family members who need support in communicating with other members of the family, (2) helping families identify community resource options and necessary changes in their environment, (3) teaching ways to prevent crises through such techniques as effective communication (for example, making assertive rather than aggressive responses to each other), (4) the use of behavior contracting as a means of negotiating behavior change among family members, (5) establishing ongoing treatment arrangements and linking clients to longer-term services. In an early report on the program, Kinney and her colleagues[67] report on a three-month follow-up of eighty families (134 family members) in which 95 percent of the families avoided out-of-home placement of a family member. The cost per client was $2331 less than out-of-home placement.

A similar program is the Lower East Side Family Union (LESFU).[68] LESFU, which operates in a low-income, predominantly minority section of New York City, developed out of a concern that the New York child welfare system relied too heavily on child placement to resolve the problems of families at risk. In an effort to reduce the number of children being removed from their homes as a result of child neglect and family breakdown, the program was started with three initial goals: (1) to strengthen families who experience extreme internal and external stress, (2) to minimize the interventions of juvenile justice and child welfare systems because of these systems' potential to break up the family, and (3) to prevent, whenever possible, the placement of children outside their own neighborhood. Teams provide a range of brief crisis intervention services and identify, locate, and contract for long-term services as needed by the family. Three of the teams include a team leader, five caseworkers, five homemakers, and a receptionist/typist. The fourth team, which does community organizing, includes a team leader and community residents, either paid or volunteer. LESFU workers are able to respond to families quickly and flexibly to assess need, locate or rearrange services from a number of service providers, and coordinate and monitor the services provided to the family. Other important tasks performed by the workers are advocacy for the client with other service providers or community agencies and networking within the community to create informal support systems for the families.

All these programs seem to be characterized by (1) service delivery in the families' home and community, (2) intensive service delivery (often available twenty-four hours a day), and (3) provision of a wide range of services. What distinguishes these home-based services from other types of family service programs is the successful implementation of these three service characteristics coupled with the neighborhood "locus" of service provision. Indeed, the most distinctive feature of home-based services is not the focus on the family as the unit of attention; it is the provision of services to the entire family in its natural home environment and the transfer of knowledge, skill, and help in this context.

It should be emphasized that many of these home-based programs are focused on families and children at risk of separation. Unlike the neighborhood or multiservice centers established in the 1960s to serve entire geographic populations, most of these programs are problem-focused and designed to serve a relatively narrow population of families in which children are likely to be removed from their home if intensive services are not provided. Hence, they cannot be construed as broad-based family service programs and could just as appropriately be described in the next chapter on services to families at risk.

Service Management

While the preceding discussion focused on new programs established specifically to enhance family functioning, it is important to remember that many programs and agencies are already in place and that there are service boundaries between them. This has resulted in development of a fragmented "nonsystem" of service delivery to families, which may be duplicative and uncoordinated. Over a number of years concern has been expressed within both professional and lay circles about the fact that the human services have generally been poorly organized, inefficiently managed, and wasteful.[69]

These beliefs have stimulated efforts within social work to improve the management and organization of the social services. They also have been responsible, at least in part, for the trend toward replacing social work administrators with top administrative personnel who have been trained outside the behavioral sciences and whose major qualification is apparently a rise to the top of a large business. Concern with the organization and management of social services may be based as much on enduring myths (for example, that there exist large-scale recipient fraud and professional negligence) as in real inefficiency or disorganization. Nevertheless, concern with the management of social services is likely to continue to receive considerable attention. This attention will, as in the past, include a range of efforts designed to influence the behavior of individual professionals as they engage in activities with and on behalf of clients, such as management by objectives[70] or the use of single-subject experimental designs to evaluate direct practice.[71]

Efforts will also continue to improve the organization and management of the entire social service system toward the end that families are better served. Currently, many such efforts are being discussed under the concepts of *service integration* and *case management.*[72] Service integration refers to efforts to coordinate or integrate services at the macro level, for example, locating representatives from a number of agencies in a single location in order to become more available to clients in a particular location. Case management refers to a service model, which is designed to promote access to services and to insure coordination of services provided to specific cases.[73]

DeWitt in a summary report on the Service Integration Targets of Opportunity (SITO) projects describes a number of service integration and case management activities which may be used to: (1) increase accessibility and availability of services, (2) increase the responsiveness of service providers, and/or (3) enhance the efficiency and accountability of services.[74] These activities, which help link individual services to each other in order to enhance service delivery for clients, include:

—*Fiscal linkages* including joint budgeting, funding, and purchase of service, which bring together service providers to prepare joint budgets or to combine funds to support or purchase services.

—*Personnel linkages* involving efforts to locate staff from different agencies together in single common locations (co-location), transferring staff who are on the payroll of one agency to the administrative control of another (staff transfer), assigning staff from one agency to work at another agency (out-posting), or using the same staff to provide service to more than one agency's clientele (joint use of staff).

—*Planning and programming linkages* that include joint policy-making, planning, programming, information sharing, or evaluation efforts among several agencies.

—*Administrative support services linkages* including consolidated or centralized record keeping, management information systems, or other support services such as auditing, purchasing, or sharing equipment.

—*Core service linkages* involving sharing access services among several agencies. These include common outreach, intake, diagnosis, referral, follow-up, and transportation services.

—*Case coordination linkages* involving efforts to coordinate services from several agencies as they relate to specific cases. These include case consultation, case conferences, or case teams. In case conferences service providers meet to discuss a client's needs and progress, determine future service plans, and assign responsibilities to each of the service providers. Case teams are made up of several service providers, often from different disciplines, providing services to a single case.

As DeWitt points out, it is not currently possible to identify which activities are most successful in assuring integration or coordination of services.[75] The reasons include lack of controlled comparisons of specific activities within single sites and the incomparability of evaluative data generated in different projects. Nevertheless, the experiences of the SITO projects do seem to suggest a number of potentially important integration activities. For example, core service linkage activities (such as outreach, referral, and intake) appear to increase accessibility of service to clients, to increase responsiveness of services provided to clients, and to facilitate interagency relationships. Case coordination linkages (case teams or case managers) also appear to increase accessibility, comprehensiveness, and the volume of services provided, but case conferences do not appear effective in this regard. Case managers appear to be effective in situations in which the manager has some power over the other agencies (for example, through the purchase of services).

In general, then, the experiences of the SITO projects do seem to suggest that various service integration or coordination activities may improve access and availability. However, further research, especially controlled comparisons of various activities, will be necessary before it is possible to identify those activities that are likely to facilitate more effective, efficient, or comprehensive service delivery. In addition to a number of policy, funding, and legislative problems that must be addressed at the federal and state levels, and the need for continued experimentation and evaluation of specific integration and coordination activities at the service delivery level, several major issues need to be considered in designing efforts to manage services more effectively or efficiently.

First, it is not at all clear that integration and coordination efforts are anything more than a partial response to the ineffectiveness, inefficiency, or wastefulness of social services.[76] Efforts to improve service integration or coordination—service management—are unlikely to do much to improve the effectiveness of services that are ineffective in obtaining the goals for which they are designed. The fundamental question raised by a concern with accountability is, "What effect does the service have on the client's life?" If, for whatever reason, services are unable to produce an effect (outcome), then no amount of integration or coordination efforts will increase the service effectiveness.

Second, at the most basic level, service delivery consists of interactions between worker and client(s). Change efforts at the policy, legislative, agency, or programmatic levels that do not deal with this basic unit of service delivery are not likely to be successful. The social worker faces a number of policy, programmatic, and organizational obstacles to effective service delivery. These include (1) confusing, contradictory, and inconsistent eligibility requirements, which place the worker in the position of being unsure of who is entitled to receive which services or being unable to provide services to cases that may be in need; (2) ever-increasing demands to complete paperwork (for example, service data, management information, case reports), much of which is of little or no help to the worker in planning or providing direct service; and (3) work in bureaucratic organizations characterized by high turnover, distance between top administration and line workers, mutual distrust between line workers and central administration, inadequate support or direction from central administration, and lack of authority in carrying out job responsibilities.

Efforts to improve the efficiency and effectiveness of social services will have to respond, in part, to the needs of social service workers. The Task Force on the Organization and Delivery of Human Services of the National Conference on Social Welfare has identified several principles that may be helpful in increasing "the front-line worker's ability to deliver efficient and effective services." These include "[giving] workers sufficient authority and resources to achieve client objectives in the context of agreed-upon agency goals, and [holding] them accountable for the results; [increasing] the availability of effective services from a variety of categorical sources and . . . the workers' access to them," and reducing the amount of time not spent directly with clients.[77]

These principles suggest a model of practice with several distinct characteristics. First, service and the evaluation of service are goal-directed. The effects of service are to be evaluated. Second, the process of service delivery (for example, the numbers of hours spent providing a specific type of service) is not as important as the results of the services. "Performance against objectives" is to be the evaluative criterion. Third, as much as possible, service to clients should not be encumbered by excessive reporting (paperwork) requirements, which take workers' time away from direct services.

In part, these characteristics describe the case management model of practice, which is receiving considerable attention of late. Although case management is being used in a number of ways, there are commonalities in how it is viewed. For example, Spitalnik refers to "case management as a service which is designed to provide access to other services and insure quality and coordination of services."[78] Pye defines case management as:

> An individualized service provided by someone acting in the role of coordinator to insure that the various needs of an individual are assessed and met. It consists of face-to-face counseling, resulting in the determination of

need, the development of a plan, the allocation of responsibility for implementation of the plan and the ongoing monitoring of the plan. Case management implies collaborative and cooperative working relationships with the individual and those relating to him with the crucial problems of his life. Case management services imply helping access to resources, helping those resources as well as helping secure rights and entitlements. The atmosphere of case management should encourage the individual to return to counseling as new or recurring needs arise.[79]

Case management includes both an individualized planning and a service coordination function.[80] The planning function requires skills in problem assessment and eliciting client cooperation. The case coordination function requires skills in administration, resource brokerage, monitoring, and advocacy. Although the actual responsibilities assigned to the case manager will depend on the type of client and agency in which the manager works, a number of general tasks have been identified:

1. Complete initial interview to assess client's eligibility for services.
2. Gather collateral information and conduct assessment of client and client's problem(s).
3. Formulate goals with involvement from client, client's significant others, and appropriate professionals, and design an intervention plan which integrates all participants.
4. Monitor adherence to the plan and manage the flow of information among participants to help insure movement toward client's goals.
5. Maintain contact with the client and client's significant others to monitor the effects of the plan and additional unanticipated problems which arise.
6. Provide counseling and information to the client and the client's significant others in the event of crisis and conflict with service providers.
7. Provide emotional support to the client and the client's significant others, so that they can cope with problems and utilize service providers more effectively.
8. Complete the necessary paperwork to maintain documentation of the client's progress and adherence of all parties to the case plan.
9. Act as a liaison between the client and the client's significant others and all relevant professionals to help the client make preferences and needs known and to secure necessary services.

10. Act as a liaison between service providers and the client to ensure exchange of information and minimize conflict between them.
11. Establish and maintain credibility and good relations with formal and informal resources to mobilize them as needed for current and future clients.
12. Secure and maintain the respect and support of those in positions of authority so their influence can be employed as needed on behalf of the clients.[81]

These tasks describe a generalist model of practice in which the social worker assumes the responsibility for assessment, development of a comprehensive service plan responding to each of the problems identified in the assessment, arranging for service to be delivered for each of the problems, monitoring and evaluating the services delivered, and conducting follow-up evaluations wtih the client to insure that problem reduction has been maintained after the client terminated from the service.[82]

Case management describes a process for assuring that clients receive the services they need. The current assumption, which awaits empirical validation, is that case management strategies offer the hope of providing services in a coordinated, effective, and efficient manner. Some of the features of the model, which *may* offer the best change of increasing the effectiveness and efficiency of services, could be helpful within both a generalist and specialist model of practice. These features appear to be (1) a concern for comprehensive assessment, identification of all client problems, and a service plan that addresses all identified problems; (2) efforts to include as many people from the client's life and the professional community as possible in resolving the client's problems; (3) an emphasis on goal-directed activities and continuous monitoring of client movement toward these goals; (4) efforts to plan service, obtain monitoring information, and establish goals in behaviorally specific language, which uses concepts at the lowest possible level of abstraction. It should be noted that the case management model of practice describes only one type of professional response to the needs of clients. The existence of a range of specialized services is fundamental, or there is little for the case manager to procure or coordinate.

The Voluntary Agency

With the increased role of government agencies in the direct delivery of social services and the increased financing of voluntary social welfare activities through government sources, the role of the voluntary sector in the provision of family social services has been questioned in recent years. There has been some discussion that the voluntary agency no longer has the financial resources to be a program pioneer or innovator[83] and that the complexity of social service needs requires "innovative, multifunctional regional social services organizations with centralized management systems and highly decentralized service delivery" arrangements.[84] It has been argued that the large number of voluntary agencies in a given city may add to the fragmentation of social service delivery and therefore increase the need for coordination and service management arrangements.

The voluntary agency has also been criticized as being unresponsive to the needs of minority groups, especially because the control of the same voluntary agency boards is in the hands of conservative social elites.[85] Furthermore, agencies in the voluntary sector have been accused of protecting their own interests as viable organizations rather than the interests of their clients. It has been said that they are elitist in their intake policies—"creaming" the most desirable clients for themselves and leaving the public sector to deal with the most difficult families. Finally, the fact that sectarian agencies may limit their intake or give priority to service their "own" has been criticized as being unresponsive to the needs of the larger community and discriminatory, since public funds are used to support most of these programs.

Many of these criticisms are undoubtedly true for some agencies, and there will probably continue to be many small agencies that continue to practice in traditional ways and to act as conservative forces in some communities. Some will continue to fight not for their clients' interests but for organizational and fiscal viability, specific sectarian interests, and/or professional vested interests.

There are also some areas in which the voluntary sector clearly should not be involved. The responsibility to see that all people are served belongs to the public sector, for only government agencies have mandated legal responsibility for all Americans. Furthermore, a number of social services involve either the investigation of illegal acts (for example child or elderly abuse) or situations that may involve state intervention under either its police power or its responsibility to act in *parens patriae*. In either case, voluntary agencies ordinarily lack the legally sanctioned authority to assume the responsibility for such interventions.

Despite these criticisms and limitations of the voluntary sector, there is a place for the voluntary agency in the delivery of social services. Moreover, because of their smaller size and local base, they can make a significant contribution to the delivery of family services. These contributions can include innovations in programs and service delivery, ability to identify needs and mobilize public opinion, and the capacity to provide preventive and developmental services without raising ethical questions about the intrusiveness of government into family life.[86] The existence of a number of small agencies providing services can also provide a degree of consumer choice.

The literature does describe a number of innovative services, many created by family service agencies. The Family Service Association of Nassau County, New York, offered a debt-counseling program, which consisted of budget and credit counseling and casework to help families who were heavily in debt understand the reasons for their problems.[87] Cutting and Prosser describe a family agency's services to military families,[88] and Vassil describes a family residential camp where disadvantaged families spent time in a recreational camp.[89] Parents assumed major responsibilities for many camp activities (such as taking care of groups of children or serving on a camp council, which made most of the decisions about the operation of the camp). Haapala and Kinney describe an intensive in-home intervention package developed in part by Catholic Community Services to prevent institutionalization of family members.[90]

These reports seem to suggest that some voluntary agencies are in fact acting as service innovators. However, if innovation is to be a primary role for the voluntary sector, more needs to be done. The most recent data on services provided by a portion of the voluntary sector is the 1970 survey of family service agencies conducted by the Family Service Association of America.[91] Although hopefully out-of-date by now, the report does not paint an optimistic picture of service innovation at that time. In terms of services provided to clients, some form of counseling was provided in 91 percent of the cases. Other services provided were: caretaking, 7.0 percent; financial assistance, 5.2 percent; referral, 28.0 percent; mental health services, 1.8 percent; legal services, 1.2 percent; adoption, 2.9 percent; advocacy, 3.0 percent; psychological testing, 1.2 percent; and family life education, 1.5 percent.

One of the factors mitigating against innovative programming in the voluntary sector may be the continued pressure to form closer relationships with public social welfare because of the decrease in voluntary funding and the increase in purchase-of-service arrangements. Indeed, Hill reports on a survey of Family Service Association member agencies indicating "widespread formalized arrangements with public agencies" which are "underwritten by governmental monies."[92] These arrangements include "consultation to extended health care facilities, group treatment for mentally retarded adolescents, family life education programs under the auspices of comprehensive mental health centers, budget counseling services in Model Cities programs, and training programs for local municipal police departments."[93]

Government financing of social services in voluntary agencies can be potentially problematic for family welfare. The advantages of these arrangements, such as increased community involvement in social welfare planning and the delivery of service and a "check" on the use of government funds[94] could be outweighed by the potentially conservative stance imposed by governmental control and/or undue influence that monetary power may provide. The recent successful congressional efforts to restrict the types of clients that federally funded legal service agencies can aid is a clear illustration of the social control risk. As Manser has suggested, the relationship between government and voluntary agency is not one of equal partners.[95] Government defines the scope of the services purchased, the unit of service to be reimbursed, and the costs to be included in calculating reimbursement rates. In addition, along with public monies come reporting, auditing, and other accountability requirements[96] that may raise professional ethical issues, especially around the concept of client confidentiality.

Another potential problem is that new services may be more difficult to plan and implement as voluntary agencies scramble to meet governmental priorities. Thus, the need to obtain government support in the form of purchase-of-service contracts in order to maintain fiscal viability may limit the voluntary sector's ability to innovate in areas that the government does not designate as priorities. Local agencies may identify changing needs more quickly than large centralized public agencies, but without public funds they may be hesitant to move into the identified areas of need. Clearly, too great a reliance on any single source of funding can threaten the innovative capacity of many agencies. Voluntary agencies should not fall into the trap of believing that only projects funded with large amounts of money can hope to generate innovative service arrangements. Relatively small investments can permit many agencies with some research capacity and originality to experiment with new service delivery arrangements and components.

In addition to service innovation, the voluntary agency can assume a watchdog function by identifying and publicizing groups whose service needs are not adequately met by the public sector. Once identified, pressure can be placed on the government to respond to the identified needs through class advocacy efforts and the mobilization of public opinion at the local level. However, this role may also be placed in jeopardy if single-source government funding becomes the norm for the voluntary sector. As Manser has suggested, it is unknown how much advocacy from voluntary agencies the government will tolerate before taking some kind of action against them through the termination of contracts and other measures.[97]

Voluntary agencies can also provide a valuable service to families whose service needs are not problem-related or whose behavior has not yet been labeled. By encouraging open intakes, reducing eligibility requirements, and maintaining flexible hours, they can provide service in a less stigmatized setting than a public agency. With proper publicity they can be viewed as concerned with developmental family problems in a noncoercive environment, which does not carry the "welfare" stigma. They can be viewed as an alternative to the public sector, offering the consumer a choice in service delivery arrangements by providing services that need not be labeled rehabilitative or problem-related.[98]

CONCLUSIONS

This chapter has suggested a number of considerations in viewing services that enhance family functioning. First, families may require services to maintain or improve their functioning for a wide range of reasons. These reasons or problems include a change in family structure, the effects of social and material deprivation and emotional isolation, and the effects on all family members of individual family members' emotional problems. Second, professional interventions should continue to be varied and to include a range of potential services such as provision of concrete resources, counseling, family life education, client advocacy, and use of social networks. What is not clear is the proper mix and range of services that should be offered to any given family. Third, questions about the effectiveness and efficiency of social work services are likely to continue. Efforts to increase or insure program accountability may offer procedures to organize services more effectively, to deliver services in locations that are more accessible to clients, and to coordinate a range of services to individual cases. To what extent inefficiency and ineffectiveness are the result of the process of service delivery or the location of traditional service delivery arrangements, and to what extent they are the result of providing services that have little or no potential for changing particular problems (for example, casework to end poverty) are questions that have not been resolved. Finally, it seems clear that social workers will continue to innovate in the area of services to families, thereby expanding the traditional family and children's services available.

This chapter has not resolved the problems of the dual focus of social work on people changing and situation changing. This dual perspective has long been a subject of debate within the profession and continues to be discussed today. For example, Cohen notes:

> One of the distinguishing features of clinical social work, as compared with other kinds of clinical interventions, is the clinician's concern with the social context within which individual or family problems occur and are altered. *Clinical social work, therefore, may involve intervention in the social situation and the person situation.*[99] (emphasis added)

This dual perspective often seems to be more a matter of intent than of actual practice. In part, our efforts are hampered by the lack of practice theory that incorporates both person- and situation-changing efforts. Certainly, the ecological perspective calls attention to the person-in-situation concept, but to date it has not developed into a full theory of practice. Both the ecological perspective and the more general issue of social work's dual nature are receiving renewed attention. Reacting to a series of papers presented at an NASW-sponsored conference on conceptual models in 1979, Briar observed,

> . . . there are differences of opinion on what words to use in labeling this process. Regardless of the label, however, person-environment interaction means that social workers *want* to perceive and analyze persons with their needs and problems in the context of the person's environment.[100]

The case management model of practice may also serve to call attention to the importance of considering both person changing and situation changing. A comprehensive assessment of all problem areas and case planning for each identified problem is certainly one avenue to reinforcing both perspectives. However, one of the greatest problems the profession faces is the limiting nature of some practitioners' self definition and some practice theory. As both Briar[101] and Meezan[102] have found, case decisions are frequently based on agency patterns or worker roles rather than specific case needs. To the extent that workers define themselves as "family therapists" or "clinicians" *and* operate on limited views of clinical practice, people changing will receive disproportionate attention. The challenge of this dual perspective is to recognize that some families have problems because of factors in the environment or the family-environment interaction, and some families have problems because of factors within individual family members or the family as a unit. To accept this challenge, social workers will need to continue to be open to both types of problems. They will need to develop services and service delivery arrangements that have the potential of effecting change in both the individual family and the family's social environment, depending on which avenue offers the greatest possibility of effecting change. Perhaps most importantly, for the foreseeable future, support of families will require efforts by social workers to reverse or impede attempts by the current administration to dismantle the American social welfare system. As was indicated in the beginning of this chapter, at this writing it is too early to foresee the full extent of these attempts. The impact upon clients has not yet been fully felt nor witnessed by social workers; nor is it clear who will give voice to the support of traditional social service values.

What is clear is that the administration's efforts to dismantle social services will have dire consequences for social work clients. Many of the budget cuts will directly affect children and families, as almost every aspect of social services is affected. The earliest history of social work seems to suggest that the profession's response should be one of political and social advocacy. Just as settlement house workers publicized the living conditions in American industrial cities in the late 1800s and worked for legislation to improve the conditions of children and families of that era, so must contemporary social workers publicize the human, economic, and social costs of the administration's programs. The traditional perspective that social work applies to human services calls attention to both people-changing and environment-changing efforts. For the foreseeable future, environment-changing efforts have taken on a new urgency.

Social workers are in an especially advantageous position to speak for children and their families, as they come in contact with them in many different settings and contexts. This writer sees nothing to support the administration's claim to a mandate to dismantle the social welfare system created during this century. The 1980 national election was hardly a direct vote on that question. The history of the United States seems to suggest that the American people have traditionally voted to support efforts to "help others help themselves." What is needed now are strong voices to articulate the need for and advantages of renewed efforts to accomplish this task through a professionally staffed, efficiently managed, and fully financed system of formal and informal social supports.

NOTES

1. U.S. Department of Commerce, Bureau of the Census, *Current Population Reports*, Series P-20, no. 336 (Washington, D.C.: Bureau of the Census, 1978).

2. *Delegate Workbook, White House Conference on Families* (mimeographed, n.d.).

3. David Finkelhor, *Sexually Victimized Children* (New York: Free Press, 1979).

4. Jon R. Conte and Lucy Berliner, "Sexual Abuse of Children: Implications for Practice," *Social Casework* 62 (December 1981): 601–6.

5. *Gallup Survey to the White House Conference on Children and Families* (mimeographed, n.d.).

6. Carle C. Zimmerman, "The Future of the Family in America," *Journal of Marriage and the Family* 34 (May 1972): 323–33.

7. Mary Jo Bane, *Here to Stay* (New York: Basic Books, 1976).

8. National Conference on Social Welfare, *Families and Public Policies in the United States* (Washington, D.C.: National Conference on Social Welfare, 1978).

9. Shelia B. Kamerman and Alfred J. Kahn, *Social Services in the United States* (Philadelphia: Temple University Press, 1976).

10. Ann Hartman, "But What Is Social Casework?", *Social Casework* 52 (July 1971): 411–17.

11. Jon R. Conte and Terese M. Halpin, "Current and Future Trends in Services to Families," in *Handbook of Clinical Social Work*, ed. Aaron Rosenblatt and Diana Waldgoel (San Francisco: Jossey Bass, in press).

12. For discussion, see Conte and Halpin, "Current and Future Trends."

13. Hartman, "But What Is Social Casework?"

14. Florence Hollis, "On Revisiting Social Work," *Social Casework* 61 (June 1980): 3–10.

15. Hartman, "But What Is Social Casework?", p. 419.

16. Carel B. Germain, "An Ecological Perspective in Casework Practice," *Social Casework* 54 (June 1975): 323–30; Carel B. Germain, "Social Context of Clinical Social Work," *Social Work* 25 (November 1980): 483–88.

17. Germain, "An Ecological Perspective in Casework Practice."

18. Carel B. Germain and Alex Gitterman, "The Life Model of Social Work Practice," in *Social Work Treatment*, ed. Francis J. Turner (New York: Free Press, 1979).

19. Carel B. Germain, *Social Work Practice: People and Environments* (New York: Columbia University Press, 1979).

20. James Garbarino, "A Preliminary Study of Some Ecological Correlates of Child Abuse," *Child Development* 47 (March 1976): 178–85; James Garbarino and Ann Crouter, "Defining the Community Context for Parent-Child Relations," *Child Development* 49 (September 1978): 604–16; James Garbarino and Deborah Sherman, "High-Risk Neighborhoods and High-Risk Families," *Child Development* 51 (March 1980): 188–98.

21. Conte and Berliner, "Sexual Abuse of Children."

22. Ellen Manser, *Family Advocacy: A Manual for Action* (New York: Family Service Association of America, 1973), p. 1.

23. Arnold Panitch, "Advocacy Practice," *Social Work* 19 (May 1974): 326–32.

24. David Hallowitz, "Advocacy in the Context of Treatment," *Social Casework* 55 (July 1974): 416–20.

25. Ibid.

26. Brian O'Connell, "From Service to Advocacy to Empowerment," *Social Casework* 59 (April 1978): 195–202.

27. Ibid.

28. Panitch, "Advocacy Practice."

29. Robert M. Rice, *A Survey of a Sample of 22 Member Agencies of the Family Service Association of America Concerning Changes in Family Problems* (New York: Family Service Association of America, 1977).

30. Brenda G. McGowan, "The Case Advocacy Function in Child Welfare Practice," *Child Welfare,* 57 (May 1978): 275–85.

31. Ibid., p. 281.

32. Ibid., p. 283.

33. Dorothy Fahs Beck, Charlotte Tileston, and Susan Keston, *Educational Programs of Family Agencies* (New York: Family Service Association of America, 1977).

34. Lucile Cantoni, "Family Life Education: A Treatment Modality," *Child Welfare* 54 (November 1975): 658–65.

35. Salvatore Ambrosino, "Integrating Counseling, Family Life Education and Family Advocacy," *Social Casework* 60 (December 1979): 582.

36. Marvin J. Fine, *Handbook of Parent Education* (New York: Academic Press, 1980), pp. 2–3.

37. Janice Prochaska and Jane P. Coyle, "Choosing Parenthood: A Needed Family Life Education Group," *Social Casework* 60 (May 1979): 289–95.

38. Dawn S. Simon, "A Systematic Approach to Family Life Education," *Social Casework* 57 (October 1976): 511–16.

39. Elaine Levin, "Development of a Family Life Education Program in a Community Social Service Agency," *The Family Coordinator* 24 (July 1975): 343–49.

40. Donald P. Riley, Katheryn Apgar, and John Eaton, *Parent-Child Communication* (New York: Family Service Association of America, 1977).

41. Betsy Nicholson Callahan, *Separation and Divorce* (New York: Family Service Association of America, 1979).

42. See, for example, Alice H. Collins and Diane L. Pancoast, *Natural Helping Networks: A Strategy for Prevention* (Washington, D.C.: National Association of Social Workers, 1976); Alice H. Collins, "Helping Neighbors Intervene in Cases of Maltreatment;" and Diane L. Pancoast, "Finding and Enlisting Neighbors to Support Families," in *Protecting Children from Child Abuse and Neglect,* ed. James Garbarino and S. Holly Stocking (San Francisco: Jossey Bass, 1980); Uri Rueveni, *Networking Families in Crisis* (New York: Human Sciences Press, 1979); Ross V. Speck and Carolyn L. Attneave, *Family Networks* (New York: Pantheon Books, 1973).

43. Collins and Pancoast, *Natural Helping Networks.*

44. Alfred H. Katz and Eugene I. Bender, *The Strength in Us* (New York: New Viewpoints, 1976), p. 36.

45. "Groups Help Those Who Help Themselves," *The Hastings Center Report* 7 (October 1977): 3.

46. Brenda G. McGowan, *Self Help and the Provision of Family Services* (New York: Columbia University School of Social Work, Cross National Studies of Social Services and Family Policy, 1979), p. 24 (mimeographed).

47. Ibid., pp. 41–49.

48. Frank Baker, "The Interface Between Professionals and Natural Support Systems," *Clinical Social Work Journal* 5 (Summer 1977): 147.

49. McGowan, *Self Help and the Provision of Family Services,* pp. 47–49.

50. Rueveni, *Networking Families in Crisis,* p. 26.

51. Collins and Pancoast, *Natural Helping Networks.*

52. Ann Hartman, "Diagrammatic Assessment of Family Relationships," *Social Casework* 59 (October 1978): 465–76.

53. Rueveni, *Networking Families in Crisis,* p. 72.

54. Ibid., p. 33–37.

55. Speck and Attneave, *Family Networks.*

56. Martin A. Kozloff, *A Program for Families of Children with Learning and Behavior Problems* (New York: John Wiley and Sons, 1979).

57. Daniel Thurz and Joseph Vigilante, *Reaching People: The Structure of Neighborhood Services* (Beverly Hills, Calif.: Sage Publications, 1978).

58. Alice Q. Ayres, "Neighborhood Services: People Caring for People," *Social Casework* 54 (April 1973): 195–215.

59. Alfred J. Kahn, "Service Delivery at the Neighborhood Level: Experience, Theory and Fads," *Social Service Review* 50 (March 1976): 23–56.

60. Frank Riessman, "A Neighborhood-based Mental Health Approach," in *Emergent Approaches to Mental Health Problems,* ed. E. Cowen, E. Gardner, and M. Zax (New York: Appleton-Century-Crofts, 1967), pp. 162–84.

61. See, for example, Sheila Maybanks and Marvin Bryce, eds., *Home Based Services for Children and Families* (Springfield, Ill.: Charles C Thomas, 1979); Marvin Bryce and June C. Lloyd, eds., *Treating Families in the Home: An Alternative to Placement* (Springfield, Ill.: Charles C Thomas, 1981).

62. Marvin Bryce, "Home-Based Family-Centered Care: Problems and Perspectives," in *Treating Families in the Home: An Alternative to Placement,* ed. Bryce and Lloyd.

63. *Workshop Materials: Home-Based Family-Centered Services: A View from the Child Welfare Sector* (Oakdale, Iowa: National Clearing House for Home-Based Services to Children and Their Families, School of Social Work, University of Iowa, 1981), p. 2.

64. Theodore Levine and Elizabeth McDaid, "Services to Children in Their Own Homes: A Family Based Approach," in *Home-Based Services for Children and Families,* ed. Maybanks and Bryce, pp. 160–71.

65. Jill McCleave Kinney et al., "Homebuilders: Keeping Families Together," *Journal of Consulting and Clinical Psychology* 45 (August 1977): 667–73.

66. David Haapala and Jill Kinney, "Homebuilders' Approach to

Training of In-Home Therapists," in *Home-Based Services for Children and Families*, ed. Maybanks and Bryce, pp. 248–59.

67. Kinney et al., "Homebuilders: Keeping Families Together."

68. Marylee Dunu, "The Lower East Side Family Union: Assuring Community Services for Minority Families," in *Home-Based Services for Children and Families*, ed. Maybanks and Bryce, pp. 211–24.

69. Robert Morris and Ilana Hirsch Lescohier, "Service Integration: Real versus Illusory Solutions to Welfare Dilemmas," in *The Management of Human Services*, ed. Rosemary Sarri and Yeheskel Hasenfield (New York: Columbia University Press, 1978), pp. 22–49.

70. Melvin C. Raider, "An Evaluation of Management by Objectives," *Social Casework* 56 (February 1975): 78–83.

71. Srinika Jayaratne and Rona L. Levy, *Empirical Clinical Practice* (New York: Columbia University Press, 1979).

72. Other authors have referred to these concepts as program coordination and case integration. See Alfred Kahn, *Studies in Social Policy and Planning* (New York: Russell Sage Foundation, 1969).

73. Deborah M. Spitalnik, "The Case Manager's Role and the Training of the Case Managers," in *Case Management: State of the Art*, report submitted to the Administration on Developmental Disabilities, Department of Health and Human Services, by the National Conference on Social Welfare (Columbus, Ohio: National Conference on Social Welfare, 1981), pp. 47–71.

74. John DeWitt, *Findings from the SITO Projects*, Human Services Monograph Series, No. 4 (Denver, Co.: National Clearinghouse for Improving the Management of Human Services, 1977).

75. Ibid.

76. Morris and Lescohier, "Service Integration."

77. National Conference on Social Welfare, *Expanding Management Technology and Professional Accountability in Social Service Programs: Final Report* (Columbus, Ohio: National Conference on Social Welfare, 1976).

78. Spitalnik, "The Case Manager's Role."

79. Edgar W. Pye, "Growth and Development of Case Management: Where Are We Headed?" in *Case Management: State of the Art*, pp. 181–203.

80. Spitalnik, "The Case Manager's Role."

81. Ann Vandenberg Bertsche and Charles R. Horejsi, "Coordination of Client Services," *Social Work* 25 (March 1980): 84–98.

82. James Itagliata, "Operating a Case Management System: A Multilevel Approach," in *Case Management: State of the Art,* pp. 98–134.

83. Alvin L. Shoor, "The Tasks for Voluntarism in the Next Decade," *Child Welfare,* 49 (October 1970): 425–34.

84. Norman V. Lourie, "Public-Voluntary Agency Relationships in the 70's," *Child Welfare* 49 (July 1970): 376–78.

85. Fred R. MacKinnon, "Changing Patterns in Public-Voluntary Relationships in Canada," *Child Welfare* 52 (December 1973): 633–42.

86. Donald L. Loughery, "Optimal Operation of Public/Private Child Welfare Delivery Systems," *Child Welfare* 49 (December 1970): 553–61.

87. John L. Laughlin and Robert Bressler, "A Family Agency Program for Heavily Indebted Families," *Social Casework* 52 (December 1971): 617–26.

88. Allan R. Cutting and Frank J. Prosser, "Family Oriented Mental Health Consultation to a Naval Research Group," *Social Casework* 60 (April 1979): 236–42.

89. Thomas Vassil, "Residential Family Camping: Altering Family Patterns," *Social Casework* 59 (December 1978): 605–13.

90. Haapala and Kinney, "Homebuilders' Approach to the Training of In-Home Therapists."

91. Dorothy Fahs Beck and Mary Ann Jones, *Progress on Family Problems* (New York: Family Service Association of America, 1973).

92. William G. Hill, "Voluntary and Governmental Transactions," *Social Casework* 52 (June 1971): 357.

93. Ibid.

94. MacKinnon, "Changing Patterns."

95. Gordon Manser, "Further Thoughts on Purchase of Service," *Social Casework* 55 (July 1974): 421–27.

96. Darrel J. Vorwaller, "The Voluntary Agency as a Vendor of Social Services," *Child Welfare* 51 (July 1972): 436–42.

97. Manser, "Further Thoughts."

98. Although this is not the appropriate place to assess recent developments in the burgeoning field of industrial social welfare, it seems clear that as social service programs for workers are ex-

panded, especially at a time when the public and voluntary sectors are experiencing severe budgetary constraints, the industrial sector may begin to assume increasing importance in the provision of family services. See, for example, Paul A. Kurzman and Sheila H. Akabas, "Industrial Social Work as an Arena for Practice," *Social Work* 26 (January 1981): 52–60; and Sheila H. Akabas and Paul A. Kurzman, eds., *Work, Workers and Work Organizations: A View from Social Work* (Englewood Cliffs, N.J.: Prentice-Hall, 1982). This development is likely to pose opportunities and constraints somewhat different from those discussed in relation to the voluntary sector.

99. Jerome Cohen, "Nature of Clinical Social Work," in *Toward a Delineation of Clinical Social Work,* ed. Patricia L. Ewalt (Washington, D.C.: National Association of Social Workers, 1979), pp. 23–31.

100. Scott Briar, "Needed: A Simple Definition of Social Work," *Social Work* 26 (January 1981): 83–84.

101. Scott Briar, "Clinical Judgment in Foster Care," *Child Welfare* 42 (April 1963): 161–68.

102. William Meezan, "Program Orientation as a Factor in Workers' Attitudes and Perceptions of the Need for Placement in Child Welfare," (D:S.W. dissertation, Columbia University School of Social Work, 1978).

CHAPTER 6
SERVICES TO CHILDREN AND FAMILIES AT RISK OF SEPARATION

Carmine J. Magazino

Much of the current debate about appropriate means to correct long-standing deficiencies in the organization and delivery of child welfare services stems from differing views on the appropriate scope and functions of the child welfare field. The strategies for reform now in vogue are directed toward the existing services although there are some attempts to redesign service delivery patterns. There appears to be no movement toward a redesign of the child welfare service system *per se* or toward broadening its responsibilities. The primary clients served by this system continue to be the most troubled and troubling families in American society, and since the problems experienced by these families are not perceived as manifestations of normal, universal needs, interventions are organized on a case-by-case basis. Such an orientation has been characterized as a "minimalist" attitude, in which services are targeted toward the most deprived families and children in society.[1]

THE MINIMALIST VIEW

This minimalist view has been challenged by those who advocate for a much broader concept of child welfare and for a broader reform agenda for the field (see Chapter 4). They begin with the assumption that all families and children need societal supports in their homes and communities and contend that the inability of families to secure the basic services and supports in their homes and communities necessary to relieve the pressures of daily living often creates the need for a residual child welfare system concerned primarily with the out-of-home care of children. They urge the development of "social utilities"—the social programs needed to enhance family functioning in modern industrial society and available to all citizens regardless of income or case-defined need—as well as the expansion of case services for families experiencing special difficulties.

Implementation of such a broad range of personal social services would constitute a true reform of the child welfare field. It assumes the existence of an adequate, viable income maintenance system and the development of a comprehensive, integrated social service system that would include social utilities such as information and referral services, day care, community centers, family planning services, and recreational opportunities; case services for families in need of counseling; supportive and supplementary services in the home; and, if needed, substitute care services. Ideally, these programs would be part of a free-standing, universally accessible, destigmatized, personal social service system designed to enhance the caretaking and socialization capacities of *all* families.[2]

However, the minimalist strategy prevails. Despite the increased recognition of the need for prevention and early intervention, services in the child welfare field continue to be organized on an individual case basis for those determined to be in the greatest need. Current efforts to improve the child welfare system are *designed to reduce the too readily available option of placement while maintaining the basic goal of protecting children at risk of serious and imminent harm.* This represents a shift in emphasis for the current system, but it does not constitute a basic reform of the child welfare field.

Prevailing Concept of Preventive Services

The field's effort to work more closely with children and families on the verge of deterioration has quickly been defined as the development of "preventive" services. This fits neatly into the current national preoccupation with prevention of costly social problems. However, it must clearly be understood that neither the newly developed services nor the new service delivery arrangements designed to prevent foster care placement constitute primary prevention, that is, activities designed to promote the well-being of all children and families and to alter their social environment, so that the prevalence of social problems will be reduced. The evolving work with families and children "at risk" might be said to approximate more closely secondary prevention activities that are aimed at early detection, diagnosis, and treatment of social problems. But even that definition of prevention is strained when one compares the numbers

of families potentially at risk of deterioration with the amount of resources allocated to address their problems and the actual services provided under the preventive service label. The range and scope of services needed to identify, reach, and help all families in trouble are well
beyond the capabilities and resources of the current child welfare system.

A forthright appraisal of the recent shift in child welfare programs can
only lead to the conclusion that these new activities are at best what
might be labeled *tertiary prevention* efforts. They are directed primarily
toward providing for children what Rapoport would call "specific protection" from inappropriate long-term foster care placement.[3] So widespread is the criticism of the alleged evils in the foster care placement
system that any activities designed to minimize or eliminate the "conta-
gion" of long-term placement in foster care are now legitimately said to
meet the criteria of a tertiary prevention activity.

To illustrate this tertiary prevention focus, New York State, in organizing its new child welfare program, clearly established the "prevention of
foster care placement" as its major goal.[4] In fiscal year 1980 New York
City's Human Resource Administration contracted with forty-eight programs to provide "preventive" services for up to 10,000 families and
14,000 children. A recent study of these programs concluded that although program staff have widely different personal definitions of prevention, the operational definitions of all programs included the
prevention and/or reduction of the need for foster care.[5] Further com-
plicating the definitional problems associated even with tertiary prevention is the fact that the state has recently introduced a case review
system designed to distinguish between "mandated" and "optional"
preventive services.[6] Mandated services are available only to those for
whom the risk of child placement is imminent (expected to occur within
sixty days) and families are asked to certify that they would need to
place their children within this time period if services were not provided.
Optional preventive services are funded on a more limited basis and are
available to families in which the threat of placement is not perceived to
be so imminent.

Such arbitrary distinctions demanding subjective judgments by workers and the subtle coercion of families in order to "certify" that placement is imminent have created a service system that is satisfactory to
neither clients nor workers nor agencies. Yet this system was implemented because, lacking a clear professional definition of prevention in
child welfare, political forces were able to focus attention on the need to
prevent foster care, and service planners were fearful that the promulgation of a broader, more rational definition of preventive services could

create a situation in which this new system, with its limited resources, would be overwhelmed by the service needs of families who are troubled but not at risk of immediate disintegration.

As the preceding discussion suggests, this author does not believe that the prevailing view of preventive services is useful at either the conceptual or the practice level. Given changing historical views regarding the types of children in need of placement (see Chapter 2) and strong research evidence pointing to workers' inability to make reliable judgments about the need for placement, and given the vague, shifting, socially defined standards of need (see Chapter 7), it seems clear that the effort to achieve clarity regarding the concept of prevention by defining this as the prevention of placement can be characterized only as a fruitless exercise in circular thinking.

If society is determined to block the gate to the foster care system, a far more rational, cost-efficient solution would simply be to close intake to all foster care settings. We are obviously not advocating such a solution, nor would the most reactionary political leader dare to make such a proposal, for there is a strong social consensus within the United States that society has some obligation to protect the welfare of children for whom parents are unable to provide adequate care. This basic premise, which underlies all the recent activity and interest in the problem of child abuse, mediates against a closed-door solution to the problem of unnecessary and prolonged use of foster care.

As a society we are committed to making some social provisions to protect children from harm, but our knowledge of what constitutes risk of harm is severely limited. And our ambivalence regarding the degree to which the state has the right and/or responsibility to intervene in family life is profound. Consequently, enormous energy is devoted to relabeling, redefining, and reorganizing services for children, but the basic policy dilemmas posed by the issue of state intervention in family life remain constant because of the lack of conceptual clarity and consensus regarding the boundaries and objectives of service for families and children.

Although on a theoretical level the author sides with those who reject the minimalist perspective of child welfare services and would like to advocate the implementation of a universal personal social service system, this seems a rather quixotic position to take in view of current political realities. Therefore, this chapter will focus more narrowly on new directions in service provision for children and families at risk of separation. However, for the reasons discussed earlier, we are loathe to term programs designed merely to prevent foster placement as "preventive" services.

Definitional Dilemma: Merger of Preventive and Protective Services

While prevention of foster care placement for children who can be maintained in their own homes is an important goal for the child welfare system, this is not possible in all cases. In order to protect some children from serious harm, removal from the home is necessary. Such decisions are often in the hands of workers delivering "protective" services— emergency services to families who have been reported for child abuse, neglect, or exploitation. However, with the adoption of a narrow, tertiary view of prevention within the field of child welfare, the distinction between "protective" and "preventive" interventions may not exist in practice. Recent research points to the lack of distinction between these two service domains.

Jenkins, Schroeder and Burgdorf recently analyzed data collected in a 1978 survey of services provided by a sample of public child welfare agencies in the first ninety days after intake.[7] They found that child abuse and neglect were the primary presenting problems in 52 percent of the cases and that one-half of all problems had been present a year or longer.[8] Although "protective" services were provided to about 32 percent of the children,[9] the most common goal (34 percent) recorded for children was "counseling to improve the child's self-image or behavior" and the most common goal (72 percent) for families was "improving family relationships or functioning."[10] One would be hard pressed to determine how the implemention of these goals constitutes "protective" services or how they differ from the goals frequently cited under the label of preventive services.

Given the lack of a clear distinction between protective and preventive services, the decision was made to focus discussion in this chapter on services for families at risk of separation, no matter what the categorical label under which these services are provided. This definition would include families where there are alleged incidents of neglect or abuse; patterns of severe interpersonal conflict; parents handicapped by mental illness, retardation, or physical disability; one or more members who are substance abusers; children demonstrating predelinquent or delinquent behavior; parents separated involuntarily from their children because of incarceration or institutionalization; children exhibiting severe emotional or school adjustment problems; parents too young to assume full child-caring responsibilities; and situations in which there is potential for physical harm because of the deprivation associated with severe poverty.[11]

There are really no clear criteria for defining what "at risk of separation" means. Some would add to the above list, while others would delete from it. The development of clear criteria has been identified as a major need in the field,[12] as the absence of clear guidelines represents a major obstacle to planning new services or redirecting current efforts. This orientation does, however, provide conceptual clarity in that it directs practice to view the *family system itself,* not simply the child, as the primary client. This implies that agency services should strive to assure that all members of the family unit participate as fully as possible in developing service plans and that, consistent with the respective civil and legal rights of each individual member, the family as a unit be viewed as the major beneficiary of services.

This focus should prevail even in situations where children cannot be protected from harm within their own homes. In such situations the state's responsibility is to protect the children's welfare by temporarily (or permanently) removing them from their families. Initially, then, the children's protection becomes the major objective and focus of service. However, once the child is protected, the focus of service should revert to the family unless it is determined that the child will never return home. This step is critical because the biological family is the primary resource for discharge of children from placement. Furthermore, it has long been clear that children served by child welfare agencies are likely to benefit most from efforts to work more systematically with and for their families.[13]

Focus of Chapter

This chapter will examine some of the implications and service potentials inherent in this shift in emphasis within the child welfare field from services for children in placement to services for children and families at risk of separation. As this focus is adopted, traditional services to families take on new meaning and existing programs are extended, reorganized, and revitalized to adapt to this new task. Social worker roles are reconceptualized, and boundary lines within and among agencies change as the field attempts to focus more explicitly on strategies of intervention designed to prevent placement. Since this mission represents new terrain for many child welfare agencies, the question becomes: "How can current services be adapted and reoriented to insure that this mandate is implemented?" To address this question, this chapter will first focus on supportive and supplementary services for families and how these two traditional child welfare services can be shifted, reorganized, and expanded to meet the new challenge of prevention of placement. Next, the chapter will look at emergency placement services and demonstrate that focusing on the needs of the family immediately after the child has been removed to insure protection from harm can prevent long-term placement. Finally, it will look at ways that the service repertoire of child welfare workers can be expanded to meet the goals of preventing unnecessary out-of-home care.

A NEW LOOK AT SUPPORTIVE AND SUPPLEMENTARY SERVICES

Child welfare services have traditionally been classified as supportive, supplementary, and substitute forms of care. The distinguishing characteristic of these services is the degree to which extra-familial resources are required to carry out the activities, tasks, and functions necessary to insure adequate child rearing. Supportive services have been described as services designed to reinforce, support, or strengthen the ability of parents and children to carry out the responsibilities of their respective roles in the family constellation more effectively. They often are thought of as services to the intact family. The agency is not assumed to have any responsibility for discharging the role functions of either parent or child.[14] Parent and child counseling, advocacy, and brokerage have customarily been viewed as the major components of supportive services. Child welfare workers have long utilized all of the traditional models of social work practice (casework, group work, and community organization) in order to help families in need. More recently many have also begun to experiment with different models of family therapy, family life education, and crisis intervention counseling as forms of supportive services.

Supplemental services have been characterized as those services or programs designed to assume some portion of the parental role responsibility, no matter how limited, within the family system. Income maintenance provisions, usually consisting of social insurance and public assistance programs, have traditionally been considered a form of supplementary service because they are designed to fulfill a part of the parental responsibility to provide adequate income for the maintenance of the family.[15] Other programs or services customarily thought as fulfilling a parental function and thus meeting this definition of supplementary services are homemaking services, day-care services, and respite care services.

Although the traditional distinctions between these different types of child welfare services provide some conceptual clarity, this classification scheme has three dysfunctional elements. First, it tends to obscure the fact that many services that could be beneficial to families at risk are not part of the customary interventive repertoires of child welfare agencies. As suggested earlier, the dream that the child welfare field could serve a primary prevention function has long been forsaken. Consequently little thought is given to the possibility of developing maternal and child health, education, employment, housing, recreation, community development, and other types of primary prevention programs from a child welfare service base. Yet applying the "supportive service" label to the limited in-home services traditionally provided by child welfare agencies tends to obscure the need for the child welfare system to develop linkages with other service sectors more capable of filling prevention functions.

A problem of more immediate concern is that this classification scheme can be used to justify the traditional boundaries between the child welfare, family service, and mental health fields—boundaries that have worked against child welfare agencies' assuming responsibility for initiating some of the newer types of service programs for families at risk (see Chapter 5). Little effort has been made within the child welfare field to develop the single-parent associations, client self-help groups, intergenerational support systems, child development and parent effectiveness courses, consumer education programs, family life education programs, and communication assertiveness training groups that are emerging in other fields of practice—any and all of which might fill significant supportive and supplementary service functions.[16] Somehow the fact that child welfare agencies offer some services under the umbrella labels of supportive and supplementary care is used to rationalize the limited interventive repertoire within these service categories, and workers who recognize the need for more innovative and specialized forms of service for their clients tend to fault agencies in other practice fields for failing to respond adequately to the needs of the child welfare population.

The final major drawback to employing the traditional distinctions between supportive and supplementary care provisions as a means of classifying child welfare services is that these distinctions imply conceptually clear, mutually exclusive, easily distinguishable service categories. While this classification may be advantageous for program planning and assessment, it tends to constrain direct service delivery because the problems of families are seldom clear, mutually exclusive, or easily definable. In practice, families often require a complex mix and blend of services that may shift as their needs and capacities change over time. Yet programs, once categorized in relation to eligibility criteria, service objectives, and arrangements, are not easily modified, integrated, or reconceptualized in order to mesh more closely with the evolving needs of specific families at risk.

Despite these caveats regarding the disadvantages of this classification scheme, we have chosen to highlight the significance of supportive and supplementary services for families at risk of separation or deterioration because the framework for these services is now in place; and given the prevailing minimalist perspective on child welfare services discussed above, it seems more realistic to consider innovative uses of these services than to propose an entirely new model for conceptualizing, organizing, and delivering services.

The inability to provide supportive and supplementary services, together with a lack of knowledge about the resources needed to maintain "problem children" in the community, has been identified as a contributing factor in the placement of children in long-term foster care. Now, as agencies become more concerned about their obligation to prevent inappropriate placement, the effective delivery of these services can be viewed as one of the crucial elements in a time-limited, case planning process that will culminate in a permanent decision regarding a child's future. In other words, the stakes for the provision of supportive and supplementary services have grown much higher as agencies recognize that these services can provide a needed barrier to foster care placement. Furthermore, if creatively used, these services can serve as a diagnostic tool to aid in selecting an appropriate placement and making permanent plans for a child in substitute care if placement cannot be avoided.

As the focus of the child welfare field begins to change, first by defining the existing family system as the primary client, and second, by placing a higher value on the avoidance of placement, new options are being developed within existing supplementary and supportive services to meet these goals. The following examination of two selected supplementary services is designed to illustrate the ways in which agencies can move from traditional modes of service delivery to more innovative service approaches for families at risk. It is important to note that these modifications are not taking shape in any systematic fashion. In fact, as the child welfare system responds to pressure to avoid placement, each agency shapes its responses in a manner that reflects its particular needs, funding pattern, and service philosophy. It is hoped that this exposition of efforts at service innovation and modification will suggest ways that other agencies within the child welfare field can develop programs that are more responsive to the needs of their target population.

Family Day Care as a Case Service

Day care means many things to many people. In the broadest sense, it refers to all arrangements for the daytime care of children, either inside or outside their own homes, when parents are unable to fulfill, or choose to delegate, one portion of their child care function.[17] Such an inclusive definition encompasses all of the various types of in-home and out-of-home care, whether voluntarily, privately, or publicly financed: the full-time "nanny" who cares for children of wealthy families; neighborhood child care cooperatives; teenage baby-sitters hired to watch children on a regular basis during after-school hours when their parents are employed; full- or part-time nursery schools and day-care centers; after-school programs; relatives or friends providing in-home care for a small fee or exchange of favors; and family day-care homes in which one or more children are placed in the home of a person hired to provide care on a regular basis.

Day-care arrangements of some type are used by a very large number of families with young children. Many are forced to arrange relatively complicated child-care "packages" to insure adequate coverage for their children at all times.[18] And as the proportion of working mothers increases, the demand for high-quality, comprehensive child care provisions expands proportionally. The purpose, functions, organization, and funding of such services continues to be a matter of widespread public debate.

From the perspective of child welfare services for families at risk, however, day-care service has a very special meaning. It is a supplementary service designed not only to help with the daily care and supervision of children, but also to insure that their developmental, educational, and health needs are met. In this sense, day care is part of an individualized case plan developed to enhance total family functioning in homes where children are at risk. For example, it may be used to keep a household intact when the primary caretaker is partially incapacitated, to give a mother who is temporarily overwhelmed respite from the responsibility of full-time child care while preserving her primary role in the family, to enhance the quality of care emotionally disturbed or retarded parents are able to provide their children, or as a means of easing parents who have been separated from their children back into their caretaking roles and teaching them more effective parenting skills.

This concept of day care as a case service is not totally consonant with the oft-cited goal of providing day care as a social utility—a basic social provision available at parental option for all children under the age of six and financed so that there is no stigma, fiscal benefit, or loss inherent in its use. Because of the lack of distinction between these two functions and the current demand for public day-care services, families at risk are often forced to compete for available slots with families who need help

with child care but do not require any other specialized servi
reason, Kamerman and Kahn note:

> It may be useful to distinguish a basic coverage child care program to meet average, ordinary circumstances, available at parental option and community capacity to supply . . . from child care as a case service, meeting special family problems or the needs of handicapped or extremely deprived groups.[19]

This suggests that the objectives, standards, eligibility criteria, and financing for day care viewed as a residual service for children in families at risk can and should be different from those implemented on an institutional basis for children in families simply seeking help with basic child care arrangements.

As Rothman has noted, the policy of expanding public day-care provisions did not derive from any special concern about the needs of families with children. The primary objective was to alleviate present and future welfare costs by encouraging and/or forcing mothers to work.[20] Although this cost-saving premise is now being questioned from several different perspectives, day care as a case service is increasingly being viewed as a cost-efficient alternative to foster care placement. As a residual child welfare service designed to address specific family handicaps or limitations, day care escapes much of the current societal debate regarding the merits of day care as a social utility. This provides an opportunity for child welfare agencies to design some innovative programs in this area. But those planning such services must be careful to specify their objectives, boundaries, and limitations clearly to insure that guidelines appropriate for day care as a case service are not arbitrarily applied to all public child care programs and that day care is not viewed as another panacea—a single, inexpensive solution to the problems of families at risk.

When day care is provided as a case service in conjunction with other supportive and supplementary services, it is essential that service delivery arrangements be flexible, comprehensive, and individualized. Only in this way can it be ensured that the individual case needs of the family are met and that the services provided are relevant to the family's situation. Furthermore, if these services are to be used to enhance family functioning, they must go beyond their traditional custodial and/or educational functions. They must be oriented toward enhancing child development and parental functioning. In this context family day care would seem to have special potential as a case service.

...is a specialized form of day-care service designed for ...g as two months and as old as twelve years of age. The ...ted toward families whose circumstances are such that ...parents are unable to provide the children with care and ...or a substantial part of the day. Like other types of day-care ...s program permits the parents to work, to obtain job training, ...day treatment or drug rehabilitation services, or to receive emotional relief from the pressures of full-time parenting responsibility, while the children are receiving adequate parental care and supervision in another family setting. But its primary goal as a child welfare service is usually to prevent or shorten foster care placement.

There are two key elements of family day care as a family-focused case service. First, it is a program designed to further children's physical, emotional, intellectual, and social development. Second, it is a supportive family social service program providing counseling, training, and advocacy services for the biological parent(s).

Family day-care programs place children needing service in a licensed "provider home." Ideally, the provider home is located in the same community as the family needing the service. Under social service supervision, the "provider" mother develops and maintains a strong relationship with the biological mother, a key ingredient in the social service plan. In addition to helping to relieve the social isolation that the mother of a child at risk often experiences, the provider mother can serve as a role model for the biological mother, teach her more effective parenting skills, and suggest linkages to other community resources.

When it works well, a family day-care program presents many positive service options not available in more traditional child care arrangements. For example, the provider home is a resource that can be selected and tailored specifically to the needs of the biological family. The service can be full or part time, the hours can be flexible, and the primary caretaker can be asked to give special attention to each child's particular developmental needs. Location of the provider home in the same community offers an opportunity for the development of other informal natural support systems for the biological family. And overhead expenses are low because the provider home can be maintained on a minimal reserve fee when not in use.

The following case presents a rather typical illustration of the use of family day care to prevent placement:

In addition to providing emotional relief from full-time care of the children, the service plan for Mrs. Y. included the following components:

Mrs. Y. first came into contact with the child welfare agency shortly after the birth of her second child, John. An unhappy relationship with her husband after eight years of marriage ended in his abandonment. Feeling alone and overwhelmed, Mrs. Y. suffered an emotional breakdown. She was unable to cope with the children, became abusive, and was hospitalized. Her children were placed in temporary foster care.

Two months later, Mrs. Y. recovered and her children were returned to her. She requested public assistance for the first time in her life as efforts through the court to secure child support payments from her husband failed. An immigrant to the United States, Mrs. Y. had no family, felt socially isolated, began to feel pressure again and found herself abusing the children. The pressure she felt was intensified by a developmental lag in her eight-month old son whom she feared was retarded. Mrs. Y. returned to the child welfare agency again, asking for help instead of placement. Foster family day-care services were provided.

—Counseling regarding child-rearing practices

—Counseling regarding issues of self-esteem, confidence, and assertiveness

—Vocational counseling to assist Mrs. Y. to explore employment options

—Referral and follow-up to a developmental disabilities clinic for her eight-month-old son

The provider mother, who lived in the same neighborhood as Mrs. Y., also served as a social support for her by sharing common experiences and introducing her to other young parents from her native country. Placement was avoided, although the environmental stresses and pathology that Mrs. Y. experienced certainly would have traditionally been viewed as indicators of the need for foster care placement.

Homemaker Services

The breakdown in the functioning of the person filling the maternal role in a family has long been recognized as a major factor in the placement of children in foster care. And the utilization of homemakers as a supplemental service to keep the family functioning through the absence or incapacity of the maternal parent has a long history in child welfare.[21] Homemakers have traditionally been viewed as temporary aids or housekeepers whose presence was necessary to maintain the household, usually as the result of illness of the mother.

However, from a family-oriented child welfare perspective, home-makers are not merely "housekeepers." The homemaker role extends far beyond the mechanics of keeping the house clean and feeding the children. It necessarily includes involvement in the interpersonal and social problems that effect the family. As the Child Welfare League of America notes:

> Families may need specific practical suggestions or authoritative information about child care, housekeeping, marketing, nutrition, budgeting, making use of community resources, job training, filling out application forms, etc.
>
> In some situations, parents may need to be taught life-styles and skills that are effective in the particular environment in which they live, and useful in coping with demands of urbanization, technological change, etc.
>
> The services of a homemaker may be used to teach basic homemaking and child-rearing skills.
>
> Staff with little or no professional training, under the supervision of a social worker, can make home visits and give guidance to parents that will help the parents become more capable of carrying their responsibilities.[22]

Child welfare programs utilizing homemakers are usually designed to prevent emergency foster care for children. They have often been used to provide either part-time respite care service for a parent at home or full-time twenty-four hour service as a temporary substitute for an absent parent. Some projects have expanded the homemaker role, asking homemakers to serve as members of a professional treatment team and to evaluate the functioning of the parent(s) in cases of suspected abuse and/or neglect, while providing temporary supportive services.[23]

There have been many reports of the value of homemaker service, and advocates for this service have often urged its expansion as a means of preventing foster care placement.[24] In evaluating the use of homemaker services, Kadushin writes:

> Homemaker service has a number of advantages over alternative plans for dealing with the problems presented by motherless families. The most important single advantage is that it permits the child to remain at home during the time the mother is incapable of fully implementing her role. Homemaker service imposes a far smaller burden of adjustment on the child than foster care, for the child adjusts to the homemaker in the comforting familiarity of his own home, his own family, his own neighborhood

Studies of the prevention of placement of children identified as being at high risk for foster care show that homemaker service is associated with increasing the child's chances of remaining in his own home . . .

Homemaker services also contribute to the efficiency and effectiveness of available medical services. Mothers are more likely to accept the necessity for hospitalization if they have assurances regarding the care of their children . . .

. . . a number of unpublished reports . . . indicate the successful use of homemakers in maintaining the family unit in cases where the mother was mentally ill but did not require hospitalization.[25]

The current effort to develop alternatives to foster care placement is likely to create added pressure for the expansion of homemaker service. However, there are a number of problems associated with this service that limit its potential usefulness for families at risk of separation.

Recruiting and training of staff is a major issue. Many homemakers deplore the working conditions that have them in what may be characterized as "unsafe neighborhoods" or working with families whose problems extend far beyond just the temporary incapacity of the parent. Homemakers are often reluctant to work in the stark environmental deprivation that characterizes the lives of a large portion of the client population served by child welfare agencies. And biological parents are quick to resent what they perceive as the invasion of their homes or the unnecessary usurpation of their parenting roles by an outsider.

Homemaker services as currently organized seem to be most useful in instances where the absence of the primary child-caring figure is temporary and limited assistance is needed to fill this parental role. For homemaker service to fulfill its potential as a case service, the nature of the family dysfunction must be clearly understood by all, the role of the homemaker must be clearly defined, and the responsibilities of the various provider agencies must be clearly allocated.

The full potential of homemaker service as a service to children and families at risk has yet to be realized. Difficulty can be anticipated if and when this service is expanded to prevent foster care placement for children in families whose interpersonal and environmental problems are so intense that they justify consideration of substitute care. Expansion of the service for this purpose must be based on a clear understanding that the role of the homemaker extends far beyond the mechanics of housekeeping to involvement in the interpersonal and environmental problems that affect the functioning of the family at various stages of intervention.

Sharp distinction must be made between "housekeeping" as a limited, temporary service and "homemaker" as a professional child welfare service. Homemakers must be helped to understand the importance of providing service within the family's normal home environment no matter how deprived it may be, and they should be given training and assistance in learning how to function more effectively in what may be, in fact, unsafe and debilitating working conditions.

Such imperatives raise questions regarding the costs, feasibility, and sponsorship of expanded homemaker service for families at risk. Issues such as public perception of the homemaker role, relatively low salary and job status, and poor working conditions must be confronted, as must the need to recruit and train more qualified personnel. Adequate funding for what is frequently, if erroneously, perceived as "free maid service" for welfare families is likely to be an ongoing problem. And turf battles can be expected if child welfare agencies attempt to administer directly a program that, for the most part, has been viewed as the province of other service sectors. Certainly the child welfare field should attempt to maximize the service potential inherent in homemaking service, but major expansion of this supplementary service will be difficult given these considerations and the present social climate. Consider, for example, the Dawson case:

The local child welfare agency was called by school officials because seven-year-old Angela often appeared with soiled clothes, was unwashed, and from all appearances seemed physically frail. An inspection of the household found two other teenage daughters and Mrs. Dawson — a single parent. Mrs. Dawson was not ambulatory as a result of a recent double amputation. She was under treatment by a visiting nurse for a diabetic condition and was emotionally depressed. The two teenage girls cared for the mother but were also experiencing depression regarding their mother's recent surgery and reacted by running from any structure Mrs. Dawson tried to impose in the home. They stayed out late and assumed no responsibility for the household. The visiting nurse indicated that her agency had requested a homemaker from the local public welfare agency. A vendor agency provided a homemaker who showed up, surveyed the apartment and Mrs. Dawson's physical handicap and stated that the apartment was too run down and the neighborhood too unsafe for her to return. The vendor agency which had contracted to provide the service indicated that no one else in their agency was willing to fill a homemaker role for this family.

The child welfare agency eventually was able to assign a caseworker to work intensively on a daily basis with the Dawson family. The caseworker focused much attention on the teenage girls, helped them work through their feelings and encouraged them to assume household responsibilities. Placement of the children was averted.

This case is instructive because the caseworker, at times, had to over-step her role and become a part-time homemaker who assisted with preparing meals and giving physical as well as emotional support to help maintain the family. Certainly it would have been preferable to assign a homemaker to work closely with the social worker in this case, as such a plan would have minimized unnecessary expenditure of professional staff time on basic social care tasks and maximized the contribution of a person especially skilled in household management. However, dysfunc-tional boundaries and resource limitations in the service network of the visiting nurse association, public assistance office, contracted home-maker service program, and child welfare agency worked against such a solution. Problems like these must be addressed if homemaker service is to fulfill its potential as a viable service for families at the brink of child placement.

EMERGENCY PLACEMENT WITH A FAMILY FOCUS

The obvious need for intervention by a legally sanctioned authority to remove a child from a dangerous or potentially harmful situation is easi-ly understood in the most severe cases of child abuse. Public emotion runs high and expressions of outrage are commonplace when society is confronted with incidents of sexually and physically abused children and children deprived of minimal medical, nutritional, and shelter care. It is generally in connection with these circumstances that the need for placement services is best understood. Intervention to protect a child from an environment that violates basic societal standards has been sup-ported consistently in this country since the establishment of the early Societies for Prevention of Cruelty to Children in the late nineteenth century. But recent close examination of these efforts has revealed that the task of building a new environment for children away from their families is far more costly and often less desirable than restoring or rehabilitating the previous environment. This recognition has led to ma-jor debates regarding the functions and scope of services to children in their own homes.

The size of the child population that needs to be removed from their homes in order to be protected from harm cannot currently be esti-mated. Definitions of both abuse and neglect are vague, and state laws vary in their definitions of these phenomena, although all laws seem to have the following elements:

1. The behavior violates a norm or standard of parental behavior —for instance the parents' obligation to the child. This in-

cludes the right to have his basic needs met, not violated. The substance of such needs is defined by cultural norms.

2. The infliction is deliberate—that is a nonaccidental—injury.
3. The abuse or neglect is severe enough to warrant intervention of some type, whether that intervention be medical, social, legal, or a combination.[26]

In addition, some laws define abuse as overt acts of commission and neglect as acts of omission.

The inability to estimate the number of children needing protection outside their own homes is further complicated by two factors: standards for intervention into family life in cases of abuse and neglect have not been uniformly adopted; and standards of evidence needed to demonstrate that a child cannot be protected in his or her own home have not been agreed upon. Because of this lack of consensus, some define responsibility in the area of child abuse and neglect broadly and advocate intervention in cases in which there is the suggestion of or the potential for child abuse. Consequently a broad target population for child welfare agencies is established, and interventive efforts are legitimately directed at all forms of child abuse and neglect.[27] Such a service philosophy runs the risk of unnecessary state intervention into family life and the possibility of removing children from their homes when they could have been protected by less intrusive means. Other groups, concerned about this excess state intervention in family life, attempt to narrow the concepts of abuse and neglect and require strict standards for intervention and the removal of children.[28] This definition narrows the target population for service but runs the risk that children who cannot be protected in their own homes will remain there and be harmed.

The practical problem faced by social workers in traditional service programs is that the alleged perpetrator of the abuse or neglect is usually the parent, and since the very concept of protection implies quick, decisive action, workers are expected to intervene immediately to prevent initial or additional harm. Often, the speediest, most obvious, and safest solution is to remove the child from the home. Consequently, services are usually delivered on a case-by-case *triage* model of treatment. Workers are mandated to protect or "rescue" the child first, then to worry about making differential assessments and ameliorating problem conditions.

Given this *triage* model of service provision, interventive efforts in this field have seldom extended much beyond the protection of the child, if it is substantiated that abuse or neglect has taken place. The very real, emergency needs of children command most of the limited program resources, leaving workers little time to become involved in the pathogenic familial and social environments that contribute to the etiology of child abuse and neglect. However, the shifting program emphasis in the child welfare field created by the desire to reduce or eliminate the use of substitute care as a service option for most children has broadened the boundaries of many traditional placement programs and forced innovations in patterns of service delivery.

Emergency Boarding Home Network

The shift from simply protecting the child from harm to protecting the child while maintaining the biological family as a resource for the child can be illustrated by considering the dilemma confronted by New York City when the decision was made to close its institutional shelters for children. The practice of placing young, dependent, neglected and abused children in temporary shelters after they had been "rescued" and "protected" from their harmful environments was attacked as "warehousing" children in environments that did not meet their needs. While the shelter operations represented the only resource for children in need of emergency protection, they did not in any way work to rehabilitate families or meet the long-term service needs of the children. Placement in one of these facilities often served as the first step into long-term foster care.

The service needs of children in the city called for twenty-four hour availability of emergency placements. The responsible city agency was satisfied that daytime emergencies could be handled by the existing system of emergency foster care facilities. What was needed was an after-hours placement mechanism.

In collaboration with five voluntary agencies, the umbrella public child welfare agency was able to shape a creative approach to emergency shelter and protective care for children while maintaining ties to biological parents. The program, known as the Emergency Foster Boarding Home Network, was hailed as a "refreshing demonstration that 'temporary' care can in fact be temporary if the responsible agencies are determined to keep it so."[29] The program incorporates features of emergency placement in the child's neighborhood, crisis intervention, and short-term family treatment. Furthermore, the program incorporates a fiscal disincentive for agencies to keep children in substitute foster care for more than sixty days.

Each of the five voluntary agencies covers a specific geographic region. Within each respective region, the agency licenses and supervises foster parents who are trained for the program. The foster parents make available a total of one hundred "emergency beds" for children under twelve years of age and are available for children who require immediate shelter care after the usual 9:00 A.M. to 5:00 P.M. working hours. All homes are available on an *open intake basis,* and a system was established to assure that foster parents are on call and available for any child placement emergency. It also insures that sibling groups can be placed together.

Upon placement, the agency initiates a short-term family treatment program with the goal of either returning the children to their own home or *appropriately* placing children in a needed longer-term substitute care program. Services are designed and implemented to prevent long-term placement for children; early return home is the primary service objective. Careful diagnostic work and appropriate treatment planning help to prevent the further deterioration of the family, which often occurs when children are hastily but inappropriately placed. Thus, several important concepts come together in this one program:

—Children are entitled to emergency protective care when they cannot be sustained in their own homes.

—Children are entitled to efforts geared toward limiting the period of time in foster care.

—The biological family is part of the client system needing services and, until demonstrated otherwise, must be considered the major resource for children.

—Agencies involved have an obligation to assure delivery of services beyond placement.

The case on page 231 provides a good illustration of the way these concepts were implemented in one emergency placement situation and demonstrates the flexibility of the program in terms of meeting both the child's and family's needs.

The significance of this illustration is that a case of this type could just as easily have developed into a situation where the mother and child remained in foster care for well over two years until the mother completed high school; or worse, mother and child could have been separated at the time of the initial placement and the infant might have drifted into long-term foster care. However, the goals of this emergency program dictated a different direction and encouraged the worker to discover more family-focused service options.

Although this program has its problems and limitations, it has been relatively effective in caring and planning appropriately, within specified time limits, for most of the children referred for emergency services. This was accomplished only after careful planning and networking by the agencies involved. The elements that contributed to the successful implementation of this program can be summarized briefly:

1. The program planners recognized the need for extensive preliminary planning to minimize the interagency conflicts that inevitably arise when the interventive efforts of a number of service providers must be coordinated. Consequently, the participating agencies were helped to develop specific guidelines regarding allocation of authority and responsibility. These included assurances that:

   —Only the public agency could authorize emergency placement with a voluntary agency

   —The voluntary agency supervising the emergency foster home would assume full planning responsibility immediately after placement

   —The public agency would assume responsibility for coordination with other municipal agencies that might be involved in an emergency placement such as police, hospitals, and the judicial system

   —The voluntary agency would maintain responsibility for the quality of care received by children in the emergency foster homes

2. The concept of a "reserve fee" for foster parents was introduced, institutionalizing the practice of paying a fee as an inducement for maintaining a bed for a child outside an institutional setting even if the bed was not in use.

3. The program reimburses agencies and foster parents at a higher rate than usual for the initial care and reduces payments after sixty days, as a disincentive to keeping children in unplanned care for a prolonged period of time. Thus, through the rate structure, the funding source rewards emergency care and discourages long-term care in the same setting.

4. The role of the emergency foster parents was essentially reconceptualized from substitute parent to specialized child care

One-year-old Jessica was placed by a public protective worker in an emergency foster boarding home after being found with her allegedly intoxicated grandmother in a subway station at 8:00 P.M. The grandmother, Mrs. Y., was arrested for possession of a hypodermic needle. Attempts were made by the Transit Police to locate the infant's mother, Susan, but she was not at home. The infant, her seventeen-year-old mother and thirty-six-year-old grandmother all live at the same address and are supported by the grandmother's public assistance budget. A neglect petition was drawn against the grandmother, who was the primary caretaker for her daughter and grandchild.

The following morning the voluntary agency's social worker located the infant's mother at her address. The apartment appeared to be sparsely but adequately furnished. The seventeen-year-old mother wanted to be with her child. The infant could not be released, at least until the initial investigation of the case was completed and the court approved the decision. However, arrangements were made to place the mother in the same emergency foster boarding home as her child, pending the outcome of the study.

Casework service was begun with the grandmother. It was determined that she had enrolled in a methadone maintenance clinic just three days prior to her arrest. She described herself as a very private person, but she was able to establish a working relationship with the agency caseworker. As the case developed, a different approach in planning emerged between the Protective Service's worker and the agency caseworker. The Protective Service's worker felt it would be in the best interests of these children (mother and daughter) to remain in care until the mother finished school and then could establish her own apartment. The agency worker suggested discharge from foster care for mother and daughter with supplemental support for the family via the provision of family day-care services.

The agency caseworker, while acknowledging the grandmother's dependence on methadone, saw strengths in this woman who visited her family regularly, had stabilized herself in her methadone program, and obviously had her daughter's and granddaughter's interests at heart.

Placement in emergency foster care lasted just over sixty days. During placement Susan continued in her school program, attending regularly. Her adjustment to the foster home was good. She responded well to the foster family whom she clearly saw as a support through an emergency situation.

Because of long waiting lists, it was learned that family day-care service would be unavailable for at least six months. No one recommended discharge without a supportive community child care program for the infant. The grandmother, however, located a neighbor who was willing to care for the child while Susan attended school. Mrs. Y. agreed to make a private payment arrangement with the neighbor. The neighbor's home was evaluated by all parties concerned, and it was agreed that it would be in the best interests of the family to use this resource as part of the discharge plan.

The family court accepted this plan and Susan and her daughter were returned home after sixty-three days in care.

worker. The foster parents were given special training to increase their understanding of issues related to child abuse and neglect and to enhance their capacity to help children cope with the trauma of abrupt separation. They were sensitized to the fact that they would provide the child's initial contact with an agency representative, thereby setting the stage for future work, and they were asked to provide reports on the child's behavior and responses that could be incorporated in the full diagnostic assessment of each case situation.

The development of the Emergency Foster Boarding Home Network has been described at some length because it serves to illustrate the way in which established patterns of care in a large, fairly rigid service system can be modified to insure that preservation of the family unit becomes the primary objective of intervention whenever appropriate. It demonstrates that children can be "protected" from both long-term drift in the foster care system and from parental abuse and/or neglect if services are defined broadly enough to encompass the provision of supportive and supplementary services as well as basic substitute care.

Community-Based Emergency Shelters

Another model of emergency care that combines a "protective" and rehabilitative function is the community-based emergency shelter. These shelters have evolved in various ways in response to the needs of different target populations. Some offer a full range of services including individual and family crisis intervention counseling, parenting classes, child care and recreation programs, medical care, and educational programs. Some serve only children or adolescents; others care for all family members. Their common characteristics are that they offer an easily accessible, immediate "crash pad" for members of families in crisis; they are time-limited; they are oriented toward reuniting family members; and they are community-based, insuring some social and cultural continuity during the period that children may be separated from their parents.

In Brooklyn, New York, St. Joseph Children's Services operates the Williamsburg Neighborhood Residence, which is a prototype of this model. It integrates services to children and services to the family while intervening actively in their social environment. Rather than offering many specialized services directly, the staff of the residence ensure that families obtain service by providing appropriate referral, advocacy, and follow-up with other community agencies. Effort is also made to connect family members with natural helping resources within the neighborhood. The basic concepts underlying the design of the neighborhood residence are:

—Early identification of family strengths, problems, and resources

—Immediacy of care, enabling family members to enter the shelter as quickly as necessary to relieve the pressure at home

—Instant (same-day) involvement of the family in working toward the primary goal of services—preservation of the family unit

—Geographic proximity, permitting children to stay in their own schools and to maintain frequent contact with other relatives and friends

—Parent participation in child care, encouraged through frequent visiting, full- or part-time residence in the shelter, and assumption of responsibility for specific child care tasks.

Although the Williamsburg Neighborhood Residence has a specific "protective" function, as the case on page 235 illustrates, the development of programs such as this can move child welfare agencies closer to the families they are intended to serve:

This case, like the emergency foster boarding home network case, illustrates that programs can provide much more than substitute care. By addressing the needs of the entire family unit, providing supportive casework services, and obtaining supplemental services through referral, case management, and advocacy activities, agencies can help to preserve the family unit for the child.

Temporary placement services have traditionally been a major gateway into foster care. Consequently, it is critical that case planning begin immediately. If the protection of the child, not the preservation of the family, is viewed as the worker's only function, part of the essential planning is likely to be ignored. But if the worker maintains a clear focus on the total family as the unit of attention, efforts will be directed toward enabling parents to participate as fully as possible in planning for their children.

The social worker's primary tasks when a child is referred for "protection" are: (1) to make suitable arrangements for the emergency care of the child if necessary, (2) to engage the parents actively in the planning process, (3) to make an accurate assessment of the child's and family's needs, resources, and limitations, (4) to identify and delineate for the family the range of options available, and (5) to enable them to participate in selecting and implementing an appropriate service plan. Because the events surrounding the opening of an abuse or neglect case tend to

Late in the evening the police requested placement for three brothers, Tom, Luis, and Joseph, ages eight, seven, and six respectively. All three children were found living in a one-bedroom apartment in a run-down apartment building without heat and electricity and with little food or furniture. Their mother Mrs. R., had walked into the police department feeling overwhelmed and frustrated, and threatening to kill the children. The boys were placed in a neighborhood shelter.

Mrs. R., a twenty-nine-year-old woman, had a history of drug addiction and for the past three years was involved in a methadone maintenance program. She was receiving public assistance. At age eighteen she became involved with Mr. R., the father of all three children, who was also a drug addict. He died when Joseph was an infant. She had no extended family resources.

Although Mrs. R. had survived on her own before and had never considered placing the children, she said she was now overwhelmed with their behavior and was especially concerned about bad behavior reports she was getting from school about Tom. The neighborhood shelter's worker tried to prevent placement by offering to provide supportive assistance for Mrs. R. through day-care services, but Mrs. R. felt too overwhelmed to care for the children and wanted them placed.

Upon placement, the neighborhood shelter arranged a contract with Mrs. R. regarding the terms of placement. A regular visiting pattern was established, and Mrs. R. was expected to stay in the residence two days a week, participating fully in the child care activities of the shelter. The child care staff worked with Mr. R. on parenting skills and handling the boys. The social worker assisted in negotiating with the school about Tom's behavior problem. Subsequently, testing and evaluation resulted in a new class placement and a more positive school adjustment for Tom. Mrs. R. maintained her involvement with the methadone clinic and kept her apartment.

The children were discharged from care within three months, their school placements intact and their mother somewhat relieved and able to handle them more comfortably. Continued supplemental support was provided to the family through after-school day-care services.

increase the social distance and distrust between client and worker, and the potential involvement of the court may heighten anxiety, special knowledge and skills are necessary to carry out these tasks.

In addition to the skills of the worker, the environment in which services are delivered is critical for effective case planning and management. A program that is true to its mission of protecting children as well as rehabilitating and treating parents must organize its operations in such a way as to facilitate the engagement of the total family in the planning and service process as soon as possible. For example, by maintaining an ongoing visible presence in the community and "reaching out" actively to families at risk, agencies should be able to minimize the potential threat posed by intervention. If agencies project a family-centered image, workers are more likely to be able to reassure clients that the service objective is preservation of the family unit. Development of programs in community-based settings should also permit staff to develop closer linkages with agencies that can provide the specialized supportive and supplementary services needed for their clients and to identify natural helping resources within the immediate social environment. By broadening the unit of attention, sharing responsibility, and expanding supportive and supplementary service options, child welfare agencies can begin to reconcile their functions of preserving the family unit while protecting the child.

NEED FOR EXPANDED REPERTOIRE OF PREVENTIVE/PROTECTIVE SERVICE EFFORTS

The prevailing minimalist perspective demands that child welfare agencies somehow endeavor to preserve family units and protect children's interests by intervening in as inexpensive, time-limited, simple, and unobtrusive a manner as possible. While such intervention may serve the immediate function of minimizing the possibility of children entering or remaining in long-term foster care (a desirable objective that lends itself easily to measures of cost effectiveness), the attainment of this limited objective is unlikely to make any real contribution to the broader service goal of enhancing the quality of life for children in families at risk. Furthermore, it could have the dysfunctional effect of obscuring subtle situations in which children who are at risk and need continued service intervention are not identified in the community.

Despite these limitations, the current emphasis on "preventive" child welfare services creates an opportunity for agencies to expand their provision of supportive and supplementary services and for practitioners to work in differential, varied, and innovative ways with families at risk. But in order to be successful in these efforts, it is essential that service providers develop as much clarity as possible about what can and cannot be accomplished by various types of specific interventive activities. It is also important that the child welfare field not fall into the trap of promising more than it can deliver given its current knowledge base, limited resources, and ambiguous service mandate. In this final section we shall summarize what is currently known about the state of the art of service provision for families at risk and examine its potential implication for the design and delivery of preventive services.

Jones, Magura, and Shyne made a major contribution to the planning base for these services by analyzing and compiling results of research that has been conducted during the past decade on the effectiveness of various service programs for families at risk.[30] Because of the difficulties inherent in measuring the elusive concept of effectiveness and specifying the critical components of comprehensive service programs, as well as the limitations of the research designs employed in many of the studies, their conclusions are necessarily tentative. Taken together, however, these findings raise questions about the degree to which the expectations underlying recent legislative and administrative initiatives related to the delivery of child welfare services can be achieved. These expectations derive from the following, generally unchallenged, assumptions:

—Given the high costs of foster care, the provision of good preventive services will greatly reduce traditional child welfare service costs.[31]

—The de-professionalization of child welfare staff will not affect the quality of services provided.

—Planned short-term service is as effective as long-term service for all families at risk.

—Careful contracting and case management alone will do much to improve the quality of child welfare services.

—Provision of specific "hard" services such as day care and homemakers will do more to preserve families than continuation of counseling services.

—The risks of permitting many allegedly abused and neglected children to remain in their own homes are minimal compared to the long-term risks of placing them in foster care.[32]

—The population of children in need of foster care can be greatly reduced by improvements in the administration and delivery of child welfare services.

—There is an identifiable population of children at risk of placement toward whom services should be targeted.

The review of research findings conducted by these authors regarding the length or duration of service and the content or methods of service provision challenge some of these assumptions and have special relevance for administrators designing new preventive service programs for families at risk and for child welfare workers attempting to identify the interventive roles they should assume in this new service arena. To summarize briefly, in regard to the issue of the desirable length or duration of service, they comment:

> Although there is little evidence of great progress with families known briefly to child welfare agencies, there is also little evidence that all families require service that extends for years. There may be a tendency to think of all child welfare cases as requiring prolonged service, since some certainly do, and the most difficult and intractable cases capture the greatest attention.
>
> It appears that the time required to achieve reasonable goals depends on the number and severity of client problems, the degree of client motivation, and the content and structuring of the service. Some families may never be able to cope with their child care responsibilities without agency support. It is clear, however, that considerable gains can be made within a few months with many families. Accomplishment of even modest objectives give both worker and client encouragement that more can be accomplished, and that is an important dynamic for change.[33]

The issue of the most effective content or methods of service provision is even more complicated. However, the research reviewers were able to identify what they considered five promising directions.

> **I.** The finding that a comprehensive program of services is more effective for families than is any single service emerges repeatedly in studies of protective services or work with multiproblem families. Although no single service can be isolated as making a crucial difference, the number of services and perhaps their complementarity are often significant factors. . . .
>
> With comprehensiveness believed to be a major factor in providing effective services, the issue becomes how to promote the delivery of comprehensive services. Studies suggest that the following factors are important:
>
> **a.** An appropriate array of services must be available—not counseling alone or concrete services alone, but a combination.
> **b.** Outreach efforts are essential; merely having the services available is not enough. . . .
> **c.** It is important to direct services to several family members . . .
>
> **II.** Service programs designed to overcome a sense of isolation and provide a supportive "extended family" are useful with overburdened, undersupported families.
>
> Several devices have been developed to facilitate the extended family concept. The establishment of a *family center* has been undertaken by several projects to provide a place where clients can meet staff members and other clients, and have a sense of a "second home" . . . The team approach is another device that has been employed. The family gets to know well more than one staff member and can call on another worker if one is away. . . .

The use of groups is another way of overcoming a sense of isolation. It appears to work if a lot of effort is put into getting the members to attend and if group leaders are skillful.

Self-help groups, such as Parents Anonymous, have been considered useful in protective services.

Lay services—that is, having volunteers, family assistants, aides, or surrogate parents spend time with the family or with individual members—were also reported helpful in protective services.

III. The worker-client relationship continues to be cited as important to effective service. A good relationship helps engage and motivate the client. It usually accompanies a high degree of agreement between worker and client on what the problems are and how to solve them, and it is related to the provision of a more comprehensive and intensive program of services.

IV. Studies suggest that it is important to have highly trained workers handling the intake, diagnostic, and service planning phases of a case. After that point, it may be that less trained or experienced staff or lay assistants can be introduced for ongoing or more intensive work.

V. A major part of work with protective service families should consist of teaching parenting skills and engaging parents in understanding the developmental tasks and enhancing the developmental achievements of their children. . . .

Deficiencies in parenting are often the primary reason the parents have been referred for service . . . Child welfare workers must be well versed in this content; it should be their stock in trade.[34]

Given this review of research on what is currently known about effective practice with families at risk, it seems possible to identify at least three different service strategies that might be implemented in child welfare settings depending on the degree and nature of the client need; the availability of family, community, and agency resources; and defined service objectives. These include: (1) crisis intervention; (2) long-term provision of continuous social supports and care for families unable to function independently; and (3) selective use of a range of coordinated supportive and supplementary services and natural helping networks.

This is not to suggest that these service strategies are mutually exclusive or that service programs should be organized on a categorical basis. Flexible, individualized use of a mix and range of services is essential for families at risk who almost by definition experience a multitude of complex, varied, often intractable problems in living. Skillful intervention at one level of service might well enable a family to function effectively on a more independent basis, and conversely a family's inability to make adequate progress while receiving limited services may provide a clear diagnostic indicator of the need to develop an alternative, more intensive service strategy. What is being proposed is that the child welfare field attempt to identify clusters of potential at-risk client populations and experiment with the development of interventive approaches designed specifically to meet different types of "preventive" service needs. This would demand increased agency innovation and risk; more worker imagination, flexibility, and skill; and greater community tolerance and support than is now available. However, these changes are essential if the field is to attain its alleged objective of improving the quality of life for children in families at risk and "preventive" programs are to represent anything more than minimal efforts to limit the harms that may be inflicted on families by a dysfunctional service system.

To illustrate, we shall describe briefly how each of these service strategies might be utilized for the different groups of families that traditionally come to the attention of child welfare agencies.

Crisis Intervention

It has been shown that crisis events provide a significant opportunity for interventions that help people make positive adjustments in their life situations.[35] As child welfare practitioners examine and test new modes of service delivery aimed at the prevention of placement, increasing numbers are finding crisis intervention theory to be of value in developing critical working relationships with parents.

In discussing the potential value of crisis intervention approaches in child welfare work, it is important to distinguish between the concepts of stress and crisis. All people experience some stress in their daily lives, and the families known to child welfare agencies often experience continuous and severe stress. Rapoport notes that stress can be considered a "pressure," a "burden," or a "chore" that one either "survives" or "cracks under"; it is enduring and has a predominantly pathological potential. On the other hand a crisis is created by a specific event that overwhelms one's usual coping resources because it poses a threat to an individual's or family's equilibrium. It tends to be time-limited and can have growth potential. A crisis can serve as a catalyst that "disturbs old habits, evokes new responses and becomes a major factor in charting new developments."[36] Stress, therefore, is something that people endure and hopefully cope with competently, while crisis presents a situation in which there must be some resolution.

Utilization of crisis intervention techniques provides an opportunity for child welfare workers to prevent placement or reduce the length of time the child spends in care if removal from the home is necessary. Often the anxiety, vulnerability, and distress that parents experience makes them very open to receiving help during the "crisis of potential placement" or the "crisis of placement." The ability of the worker to be sensitive and supportive to the family at this time can be essential in engaging the family in a successful planning process. The involvement of parents as early as possible in work focused on the precipitating crisis event is critical in facilitating future treatment. When agency policies and procedures or workers' lack of understanding and skill in handling crisis situations lead to a prolonged, complex, unfocused intake study, parents are likely to become confused, distrustful, and defensive. They may even withdraw from the planning process.

Intervention at the point of crisis should be focused on helping the family reorganize and focus on the trauma of imminent or actual placement. Once the family has gained cognitive mastery of the situation and developed some confidence that the worker will help them to cope with the situation that lies ahead, they may be ready to identify their service needs and to begin contracting with the worker regarding goals, strategies, interventions, and reciprocal roles and responsibilities.[37]

When a complaint of neglect or abuse has been filed and a family is in crisis because of the potential or actual placement of their child, the worker should give priority to the following practice tasks:

—The worker should be available to help the family confront the situation immediately by providing information, support, and an opportunity to talk about their fears and concerns. Parents often do not know who their accuser is or understand the allegations that have been made against them. They need assurance in examining and coping with what is likely to be perceived as an unfair attack by a relative, neighbor, or professional adversary, for example, physician, teacher, public assistance worker.

—The worker should assist the family to perceive events correctly and to understand their potential implications. Here the task is to destroy the mythology surrounding the situation while clearly spelling out the real nature of the charges and events occurring outside their control. Clarity is essential at this point.

—The worker should then attempt to help the parents express and deal openly with their incapacitating feelings of doubt, guilt, self-blame, anger, and hopelessness. Realistic assurances and confidence in the family's capacity to cope with the situation should be demonstrated insofar as possible. Unhealthy defenses should not be encouraged; the family members must be helped to acknowledge that they are in trouble.

—The worker should help the parents deal with their feelings of grief and mourning stimulated by the potential or actual separation from their child. By providing information about the child and the treatment plan, the worker may be able to relieve some of the parents' anticipatory anxieties regarding the type of care the child might receive.

—Once the parents have gained some mastery of the situation, they can be helped to identify and begin to use the services available to them. The provision of concrete resources designed to help with the practical demands and necessities of everyday living may enable the parents to mobilize their own capacities more fully and to engage in purposeful long-term, problem-solving activities.

The use of crisis intervention as part of a service strategy for families at risk can prevent placement or minimize its length. But it is important to note that work focused around the "crisis of potential placement or placement" is limited. Crises do not last forever. Families adapt to new realities after the immediate crisis subsides. If needed supplemental and supportive services are not available to parents when they are receptive to receiving them, an opportunity is lost. If no clear service plan has been established once the crisis situation has run its course, both parents and child are likely to adapt to the new reality and more readily accept placement—thus initiating or prolonging the time spent in foster care.[38] Knowledge of this risk ought to increase the workers' efforts to intervene appropriately at the time of crisis.

The Welch family case on page 243 illustrates effective use of crisis intervention techniques to prevent long-term foster placement and to enhance parental functioning.

Long-Term Provision of Continuous Social Support and Care

Other families in which children are at risk may require more long-term continuous support services if children are to be sustained and given adequate developmental opportunities in their own homes.

Robert Morris has commented that there is:

. . . a flaw in the social arrangements in the United States, namely, the persistence and even the increase in the number and proportion of persons who need the social supports of continuous care to survive. This phenomenon has been obscured because social work, along with many other professions, has chosen to concentrate on treatment and therapeutic skills whose aim is to "cure" or remove handicapping and dysfunctional conditions. This remnant of the nineteenth-century confidence in science and technology has led the medical profession to believe that the alleviation of health problems can be achieved mainly by the conquest of infectious

An anonymous call to police led them to find five-year-old Vincent and three-year-old Sara alone in an apartment that seemingly had been ransacked. With no adults on the scene and no neighbors or relatives present, the children were placed on an emergency basis by the child protective agency.

Shortly after placement Mrs. Welch, very upset, called requesting the return of her children. Upon investigation it was learned that Mr. Welch, the father of both children, had been an alcoholic for about three years. He ceased supporting the family but would come and go as he pleased. He was given to rage and beat Mrs. Welch regularly. On the night the children were placed in emergency care, Mr. Welch had broken into the apartment, destroyed the furniture and stolen money and household goods. Mrs. Welch had left the children temporarily to visit a relative to obtain food and money.

Mrs. Welch stated she had not called the police because "he is the children's father and my husband and he would never hurt the children." Mrs. Welch then broke down and cried about how she had tried to keep the family together often subjecting herself to beatings and abuse at the hands of her husband to accomplish this. This was the first time the children were taken away from her and the first time the police had been called.

The crisis around the placement led Mrs. Welch to see how her dependence and attitude toward Mr. Welch were threatening the functioning of the family and the welfare of her children. Mrs. Welch was helped to identify her priorities and use her strong desire to care for her children to mobilize herself. She got legal protection from her husband and arranged day care for her children while she sought and gained part-time employment. The children were returned home within thirty days of placement. Mrs. Welch subsequently moved to another apartment, joined a single parents' support group, and requested counseling from a family service agency in order to "help her develop a more positive self-image and find ways to engage in less self-destructive relationships."

diseases, when in fact the opposite has occurred. . . . Social workers have followed the same line of reasoning, and social conditions have proved to be even less amenable to therapeutic correction.[39]

Although Morris was referring to the full range of physical, psychiatric, developmental, and social disabilities that affect "approximately 10 percent of the population for whom therapeutic means are ineffective and who must be maintained by continuous supplementary social supports,"[40] it is clear that his comment is equally applicable to a segment of the population traditionally served by child welfare agencies, that small group of families well known to experienced practitioners who "may never be able to cope with their child care responsibilities without agency support."[41]

Child welfare agencies have traditionally handled such situations by placing the children in foster care and perhaps seeking termination of parental rights and subsequent adoption. More often, because of the difficulties inherent in terminating parental rights when there is even a "flicker of interest," children of such parents have simply been allowed to grow up in foster care. (See Chapters 1 and 7 for further discussion of this issue.)

An alternative to foster care in such situations would be for agencies to make more concerted efforts to supply whatever supports are necessary to sustain these children in their own homes. This might demand the provision of an extensive combination of financial, child care, household management, counseling, educational, respite care, nursing, child development, recreational, and adult socialization resources to ensure that the children are protected and are receiving a minimal level of adequate care. All of this would be a costly venture, one that certainly is more aptly labeled "social care" than preventive service. However, it would insure that children grow up in a home where they know they are loved and belong, no matter how severe the limitations of their parents. Consider, for example, the case of the Britton family on page 245.

This case clearly illustrates the use of supplementary and supportive services as a long-term plan to prevent foster care placement. By monitoring and supplementing the boys' care, while attempting to enhance the mother's parenting capacities, the family is sustained in the community. It is clear that this family could not care adequately for the children at home without this intense support on a regular basis.

Child welfare and mental health experts could spend many hours debating the merits of this case plan. Despite extensive research efforts, simply not enough is known about the various forces shaping child development to predict with any certainty the outcome of a particular set of life circumstances and events for individual children. Some children are amazingly resilient and seem to survive horrendous family situations. Others may be severely damaged by what could appear to be relatively minor threats to their healthy development. There is now a relatively high degree of consensus regarding a child's need for a sense of belonging and permanence, but whether this sense of continuity is best provided by biological parents who care deeply about their children, no matter how severe their personal disabilities, or by substitute adoptive parents, is still an open question.

Leslie Britton is a seventeen-year-old, mildly retarded mother of three out-of-wedlock children, ages four, two, and three months, all with different fathers. A recent psychological evaluation registered Leslie's IQ at 60 with an estimated mental age of eight.

Leslie, who lives with her mother, gave birth to her first child at thirteen years of age. All the children and their mother are dependent on the grandmother and are being supported through her public assistance allowance. While housing conditions are overcrowded and finances are limited, they do permit the provision of minimal care for the children.

The grandmother is unable to care fully for the boys, but will not consider placement in foster care. Adoption has been suggested, but both mother and grandmother refuse to consider this an option. Family day-care services were offered as a supplemental service to assist the family in learning sound child-rearing practices while allowing the children to develop normally. Since current funding guidelines in the area where this family lives permit the provision of family day care until the youngest child is twelve, this means the agency can, and probably will, be involved with this family for almost twelve years or until the oldest child's sixteenth birthday.

The social worker responsible for the case succeeded in convincing Leslie, with support from her mother, that it would be helpful to obtain an IUD to prevent further pregnancies. He also made arrangements for Leslie to enter a training program where she is improving her life skills, with a view toward making her capable of independent living.

Day-care services are assuring that the nutrition, health, and socialization needs of the boys are being met. This eases tensions in the family that might result in the need for placement. However, long-term prognosis calls for continued supplemental services for many years as the children grow and develop.

Given these limitations in our knowledge base, decisions regarding the degree to which society will subsidize the provision of continuous social care and supports designed to preserve family unity are likely to be resolved in the political arena. Child welfare personnel must certainly retain responsibility for individual case assessment, planning, and service provision. But they can also help to clarify the issues inherent in the larger social debate by experimenting with various types of social support arrangements, discovering ways to involve other community members in the provision of care, and analyzing the fiscal, social, and personal costs inherent in different service strategies.

Comprehensive Array of Service Provisions

It is rather disquieting to portray this third proposed approach to service delivery as a specific interventive strategy, as the notion of a "comprehensive array" seems to be the key to effective service provision for all families at risk of separation or deterioration as well as for the wider range of families served by family and child welfare agencies. Yet the fact that so few traditional agencies are able to offer such an array of services forces us to describe this as a special approach to service provision for children at risk. The service directions suggested by the research review of Jones and her associates, cited earlier, offer the most obvious starting point for the design of effective preventive programs: availability of a range of services involving all family members and emphasizing outreach, advocacy, case management, and community resource utilization; use of the agency as an "extended family" support system in which various staff, other clients, and volunteers all help to share the family's burden and enhance their sense of belonging; employment of practitioners able to establish and maintain positive working relationships with families who are frequently overwhelmed, hopeless, and demanding; availability of staff who have thorough knowledge of children's developmental needs and tasks and are able to teach good parenting skills; and planned differential use of staff designed to maximize professional decision making and participation by other staff and informal helping resources in the provision of social supports.[42]

While space limitations prevent a full discussion of each of these individual components here, the program of the Center for Family Life in Brooklyn, New York, provides a clear illustration of the array of services and activities that might be offered in a comprehensive, community-based preventive service agency for families at risk. The program activities, which are family focused and emphasize the provision of opportunities for individual and community development, include the following:

—Accessibility on a seven-day-a-week, 8:00 A.M.–11:00 P.M. basis to all children and families in the target community

—Comprehensive case assessment and evaluation services including psychological and psychiatric evaluation as needed

—Crisis intervention counseling for families and youth

—Open-ended, long-term individual, family, and group counseling services

—Referral, brokerage, and advocacy efforts on behalf of families needing help from other medical, legal, vocational, psychiatric, and special service agencies

—Provision of regularly scheduled family life education programs, parent and youth discussion groups, and therapeutic activity groups for children

—Planned social activities such as weekly parents' nights, after-school drop-in programs for children and youth, teen nights, and special recreational programs such as dances, attendance at sports events, and cultural activities

—Summer day camp program for elementary school-age children

—Foster grandparents program to provide parenting assistance in homes where children are at risk

—Volunteer Big Brothers/Big Sisters program for children with special emotional and social needs

—Training of volunteers to staff agency advocacy clinics located in several community facilities. Needed assistance is provided to any community person requesting help with income maintenance, housing, and/or medical problems

—Active participation in a consortium of community agencies and churches that have developed an emergency food bank for families in need

—Development of a neighborhood thrift shop, which also serves as a site for an advocacy clinic, and the storage and distribution of emergency food supplies

—Development of special projects in two neighborhood public schools designed to enhance community-school relationships by the provision of family life education, tutoring, recreational, and cultural enrichment programs

—Active participation in a "Human Service Cabinet" convened by the local planning board and composed of representatives of all the major public and voluntary services in the community

—Establishment of a community advisory board composed of a cross section of neighborhood residents, clients, professionals, and community resource persons.[43]

No two comprehensive preventive service programs can or should look exactly alike. Specific service provisions must be shaped by community needs and resources. However, the components that seem to contribute to the effectiveness of this and other similar programs include the emphasis on flexible and varied interventive strategies; easy, quick, destigmatized points of access and outreach; provision of integrated, family-focused services; careful immediate attention to concrete service needs; extensive community involvement; clinical training and consultation for staff providing case services; and a service philosophy that reflects a strong belief in the potential for individual, family, and community development.

The following case illustrates what can be accomplished through the thoughtful provision of a range of services to a family in which a child is at serious risk of placement. The agency arranged placement as part of a continuum of care that is likely to serve a more significant long-term preventive function than would have been possible if its only objective had been prevention of out-of-home care.

Mrs. Hamton, now twenty-five years of age, the mother of a six-year-old boy, admitted that her tensions and frustrations made it extremely difficult for her to cope and that she had beaten her son until he was unconscious. Don himself is a child given to tantrums, fighting, throwing objects, hitting, and biting both children and adults. Because of her readiness to receive help, the worker tried at first, to set up a support system at the center. This was insufficient to maintain the child at home. The center was able to locate a foster home a few blocks away from the mother. Mrs. Hamton visits Don daily and uses the center herself frequently throughout the week. She is receiving educational and employment counseling and also attends parents' night regularly. Her own emotional needs are met through a variety of contacts, including individual casework and group activities. For example, a birthday party for her was arranged recently by the members of parents' night.

Don is now attending special day school found for him, where individualized help is provided. His behavior is improving steadily in his foster home, which is so near his mother and the center that separation and loss have been minimized.

Both need continued help to achieve the growth that will permit successful reunion, but it is expected that as Mrs. Hamton's sense of self-worth and competency is increased and her isolation is diminished, she will gradually be able to resume responsibility for the care of her son and handle him more effectively. The center will continue to provide supplementary and supportive services after the family is reunited.

As suggested earlier, the range of services offered in any comprehensive preventive service program should reflect the needs and resources of the target population as well as the expectations and potential contributions of the surrounding community. The specific array of services and supports offered to different families in need must be based on carefully individualized case assessments. However, the supportive service options identified in Figure 6.1 suggest the array of potential service provisions that should be considered by agencies attempting to design and deliver preventive services to families at risk.[44]

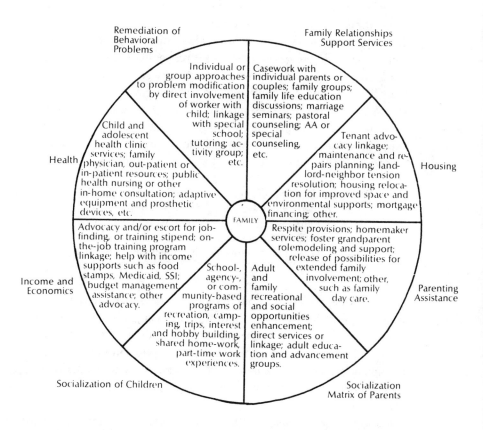

FIGURE 6.1. SUPPORT SERVICE OPTIONS FOR FAMILIES AT RISK.
Source: Sr. Mary Paul Janchill, *Guidelines for Decision-Making in Child Welfare.* NY: Human Services Workshops, 1981, p. 13.

A FINAL COMMENT

A major function of the child welfare service system is to provide services to families under stress that either support, supplement, or substitute for the caretaking functions of the parents. Much attention has been drawn recently to the failure of this system to perform adequately. Major criticism has been focused on the imbalance between substitute care services and services designed to keep children out of care. Consequently, the field is experiencing a shift in emphasis. More attention is now being given to services directed to families "at risk of separation" with the hope that this change in focus will minimize the need for placement services.

Unfortunately, the primary concern underlying this shifting emphasis is diverting children "at risk of placement," not enhancing the quality of life for children in families at risk. While this change in focus for child welfare service provision poses as "preventive" service, it actually represents minor tinkering with a residual service system. In fact, most of the clients served by child welfare agencies have experienced such severe deprivation and present such a myriad of complex personal and environmental problems that it is questionable whether the actual concept of prevention can convey a realistic service objective for this population. As Richard de Lone has noted:

> Tragically, disaster and breakup can and do afflict families in all social groups, so there will always be a child welfare system and always be an imperative to improve it. But this system exists in good measure to handle the most severe casualties of inequality, children whose families crack under the pressure of poverty, disease, unemployment, racism or for that matter, welfare.[45]

Thus, while the current shift in emphasis offers opportunities for child welfare agencies to enhance their provision of supportive and supplementary services to children and families in their own homes, the difficulties inherent in identifying the service population at risk and the ambiguity of the child welfare field's service mandate create major impediments to the development of an organized, coherent service delivery strategy.

Some families survive and function so well under the most adverse conditions that placement is never considered an option. In other families the caretaking functioning of the parents is so impaired that intervention must be ordered by the state for the protection of the children. In both instances the families need help. A serious prevention effort ought to be aimed at the eradication of the problems of poverty and its related effects on families and children. Yet this is not the strategy underlying current reform efforts in the child welfare system. The goal at present is primarily to move toward the "prevention of placement."

Time alone will determine the wisdom of the current movement toward reducing or eliminating the need for foster care placement whenever possible. Short-term outcome measures and cost-effectiveness studies cannot provide the answer to what is ultimately a policy question. What is clear, however, is that the shifting emphasis, if not accompanied by adequate provision of supportive and supplemental services, poses the risk of simply shrinking the total network of child welfare services—a residual but very essential service system—at a time when families are under more economic and social stress than at any time in recent history.

In the past, the child welfare field clearly erred in the direction of an overemphasis on substitute care provisions. Its goal was primarily to protect children, regardless of the threat to family integrity. Therefore, current initiatives designed to preserve families at risk must be viewed as a needed corrective for past inequities and imbalances in the system. But underintervention can be as harmful to family life as overintervention. One can only hope that the very limited solutions proposed now will not create a new set of injustices. The balancing of children's needs with parents' rights in the context of changing expectations and limited public resources is indeed a very delicate act.

NOTES

1. Alfred Kadushin, "Child Welfare Strategy in the Coming Years," in *Child Welfare Strategy in the Coming Years* (Washington, D.C.: Department of Health, Education and Welfare, 1978), pp. 14–17.

2. See, for example, Sheila B. Kamerman and Alfred J. Kahn, *Social Services in the United States* (Philadelphia: Temple University Press, 1976), pp. 141–97.

3. Lydia Rapoport, "The Concept of Prevention in Social Work," *Social Work* 1 (January 1961): 11.

4. Child Welfare Reform Act of 1979, New York State Session Law (1979), Chapters 610 and 611.

5. *An Ounce of Prevention: A Survey of Preventive Service Programs Contracted by New York City Special Services for Children* (New York: Interface, 1980).

6. See New York State Department of Social Services Administrative Directive, "Client Eligibility for Mandated Preventive Services and

District Qualifications for Reimbursement," January 12, 1981, and Official Regulations of the State Department of Social Services, Sections 430.8–430.13 as amended, effective April 1, 1982.

7. Shirley Jenkins, Anita G. Schroeder, and Kenneth Burgdorf, *Beyond Placement: The First Ninety Days* (Washington, D.C.: U.S. Department of Health and Human Services, 1981).

8. Ibid., p. 87.

9. Ibid., p. 63.

10. Ibid., p. 88.

11. Sister Mary Paul Janchill, *Guidelines to Decision-Making in Child Welfare* (New York: Human Services Workshop, 1981), p. 21.

12. Eileen Gambrill and Kermit T. Wiltse, "Foster Care: Prescription for Change," *Public Welfare*, 32 Summer 1974, pp. 39–40.

13. See, for example, David Fanshel, "The Exit of Children from Foster Care," *Child Welfare* 50 (February 1971): 65–81; David Fanshel and Eugene Shinn, *Children in Foster Care: A Longitudinal Investigation* (New York: Columbia University Press, 1978), pp. 488–90; Shirley Jenkins and Elaine Norman, *Beyond Placement: Mothers View Foster Care* (New York: Columbia University Press, 1975); Shirley Jenkins and Mignon Sauber, *Paths to Child Placement* (New York: Community Council of Greater New York, 1966).

14. Alfred Kadushin, *Child Welfare Services,* 3rd ed. (New York: Macmillan, 1980), pp. 75–108.

15. Ibid., pp. 115–47.

16. There are, of course, some notable exceptions. See, for example, Jane Knitzer, Mary Lee Allen, and Brenda McGowan, *Children Without Homes* (Washington, D.C.: Children's Defense Fund, 1978), pp. 153–60; Sheila Maybanks and Marvin Bryce, eds., *Home-Based Services for Children and Families* (Springfield, Ill.: Charles C Thomas, 1979); Harold Weissman, *Integrating Services for Troubled Families* (San Francisco: Jossey-Bass, 1978).

17. Kamerman and Kahn, *Social Services in the United States,* p. 37.

18. Sheila Kamerman and Alfred Kahn, *Child Care, Family Benefits and Working Parents* (New York: Columbia University Press 1981).

19. Kamerman and Kahn, *Social Services in the United States,* p. 132.

20. Sheila Rothman, "Other People's Children: The Day Care Experience in America," *The Public Interest,* 30 Winter 1973, pp. 11–27.

21. Kadushin, *Child Welfare Services,* pp. 235–37.

22. *Preliminary Statement on Social Work Services for Children in Their Own Homes* (New York: Child Welfare League of America, 1968), p. 30.

23. Children's Aid Society, "Nine to Twenty Four Hour Homemaker Service Project," *Child Welfare* 41 (March 1962): 99–103; Children's Aid Society, "Nine to Twenty Four Hour Homemaker Service Project—Part II," *Child Welfare* 41 (April 1962): 153–58.

24. Joseph Reid, "Homemaker Service for Children," *Children* 5 (November/December 1958): 210–12.

25. Reprinted with permission of Macmillan Publishing Co., Inc. From *Child Welfare Services*, 3rd ed. by Alfred Kadushin. Copyright © 1980 by Alfred Kadushin.

26. Kamerman and Kahn, *Social Services in the United States*, p. 146.

27. *Standards for Child Protective Services* (New York: Child Welfare League of America, 1974).

28. Defining abuse, neglect, and maltreatment legally falls to the individual states. For a discussion of issues involved in arriving at such legal definitions, see David Schwartz, "A Reappraisal of New York State's Child Abuse Law: How Far Have We Come?" *Journal of Law and Social Problems* 13 (1977): 105–8.

29. *Emergency Foster Boarding Home Network* (New York: Citizens' Committee for Children, 1979).

30. Mary Ann Jones, Stephen Magura, and Ann W. Shyne, "Effective Practice with Families in Protective and Preventive Services: What Works?" *Child Welfare* 60 (February 1981): 67–80.

31. Gertrude Halper and Mary Ann Jones, *Serving Families at Risk of Dissolution: Public Preventive Services in New York City* (New York: Human Resources Administration, 1981), p. 174.

32. Ibid., p. 176.

33. Jones, Magura, and Shyne, "Effective Practice with Families," pp. 71–72.

34. Ibid., pp. 72–75.

35. Lydia Rapoport, "Working with Families in Crisis: An Exploration in Preventive Intervention," in *Crisis Intervention: Selected Readings*, ed. Howard J. Parad (New York: Family Service Association of America, 1971), pp. 129–39.

36. Lydia Rapoport, "The State of Crisis: Some Theoretical Considerations," *Social Service Review* 36 (June 1962): 211–17.

37. For further discussion of this concept, see Anthony Maluccio and

Wilma D. Marlow, "The Case for Contract," *Social Work* 19 (January 1974): 28–36.

38. Shirley Jenkins and Elaine Norman, *Filial Deprivation and Foster Care* (New York: Columbia University Press 1972).

39. Robert Morris, "Caring For vs. Caring About People," *Social Work* 22 (September 1977): pp. 353–59.

40. Ibid., p. 354.

41. Jones, Magura, and Shyne, "Effective Practice with Families," p. 72.

42. Ibid., pp. 72–75.

43. Progress Report, Center for Family Life, Brooklyn, N.Y., April 1, 1981, pp. 2–4.

44. This diagram is a slight modification of one developed in Janchill, *Guidelines to Decision-Making*, p. 13.

45. Richard de Lone, *Small Futures* (New York: Harcourt Brace Jovanovich, 1979), p. 85.

DIRECTIONS FOR CHILD WELFARE SERVICES

The six chapters in Part III discuss the current child welfare system and point to new directions for service delivery. For the most part, these chapters are cast within the concepts of permanency planning. All the chapters view the system of substitute care as a temporary system which, when appropriately used, should result in permanent living arrangements for children.

Chapter 7 reviews decision making in the field of child welfare. It notes that the decision-making power of individual workers is restricted by policy, the availability of resources, and the actions taken by others. After reviewing the literature on decision making, the chapter discusses the various factors that influence individual decisions. The authors conclude that the current standard used for decision making—the best interest of the child standard—is too broad and vague to allow consistent decisions to be made within the field. They propose a new decision-making standard based on the concepts of "imminent harm" and "minimum standards of parenting." The chapter concludes by showing how such a standard could be applied in the field and how it might focus service delivery efforts and better protect the rights of clients.

Chapter 8 is concerned with foster family care. The author stresses that the use of this service should be planned and time-limited and that this service should be used only when children cannot be maintained within their own homes. The chapter focuses on the service needs of the biological parents, the child, and the foster parents during the preplacement, service planning, and placement phases of foster family care. It concludes with a discussion of the role of the agency in assuring that appropriate services during each of these phases and to each of these parties is provided.

Chapter 9 stresses the importance of case assessment in determining the appropriate resources to be used in serving special populations of children. It also discusses special considerations to be taken into account when serving these children. It then applies these ideas and focuses on the appropriate use of in-home specialized care, day treatment, study homes and diagnostic centers, foster family homes, and group residential facilities. It concludes with an example that demonstrates how these considerations can be translated into more appropriate service delivery and practice.

Chapter 10 is concerned with achieving permanence for children who enter the substitute care system. It begins with a discussion of the children for whom special efforts to achieve permanence might be needed and the mechanisms that might be used to identify them. It then discusses the various ways of achieving permanence—return home, return to relatives, adoption, and planned long-term foster care—and the program and practice conditions necessary to achieve each of these outcomes. It concludes with a discussion of the important role that the worker plays in achieving permanent plans for children.

Chapter 11 is concerned with the adoption of children who have spent a period of time in substitute care and may have special needs. It argues that if the needs of these children are to be met, agencies must pursue a number of strategies simultaneously. These strategies include the active, continuous recruitment of adoptive homes, the elimination of agency eligibility requirements that are not predictive of the ability to parent special needs children, the expansion of adoption opportunities to groups not traditionally considered appropriate for adoptive parenthood, the elimination of barriers to special needs adoption within the service delivery system, and the provision of meaningful services to the various parties involved in the adoption. The chapter concludes by noting that adoption must be seen as a child-centered service if children with special needs are to be adequately served.

The final chapter is concerned with the personnel needs of the child welfare system. It notes the current variation in skill levels, training, and expertise of child welfare staff and argues persuasively for the differential use of staff based on the task to be accomplished. The chapter delineates roles and responsibilities for professionals of various skill levels as well as nonprofessionals within the major areas of child welfare work. It then presents models for staffing child welfare agencies. The chapter concludes with a discussion of staff training and notes the importance of such training to worker morale.

CHAPTER 7
DECISION MAKING IN CHILD WELFARE: CURRENT ISSUES AND FUTURE DIRECTIONS*

Theodore J. Stein and Tina L. Rzepnicki

Child welfare means different things to different people. Broadly defined, the concept of child welfare embraces all policies and programs related to the well-being of children. However, such a perspective is too broad to be of practical use to the reader attempting to conceptualize current issues in decision making within the field. It requires a context that includes the social values that support a child welfare system, the goals of the system, and the methods that are used to realize goals, as well as consideration of the structural variables that affect decision making such as child welfare policy and statutory law.

A more restrictive view of child welfare emphasizes services and professional practices that protect children at risk, that place children in out-of-home care, and that find permanent homes for children whose parents cannot or will not provide ongoing care. This latter view of child welfare is what concerns us. This narrower perspective has generally prevailed in practice (see Chapters 1, 2, 4, and 6), and the issue of decision making assumes special significance when considered in the context of a field of practice designed to serve a small, vulnerable segment of the population. Therefore, this chapter will focus specifically on decision making in preventive/protective services,[1] foster care,and adoption services, the three programs through which most child welfare services are provided. Taken together, these programs account for over 70

*This chapter is based, in part, on research conducted under a grant received from the United States Children's Bureau, U.S. Department of Health and Human Services, grant number 90-CW-2043 (02).

percent of all services that child welfare staff provide for children and their families.[2]

In the process of providing services, child welfare workers undertake a variety of tasks on behalf of their clients, perhaps the most critical of which is decision making. The choices made at any single point can set the course for future transactions between worker and client as well as those between members of a family. For example, the accuracy and quality of data are conditioned by whether workers decide to conduct assessments in the office, in the client's home, or both; whether they elect to gather information through verbal exchanges during interviews, through client self-reports, through direct observation of family members, through reports by third parties, or a combination of these methods.[3] Information gathered during assessment serves as the basis for deciding whether to open a case in an agency and determines, to a large extent, what services will be provided. Thus, choices made at the outset may have serious ramifications for all future decisions.

Likewise, if a child must be placed in out-of-home care, ongoing contact between family members may be contingent upon the geographic proximity of the placement facility to the home of the child's biological parents. The distances to be traveled can affect the frequency and duration of parent-child visits which, in turn, may affect the likelihood of children being reunited with their families of origin.

Child welfare workers do not have unlimited decision-making power. The options available to a worker are, as a rule, limited by eligibility requirements established in agency policy or by statutory law and by the availability of resources. For instance, a protective service worker may suspect that a child is suffering from emotional neglect. Whether he or she can open a case on this basis is contingent upon the conditions covered in a state's statutes and the evidentiary requirements for sustaining allegations in court. Eligibility rules can limit a client's access to voluntary services. Resource deficits may force choices—children who might otherwise be maintained in their own homes may have to enter foster care if day care, homemaker, or emergency caretaker services are not available. And some decisions are made by others before a worker receives a case. For example, a juvenile court judge may require parental involvement in a treatment program. While the worker may disagree with this judicial ruling, she or he has little power to effect change in it.

Thus, decision making at the line level is a restricted enterprise. Choices made by others set boundaries governing the options available to the worker. Any effort to understand the decision-making process and to develop guidelines for decision making must take these limitations into account.

This chapter begins with a brief review of the literature on decision making in child welfare. Next, we discuss environmental influences, including social values, statutory law, social science knowledge, and program variables that affect decision making. A review of legal issues and their implications for decision making in child welfare concludes this chapter.

DECISION MAKING: RESEARCH FINDINGS ON THE STATE OF THE ART

For over two decades researchers have made efforts to discern the processes that child welfare workers engage in when making decisions for children. This research proceeded on the assumption that if key decision-making points could be identified and the decision-making process described, a decision-making framework to guide child welfare staff in making critical choices could be developed inductively from practice knowledge.

Over time, investigators have sought answers to a series of questions such as "How do workers make intake decisions?",[4] "How do they assess parental adequacy?",[5] "What is the basis for deciding whether children should be placed in out-of-home care?",[6] "Should children be placed in institutions or in foster family homes.?",[7] "When should children who are in placement be reunited with their biological parents?",[8] "What are the criteria for selecting foster parents[9] and adoptive applicants?"[10] In more recent years, attention has turned to questions of how workers decide whether a child has been abused or neglected.[11]

Unfortunately, consistent decision-making principles have not been identified. For example, both Boehm[12] and Shinn[13] inform us that decisions to place children out of their own homes are based mainly on a diagnosis of the mother's pathology, whereas Phillips and associates[14] report that the single most important combination of factors pointing to a placement decision were traits of the father and that neither the mother's functioning nor her relationship to the child was an important consideration. By contrast, Ryan and Morris[15] inform us that diagnostic criteria play no role in critical intake decisions, a position that is reinforced in data reported by Stein.[16]

If decision making is guided by the application of rules induced from practice and if these rules are consistently applied to cases, one would expect that social work judges, who are experienced child welfare practitioners, when asked to evaluate case material independently, would reach some degree of consensus on what the case decision should be as well as on the most salient factors affecting the decision. This has not been the case. Phillips and colleagues[17] compared decisions reached by social workers with those of three independent judges, each of whom had more than five years of experience in making child welfare decisions. The judges agreed with each other and with the workers on less than one-half of the cases. When they did agree, they did not identify the same factors as affecting their decision.

Wolins, reporting data from his study of how foster parents are selected, found that the amount of information that was available in a case record had a significant impact on interjudge agreement. Concurrence among judges climbed from a low of .47, when the entire case record was used, to a high of .81 when the judges were given only that information deemed most relevant to the decision. Of particular interest is the fact that when 80 percent of the material in the case record was *randomly discarded,* the level of agreement between judges was nearly as high or better than that achieved when the entire case record was read.[18]

It thus appears that decision making is not governed by the application of constant rules to case materials. What then, are the primary variables that affect worker decision-making behavior? The suggestions are many and varied. As previously mentioned, deficits in the resources needed to assist parents with problem solving are said to constrain the options available.[19] The fact that some decisions are made by others before a worker receives a case also constrains this function. There is also evidence that accepted practices within a given agency, rather than principles of practice derived from theory or accumulated practice knowledge, guide decision making.[20] Some of the more unsettling explanations for the way decisions are reached focus on the worker and highlight the role played by subjective factors such as the practitioner's personal values and biases and the idiosyncratic assumptions that he or she makes, as well as his or her "ideals" of family life.[21]

Practical constraints in the form of resource deficits and decisions made by others are to be expected in child welfare. They have, and will no doubt continue, to limit workers' options. And it would be naive not to expect personal judgments to enter into the decision-making process. However, one would expect research to uncover a core data set, in the form of constant items of information, that workers gather. These would, of course, differ in relation to the decisions to be made, but insofar as accumulated practice knowledge exists, this core data set should inform decision making, and its elements should be discoverable. It is to such a core data set that one would expect individual judgment to be applied. The absence of this central base of information is what is so distressing. If external influences such as the availability of resources and decisions made by others were eliminated from an analysis of decision making in child welfare, one would have to conclude that individual discretion is the major force in selection of options. The question then becomes, "Why?"

In order to address this question we must turn our attention to the environment in which decision making occurs and review ways in which various elements in this environment support or constrain the decision maker's tasks.

THE DECISION-MAKING ENVIRONMENT

The decision-making environment is comprised of three domains: the social environment, the professional environment, and the program environment. The social environment includes a system of values that are articulated in social policy and statutory law. These values are given expression by legislators when they fund the social programs through which child welfare services are provided. The professional environment is shaped by social science knowledge and the technology derived from that knowledge. These guide social work practice and provide a means for achieving program goals. The professional environment also includes a system of values that are inextricably linked with social values (if not wholly synonymous with them), yet reflect the particular ideals and subculture of the social work profession.

Just as goals must be viewed in relation to the technology that is available to achieve them, so must values be weighed against current knowledge if they are to provide useful guides to action rather than ideal statements of purpose. While separable for the purposes of discussion, these variables within the social, professional, and program domains interact with each other. In the following pages, we will concern ourselves with the social and professional environments. Issues related to the influence of values and knowledge on decision making are addressed. The resulting effects on the program environment are described later in this chapter.

THE SOCIAL ENVIRONMENT

Values

There are two social values that are closely linked with the provision of children's services. The fact that child welfare services exist at all is a statement of the value that our society places on young people and an expression of society's willingness to fund programs for the care and protection of those youngsters whose parents cannot or will not provide for them. This value is expressed in the concept of the *best interests of the child.* This decision-making standard, as it is called, expresses the concern that all actions taken on behalf of children seek to maximize their full potential for growth and development.

The second value is embodied in the concept of *family sanctity,* which expresses the state's interest in preserving the family unit as the basic framework for raising children. Family sanctity also refers to matters of privacy which, by custom, hold that family privacy should not be violated unless intrusion by an outside authority is necessary to protect the rights or to safeguard the well-being of family members.

These two values provide a context in which the decision maker, be it a juvenile court judge or child welfare worker, must weigh and balance choices. The right of parents to raise their children free of state interference is a well-embodied principle of American law. Thus, in theory, the worker who must decide whether to provide services to children in their own homes or in out-of-home care must, in keeping with the values expressed in the concept of family sanctity, make every effort to preserve each family unit unless there is compelling evidence that a child's best interests cannot be served in that environment. When such evidence exists, the child's right to be safeguarded from harm is balanced against the parent's right to privacy. The latter is upheld to the extent that parents meet their responsibilities to care for and to protect their children. Depriving parents of their rights and depriving children of the right to be raised by their biological parents are justified only when it can be shown that parents have violated their social contract regarding protection of their children.

The question of interest is: "How does one judge when parents have violated their social contract?" There are situations where a child has been so severely maltreated that the question becomes moot. However, such cases are in the minority; hence, this question has significance in a majority of cases that come before child welfare workers.

As discussed earlier, values inevitably influence the decision-making process. However, values are too abstract to be useful guides for action. Values can inform the decision-making process only to the extent that they yield criteria that the decision maker can use to evaluate which of the available options in any situation are most likely to promote goal attainment. The decision maker must be able to point to observable phenomena that permit inferences that a specific value is being upheld. These observable phenomena become the criteria for decision making.

Thus, criteria for child welfare decisions may be derived from statutory laws, which embody social values and which provide a mechanism for state intervention to uphold these values. They may also be derived from social science knowledge and from the policies of child-caring agencies. The relationship between statutory law, social science knowledge, and decision-making criteria are reviewed next. The importance of agency policy in decision making is considered when we discuss the program environment.

Statutory Law

Juvenile court hearings are bifurcated into jurisdictional and dispositional phases. At the jurisdictional phase a judge must decide whether the evidence presented to the court is sufficient to sustain an allegation that a child has been abused or neglected as defined by state law. An affirmative answer gives the court the right to assume jurisdiction over the child. If jurisdiction is taken, a dispositional hearing is held; at this time it must be decided whether the child can remain at home or should be placed in substitute care. Whether the decision is jurisdictional or dispositional, a judge needs criteria to guide the process of making choices.

Criteria for jurisdictional decisions are derived from states' neglect, abuse, and dependency statutes. These laws identify conditions under which the state may intervene in family life. Dependency refers to the inability of parents to provide for their children due to monetary deficits. Unlike abuse and neglect, there is currently no imputation of parental fault in matters of dependency. Neglect generally refers to the chronic failure of adults to protect children from physical danger. In some states, the concept has been expanded to include "failure to provide for the positive social and psychological development of the child."[22] Abuse refers to parental actions that cause a child to suffer physical or emotional harm.

Abuse and neglect statutes are vague, allowing for a broad interpretation of the exact conditions that constitute either condition. It has been argued that the breadth of these statutes is important, that a juvenile court judge must have the latitude necessary to exercise discretion in determining whether any given case fits within the law. Broad statutes are said to permit the expression of local community attitudes and to encourage flexible use of community resources.[23]

However, such breadth creates problems of two sorts. First, broad statutes provide no guidelines for determining whether behavior falls within or outside socially acceptable boundaries. Thus, the generally accepted doctrine in criminal law, which requires that the law give "notice of what is proscribed . . . in a language that the common world will understand," is not applied to the civil laws governing the maltreatment of children.[24] Hence, it is extremely difficult to articulate criteria for determining whether maltreatment exists. It has been suggested that the ambiguity of the law may "encourage intervention by many well-intentioned persons who ignore the negative consequences of their acts."[25]

A second, closely related problem is that vague laws create a framework for indiscriminate social control of behaviors that a community finds distasteful. Critics of the juvenile court have pointed out that judges as well as child welfare workers exercise a great deal of individual discretion in making decisions.[26] Since a majority of the clients of child welfare agencies are poor and/or minority families, vague laws may be used to reinforce other forms of discrimination.

The desired outcome of a dispositional decision is to choose a living arrangement that will promote the child's best interests. To determine whether a child can be protected in his or her own home, or whether out-of-home placement is necessary, one must endeavor to predict which alternative is most likely to further the goals implied by the best interests standard. The ability to predict outcomes is related to the professional environment and the state of social science knowledge. This issue is an important one and will be reviewed in some detail.

The Professional Environment

Social Science Knowledge

Decision makers are concerned with the consequences of their actions. Exact outcomes, however, are rarely known. Individuals make predictions as to the most likely outcome of a given course of action, but all predictions are essentially hypotheses. One hopes, but cannot be sure, that the course of action selected will further movement toward an identified goal. It follows, then, that all decision making involves an element of risk taking as to whether one's predictions are accurate.

Predictions can have short-term or long-range consequences; their risks may be minimal or great. The bulk of choices that we make as individuals involve short-term predictions for which we incur minimal risk. Decisions where the consequences are difficult to predict and/or where outcomes may not be known until far into the future can be extremely troublesome because answers are needed to what are essentially unanswerable questions. One either accepts the risks involved or becomes hopelessly mired in indecision.

The accuracy with which professionals are able to predict what is in any child's best interest is contingent, in part, upon whether they focus on long-range or short-term outcomes. It can be argued, for example, that what is in a child's best interest is to provide all that is possible within the limits of social science knowledge at any given time. Interpreting the standard in this way focuses the decision maker's attention on ideals—on what the child welfare field would like for all children in the long run, not necessarily on what it is able to obtain for children now. Stein has expressed this problem in the following way:

> If we could specify all or most of the conditions that further [a child's best interest], these specifications would serve as criteria to guide us in assessing whether the conditions under which a child is living further or impede progress toward this goal. We can, of course, specify minimum conditions. For example, immunizing children against disease, providing a balanced diet, and requiring a minimum amount of schooling are viewed as serving a child's best interests. In any given case, we can determine whether this interest is furthered by checking medical and school records for information regarding immunizations and classroom attendance and by testing a parent's knowledge of nutrition and meal planning. We encounter difficulties when trying to specify conditions at the other end of the continuum—those under which a child will feel loved, wanted, and secure. If the conditions cannot be identified, criteria cannot be specified. Without criteria, decisions are not likely to be made nor case plans formulated. If they are, the criteria used are apt to be highly subjective.[27]

Child welfare practitioners have long assumed that long-term predictions for children could be made on the basis of information describing family dynamics, such as how parents interact with their children, what their attitudes are toward their children, and so forth. Essentially, workers have felt confident in their ability to predict the type of adult a child would become given knowledge of family dynamics and child-rearing practices. In recent years, this confidence has been severely undermined by data from a variety of sources, including longitudinal studies of child development and exhaustive reviews of child development research.[28] One such study will serve to illustrate this point.

In 1929 a thirty-year longitudinal investigation was undertaken by investigators at the University of California at Berkeley. With the objective of observing physical, mental, and emotional growth in average people, 166 infants were tested and later interviewed over a period of thirty years. Based on early observations, the children's homes were classified as troubled and untroubled. The predictions made by the researchers were straightforward: The children coming from troubled homes would become troubled adults; those whose homes were untroubled would become untroubled adults. Jean MacFarlane, in reporting the results of the study, informs us that the predictions made by the researchers were incorrect two-thirds of the time.[29]

At the end of the study period, many of the youngsters from troubled homes were "some of the most outstandingly mature adults in the entire group. They were well integrated, highly competent and/or creative . . . clear about their values . . . understanding and accepting of self and others."[30] The young people whose homes were viewed as trouble-free provide a sharp contrast. As adults, these children were "strained and dissatisfied, wondering what went wrong and longing for the good old days."[31]

There are several reasons why efforts to make predictions have proved so fruitless. First, there is a tendency to overemphasize the importance of experiences that occur in the first five years of life. It is assumed, for example, that most of the adult behavior is determined during this time. Hence, there is a failure to take into account the modifying effects of subsequent experiences. Thus, the influence of peer groups, teachers, and other adults and the effects of television programming on a child's socialization are largely ignored. Furthermore, few theories of child development take into account the effect of a child's perception of events and how perceptions can influence development.[32]

The fact that many ideas about child development come from research conducted in clinical settings where troubled individuals describe their experiences to clinicians or researchers also inhibits the ability to make accurate predictions of future development. To assume that data gathered from a clinical population can be generalized to the population at large or to the population with a given problem is an error. Persons who seek help may differ in significant ways from those who do not. Finally, the fallibility of memory, the fact that impressions become concretized over time and that these may differ from the events from which they were formed, and the fact that a therapist can influence the content of a client's verbal reports, all cast doubt on the accuracy of ex post facto recollections.[33]

Practice Knowledge.   What are the consequences for the decision-making process of trying to select options without criteria to serve as guides for data collection and for evaluating choices? The worker who is assessing the safety of a child's home must have ways of discriminating safe from unsafe conditions. The worker who is confronted with deciding whether a child can be reunited with biological parents must have criteria for assessing parental adequacy.

Here, the knowledge base of the profession, which is a subset of general social science knowledge, and the profession's standards of practice emerge as critical guides for information gathering and decision making. Questions as to what comprises this body of knowledge and the ways in which it informs decision making are the issues that investigators sought to uncover in the studies reviewed at the beginning of this chapter. Unfortunately, as Phillips and associates noted in discussing their efforts to discern how workers make choices, practice knowledge has not been "articulated in sufficiently specific terms to meet the needs of practitioners."[34]

Decision making is a complex activity. Unlike the laboratory, the real world abounds with diverse stimuli, which must be categorized in terms of their relevance to the decision at hand. Variables must be weighted to suggest a rank ordering of importance within and across each category and weights must be flexible, since the significance of any single factor can fluctuate in relation to the presence or absence of other factors.

For example, it is axiomatic to state that a child's well-being is affected by interactions with significant others. Now, if a preschool age child is being raised by a single parent who is isolated from family and friends, great emphasis would be placed on the parent's child-caring skills, his or her knowledge of what to expect of children of different ages, and the nurturance and stimulation that the parent provides. But what if there are two parents? What if relatives reside in the child's home and the family has a strong friendship network? What significance is assigned to the effects on children of interactions with teachers and peers, and how is the burden of responsibility for the child's well-being, in the present and the future, distributed across all of those persons who may influence a child's development?

Research findings have, as already noted, undermined confidence in the ability to predict adult development based primarily on knowledge of parent-child interaction. But this has left a knowledge void that has yet to be filled in a manner sufficient to inform the decision-making process.

As the field becomes more cognizant of the variety of factors that affect a child's well-being, the decision maker's tasks become increasingly complex. The universe of factors to be considered is great, but precise ways of determining the relevance of these factors have not been articulated.

Students of child welfare learn that they are to elicit information from clients in diverse areas related to family functioning and to draw inferences regarding parental interest in and ability to provide ongoing care for their children. What one wants, but does not find, are instructions for using this information to make informed choices.[35] Thus, there is no way to sort the relevant information from the irrelevant, and workers become mired down with copious amounts of data, the use of which is not clear for decision making.[36] Without guidelines, it is easy to view everything as having potential relevance. It is not surprising, then, that in a study of protective service workers, public health nurses, and other professionals who work with abused and neglected children, 69 percent strongly agreed or tended to agree with the statement, "It is difficult to know what is and what is not child maltreatment," and 79 percent responded in a similar manner to the statement, "It is difficult to know when parents should have their children returned [from foster placement]."[37]

In a very real sense, the problems that are created by the absence of guidelines for gathering and using information are sufficient to explain the decision-making problems that have been uncovered by investigators and reviewed at the beginning of this chapter. Without criteria to guide data gathering, the process breaks down in its earliest stages.

The Dilemma

The decisions that confront child welfare workers are among the most difficult decisions made in a clinical context. Certainly, many clinical decisions have far-reaching implications for clients, and in most instances knowledge of human behavior is so restricted that professionals cannot make the long-range predictions which would ease the process of making decisions. However, when clinical transactions occur between two adults, the practitioner always has the choice of forcing the final decision on the client whose "right to self-determination" provides a convenient framework for opting for client choice.[38] This is not the case in the child welfare field where some clients may be considered too young to be active participants in the decision process and where parents, because they are said to have maltreated their children, are often viewed as having abrogated their right to make choices for their children.

The dilemma that confronts the child welfare worker can be expressed as follows: Decisions must be made for a very vulnerable population of clients, using a decision-making standard that does not lend itself to specification. Workers must formulate long-range predictions without support from social science knowledge, and they must frequently operate within a framework of statutory laws that are deliberately vague. Since professional standards and principles of practice are not specific,[39] one cannot assume that professional education will provide workers with the skills necessary to undertake the decision-making responsibilities they confront. While the development of a professional knowledge base can help workers to make more sophisticated assessments of case need and to draw more reasoned inferences based on the data they have collected, professional education is unlikely to give workers the specific guidelines needed for reliable decision making.

Earlier, we raised the question: Why does individual discretion play a major role in decision making? It appears that vague laws and knowledge deficits create a void for decision makers, which they tend to fill by interjecting personal values and biases. Further, in the absence of specific decision-making criteria workers will, understandably, opt for the safest choice. For instance, workers may choose to leave a child in foster care if this situation meets the child's minimal needs rather than returning the youngster to biological parents, since it cannot be predicted whether a child will be abused or neglected once again.

Finally, decisions are often made by default. For example, some biological parents do not receive the services that might enable them to resume care of their children, and the children are allowed to drift in foster home placement. There is strong evidence that case plans are not formulated for a significant number of children served by child welfare agencies.[40]

It is important to recognize that the situation in which child welfare workers find themselves reflects a general ambivalence on the part of society toward the issue of how to treat parents who mistreat their children. For example, despite the value placed on family sanctity and on the right of parents to raise their children free of outside interference, federal funds for programs to prevent placement of children or for services to reunify families after children enter care have historically been very limited, while funds to maintain children in placement have been relatively unlimited.[41] (See Chapters 2 and 3 for further discussion of this issue.) The fiscal incentives in federal policy have a direct influence on the policies and actions of state-level administrators, and these, in turn, shape the professional decision-making environment in which child welfare practitioners must function.

An Alternative Standard for Decision Making

In order to overcome some of the current problems in decision making, some have argued for a new decision-making standard and for delineating the statutory conditions that constitute abuse and neglect.[42] The rationale for this position, some elements of which have already been reviewed, are discussed next.

Critics of the *best interest* test argue that a child's caretaker has the right to know which of his or her behaviors are proscribed by law. They posit that vague laws permit discretionary decision making and encourage intervention under arbitrary conditions. As such, they violate the value this society places on family privacy.

They further argue that intervention into family life under broad standards may do more harm than good. Except for situations of severe maltreatment, where sheltering a child from further harm is in and of itself a sufficient justification for state action, it is appropriate to ask, "What good will come from state intervention into family life?" Since state action undermines family privacy and since it may disrupt the bonds that exist between parents and their children, the state has an obligation to provide assistance to help families resolve their problems once it has decided to intervene. Such assistance constitutes a balance against unwarranted invasion of privacy. As noted previously, evidence suggests that assistance is not always forthcoming.[43]

It is unfortunate, but true, that the state frequently fails to provide services to families once an intervention decision has been made. There are many reasons for this, including lack of worker skill and large case loads, which restrict the amount of time a worker can devote to any one family.[44] More importantly, perhaps, the current technology for solving many difficulties that confront families is limited and problem-solving resources are in short supply. The shortage of resources is most apparent when one considers the lack of concrete services such as housing and financial assistance needed by many of the clients served by the child welfare system. Further, there is a growing body of evidence that children in state custody are not safe from abuse and neglect while in substitute care arrangements.[45]

Another argument in favor of a revised standard for intervention is highlighted by recent evidence suggesting that in cases where the failure of the parent to provide adequately for the child is the primary or sole allegation, poverty is a common factor.[46] While those advocating for an alternative standard of decision making do not believe that its adoption can resolve intractable problems such as poverty, they do believe that a narrower, more specific standard for state intervention would reduce the chances of coercive intervention in family life when poverty is the main source of a client's difficulties.

The final argument for change in the standard for intervention rests on the fact that we are not able to make the long-range predictions that are called for when we attempt to determine what is in the "best interest" of a child. Our current knowledge does not allow us to do so accurately or reliably.

Much of the criticism of the "best interest" standard has centered on situations where intervention is coercive—where court action is evoked because parents will not accept services on a voluntary basis. However, some requests for assistance from child welfare agencies are initiated by parents, and these voluntary cases may not, initially, involve the court. Criticisms that center on violations of family privacy are not usually viewed as applicable when services are voluntarily requested, for unlike situations where intervention proceeds on the basis of a court assuming jurisdiction over a child, voluntary clients may, in theory, withdraw from services at any time.

We strongly support the suggestion that services be made available to any family requesting assistance with their difficulties. However, we take the position that a revised standard for intervention is as pertinent to voluntary cases as it is to involuntary cases. As discussed earlier, child welfare workers, as well as juvenile court judges, need guidelines for decision making, which they presently endeavor to derive from the "best interest" standard. Thus "voluntary" families may be evaluated against the ideals embodied in this standard, which may, in turn, result in workers' setting unrealistic expectations for family functioning. This may result in an evaluation of the family as inadequate and lead to court intervention if and when the "voluntary" client decides to withdraw from services. There is also evidence that many children in out-of-home placement entered care via voluntary requests for services.[47] Once children are in a substitute placement, parents who placed their children voluntarily are at risk of having their behavior evaluated using the "best interest" standard and of finding, when they ask to have their children returned, that court action is taken.

An acceptable alternate decision-making standard must lend itself to the development of operational criteria that can be reliably applied on a case-by-case basis to determine whether child care meets minimally acceptable standards, and it must lend itself to setting attainable goals. It should also respect the ethnic and cultural diversity of American society by being specific enough to limit the use of individual discretion by the court and child welfare workers. This is best accomplished *if intervention decisions require evidence that a child has been harmed or is at risk of harm in the near future.* This evidentiary requirement serves a dual purpose. First, it recognizes that efforts to make long-term predictions are not fruitful. Second, it represents an effort to reduce the chances that intervention will occur for moral reasons alone.

Previously, we mentioned that the ambiguity of current statutues provides a framework for indiscriminate social control of behaviors that a community finds distasteful. Under the guise of protecting children, parents are often punished for behaviors that are deemed immoral. Children have been removed from the care of their parents because the court does not approve of their life-style. Thus, children have been placed in substitute care because a mother frequented taverns or had male visitors overnight, because of their religious beliefs or because they lived in a communal setting, or because the parent was a lesbian or male homosexual.[48] None of these cases involved evidence of harm to a child.[49]

While the state can elect to intervene for such reasons, it must be recognized that under such conditions, establishing objective criteria for reuniting children with their parents is all but impossible.[50]

Using the proposed revised standard, which focuses on demonstrable or potential harm to the child, the decision maker's concern would be to show the ways in which "immoral" behavior was currently affecting the child or to posit a reasonable hypothesis of harm in the near future. To illustrate, if the mother who frequents taverns or has overnight visitors is not arranging for adequate supervision or is not feeding her child, intervention would occur for the latter reasons, not because her personal behavior violates community norms.

Thus, the decision maker's attention is drawn to the child. The focus of concern during an investigation or case assessment is the youngster's physical condition and behavior in different situations. If the data gathered suggest that these are inappropriate, this information might be used to support inferences that the child is experiencing emotional, psychological, or physical difficulties.

Assume, for example, that during a home visit a protective service worker observes a youngster sitting in a chair in a corner of the room. The child will not, when asked, come over to sit by the worker and his parent. Assume further that the child's response to questions are hesitant and that his affect is flat, that is, his voice is monotonic, and he does not look at the person to whom he is speaking.

Hypothetically, the child's behavior could be caused by nervousness in the interview situation; it could be indicative of behavioral norms of a subculture different from that of the workers; or it could reflect a more generalized problem. To confirm which of these hypotheses is correct, workers would seek assessment information from different sources. They may contact the school to inquire about the child's behavior in and outside of class; they may make inquiries of relatives and friends of the family; and they may observe the child at school, at play, and in interaction with others including parents. They may also arrange for psychological testing. If additional information indicates that the behaviors observed during the initial interview are representative of the youngster's behavior elsewhere and that they are not normative behaviors for the child's peer group, the suggestion that assistance is needed is reasonable.

Whether intervention should proceed on a voluntary or an involuntary basis would be contingent upon the parent's response to the suggestion that help is needed. If the suggestion is accepted, assuming that the parent has not previously withdrawn from a program designed to assist the family with this difficulty, services could be provided on a voluntary basis through a child welfare or other community agency. In such a situation, the worker would want to monitor whether or not the parent follows through with the referral and with the subsequent service program.

If assistance is offered and refused, or if the client's service history raises questions about the likelihood of continuing with services on a voluntary basis, there would be sufficient grounds to open the case on an involuntary basis. A refusal to accept help, in the face of evidence that it is needed, lends support to the hypothesis that the parent's concern for the child is below what is expected.

It should be noted that there are situations where intervention may be indicated even though the parent's behavior is not having an immediate, observable effect on the child. The most notable of these are situations in which there is inadequate supervision of the child. If the worker's assessment indicates that the child should not be left unsupervised (either because the child is too young to seek help, if needed, or because the child does not know how to seek help and is not able to develop sufficient self-help skills) and if the parent will not arrange for supervision or accept services, then it is reasonable to posit that that child is in danger in the near future if left unsupervised.

An important element of a revised standard for decision making is the notion of holding caretakers accountable for *minimum standards of parenting*. This does not appear to be the expectation under the current "best interest" standard. There is evidence that workers using the current standard assess parental adequacy against an ideal.[51] Thus, parents are at risk of having their behavior evaluated using a referent that would not be found in the community at large. Additionally, while intervention may be justified to safeguard children, regard for family autonomy directs the worker to retreat from involuntary interference in family life at the earliest possible moment. Even if ideals were attainable—if they could be translated into observable phenomena and sufficient resources were available to attain them—intervention toward such ends would require a rethinking of our society's philosophy regarding the right of parents to raise their children free from outside interference. Moreover, there is a strong probability that if ideal standards were applied to the community at large, a majority of families would be found wanting and state intervention in family life would increase to a wholly unacceptable degree.

Over time, with the accumulation of knowledge and with an increased willingness on the part of society to fund a greater array of services, the proposed standard can be expanded. Society must ultimately aim for what is best for children, but ideals must be tempered by what is attainable. To insist on an ideal that is not compatible with the current state of knowledge, with current technology and resources, and with the realities of the world in which child welfare workers practice is to ask that the minority of families served by child welfare agencies bear the brunt of society's good intentions.

Summary

For several decades professionals in social work have argued for the importance of developing a decision-making framework to guide child welfare workers in making critical choices. Efforts to develop such a framework inductively from a study of practice have not borne fruit. The assumption that practice knowledge was sufficient to guide child welfare workers in making critical choices has not held up under close scrutiny. A full comprehension of the difficulties that confront practitioners forces one to consider the larger social and professional environments in which child welfare programs are embedded and to review certain elements in these environments that give direction to the day-to-day activities of child welfare personnel.

As the preceding review has shown, the social values that underpin child welfare programs, and the statutes that embody these values, are couched at a level of abstraction that precludes the identification of criteria that can be used as guidelines for making critical choices. Furthermore, the state of social science knowledge is such that the ability to predict outcomes is severely restricted. For these reasons, the movement to articulate a new decision-making standard, one that focuses on minimum standards of parenting and a showing of harms to a child, is gaining support. So, also, are efforts to reduce the ambiguity in neglect and dependency statutes. Now we will endeavor to add perspective to this discussion by describing the program environment in which child welfare decisions are made.

The Program Environment

The program environment for making decisions in child welfare is embedded in the social and professional environments. The variables in these domains interact with each other. Program goals and the processes used to realize goals are derived from social values and social science knowledge. Practice knowledge should, in turn, feed into and expand the base of social science knowledge. In the following pages the main elements of the program environment as they relate to decision making are described. These elements are summarized in Figure 7.1.

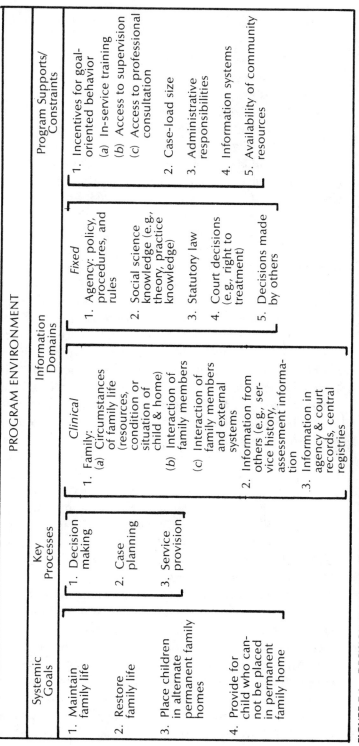

FIGURE 7.1. DECISION ENVIRONMENT This diagram represents a partial model. All the variables external to the program environment are not shown. Political considerations that influence funding decisions are a notable omission.

Goals

In order to gather the data necessary to implement a decision-making standard focusing on specific harms to the child and minimal standards of parenting as the prerequisite for state intervention, we suggested earlier that the worker's assessment should focus on the child's actual physical condition and behavior in different situations, not on vague indicators of family functioning. However, the model shown in Figure 7.1 is explicit in identifying the family unit, not the child in isolation, as the unit for service—the focal point around which all child welfare decisions must initially revolve. As already noted, American law and social custom direct that biological parents have a right to the custody, care, and control of their children, and all initial decision making must reinforce this right. When parental actions yield evidence that they cannot or will not continue to care for their children, attention must shift to the child's right to be raised in the continuous care of another set of adults. Thus, the model supports what have long been cited, in principle, as goals of the child welfare system. In descending order, these are maintaining family life through the provision of services to children in their own homes, restoring family life when children have been placed in out-of-home care, and the placement of children in permanent family homes through adoption or court appointment of a legal guardian when neither of the first two options is possible. Planned long-term foster care is an alternative, although a less desirable one, given the absence of legal safeguards for such arrangements.

These goals provide a reference point against which the decision maker must evaluate or balance all choices. Stated otherwise, each time a decision is made the decision maker must ask the question: To what extent will this particular alternative further the attainment of a systemic goal? For example, when a child enters out-of-home care (assuming that the youngster does not have special needs that require placement in a residential treatment facility), the decision where to place, when made in the context of the goal of restoring family life, may force a different set of choices than when the goal centers *primarily* on the child's well-being. The former goal narrows the range of alternatives by focusing the decision maker's attention on selecting a placement that is geographically close to the child's biological parents, since research evidence suggests that parental visiting is a key variable in family restoration.[52] Since a majority of parents served by public agencies are poor and presumably unable to afford costly transportation and assuming that there is an inverse relationship between the probability of frequent visits and the distances to be traveled, it is possible to rank-order placement alternatives based on their geographic proximity to the home of biological parents. Selecting an initial placement where the concern is solely with the child's needs may result in choices that mitigate against family reunification. This may be justified if there is persuasive evidence that the child has special needs that cannot be met in the community where the parent resides. In considering whether the child's needs demand a special placement, the hypothetical costs in terms of long-range goals must be taken into consideration. Further decisions based primarily on the child's well-being may be correct once evidence shows that reunification is not possible, in which case the decision maker directs attention to finding an alternative permanent home for the child.

Key Processes

What are the key processes by which systemic goals are achieved? Our position is that *managing information in order to reach decisions that will result in permanency in a child's living arrangements and formulating these decisions into case plans, the objectives of which are realized through the provision of services, are, in that order, the key processes through which systemic goals are attained.* The suggestion that decision making to achieve permanency is the key process differs markedly from the position that treatment and nurturance of children are the main objectives of child welfare.[53] Treatment to remediate the conditions that led to a family's involvement with a child-caring agency is clearly necessary; however, in this proposed model of practice, treatment is given for the purposes of decision making, not as an end in itself. Thus, given a goal of family reunification and recognizing the relationship between the probabilities of attaining this outcome and the length of time a child is in care, the range of problems to be addressed by the worker and the level of family change that can be expected to occur before the child can be returned home will be determined in relation to the primary objective of family reunification. This sets a ceiling on the change demands that child welfare workers can make of parents, supporting a focus on minimal standards of parenting.

This position should not be construed as suggesting that families be left with unresolved difficulites. It does, however, suggest that child welfare agencies are only one part of a community's total family service system and that distinctions must be made between the objectives of child-caring agencies and other community systems such as family service and community mental health agencies. If such distinctions are not made, the current practice of using child welfare agencies as a "dumping ground" for cases that other community agencies do not want to serve is reinforced. The irony of this should be readily apparent. Child welfare staff, given their reliance on community agencies to assist in resolving family difficulties, are put in the position of having to refer families to the very community agencies that rejected them and referred them to the child welfare system in the first place.

Limiting the range of problems that are the proper concern of child welfare agencies and setting limits to the changes demanded of families sets boundaries on which aspects of a client's life space are the proper subject for inquiry, an issue that traditional treatment models leave open-ended. Setting such boundaries is critical if criteria to guide child welfare workers in their data-collection and decision-making activities are to be specified. Such guidelines for data collection are derived from knowledge of how the collected information will be used. Additionally, a respect for family privacy demands that workers justify their information-gathering activities; again, such justification comes from knowledge of how information will be used. Also, time constraints imposed by case-load size and administrative paperwork demand that limits be set. Finally, since approximately 75 percent of the children in the care of public welfare agencies are being served by persons with no academic training in social work (of the 25 percent with social work degrees 16 percent hold bachelor's degrees, 9 percent graduate degrees),[54] even if more traditional treatment models were appropriate in the past, the realities of current practice indicate that this is no longer feasible.

Information

This model identifies two information domains. The first is labeled *clinical,* the second, *fixed.* Information in the clinical domain requires worker judgment in deciding which items of information, out of a defined range, are relevant to any case, how best to gather relevant information, and how it is to be interpreted. Fixed information remains relatively constant over the life of any case although it may change over time. Agency policy and court decisions, such as those dealing with a client's right to treatment, are examples of information in the fixed domain.

As is the case with clinical information, there is some degree of flexibility in applying fixed information to inform the process of making case decisions. For example, statutory law sets boundaries on the type of child over whom the court can assume jurisdiction. However, the inexactness of the concepts of neglect and abuse provide flexibility when considering whether any child fits within these definitions. Also, some agency policies should not be considered entirely fixed. Dysfunctional policies are an appropriate target for social work intervention.[55] However, such change can be a lengthy process, and because of the time constraints inherent in making appropriate decisions under a model of practice that focuses on specific harms to the child, agency policy is identified here as a fixed element in the information domain.

The central point is that decision making in child welfare is rarely, if ever, a wholly clinical phenomenon in the sense that decisions made by private practitioners may be. From the worker's viewpoint, there is continual interaction between these two information domains wherein fixed information sets limits to the options the worker may select. For example, agency policy may require a court order before a child can be placed in out-of-home care. If the facts of a case do not provide a basis for the court to assume jurisdiction over a child, placement may not be possible even if the worker deems it necessary.

Dichotomizing information into clinical and fixed domains and identifying the variables in each domain can facilitate the development of decision criteria. For example, if the decisions that workers make are isolated and each decision viewed in relation to clinical and fixed information domains, the general data base for the decision can be identified. The data base for some decisions, eligibility for services for instance, may be derived solely from agency policy. For other decisions clinical and fixed domains must be viewed in tandem.

Consider the decision, Should a child be placed in out-of-home care? Agency policy and statutory law may set boundaries for the clinical data base by limiting out-of-home placements to situations where a child has been harmed or is at risk in the near future and where there is evidence that the child cannot be protected in his or her own home.

By focusing on harms to a child, the clinical data base required for decision making is greatly restricted in comparison to situations where parental behaviors or conditions, absent any showing of harm to the child, are sufficient grounds for removal. Rather than focusing on parental behaviors *per se,* the concept of specific harm directs the practitioners' attention to the child's physical and emotional condition. This becomes the starting point for assessment. Bearing in mind that this model of practice is not concerned with long-term prediction, it becomes possible to isolate criteria of harm in both the physical and emotional realm.

The requirement for evidence that a child cannot be protected at home would direct the worker to seek information from case records and collaterals regarding prior efforts to provide at-home services. It would also direct the worker to identify those parental actions that create risk. This assessment would focus on a parent's knowledge of child care including parental expectations for children, behavioral excesses (in terms of discipline, for example), and on behavioral deficits that may have caused an injury or could reasonably be expected to create risk. If harm is identified and those parental actions that create further risk are isolated, the availability of resources and parental willingness to accept services then influence whether the child should be placed.

Program Variables

Program variables that support or constrain a worker's decision-making tasks are shown in the far righthand column of Figure 7.1. Shared consensus on the goals of the child welfare system, on the main processes of realizing goals, and the availability of decision-making criteria are necessary but not sufficient to insure goal-oriented worker behavior. Without support systems that facilitate their use, the development of decision criteria is little more than an academic exercise.

Many facets of social work in child welfare settings are punitive. High case loads, excessive administrative work, demands created by the crisis nature of many worker-client contacts, limited access to supervisory and other professional consultants, and the absence of in-service training programs that focus on development of worker skills (as opposed to those that train for procedural matters) are factors that may negatively affect worker behavior. These difficulties no doubt contribute to the high turnover of child welfare staff, which mitigates against realizing permanency objectives. It can also contribute to staff "fudging" on paperwork by reporting insufficient or incorrect information and to an unwillingness to terminate cases where maintenance is a major activity, since such cases are less demanding of worker time than are new ones where the activity level is relatively high. Recognizing that fiscal incentives are not available and that budgetary constraints may limit the hiring of new staff, it is essential to look elsewhere for incentives for child welfare workers.

Consideration should be given to ways in which administrative paperwork that staff must undertake can be reduced. All data-gathering requirements should be reviewed, and those that are redundant should be eliminated. Computers could be programmed to provide feedback on a selected range of case-specific variables, such as whether there is a written case plan, the date of the next case review, the length of time that children have been in care, and so forth. Or using office-based terminals, workers could use access to an agency's main computer to retrieve case-related materials, thus reducing the amount of time needed to retrieve data from case records.[56] Computerized feedback could also facilitate supervisory case review.

Varying work schedules and rotating job assignments, time off for educational advancement, tuition reimbursements, and opening paths for career advancement to persons whose positions have been considered dead ends have all been used as incentives for public sector employees.[57] Different approaches to case-load management might be an incentive for some staff. For example, case assignment could be predicated on the basis of case activity, where workers carrying new cases would have smaller case loads than workers carrying cases where maintenance is the major activity. Additional consideration should also be given to more differential use of staff and to the use of team or work group methods for allocating responsibility and implementing service plans. (See Chapter 12 for a full discussion of current staffing dilemmas and potential solutions.)

Summary

Decision making in the context of a finite range of systematic goals and the implementation of these decisions is the main business for child welfare personnel. Decisions are formulated in case plans and objectives pursued through the provision of services to children and their families. The information base for decision making involves both clinical and fixed domains. Requiring evidence of harm to a child restricts the clinical information base so that criteria for decision making can be articulated. Such articulation is very difficult if not impossible when concern centers on attaining global goals, due to current limits in social science knowledge, and funding and service resources. Fixed information, such as agency policy and statutory laws, interacts with and sets boundaries around the clinical domain. Agency support systems, including incentives for goal-oriented staff behavior, are essential to attaining systemic goals.

LOOKING AHEAD

Many of the decisions that child welfare workers make have profound consequences for children and their families. Parents may be deprived of their right to raise their children according to their own conscience, and children may be deprived of the right to be raised by their biological parents. Interfering in family relationships is justified when there is evidence to show that parents have violated their social contract to protect their children. When this occurs, a young person's right to safety supersedes the prerogative of parents to retain care, custody, and control of their children. Thus, child welfare staff members must strive to create a balance between the right of parents to raise their children free of outside interference and the right of children to be safeguarded from harm.

When parental autonomy is reduced, a void is created for the child that has typically been filled by the state, which under the doctrine of *in loco parentis* assumes the legal position of a child's parents. Parents do not lose all their rights with respect to their children. Rather, a new balance is created wherein the state assumes the authority to make major decisions for children over whom it has jurisdiction. Historically, children have not been accorded rights independent of those of their parents nor have foster parents had any prerogatives relative to the children in their care. Agencies have been free to place and remove children at will.[58]

As a consequence, until recently, persons in whom the state has vested the authority to act on behalf of children have functioned with relative impunity. The courts and child-caring agencies have been viewed as benevolent, acting to protect children and to further their best interests. The possibility that state action could have negative consequences for youngsters and their families was not seriously entertained. The effects of state action have not been systematically monitored.

Evidence gathered in recent years has shown that intervention by child welfare agencies may exacerbate, rather than ameliorate, family difficulties. Some children have been removed from the care of their parents only to be forgotten—allowed to drift from foster home to foster home with no permanent plans for their future. Services to biological parents have been the exception.[59] While recognizing that many children have benefited from state intervention, there is growing evidence that some youngsters have been maltreated while in state care,[60] despite the fact that they have been placed in state custody for their own protection. This evidence forces a reconsideration of the previously unquestioned assumption that actions taken by state agencies are *ipso facto* beneficial.

Concomitant to the unfolding evidence of state neglect and of maltreatment of children while in state care has been the growth of social movements that are concerned with individual rights. Legally, the concept of rights refers to "enforceable claims to the possession of property or authority, or to the enjoyment of privileges or immunities."[61] This definition sets boundaries on children's rights issues, since it excludes those claims that center on a child's right to continuous loving care or to being raised in a sympathetic community. Despite the importance of such claims, they do not constitute legally enforceable rights. We do not have standards for evaluating whether children are receiving continuous loving care, and it is questionable whether acceptable guidelines could be developed in so heterogenous a society as ours.

The civil rights movement of the 1960s created a *zeitgeist* in which child advocates could assert the notion that children have rights that may be independent of those of their parents. The United States Supreme Court has extended a series of constitutional guarantees to young people. These range from a recognition that children have a right to free speech and a right to privacy to the acknowledgment that young people have the right to certain due process safeguards at the jurisdictional phase in delinquency proceedings including the right to counsel and the right to confront and cross-examine witnesses.[62]

The trend to what has been labeled the constitutionalization of children's rights has provided a framework for litigation against child-caring agencies. The courts "have held that the *in loco parentis* status cannot be used to overcome a child's constitutional rights. Juveniles incarcerated in training school, for example, have a number of constitutional protections including the right to contest confinement, to be free of arbitrary punishment and to receive treatment."[63]

Of special significance for child welfare services has been the suggestion that children have a right to a permanent home and that the psychological bonds that develop over time between a child and his or her substitute caretakers may take precedence over blood ties.[64] The Supreme Court of California made specific reference to the development of psychological bonds when it ruled that foster parents may "appear as parties to assert and protect their own interests in the companionship, care, custody and management of [a] child . . . [for whom they have been providing ongoing care]."[65] While decisions have been equivocal, other courts have recognized a similar right.[66]

Moreover, mechanisms are being established to ensure that agencies take action to facilitate permanency planning for children. For example, the Adoption Assistance and Child Welfare Act of 1980 (see Chapter 3) requires each state to establish a system for case review to ensure that permanent plans are made for children in a timely manner. In an effort to make review an impartial process, the act requires that it be "open to the participation of parents of the child, conducted by a panel of appropriate persons at least one of whom is not responsible for the case management of, or the delivery of services to, either the child or the parents who are the subject of review."[67] To make review more substantive, thus reducing the chances that it will be the "rubber stamping" process that has characterized many review procedures in the past, the act also requires that case plans be formulated and sets specifications for case planning.[68]

Other examples of efforts to safeguard client rights can be cited. The Juvenile Justice Standards Project of the American Bar Association has promulgated guidelines for presenting evidence in court, which, if adopted, would require workers to present factual information in support of their recommendations rather than the uncorroborated, inferential documentation that has long characterized social reports.[69] In a similar vein, the National Council of Juvenile and Family Court Judges has set forth procedural guidelines for judges to follow during review hearings including standards for workers to follow in presenting information in the court.[70] Add to this the efforts to articulate a more restrictive standard for decision making, and one is left with a picture of systemic changes that constitute a dramatic departure from the usual reporting, review, and decision-making practices. These changes portend to alter social work practice in child welfare radically.

Implications for practice are not difficult to discern. The increased formality of the juvenile court occasioned by the extension of due process rights to young people, the willingness of the court to accord rights to foster parents and to recognize that children have rights that may be independent of those of their biological parents, plus the mechanisms that are being put in place to monitor the actions of child-caring agencies all point to the creation of a legal framework around this area of social work practice.

Workers can expect that "guidelines for gathering and recording data during assessment and investigation, case planning and service delivery will stress the acquisition of factual, rather than impressionistic, information and will emphasize recording in a descriptive, as opposed to an inferential manner. Workers will have to become familiar with legal rules regarding evidence in order to determine what to look for during investigations and what will be admissible in court."[71] The personal discretion that has typified social work and judicial decision making can be expected to yield to requirements that recommendations be supported by factual evidence. Practitioners will have to consider the respective rights of each party involved in a case and to consider that the interests of these parties may differ. The negotiations that workers will have to undertake when the goals of biological parents, foster parents, and children differ will require a very different set of skills than are commonly associated with practice. Child welfare workers will have to sustain their positions with objective information showing why any one recommendation is more sound than any other.

CONCLUSION

For more than two decades professional social workers have highlighted the need to articulate procedures for decision making in child welfare. It is paradoxical to consider that efforts to respond to this imperative have been hindered by good intentions. We have pursued objectives in serving children and their families that reach beyond current knowledge and resources. And there is reason to question society's willingness even to develop policies and fund basic programs designed to ensure that the objectives currently within our grasp can be attained.

Today, given the emergence of a legal framework around practice, the issue of developing guidelines for decision making assumes a greater urgency than at any time in the past. A willingness to recognize our limitations and to proceed to assist families within recognizable limits may, in the final analysis, increase the likelihood that our efforts will indeed serve the best interest of children and their families while simultaneously respecting their rights.

NOTES

1. The future of social work services to children in their own homes as distinct from protective services is not clear. It is plausible that all social work services to children in their own homes will be provided through protective service units. See *Preliminary Statement on Social Work Service for Children in Their Own Homes* (New York: The Child Welfare League of America, 1977), Foreword.

2. Ann W. Shyne and Anita G. Schroeder, *National Study of Social Services to Children and Their Families* (Washington, D.C.: United States Children's Bureau, DHEW Publication No. (OHDS) 78-30150, 1978), p. 62.

3. See Theodore J. Stein, *Social Work Practice in Child Welfare* (Englewood Cliffs, N.J.: Prentice-Hall, 1981), Chapter 5.

4. William Ryan and Laura B. Morris, *Child Welfare: Problems and Potentials* (Boston: Massachusetts Committee on Children and Youth, 1967); Theodore J. Stein, "A Content Analysis of Social Caseworker and Client Interaction in Foster Care" (D.S.W. dissertation, University of California, Berkeley, 1974).

5. Bernice Boehm, "An Assessment of Family Adequacy in Protective Cases," *Child Welfare* 41 (January 1962): 10–16.

6. Bernice Boehm, "Protective Services for Neglected Children," in *Social Work Practice: Proceedings of the National Conference on*

Social Welfare (New York: Columbia University Press, 1967), pp. 109–25; Eugene B. Shinn, "Is Placement Necessary?: An Experimental Study of Agreement Among Caseworkers in Making Foster Care Decisions" (D.S.W. dissertation, Columbia University, 1969); Michael H. Phillips et al., *Factors Associated with Placement Decisions in Child Welfare* (New York: Child Welfare League of America, 1971).

7. Scott Briar, "Clinical Judgment in Foster Care Placement," *Child Welfare* 42 (April 1963): 161–69.

8. Kenneth Cross et al., "Decision Making Processes Utilized by a Selected Agency in Placing Children Referred for Neglect" (M.S.W. thesis, Arizona State University, 1966), as cited in Edmund V. Mech, "Decision Analysis in Foster Care Practice," in *Foster Care in Question: A National Reassessment by Twenty-One Experts,* ed. Helen D. Stone (New York: Child Welfare League of America, 1970), pp. 26–51.

9. Martin Wolins, *Selecting Foster Parents* (New York: Columbia University Press, 1963).

10. Donald Brieland, *An Experimental Study in the Selection of Adoptive Parents at Intake* (New York: Child Welfare League of America, 1959).

11. Joan W. DiLeonard, "Decision Making in Protective Services," *Child Welfare* 59 (June 1980): 356–64; Saad Z. Nagi, *Child Maltreatment in the United States: A Challenge to Social Institutions* (New York: Columbia University Press, 1977).

12. Boehm, "Protective Services for Neglected Children."

13. Shinn, "Is Placement Necessary?"

14. Phillips et al., *Factors Associated with Placement Decisions.*

15. Ryan and Morris, *Child Welfare: Problems and Potentials.*

16. Stein, "A Content Analysis."

17. Phillips et al., *Factors Associated with Placement Decisions,* p. 84.

18. Wollins, *Selecting Foster Parents,* pp. 72–73.

19. Nagi, *Child Maltreatment in the United States,* pp. 89–93; Shyne and Schroeder, *National Study,* p. 156.

20. Briar, "Clinical Judgment."

21. Ibid., p. 167; Phillips et al., *Factors Associated with Placement Decisions,* p. 84; Hillary Rodham, "Children Under the Law," *Harvard Educational Review* 43 (1974): 1–28; Robert H. Mnookin, "Child Custody Adjudication: Judicial Function in the Face of Indeterminancy," *Law and Contemporary Problems* 39 (Summer

1975): 226–93; Michael Wald, "State Intervention on Behalf of 'Neglected' Children: A Search for Realistic Standards," *Stanford Law Review* 27 (April 1975): 1034; Arthur Emlen et al., *Overcoming Barriers to Planning for Children in Foster Care* (Portland, Ore.: Portland State University, 1977), pp. 43–44; Boehm, "Family Adequacy," p. 10.

22. Sanford N. Katz et al., "Child Neglect Laws in America," *Family Law Quarterly* 9 (January 1975): 5.

23. Rodham, "Children Under the Law," p. 4; Sanford N. Katz, *When Parents Fail: The Law's Response to Family Breakdown* (Boston: Beacon Press, 1971), pp. 62–63.

24. Walter Barnett, *Sexual Freedom and the Constitution: An Inquiry Into the Constitutionality of Repressive Sex Laws* (Albuquerque, N.M.: University of New Mexico Press, 1973), p. 21.

25. Michael S. Wald, "Thinking About Public Policy Toward Abuse and Neglect of Children: A Review of 'Before the Best Interests of the Child,'" *Michigan Law Review* 78 (March 1980): 650.

26. Wald, "State Intervention," p. 1034; Rodham, "Children Under the Law," pp. 4–5.

27. Theodore J. Stein, *Social Work Practice in Child Welfare,* © 1981, pp. 136–137. Reprinted by permission of Prentice-Hall, Inc., Englewood Cliffs, N.J.

28. Arlene Skolnick, *The Intimate Environment: Exploring Marriage and the Family,* 2nd ed. (Boston: Little, Brown, and Co., 1978), p. 354; Sheldon H. White et al., *Federal Programs for Young Children: Review and Recommendations,* Vol. 1: *Goals and Standards of Public Programs for Children* (Washington, D.C.: Superintendent of Documents, 1973), p. 130; Joseph Goldstein, Anna Freud, and Albert J. Solnit, *Beyond the Best Interests of the Child* (New York: The Free Press, 1973), p. 6.

29. Skolnick, *The Intimate Environment,* p. 353.

30. Ibid., p. 354.

31. Ibid.

32. Jerome Kagan, "The Parental Love Trap," *Psychology Today* 12 (August 1978): 54–61, 91.

33. For a review of this subject, see Albert Bandura, *Principles of Behavior Modification* (New York: Holt, Rinehart and Winston, 1969), Chapter 9.

34. Phillips, et al., *Factors Associated with Placement Decisions,* p. 2.

35. See, for example, ibid.; Rita Dukette, *Structured Assessment: A*

Decision-Making Guide for Child Welfare (Chicago: U.S. Department of Health, Education and Welfare, Region V, April 1978).

36. Brieland, *An Experimental Study;* Stein, "A Content Analysis," p. 278; Naomi Golan, "How Caseworkers Decide: A Study of the Association of Selected Applicant Factors with Worker Decision in Admission Services," *Social Service Review* 43 (1969): 289–96.

37. Nagi, *Child Maltreatment in the United States*, p. 15.

38. Scott Briar and Henry Miller, *Problems and Issues in Social Casework* (New York: Columbia University Press, 1971), p. 42.

39. Kermit T. Wiltse, "Current Issues and New Directions in Foster Care," in *Child Welfare Strategy in the Coming Years* (Washington, D.C.: U.S. Department of Health, Education and Welfare, DHEW Publication No. (OHDS) 78-30158, 1978), pp. 61–64.

40. See, for example, Shyne and Schroeder, *National Study*, p. 58; Report of the Comptroller General of the United States, *Increased Federal Efforts Needed to Better Identify, Treat and Prevent Child Abuse and Neglect* (Washington, D.C.: General Accounting Office, HRD-80-66 (April 29, 1980), p. 36. For a review of additional studies on this subject, see Theodore J. Stein, Eileen D. Gambrill, and Kermit T. Wiltse, *Children in Foster Homes: Achieving Continuity of Care* (New York: Praeger Publishers, 1978), p. 13.

41. Jane Knitzer, Mary Lee Allen, and Brenda McGowan, *Children Without Homes: An Examination of Public Responsibility to Children in Out-of-Home Care* (Washington, D.C.: Children's Defense Fund, 1978), p. 123; Jessica S. Pers, *Government as Parent: Administering Foster Care in California* (Berkeley, Calif.: Institute of Governmental Studies, University of California, 1976), p. 83; The Adoption Assistance and Child Welfare Act of 1980, P.L. 96-272, holds promise for correcting this situation. The law places special emphasis on the prevention of placement and on reunifying children with their biological families, and it allows for federal funds to support voluntary placement without a judicial order. See John A. Calhoun, "The 1980 Child Welfare Act," *Children Today* 9 (September–October 1980): 2–4, 36.

42. See, for example, Mnookin, "Child Custody Adjudication"; Institute of Judicial Administration, American Bar Association, Juvenile Justice Standards Project, *Standards Relating to Abuse and Neglect: Tentative Draft* (Cambridge, Mass.: Ballinger Publishing Co., 1977); Goldstein, Freud, Solnit, *Beyond the Best Interests of the*

Child; Joseph Goldstein, Anna Freud, and Albert J. Solnit, *Before the Best Interests of the Child* (New York: The Free Press, 1979).

43. For a review of this subject, see Stein, Gambrill, and Wiltse, *Children in Foster Homes,* pp. 12–14.

44. Ibid., pp. 14–15.

45. *Child Abuse and Neglect in Residential Institutions: Selected Readings on Prevention, Investigation, and Correction* (Washington, D.C.: National Center on Child Abuse and Neglect, U.S. Department of Health, Education and Welfare, DHEW Publication No. (OHDS) 78-30160, 1978); Knitzer et al., *Children Without Homes,* Chapter 2.

46. Jeanne M. Giovannoni and Rosina M. Becerra, *Defining Child Abuse* (New York: The Free Press, 1979), p. 235.

47. See, for example, Alan R. Gruber, *Children in Foster Care: Destitute, Neglected, Betrayed* (New York: Human Sciences Press, 1978), p. 37.

48. Robert H. Mnookin, "Foster Care—In Whose Best Interest?" *Harvard Educational Review* 43 (1974): 158–97; Wald, "State Intervention," p. 1023.

49. Ibid., p. 1033.

50. It is possible to return a child contingent upon the parent's not having male visitors overnight or not frequenting taverns. However, it is all but impossible to establish a satisfactory level of proof that these changes are permanent.

51. Boehm, "An Assessment of Family Adequacy."

52. David Fanshel and Eugene B. Shinn, *Children in Foster Care: A Longitudinal Investigation* (New York: Columbia University Press, 1978), Chapter 4.

53. Wiltse, "Current Issues," p. 61.

54. Shyne and Schroeder, *National Study,* p. 77.

55. For further discussion of this topic see, for example, Brenda G. McGowan, "Strategies in Bureaucracies," in *Working for Children: Ethical Issues Beyond Professional Guidelines,* ed. Judith Mearig (San Francisco: Jossey-Bass, 1978), pp. 155–80: George Brager and Stephen Holloway, *Changing Human Service Organizations: Politics and Practice* (New York: The Free Press, 1978).

56. Dick Schoech and Lawrence L. Schkade, "Computers Helping Caseworkers: Decision Support Systems," *Child Welfare* 59 (November 1980): 566–75.

57. National Commission on Productivity and Work Quality, *Employee Incentives to Improve State and Local Government Productivity* (Washington, D.C.: U.S. Government Printing Office, stock number 052-003-00090, March 1975).

58. *Legal Issues in Foster Care* (Raleigh, N.C.: National Association of Attorneys General, Committee on the Office of Attorney General, 1976), pp. 21–27.

59. For a review of studies on these subjects, see Stein, Gambrill, and Wiltse, *Children in Foster Homes,* Chapter 2.

60. See *Child Abuse and Neglect in Residential Institutions.*

61. See Rodham, "Children Under the Law," p. 2.

62. Donald Brieland and John Lemmon, *Social Work and the Law* (St. Paul, Minn.: West Publishing Co., 1977), p. 154.

63. Carol M. Rose, *Some Emerging Issues in Legal Liability of Children's Agencies* (New York: Child Welfare League of America, 1978), pp. 5–6, 8.

64. Goldstein, Freud, and Solnit, *Beyond the Best Interests;* Goldstein, Freud, and Solnit, *Before the Best Interests.*

65. *Children's Rights Report,* vol. 1., no. 4 (New York: Juvenile Rights Project of the American Civil Liberties Union Foundation, December 1976–January 1977), pp. 4–5.

66. *Legal Issues in Foster Care,* Chapter 3.

67. *Adoption Assistance and Child Welfare Act of 1980,* P.L. 96-272, p. 11.

68. Ibid., pp. 3, 10.

69. Institute of Judicial Administration, American Bar Association, Juvenile Justice Standards Project, *Standards Relating to Juvenile Records and Information Systems: Tentative Draft* (Cambridge, Mass.: Ballinger Publishing Co., 1977), p. 71.

70. Roberta Gottesman, *Bench Book: Post-Dispositional Periodic Review* (Washington, D.C.: unpublished manuscript, 1979), pp. 54–55; John P. Steketee, "The CIP Story," *Juvenile Justice* 28 (May 1977): pp. 3–14.

71. Stein, *Social Work Practice,* p. 265.

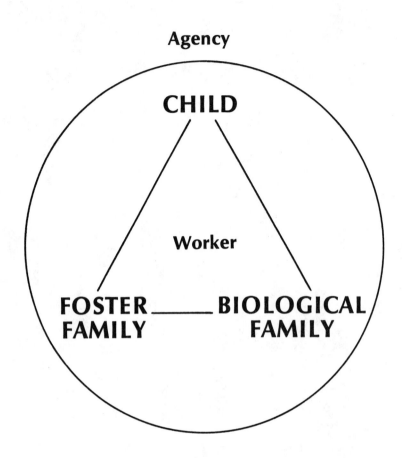

CHAPTER 8
MAKING FOSTER FAMILY CARE RESPONSIVE

Karen Blumenthal

In earlier chapters a number of strong arguments were presented for the development and utilization of services that maintain family integrity and keep children within their own homes. However, it must be recognized that this is not always possible or desirable. In some situations children, if left within their family units, will suffer severe physical and emotional harm. In other situations children need specialized help, which cannot be provided within their family environments. In these situations foster family care can be an appropriate service for children and their families.

When the term "foster family care" is used in this chapter, it refers to the provision of *planned, time-limited, substitute family care for children who cannot be adequately maintained at home, and the simultaneous provision of social services to these children and their families to help resolve the problems that led to the need for placement.* A number of critical concepts are embodied in this definition.

1. Foster family care is planned. What happens while children are in care is not left to chance. Decisions are made by foster care workers, parents, children, and foster parents about their mutual goals, tasks, and responsibilities.
2. Foster family care is time-limited. Children should not, under most circumstances, remain in foster care indefinitely. It is a temporary service provided to children and their families for a limited, agreed upon period. At the end of this period the children should be living in a stable, permanent home in which the potential for support, love, and ongoing commitment is present.

3. Foster family care is provided only when children cannot be adequately maintained within their own families. It should be utilized only when less disruptive alternatives have been explored and have been found to be unworkable or when specific conditions exist in the home that are dangerous to the children.

4. Foster family care is not limited to the provision of physical care and should not be conceptualized as a service for children alone. A range of services should be available to children and their families that help to remediate the situation that led to the need for placement and result in the reunification of families or the development of alternative permanent plans for the children.

If foster family care is to conform to this definition, several requirements must be met. The family and child should be involved in planning with the worker, so that their individualized needs can be identified. This should result in the formulation of a service plan in which these needs are articulated and the goals of placement are established. Services should then be provided to both children and their families. Families should be helped to enhance their functioning and maintain their ties to their children in placement, so that parental care can be reestablished as quickly and expediently as possible. If it is determined that parental ties cannot be maintained, services leading to the termination of parental rights should be initiated, so that an alternative permanent home can be established.[1] (See Chapters 7, 10, and 11 for further discussion of this issue.) Children should be provided with services to insure that both their basic (supervision, education, health care, recreation, and other) and specialized needs are met. There should be continuous monitoring of the service plan and the services provided. This helps to insure that the needed services are delivered, that progress toward goals is evaluated regularly, and that revisions in the service plan are made when appropriate and necessary. Finally, foster care should result in the establishment of permanent homes for children, either with their biological parents or in new families. It is generally believed that foster care must be predicated on the principle that *foster care workers, biological parents, foster parents, and children form a team of individuals who are all working together toward a common goal: a permanent plan for a family.* All should understand as fully as their individual capacities permit the objectives and goals of foster care, the services needed and available to meet these goals, their respective rights and responsibilities in attaining these goals, and the consequences if these goals are not reached. Open communication between the various parties is essential so that important information related to objectives, goals, and responsibilities is shared.

Unfortunately, the child welfare literature is replete with books, reports, and articles indicating that these practice requirements have often been ignored in the past. Some children entered the placement system too easily[2] because alternative resources did not exist or were not utilized. Foster home care was generally not utilized as a short-term service; children remained in foster homes for unconscionably long periods of time.[3] The focus of services was rarely on the biological family; parents were virtually discouraged if not prohibited from having anything to do with their children once they were placed in a foster home.[4] Case records frequently did not contain written case plans that identified clear goals, tasks, and responsibilities; moreover, if goals and expectations existed, they were rarely shared with parents.[5] The fact that foster care required timely decision making went virtually unrecognized.

The tendency in the past was to focus agency attention on the children in care and their foster parents. Traditionally, large portions of workers' time were spent attempting to insure that the foster parents were providing a nurturing environment for the child and that the child was making an adequate adjustment in care.[6] Despite these efforts, stability in placement and continuity of care were not achieved; many children experienced multiple placements.[7] The needs of biological parents were often ignored by foster care workers and foster parents. As a result, the conditions that led to placement did not change, and many parents were neither encouraged nor provided with the services which would enable them to reunite their families. Their children languished in care, experiencing foster care "drift."[8]

The foster care picture appears much brighter today as a result of the impact of several research efforts and demonstration projects.[9] Major attitudinal, policy, and programmatic changes have occurred throughout the country.[10] The changes, which have affected agency practice with biological parents, foster parents, and children, will be discussed in this chapter.

THE BIOLOGICAL PARENTS

Biological parents are critical to the success of foster care service. Without their active involvement in services, it is unlikely that the family unit can be reestablished within a reasonable time period or that an alternate permanent plan will be achieved for their child. This section addresses the ways in which biological parents should be involved in preplacement planning, service planning after entrance, and ongoing service provision.

Preplacement Planning

Parents experience a variety of feelings at the point when their child enters the foster care system. These can range from relief to sadness to anger.[11] No matter what their particular feelings, it is essential to provide parents with the help needed to resolve their conflicts about the placement and their feelings about separation from their child. Developing a trusting, supportive relationship at this early point, while often difficult, enables the worker to carry out important tasks during the preplacement period and facilitates constructive work during the placement.

During the preplacement period, information concerning foster care services, agency policies and procedures, and the respective rights and responsibilities of parents and agency should be reviewed. Biological parents should understand what is involved in the use of foster care service and the importance of their continued involvement and contact with their children while they are in care and with the continuing service worker. They should also be cognizant of the possible consequences of their inaction, including termination of parental rights. Only then can they be informed consumers of foster care service.

In order to accomplish this, some foster care agencies have prepared handbooks designed specifically for biological parents. Figure 8.1 is the table of contents from such a handbook. It answers the important questions that many parents have about foster care. Parents cannot be *made* to read such handbooks. However, by distributing them to parents and taking the time to highlight their contents, and preparing them in all relevant languages, the worker can at least be assured that parents have been informed that they retain specific rights and that they are expected to assume certain responsibilities while their children are in care.

A typical list of these parental rights and responsibilities is displayed in Figure 8.2. These rights are aimed at fostering a continued relationship and involvement between the parent and child—a necessary prerequisite to the child's return home. Parental responsibilities are also directed toward the goal of returning the child home.

During the preplacement period, discussion should also focus on the responsibilities that the agency carries while a child is in foster care. These include the provision of food, clothing, shelter, education, medical care, and supervision to the child and most importantly, the provision of services to the parents to help them resolve the problems that

FIGURE 8.1 SAMPLE CONTENTS OF HANDBOOK FOR BIOLOGICAL PARENTS
Source: *The Parents' Handbook: A Guide for Parents of Children in Foster Care,* New York City Special Services For Children, January 1977.

resulted in placement. Such services are designed to insure that timely decisions are made concerning the child's future. Ensuring that the child returns to a permanent, stable home as expeditiously as possible should be acknowledged as the goal of foster care. In conjunction with this,

1. Your Rights

- To work together with your caseworker in making the plan for your child.
- To be consulted whenever a change in the plan is being considered.
- To know what the agency expects you to do before your child is returned to you.
- To visit your child. You and your caseworker together will decide how often, when and where you should visit your child. You have the right to be alone with your child, and perhaps to have your child spend an afternoon with you outside the agency or visit you at home if that is part of the plan. Family Court Judges and SSC have the right to limit visiting if they decide that it will not be good for your child.
- To appeal a decision limiting your visiting rights.
- To be given carfare for your visiting, if you are financially eligible for it.
- To meet the people who directly care for your child, such as counselors, houseparents or foster parents.
- To get reports from your caseworker on your child's health and development, progress in school, and behavior.
- To receive help and/or counseling for problems which need to be resolved before your child can return home.
- To receive help, if needed, for your children who remain at home with you.
- To have your child receive religious training if you have asked for it.
- To approve surgery or serious medical care if needed by your child, except when you cannot be reached in an emergency.
- To be notified as soon as possible of any serious medical emergency, and if any major treatment is given without your consent.
- To have your complaints listened to and responded to by the agency.
- To receive notice of and to attend any Court action held about your child or about your parental rights, except if the Court acts in an emergency.
- To consult with a lawyer at any time, and to be represented by a lawyer in any Court action concerning your child or affecting your parental rights. (If you want a lawyer, see Section G.)

2. Your Responsibilities

- To work with your caseworker in setting up the plan for what **you** must do while your child is in care, and for what will be best for your child's future.
- To work toward solving the problems which prevent your child from coming home to you. If your caseworker advises you to go somewhere to get help for a problem, you should follow up on that suggestion.
- To visit your child regularly, at a time and place agreed upon with the agency caseworker. This is so important that the law says that if you are able to visit your child but make infrequent visits, you could lost your parental rights. If you cannot visit, you must tell the caseworker why, and make every effort to call your child or write regularly.
- To talk about your child's care and progress with your caseworker.
- To tell your caseworker about major changes in your life, such as change of address, telephone number, job, income, marriage or other living arrangements and changes affecting other members of your family.
- To keep appointments with your caseworker. If you cannot keep an appointment or must cancel a visit, let your caseworker know.
- To answer letters that agency workers send to you. If your worker asks for information about your child, it is very important that you provide it.
- To pay toward the cost of your child's care, if you are found to be able to do so. You must tell your caseworker if your income changes.

FIGURE 8.2 RIGHTS AND RESPONSIBILITIES OF BIOLOGICAL PARENTS OF CHILDREN IN FOSTER CARE
Source: *The Parents' Handbook: A Guide for Parents of Children in Foster Care*, New York City Special Services for Children, January 1977.

parents should be aware that there will be careful monitoring of progress toward goals; for example, there will be continuous review of the service agreement between the parents and worker, and there may be an administrative, citizen, and/or judicial case review to insure that goals are met. While this should be conveyed in a sensitive, nonthreatening way, the parents must understand agency expectations clearly regarding their continued contact and involvement with their child and the agency.

When the parents agree that foster care is necessary, a voluntary placement or entrustment agreement is discussed and signed. This agreement, often a standardized form, transfers the care and custody of the child from the parent to the agency or public department of social services. It is becoming increasingly common for agreements of this type to stipulate a time period during which care will be provided and to provide a list of general rights and responsibilities of the parents and agency. The parents should be informed at the time the agreement is signed that a service agreement will be drawn up at a later date that will be concerned with their specific situation and needs of their family.

Although parents of children who are placed in foster care as a result of a court order do not sign a voluntary placement agreement, it is equally important for them to understand their rights and responsibilities. It should be made clear that court placement does *not* mean that the child cannot go home; the initial goal of foster care remains the reestablishment of the family through the provision and utilization of needed services.

The process of finding the right foster family for a particular child can be very time-consuming. While the child's needs and the availability of foster families are the most important factors guiding the placement decision, parents should be assured that their desires related to the care provided to the child will also be taken into account whenever possible. When possible, they should be involved in the process of choosing the foster family and should be informed about the progress made toward identifying the best foster family.

Whenever possible, parents should be encouraged to make a preplacement visit to the specific foster home chosen for their child. This allows them to have a firsthand view of the foster family and the home environment and provides them an opportunity to share information about their child. Furthermore, a successful preplacement visit can pave the way for a positive relationship between the biological parents and the foster family while the child is in placement.

Finally, the parents should be encouraged and helped to talk with the child about the decision regarding placement, for example, why it is necessary, what it will be like, how the parent will continue to see the child and take an active interest in his or her activities.[12] Such a dialogue can help to relieve the child's anxiety and confusion about placement and sustain the child in the transition from own home to foster home.

It should be pointed out that the process described here is the ideal. A substantial proportion of children in foster care enter under emergency conditions where there is no time to engage in preplacement planning. In other instances, children are placed in care by local juvenile and family courts. Foster care workers may not become involved in these cases until after the child is placed. In such cases, much of what has been discussed above needs to be done as soon as possible after the placement, since parents whose children are placed involuntarily also need to know and understand their rights and responsibilities.

Service Planning

Either before or shortly after children are separated from their parents, a service plan for the family needs to be developed and recorded in the case record. Early case planning enhances the possibility that permanence will be achieved, since parents will not yet have adjusted to their loss and may be more highly motivated to resolve family problems, and children will not yet have settled into relationships with their foster parents. Such early planning may facilitate the reunification of families.

The placement service plan is developed as a result of meetings involving the biological parents, the agency worker, and the children. Foster parents, members of the child's extended family who might play a significant role in the child's future, and other service providers who will work with the family may also be involved in this process. Every effort should be made to encourage parents and children to discuss their situations, the goals of foster care, and how these goals can be accomplished. To this end the worker can act as an adviser, teacher, and facilitator to the family and can identify possible options for them. Insofar as possible the plan should reflect their views and desires.

The essential components of a service plan include:

—The specific circumstances/problems that necessitated the child's placement in foster care

—The changes that must take place before the child can return home; these must be specific, realistic, measurable and/or observable

—The anticipated length of the placement

—The specific actions to be taken and/or services to be provided by the agency in correcting the conditions that led to placement

—The specific actions to be taken by the parents in correcting the conditions that led to placement

—The specific actions to be taken by the child in correcting the conditions that led to placement

—The services to be provided by other community resources to help bring about the necessary changes

—The parent-child visiting arrangements including frequency, location, length, timing, and participants

—The approximate duration of services and the dates by which it is reasonable to expect the necessary changes to occur. (This sets the parameters for the service program and insures that all concerned parties are cognizant of these time frames.)

—A time schedule for periodic assessment of the progress that has been made toward established goals.

Although placement service plans are recorded in the case record, modifications can be made as circumstances change. Furthermore, parents should have their own copy of the plan, so that they can refer to it whenever they wish to review specific provisions.

Service plans in the case record can be complemented by a written service agreement or contract between the biological parents and the agency. However, there has been considerable debate concerning the value of these agreements within the field. Proponents view their use positively for several reasons. First, the agreement is seen as an affirmation of the agency's desire to bring about the child's return home. Second, it clearly presents the agency's expectations of the parents and of its own staff. Third, it is a tool that allows the parents and worker to measure movement toward case goals because it is change-oriented, service-specific, and time-limited. Fourth, it provides a mechanism by which the parent can hold the agency accountable for the provision of services. Finally, it provides a means through which the agency can assess parental commitment to the goal of return home. Such contracts have been a component of several major successful permanency planning projects.[13]

However, others feel that formulating service agreements in writing is counterproductive and inconsistent with the cultural norms of many of the families involved in foster care. The opponents of written contracts feel that a person's word should be sufficient and that written agreements may demonstrate a lack of trust by the worker.[14]

As written contracts have been a helpful tool in many situations, it is probably sensible to encourage their use. However, discussion about this should take place, and the decision to develop a written service plan should respect individual and cultural differences. If used, written contracts need to be time-limited and phrased in clear, concise, and understandable language. The fact that provisions of the agreement can and should be modified as necessary should be stressed. This insures that the agreement continues to reflect the reality of the situation and the current needs of the parent and child. Also, the parents' right to have someone they trust (a friend, relative, or lawyer) review the contract with them to insure that they understand their rights and responsibilities in its implementation should be protected.

The worker should consult with other service providers before the service contract is signed, if these providers have agreed to assume specific responsibilities in carrying out the terms of the agreement. Consultation can help insure that services needed by the family and agreed to in the contract are actually delivered. Figure 8.3 is a sample of the type of service agreement form that can be utilized.

One element of the service planning process which deserves special attention is parent-child visiting. Research has demonstrated that the well-being of children in foster care is often related to patterns of parental visiting and that visiting is not only the best predicator of discharge from care, but that it is positively related to the amount of service a family receives.[15] Such findings demand that attempts be made to influence the frequency and quality of visiting and that visiting begin as soon as possible after placement. Because of its importance, parental visiting can be seen as the cornerstone of service planning. Regular visits provide children with the opportunity to see their parents realistically. It can reassure them of their parents' love and concern, and provide their parents with the opportunity to see and learn about their progress and development. It can also serve as a positive force in enhancing parental cooperation and efforts to change.[16]

The facilitation and encouragement of visiting thus becomes a crucial task, and the removal of artificial barriers to visiting becomes a major goal for supervisors and administrators. While visiting sometimes may be problematic,[17] its importance requires that an atmosphere be created that supports visiting by parents and other members of the nuclear and extended family. Agency workers need to act as enablers to the parents in matters of visiting, and administrators should not allow visiting to be circumscribed, limited, or prevented by staff passivity or resistance, the use of foster homes in geographically inaccessible areas, or by resource limitations including lack of funds for transportation.

Agency policies in this area must be flexible enough to accommodate

I (We) _____ , the parents(s) (guardian)(s) of

_____ want my (our) child(ren) returned home

permanently by _____
                     specific date or achievement of

_____
                     specific condition(s)

I (We) know there are the following problems that must be resolved before
my (our) child(ren) can return home:
1.
2.
3.
4.
In order to work toward the goal of having my(our) child(ren) return home,
I (we) will:
1.
2.
3.
4.
5.
To help me achieve the goal of return home, _____
will: DSS social worker
1.
2.
3.
4.
5.
I(We) _____ understand that if I(we) fail
          name of parent(s) or guardian(s)
to meet the terms of this agreement, I(we) may be asked to relinquish
my(our) parental rights to my(our) children or the Department of Social
Services may petition the court for guardianship with the right to consent
to adoption.

My(Our) efforts at successfully completing the tasks will be evaluated with

me(us) and _____ at our regular meetings. We
                     worker
may modify specific terms of the agreement if we agree that doing so is
indicated.

This agreement will continue in effect until _____.

Signature:

Date:

FIGURE 8.3. SAMPLE WRITTEN AGREEMENT FORM
Source: Author

a wide range of parental situations. Rigid requirements and prohibitions (for example, that visiting may only take place once a month; visits may only last one hour; visits may only occur in the foster parents' home; visits may not take place during the evening, on weekends, or holidays; or visiting may not begin until the child has been in care for three months) should be prohibited because flexibility in visiting can enhance the relationship between parents, child, and agency.

In order to enhance the parent-child relationship during placement, visiting should be as natural an interaction as possible. While observation of an occasional visit may be an important aspect of placement planning and monitoring, supervision of every visit should be avoided unless it is determined that visits could be dangerous to the child. When information is obtained during observation of visits it should be placed in the case record, for it can be used to assess the quality of interaction between the parent and child and to monitor the service plan. Frequency and consistency of parental visits, cancellations of visits, reactions to visiting, problems during visiting, responses to agency attempts to encourage and enhance visiting, and the necessity to supervise visits can all be indicators of the level of goal achievement in foster care.

In addition to visits, other contacts between parents and their children should be encouraged. Phone calls, letters, and cards are important "reminders of caring" for all children in foster care. They are especially important when parents are hospitalized or incarcerated, although in such cases appropriate special efforts to have children visit these parents should also be made. Consideration should also be given to transporting the children to their parents' homes when parents are unable to visit, or when there are other children in the home who require the presence of the parents.

Visiting is not an end in itself but a means to an end. Therefore, parents should understand that visiting is a responsibility as well as a right, and workers may have to make extraordinary efforts to encourage and facilitate it. Workers may also need to remind some parents that their failure to carry out this responsibility endangers their continuing relationship with their child.*

Ongoing Service Provision

Competent, conscientious provision of services to biological parents is a critical aspect of the foster care process. Without such services paren-

---

*For further discussion of the many issues involved in parental visiting, see Anita Weinberg and Karen Blumenthal, "Issues Relating to Parental Visitation of Foster Children," in *Foster Children in the Courts,* ed. Mark Handlin (Newton Upper Falls, Mass.: Butterworth Legal Publications, in press), Chapter 14.

tal change is less likely, and the foster care service can continue indefinitely. Service planning is an empty exercise when responsibilities are not carried out and there is no ongoing evaluation of progress.

The first task that must be attended to if service provision is to be effective is the development of the worker-parent relationship.[18] Callard and Morin comment:

> A cooperative and trusting relationship with the client is an essential precursor of successful service. Although the establishment of the relationship and the commencement of service may overlap . . . no substantial progress is made unless the counselor's perception of the need for change agrees with that of the client. . . . During the first month of client contact, counselors work toward laying the foundation for this relationship. . . . The counselors convincingly convey to the client that he or she and the family are valuable, and establish rapport with the client. . . . An optimistic posture toward the client's interest in progressing is essential.[19]

The task of developing the worker-parent relationship is often complicated by the fact that many of the children in foster care come from families where there are severe problems and where the parents are described as "hard to reach" because "they avoid or reject the services that hold some promise of helping them to deal more effectively with the problems that led to placement."[20] But as Horejsi and associates note:

> Despite the difficulties involved, it is possible to reach most of these parents and engage them in a helping process; however, it takes much time, effort and an application of techniques that make social workers rather uncomfortable . . . aggressive casework.[21]

Workers often have divergent views about the most effective means of reaching such families, and successful outreach programs have utilized a range of practice approaches. The following principles for developing working relationships with parents of children in foster care, originally identified by staff of the St. Paul Family Centered Project as related to the success of programs dealing with hard-to-reach families, are suggested:

—Direct and relentless outreach to families, even when they [are] not asking for help and even when they actively [resist] professional intervention
—Steadfast conviction and optimism that even the most troubled and chaotic families [can] make positive changes
—Frank and completely aboveboard communication with the families, including the sharing of agency records and agency reports
—Giving more attention to the needs of the parents than to those of the children

—Focusing on what the family [want], not on what the worker, agency, or community [want] for the family
—Building a working relationship by demonstrating to the family that a professional [can] be of use to them in practical and tangible ways
—Extensive use of home visits, family interviews, and extraordinary efforts to involve the fathers
—Emphasis on the family as a system in assessment and treatment
—Designation of one professional person as the coordinator of all services received by a family even when those many services [are] coming from a variety of different agencies[22]

Once a relationship is established, there are many ways in which the worker can assist parents while their children are in foster care. The first involves implementing the assumption that all parents have some capacity to "parent." It is essential for agencies to demonstrate a belief in this capacity and to provide parents opportunities to demonstrate it. These opportunities might include shopping for toys, clothing, and educational supplies for their children; arranging for and accompanying children to medical and dental exams; meeting with teachers, making decisions about school curriculum, and signing report cards; involving the parents in decisions concerning discipline; and arranging picnics, parties, and social activities involving parents and their children.[23] The opportunity to perform these tasks should be based on parental capacity and a clear understanding of the differential roles of biological and foster parents. As parental capacity increases, so also should child-caring opportunities. With the resolution of the problems that led to placement, parents should be encouraged to fulfill as many parental roles as possible in order to facilitate children's transition from foster care back to their own homes.

Parents should also be provided with ongoing meaningful services during the placement.[24] The degree of support provided depends on the severity of the family's problems, the resourcefulness of the parents in locating services, and the capacity of the parents to use services. The less capable the parents are, the more help they will need with concrete services such as transportation, housing, and appointment-setting. The worker and parents need to determine together which steps the agency should take to support parents and which should be left to the parents' initiative.

According to Callard and Morin, the day-to-day delivery of services, that is, the implementation of the service plan, includes:

Frequent face-to-face contact with the client and family; the provision of direct services such as transportation to and from clinics, agencies and foster homes; . . . arranging for donations and home repairs as warranted;

and advocacy vis-à-vis the public, social, legal, and medical services, the schools and the courts.[25]

Ideally, worker-parent contacts should occur weekly; if that is not possible, then at least once every two weeks.[26] These contacts serve five important purposes. They can be used to (1) provide counseling and other casework services related to improving parental functioning, the parents' own behavior and emotional adjustment, the parents' relationship with the foster parents, financial management, household management, and marital functioning; (2) share information and concerns about the child's adjustment, health, schooling, progress, and so on; (3) discuss parent-child visiting and the appropriateness of the visiting plan; (4) elicit feedback about services provided by other community resources; and (5) evaluate progress. During these contacts the worker provides guidance and direction, offers emotional support, seeks information, and promotes client understanding.[27]

Another way the worker can assist parents is by facilitating the utilization and coordination of community resources. The successful provision of foster care services requires that parents use all possible community resources that can help the family resolve the problems that led to placement. Such resources might include: financial assistance; medical services; housing assistance; family life education; psychiatric/psychological evaluation; education in home management; vocational counseling, training, or placement; tutoring or remedial education; psychiatric/psychological treatment; day-care and homemaker services; and recreational services. More imaginative and less traditional ways of helping families have also been identified,[28] and workers can act as a catalyst for their use. For example, a large company might be able to loan a resource, such as a company bus, to facilitate parental visiting. Service groups could be approached about special projects, such as winterizing a client's home. A school of nursing might be asked to provide child care seminars to parents of children in care, and universities could be asked to arrange for their medical and dental students to offer free services to parents.

Special attention also needs to be given to identifying and utilizing informal helping resources. Such help consists of self-care and self-help groups.[29] Identifying potentially effective informal helpers, approaching informal helpers to enlist their aid, and providing assistance and support to these informal helpers might all be roles for the worker.[30] However, the responsibility for helping parents of children in foster care cannot be completely transferred to members of the informal helping system. Workers need to (1) assess carefully the potential benefit of incorporating the informal helping system into a plan of intervention; (2) ensure that the informal helper(s) and clients have a clear idea of their tasks and respective responsibilities; and (3) monitor carefully the informal helping process.[31]

Self-help groups can be an effective resource to many parents with children in foster care. Unfortunately, self-help groups organized exclusively for parents of children in foster care are rare.[32] However, when such groups are available and used appropriately, they can be an important resource for parents.[33] Other self-help groups, such as those for abusing parents, battered women, alcoholics and substance abusers, and former psychiatric patients can also provide significant support and assistance for these parents.

The foster care worker must assume the responsibility of coordinating the multiple services the family may be receiving and of regularly assessing their value. The various service providers need to know that these clients have children in foster care and must understand that the effectiveness and pace of their work may have major implications for these families and their children. The worker might also need to convene case conferences at appropriate intervals, so that all those involved with a particular family can share information, evaluate the status of the situation, and determine future directions.

Finally, if foster care is to be a time-limited service, it is essential that progress toward goals be regularly evaluated. The written service agreement is a good tool to use in this process. The worker needs to verify (either directly from the parents or from other services providers) parental efforts to meet the terms of the agreement. How well the worker and the agency are carrying out their obligations must also be reviewed.

Modifications in the service plan and the written service agreement should be anticipated during the evaluation process. Because of faulty assumptions in the initial agreement and/or changed circumstances, the worker and parents may wish to amend or change certain terms or extend the time frame. However, the importance of meeting the established permanency planning goals within a reasonable length of time should always be emphasized.

THE CHILD

In order to achieve permanency planning goals, a great deal of attention has recently been focused on working with the parents of children in foster care. However, the needs of the children entering this system cannot be overlooked. All children need permanence, stability, continuity, and nurture, the provision of which cannot be indefinitely delayed;[34] and the needs of foster children can be especially intense in these areas.

There is evidence that a large proportion of the children currently entering the foster care system are adolescents,[35] and while some are placed in group homes and other congregate care facilities, substantial numbers are still placed in foster homes. The service needs of this population are, in some instances, dramatically different from those of a younger population. These adolescents present new challenges to foster care agencies; while they may require more therapeutic services, they are also more capable of contributing to service planning and delivery than their younger counterparts.

Children of all ages share common concerns about being placed in foster care. They often wonder why they must enter foster care and why their own parents cannot care for them. They frequently believe that they have done something wrong, which has caused their parents to place them. They may question whether their parents still care about them and are often concerned about the possibility of living with their parents in the future.

The more completely children understand what foster care is, why they are there, and what will happen to them, the easier their adjustment and the more valuable the entire substitute care experience can be. Fostering this understanding is an ongoing process that requires the worker to use many different individualized intervention techniques and tools.

Preparing Children for Placement[36]

Children about to be placed in foster care often need help in accepting the changes in their life situations and in understanding why these changes are occurring. Providing this help can facilitate their transition to a foster home and can dispel some of their fears of the unknown. When the parents can assume this responsibility, it is best that they do so because the children may be better able to accept placement if they believe that this is the best arrangement their parents can make. Several basic principles should guide the work of preparing children for placement.

First, appropriate information about the particular foster home which has been selected should be furnished to children. This gives them some idea about their new living situation and what can be expected. Such information should be given in a forthright manner appropriate to the child's age. It should be presented in realistic terms, so that the child's expectations of the foster home are reality-based. During this process children should be given the opportunity to raise whatever questions, doubts, and fears they may have. Preparing children for foster care in this manner should enhance their ability to take advantage of their new situation and reduce problems in their ability to relate to their foster parents.

Second, whenever possible, children should visit the foster home prior to their actual placement. This allows them to meet the foster parents and to see their new environment. It may also reduce their anxiety about the move. Children's reactions to the visit and to the prospective family can be indicators of future adjustment in the home and should, therefore, be considered in the final decision to place them in a particular foster home.

During this preparation period, children should be assured that agency contact will be maintained with them and their parents during placement, and that they will have the opportunity to discuss how the placement is working out. Such assurances allow children to feel that there will be some continuity in their lives despite the disruptive effects of the placement. It also demonstrates the worker's commitment to maintaining the biological family. For these same reasons, children should be helped to understand the nature of their expected contact and involvement with their parents during the placement and the importance of parent-child visiting, as well as the visiting plan and its importance.

During the preparation period, criticisms of the child's own home and parents should be avoided. It should be recognized that children have a strong need for parents they can respect and love and whom they feel love and respect them. Diminution of their parents or their relationship with them can cause poor adjustment in the foster home and intensify negative feelings and anxiety about the placement.

In addition to direct preparation of the child by a worker, some agencies have developed a handbook to help prepare children for foster care. These handbooks are short, easily readable, and attractive. They convey, in a general way, information about foster care that children need to understand if they are to make the most of the placement. Having this tangible item can be useful, since children can refer to it when they feel the need and can incorporate the information it contains at their own pace. Also, it is often helpful for children to be given the worker's address and telephone number in writing so they know they can make independent contacts if they are worried or troubled about anything.

Service Planning

To the extent appropriate for their age, children should play an active role in service planning. They should have an opportunity to share their view of the situation that led to placement and to express their opinions about the situation. Only an inexperienced or incompetent worker would dismiss these observations lightly; they are often profound and should be taken into account as planning decisions are made.

It is equally important for workers to discuss with children the important aspects of their service plans once they are finalized. Children should be helped to understand the activities that will be carried out on their behalf and the services that will be provided to insure that they receive needed care and treatment. They should also understand the role that their biological parents will play during the placement period and the actions necessary to bring about the reunification of the family; the foster parents' part in implementing the placement service plan; and their own responsibilities for making foster care a helpful experience. The way in which these understandings are reached will vary in accordance with the child's age and maturity.

The value of developing a written service agreement with any youngster old enough to understand its meaning should also be weighed. This agreement can be a valuable tool in many situations, especially in view of the number of older adolescents with serious problems of their own who are currently entering care. The provisions of the agreement must be consistent with the agreed-upon planning goal—return home, adoption, emancipation after foster care. For example, when the projected permanency planning outcome is emancipation/independent living, the agreement should contain provisions that specifically relate to the achievement of that outcome, such as job training, education, housing, and income supports.

Implicit in all that has been stated thus far is that prior to the placement a relationship should be established between the child and the worker who will carry case responsibility during the placement. Building this relationship may involve several contacts—interviews and/or observations—and may require varying periods of time depending upon the specific circumstances of the child. Again, it should be noted that this is not always possible, since many children enter foster care in emergency situations, and some children who enter foster care are too young to understand what is occurring. But when children are placed on an emergency basis, it is important that the information that is ideally conveyed during the preplacement period be conveyed as soon as possible after the child enters care.

Ongoing Service Provision

Standards for Foster Family Service of the Child Welfare League of America includes this description of service to the child:

Service to the child is provided by working with the adults in his life, particularly his parents and foster parents, by direct social services such as casework and group work with the child, and by use of related professional services and other resources.[37]

Although many children do require special, individualized services, much of the work done by the agency with the biological parents and foster parents has a very significant effect on the child. This effect must not be overlooked. For example, when workers help parents assume some ongoing responsibilities for their child's daily care, they are providing service not only to the parent but also to the child.

The agency's provision of service to the child can essentially be divided into two broad groupings: (1) care and treatment, including health services, psychiatric or psychological services, educational opportunities, vocational counseling and training, and so on;[38] and (2) casework counseling regarding the child's acceptance and understanding of the new situation and new relationships with biological and foster parents, and resolution of the problems that led to placement.[39] Despite the current emphasis on working with biological parents to bring about permanence for children, the multiple service needs of some children entering foster care cannot be overlooked. This is especially true for older adolescents who must be prepared for independent living,[40] and emotionally disturbed, developmentally impaired, and physically handicapped children who may be placed in foster homes.

Workers carry many responsibilities in relation to children in placement. Through maintenance of continuous relationships they help children understand the need for separation from their biological parents, discuss parent-child relationships and visiting, and monitor progress toward goals specified in the service agreement. They also are responsible for making plans with the foster parents regarding supervision of the children's daily living situations and assessing the degree to which children's physical, emotional, cognitive, social, and educational needs are being met. Workers may also have to coordinate community resources utilized on behalf of the children under their supervision, and, if necessary, they may provide individual and/or group therapy to children experiencing special emotional problems.[41]

Workers must also attempt to insure stability in foster home placements, so that no child experiences unnecessary multiple moves within the foster care system. Although replacement is sometimes necessary and unavoidable, professionals agree that it is undesirable and should be avoided, if at all possible.[42] A number of steps can be taken to reduce this phenomenon. Agencies can examine why foster families terminate placement early[43] and develop methods to sustain or increase motivation for foster parenting.[44] When a particular problem is developing in a foster home, agencies need to provide specific help to the foster family in a timely fashion, so that the problem does not escalate and the family situation does not deteriorate. Any foster family request for removal of a foster child from the home should be explored fully by the worker with the foster parents and foster child. When appropriate, the biological parents should also be involved. Discussion and counseling can frequently serve to resolve problems that might otherwise lead to a final decision by the foster parents that replacement is necessary.

While emergency removals must be arranged in situations where it is apparent that without immediate action serious harm could come to the child and/or the foster family, other replacements should be carried out in ways that minimize the potential damage to the foster parents' and the child's self-image. Preferably, replacements should occur as the outcome of a series of discussions in which foster parents, child, and worker all arrive at the decision that the move is necessary and desirable.

Agencies should also consider the value of reviewing systematically the situations of children who are vulnerable to replacement. For example, if a child has been in care less than two years and has already experienced two replacements, a special administrative case review might be conducted involving all of the direct-service and supervisory staff familiar with the case. The purpose of such a review would be to determine the causes of the replacements and to decide upon the plan of service most likely to stabilize the child's experience in foster care.

From this discussion it becomes evident that, as with services to parents, services to children in foster care need to be provided in a planned, goal-oriented, time-limited fashion. Such an approach should help prepare children to cope more effectively with the outcome of placement, no matter whether this is return home, adoption, or planned long-term foster care.

THE FOSTER FAMILIES

Ultimately, the primary resource in any program of foster family care is the foster family. Only when there is a substantial pool of foster homes to draw upon can the best possible match be made between children and foster parents. Yet agencies often have difficulty in maintaining an adequate number of foster homes, in part because they have tended to define the foster parent role in very ambiguous ways. As Kadushin has noted:

In one sense, foster parents are "clients" of the agency because the agency has a resource—foster children—that can help to meet some of the foster parents' needs. In another sense, they are non-professional volunteer members of an agency staff, offering their homes and their services to meet the needs of children. In one sense, they stand in a supervisee relationship to the supervisor-worker assigned to the home. In another sense, they are colleagues cooperatively engaged with the worker in helping the child, each providing different kinds of help, offering skills at different professional levels.[45]

This issue of role ambiguity is a long-standing, complex one, which results from an inability to define expectations and responsibilities of foster parents carefully.[46] Horejsi comments that "given the national organization of foster parents, the expansion of training programs for foster parents and other moves toward professionalization, it is likely that the emerging role of the foster parent will be that of an agency employee having specialized skills and providing a particular type of service."[47]

Given this role definition, foster parents should understand that foster care is a temporary, time-limited, goal-oriented service and that they play a major part in achieving service goals. They have a pivotal role in the maintenance of the ties between children and their parents, in the process of rebuilding the biological parent-child relationship, and in the reestablishment of the biological family unit. But they must also be advised that if the biological family cannot be reunited within a reasonable period of time and the child is freed for adoption, they may be asked to commit themselves permanently to the child through either adoption or planned, long-term foster care. Workers can play an important part in reconciling these contradictory expectations by helping foster parents understand that their commitment is to the achievement of whatever is best for children and their families. This message should be conveyed during the process of selecting and training new foster families, and its implications should be explored fully with foster parents each time a worker is considering the placement of a specific child in the home.

Preparing Foster Families

The first step in preparing foster parents for their new role is to educate them about foster care in general. This requires that agencies discuss with the prospective foster parents the goals and objectives of foster family service, the purpose and method of the study process, the special characteristics of foster family service and the children who are now entering care, the relationship between the agency and the foster parents, the relationship between foster children and their biological parents, and the legal ramifications of foster family service.

Much of this education can be accomplished during the assessment process. But this requires that agencies reevaluate the purpose of foster home studies[48] and develop assessment procedures that emphasize the family's ability to: (1) provide for the needs of children placed in their care, (2) relate to biological parents in a helpful way and assist foster children in their relationship with them, and (3) work as a team member with social service staff. Rather than placing an emphasis on evaluation of the home, the study should be viewed primarily as a method of preparing applicants for foster parenting. Horejsi remarks:

> Most of those who are unsuitable will withdraw their applications once they have been presented with a realistic picture of foster parenting and an opportunity to examine their motives for wanting to become foster parents and their abilities to deal with foster children. Various techniques are used in the home-study approaches that emphasize preparation rather than evaluation. These include presentations by experienced foster parents, foster children and natural parents, discussions of case vignettes, films, video tapes and role play, question-and-answer sessions, etc. The purpose of these techniques is to help applicants understand common problems in foster care and learn methods of dealing with these problems.[49]

Workers should continue their role as educators even after the home has been approved. For example, during the initial visit, many of the important points about foster care that were discussed during the selection process can be reviewed, and any questions that the foster parents have in these areas can be fully answered. In this way the family can begin to feel comfortable with their new role.

One tool developed to provide this information is the foster parent handbook.[50] According to Stone and Hunzeker, this handbook has three basic purposes:

> —To provide in one source the policies used in administering the foster family care program;
> —To give the information foster parents need to have about their responsibilities to the foster children, the agency, the natural family, and the community;
> —To offer in a convenient way informal resources and suggestions on solving some of the daily problems in foster care.[51]

Figure 8.4 contains a list of those topics usually included in a handbook for foster parents. It includes the rights, roles, and responsibilities of the foster child, biological parents, foster parents, and worker; the importance of teamwork and of keeping biological parents involved with their child; agency policies that impact on foster parents; the importance of training; and the availability of resources for foster parents.

1. Definitions of foster care
2. National Foster Parents Code of Ethics
3. Rights and responsibilities of foster child
4. Rights, responsibilities, role of social worker
5. Rights and responsibilities of natural parent
6. Rights, responsibilities, and role of foster parent
7. Information on agency licensing and home study procedures
8. Importance of confidentiality and principles that apply to the foster parents and the social worker
9. Importance of teamwork and cooperation between foster parents and agency
10. Description of educational/training opportunities available to or required of foster parents
11. Explanation of agency policy and provisions related to foster care payments; transportation and clothing for child; personal allowances for child; medical, dental care, and education costs for child; vacations; record keeping; child discipline, and so on
12. Information on and explanation of agency policy related to liability, insurance, taxes, travel out of state
13. Explanation of legal procedures and basic legal terminology (for example, custody, guardian *ad litem,* neglect, abuse, and so on)
14. Descriptions of foster parent associations
15. Sources of useful information for foster parents
16. Explanation of channels of appeal or complaint that may be used by foster parents
17. Explanation of agency purpose, structure, organization, and funding
18. Importance of keeping natural parents involved with their child and explanation of how visits by parents can be handled

FIGURE 8.4 TOPICS IN FOSTER PARENT HANDBOOKS
Source: *Foster Family Care: A Handbook for Social Workers* by Charles Horejsi, pp. 229–30.

Foster parents should read, discuss, and sign a foster home placement agreement during this preplacement period. This agreement, generally a standardized form, specifies the agency's expectations of the foster parents and the agency's commitments to them.[52] Once the agreement is signed, the family should be assisted in making an informed decision regarding their desire to accept a *particular* child into their home and should be helped to anticipate problems that might occur with different types of children. Having decided on the type of child they would feel most comfortable with, discussions about specific children can begin.

Families should discuss the needs of specific children and the family resources necessary to meet these needs. In order to accomplish this, the foster parents must be provided with substantial information about the child and and his or her family. They need to be aware of the established objective of foster care service for this particular child, the time limits for reaching these objectives, and the services that will be provided to accomplish them. The visiting rights of the biological family and the specific visiting plan for this child must be discussed. The foster parents need to have an understanding of the parent-child relationship and should be helped to anticipate the problems that may arise during placement as a result of parent-child interaction. Finally, the foster family must know about the child—unique behaviors, interests, hobbies, health, school performance, special problems, eating, and sleeping habits, and so on.

The foster father should be included in these discussions, for research has suggested that his views, feelings, and motivations may be more predictive of placement success than those of the foster mother.[53] Furthermore, placement stability has been found to be enhanced when discussions about this information have occurred with both foster parents during separate interviews.[54]

Past practices have often excluded the foster father from involvement with the worker and the agency. Practical problems, such as work schedules, and assumptions regarding the father's role in child care have meant that he was often seen as secondary in this process. With the knowledge now available about his importance, workers and agencies must make special efforts to overcome these barriers to the foster father's involvement with the agency, worker, and child.

While it is essential for the foster parents to treat information about the child and his family as confidential, it is important that they be given the opportunity to discuss their feelings about a prospective placement with the worker. As one commentator has stated:

> The foster parents are good judges of whether or not a particular child will work out in their home. Even though they may not be able to verbalize the reasons for their beliefs, more often than not they seem to know what will and what will not work. . . . If the foster parents and the child seem to hit it off and/or if the foster parents are of the opinion that it will work, the match is likely to succeed. If, on the other hand, the foster parents are doubtful about the match or express fear of the placement, chances are good that the placement, in fact, would fail.[55]

Service Planning

The nature and extent of the foster parents' involvement in the development of the service plan for family and child should be considered on a case-by-case basis. Such involvement can lead to a greater understanding of the family situation and can enhance the foster parents' commitment to the service goals. However, the involvement of the foster parent in this activity may also inhibit the biological parents' and child's discussion of personal, family matters. Whatever the nature of their participation in this process, the placement service plan, especially the permanent planning goal and those aspects of the plan that could affect the child's activities and behaviors, should at least be discussed with the foster parents. Only when they have an understanding of the placement service plan can they be expected to play a facilitative role. It is imperative that they "not be left out or confused by the activities of the worker with them or . . . with the child."[56] Sharing as much as is known about the family and child is a major responsibility of the worker and should be stressed.[57]

Since service planning is an ongoing process, the worker should actively solicit information and advice from foster parents that might affect planning. The foster parents spend the greatest amount of time with the child and "should be treated with respect and appreciation and viewed as members of the team. Their ideas should be sought. They must be trusted."[58]

As previously indicated, the foster parents must recognize the importance of parental visiting to the child, and planned visiting should be discussed thoroughly with them. Foster parents should be helped to encourage frequent and lengthy visits, to permit visiting in their homes, to bring children to the biological parents' homes and to the agency's office for visits, and to comply with agreed-upon visiting schedules. If visits are problematic or children have negative reactions to them, an assessment should be made of the probable causes and suggestions about possible solutions be offered. However, such reactions should not necessarily lead to limitations on visiting.

A written service agreement could also have some utility for the foster parents by clarifying their roles and responsibilities in individual case situations. When discussing common concerns and complaints of foster parents, Horejsi states, "Foster parents frequently complain that they are not informed about or helped to understand their rights and responsibilities. Many are confused about their role and unsure of exactly what is expected of them."[59] A written agreement patterned after, but not duplicating, the one developed between the parents and the worker could help to remedy these complaints. However, there may be foster parents who are uncomfortable with this kind of agreement. Therefore, the decision to develop it should be made on an individualized basis. Whether or not a written plan is developed, it is important for the foster parents to be clear about their responsibilities.

Perhaps the most important, though currently most neglected, aspect of the service planning process is provision for a working relationship between the foster parents and biological parents. Although agencies have not traditionally encouraged this relationship, it is clear that its development is consistent with current views about the goals of foster care. Caseworkers and/or foster children should not serve as the "go-betweens" for foster parents and biological parents. Biological and foster parents should be encouraged to discuss matters of mutual concern directly with each other—especially the progress, growth, and development of the child. They should also plan joint activities that will benefit the child. Building this relationship may be difficult and time-consuming. It may require the foster parents to be aggressive in their attempts to reach out to parents who may resist or fear such efforts.[60] But it may ultimately be a rewarding experience for the foster parents and an important element in the success of the placement.

Service Provision

Foster parents are in a unique position in the agency. Not only are they the *recipients* of services from the agency, but they also *provide* services to biological parents and the child in their homes. Both of these are vitally important to the well-being of children and families.

It is through contacts with the agency that foster parents receive support, consultation, and reinforcement for their role and obtain information about children and their families vital to the performance of their functions. It is also through these contacts that the agency insures that the child's needs are being met.

According to the Child Welfare League of America *Standards,* agency –foster parent contact has two interrelated purposes:

—The agency has the obligation to ascertain whether the child is receiving care in accordance with acceptable standards, and in relation to his needs. To do this, the social worker must keep informed about the child's adjustment and development in the foster home, and the manner in which the foster parents carry their responsibilities toward the child. This information then serves as the basis for planning help with the foster parents to enable them to carry out their responsibilities toward the child, and as a guide to provision of additional services the child needs.

—The agency has the obligation to promote the competence of the foster parents in their care of the child by relieving anxieties aroused by the presence or behavior of the child; by increasing the foster parents' understanding of the child's behavior; by giving information, learning opportunities and guidance in meeting the needs of the individual child;

and by prompt provision of supportive help during difficult periods of placement.[61]

Research has shown that it is very important to provide support and consultation to foster parents and to be accessible to them, especially during the first three months of placement.[62] If possible, regular meetings should be scheduled, supplemented by telephone calls.[63] Foster parent motivation is more likely to be sustained when the parents believe the worker is both accessible and helpful.

The worker's role in relation to the foster parents is basically that of an enabler and a facilitator. By providing needed advice and knowledge, the foster parents can, in turn, provide appropriate care for the child. An ongoing working relationship allows the foster parents to become involved in service planning and provision. Evelyn Felker, a foster parent herself, calls this a "matter of sharing responsibility"[64] and mentions the critical areas where responsibility should be shared: planning for children, decisions concerning discipline and privileges, and relations between the children and their parents.[65]

Foster parents have many skills that can be usefully taught to the biological parents such as child rearing, housekeeping, appropriate ways of handling feelings, and knowledge of community resources and how to use them. They can also involve the biological parents in important planned activities such as school conferences, shopping trips, holiday planning, special events, and doctor and dental appointments. And, they can encourage biological parents to participate in day-to-day decision making with their child.[66] By engaging in these activities they enhance parental competency and demonstrate their belief in the importance of the biological parents to the child.

In most instances, foster care should be a temporary service that results in reestablishing the biological family unit. However, there are times when the child cannot go home and parental rights to the child must be terminated. There are also times when these ties cannot be severed and the child cannot return home. The legal status of foster parents in such cases has been changing.[67] The right to a hearing, under certain circumstances, before a child is removed from the foster home at the agency's request is being discussed and debated in agencies and the courts.[68] Preference in adoption is now being granted to foster parents in new laws and regulations. (See Chapters 10 and 11.)

The changing picture of foster family care, especially as it relates to the assumption of new roles and responsibilities by foster parents, underscores the increased importance of foster parent training and foster parents' groups. Foster parent training should include preservice and in-service training. It should relate to the everyday concerns of the foster parents and should be practical. Foster parents must have the opportunity to discuss, share, and compare their experiences and perceptions during a structured training session. The Child Welfare League of America has developed a basic curriculum for foster parent education, as well as specialty curricula which focus on children with special needs or characteristics.[69] Curricula have also been developed by a number of universities.[70]

Self-help groups for foster parents can also be useful. As with formal training, they can help increase knowledge and skill, offer foster parents an opportunity to discuss problems of mutual concern, help enhance the status and satisfaction of foster parents, enable foster parents to understand what is involved for the biological parent and the child in the experience of separation, provide a forum for expression of dissatisfaction with different aspects of the job, plan recruitment programs, and give prospective applicants a clearer idea of what is involved in foster parenthood. They can also provide a strong voice for their constituents and serve as a force for change for themselves and the children and families they serve.

THE ROLE OF THE AGENCY

Throughout this chapter, we have alluded to the numerous responsibilities of the workers during the foster care process. For example, during the preplacement period, they ensure that the biological parents, children, and the foster parents have a good understanding of various aspects of the foster care service and establish working relationships with all the parties concerned. During service planning, they discuss with the biological parents the problems that led to placement, specify necessary changes, and identify services and supports to be provided. Where appropriate, they involve children in the planning process. They also insure that the foster parents are informed of the planning decisions that are made. While the child is in the foster home, workers provide support and services to the biological parents, child, and foster parents and coordinate and monitor services provided by other community agencies and informal helping resources. They must also maintain careful records that can be subject to external review and may be used in court proceedings. Finally, workers must participate in and often take primary responsibility for the critical decisions regarding the child's readiness to return home, termination of parental rights, and/or adoption placement. Carrying out these responsibilities is a herculean task no matter whether the case load is 20 or 50 or 150, and agencies must provide the supports necessary for workers to carry out these tasks.

Needed Resources

To serve families effectively, the foster care agency must have a variety of resources at its disposal. The first is adequate staff at all levels—supervisors, social workers, and case aides—with clearly delineated responsibilities, a range of professional and technical skills, and the personal qualities and commitment that enable people to work effectively with this population. Preservice and ongoing in-service training are essential if foster care services are to protect the child's right to permanence, continuity, and stability. For example, workers and foster parents should be familiar with current theory and knowledge of child development, parent-child relationships, and permanency planning. Attitudes about the importance of biological parents to their children in care and the appropriate role of each party in the foster care system need to be examined. Skills in handling difficult situations within foster homes that might lead to the replacement of the child must be developed.

Continuous, meaningful training can impact on every aspect of foster care service, and revitalized child welfare education programs in undergraduate and graduate schools of social work are potential resources that agencies can explore for training purposes. However, it is essential that training be integrally related to agency program. Without the ability to apply knowledge, worker training can be a futile exercise. (See Chapter 12.)

The second critical agency resource is a substantial pool of foster families that can meet the varying needs of the children currently entering care. There has been a continuous problem in finding a sufficient number of adequate foster homes. Kadushin offers one explanation as to why this problem is likely to become more severe in the future:

> Women's liberation, zero population growth, the increasing percentage of working mothers—all contribute to the devaluation of parenthood and the child-rearing functions. The competition of the employment market, for which many more women can now qualify, and its substantially higher economic returns will further reduce the number of women likely to be interested in foster care. The large families that once served as the training ground for many foster mothers are a thing of the past, and limited house space makes the addition of another family member difficult.[71]

The lack of resources is exacerbated by the fact that there is a greater need today for homes for older, developmentally disabled, and emotionally disturbed children.

While there are no simple answers to the problems of insufficient resources, several changes in current agency policies and practices can lead to improvement in this situation. First, agencies can make greater use of relatives and family friends as foster parents. An interested friend or relative, who has demonstrated concern for the child and expresses a willingness to cooperate with the agency, should be given careful consideration as a potential foster parent. And it is important that home studies in these situations be completed expeditiously, so that a potential resource is not lost and the friend or relative can receive the agency benefits attached to the status of licensed foster parent, including board payments and agency supports. By using friends and relatives as foster parents, children may be provided with the continuity and stability that would otherwise be missing in their relationships.[72]

Second, the rewards for foster parenting can be made far more attractive than they currently are. Foster parents must be adequately reinforced for the critical functions they perform. These supports can be both monetary and socio-emotional, including praise from agency staff, happiness expressed by the foster child, recognition from outsiders, participation in special events, and opportunities to secure training.[73] It is generally easier for agencies to develop means of expanding nonmonetary supports than to raise foster parent payment levels, as the latter are usually established by state legislatures or administrative bodies. However, if Kadushin's assessment of the reasons for the declining population of potential foster parents is correct, it seems clear that agencies must devote more effort to securing more adequate financial payments for foster parents.

This also suggests that the foster parent role needs to be reconceptualized as a specialized role deserving greater social status and financial reward. Given the changing nature of the population requiring foster care and the shifting role of women in society, it seems obvious that the time of viewing foster mothers simply as warmhearted, generous, maternal, volunteer types is over. So also is the view of foster parents as "needy" individuals who seek the agency out in order to work through their personal problems. (See Chapter 12 for different ways of conceptualizing foster parents as integral members of the agency staff.) Such a reconceptualization of the foster parent role demands that foster parent recruitment efforts be intensified and targeted to different audiences.

Recruitment involves "a program of interpretation to the public of the need for foster homes for children and the satisfactions to be derived from fostering a child."[74] There are several essential aspects to such a program.[75] Recruitment efforts need to be continuous; sporadic bursts of intensive recruitment are not very effective. There should be specific staff assigned to recruitment activities who coordinate and organize recruitment efforts and secure the assistance of foster parents, foster parent organizations, and foster children. Cooperative multiagency efforts seem to be most successful and cost-effective. Recruitment efforts should be concentrated on those groups or neighborhoods containing large numbers of women who might be interested in assuming this new foster parent role. Moreover, attempts should be made to reach out to those communities where children in need of foster care service reside. Numerous strategies should be used to recruit foster parents, and there should be a balance between media campaigns, written materials (posters, leaflets, shopping bag stuffers), and face-to-face communication through community groups. Finally, if campaigns are to be successful, inquiries about foster parenting should be responded to in a timely manner, preferably in person.

It is important for agencies to present a realistic picture of foster care in their recruitment message. To accomplish this, agencies have successfully used foster parents to present a balanced picture of the rewards and frustrations of foster parenting. Visual presentation of parent-child interactions in foster homes can provide a positive yet realistic image of foster care. Professional staff members should also be available to answer individual questions, discuss the technical aspects of foster parenting, and describe the numerous types of homes, both short-term and long-term, which may be needed for the variety of children requiring placement (adolescents, infants, sibling groups, disturbed, or physically handicapped children, and so on). Small-group discussion can be an effective means of helping potential foster parents express their aspirations and fears about foster care, clarify expectations and responsibilities, and encourage women who have not been employed outside their homes to assume new, more potentially challenging and rewarding roles.

A third resource that should be present if agencies are to provide effective foster family care is the availability of a range of appropriate services for all the parties concerned. Such services are necessary to help parents and their children resolve the problems that led to placement. These services might include counseling, family life education, drug or alcohol treatment, medical care, financial assistance, housing assistance, and so forth.

While some of these services should be provided directly through the child welfare agency, others can only be provided by agencies currently outside the boundaries of child welfare. Thus, it is crucial that agencies develop appropriate referral and advocacy resources so that families are assured of needed services. The development of formal linkages and the

use of purchase-of-service contracts with other agencies can facilitate the worker's job of identifying, assessing, coordinating, and monitoring the provision of services to both families and children. (See Chapter 5 for a discussion of linkage mechanisms.)

The final resource needed by agencies to insure effective service is the ability to create and help sustain informal helping networks for the various parties involved in foster care. Horejsi and associates state that "a proper blend of formal and informal services [provided or coordinated] by the worker improves services."[76] These informal networks can include persons involved in foster care; their relatives, neighbors, and friends; and nonprofessional individuals and groups that provide assistance.[77] Self-help groups have been an important resource for many foster parents, and if organized on a more widespread basis, they could service a similar function for many parents with children in foster care. Such groups can produce desired social and personal changes through the provision of mutual aid, emotional support, and material assistance, and they provide a reference group for parents in similar situations, allowing them to feel less isolated.

Decision-Making Guidelines

In addition to providing necessary resources, agencies should develop written policy statements to guide the decision-making processes essential to the provision of effective foster care service. As mentioned in previous chapters, workers make a number of critical decisions for each child. Without appropriate guidelines these decisions can be haphazard and result in inappropriate plans and placements for children.

One of the first decisions a worker must make is whether a child can remain at home or needs an appropriate placement. The decision to place a child is justified only when certain conditions are present and when other alternatives have been explored and have been found unworkable. (See Chapter 7.) This means that a careful assessment must be made in which appropriate information is gathered. If unnecessary placements are to be avoided, alternative resources must be available, and workers must have the knowledge and motivation necessary to use them effectively. A viable system of foster care requires that the "gate" be open only to those who need this service and cannot be protected or helped in a less disruptive manner.

A second important decision that must be made is the type of placement that will best meet a child's needs. Many factors must be considered including the child's age, the child's relationship to parents and siblings, the biological parents' preferences, and the availability of resources. The guiding principle in arranging placements is that children should be placed in the least restrictive, most family-like setting that is appropriate to their needs and within reasonable proximity of family and home community. Workers need to have extensive knowledge of the placements available and the assets and liabilities of each service option. (See Chapter 9 for a full discussion of service options for children with special needs.)

Related to the decision regarding the appropriate type of placement is the choice of a specific foster home for a child. Agencies need to develop criteria to be used in "matching" a child with a potential foster family. Under ideal conditions, a foster family with specific capabilities is sought for each individual child; that is, there is an attempt to locate a home suitably matched to the unique strengths, needs, and problems of each particular child. Specific criteria are identified in the American Public Welfare Association's *Standards for Foster Family Services Systems*[78] and include, for example, the family's ability to relate to the child's needs; to preserve the child's racial, cultural, and religious heritage; to accept the child's biological parent relationship; and to deal comfortably with problems that may arise during the placement.

Horejsi provides helpful guidance concerning ways social workers can assess a foster family's capacity for parenting a particular foster child and suggests a list of questions that are relevant to many selection decisions. These questions include whether the family can provide care, affection, warmth, and trust for this child; whether the family can relate to the child's biological parents; whether the family can incorporate this child and be realistic in its expectations and flexible in meeting the child's individual needs; whether the family has the strengths and supports necessary to parent this child; whether the family will cooperate with the agency and assist in carrying out the service plan; whether the child will react positively to the family and not seriously disrupt the family equilibrium; and whether the services needed are available in this family's community and the family will facilitate their use.[79]

The research of Aldridge, Cautley, and Lichstein also provides some useful insights into the matching process[80] and suggests that it is better to delay a placement than to make a bad matching decision that creates frustration for all concerned.

Criteria for decision making related to the development and implementation of permanent plans for children are also critical. Workers need to be thoroughly familiar with the different ways in which permanence can be secured for children and under what circumstances return to the biological home, adoption, or planned long-term foster care is to be preferred. Also workers must be helped to recognize the importance of *time* in decision making and should be committed to the movement of children into permanent homes as quickly as possible.

Case-Load Management

A common complaint heard in foster care agencies, especially in the public sector, is that large case loads create an impediment to effective service delivery and that case-load size inhibits workers from performing all of their assigned tasks—especially work with biological parents.[81] But Pike suggests that "large caseloads, per se, are not constraining; for demoralized staff who need rationalization, it's perfect."[82] Stein, Gambrill and Wiltse also take issue with this argument, stating:

> Although we do not suggest that no relationship exists between caseload size and time available for service delivery, it should be clear that caseload size alone is not a significant determinant in decisions concerning who will receive services. . . . It is our position that arguments to reduce caseload size are spurious, because type of activity, not size per se, is the crucial dimension.[83]

Clearly type of activity and case-load management skills are critical dimensions in effective foster care work. However, it seems obvious that workers will be able to provide more intensive services to parents and their children when case-load size is manageable, not overwhelming. It may be unrealistic to recommend, as one report has, caseloads of ten to twelve families, "to permit close contact with families—nuclear and extended—and ample time for extensive work with other agencies and organizations."[84] But if permanency planning goals are to be pursued for all children, timely decision making, aggressive intervention, and follow-up will be needed in many, if not most, cases. Case loads of unmanageable size are not conducive to such efforts.

Workers need to make daily decisions about which cases require immediate attention:

> In order to achieve permanence for the largest number of children in the shortest length of time, it is necessary to set clear priorities, schedule [worker] time, and channel [worker] efforts. Sometimes caseworkers become caught up in the demands of agency priorities and departmental regulations and overlook the need to make, and review, decisions about their own caseloads. Frequently, decisions are made under stress, without adequate consideration. Devoting a day each month to caseload organizing and review may save . . . many hours of misspent time and effort and will give [workers] greater control over [their] caseload.[85]

The key steps to case-load control are screening cases, grouping cases, setting priorities, planning, and scheduling.[86] Although agencies utilize different techniques for case-load management and establish different strategies for setting priorities, it is essential that the established procedures be communicated to workers through understandable policies, procedures, guidebooks, and training.

Case Management

Agencies must decide who will take responsibility for assessing, planning, implementing, and monitoring cases. In some agencies, a single worker has responsibility for everyone who is involved in a case: the biological parents, the child, the foster parents, and any other service providers. In others, these responsibilities are divided between two or more workers.

There is little research to guide agencies. In one article, Stein and associates observe:

> . . . there was greater movement of children out of the foster care system when management of cases was divided between special project workers and county workers, compared with the usual pattern of service delivery, and . . . this was achieved without a greater reduction in caseload size. . . . This advantage was attained without undue cost in time spent in joint contacts between project and county workers, and without severe problems.[87]

Although this would appear to be a strong argument for division of case responsibility, these authors conclude:

> However, justification for adopting such a procedure [division of case management] would have to rest on empirical evidence that such a process was necessary for providing intensive services to parents. If a single worker can manage the entire case, and provide intensive services to biological parents, there is little to recommend a division of labor.[88]

Pike has a somewhat different perspective on this issue:

> I believe that a worker who has maintained status quo for two years will usually be incapable of objectively pursuing a return home. Upsetting the equilibrium is too threatening, and a "parents only" worker is indicated. However, the plight of the child is one of the strongest internal motivators in laboring with parents and the parents' worker must have sufficient contact with the child to have a sense of mission through the empathy with the child's situation. Theoretically, the worker with total case responsibility may have a more comprehensive perception of the situation and be more time efficient when fewer conferences with other staff are required, but the plethora of detail responsibilities in the management of the foster

care placement often overwhelm and obscure the work with the parent. I believe that, unless cases are new and few, two workers are more effective with even a third worker functioning as a paralegal, if TPR [termination of parental rights] is indicated.[89]

Since there is no clear evidence as to which is the most successful approach, agencies might want to experiment with different possibilities and determine which approach works best for them. No matter which system is endorsed, one person should be designated the case manager —the person who takes responsibility for coordinating the work of all the individuals involved in a case and monitoring their ability to carry out their designated tasks.

The creative use of teams of workers may provide a possible solution to the problems of case-load size and worker responsibility. There are many ways to constitute a team.[90] One possibility is a team consisting of a supervisor, caseworker, and case aide all working with a single family. Another model uses several caseworkers, supported by a supervisor and case aides. All of the workers are familiar with all of the families in the team's case load. Multidisciplinary teams, consisting of a social worker, homemaker, mental health specialist, legal specialist, and medical specialist, have also been utilized. Foster parents can also be included as part of a team. (See Chapter 12 for further discussion.)

The agency's willingness to sanction and encourage differential roles for workers can also have a positive impact on the worker's ability to carry out responsibilities. Jones, Neuman and Shyne commented that "skillful case management and advocacy are as important as emotional support, advice on practical matters and counseling on interpersonal problems."[91] In some cases, workers are expected to fulfill all of these roles. In others, the worker functions almost exclusively as a case manager/coordinator, while direct services are provided by other staff. Pike provides a compelling argument for the latter approach:

> I would stress the role of case manager and de-emphasize the counselor or "psychotherapy" role. The latter leads to unilateral decision making. [It] clouds issues of confidentiality, and requires another set of skills that further dilute the focus. Being a skillful case manager is achievable but the responsibilities are great and the demands wearing. Adding a therapy role is counterindicated.[92]

The delegation of the therapeutic role requires that there be another person or agency to provide this service. Before an agency decides to delegate this or any other responsibility, it must carefully assess who within the agency and/or the community can assume these delegated functions.

No matter which model of service delivery is ultimately chosen by the agency, recognition should be given to the need for shared decision-making responsibility and expert consultation.[93] By providing this support, agencies help to insure that workers feel less isolated and over-whelmed in their work.

Monitoring Service Provision

In addition to developing criteria for decision making, agencies should have the ability to monitor progress toward the goals set out in service plans. If children are not to continue to drift in foster care or experience unnecessary multiple placements, responsibility must be lodged not only with the individual worker, but also with the agency and with the child welfare delivery system as a whole. A working information system, coupled with a formalized internal review system, is an essential component of sound foster care service. Through these mechanisms, useful information about children and their parents can be collected,[94] and events that should be occurring at specific times can be tracked; consequently the progress or lack of progress toward achieving case goals can be monitored and the data gathered can be used to insure that necessary contracted and in-house services are being provided.[95] External review systems, discussed in Chapter 10, can be helpful in this regard.

Information systems and review procedures can also lead to increased knowledge about the foster care system and can impact positively on agency policies and practices. For example, an individual agency or the entire foster care network in a given area could undertake the study of a particularly troublesome phenomenon such as the multiple replacement of children. Factors associated with this phenomenon could be identified through the use of the aggregate data base available through an information system. This information could add to the knowledge base within the community and influence the delivery of services.

Grievance Mechanisms

An important administrative prerequisite to a viable foster care system is a grievance mechanism that can be utilized by biological parents, foster parents, and age-appropriate children. The availability of such mechanisms can help to alleviate some of the problematic situations that arise frequently in foster homes. The presence of such mechanisms also reinforces the agency's commitment to the various parties in foster care and allows them a resource beyond their individual worker if they believe they are not being properly served.

A number of factors have been identified as contributing to the successful operation of an internal grievance mechanism:

—A written description of policies and procedures that is distributed automatically to all who are entitled to use the grievance mechanism

—Individual discussion by workers with clients at the point of intake about the grievance procedures available to them

—Easy accessibility to clients, for example, telephone and walk-in service

—Prompt response to individual complaints

—Staff who are open-minded, objective, and committed to the concept of clients' rights

—Administrative authority to enforce decisions rendered under the grievance procedure

The Parents' Rights Unit within New York City's Special Services for Children might serve as a model for such a mechanism.[96] This unit allows biological families and children the opportunity to challenge agency decisions that they feel are not in their best interest. It provides an ombudsman for the person filing the complaint. This ombudsman explores the problem with the various parties involved and gathers available information about the situation. This results in a recommendation of needed changes. The parties are informed of these recommendations and are told of their legal rights if the recommendations are not satisfactory or are not implemented. Hence, a mechanism based on this model can allow families the essential opportunity to raise their concerns, obtain clarification regarding their rights and responsibilities, and seek redress for their grievances without fear of punitive response from the agency or unnecessary court involvement. Such a mechanism might also be helpful in resolving differences between foster parents and agencies.

CONCLUSION

This chapter has identified the critical philosophical, policy, and programmatic elements that are needed for an effective foster care system. It is heartening to be able to write that many of these elements are now in place in various programs in different parts of the country and are in the process of being implemented elsewhere. Although no one can be certain that a foster care service characterized by these elements will help to preserve families and meet children's needs for continuity, stability, nurture, and permanence, certainly the introduction of these elements should help to correct some of the problems of the past and make the future outlook more promising.

In the near future, foster care programs will have to make changes consistent with many of the ideas presented here. When implemented, P.L. 96-272, the Adoption Assistance and Child Welfare Act of 1980 (see Chapter 3 for a full discussion of this law) will require foster care agencies to move in these directions if they are to continue to receive public funds. Preservice and in-service training of staff at all levels will be necessary if these mandated changes are to be implemented properly. State laws and regulations will also have to be reexamined and brought into conformity. Hence, there is much to be done before the gap between the promise of this law and actual agency performance is narrowed.

There is reason for optimism, but this needs to be tempered because the conservative outlook sweeping the country is exacting a toll on all service programs, including foster care. In the long run, the implementation of the ideas described in this chapter should be cost-effective. But initially, many of the costs associated with these changes (provision of services to biological families, management information systems, and case review) will be considerable. It remains to be seen if the required funds will be forthcoming.

In a recent statement the Child Welfare League of America affirmed its position that "foster care services administered and delivered according to standards are vital to the growth and development of some children and necessary to maintain many families beset by crisis and chronic problems."[97] The statement includes this description of "good foster care":

> continuous involvement of the biological parents (or legal guardians) in planning for and maintaining contact with their children; provision of resources and rehabilitation supports to parents to help them assume or terminate their child-rearing responsibilities; and an individualized plan of service for each child, showing purpose, method of implementation and desired outcome, with careful and periodic monitoring.[98]

This chapter has attempted to describe what is involved in the above. Quality foster care services *are* possible when there is philosophical, legislative, and financial commitment. It remains to be seen if the current commitment is sufficient to permit the achievement of this objective.

NOTES

1. For a discussion of standards for termination of parental rights, see Michael Wald, "State Intervention on Behalf of Neglected Children: Standards for Removal of Children from Their Homes, Monitoring the Status of Children in Foster Care and Termination of Parental Rights," *Stanford Law Review* 28 (April 1976): 623–706.

2. Mary Ann Jones, Renee Neuman, and Ann Shyne, *A Second Chance for Families: Evaluation of a Program to Reduce Foster Care* (New York: Child Welfare League of America, 1976); Jane Knitzer, MaryLee Allen, and Brenda McGowan, *Children Without Homes* (Washington, D.C.: Children's Defense Fund, 1978); Joseph Persico, *Who Knows? Who Cares? Forgotten Children in Foster Care* (New York: National Commission of Children in Need of Parents, 1980); Wicomico County Department of Social Services, "Toward a Theory of Rational Gatekeeping," Wicomico County, Maryland, n.d. (mimeographed).

3. David Fanshel and Eugene Shinn, *Children in Foster Care: A Longitudinal Investigation* (New York: Columbia University Press, 1978); Alan Gruber, *Foster Home Care in Massachusetts* (Boston: Governor's Commission on Adoption and Foster Care, 1973); Henry Maas and Richard Engler, *Children in Need of Parents* (New York: Columbia University Press, 1959).

4. Comptroller General of the United States, *Children in Foster Care Institutions—Steps Government Can Take to Improve Their Care* (Washington, D.C.: U.S. General Accounting Office, 1977), reported in Judith Schaffer, *Compendium of Research on Foster Care in New York City* (New York: Office of the City Council President, 1979), p. 13; Gruber, *Foster Home Care in Massachusetts*, p. 50; Maas and Engler, *Children in Need of Parents*, pp. 390–91; Deborah Shapiro, *Agencies and Foster Children* (New York: Columbia University Press, 1976), p. 195.

5. David Fanshel and John Grundy, *CWIS Report* (New York: Child Welfare Information System, 1975), p. 8; Edmund Sherman, Renee Neuman, and Ann Shyne, *Children Adrift in Foster Care: A Study of Alternative Approaches* (New York: Child Welfare League of America, 1974), pp. 49–95; Kermit Wiltse and Eileen Gambrill, "Foster Care 1973: A Reappraisal," *Public Welfare* 32 (Winter 1974): 8.

6. Donald Brieland et al., *Differential Uses of Manpower: A Team Model for Foster Care* (New York: Child Welfare League of Amer-

ica, 1968), p. 17; Draza Kline, Helen Overstreet, and Mary Forbush, *Foster Care of Children: Nurture and Treatment* (New York: Columbia University Press, 1972); Theodore Stein, Eileen Gambrill, and Kermit Wiltse, *Children in Foster Homes: Achieving Continuity of Care* (New York: Praeger Publishers, 1978).

7. Fanshel and Shinn, *Children in Foster Care;* Knitzer, Allen, and McGowan, *Children Without Homes.*

8. David Fanshel, "The Exit of Children from Foster Care: An Interim Research Report," *Child Welfare* 50 (February 1971): 65–81; Helen R. Jeter, *Children, Problems and Services in Child Welfare Programs* (Washington, D.C.: Children's Bureau, 1963); Maas and Engler, *Children in Need of Parents;* Paul Mott, *Foster Care and Adoptions: Some Key Policy Issues* (Washington, D.C.: U.S. Government Printing Office, August 1975).

9. Fanshel and Shinn, *Children in Foster Care; Issues and Experiences in Permanency Planning: A Report on Seven Regional Work Sessions on Foster Care Reform* (Portland, Ore.: Regional Research Institute for Human Services, Portland State University, 1980); Stein, Gambrill, and Wiltse, *Children in Foster Homes.*

10. This author has recently been involved in research that requires contact with many public and voluntary agencies throughout the United States. Through this work it has been discovered that many states have implemented new policies for their foster care programs and that attitudinal changes about the role of the biological parent have occurred.

11. Shirley Jenkins and Elaine Norman, *Filial Deprivation and Foster Care* (New York: Columbia University Press, 1972).

12. For discussion of how this can be accomplished, see Barbara Rutter, *The Parents' Guide to Foster Family Care* (New York: Child Welfare League of America, 1978).

13. Victor Pike et al., *Permanent Planning for Children in Foster Care: A Handbook for Social Workers* (Portland, Ore.: Regional Research Institute for Human Services, Portland State University, 1977); Stein, Gambrill, and Wiltse, *Children in Foster Homes.*

14. Mary Ann Jones, James Mann, and Sister Mary Paul Janchill, personal correspondence.

15. David Fanshel, "Parental Visiting of Children in Foster Care: Key to Discharge?" *Social Service Review* 49 (December 1975): 493–514; Shirley Jenkins and Elaine Norman, *Beyond Placement:*

Mothers View Foster Care (New York: Columbia University Press, 1975).

16. For discussion, see Rutter, *The Parents' Guide to Foster Family Care.*

17. *Policy Statement on Parental Visiting* (New York: N.Y. City Department of Special Services for Children, September 1975).

18. Charles Horejsi, Anne Vandeberg Bertsche, and Frank Clark, *Parents with Children in Foster Care: A Guide to Social Work Practice* (Missoula, Mont.: University of Montana Department of Social Work, September 1980), pp. 55–87.

19. Esther Dean Callard and Patricia Morin, *Parents and Children Together: An Alternative to Foster Care* (Detroit, Mich.: Wayne State University, Department of Family and Consumer Resources, 1979), pp. 29–30.

20. Horejsi, Bertsche, and Clark, *Parents with Children in Foster Care,* p. 65.

21. Ibid.

22. Ibid., pp. 70–71.

23. Ibid., pp. 98–99; Hugh E. Saville, "Restoring a Balance: Parental Care—Foster Care" (paper presented at the Child Welfare League of America Regional Conference, Edmonton, Alberta, Canada, June 1, 1973).

24. This section of the chapter draws from Pike et al., *Permanent Planning for Children in Foster Care;* and John McGowan and Christine Deyss, *Permanency Planning: A Casework Handbook* (Albany, N.Y.: Welfare Research, Inc., 1979).

25. Callard and Morin, *Parents and Children Together,* p. 19.

26. For a discussion of the issue of the frequency of worker-parent contact, see Karen Blumenthal, "Worker–Biological Parent Contact in Foster Care: A Discussion Paper," (New York: Child Welfare League of America, August 1980), pp. 14–16 (draft).

27. Jones, Neuman, and Shyne, *A Second Chance for Families,* pp. 67–68.

28. McGowan and Deyss, *Permanency Planning,* p. 58.

29. Horejsi, Bertsche, and Clark, *Parents with Children in Foster Care,* p. 146.

30. Ibid., pp. 152–69.

31. Ibid., pp. 169–71.

32. See, for example, Hanni Edinger, "Reuniting Children and Parents Through Casework and Group Work," *Children* 17 (September/

October 1970): 183–87; Dorothy Murphy, "A Program for Parents of Children in Foster Family Care," *Children Today* 6 (November/December 1976): 37–40; Neil Silever, "Mothers' Group," *Children's Village Bulletin,* June 1976, p. 14.

33. Sister Mary Geraldine, Sister Mary Paul, and Carol Heiney-Gonzalez, Center for Family Life in Sunset Park, Brooklyn, New York, November 1980, personal interview.

34. See Joseph Goldstein, Anna Freud, and Albert Solnit, *Beyond the Best Interests of the Child* (New York: The Free Press, 1973).

35. See, for example, *Planned Permanency for Children* (Springfield, Ill.: Illinois Department of Children and Family Services, 1980 Plan: Phase II, vol. 1, 1979), pp. 83–84; Virginia Sibbison and John McGowan, *New York State Children in Foster Care* (Albany, N.Y.: Welfare Research, Inc., 1977), pp. ix, 23; *Your Neighbor's Kids* (Augusta, Maine: Governor's Task Force on Foster Care for Children, 1980), pp. 16, 20, 78–81.

36. This material is based upon *Standards for Foster Family Service* (New York: Child Welfare League of America, 1975); and Rutter, *The Parents' Guide to Foster Care.*

37. *Standards for Foster Family Service,* p. 36.

38. Ibid., pp. 44–48.

39. Ibid., pp. 42–44.

40. For a discussion on preparation for emancipation and independent living, see Paul Kuczkowski, *Permanent Planning in Maryland: A Manual for the Foster Care Worker* (Baltimore, Md.: Maryland Foster Care Impact Demonstration Project, August 1978), pp. 47–52.

41. *Standards for Foster Family Service,* p. 38.

42. For a discussion of the negative effects of replacement, see Charles Horejsi, *Foster Family Care: A Handbook for Social Workers* (Missoula, Mont.: University of Montana, 1978), pp. 157–58.

43. Patricia Cautley and Martha Aldridge, "Predicting Success for New Foster Parents," *Social Work* 20 (January 1975): 48–53.

44. Horejsi, *Foster Family Care,* pp. 256–58; Martin Sundel et al., *Local Child Welfare Service Self-Assessment Manual,* Part II: *Resources* (Washington, D.C.: The Urban Institute, 1979), pp. V-26–V-32.

45. Reprinted with permission of Macmillan Publishing Co., Inc. from *Child Welfare Services,* Third Edition by Alfred Kadushin. Copyright © 1980 by Alfred Kadushin.

46. Horejsi, *Foster Family Care,* pp. 220–21.

47. Ibid.

48. Patricia Cautley and Diane Lichstein, *The Selection of Foster Parents: Manual for Homefinders* (Madison, Wisc.: University of Wisconsin Extension, 1974); Horejsi, *Foster Family Care,* pp. 175–210; *Standards for Foster Family Services Systems for Public Agencies,* rev. ed. (Washington, D.C.: American Public Welfare Association, 1979), pp. 55–62.

49. Horejsi, *Foster Family Care,* p. 194.

50. See Helen Stone and Jeanne Hunzeker, *Creating a Foster Parent–Agency Handbook* (New York: Child Welfare League of America, 1974).

51. Ibid., p. 5.

52. For a discussion of format, wording, and content of these agreements, see Trudy Festinger, "Placement Agreements with Boarding Homes: A Survey," *Child Welfare* 53 (December 1974): 643–52.

53. Martha Aldridge, Patricia Cautley, and Diane Lichstein, *Guidelines for Placement Workers* (Madison, Wisc.: University of Wisconsin Extension, Center for Social Services, 1974), pp. 24–26.

54. Ibid., p. 7.

55. Horejsi, *Foster Family Care,* p. 214.

56. *Standards for Foster Family Service,* p. 65.

57. Aldridge, Cautley, and Lichstein, *Guidelines for Placement Workers,* pp. 20–21.

58. Horejsi, *Foster Family Care,* p. 245.

59. Ibid., p. 221.

60. See Patricia Ryan, Bruce Warren, and Emily Jean McFadden, *Seventeen Course Outlines for Foster Parent Training* (Ypsilanti, Mich.: Eastern Michigan University, 1978).

61. *Standards for Foster Family Service,* p. 66.

62. Aldridge, Cautley, and Lichstein, *Guidelines for Placement Workers.*

63. Horejsi, *Foster Family Care,* pp. 247–54.

64. Evelyn Felker, *Foster Parenting Young Children: Guidelines from a Foster Parent* (New York: Child Welfare League of America, 1974), p. 53.

65. Ibid., pp. 53–56.

66. Emily Jean McFadden, *Working with Natural Families: Instructor's*

Manual (Ypsilanti, Mich.: Eastern Michigan University, Foster Parent Education Program, 1980).

67. See, for example, Sanford Katz, "Changing Legal Status of Foster Parents," *Children Today* 6 (November/December 1976): 11–13; Carol Rose, *Some Emerging Issues in Legal Liability of Children's Agencies* (New York: Child Welfare League of America, 1978), pp. 41–43.

68. Rose, *Some Emerging Issues,* pp. 41–43.

69. Helen Stone, *Foster Parenting an Adolescent* (New York: Child Welfare League of America, 1978); Helen Stone, *Foster Parenting a Retarded Child* (New York: Child Welfare League of America, 1979).

70. Gretchen Heinritz and Louise Frey, *Foster Care: How to Develop an Educational Program for Staff or Foster Parents* (Boston: Boston University School of Social Work, 1975); Pam Marr, *Introduction to Foster Parenting,* vols. 1 and 2 (Manhattan, Kans.: Kansas State University, Department of Family and Child Development, 1976); Ryan, Warren, and McFadden, *Seventeen Course Outlines.*

71. Kadushin, *Child Welfare Services,* p. 390.

72. Knitzer, Allen, and McGowan, *Children Without Homes,* pp. 20–21; Joan Laird, "An Ecological Approach to Child Welfare: Issues of Family Identity and Continuity," in *Social Work Practice: People and Environments: An Ecological Perspective,* ed. Carel Germain (New York: Columbia University Press, 1979), p. 190.

73. Horejsi, *Foster Family Care,* pp. 256–57.

74. Kadushin, *Child Welfare Services,* p. 328.

75. Robert Friedman et al., "The Difficult Job of Recruiting Foster Parents," *Public Welfare* 38 (Summer 1980): 10–17; Michael Garber, Sister Mary Patrick, and Lourdes Casal, "The Ghetto as a Source of Foster Homes," *Child Welfare* 49 (May 1970): 246–51; Horejsi, *Foster Family Care,* pp. 167–74; *Standards for Foster Family Services Systems,* pp. 48–49.

76. Horejsi, Bertsche, and Clark, *Parents with Children in Foster Care,* p. 163.

77. Ibid., p. 141.

78. *Standards for Foster Family Services Systems,* pp. 68–69.

79. Horejsi, *Foster Family Care,* pp. 216–19.

80. Aldridge, Cautley, and Lichstein, *Guidelines for Placement Workers.*

81. Stein, Gambrill, and Wiltse, *Children in Foster Homes,* pp. 108–9.

82. Victor Pike, personal correspondence concerning Blumenthal, "Worker-Biological Parent Contact."

83. Stein, Gambrill, and Wiltse, *Children in Foster Homes*, pp. 108–9.

84. Jones, Neuman, and Shyne, *A Second Chance for Families*, p. 126.

85. McGowan and Deyss, *Permanency Planning: A Casework Handbook*, p. 114.

86. Ibid., pp. 115–23.

87. Theodore Stein, Eileen Gambrill, and Kermit Wiltse, "Dividing Case Management in Foster Family Cases," *Child Welfare* 56 (May 1977): 326–27.

88. Ibid., p. 330.

89. Victor Pike, personal correspondence.

90. Brieland et al., *Differential Uses of Manpower;* Donald Brieland, Thomas Briggs, and Paul Leuenberger, *The Team Model of Social Work Practice* (Syracuse, N.Y.: Syracuse University School of Social Work, Division of Continuing Education and Manpower Development, 1973); Callard and Morin, *Parents and Children Together,* p. 20; *Annual Report* (New York: Lower East Side Family Union, 1977), pp. 4, 6, 11–13, 60–62; Bernice Madison and Michael Schapiro, *New Perspectives on Child Welfare Services: Services, Staffing, Delivery Systems* (San Francisco: Foster Family Care Project, 1973), pp. 138–58.

91. Jones, Neuman, and Shyne, *A Second Chance for Families.*

92. Victor Pike, personal correspondence.

93. Pike et al., *Permanent Planning for Children in Foster Care.*

94. For example, Child Welfare Information Services, Inc., in New York City collects and disseminates information about foster care in New York City. See also Joseph Combs, "An Information System that Measures Foster Casework Effectiveness," *Children Today* 9 (May/June 1979): 15–17, 36; John Poertner and Charles Rapp, "Information System Design in Foster Care," *Social Work* 25 (March 1980): 114–19.

95. W. Eugene Claburn, Stephen Magura and William Resnick, "Periodic Review of Foster Care: A Brief National Assessment," *Child Welfare* 55 (June 1976): 395–405; Arthur Emlen, "The Value of Caseload Screening and Periodic Case Review in Permanent Planning for Children in Foster Care" (Portland, Ore.: Regional Research Institute, Portland State University, mimeographed, n.d.).

96. For additional information, see *The Parents' Rights Unit: Respond-*

ing to Grievances of Parents with Children in Foster Care (New York: Citizens' Committee for Children, October 1977).

97. "CWLA's Statement on Foster Care Services," *Child Welfare* 58 (January 1979): 49.

98. Ibid., p. 50.

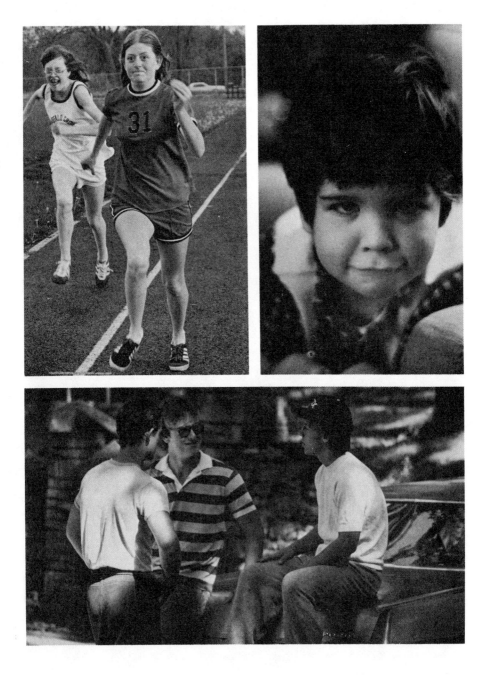

CHAPTER 9
SERVICES FOR SPECIAL POPULATIONS OF CHILDREN*

Sister Mary Paul Janchill

With the increasing recognition of the unique contribution of family membership to the child's sense of identity and the understanding of the difficulties involved in finding new "psychological parents" for children removed from their homes, child welfare agencies are expending new energy on working with families of children in or at risk of foster care placement.[1] As a result of this laudable movement there is beginning to be an attenuation of the need to weigh the "best interests of the child" against those of parents. Historically, these polarities were most in evidence in situations where parents were seen as "neglectful." Removal of children was *presumed* to be justified by the emotional and environmental advantages that they would experience after placement. However, increased reporting of the psychological burdens placed on both the children and their parents as a result of placement, the many negative effects of abrupt, insensitive, and even punitive placements, and a recognition of the social and fiscal costs of placement have led to a reduction in the blaming of parents who were once labeled as resistant or deficient[2] and thereby excluded from treatment planning. Recently a new appreciation of working with individuals and families within an ecological frame of reference has led to the design of family support systems aimed at improving dysfunctional home environments and releasing adaptive capacities in parents that affect the care of their children.[3] However, in this commendable search to provide help to children by means of helping their parents and siblings, there is some risk that

---

*This chapter is based in part on Sister Mary Paul Janchill, *Guidelines to Decision Making in Child Welfare* (New York: Human Services Workshop, 1981).

some of the special problems of children and youth, associated either with selective environmental stresses or particular handicaps, may be minimized.

The unfortunate fact that most children entering placement do so in "emergency" situations that allegedly require same-day or very early removal complicates the problem of properly identifying children with special needs and appropriately planning for them. Planning and preparation, so that the child and placement resource are suitably matched, may be as minimal as one or two telephone conversations with a "homefinder" in the social agency or a telephone call to the intake worker of an agency providing group care. Neither preplacement visits to foster care settings nor individualized and holistic assessments of child and family needs influence a majority of placements. It is obvious that this must be corrected if any reform in the foster care system is to be achieved.

Outside the foster care system, too, there is regrettable inadequacy in case assessment. A recent federal study of social services intake activity by 198 agencies, representing 474 access points, showed that diagnosis was completed at the worker level in 86 percent of the units and at the supervisor level in 4 percent, while a minority of assessments were accomplished through an interdisciplinary or case team. The researchers pointed out that where a case team was involved, more sources of information (psychiatric, psychological, school, and medical reports, for example) were used.[4] The fact that child welfare agencies nationally are staffed predominantly by workers holding only a bachelor's degree and whose "experience" and/or in-service training is their main source of preparation for this field of practice aggravates haphazard planning and poor methods of error correction.

The problem of inadequate case assessment can be as severe in mental health clinics or even hospitals! Reports from such settings are often limited to an examination of the individual in relation to the presenting condition or symptomatology along with very general, even global, goal setting. A comprehensive assessment of the bio-psycho-social needs and resources of the child and family is the exception. Accordingly, it becomes a practical and professional necessity for most social workers to re-tread the paths of case assessment in order to shape, with the client, an appropriate, responsive service plan.

Elsewhere this author has presented a methodology to complete the interlocking processes of case assessment and planning.[5] It involves the systematic review of the cultural, economic, educational, social, and physical environment of the family as well as the health, values and perspectives, communication patterns, and interpersonal functioning of its members. Such assessments are necessary, since no mere listing of problems or designation of handicaps can point the direction for service. No diagnostic label can tell one what the appropriate social service or therapeutic strategy should be, in contrast with physical medicine where this is sometimes possible.[6] There is rarely a one-to-one correspondence between a social or psychological problem category and a service solution. Rather, holistic assessment and differential intervention choices are essential in all situations involving handicapped children and their families.

This is especially relevant in the field of child welfare, which has been undergoing significant changes in the composition of client populations. Many child welfare agencies report a decline in intake and admissions of the more "normal," young or latency-aged child, needing placement predominantly because of family neglect or incapacity. It is very common to find social workers and program directors in public and voluntary child welfare agencies describing their children as "more disturbed," "more behaviorally troubled," "more retarded," or even "more multiply handicapped" than in the past. The de-institutionalization movement, which has cut across a variety of human service systems, has undoubtedly contributed to a shift of responsibility from these more specialized service systems to the more generic services of the child welfare field. Placement of children in psychiatric centers, mental retardation institutions, state youth facilities, and other categorical programs is being discouraged. Such facilities are seen as "too restrictive" due to the segregation they impose on their client population and are viewed as stigmatizing. Consequently, even the sponsoring agencies often declare placement in these facilities to be the "solution of last resort."

Because of these trends mental health, mental retardation, and juvenile justice/youth service departments have generally been showing decreased admissions of children to institutional and other group care programs under their auspices. While some have opened small group homes and developed family foster care homes, there has been an even larger shift to the utilization of facilities in the child welfare system as these departments have changed intake policies and have simply declined admissions. In addition, children with medical or physical complications, including sight or hearing loss, epilepsy, cerebral palsy, heart ailments, or even such precarious conditions as hemophilia and serious respiratory problems are now being cared for by child welfare agencies instead of "children's convalescent homes" and medically sponsored agencies, which were formerly in use throughout the country. Most recently, the mission of the juvenile court is being put to question, with increasing demands that child welfare and social service systems take responsibility for many of its clients including runaways and other children with behavioral problems who have not committed criminal offenses. Probation departments are increasingly referring children and youth to child welfare agencies for assessment and service, and in many areas, child welfare agencies have assumed reponsibility for preventing or diverting children from deeper penetration into the court process. And judges' orders for service very frequently obligate child welfare agencies to provide help for these youngsters.

The removal of children from rehabilitation systems that carry heavy burdens of stigma and social segregation for their enrollees and clients could be a radically progressive and promising movement. However, the realization of this potential depends on the capacity of child welfare programs and personnel (1) to acquire the skills for affecting bio-psycho-social development and change through the healthy normalization of these children's activities and relationships regardless of their presenting symptomatology, and (2) to incorporate family and community involvement in the very design of the services provided. Holistic case assessment, as emphasized above, is at the heart of this kind of program development. Therefore, child welfare agencies generally, and foster care agencies in particular, face outstanding challenges in taking on more handicapped and marginalized children, on the one hand, and surpassing the custodial, residual and unsuccessful approaches which have made psychiatric, mental retardation, juvenile justice, and other categorical settings unwanted, on the other.

CONSIDERATIONS IN SERVING SPECIAL POPULATIONS

Issues of program specialization are often implicated as child welfare agencies are pressed into service or take contracts (if they are voluntary organizations) from the public sector to serve new client groups. While funding patterns and external demands sometimes govern how programs develop for specific groups or new categories of clients, a number of practice principles should be adhered to if service provision is to be effective.

First, remediation or control of a child's handicapping condition should not be permitted to obscure or diminish the promotion of familial ties and cultural identification. Programs should also promote physical, educational, and social development through interchanges with the community and its resources. Specialized services that significantly inhibit access to these sources of development should bear great public, professional, and citizen scrutiny.

Commonly there has been the tendency in more "specialized" settings such as psychiatric hospitals, residential treatment centers, group care settings, and institutions for the retarded to regard the child as client and recipient of service, with family members "allowed" limited "privileges" of visitation and contact. Child welfare agencies, which often have similar orientations, need a great deal of help if they are to avoid isolating children from their families and communities because of the perceived service requirements of these "more handicapped" or "more disturbed" children. Since children of poor and minority group families are overrepresented among those placed outside the home and those diagnosed as psychiatrically disturbed, mentally retarded, learning disabled, delinquent, and the like there is a great risk of reinforcing conditions of familial and social deprivation in the very process of making these children the recipients of "special" services.[7]

Second, remediation of a handicapping condition should not exonerate the child welfare agency or its personnel from the responsibility of achieving permanent plans for children, including arrangements for adoption when biological families cannot or do not take responsibility for planning for their children or maintaining continuous, helpful relationships with them. Unfortunately, children in the care of psychiatric hospitals, residential treatment centers, mental retardation institutions, group settings, medical facilities, or juvenile justice agencies have rarely had the kinds of services that insure permanency planning. It would be unfortunate if child welfare agencies were to assume that the existence of handicaps in the psychological, behavioral, or physical realm justified peripheral attention to the support or creation of a permanent family/home context for the child.

Third, specialization of service should not necessarily be tied to the homogenous grouping of children by age, IQ, sex, physical size, nature or degree of handicap, or kind of behavior. Diagnostic classifications need not, and often should not, be the basis of grouping children to insure that services are more "specialized." By way of a general developmental principle, Bronfenbrenner has pointed to the disadvantages of age and sex segregated environments for children by recognizing the basic human need to learn and master skills in an ecological context that provides both role modeling and adaptive challenges.[8] While the intake policies of many service systems involved with categorically grouped populations of children assume that "segregation" results in better programming, such assumptions warrant careful examination. For example, this writer knows of no research that demonstrates that schizophrenic children get better when placed with other schizophrenic children rather than with children demonstrating diverse psychiatric disabilities and degrees of health. When homogeneous groupings of children are made for funding or management reasons, serious attention needs to be given to the provision of additional services that compensate for the disadvantages that may accrue to the children.

Fourth, specialization of service can be justified only when it is directly associated with the individualization of the specific children within the program. The specialist's knowledge of a particular field should be extensive enough to insure that individual differences between clients become more significant and intelligible. When a given child welfare or human service agency agrees to assume care of mentally retarded, delinquent, runaway, or emotionally disturbed children in a categorical fashion, specialization of service cannot be assumed unless individualization shows itself conspicuously in the design of the service plan, the helping process, and the choices allowed the child and family.

The considerations expressed above come from the observation that the specialized programs and organizations tend to focus a great deal of energy on "boundary maintenance." Such programs attempt to hold to their distinctiveness by controlling client selection, delineating special treatment methods and techniques, restricting the movement of clients in and out of the program, as well as staffing pattern exclusiveness. Specialized programs often claim that the very handicaps of the clients require these special measures. However, excessive boundary maintenance can diminish the constructive effects that other relationships and interactions can have on the specialized program and its clients.

When handicapped children are cared for in a specialized but insulated program or setting, there is considerable risk of reinforcement of handicap or of atypical behavior. Most readers could easily verify this from knowledge of what happens in psychiatric institutions, detention centers, institutions for the retarded, and similar settings. The fact that the broader environment may be noxious and threatening to an individual or family system, or that it may have caused risk of damage to them, is not an argument for program insulation. Rather, it suggests the need to stimulate change in the environment by enhancing intergroup relations, improving communication with potential sources of support, and striking firmer stakes in systems such as schools, community centers, churches, neighborhood organizations, or agencies belonging to different funding/governmental auspices, in order to induce a healthier context for the client.

Attention to these principles appears to be critical if the needs of the "special child" are to receive an appropriate response from the child welfare system. Without respect for these principles, child welfare agencies can fall into the trap of lowering expectations of both their clients and their programs and reverting to the provision of maintenance or custodial services. This would hardly be different from what other service systems have provided in the past and discarded through the deinstitutionalization movement.

Another set of considerations in the selection of resources for children with special needs (especially when out-of-home care is necessary) has been popularized within the principle of *least restrictive alternative.* When this principle is properly applied, it is more than a civil liberties mandate; it is a genuine criterion of appropriate service planning. In general, this principle directs one to avoid service plans that unnecessarily restrict children's opportunities for normalization and socialization because of their problems or handicaps. It argues that the logic of interventions should be based on "what it takes" to manage selected case goals and tasks and to avoid interventions that "do too much" for the child and family and thus diminish their opportunities.

In some instances the meaning of this phrase has suffered by oversimplification, excessive concreteness in the understanding of the term "restrictive," or even vagueness. The principle should not be interpreted as mandating a hierarchical order of different types of service ranging from more to less normalizing. A foster family home, for example, may actually be more restrictive (less normalizing) for some adolescents than a staffed apartment or group home setting, especially if the locale, living design, and supporting staff of the group setting make this "home" more congruent with the ethnic and socioeconomic context of the client and provide experience and activity levels that better fit individual needs. Neither should the size of a facility be a final criterion of the degree of restrictiveness. And most important, respect for the principle of least restrictive environment should not be confused with opting for the least *intrusive* intervention in which less special help than needed may be offered.

In some instances the necessary and appropriate guard against an improperly restrictive service option (for example, a placement in a segregated locale from which reentry problems on return to one's home environment become severe) is to find and support several kinds of help within the community and to provide needed case integration (see Chapters 5 and 6). For example, the care of a mentally retarded or multiply handicapped child within a biological or foster family home will meet the criterion of least restrictive alternative only if this service option includes the concurrent provision of supportive services commensurate with the child's needs. This may mean providing respite services, a part-time home aide, a therapeutic day program in which physiotherapy and occupational therapy are part of the educational design, or a similar "package" of services selected according to the individual's need for remediation and development. Ideally, some, if not all, of these supportive services should be provided within the community rather than *brought into* the home site to enhance normalization. In rural areas, where it is more difficult to locate and use some professional services, caution should be exercised in choosing the locations of foster family homes unless the specific caretakers are specially trained and recruited and are willing to aid in the transportation of children to educational, recreational, and therapeutic programs. Otherwise, even a family home can become a mini-institution—custodial and underservicing.

There is a general understanding that institutional programs in any system of care require special justification for the placement of any child because they tend to *bring in* most of the social contacts, therapy, education, and activity that comprise the child's living milieu and life space. Because of the hazards to individualization and normalization inherent in these programs and the questions that have arisen about the sufficiency of service they provide, institutional placement will always need to pass the test of the principle of least restrictive alternative. This test can be initiated in a case assessment that asks: "What are the special needs of this child and his or her family which *cannot be met by community resources* and therefore justify the provision of a setting that brings in services not otherwise available?" If appropriate resources can be provided within the community and the need is for a catalyst agent (family caretaker, a group home or residence staff, or other home-connected program) to select, organize and integrate services to meet the identified treatment needs, then one looks to this less restrictive (more appropriate) agent rather than an institutional setting. Thus, choosing the appropriate *degree* of structure to accomplish goals is linked to the selection of understanding and qualified personnel trained in matching children with special needs to programs that provide adequate, appropriate, normalizing sources of help (see Chapter 12).

OPTIONS IN CARE

Given these considerations, it becomes logically possible to provide the child with a variety of special services and remedial, rehabilitative, and developmental interventions from the base of a family home. The assumption that family care can meet the criterion of least restrictive alternative is held most firmly in the cases of preschool-aged children, given their need for nurturance by a small number of primary caretakers and "handlers" who can provide continuity and consistency. In such cases it is generally desirable that the biological or foster family be provided ready access to the therapeutic and specialized services needed by a handicapped child and that the child welfare agency deploy its staff in such a way as to ensure this access. While family care may also be appropriate for many older children, the practical needs and growth requirements of *particular* school-aged or adolescent youngsters may point to the need for group approaches. With these principles in mind, certain organizational forms of service are now highlighted for their potential in providing appropriate help.

In-Home Specialized Care

Child welfare agencies are currently modeling a variety of in-home supports to children with special needs. While these services are most readily available for children who are mentally retarded or physically handicapped, there are some programs targeted for children who are learning disabled and behaviorally disordered. Perhaps the most familiar of these services is the use of home health aides, home instructors, and homemakers who are sent to individual homes and children in order to support family care and functioning.[9] Training-for-living programs, in which professionals go to the homes of retarded children to help with life skills development and provide parent training in motor, cognitive, and physical stimulation, while far from universally available, are now found in some communities. Providing families with physical adaptations in the home, such as lifts in the bathroom and bedroom of a handicapped or nonambulatory child, as well as other adaptive chair and bed equipment, has made family care a greater possibility for many children with serious physical problems as well as for those who have disabilities associated with severe to profound mental retardation. Visting nurses are sometimes available to supplement the services of child welfare agencies in monitoring cases of children with "failure-to-thrive" syndrome or developmental disabilities. Maternal and child health stations may also supplement the work of child welfare agencies when called upon to assist through consultation, service planning, and cooperative monitoring of a child's needs.

In-home family supports, such as casework services, the employment of foster grandparents, or family group sessions, are becoming more available through community-based child welfare programs. Many of these services are focused on the amelioration of symptoms associated with behavior disordered children or children reacting to anxiety-producing situations within the family. Similar kinds of home-based services are also being used in some areas of the country to maintain children in a foster family home as an alternative to institutional care. For example,

Nebraska and Michigan have been prominent in creating small alternative living units, which receive the special supports of trained foster parents and visiting professionals for children who would have otherwise been institutionalized as severely retarded.[10]

There are a number of problems that may be encountered in providing in-home specialized care to children. Some services may be over-specialized and available only in central locations. Others may be available only to special categories of children. Still others may be informal, making access difficult. Some services that are "targeted" to children and adolescents, while excellent, do not provide help to parents or siblings. Some are limited to personal social services and do not address financial, housing, education, employment, or legal needs, nor do they provide advocacy, brokering, or linkage to these systems. Some available social supports are not linked with the specialized resources that some handicapped children need. And so, for families and children with serious life management difficulties and multiple-level problems, there can be starvation amidst plenty, given the diffuseness and fragmentation of the service system.

In cases that come to the attention of social agencies because children may be separated from their families, it is most important that the selection and offer of help be relevant to the carefully assessed needs of families and their children. It is imperative that the services offered are acceptable to the service recipient and are meaningful to a comprehensive and integrated service plan—a plan that articulates and brings together the interpersonal and ecological dimensions of family-child problems. The span of help offered is critical because *simplistic solutions to complex life stress situations fail.* Case integration is also critical, for it is not reasonable to have a very troubled family assume the full burden of locating all the basic and specialized helps needed from agencies and groups, which may have inconsistent access requirements, goals, and objectives.

The "packaging" of services at the neighborhood (local) level in comprehensive personal social service centers where the helping includes advocacy and brokering as well as sustained, direct services for as long as needed, has much to offer (see Chapter 6). At the local level the impinging systems affecting the lives of children can be drawn together. Generic social services and community-based support coupled with timely responses from specialized agencies, schools, medical institutions, welfare centers, churches, youth centers, housing groups, employment programs, police, and courts are fundamental if effective in-home care is to be provided to "special" children and their families.

New resource development for these children and their families can occur by working at the point of "interface" between two human service systems, for example, schools and the health system or hospital, the family and the school, or the police and the youth gang systems. In the future the "community school" model of services, in which a variety of community groups participate in a range of programmatic services—social, recreational, family education, child development education, and so on—may be a promising way of maximizing this principle of interface and building the capacity of a community to sustain children and families.

Day Treatment Centers

While most *day-care* centers are either neighborhood-based or designated for a particular local population of preschool children, few have taken on the remediation of handicaps as a responsibility. Most see themselves as meeting developmental rather than remediation needs. *Day treatment* centers, on the other hand, usually incorporate activity and educational programs with social and psychological services for children and adolescents. In the past day treatment programs were apt to be extensions of psychiatric hospitals or institutions for others who were disabled. Recently, however, child welfare agencies have sponsored such programs as an alternative to institutionalization and as a "preventive" strategy for children at risk of placement. Some day treatment programs have grown out of court diversion projects in which child welfare and other community organizations have been funded to sustain children within the community who are out of school and behaviorally troubled. Remediation of learning deficiencies, amelioration of alienation through the creation of therapeutic environments, and the shaping of academic, vocational, and social competencies are the primary goals of such day treatment centers.

One also finds models of day treatment programs for preschool children, but the funding tends to come categorically for such groups as the cerebral palsied, neurologically or orthopedically impaired, or developmentally disabled children. These programs provide sensory-motor stimulation, ambulation, and other self-care training for these groups and where appropriate, may include an educational and/or therapeutic component.

Although some day treatment programs are sponsored by mental health centers, agencies in the mental retardation/cerebral palsy/epilepsy and neurological impairments fields of service, and medical hospitals, these programs may be called upon by the child welfare field to provide some of the services that would allow children to remain at home, in substitute family care, or in a community-based group home. Thus, they can play an important role in keeping children out of more restrictive placement.

It should be noted that day treatment programs under such auspices vary in their supports and the outreach they provide to families and siblings. Generally, they tend to be more child-focused than family-focused, and the child is seen as the primary client and the recipient of the basic, direct services. Because of the amount of "life space" affected by day treatment programs providing therapeutic management and services over five days a week, they can be a very important resource for children with serious psychological, physical, behavioral, or social needs. They should thus be considered for appropriateness before recourse is made to residential care or hospitalization, particularly if the family is able to maintain a child at home with this and any other needed supports. Interdisciplinary team involvement within these programs can contribute to appropriate programmatic individualization and specialization. In some instances dual sponsorship by a child welfare agency and a local school system can also have this effect—licensed teachers providing appropriate educational opportunities and programs and child welfare agency personnel supplying case services, family-related supports, and other appropriate activities.

Study Homes and Diagnostic Centers

The use of designated foster homes, group homes, or small diagnostic centers for holistic assessment, crisis management, and service selection and planning needs more extensive incorporation into the child welfare system if the problems of haphazard placement and service management mentioned at the outset of this chapter are to be ameliorated. The sense of "emergency," often present in planning for a child in out-of-home care, must also include the urgency of knowing the child and family as fully as possible. Without this knowledge, the field will continue to place children in foster homes, group homes, or institutional settings in a virtually random fashion, basing their decisions on "what is available" rather than what is needed. This problem, endemic in the field, leads to the need to correct any initial errors in the child-facility "match" through the replacement of children, a process that is often traumatic and dysfunctional. Unless there has been an opportunity to assess the needs of children systematically, taking into consideration not only their presenting symptomatology, handicapping condition, and functioning levels, but also the familial and ecological context in which these have evolved, one is saying that any given solution is interchangeable with another—a premise few would hold.

Small diagnostic centers, staffed by an interdisciplinary team of personnel from the fields of social work, psychology, psychiatry, education, and health, have come into some increasing use in the larger cities. Many of them have developed in proximity to juvenile courts, and some have been staffed by probation departments attached to such courts. Others have been developed by county or city child welfare departments, and in some areas of the country they have come to supplant congregate "shelters" for new entrants into the placement system. When diagnostic centers fulfill their potential, they are more than new forms of shelter or temporary care. They exercise strict time limits in the study and evaluation services they provide. They offer crisis services aimed at the resolution of problems and placement diversion, and often they become an access point leading to community-based helps (see Chapter 6). In cases where placement cannot be averted they are often a locus from which extended planning can be made, preplacement visits to a foster home or group home arranged, and other preplacement services can be provided.

While diagnostic centers offer the presence of interdisciplinary staff representation and expertise for comprehensive assessment within the agency, off-grounds staff with similar qualifications could perform the same functions for a public or voluntary agency wanting to use family care homes as study homes. Virtually any foster care agency could develop such a study home to ensure relevant planning for children whose problems and symptomatology have not been fully assessed and whose bio-psycho-social needs and the environmental context in which these needs have occurred are not fully known.

Foster Homes

Ordinarily, because of the opportunities for normalization and the availability of primary relationships within a family context, foster family homes are considered to be a primary option for children who cannot be sustained in their own family homes. Foster family care is the only appropriate kind of care for infants and preschool-aged children; it is also appropriate for many latency-aged and adolescent youngsters depending on their characteristics and needs and the service plan developed for them. Foster family care can also be helpful for some children with special needs who are ready to leave a psychiatric hospital, residential treatment center, or other institutional facility.

However, it must be recognized that there are some children who should not be in foster homes. These include children who refuse to accept substitute parents and reject living with a substitute family, children who are a danger to themselves or others, youngsters who cannot find acceptance in or adjust to a community school, or children who, because of fragile ego development and/or extreme impulsivity, need a more structured setting and program with some amount of peer and adult role modeling and on-site professional help. There are some latency-aged or adolescent youngsters who appear not to have much "glue" with which to organize behavior and activity and who need supervision and more professional help than is available in a family setting.

However, it is sometimes possible to sustain children with special problems or handicaps within foster homes when this resource is joined to other supports, for example, a day treatment center, which could provide special education as well as individual counseling or therapy. Alternate educational programs, medical services in the community or provided by a visiting nurse, after-school recreational programs, and a variety of forms of counseling or therapy are some of the most frequently used community supports that may make it possible for a foster family to sustain a child with particular needs. Provision for the foster parent to have ongoing consultation with a child care specialist, an experienced social worker, a psychologist, or a psychiatrist may also enable such a foster parent to deal with special tasks.

The kinds of help given to the foster parents that enable them to relate to the child's biological parents and siblings, as well as the child's own feelings and experiences in relation to their situation, may make a difference in their capacity to sustain the youngster "in care."

Matching child and foster family inevitably means taking into consideration the motivations, characteristics, and personality of each individual. For example, a foster mother might do well with infants and young children but have difficulty with an adolescent because of her own experiences during this developmental stage. Similarly, some foster parents may do well with emotionally handicapped children but not with children who are physically handicapped. In a rural area, where proximity to organized recreational, social day treatment, or other services may not exist, the adequacy of a foster home for school-aged children and adolescents with disabilities or handicaps may be diminished. This may not be true for youngsters with similar characteristics in urban settings where foster homes can be linked to such resources. There are a number of different types of foster homes that could serve the child with special needs.

Foster boarding homes. Foster boarding homes are homes belonging to persons who are licensed by a public or voluntary child welfare agency to care for a child or a specified number of children, under conditions and regulations governing the quality and range of that care. These homes are under the continuing supervision of the sponsoring agency, and the latter makes payments to the foster parent(s) for the care and special needs of the child(ren). The number of children who may be cared for in a particular family home will depend on the characteristics of the caretakers, physical space available, number of own children, experience in foster parenting, and other such factors. An entire sibling group may go into a single foster boarding home.

Agency-operated boarding homes. Group foster homes for which a larger range of operating costs and expenses are paid for by the sponsoring agency are known as agency-operated boarding homes. In some instances the actual home site for this kind of family boarding home is rented and/or furnished by the sponsoring agency in order to give the caretakers the facility to provide for a group of children. The home site may be a detached dwelling or apartment. The aim is to maintain a family atmosphere similar to that in a foster boarding home, although the agency-operated boarding home will, in some respects, resemble a small group home. Agency-operated boarding homes are sometimes ideal for a sibling group or for a group of children/adolescents having some commonality of service needs in which a "peer group" may be of some value. The use of an agency-operated boarding home may, in these instances, enhance the the provision of services and linkages to community resources.

Wage-work homes. Homes in which an adolescent is accepted for family care in return for some personal services such as some baby-sitting, help with housework, or "mother's helper" role are called wage-work homes. Although planning for such placements has to be done very cautiously and with full assessment in regard to all the parties to the arrangement (because of the risks of exploitation or neglect of some basic developmental/social/educational needs), certain adolescents who need to emancipate themselves and who are able to handle themselves in a community have profited from this type of foster care. For example, such homes have been used quite successfully for single expectant mothers. Those who are considered for such wage-work homes should be sixteen years of age or older and should normally be involved in a school or vocational training program at least part-time while living in the home. However, youngsters who are emotionally disturbed, who are a danger to themselves or others, who need the patterning of a more structured or professionalized setting or a closer link to a supervising child welfare agency and a particular plan of permanence, or who are vulnerable to exploitation because of mental retardation or other handicaps should not be placed in wage-work homes.

Group Residential Care

When the special service needs of handicapped, emotionally disturbed, or behaviorally disordered children exceed what can be recruited as supports to their own or kinship homes, or foster family homes (including such supplementary assistance as alternative schools or day treatment), group care settings may be valid and valuable options. The various forms of group residential care are almost always administered directly by a social agency and that agency's employees, whereas foster boarding home care is generally purchased from families who use their own homes or occupy a home site provided by the agency.

Group care settings vary in their approximations to family-style living. There are some group homes in detached dwellings or apartments where group home "parents" or counselors act as surrogate parents and live in part or all of the week. At the other end of the continuum of group residential care, caretaking may be the responsibility of three shifts of staff who cover a twenty-four-hour period, along with a variety of other part-time or full-time staff in disciplines such as education, recreation, vocational training, social work, psychology, psychiatry, nursing and medicine, and sometimes with in-house chaplains as well.

Group care settings incorporate community resources to varying degrees. Some, including many institutions, rely almost entirely on in-house services to the children or adolescents in residence. Such institutions, whatever their goals for therapeutic management, role modeling, and "parenting" responsibilities, least approximate family care, although an individual staff member may in some instances be perceived by a youngster as a parental surrogate.

Group homes. Like other group care settings described below, group homes are entirely supported by a public or voluntary child care agency under conditions and regulations set forth by a state government department. These regulations in some ways define the setting in terms of capacity or size, for example, six to twelve children. Most often group homes are either for boys or girls; unless they are for large sibling groups, few are coeducational. In some areas a group home population of children lives in an apartment or house rented or owned by an individual or family who is reimbursed for the care of the children. In other instances the group home is a facility owned or rented by the child welfare agency, with the adult caretakers regarded as salaried employees who come to live in with the children or spend one "shift" of the day or evening with them.

A major consideration in the use of group homes is their "community base," which can contribute to normalization of relationships with social, educational, familial, religious, ethnic, and other social institutions. Group homes are normally located in residential areas. However, in some instances the location may be remote from the community in which the child originally lived. Some are located in suburban or rural areas in which children need to ride to school, medical facility, recreational resource, church, and so on. Still others are "neighborhood-based," that is, located in the neighborhood from which the children come or close to it, in an urban area.

Children who can profit from group home placement include those who may have affectional ties with their own parents, which preclude their acceptance of the more intense emotional involvement characteristic of foster family care. They may be children with intense emotional problems or physical/behavioral/learning disabilities that require more professional help than would be available within a foster home placement. Older children and adolescents may be found to do better in group homes (or group residences as described below) than in foster homes if, even with adequate preparation and exposure, they are resistive to foster family care. In this regard it should be noted that for some adolescents with strong needs for emancipation, group home or group residence placement may actually be experienced as a *less restrictive* placement than foster family care, which may be perceived as more controlling and limiting. This would need evaluation in the context of full case assessment.

In some instances a group home may be more appropriate than foster family care because of the more "troublesome" characteristics of one or both parents of the youngster. The parent's behaviors may be better managed by the agency staff attached to the group home.

Children leaving institutional care may also benefit from a group home. A group home or group residence may provide more "transitional" help than direct placement in a foster family home, although adequate preparation for the latter may make it quite feasible and profitable for a youngster.

The location of the home and the characteristics of caretakers and staff should be considered in determining the appropriateness of a particular group home for children and youth with observable handicaps and behavioral disturbances. The behavior and needs of the child must be manageable by the program and the community in which it is placed. Some group homes have been able to sustain young people with particular kinds of "acting-out" or unconventional behaviors more than others. Much of this depends on the capabilities, attitudes, and resources of the staff and the supports they can call upon in promoting positive, goal-directed behaviors of the children in care. In other instances acceptance of the neighboring community will be a determining factor, for example, whether homosexual youth or those with other unconventional behaviors will be tolerated and responded to.

Group residences. While the terms "group home" and "group residence" may reflect semantics, the difference between them is usually based on definitions provided by governmental regulations based on the size of the facility. While group homes are usually said to be "family-like" residences and programs for six to twelve children, the "group residence," so called, is "set" for thirteen to twenty-five youngsters. Group residences are much less available as an option because locating the physical facilities and space for this number of children within a community is more problematic.

Group homes may be too small (especially because of economic factors) to permit the assignment of a discrete clinical staff on site, whereas group residences normally provide for social work and/or other clinical staff to work directly at the facility. Group residences, like the group homes described, are usually for boys or girls rather than coeducational.

In general, group residences are often appropriate and helpful for the following types of youngsters:

—Adolescents who have had disabling emancipatory struggles with own parents or foster parents, and who need more professionally-toned relationships with adult authority figures as well as a positive and supporting peer structure

—Adolescents returning to the community after institutionalization, with residual problems that require on-site continued professional help

—Adolescents who come from homes where cultural backgrounds and/or restrictive religious practices may have contributed to acute intergenerational conflicts or conflicts with recognized norms, so that such youngsters need neutral, supervised settings to test out freedoms and heterosexual friendships

—Adolescents with behavioral and/or emotional problems or psychological impairments which require help in a therapeutic milieu directed by an interdisciplinary staff—a milieu which is, at the same time, open to frequent transactions with friends, relatives, schools, and community social systems and organizations

—Adolescents who have been drug or alcohol abusers or repeated runaways, who profit from a group care setting encompassing, along with other therapeutic resources, positive peer pressures as well as individualization of helps and services

—Adolescents who have had repetitive experiences of failure in family-type or group homes

—Adolescents whose plan for permanency is independent living, particularly if the program includes linkages for work experiences, vocational training, and/or college placement.

Institutions. For a "first cut" at classification, institutions are defined in regulations on the basis of population capacity, that is, programs with a residential population of twenty-six or more. Within these settings there may be some physical divisions, such as separate cottages or "units," which may be apartments set off in a large building or even separate buildings. Institutions with these multiple units have child-care staff who are usually assigned to work with the children of a discrete grouping. The staff of these units may also include social workers, recreation workers, psychologists, psychiatrists, nurses, and others, working in "teams" with the child-care workers or counselors. The team assignment is increasingly becoming a matter of governmental recommendation or even regulation, for it is seen as a way of insuring individualization of need and effective therapeutic management.

Placement in institutional care is to be regarded as a restrictive measure to be called upon when the needs of a child cannot be assured by other forms of care. Institutional placement should *never* be determined by family-related characteristics. The use of this service option should always be based on the level of services required by the youngsters themselves. The justification for institutional placement, then, would require a very special assessment of need, including answers to the question: "What tasks are required to help this youngster which either could not be achieved in the community, or could be better achieved in an institution than elsewhere?"

Although the child's special problems and needs should constitute the rationale for this kind of placement, it is very important to examine the presenting behavioral or psychological problems in relationship to family members, peers, school, and relevant social systems. One should determine if relief in any of these areas might reduce the need of the youngster to "act out" and see if some reconstitution of social experiences through new learning, new relationships, and developmental activities could become the substance of "rehabilitative" or "corrective" work closer to the community. However, youngsters whose behavior and/or psychological disturbances indicate that they could endanger themselves or others may need institutional care. In such cases the service plan for each child must also ensure services to the family so that needed intrafamilial and environmental interventions will be adequate and relevant.

The advantages of institutions are their capacity to garner multiple services and to integrate them to respond to the physical, emotional, educational, social, vocational, and spiritual needs of youngsters who lack the control needed to live in a family-type or less restrictive group setting; they may also lack the control to attend and use a community school. Youngsters who have such severe behavioral and/or psychological handicaps may need to have services *brought into* a therapeutically planned milieu and a contained environment, though not necessarily in a secure facility. The use of the latter would be justified only on behalf of a youngster who has committed serious assaultive behavior or who, by reason of psychosis, is incapable of self-protection.

When the very intrusive and restrictive option of institutionalization is called for, there should be an assumption of the need for a planned, specially staffed therapeutic program consisting of services that are selected and integrated by an interdisciplinary team. Favorable ratios of staff to children to assure individualization, the selection of focused tasks that have direct relevance to the identified developmental and rehabilitative needs, service plans that are constituted by the team with child and parent(s) and monitored in regular progress reviews will allow a certain diversity of program models and specializations among centers.

Placement in an institution for the advantages of more comprehensive or controlled programming, on-site therapy, on-site schooling and training, and so on would be very inappropriate if children could use these services within their communities. Youngsters who are able to obtain acceptance in a community school should not be educated in an on-grounds school of an institution, and in fact, it would usually be inappropriate for such a child to be in an institution rather than a group home or group residence. Unfortunately, some institutions continue to accept children who could be better served in community facilities. These facilities continue to *bring in* a larger range of services than is required by the child population including for example, a school, medical clinic, chapel, gym, and social activities. As a result the children live in an environment dysfunctionally segregated from the community.

To illustrate some of the possibilities for residential treatment programs, based on a broad sketch of population needs, three examples are given below:

Centers that are appropriate for and serve children whose disturbance are manifested by deviant behavior, impaired socialization, or lack of impulse control: Such children require not only individualized treatment but strong patterning of behavior through new relationships, well-organized activity programs, special education, and skill building. Some of these centers may be designed around a particular group of youngsters, such as those susceptible to drug or alcohol abuse, or autistic children who have complex developmental, learning, and behavioral problems and need a strong psycho-educational program, one-to-one staff support, and an emphasis on skill and competency training, communication, attention building, and so on.

Centers for children who are emotionally conflicted or disturbed as manifested in destructiveness to themselves or others or to property, or may be so lacking in reality orientation that twenty-four-hour supervision would be called for. These settings would need to have capacity for strong psychiatric consultation to manage children with suicidal orientation, those with serious thought or affect disorders, or who manifest very rageful behavior. Although the symptomatic behaviors of some of these children may appear to reflect unusual pathology (self-mutilation, deviant sexual behavior, fire-setting, anorexia, severe accident proneness, continual disruptive confrontations, and so on), there is great need to "treat" such children on the basis of a careful understanding of rejections and deprivations, which may have fed into a "vicious cycle" of acting out. Such programs should assure that institutionalization does not come to reinforce the rage of abandonment or self-definition of being bad, evil, and so forth.

Centers that serve multiply handicapped children where there may be medical dimensions to their needs, such as neuromuscular, orthopedic, or other organically related handicaps: Included here would be children with severe developmental lags, which require highly specialized programming in order to prepare them for progressive movement to less restrictive, more normalized community living options. Such centers may also serve, for a limited time period, severely retarded children where such youngsters' handicaps are either secondary to another disability (medical or psychological) or associated with unusual neglect or abuse.

Summarizing some major points to be observed in the use of institutional care:

—This represents an option at the most restrictive end of the continuum of residential services; therefore, use must be justified by the severity of the need as well as the particular specializations and resources offered by the institution. Institutions should not be used to accommodate neglected or dependent children who could be served in other forms of group care or family-type boarding homes with special supports and services obtainable in the community or supplied by a sponsoring agency.

—Although the child's special needs lay the base for the selection of a residential treatment program, the services provided must always have in view a plan of permanency and the provision of helps to the family to enable them to supply a sustaining environment for the child. Services to the family should be provided to relieve any factors contributing to the child's disabilities and/ or to participate in progressive planning on behalf of the youngster.

—Residential treatment centers may vary in program design, activities, and specializations, based on the best defined professional knowledge (to which licensing and accreditation organizations can contribute) about how remediation and developmental gains are enhanced. Program design should include commitments to utilize community resources and linkages, generic social supports, and/or graduated reduction of physical controls, as appropriate, so that institutional care is regarded as a strictly time-limited service that is preliminary to a clearly designated, less restrictive form of care.

Reflections on Group Care

Group care settings are often conspicuous to the communities in which they are situated, making normalization and integration of their residents difficult. The very existence of the group care setting in the community is most often explained by the distinctive characteristics of the residents, which mark them as atypical. Consequently, the processes of positive identity formation and competency acquisition are often hampered. This can only be compensated by the special efforts of the agency and its staff to maximize the individualization of the residents in relation to their participation in the group care program and in respect to their contacts with family, friends, neighbors, school, church, and access to other developmental opportunities.

The physical location of the group care setting is often a controlling variable in making this individualization and normalization possible. By public policy (and the support of advocates recruited from as broad a base as possible) group care settings should not be developed outside residential areas and the reach of ordinary public transportation. They must be accessible to family and community. Group care facilities in segregated or remote areas can rarely be effective in the developmental and therapeutic management of handicapped or troubled children.

Strong resentments are often generated by communities about allowing group homes, group residences, or residential treatment centers in their midst. Child welfare agencies meet strong obstacles in site selection within residential communities. Fortunately these obstacles can be somewhat reduced if agencies choose smaller houses or units within the community or apartments within a complex large enough to make one or two units less imposing. Agencies can also reduce opposition to the facilities by properly preparing and organizing the community in which they will be located. The fact that a community can test and verify the good track record and responsible performance of the sponsoring agency can go far in winning community acceptance. While these efforts may be time-consuming and difficult, it must be remembered that when opposition must be met by court litigation, the process of starting a group facility is drawn out and presents potential stress for the children as well as the staff of the program.

To the extent that residential treatment centers might be needed for children or adolescents whose behavioral and psychological impairments render them dangerous to themselves or to others, and therefore, in need of a program that is relatively more encompassing and structured, we may be more accepting of their location in less normalized residential areas for practical reasons. Ideally, however, these too should be community-based.

Customarily, justification for incorporating *more* children in a residential setting is based on the youngsters' needs for a more intensive level of service provided by a more professionalized staff. Sometimes cost-effectiveness is also cited as a reason for larger units. However, this cost-effectiveness argument deserves more study and critique, since program design, service arrangements, and staffing are amenable to a variety of factors that influence costs. For example, one method of deploying staff and support services that protects specialization and intensity of care within small facilities is being tried with a number of populations. This program model, which was first used in the de-institutionalization of the mentally retarded and other developmentally disabled individuals, has been called the *core-satellite design*. In this model several family care homes, staffed apartments, or supervised residential units of very modest size are programmatically and administratively staffed by a *core* facility or office. Caretakers and professionals are deployed from this core facility in a ratio based on the specific kinds and amounts of help that individual residents need. The core-satellite composite may consist of one group home for six children and three nearby staffed apartments, each housing three youngsters, for a total population of fifteen. Alternately, the core-satellite composite could be made up of six three-bedroom houses, or a group home for eight and a few family care homes, or varying combinations of group and individual homes with the maximum population usually not exceeding twenty-five.

Depending on the nature of the developmental and remediation needs of the children, the administering child welfare agency should decide what caretaking and professional disciplines would be encompassed in the staff, how many staff to employ, and for what hours they should be employed. Live-in child-care personnel would be assigned to individual apartments or to the core group home, while certain professionals (social worker, occupational therapist, psychologist, and the like) would share time with all units.

This is a way of providing an appropriate level of professional and specialized help to children without diminishing the normality of the home itself. A core-satellite program design can provide a capacity comparable to a group residence for up to twenty-five children without reverting to the near-institutional form that the latter might come to resemble. The provision of specialized professional assistance and services to children and youth who might then be able to live in a style resembling that of a family has many other advantages, which may be easily discerned by the reader in terms of avoidance of negative labeling in the community and so on. Such programs can be designed for emotionally disturbed, behaviorally disturbed, or other handicapped youngsters such as those who are autistic, physically impaired, or mentally retarded. They can provide the necessary individualized services in a cost-efficient way, as there are often many economies in this design as compared with the financial obligations accompanying the maintenance of a discrete plant or facility to house a similar number of children.

Whether by the use of such a core-satellite design or the pulling in of community resources, there is often the possibility of reducing the need to call on institutional care for children with special needs. Combining an alternate school or day treatment program with a home support arrangement, a family-centered treatment program, intervention in any one of the systems impinging on a child or family, or strengthening an area of special promise or competence may make a strategic difference. Going outside one's own agency boundaries to locate and use supports and resources is a rewarding method of upgrading services to children and to those most psychologically significant to them—their families. Consideration should be given to the use of valuable resources such as neighborhood friendship groups, self-help groups, skill-exchange cooperatives, recreation and socialization programs, school-based clubs, open lounge activities, and many other interest-based activities. While lack of resources is a frequent complaint of social workers aiming to help children with special needs, there is little doubt that in the search for the remedial and the correctional, we frequently underestimate a variety of informal or relational contexts in which remediation and therapeutic management could be addressed.

One recent survey of the theories and strategies underlying services to behaviorally disordered or delinquent youngsters comes to the following conclusions, which have relevance for others:

> The most direct and immediate implication of the well-supported delinquency theories is that there are arrangements and processes in contemporary social institutions that generate delinquent behavior. To reduce delinquent behavior, these arrangements and processes should be altered. The most fruitful arenas for delinquency prevention initiatives are education, work, and community service broadly defined, *and their interaction with each other and with families.*[11] (emphasis added)

It is possible, then, that growing recognition of the salience of social systems and the dynamics of human ecology will draw practitioners and program administrators to be catalysts in the use of these various possibilities on behalf of troubled and handicapped children. There is so much openness to methodology that new "program design" should become an attractive challenge. Beginning research that explores connections between a given handicap and the ecological context for helping is emerging.[12]

An Application of the Ideas

One descriptive example is now presented to demonstrate how the above ideas can be translated into practice. In this example certain structures are developed side by side with freedoms and individualization in an urban residence in a major city.[13] One of the accomplishments of this group care setting for emotionally disturbed and behaviorally troubled adolescent girls has been its harmonious relationships in a section of the city that contains a university and a variety of social/cultural organizations as well as businesses and churches. The community is otherwise typical of many areas of that city. The group residence itself has not attracted very much notice, as its occupants go and come as they would from a variety of other types of buildings. The vicinity is mixed as to ethnicity and social class.

S.H.R. is a treatment-oriented group residence for twenty adolescent girls who are emotionally disturbed and neglected, and who manifest a range of behavioral disorders. Their problems are rooted in family breakdown and complex socioeconomic dislocation. Placement of these young people originates with one of the family courts or the city's child welfare department. In each case the recommendation for residential treatment and care on a year-round basis has resulted from psychosocial study by the referring agency, as well as psychiatric and psychological evaluations. The population of the residence represents a variety of ethnic groups and races. The girls come from multiproblem families from depressed areas of the city and give evidence of marked social and emotional deprivation. Motivation for education has been seriously affected, and their social exposures have been limited.

The staff goes on to say:

> Specifically our youngsters are in need of developing warm, rewarding, growth-producing relationships with peers and adults; to become aware through the medium of individual and group therapy in addition to the therapeutic milieu of the residence, of their own potential for growth, self-becoming and self-awareness; to receive guidance and direction in broadening their educational and social experiences and opportunities; to be provided with a group living experience rich in nurturance and support which also has necessary structure and ample room for the teenager to test out her need for independence and to achieve a sense of mastery over her own life; to receive support and intervention in dealing with their fractured and fragmented families; to have easy access to their families who live nearby, as well as access to friends; to participate in the community's educational systems as well as its social and recreational activities; to receive all necessary and appropriate medical services; to live in a setting where the religious and cultural perspectives of each child are respected and fostered. . . .

With regard to daily activities and structure:

> Daily activities reflect the diverse school work, social and recreational needs of our youngsters. Rising time varies for each resident and is dependent on her school program. Work, tutoring, and recreational experiences are coordinated with appointments for group and individual therapy sessions which are given priority.
>
> Each girl is free to send and receive mail in complete privacy. In addition there are two phones for the use of the residents who are free to make and receive phone calls unmonitored by the staff.
>
> The residence director, together with child care and social work staff, sets appropriate curfews for each girl. These are flexible and age-appropriate

and reflect the desire of the staff to encourage personal responsibility and accountability on the part of each youngster. In general, high school seniors and older adolescents must be home on weekends by 1:30 A.M., and younger residents from between 11:00 P.M. and 12:30 A.M. During the week all must be in by 10:00 P.M. in preparation for the next school day. A tradition has been established whereby the girls informally notify a child care staff member whenever she leaves the residence—modeling this after normal family living where children greet parents upon arriving and leaving their homes. The residence director or her assistant is available to welcome the girls' dates and friends and to share their evenings' experiences by waiting up for their return. Youngsters are able to extend their curfew upon request when this seems appropriate.

Each girl is personally responsible for maintaining her room in good order and is assigned some routine duties as washing the dishes after a meal, setting tables, etc. Tasks are rotated and are scheduled so as not to interfere with schooling, recreation, normal community contacts or family visiting. A housekeeper, cook, and maintenance man share responsibility for the general upkeep and maintenance of the residence.

On provision for education:

Wherever possible the residents are encouraged to continue in their former school. However, distance, an inappropriate educational setting or poor adjustment there may necessitate a transfer. Educational planning is thus made, before admission to the residence, with the girl and her parent(s). Each girl is encouraged to participate in the selection of her school and course and for this purpose educational and vocational aptitudes are tested initially and reviewed according to need. Both public and parochial schools are utilized in an effort to ensure each resident a school program designed to meet her needs. Schools offering special remediation, nongraded classes, high school equivalency as well as those offering academic courses may be selected.

The residence director is responsible for coordinating and supervising school attendance, e.g., by weekly checks on attendance, representation at parent-teacher conferences and periodic meetings with school guidance counselors and program coordinators. At "treatment and review meetings" and the daily informal sharing between caseworkers and the director, the educational needs of each girl are frequently discussed and evaluated. . . . A strong tradition of daily school attendance has been built into the residence (with strong peer support and offers by older residents to assist younger children with their work).

Guiding the use of leisure time:

Each girl is encouraged to participate in school activities such as athletic teams, cheerleading, band, etc., to participate in church-related activities, and resources at community facilities. The residence also sponsors trips to places of historical and cultural interest and to other cities. Girls make use of bowling, plays, ice and roller skating and movies, and residents are encouraged to make use of many free or low cost activities occurring in the city.

The girls are welcome to invite their friends and dates to share in the activities at the residence and also to go with them on outings. Recreational areas within the residence include a roof, pool room, and a living room equipped with stereo and TV, in addition to a larger lounge area. Often trips and activities are open to the girls' friends and family members. At the residence itself there are informal arts and crafts sessions; also bicycles, ice-skates, softball equipment, etc., are available for continual use. There are some planned camping outings as well, and the girls are encouraged to participate in recreation and vacations of their families.

Introduction to the work world:

Each girl for whom it is age appropriate is encouraged to seek part-time employment and helped to budget her savings. Staff assist the girls in contacting and locating job situations which might expose the residents to future vocational and career openings. . . .

Home and family visits:

Parents are encouraged to call, visit, and come to dinner any time; often a younger brother or sister is invited to sleep over. Proximity to their old neighborhoods enables our youngsters to visit families and friends as frequently as they wish. Special invitations go to their families and friends at the time of a girl's birthday or special celebrations at Christmas Eve, Thanksgiving, Easter and graduations. Siblings and friends are invited to join the girls on outings and trips to the beach, sports activities and other events.

Medical services:

Each girl is enrolled at the child and youth clinic at the nearby hospital, where initial and annual screenings as well as follow-up are provided. Private specialists in the community are used for visual, dental, and other special medical needs of the residents. Since each resident has an individual bedroom, there is no isolation at the time of illness, but hospitalization within blocks of the residence location can be called upon as appropriate. The family would be notified immediately, their consent obtained, and close contact maintained between the girl, her family and the residence.

Other:

Meals and snacks meet the nutritional standards recommended by the National Research Council. Menus are planned by the cook in conjunction with our youngsters who are encouraged to help plan and especially on weekends participate in cooking. . . . Cultural dishes are a favorite and enable the girls to share their heritage and experience a variety of foods. The kitchen is always available for their use; supervision and guidance in food preparation are provided by the cook and child care staff. The full time cook prepares lunch and dinner Monday through Friday, while the girls and child care staff prepare meals on the weekends, along with daily breakfast and snacks.

All residents receive a monthly clothing allowance of $40.00 (in addition to a weekly expense allowance of $10.00 plus carfare for school, medical appointments, home visits and recreation). A supplementary clothing allowance is provided at the time of admission, discharge, and when winter coats need to be purchased. Each girl is free to spend her weekly personal allowance without accounting to the staff.

Any corporal punishment of youngsters, use of isolation, or the deprivation of meals, mail or family visits as a means of discipline is prohibited.

Psychotherapy:

Each girl has a weekly individual psychotherapy appointment at the residence; as well, she participates once weekly in group therapy. A condition of admission to the residence is the girl's agreement to participate in these ways of becoming more self-aware, autonomous and able to make responsible choices in relation to her family, friends and activities.

Individual sessions are provided by experienced and skilled clinical social workers. Group therapy is co-led by one of the latter with the staff psychiatrist; a second group is led by a worker with a clinical psychologist who is also a staff member.

Direct social services are also provided to parents and siblings as needed to make the family unit more functional for its members and to provide concrete assistance in their social and environmental needs.

Thus both experiential and reflective methods are used to help the girls and their families to a better understanding and use of the dynamic systems impinging in and on their lives.

While this description of one residential treatment program for troubled adolescents illustrates one approach to specialization, adaptations of many other types may be made through the interplay of structures, boundaries of service, use of community and involvement of family, in designing services for other kinds of needs and the situations of other handicapped children. In the future, child welfare agencies' responses to troubled and handicapped children will surely lie in the direction of joining the developmental with the remedial, the personal with the social, the individual with a sustaining family and community—as our best understanding of how to help.

NOTES

1.   Charles R. Horejsi, Anne Vandeberg Bertsche, and Frank W. Clark, *Social Work Practice with Parents of Children in Foster Care: A*

Handbook (Springfield, Il.: Charles C Thomas, 1981). This guide to practice rests on principles derived from research; it combines salient standards with selected methodologies. See also Anthony N. Maluccio and Paula A. Sinanoglu, "Social Work with Parents of Children in Foster Care: A Bibliography," *Child Welfare*, 60 (May 1981): 275–303.

2. Ruth Hubbell, *Foster Care and Families: Conflicting Values and Policies* (Philadelphia: Temple University Press, 1981). See also Shirley Jenkins and Elaine Norman, *Filial Deprivation and Foster Care* (New York: Columbia University Press, 1972).

3. Sister Mary Paul Janchill, *Guidelines to Decision Making in Child Welfare* (New York: The Human Services Workshops, 1981).

4. Shirley Jenkins and Anita Schroeder, *Intake: The Discriminant Functions: A Report on the National Study on Social Services Intake for Children and Their Families* (Washington, D.C.: Office of Human Development Services, U.S. Department of Health and Human Services, 1980), p. 35.

5. Sister Mary Paul Janchill, *Guidelines to Decision Making,* pp. 3–34.

6. This author takes the position that terms such as "severe affect disorder," "moderate thought disorder," and the like are in and of themselves not justifications for institutionalization, since the accompanying distress to the individual, family, and community may be treatable by a wide range of methods and in a variety of community or residential settings. A comparable thesis is also maintained in E. T. Heck and A. R. Gruber, *Treatment Alternatives Project: Final Report and Evaluation* (Boston: Boston Children's Association, 1976).

7. See, for example, Murray L. Gruber, "Inequality in the Social Services," *Social Service Review* 54 (March 1980): 59–75; and Shirley Jenkins, "Child Welfare as a Class System," in *Children and Decent People,* ed. Alvin Schoor (New York: Basic Books, 1974), pp. 3–23.

8. Urie Bronfenbrenner, *The Ecology of Human Development* (Cambridge, Mass.: Harvard University Press, 1979).

9. See, for example, P. W. Soyka, "Homemaker-Home Health Aide Services for Handicapped Children," *Child Welfare* 55 (April 1976): 241–51.

10. Martha Ufford Dickerson, *Social Work Practice with the Mentally Retarded* (New York: The Free Press, 1981), pp. 184–93.

11. Grant Johnson, Tom Bird, and Judith W. Little, *Delinquency Prevention: Theories and Strategies* (Washington, D.C.: Law Enforcement Assistance Administration, U.S. Department of Justice, April 1979), p. 4.

12. See, for example, Suzanne Salzinger, John Antrobus, and Joseph Glick, eds., *The Ecosystem of the "Sick" Child: Implications for Classification and Intervention for Disturbed and Mentally Retarded Children* (New York: Academic Press, 1980).

13. The residence offering this residential treatment program is not named here, by agreement with its director, in order to spare the residents publicity.

**Return
Home**

**Return
to
Relatives
Home**

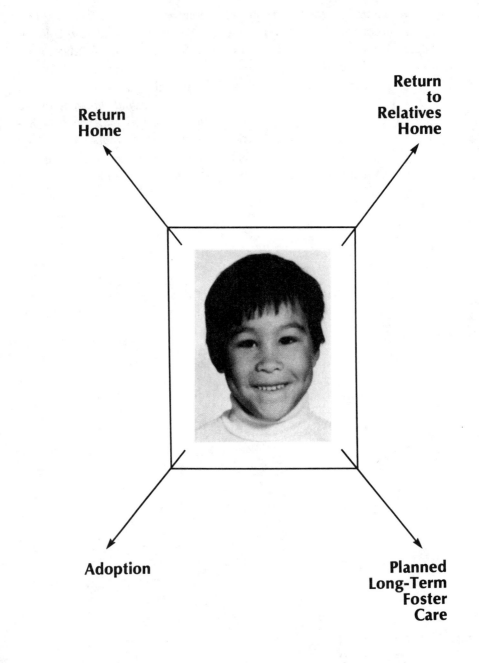

Adoption

**Planned
Long-Term
Foster
Care**

CHAPTER 10
ACHIEVING PERMANENCE AFTER PLACEMENT

Joan F. Shireman

There is a "watchword" in our current child welfare service system—permanency planning. The meaning of the term is simply that children deserve to receive careful, thoughtful planning for their future. When children are not at home, the responsibility for such planning rests with the state and, in a practical sense, with the child welfare system responsible for their care. Such planning begins with the decision as to whether a child should enter foster care, and there is no doubt that for many children this is a needed, necessary, and valuable service. Once children enter care, the need is for planning and work so that they may have permanent homes of their own. This need has long been recognized within the child welfare system, although changing assumptions about the goals of child welfare and what constitutes good planning have, at times, tended to mask this historical concern. (See Chapter 2 for a discussion of how foster care was originally seen as a way of achieving permanent homes for children.)

Who are the children for whom permanency planning is needed? First, they include those children still in their own homes and "at risk" of placement. Second, they include children whose custody is at issue as their parents separate or form new families. Third, they may or may not include children growing up with relatives or in "informal" adoptive homes, arrangements particularly common among some minority groups. Finally, they include children currently being cared for outside their own families in foster homes or group settings. This chapter focuses on this last group.

Not all children in foster care are in need of special permanency planning services. For many children, the current foster care system provides appropriate service, meeting their need for good care in a comfortable setting during the period of time when their parents are not able to care for them. For these children, placement is the temporary, time-limited, goal-directed service described in the preceding chapters.

However, studies done as early as 1959 began to call attention to the problems of some children living away from home. In that year Maas and Engler published the first systematic study of children living in foster homes and institutions, and the child welfare field was startled to learn that more than half of the placed children seemed destined to grow up in care. Perhaps the most important discovery was that once children had been in foster care or institutional care for eighteen months, they were likely to remain.[1] Temporary foster care became permanent by default.

In the more than twenty years since this publication, there have been continued efforts in the child welfare field to correct this situation. Many projects, some of which will be reviewed in the following pages, have demonstrated a variety of approaches to achieving permanency for children. Nonetheless, studies of foster care case loads in assorted states during these years continued to reveal that large numbers of children were "drifting" into permanent foster care without assessments, plans, or efforts to work with them or their families toward permanence. Finally, following a study in 1978 came the indictment:

> Children placed out of their homes are not only likely to be cut off from families, but also abandoned psychologically and sometimes literally by the public systems that assume responsibility for them. They are, in effect, children in double jeopardy.[2]

As a result, attention has currently turned to the study of ways in which the child welfare system itself can facilitate workers' efforts to plan for children in care. The resulting system characteristics and programs developed to facilitate permanency planning are the subject of this chapter.

What Constitutes Permanency?

"Permanency" in a child's life is difficult to define, for who knows what circumstances may suddenly disrupt the most seemingly stable situation? Pike's definition is perhaps the most useful: "*Permanency* describes *intent*. A permanent home is not one that is guaranteed to last forever, but one that is *intended* to exist indefinitely."[3] Intent creates commitment between the child and the family unit, and thus continuity in a single home evolves. Intent bespeaks conscious and careful planning.

Many authors write of a sense of "belonging," rooted in cultural norms and definitive legal status. One wonders if legal status may not be the least important of the elements of permanence. Informal adoption, which has no legal basis, has been repeatedly identified as a major and culturally sanctioned way of providing homes for black children within their own community. Legal classifications can be relatively meaningless to children and their families and may be important only insofar as they reinforce existing commitments.

Permanence is usually achieved for the child "drifting" in foster care through: (1) rehabilitation of the biological home and restoration of the child to it, or (2) termination of parental rights and subsequent adoption of the child by relatives, foster parents, or new adoptive parents. There are also some instances in which neither of these solutions is feasible. In such cases a third alternative is being tried, which seems to give promise of permanence, though with uncertain legal status: *planned* long-term foster care. This option is differently implemented in different settings and may take the form of contractual agreements among foster parents, biological parents, and the agency. Such agreements may be reinforced by the foster parents taking guardianship of the child.

Each of these living arrangements is more difficult to attain than it seems reasonable to expect. Each has its own problems, and each demands sustained casework activity. A number of demonstration projects have been successful in implementing permanency planning for a high proportion of the children on their case loads. Typically these projects report high morale, enthusiasm, and concern about the lives of children on the part of project staff; most have worked with relatively small case loads to enable intensive work. Even so, the process is often lengthy. One project has suggested that intensive *permanency planning begun when a child has been in care for some years takes an average of sixteen months,*[4] an estimate that seems congruent with the reporting of other projects.

Difficult though it may be to achieve, the importance of permanent homes for children justifies the necessary effort, as the possible destructive effects of foster care are well known. Primarily, these concern: (1) children's difficulties in forming a positive sense of self when they are separated from their own parents and have not settled into other homes of their "own," and (2) the damage that may be done to children's ability to learn and to trust in new relationships when continuity of care is not provided. These concerns form the basis for the current efforts to achieve a permanent home for every child in foster care.

IDENTIFYING THE CHILDREN

The Children in Jeopardy

It is difficult to estimate the number of children for whom permanency planning services are needed. The available data can be misleading. For example, Kadushin noted that in a cross-sectional analysis of the foster care population at any time, children in care for extended periods are overrepresented. This yields an exaggerated estimate of the average length of time in foster care. He suggests that:

> A longitudinal study, then, is a more accurate procedure for analyzing the question of whether the foster family care system offers temporary care. Such studies, unlike the studies reviewing the population in care at any one period, tend to show that, for many children, the system is working as it was intended to work—providing substitute care during a temporary crisis in families when care of children in their own homes was impossible or hazardous or when the children's behavior made maintenance at home difficult.[5]

This author concludes that about 25 percent of the children entering care are likely to remain in care indefinitely and thus need some structured provision for permanence.[6]

On the other hand, a 1979 report concluded that because of poorly kept statistics, it was not even possible to obtain an exact count of children in foster care. The report estimated that there were more than 500,-000 such children, that the "system" discouraged permanent planning for these children, and that children virtually became "lost" in care.[7] Another study concluded that parents were often discouraged from maintaining contact with placed children and received little help with problems that led to placement, while at the same time there was a reluctance to terminate parental rights and move toward adoption.[8] Still a third study estimated that of the more than 350,000 children in foster care, about half would remain "for a long period," many until adulthood.[9]

At the very least, one must be aware that almost every census of the foster care population of any county or state reveals large numbers of children who have been in foster care for long periods of time. Many of them are older children, and many have very little contact with their own parents. Whether their numbers are proportionately many or few, it is necessary that they be helped through purposive planning efforts. As a first step, methods of identifying these children need to be developed.

Children in Need of Planning

The information that should be used to "flag" children in need of concentrated efforts toward permanency planning includes: (1) length of time in foster care, (2) number of placements, (3) age of the child, (4) minority status, and (5) special needs or circumstances. Even with the information readily available, however, its interpretation and use require thoughtfulness and imagination.

In identifying children already in the child welfare system for whom special planning is necessary, time in foster care is probably the most often used criterion. This makes sense; the data are the most consistently available and readily obtainable. But it is difficult to assess what period of time is appropriate for temporary care and when that care begins to drift toward unplanned, long-term care. The rapid development of children and their truncated sense of time mean that their "time clock" allows them a relatively short period of instability before developmental damage may take place[10] or they become "embedded" in a new home. Thus, planning for the child must begin as soon as possible. One author notes:

> The chances of success for any permanent plan are greater if you start early. A structured treatment plan initiated immediately after placement, provides the best opportunity for the child to return home. . . . Immediately after the child has been placed in foster care, parents and worker can more easily identify and agree on the reasons that the child was removed. Parents have not yet adjusted to their loss and are motivated to change in order to regain their child. . . . If the parents have deserted, it will be easier to find them and make a plan with them about the future of their child. If you wait, they may disappear altogether. . . . The child hasn't yet settled into a relationship with his foster parents. . . . If the restoration plan is unsuccessful, the documented effort to treat, and failure of the parents to respond, become part of the case for terminating the parents' rights so that the child can be adopted. If the foster placement has been successful and the foster parents want to adopt, an early adoption in that setting is better for the child than the status of foster child. If adoption in another home is indicated, the move for the child is easier, because he spent only a brief time in foster care.[11]

In an attempt to force planning for permanency, it has been suggested that juvenile court judges be required at the end of a fixed period of time—perhaps twelve or eighteen months—either to return children to their biological parents or legally free them for adoption.[12] This is a powerful idea that seems to make sense. But how difficult would this be to implement given the complexities of practice? Agencies may fail to provide services for a variety of legitimate reasons. Courts may delay termination of parental rights for reasons that seem sound to individual judges and may be highly idiosyncratic. Parents may have severe environmental and personal problems, which, with all goodwill, are difficult to resolve. For example, it has been suggested that a two- to four-year period may be necessary for resolution of some family difficulties.[13] Clearly this is too long a time for young children to remain in "temporary" care.

The right of children to permanence needs to be protected; this is the thrust of the idea behind time limits. But rigid time limits may conflict with the need for individual attention to the particular circumstances of a given child and family, which are the traditions of our social work and juvenile court systems. And, it should be remembered that no matter what time span is set, there will be error, either in identifying a high proportion of cases for which planning is already underway or in omitting cases that are actually "drifting."

The age of the child is another commonly used criterion for identifying children in need of permanency planning services. Older children—over ten, twelve, or fourteen—are often considered difficult to plan for. They may be close to achieving independence or at a developmental stage where they rebel against the controls of family life. However, failure to work on permanent plans for them may be a real disservice. Although adoption in a new home may not be feasible, reacquaintance with biological parents or formalization of long-term foster care arrangements might be expected to have a positive impact on the identity crises of adolescence.

On the other end of the age continuum, infants are often not identified as needing planning services. It is often believed that they are easy to move into permanent homes. However, a few months of unplanned time in foster care soon moves an infant into a "harder to place" category.

Repeated replacement within the foster care system may almost automatically be taken as an indicator that a child is experiencing difficulty and should receive special attention. Given the difficulties of separation, one foster care placement is all that any child should experience.

A review of studies indicates that more than half of the children in care do indeed experience only one placement.[14] Two placements—first a short-term "emergency" placement and then a long-term placement—are not an uncommon pattern. Perhaps three placements indicate trouble. This number is lower than the one commonly used; yet, less than a quarter of the children in placement would be identified through application of such a criterion.

Minority status may also be used as a criterion to identify children for whom special efforts to achieve permanence should be undertaken. There is evidence that children of minority backgrounds do not find the child welfare system as responsive to their needs as do other children. Agencies have traditionally had difficulty recruiting foster homes and adoptive homes for minority children, particularly those with handicaps. Consequently, once placed away from home, minority children do not have plans for permanent living accomplished for them as expeditiously as other children. They tend to remain longer in care and to have more placements than do other children. A smaller proportion return home; a smaller proportion are adopted.[15]

It is not clear whether the cause is neglect by workers or whether plans are simply more difficult to implement for minority children. The disadvantages under which minority families live may make it harder to plan children's return home, and controversy has surrounded the unconventional approaches to finding adoptive homes for minority children that have been tried.

The need for appropriate planning for children with special needs, be they physical, emotional, or developmental, was stressed in the previous chapter. Such children present a special challenge to agencies' permanency planning efforts. Location of appropriate resources is critical, yet difficult.[16] Fewer families are able to cope with the demands such children make, and the cost of caring for them is high. Yet, without permanency planning efforts, these children are probably the most likely to "drift" in the foster care system and to suffer replacement within it.

Mechanisms for Identifying Children in Need of Permanency Planning

In a large child welfare system, there must be a system of record keeping if those who provide service are to be held accountable to those they serve and to the community that finances the service. Part of the difficulty in evaluating the seriousness of allegations of aimless "drift" in foster care is that there are few satisfactory information systems operative in child welfare. Thus, there is little capacity to compile systematic nationwide statistics or for agencies to retrieve information about the children and families they serve. Without information, it is not possible to monitor the progress of children, to understand their circumstances, or to identify them as needing special attention. The most promising pathway to systematic data bases, both for assessing the scope of the child welfare problem and for individual case planning, would seem to be the introduction of automated data systems.

To date, information systems have predominantly provided those "hard" data that can "flag" the need of a child for planning efforts.

However, workers are accustomed to the judgments made in conventional record keeping and use this material in decision making. The inclusion of more qualitative material in information systems seems quite possible and is a way of incorporating these judgments on a systematic basis. Recently, for example, work has begun on increasing the capacity of the Child Welfare Information System in New York to provide descriptive data in areas crucial for permanency planning—the nature of the child's relationships with biological and foster parents, visiting patterns of biological parents, foster parent reactions to the idea of adoption, and the social worker's assessment of the foster home. The pilot tests indicate that this type of information can be categorized by social workers and routinely entered into the data system.[17] This would provide the information needed for more sophisticated decisions in directing permanency planning efforts.

Automated data systems currently in use usually provide data on time in care, number of placements, age, minority status, and handicapping conditions. Once criteria are established for the use of these data, these systems can provide a means of identifying children for whom permanency planning services are needed. When data such as contacts with biological parents, relationship with foster parents, and casework goals can also be added to these automated systems, needed intensive services will be more easily and accurately allocated.

In addition to automated data systems, it has been suggested that periodic review of the cases of children in care can be used to identify those who may be "drifting." When first instituted, such review may be resented as a "policing" action, which demands much time but offers little return. Indeed, if the chief problem in carrying out plans for children is lack of time and resources, it is difficult to justify extensive demands on already overburdened workers. However, case review has been shown to accelerate the pace of planning for children. A variety of types of mechanisms to carry out these reviews have been developed. Imaginatively used, they can become a means of support and teaching, and thus facilitate the work of social agency staff.

The most traditional of the review procedures that have developed in the last ten years is that of a periodic case review within the agency itself. In 1976 more than half of the respondents to a survey of statewide public agencies reported such a review plan.[18] Review can occur either at a supervisory or at a central administrative level.

Such administrative reviews impose demands on social agency staff both for preparation of the case for review and for the review itself. However, they offer no impetus for change either from an outside authority or from the stimulation of outside ideas. Agency case review may alleviate organizational impediments to planning, as it logically would be expected to do.[19] However, there are few data by which one can evaluate whether such review actually does facilitate planning for children. Good staff training and supervision within an agency should improve all services to children. One wonders whether systematic internal review can add much more.

Review by the court system has become an increasingly popular idea in recent years. The logic behind this trend seems to be that if the state has taken custody of a child, the juvenile court, in its role as protector of the child, has a responsibility to oversee this child's care. It is somewhat difficult to see why the juvenile court is necessarily a better protector of the child than the child welfare agency; both were established for this purpose. However, there is merit in the idea of external monitoring of any agency to whom the lives of relatively powerless persons are entrusted.

Court review has been demonstrated to have an impact on planning for children. A careful evaluation of the impact of mandatory review of all children in voluntary placement for more than twenty-four months showed that the need to prepare a case for court and the need to carry out the court's orders increased the pace of planning for children.[20] Generally the court and the agency agreed on goals for the case; the court often directed specific and immediate actions toward implementing these goals.[21]

However, one problem with court review is that the juvenile courts themselves are often understaffed and unable to keep up even with reviews that are a specific part of their own initial commitment of children to foster care. In New York, for example, extra judges were assigned from the civil court to expedite initial reviews; even then, apparently, at least three years passed before some cases were initially reviewed.[22] Since the court system itself is often overwhelmed and since the element it brings to reviews is authority—not new ideas or special expertise—one might question whether these reviews will be, in the long run, much more effective than internal agency review.

A more promising approach is the citizen review boards, sometimes attached to the court and sometimes not. In some states they have been introduced because the court system was too overloaded to take on the review function.[23] Typically such boards are composed of groups of professionals and citizens who are concerned with the lives of children in care. As such, they often bring a different perspective and new ideas to the review of cases. Sometimes these boards add members from specific fields to fill gaps in knowledge.[24] As they learn more about children in care, they can become a powerful advocacy group.[25] Periodic review by such boards seems to generate case activity just prior to review as written case plans are prepared. Workers often report they feel supported by the opportunity to share decision making with review board members.[26] The review ensures systematic planning for all children in care and should facilitate staff training through the input of new ideas.

Review boards can have an additional function. When "interested parties" (biological parents, foster parents, or children) are invited to attend, they provide these participants an opportunity to have input into case planning. Foster parents particularly seem to value this.[27]

Review mechanisms force attention to systematic planning for all the children in the foster care system and thus may reduce the problems of delayed planning and "drift." It is apparent that the foster care system has neglected some children and thus demonstrated the need for external monitoring. This is seen as particularly appropriate since the children and families served are relatively powerless in our society. However, review mechanisms seem, in general, to rely on summaries obtained from the agency and to accept the agency's evaluation of the situation and plans for the child. Given the many other pressures within the system, one wonders if the need for review is the central issue. At a minimum, if case reviews are implemented, they should be structured so as to be as helpful as possible in case planning toward one of the three identified goals of permanency planning—return to the biological home, adoption, or planned long-term foster care.

RETURN TO THE BIOLOGICAL HOME

All things being equal, the assumption of the child welfare field is that the best plan for children in foster care is to return them to their families of origin. There they will grow up "like everyone else" with only the developmental tasks common to all children to master. Their loyalties to their own families will be unconflicted, and their sense of who they are will be rooted in family continuity.

Most children do return to their own homes. In a two-year longitudinal study in New York City, 54 percent of the children were found to return home within the first three months of placement.[28] Another five-year longitudinal study, also in New York, excluded children in care less than ninety days. Even so it found that 56 percent of the children returned home over the five-year period.[29] If these figures are representative of other localities, and there is no reason to believe they are not, they are clear indicators that the child's own home is the primary resource in permanency planning.

Even when return home seems highly improbable, a child's own home can be an important resource. To illustrate, in a survey of 1300 children in foster care for an average of eight years, the parents were found to be "out of the picture" or to have such limited capacity that only 10 percent of the children were thought likely to return home. Yet, after two years, 18 percent had been discharged to their parents.[30] A major permanency planning project in Oregon, which sought to demonstrate that plans could be made for children who were indeed "drifting" without parental ties in the foster care system, selected a sample of 509 children who were thought extremely unlikely ever to return home. For each of these children, the social worker first ascertained the current whereabouts, capacities, and interest of the biological family. As a result of a commitment to return these children to their own homes whenever possible, 26 percent returned home.[31]

It is evident that the child's own home must first be explored as permanency planning begins. If the child is to return home: (1) the bonds that unite a family must be maintained; (2) parental capacity to care for the child must be assessed and, if necessary, enhanced; and (3) services to facilitate the movement home must be offered.

Maintenance of Parent-Child Bonds

Data from both cross-sectional and longitudinal studies show the highest rate of return home during the first year of placement.[32] The tendency of a family to reestablish an equilibrium, which excludes the child in foster care within a few months has long been observed by child welfare workers and is manifest in the diminished visiting that occurs as the child remains longer in foster care.[33] Prompt action to attempt to remedy the problem that brought the child into care is desirable, of course. The faster a family is helped to be ready for a child's return, the less disruption there is for both child and family. However, it must be recognized that some problems simply take time to resolve.

Considerations of family structure and networks of relationships may also explain the finding that older children return home in higher proportion than younger children.[34] These children have an established place in their biological families, and when they are away, the "gap" may close more slowly.

Most important among the correlates of discharge are those factors that indicate strong family attachment to the child and the maintenance of these bonds during placement. Visiting by parents has been reported to be associated with discharge, being perhaps the strongest predictor thus far identified.[35] Repeated studies have shown shockingly low percentages of children visited and amazingly infrequent visits. In fact, the majority of children in care for more than two years are rarely visited.[36]

There is probably a "mix" of responsibility for this lack of parental visits. A national study "found over and over again" policies and practices that made it difficult for parents to visit. The authors reported a general failure of agencies to articulate specific policies about visiting and an attitude that visits are a "nuisance." When there were policies, they were often found to be restrictive. Finally, the authors note a failure by agencies to provide transportation, or to reimburse needy parents for transportation, when they do visit.[37]

Such policies work against the child's return home in that they disrupt one of the few bonds that tie together the separated child and parent. However, there is not universal agreement that agency policy is a major contributor to parents' failure to visit. Kadushin's review of available research indicates that agency restrictiveness seems to be a factor of only limited importance to parent-child visitation.[38]

Other factors shown in various studies to predict return home also appear to be indicators of parents' investment. For example, one study found that signing a contract to work with an agency on problems preventing return (as opposed to entering into a verbal agreement only) was associated with the child's return home.[39] Frequency of contact with the caseworker is also a predictor of return home.[40] This factor probably indicates the worker's availability to the parent in addition to indicating parental investment in the child.

While most children who go home do so within their first year of placement, there is a continuing pattern of discharge through the following years in care. The reasons children enter foster care show a range in complexity and difficulty of resolution. The data indicate some association between the complexity of the presenting problem and the length of time in care. In a sample of 577 children followed over five years, Fanshel and Shinn found a low rate of discharge during the first year in care for children with behavior difficulties, but by the end of five years only 24 percent of these children remained in care.[41] Children who enter care due to the physical illness of a parent or other situational stress are likely to be discharged earlier.[42] Children who are deserted, neglected, or abused, or whose parents are drug abusers remain longest in foster care.[43]

These data make sense when one considers the varied complexity and extent of services necessary to alleviate different types of family problems. For example, a child's behavior problems most often improve slowly, over a period of years, unlike physical illness, which can often be relatively quickly cured.

Assessing Capacity to Care for a Child

If parents are to care successfully for their children, they not only must be motivated to maintain the necessary family bonds, but also must have the capacity to care adequately for them. Assessment of this capacity, and enhancement of it, is one of the most difficult tasks of the child welfare worker. Placement is generally a "last resort"; the difficulties that must be overcome before a child can return home must not be minimized. According to social worker assessments, parental unwillingness or inadequacy in carrying out parental functions accounts for 70 to 80 percent of placements.[44] Thus, the central family problems need to be identified as return home is considered. These problems must be sufficiently resolved so that the child will receive at least a minimal level of care upon return.

Parents must have sufficient maturity to be able to provide reasonably consistent nurture and guidance for a child. Assessing whether this capacity is present is difficult, given the enormous variability in cultures, life-styles, and patterns of child care that exist in our country today. And it is always difficult to evaluate a home for a child when the child is not in it. Nevertheless, it must be done and done well, for the child has a right to a home where the basic conditions for growth are present.

Having located a parent (for which an extensive search is often needed) and completed a full assessment, the worker's actions in helping to remedy the problems of the family will be as varied as the problems themselves. There have been several attempts to ascertain what specific patterns of service are most effective in enabling parents to take their children home from foster care. The first studies in this area tested the impact of monitoring systems and the provision of intensive services. More recent work has monitored the effects of time-limited casework and use of specific contracts.

A study by the Child Welfare League of America in 1973 attempted to address the dual problems of children "lost" in foster care and the lack of effort to maintain contact with their biological parents. In order to counteract the first problem, a unit in which workers reported every three months on the status of children in their case loads and their efforts to develop and implement case plans was established. In order to deal with the second problem, another experimental unit was established to provide intensive and well-conceptualized casework services directed primarily at the parents, both before and after the child returned home. Neither approach led to a statistically significant increase in the number of children returned home. Small numbers in the sample, the limits of time, and the impact of antecedent variables may, in part, explain this.

However, plans for the children in the newly established units did remain more stable over a four-month period, indicating either that planning was better or that follow-up services were important.[45]

An approach using behavioral treatment methods, written contracts, and intensive service to biological parents in Alameda County, California, yielded greater success in returning children to their own families. At the end of two years, comparisons of the 145 experimental group children and the 148 control group children, matched on several relevant variables, showed that 70 experimental group children had been returned to their own homes or were about to be returned, while only 45 control group children were so directed. Although there may be confounding variables, the results are impressive. A basic appeal to the health and areas of competent functioning in the biological parents, expressed in written contracts detailing what they and the agency were to do to effect restoration, seems in large part responsible for this success rate. Follow-up after one year indicated that most plans had remained stable.[46]

For many of the specific problems of these families, specific resources may well be available in the community. For example, homemakers may be able to teach basic housekeeping skills; parent education classes may teach parenting skills. Medical resources to treat chronic, debilitating conditions, as well as more acute illnesses, can be found for parents. Mental health clinics can help in the assessment and management of emotional illness. Many parents are single; for them, parent support groups can provide needed social contact and support of parenting efforts. The self-help groups that focus on serious problems such as alcoholism or child abuse seem also to have some success in treatment. Child welfare workers cannot provide these services directly but can be invaluable to parents in providing information, developing and supporting motivation for the use of available services, and making effective referrals.

A special note needs to be made of income maintenance services. Poverty is commonly identified as a basic, underlying problem of families whose children come into placement. In a review of the data concerning children in foster care in five states, Vasaly found the income of most biological parents to be below poverty level.[47] Poor education, unemployment, and poor housing tend to be accompanying problems. Several studies note that white children are discharged from foster care earlier than nonwhite children.[48] A partial reason may be added economic and situational stress that minority families often experience. The child welfare worker may often have to act as advocate for these families, helping them negotiate the intricacies of our public welfare system.

These intricacies are particularly difficult when plans are being made for a child not yet in the home.

Social Worker and Biological Parents

Biological parents usually have fewer contacts with social workers than do the foster parents or the child during the period of foster care. A good working relationship between biological parents and workers is important if children are to be discharged and maintained in their own homes. Positive worker attitudes toward the parents and accurate parental perceptions of the role they are expected to play are major concomitants of these relationships.

The evidence available on worker attitudes toward biological parents is fragmented. The worker's positive assessment of the mother's child care abilities, attitudes toward placement, and attitudes toward the worker have been found to be associated with discharge.[49] Mothers whose children were placed for "socially acceptable" reasons and who viewed placement with "thankfulness" have evaluated foster care more positively and rated worker helpfulness higher than did those parents whose children were placed because of abandonment, severe neglect or abuse, severe family dysfunction (including substance abuse), and unwillingness to continue care.[50] Service delivered over a two-year time span was found to be associated with parental maintenance of visits to the child and worker assessment that the mother had good capacity for service involvement.[51] All of this may indicate that staff tend to work more productively with those parents whom they think demonstrate potential for problem resolution.

Social workers of 584 children in foster care who had had some contact with the parents of the child in the preceding two years were queried about the reasons for diminished parental contact. The workers perceived that three-quarters of the parents manifested problems of low motivation. This same study found over 40 percent of the mothers to be severely depressed. Circumstantial factors were also identified as causing low use of available casework service: distance, illness, financial limitations, and, for fathers, employment hours.[52] However, an index of capacity for service involvement showed only a small partial correlation with discharge status.[53] This can in part be explained by technical factors, but is an interesting comment on the complex and little understood interrelationships among attitudes, help offered, help used, and outcome.

Parents may tend to be placed in a passive role during the time their children are in foster care. Expectations that they become active in working toward the return of their children may conflict with this passivity. This tendency may be accentuated by the fact that parents do not routinely receive progress reports about children in foster care, do not participate in major decision making, and are generally not expected to raise questions about what is happening.[54] Jenkins and Norman found that mothers had "very definite ideas as to how they were supposed to behave in relation to workers." The major categories into which these perceptions fell included "to be undisguised," "to be controlled," and "to be acquiescent."[55] Another study reports a high incidence of passive resistance—failure to keep appointments and lateness, refusal to discuss personal problems, defensiveness, and excessive dependency.[56] All of this indicates that when return home is the goal, not only must severe family problems be resolved, but attitudes of both worker and parent that may impede the resolution must be managed.

The decisions made around the possible return of children to their own homes are perhaps the most agonizing of those made in permanency planning. In many instances, the biological home has once been devastating for the child. Yet, it is their "own" home, where they "belong" and the alternative plans are neither easy to implement nor problem-free. Any decision has serious consequences; so does no decision.

Under these circumstances, it is imperative that the child welfare worker be able to share perceptions and decision making with others. Some demonstration projects have used a "team" to share decisions and their implementation. The opinion of experts in other fields—physicians, psychologists, and psychiatrists, for example—may also be necessary. Other professionals who have worked, or are working, with the family can provide useful information. Finally, supervisory consultation and administrative support are necessary if these difficult decisions are to be made and implemented (see Chapter 12 for further discussion).

Maintenance of Children in Their Own Homes

Very little is known about the process of going home. It seems such a "natural" event that it is hard to realize that for this move, too, there must be preparation. Depending on the length of time children have been away from home and the visits they have had, their own family may seem either familiar or very strange. Many of the preparatory activities detailed in the materials relating to the introduction of a child to an adoptive family may be very appropriate in the introduction of children to their own families. These procedures are reviewed in the following section of this chapter.

Practice wisdom dictates that, at the very least, frequent visits between children and their parents should precede a move back home. In this way they can become reacquainted and the customs of each can become familiar to the other. This is a time of reestablishing old affectional ties and working through the process of giving up ties that may have become meaningful during foster care. It is also a time of testing, for both children and their parents, of whether there is capacity to cope with the stresses of the family's life. Much additional work should go on between worker and client as preparations are made for return: evaluating the factors that made placement necessary and how these have changed, delineating the tasks to be accomplished to enable the child to return, assessing the current capacity to care for the child, continuing support and encouragement through troubled times, and sharing the feeling of accomplishment when the work necessary to bring a child home is achieved.

There are few available data on the frequency with which this pattern of work and shared experiences occurs. Fanshel and Shinn report in their longitudinal study that 12 percent of the returns were precipitous, and another 12 percent "somewhat sudden."[57] Whether these precipitous returns resulted in lower success rates is not known. Given the current pressure to return children home as quickly as possible, there is a clear need to examine what, if any, are the outcome differences between planned and precipitous return. One wonders if this area is largely unexplored due to an underlying assumption that "of course" a biologically related family will get on well together.

Workers are apparently astute in assessing the capacity of homes. Asked to judge the probability of a returned child's remaining at home, workers make assessments that are often correct. Children in situations about which workers were pessimistic have a much higher rate of reentry into foster care than those returned to homes that workers thought would succeed.[58] Asked what they were concerned about, workers identified personality problems of the parents, mental illness, poor child-rearing capacity, worry about the child's adjustment, and marginal family finances, in descending order of importance.[59] Such findings are useful, but they deal with fairly large and abstract areas of concern. A detailing of more concrete concerns, with follow-up to see if they were justified, would be of interest.

Provision of services to these families after the return of their children should assist them in reestablishing positive patterns of living together. "Rarely, however, is anyone fully prepared for the child's return, whatever the reason. Some families, because they are strong and resilient can readjust even if they have had minimal or no contact. Others do not fare so well."[60] Typically, as would be expected from a review of the problems at placement and the modest changes occurring during placement, families seem to need assistance in attaining such immediate resources as shelter, income, and medical care. They need support and encouragement as they struggle to meet the ongoing demands of life with their newly returned child.

Support and encouragement seem to come chiefly from continued casework contacts, mentioned repeatedly as an important service. The fullest information about this service is presented in the report of a 1976 study of 549 families, of whom 373 received intensive service in a demonstration unit. Unfortunately the analysis of these data did not separate those children who had returned from foster care from those in which the goal was the prevention of a first placement. One must make the assumption that the same casework services were provided to both groups. Workers themselves tended to consider casework the most important of the follow-up services; there are no comparable data about client perceptions. The worker's predominant role was seen as giving advice and guidance. Parental and child functioning within the family were the most frequently discussed topics.[61]

Support and encouragement also come from relatives[62] and from organizations such as church groups and community centers, which mothers report they find helpful.[63] There is little information available on the extent to which these parents are isolated from support systems. However, this is a common observation of those who work with abusive and neglectful families, and one would assume this may be a problem for many of these families. It is certainly an area that deserves additional study.

The array of concrete services needed and used by families whose children have returned home is long. Medical care, financial assistance, and housing seem to be most important. In a study of families receiving services designed both to prevent placement and to assist in restoration, over half of the sample received financial assistance (78 percent) and/or medical service (60 percent), over a third received help with housing (45 percent), family life education (41 percent), psychological evaluation (38 percent), education in home management (37 percent), and/or vocational counseling or training (35 percent). Only 19 percent used day care and 19 percent homemaker service.[64] Assistance with income and housing was found to be associated with the continuation of children in their own homes.[65] This distribution of services seems fairly typical, though when the intensive services of a demonstration project are not available, the percentages of families receiving such help are probably much lower. It is important to note that even the services used by only a small portion of parents are not unimportant. When they are needed, they may well make a big difference.

There is relatively little material available on parental perceptions of the stresses of the child's return home. Mothers report that children are often difficult to care for and relate to immediately after their return home—they seem "changed."[66] A reported discussion group of parents notes that they were "very explicit in describing problems of a return home." The only problem detailed, however, was parental anger and distress when children talk about the material advantages of the foster home.[67] Perhaps that illustration is indicative of the feelings of frustration and anger which must frequently occur as families adjust to living together again, feelings that make positive interaction difficult.

In the follow-up of a large demonstration project in Oregon, 25 percent of the children were reunited with their biological parents although they were originally referred to the project for adoptive placement. These parents reported that they were "well prepared" for the child's return. A few had attended parenting classes; more had read books on child rearing. Advice from the child welfare worker was considered useful. Most parents reported that adjustment to the child was "easy," and the majority denied that events in the past had created any problems.[68] There is no report on how the child's memories of foster care were being handled. Reading this, one has a sense of denial of the past and refusal to discuss it. It is not clear whether the children were being given a chance to handle the difficult experiences they have undergone.

Outcome

Return home is not the final goal of permanency planning. The home must be such that it meets the "minimum sufficient level" of care that is adequate for the particular child involved.[69] The child must be able to remain in the home and to thrive there. There are few estimates of the number of children who leave foster care only to return. In a four-and-a-half-year period during which children who had spent at least one week in foster care were followed, 19 percent had at least one case reopening.[70] Following children who entered foster care for a five-year period, another study found that 16 percent of the children discharged home returned to foster care at least once.[71] A one-year follow-up study found 27 percent of the children who went home returned to foster care.[72] Of the seventy-three children returned to their homes in a California study, only two reentered care in the following year—one from the control and one from the experimental group. This is by far the lowest report of reentry into the system.[73]

The Oregon project attempted to account in some detail for the experiences of the seven children who returned to foster care after discharge home. They found these seven children to have spent more than twice as long in foster care and to have had fewer visits than the children who remained at home. They were older, had had more placements, and had not had as strong bonds to foster parents (perhaps indicators of difficulties in forming relationships). Income level of their mothers was also lower.[74]

Aside from the statistics of return to foster care, there is little "outcome" data on return to the home of biological parents as a form of permanent planning. One follow-up study did indicate that the children returned home were not doing as well as children in other placements. However, these children did show limited improvement in all categories assessed, and their parents had found the return home "easy" and expressed satisfaction with the outcome. Interestingly, some of these parents expressed initial uncertainty about how the return home would work out, but by the follow-up time 83 percent thought the plan was permanent.[75]

RELATIVES: EXTENDED FAMILY RESOURCES

Discussion to this point has centered on the children's return to their own parents. When this is not possible, relatives may provide a valuable placement resource. They are usually familiar to the children, "feel" like family, and may have more capacity to parent than biological parents. In the five-year longitudinal New York study, grandparents eventually made homes for 7.5 percent of the children and other relatives for an additional 7 percent.[76] The acceptance of children by relatives is extremely common among black families[77] and is so successful that many of these children never enter the child welfare system. One project in California found that children placed with relatives were unlikely to be adopted, but relatives often assumed legal guardianship.[78]

When relatives do take children into their homes, the procedures for placement and supervision after placement should be similar to those used when children return to their biological parents. Since children usually know their relatives, allaying of fears about the home and extensive preplacement visits are usually not thought necessary. But as in return to parents, children may have little opportunity to work through the emotions connected with their placement experiences. Relatives may be reluctant to ask for the help they need in managing a child's adjustment to their home. The procedures followed in nonrelative adoptions are detailed in the following section. Many of them might be appropriate when relatives adopt or assume guardianship of a child.

When children are unable to return to parents or relatives and, either because of bonds to the biological family or for other reasons must remain in foster care, relatives may serve as an important link for them to their family of origin. Sometimes relatives even form a part of an adopted child's life. Continuing contact with relatives can foster a firm sense of self-identity and can help children retain a realistic perception of their families and the reasons for their placement.

As children attain independence, relatives may form the family that they come to consider their "own." This is particularly true if for some reason the foster home that has been most meaningful was disrupted prior to their last years in care. Thus, contact with relatives seems generally to be helpful to children and should be preserved if at all possible.

A NEW ADOPTIVE HOME

When it is clear that children cannot grow up in their biological parents' home, adoption becomes the alternate way of providing them with a permanent home and parents of their "own." Easiest for the child, in that persons who are already psychological parents become legal parents also, is adoption by the foster family with whom the child is living. This is discussed in greater detail later in this chapter. However, such adoptions are not always possible. In these cases a different adoptive home must be sought, assessment made of the capacity of this child and family to live together, an acquaintance between child and family established, and a placement made, supported, and legally ratified.

> By far the most important thing the social agency does for the child is to provide him with an adoptive home. All else is commentary. All the casework preparation, all the casework efforts in easing transition, all the casework in follow-up during the post-placement year is frosting on the cake of the potential for changes provided by a different environment.[79]

The problem of finding adoptive homes for children who need them remains crucial. Recent estimates show that there are 102,000 children free for adoption and in need of homes in the child welfare system. Of 97,000 on whom data are available, 63 percent of these are white, and 28 percent black. The median age is seven years.[80] Adoption services are apparently not being offered equally to all children.

> The data seem fairly clear. There are groups of children free for adoption currently in the child welfare system who are not being adequately served. These tend to be children who are older, handicapped, or who belong to minority groups.[81]

The Decision that the Child Cannot Return to the Biological Home

The first step in the movement of children toward adoption is the clear determination that they cannot live with their own parents, either now or in the future. This determination is difficult; it requires a willingness to make predictions based on current knowledge and a willingness to make an unequivocal decision that has great importance in the lives of several people. The question asked is whether this set of biological parents will ever be able to make a home for this specific child.

The first part of this assessment is to determine parental capacities. A number of barriers to a child's return home have been identified and include: (1) parental absence, the lack of consistent contact between parent and child over a period of time; (2) parental condition, the qualities within the parent that prevent adequate nurturing; and (3) parental conduct, the observable behavior of the parent that indicates inadequacies in parenting ability.[82]

Parental absence is frequently documented. Most of the studies of children in foster care note the large numbers of children who have no contact or very limited contact with their parents.[83] "Meaningful ties with biologic parents," which is not quite the same as parental visiting, were identified for only 14 percent of the children in foster care in one study.[84] Parents "drift away," and their whereabouts become unknown, or they make only sporadic contact with children in care. Responsible social work dictates that an aggressive search must be made for these parents. If determined efforts to reinvolve them do not succeed, adoption may become the only way that children can have involved parents of their "own." The documented record of the attempts to find and involve the parents also becomes a crucial document for the court in a petition to terminate parental rights.

Assessment of a diagnosable parental condition, or pattern of parental conduct, such that the child cannot ever return home, is more complex. Shared decision making is as imperative at this point as it is in deciding that the child can return home. Varied points of view are expressed, bias is minimized, expert knowledge is tapped, and responsibility is shared. Even so, these very final and complex decisions are extremely difficult to make, for we do not know enough to predict human behavior with any certainty. (See Chapter 7 for a full discussion of the complexities of decision making.)

The Adoptable Child

In order to be the subjects of adoptive planning, children must be "adoptable." This means that they must have resolved emotional ties to their biological family and must be able to benefit from family life. The only children who are not adoptable are those whose emotional or physical state is so deterioriated that they can only thrive in a specialized institutional or group setting; or occasionally, those adolescents whose thrust toward independence is so great that they are not able to form new family ties. All other qualifications on adoptability simply restrict the child's chances for a permanent home.

Few persons would currently argue that there are any classifications of children, other than those who cannot benefit from family life, that are unadoptable. Children with a wide range of handicapping conditions have successfully become family members. The story of the placements made by Spaulding for Children, an agency specializing in the placement of "hard-to-place" children—"children older than eleven years, children with physical, educational, or emotional handicaps that are moderate to severe in nature, multiple-handicapped children, or brothers and sisters who should be placed in the same family"—amply demonstrates this.[85]

It has been argued that since the legally freed children have no legal parents of their own, termination of parental rights should not be undertaken until it is known that there is an adoptive home available.[86] However, termination of parental rights takes time, and during that time a waiting adoptive family, unless they are willing to risk placement when adoption is uncertain, may be lost to a child. More importantly, unless a child is identified as adoptable and prepared for adoption, it is unlikely that an energetic effort will be made to find an appropriate adoptive home.

Termination of Ties to the Biological Home

A major step in adoptive planning for children is the termination of parental rights. This is a point where permanency planning, unless goal-directed and strongly supported, often falters. Child welfare workers are often reluctant to take this very final step. They are acting on a prediction about the child's biological family and often argue that given more time and opportunity, this family might change. Discomfort with the court adds to this reluctance to act. A project in Oregon demonstrated what was already suspected; workers tend to see the court and its unfamiliar legal demands as major obstacles in permanency planning.[87] The system of the court and the evidence it demands are unfamiliar to many child welfare workers. Unless they have specific training in the law and implementation of legal processes, these demands can be very intimidating.

Additionally, two recent nationwide studies suggest that courts themselves exhibit extreme reluctance to terminate the rights of biological parents. Criteria for termination are not explicit, searches for long-absent parents are often extended, and a brief show of interest or protest may cause a judge to give a biological parent more time before a final decision is made.[88] Courts very properly insist on careful documentation of the child welfare agency's attempt to work with the family. Here, special training, consultation, and administrative support prove crucial, for it has been demonstrated that as methods of working with the court have been developed and workers feel comfortable with them, worker reluctance diminishes.[89]

If children are to move into adoption, their emotional ties to their biological homes, and to the foster homes that have cared for them, must also be resolved. Ties to a biological home may be fostered by anger, hurt, resentment, or belief in a fantasy parent who is all-giving and who will "rescue" the child any day. Ties to the foster home may be predominantly affectional and may be intensified by the child's fear of a move to another home.

Just how these ties are to be resolved is not clear. There is considerable literature concerning the role of the caseworker in discussing with children the reasons for their placement and helping them bring to consciousness and evaluate unrealistic perceptions of their biological parents. The child who understands the reason for placement apparently adapts better to foster care.[90] One study found frequency of caseworker contact to be associated with lessening attachment to biological parents.[91]

It is difficult to conceptualize what a "good" working-through process might be. Behavioral disturbance in a child may be evidence of grappling with formerly repressed feelings,[92] or may instead be evidence of unmanageable tensions. Fanshel and Shinn found casework intervention in the foster home to be associated with increased problems in coping on the part of the child, though these authors point out that caseworkers may visit the already disturbed child more frequently than others.[93] Visits by biological parents have been found to be associated both with greater disturbance[94] and with a better self-concept,[95] and they may aid children in making realistic assessments of their biological homes[96] and in becoming ready to form new attachments.

Concrete communication aids, such as building scrapbooks that detail the major experiences of the child's life, are reported to be helpful in building a relationship between child and worker. Through such aids, children are helped to master the information they need and are free to react to the memories of past events.[97]

Ties to the foster home must also be recognized, and the child's fears about a move to a new home must be resolved. Children must be helped to understand what adoption means. Doubts about permanence must be allayed. Children need to realize that they do not need to give up loyalties and affections developed in the foster home. They must also understand why they cannot continue to live with their foster parents. Often, contact with a foster home, through letters or occasional visits, can be continued after adoption.

Recruitment of Adoptive Homes

The procedure through which adoptive homes are recruited and evaluated are detailed in the following chapter. There seems to be no doubt that homes can be found for most of the children who have spent time in foster care, despite their age, handicap, minority status, and history. Demonstration projects and agencies which specialize in adoptive placement of these children have placed a high proportion of the referred children.[98] The common threads in their practice seem to be relatively small case loads so that intensive work is possible, a thorough knowledge of the children, accepting and liking the children, and commitment to finding them homes. Reading the project reports, one senses high worker morale and persistence in searching for homes for the children.

Subsidy, the payment to the family of some of the expenses of child care, has been one of the tools used in the development of adoptive homes. Subsidy payments may be monthly payments to assist in the day-to-day care of the child, payments for extraordinary medical expenses necessitated by the treatment of some handicapping condition, or single payments for some particular expense connected with adoption. Early advocates of the use of subsidy projected their extensive use and great savings to the community. Later experience has indicated that there are many factors other than economic ones impeding adoptive placements, though subsidies continue to be thought a valuable tool.

Adoption exchanges have also been established to facilitate "matching" children with special needs with families who think they might be able to adopt them. Organized on a local, state, regional, and national basis, these exchanges list children available for adoption for whom an agency does not have a home. The listings are circulated, in the hope that another agency will have a waiting home. Some exchanges also list waiting homes. These tactics have not worked as well as logic would suggest they might. In general, only small numbers of children have been placed through exchanges.[99] It is quite possible that this medium does not provide the degree of knowledge of the children that is necessary if there is to be work toward their placement. There may also be some distrust of another agency's evaluation of a child or family.

Direct recruitment of adoptive homes for these children can take place through the use of two strategies: (1) publicity to make the community aware of the needs of groups of children for adoptive homes, and (2) focused efforts to find homes for specific children. These two strategies can be effectively used together.[100] Applicants are commonly urged to consider the wide range of children needing homes. Most applicants can only consider adopting children with certain clusters of characteristics; luckily these clusters vary among adoptive applicants.

Preparation and Matching

Part of the adoption study consists of exploration of the extent to which families can extend themselves to meet the needs of waiting children and the range of problems that the family can handle. Relatively little is known about the factors that will enable any specific family to make a home for a particular child. The "magic" of a parent-child relationship that works is not unlike the magic of marriage. Differing practices in bringing parents and children together are reported. The traditional process of agency selection of a child for a family does not seem appropriate for children with special needs. Certainly in the adoption of an older child with potentially handicapping experiences, and perhaps actual handicaps, the potential adoptive parents should play a large role in deciding whether a particular child will "fit" into their home. They have a right to all the information an agency has about a child. It is essential that agency and family communicate freely. To facilitate this, agencies are changing their traditional practices with adoptive applicants. For example, one agency let applicants select, from a "picture book" of waiting children, the child they thought would fit their family; the adoptive study then focused around evaluation of the projected "match."[101] Another agency reports making the selection for applicants, but giving them great freedom to say "no" and to move on to the selection of another child. Detailed information is shared, and if the family expresses interest, they are given the child's complete record to read.[102]

Preparation of children for a move to an adoptive home is twofold. The first task, already discussed, is to help them have a realistic understanding of what has happened in the past and to help them react to it. Secondly, children's fears about a move to a new home must be resolved. Specialists in preparing older children for adoption have found that the children must be involved in helping to plan what kind of home they would like and must have specific information about the new family and its expectations.[103]

The first meeting between children and their potential adoptive parents is one of the most sensitive points in the adoption process. Children must be protected from the possibility of rejection while, at the same time, they and the adoptive family have a chance to become acquainted. The best safeguards in this situation lie in extensive sharing of information with the potential family prior to their meeting the child. In this way as many doubts and questions as possible can be worked through. While it is sometimes possible to allow parents to see children first in situations where they do not know they are being observed, this can really only be done with very young children—older children "catch on" quickly. Older children, it has been found, can handle the introduction and the possible decision not to proceed with the adoption if there is careful explanation that there is no way to be sure what the outcome of a meeting will be.[104]

Preplacement visits are the next step in the formation of an adoptive family. These visits must be extensive enough to allow the child and family a chance to test their ability to live together. They must also allow the child to develop a sense of trust so that the move to a new family can be accomplished with confidence. The demonstration that the foster family remains intact and interested is important in helping children resolve their sense of loss without damage to their self-concept. Often, it is the children themselves who declare their readiness to make a final move.

Maintaining the Placement

To a greater or lesser degree, all agencies maintain contact with families for a time after placement. All states have a period, varying between six months and one year, during which agency supervision is mandatory; legal adoption cannot be completed until after this period. Early recognition of developing problems and work with them is important, and the supervisory period gives sanction to this. A diminishing need for contact with the agency, as the crisis of placement is resolved and homeostasis of the family restored, has been noted.[105]

There is evidence that families' wish to maintain contact with an agency worker after adoption varies with the "differentness" of the adoption. In a six-year follow-up of 160 two-parent families who had adopted young infants, almost no wish for continuing contact with the agency was expressed.[106] On the other hand, people who have adopted children of other races have enthusiastically formed self-help groups, which continue for years after the adoption. In one agency, parents who adopt older and often handicapped children often have intensive contact with the agency in the months following the adoption, and 80 percent remain in contact with the agency through the following years.[107] Probably most of those parents who adopt older children who have "drifted" in foster care fall into the group of parents who wish to receive assistance from the agency.

The problems that must be resolved if an adoption is to be maintained have been identified as falling into four categories: (1) difficulties resulting from the child's reactions to former circumstances, (2) the family's unexpected reactions to the child, (3) a breakdown in the worker's effectiveness, and (4) unexpected circumstances in the home. Services are principally delivered by the caseworker, but team evaluations are used to assist, as are contacts with other families who have adopted and other community resources.[108]

Outcome

There is evidence that families with a strong commitment to permanence emerge from the process of preparation and matching. Most adoptive families remain intact, and most families express great satisfaction with their situation.

Without question, the rate of failed adoptions is higher for older children than for infants. A study of failed adoptions in northern California showed that the older the child, the greater the hazard in the placement.[109] Overall, only about 2 percent of adoptions end in removal of the child from the adoptive home.[110] The reported failure rate nationally for adoptions of children "with special needs" is 15 percent.[111] Intensive services may diminish this rate.[112] It should be noted that the children involved in many of these "failed" adoptions are successfully replaced in other adoptive homes.[113] Given the complexity of these adoptions, the percentage that does not work out is not surprising.

More surprising is the high proportion of families expressing contentment following the adoption of an older child. In 1970 Kadushin interviewed parents in ninety-one families who had adopted children over five years of age. He found 78 percent expressing satisfaction with the adoption, an outcome similar to other adoption studies.[114] In a follow-up of older children placed in adoption at least nine months previously by the demonstration project in Oregon, the adoptions were described as follows:

The picture of adoption by new parents is undoubtedly a positive one. The parents seem materially and psychologically stable, with a deep commitment to the success of the adoption and the adjustment of the children. They all voice improvement and satisfaction with the results at interview time. The children seemed to feel permanent in their new positions and valued the situation as an improvement over the past . . . adoptions by new parents seem highly successful.[115]

This summary seems representative of the descriptive material reported by others who have worked with the adoption of "special needs" children.

There are signs indicating that adoption is a resource that is increasingly used in planning for children in foster care. There are now twice as many children receiving adoption services as there were in 1961.[116] The use of nontraditional families, such as single-parent homes, is increasing.[117] There is an increasing literature about flexible and imaginative assessment of adoptive applicants. Finally, it is noted that the nature of the children referred to the adoption exchanges, or to agencies specializing in the adoption of "special needs" children, has shifted over the last years. Such children now tend to be older and more severely handicapped.[118] Apparently children once perceived as needing special services are now being placed as part of the routine adoption service of a number of agencies.

LONG-TERM CARE IN THE FOSTER HOME

The foster home is, of course, a primary resource for children who cannot return to their own homes. If they have been in a single foster home for a long time, a "psychological parent-child relationship" may have developed. For the majority of children in foster homes for several years, the foster home has become a "real home." Prolongation of this relationship is certainly to be preferred to its disruption.

Foster homes can become legally recognized permanent homes if it is possible for the foster parent to adopt the foster child. When this is not possible, other arrangements such as legal guardianship for foster parents, formalized long-term contracts or agreements between agency and foster parents, or informal agreement that a placement will continue unchanged are used to secure long-term care for children.

Adoption by Foster Parents

Adoption of the child by the foster parents with whom they live seems an obvious means of securing a permanent home without disrupting an ongoing relationship. Although not formalized by legal adoption, this concept of permanency was part of the beginnings of foster care. Yet, there was a period of years when such adoptions were not considered. Emphasis in foster home studies was often on the ability to "give up" a child. Placement agreements between agency and foster parents, which vested decision-making power in the agency, often reinforced the passive, temporary nature of the foster home. This concept of the foster home as a temporary shelter for children predominated in child welfare agencies until the past decade. In 1973, the following comments appeared in a book that has had great impact on the field:

> Nevertheless, agreements generally made with foster parents are consistent in being emphatic on two main conditions: that the child in question is placed on a temporary board and care basis only and is not placed with the foster family for adoption; that the welfare commissioner or agency reserve the right to remove the child at any time from the foster home and that upon such removal the initial agreement is cancelled immediately. Adherence to these terms has unquestionable consequences for the child/ foster parent relationship.[119]

It was not really until the 1970s, when agencies became increasingly concerned about making formalized permanent plans for children, that foster homes began to be considered for adoption. In numerous states, case-load censuses revealed that there were large numbers of older children, often of minority races, who had no contact with their biological families for years and yet were continuing to live in foster homes. What could be more natural than to suggest that foster parents adopt them? The concept of the foster parent/adoptive parent continuum emerged.[120] For the first time in many years, caseworkers approached foster parents about adopting their foster children.

Whether adopted by their foster family or by a different family, children's ties to their biological families must be legally terminated—they must be "freed" for adoption. This process may be simplified in some jurisdictions by the fact that an adoptive home, the foster home, has already been "found" and is "waiting" for the child. It has been observed that termination is quicker and apparently more comfortable for the courts and the biological parents when children are already in the home where they will remain.[121] However, the legal processes necessary and the time they take are generally the same as those detailed earlier.

Ties to a biological family are not only legal; they are also emotional. Hence, just as in adoption by a new family, children adopted by their foster parents must be helped to resolve these emotional ties. In addition, children may need help in coping with the loyalty conflicts they may experience between foster/adoptive parents and biological parents. The complexities of the tug-of-war between loyalties to a biological family and to a foster family are illustrated by a study that examined the relationship of 352 foster children, most of whom were in long-term foster care, to their own and their foster families. Caseworkers reported that half of the children had no attachment or minimal attachment to their own families. Over three-fourths of the children were thought to be strongly identified with the foster family. Almost half were considered to be "at peace" with their living arrangements. However, age was a differentiating factor in all these relationships. Younger children tended to have less attachment to their own families, be more deeply integrated into foster homes, and more "at peace." Older children, despite their increased years in the foster home, demonstrated more conflict.[122]

Interestingly, the presence of other biological relatives in the child's life does not seem to complicate adjustment; indeed, it may facilitate it. Brothers and sisters, particularly if they are in the same foster home, can be a source of support and mutual assistance in working out the problems of foster care. One study showed an appreciably smaller percentage of children displaying problems when siblings were in the same foster home.[123] Grandparents who are interested in children but cannot care for them are often accepted by the foster family and child. While recognized as concerned people, they apparently have little impact on the developing foster parent-child relationship.

As agencies began to encourage formal adoption by foster parents, it quickly became apparent that one impediment to this type of permanent planning was that foster parents often could not afford to adopt. One of the reasons for caring for foster children was the need to earn money, and the foster care board payments were a part of the family economy. Additionally, some of the children needing homes had extensive medical or psychological problems for which heavy expenses could be incurred in subsequent years. The economic barrier had to be removed to facilitate adoption of these children by foster parents. Subsidies have been particularly useful in facilitating adoption by foster parents. However, as will be discussed in the next chapter, there have been some problems in the use of subsidies when foster parents have chosen to adopt children in their care.

The formation of the "bond" between foster parents and foster children that facilitates successful adoption remains one of the most mysterious, and important, factors in permanency planning. That it is formed through the day-to-day interactions of caretakers and children is unquestionable. Isolating the elements of this bond is difficult. Goldstein and colleagues write of a relationship in which the child is "truly wanted" and "feelings are totally involved" so that there is in effect a "common law adoption."[124] The bond is akin to the sense of "total commitment" of which Pike writes.[125] Ward isolates factors of "entitlement" to the child and "validation" of parenting—the sense that "parenthood is ratified or confirmed both by societal attitudes and experiences with the child."[126] When foster parents are interviewed, they speak of a very early absorption of the child into the family with a continuing intent to adopt[127] and a sense of "likeness" between child and foster family.[128]

In a study of sixty foster families, about half of whom adopted children in their care, caseworkers identified enjoyment of children (particularly on the part of the mother) and sensitivity to their needs as attributes of foster parents who adopted and identified "a combination of child-centered motives and narcissistic investment in raising children" as reasons for taking children into the home. Attitude-scale responses of foster parents who had adopted expressed strong interest in children and an ability to respond to the differing characteristics of their children.[129] However, these terms all lack specificity. One is left with very few concrete indicators of the factors that go into bonding between parents and children.

Time has been identified as an important dimension. Children who enter foster care young and have little memory of any other home will quickly become members of what seems their "own" home. Measures of "embedment" in foster care show this clearly, children under two at entry appearing "deeply embedded" in their foster homes.[130] Many writers have noted, and common sense agrees, that length of time in the foster home is associated with the foster parent becoming the "psychological" parent to the child; the data of the New York longitudinal study showed increasing "embedment" in foster family as time progressed.[131] In another study in New York, it was noted that foster parents tended to be approached by the agency and asked to consider adoptions six or seven years after the child entered their care.[132] Thus, one would expect the younger child who has been in the same foster home for a number of years to have relatively little difficulty in becoming part of the foster family.

Logically, adoption by foster parents makes a great deal of sense, for the child achieves permanence without disrupting an existing set of relationships. New concepts such as that of the foster care/adoptive family[133] blur distinctions between the two types of homes. However, a finding of a recent study, in which foster parents who had expected to adopt from the start of a placement were distinguished from foster parents who did not intend to adopt, gives rise to some concern. The number was small, but the fourteen foster parents who adopted when they had not originally expected to found the adoption less satisfactory, and their children did less well as adults. Many reported that a distance between child and family was always maintained.[134] This finding is troubling and deserves further exploration.

Long-Term Foster Care

There are circumstances when neither return home nor adoption can become a reality for a child. Our court system is often reluctant to terminate parental rights. When parents will not voluntarily surrender their children, judges may refuse to free the children for adoption, even in situations in which it seems unlikely that they will ever return home. Children may retain strong emotional ties to their biological families and be unwilling to invest emotionally in an alternate family, even explicitly refusing adoption if they are old enough. An adoptive home may not be found for some children, and their foster parents may not want to adopt.

Attempts to identify the characteristics of those children who remain in foster care without adoption show that they are in general older and nonwhite, and have no functioning homes to which they can return.[135] Presence of a severe handicap or being close to or in adolescence have been identified as deterrents to adoption by foster parents.[136] There is little descriptive literature on the characteristics of children for whom long-term foster care is planned. Stein, Gambrill, and Wiltse identified being in a foster home over three years as a determining characteristic.[137] In examining planned long-term foster care in one agency, Rothchild found half the group for whom this was the plan to be severely emotionally or physically handicapped.[138] Long-term foster care is thought to be particularly appropriate if children have established roots in a foster home where there is indication that they can remain.

When long-term foster care is planned, the intent of permanence should be as explicit as possible. Every child should have a guardian, and when state statutes permit the foster parents to be the judicially appointed guardian, the placement will be strengthened. As guardian, the foster parent can take the child out of state, consent to medical treatment, and make other major decisions about the child's life. The foster parent's role thus resembles much more closely that of a "real" parent, and some of the factors of agency intrusiveness, which may distort formation of a cohesive family, may be minimized. Guardianship by foster parents may not be possible in some states where statute prohibits payment to a guardian.[139] When feasible, however, logic suggests it should be implemented.

An explicit contract between foster parents and agency is another way of planning long-term foster care. In such contracts, the agency usually agrees that the placement will be maintained unless new circumstances arise, and the foster parents declare their intent of keeping the child in their home until maturity. The child welfare agency retains responsibility for major decisions and for financial support. This is not a legal document, but an expression of the intent of both parties. Disruption is less likely if the biological parents also agree.

Since long-term foster care is the most problematic and "last choice" of the options in making permanent plans for children, it seems worthwhile to review briefly what is known about the experiences and outcomes of such care. In doing so, one must look at the studies of children who have grown up in foster care. However, these provide little more than evidence of the problems and usefulness of all kinds of long-term foster care. Emphasis on planning and the use of contracts and other agreements are developments of such recent origin as to render impossible the evaluation of their long-term impact.

Children remaining for extended periods in foster care may experience repeated replacements. These replacements, coupled with the original separation from the home, may well lead to the extensive personality damage of which the literature warns.[140] However, as we have seen, most children settle into a single home in which they remain. About 25 percent experience replacements. As the years go by, most lose contact with their biological parents. The foster home becomes their only home. It is to consideration of the impact of long-term single-family care that we now turn.

In the most detailed and sophisticated study of foster care to date, Fanshel and Shinn followed a cohort of 227 children entering foster care and remaining over a five-year span. Their study provides a wealth of data about various facets of adjustment. Overall, neither improvement nor deterioration in children's functioning was found. Social workers identified the provision of an environment in which growth and development could take place as beneficial in 91 percent of the cases. Detrimental effects were identified in 43 percent of the cases; the child's sense of "insecurity" was prominent in the examples cited.[141]

Growing up as a foster child apparently has its problems, but available data also suggest some ways to ameliorate these. Adults looking back on the experience speak of resentment at being "different" and somehow "second class." "Foster child" appears to have negative connotations— adults report that as children they thought others believed they were "bad" and were in foster care for that reason.[142] Foster parents may be viewed very negatively by adults who were foster children, or may be fondly recalled as one's "own" family; as would be expected, the quality of the relationship with foster parents seems to be a determinant.[143] Lack of information about reasons for foster placement is mentioned by adults as a source of resentment.[144] The misery of children who do not understand what has happened to their own home has been described poignantly.[145] Possession of a good understanding of the reasons for foster care is associated with a good sense of self.[146] Continuing contacts with biological parents and with relatives can also be helpful. Thus, again in this context, it seems that providing help to children so that they understand why they were placed and retain good feelings about themselves and their biological parents may do much to make long-term foster care a more positive experience.

There is some evidence that long-term foster care may "feel" like adoption to the foster family and child. Weinstein found that over two-thirds of the children he interviewed expected to remain permanently in the foster home (even if biological parents were visiting).[147] However, children for whom a move was imminent were excluded from this sample; and in another study, a small sample of adults reported remembering that fear of change and of what would happen next was prominent.[148] Foster parents tend to see themselves in a role similar to biological parents and to be so defined by others in the community.[149] Many apparently have hopes and even expectations of adopting as they begin foster care.[150] Thus, there may be a sense of permanence in many foster homes, which can be enhanced by long-term agreements when adoption is not possible.

The impact that these childhood experiences have on the adult lives of former foster children is also important in evaluating long-term foster care. After review of eight major outcome studies, Kadushin concludes:

> Children who were in foster care for long periods have in 70–80 percent of the cases, grown up satisfactorily. Some of the associations usually thought to be related to outcome, such as age at placement and number of replacements, are not unequivocally supported in the studies. Outcome seems to be differentially related to the sex of the child and directly related to the interpersonal quality of the foster home.[151]

Comparisons of outcomes of long-term foster care and adoptive care have produced contradictory findings. In an elaborate study in which worker judgments on the child's experiences with family life were the primary data, 77.6 percent of those children adopted by foster parents were found to have no problems, as were 72.8 percent in regular adoptive homes and only 51.5 percent of those in long-term foster care. However, as over half the problems were medical, it is unclear whether this reflects poorer adjustment or a higher proportion of handicaps.[152]

The percentage of satisfactory adjustments reported by Kadushin above is similar to the percentage reported in adoption follow-up studies.

How does one connect troubled memories of foster care with the successful lives former foster children seem to lead? One thread may be in the repeated findings of some of the studies that former foster children do not feel as secure about themselves as their outward lives would warrant—though there is little basis on which to compare these feelings with those of children who have grown up in more permanent homes. It is perhaps best summed up in the concluding paragraph of one of Meier's reports:

> The vast majority of the subjects have found places for themselves in their communities. They are indistinguishable from their neighbors as self-supporting individuals; living in attractive homes; taking care of their children adequately, worrying about them, and making some mistakes in parenting; sharing the activities of the neighborhood; and finding pleasure in their association with others. They do not always regard themselves as being indistinguishable, however, because they remember that, as foster children, they were different from their peers.[153]

THE CHILD WELFARE WORKER

Failure to act aggressively to secure permanent plans for children is sometimes excused with the statement that child welfare workers are overwhelmed by the demands of their work load, and it is easy to support the statement that workers may be overwhelmed. Typically, caseworkers in the child welfare system carry case loads of seventy to ninety cases, and paperwork is extensive, consuming up to 30 percent of worker time.[154] That is hardly enough time to implement plans for permanency. While the pressure to "do something" is intense, supports are lacking. Child welfare workers typically have a bachelor's degree in a field other than social work.[155] There is little emphasis on in-service training, and supervisory staff are often as overwhelmed as the casework staff.[156] Thus, workers are expected to make complex decisions without a knowledge base to guide them. Under these conditions, staff turnover is frequent, adding to the difficulty of making and implementing long-range plans.

But there may be ways of managing this work load so that the results of efforts expended are maximized. A review of the projects that have demonstrated success in achieving permanent plans for children shows that they have in common: (1) regular review of children in care, which includes extensive knowledge about each child; (2) casework oriented toward the goal of permanency planning; (3) consultation when needed around assessment of children and families, and legal consultation; (4)

support to the caseworker in decision making through supervision or team discussion; (5) the capacity to give intensive service during a relatively brief period of time; and (6) high staff morale and an intense staff commitment to the welfare of the children. These elements may be relatively difficult to implement, given the conditions cited in the preceding paragraph. Their identification outlines a goal for the organization of services.

Some elements of this organization have been implemented in large agencies. Stein and associates report the following as being evident in some:

> . . . clearly articulated agency objectives to reduce job ambiguity, particularly for new workers who are unfamiliar with agency goals; ongoing in-service training programs, clerical support to reduce the amount of time workers spend completing forms, feedback from administration about the purposes and outcomes of information that workers are asked to supply; involving staff in decision making that affects their day-to-day work; and support from legal staff to facilitate moving children through court termination proceedings and to subsequent adoption or legal guardianship.[157]

Training manuals that detail effective methods of case management are increasingly available. Some deal most completely with return home,[158] while others focus on adoption.[159] Their use should facilitate learning and applying effective methodology.

Increased coordination between the child welfare agency and other community agencies is another way of improving existing services. If the child welfare worker has neither the training nor the time to supply the services needed with the appropriate degree of intensity, perhaps someone in another agency can. The problem is to communicate case goals and time lines between agencies.

The role of the child welfare worker as advocate for the children and their families should not be ignored. Many of the biological families of children in need of planning may be severely deprived. They may be depressed, timid, and particularly if members of a minority group, accustomed to being ignored by the community. With aggressive intervention on behalf of a client, the child welfare worker can sometimes induce the income maintenance, medical care, and other social service systems to be more responsive to client needs. Foster and adoptive parents, too, sometimes need guidance in dealing with an unfamiliar array of services, particularly if they are caring for a handicapped child. Workers can be effective in finding and mobilizing community (and relative) support systems for families. All of this can give the family a better chance to function effectively.

Without question, however, the most important element in the organization of child welfare services lies in the provision of focused training and opportunities for case discussion and consultation. Social workers are called on to make complex decisions that have a profound effect on other lives. They need a knowledge base on which to make those decisions. And they need the support of other staff, some with different areas of expertise and some with longer experience, as they work to implement the decisions.

CONCLUSION

Through the years, the child welfare system has probably assured that most children whose families could not care for them had wholesome growing-up experiences. However, current studies indicate that while permanent family living experiences have been a goal for many years, an undetermined but large number of children are "drifting" in foster care. This is contrary to the intent of the child welfare system and the people who staff it. It is thus imperative to examine the factors that may remedy the problem.

Knowledge about the children in care is crucial. An information system should provide basic descriptive information, including dates and locations of placements, use of other agencies, dates of reviews, and goals with a time framework for their accomplishment. Computerized information systems become increasingly useful as the size of child welfare agencies expands, and as computer technology develops. But more important than systematized stored information is the individualized knowledge that workers have about each child in their case load and their interest in using that knowledge to make the best possible plans for that child. If children can benefit from family life, it is important that the worker be committed to finding them a permanent family of their own.

Casework services must be organized in such a way that the worker is able to provide the intense, relatively short-term, and goal-directed services that the child needs. Most promising in restoring biological homes are those services that appeal to the "health" of biological parents, contracting with them to accomplish a series of tasks directed toward the goal of attaining a "minimum sufficient" home for the child. When children cannot return home, adoptive planning can often be arranged. The children must first be helped to become psychologically as well as legally free of close ties to their biological home. If they have formed a close bond with the foster family with whom they have lived, this may be the adoptive placement of choice. If not, it has been demonstrated that new adoptive homes can be found for children with special needs, children can be helped to move, and in most cases the adoptions can be sustained. If adoption is not possible, the worker's task is to make explicit the intent of permanence in the foster home and develop any possible safeguards to that permanence.

Children also need the protection of a system that provides support and expert consultation to the worker in decision making and assures the children of periodic review of their status. The work of any agency serving relatively helpless persons probably needs outside monitoring. Citizen review boards, with their input of new ideas and support in decision making, seem a particularly promising new structure. Such boards seem generally to contribute to the achievement of the agency's goals.

It is doubtful whether there is any one "best" plan for children in foster care. Each good plan is the result of a careful matching of the child's characteristics and the characteristics of the alternative families potentially available. The "outcome" data for all the plans examined in this chapter indicates about 15 percent of the returns to the biological home and about 15 percent of the adoptive placements of the older children end in replacements. Apparently 25 percent of the children in long-term foster care experience replacements. The figures are all approximations and are not far apart. Follow-up studies show that most children in foster care and adoption grow up into reasonably adequate adults.

Each child deserves a carefully developed and implemented plan. Whatever the legal and social sanctions of that plan, the commitment of family members to each other and the intent of permanency are crucial to the child. This much we owe each child, and this the child welfare system is attempting to provide. If the child welfare system has faltered in providing these services, there is at least some knowledge of what remedies are needed. Now they must be put in place.

NOTES

1. Henry Maas and Richard Engler, *Children in Need of Parents* (New York: Columbia University Press, 1959).

2. Jane Knitzer, MaryLee Allen, and Brenda McGowan, *Children Without Homes* (Washington, D.C.: Children's Defense Fund, 1978), p. 5.

3. Victor Pike, Susan Downs, Arthur Emlen, Glen Downs, and Denise Case, *Permanent Planning for Children in Foster Care: A Handbook for Social Workers* (Portland, Ore.: Regional Research

Institute for Human Services, Portland State University. Copyright U.S. Department of Health Education, and Welfare Children's Bureau, 1977), p. 1.

4. Arthur Emlen et al., *Overcoming Barriers to Planning for Children in Foster Care* (Portland, Ore.: Regional Research Institute for Human Services, Portland State University, 1977), p. 26.

5. Alfred Kadushin, "Children in Foster Families and Institutions," in *Social Service Research: Reviews of Studies,* ed. Henry Maas (Washington, D.C.: National Association of Social Workers, 1978), p. 99.

6. Ibid., pp. 99–100.

7. Joseph Persico, *Who Knows? Who Cares? Forgotten Children in Foster Care* (New York: National Commission for Children in Need of Parents, 1979).

8. Knitzer, Allen, and McGowan, *Children Without Homes,* pp. 22ff.

9. Pike, Downs, Emlen, Downs, and Case, *Permanent Planning for Children in Foster Care,* p. i.

10. Joseph Goldstein, Anna Freud, and Albert Solnit, *Beyond the Best Interests of the Child* (New York: The Free Press, 1973).

11. Pike, Downs, Emlen, Downs, and Case, *Permanent Planning for Children in Foster Care,* pp. 4–5.

12. Robert H. Mnookin, "Foster Care: In Whose Best Interest?", *Harvard Educational Review* 43 (November 1973): 599–639.

13. Deborah Shapiro, *Agencies and Foster Children* (New York: Columbia University Press, 1975).

14. Kadushin, "Children in Foster Families," pp. 100–101.

15. David Fanshel and Eugene B. Shinn, *Children in Foster Care: A Longitudinal Investigation* (New York: Columbia University Press, 1978), pp. 112ff; Knitzer, Allen, and McGowan, *Children Without Homes,* pp. 50–51.

16. Blanche Bernstein, Donald Snider, and William Meezan, *Foster Care Needs and Alternatives to Placement* (Albany, N.Y.: New York State Board of Social Welfare, 1975).

17. David Fanshel, *Computerized Information for Child Welfare: The Availability and Capacities of Parents and Children in Foster Care for Service Involvement* (New York: Columbia University School of Social Work, November 1978); David Fanshel, *Computerized Information for Child Welfare: Foster Children and Their Foster*

Parents (New York: Columbia University School of Social Work, 1979).

18. W. Eugene Claburn, Stephen Magura, and William Resnick, "Periodic Review of Foster Care: A Brief National Assessment," *Child Welfare* 55 (June 1976): 397.

19. Ibid., p. 402.

20. Trudy Festinger, "The New York Court Review of Children in Foster Care," *Child Welfare* 54 (April 1975): 211–45; Trudy Festinger, "The Impact of the New York Court Review of Children in Foster Care: A Follow Up Report," *Child Welfare* 55 (September/October 1976): 516–44.

21. Festinger, "The New York Court Review," pp. 230ff.

22. Ibid., p. 216.

23. Barbara Chappel, "Organizing Periodic Review in Foster Care: The South Carolina Story," *Child Welfare* 54 (July 1975): 483.

24. Trudy Backus, "Foster Care Review: An Ohio Example," *Child Welfare* 57 (March 1978): 161.

25. Jon Conte, *A Qualitative Evaluation of Citizen's Review Boards in Four States* (Chicago: Jane Addams Center for Social Policy, University of Illinois at Chicago Circle, mimeographed, 1981), p. 180.

26. Ibid., p. 130.

27. Ibid.

28. Shirley Jenkins, "Duration of Foster Care—Some Relevant Antecedent Variables," *Child Welfare* 46 (October 1967): 451.

29. Fanshel and Shinn, *Children in Foster Care*, p. 115.

30. Fanshel, *Computerized Information . . . The Availability and Capacities*, p. 62.

31. Janet Lahti et al., *A Follow Up of the Oregon Project* (Portland, Ore.: Regional Research Institute for Human Services, Portland State University, 1978), p. 5.1.

32. Kadushin, "Children in Foster Families and Institutions," p. 99.

33. Ibid., p. 188.

34. Fanshel and Shinn, *Children in Foster Care*, p. 126.

35. Ibid., pp. 88ff.

36. Ibid.; Shirley Vasaly, *Foster Care in Five States* (Washington, D.C.: Social Work Research Group, George Washington University, June 1976).

37. Knitzer, Allen, and McGowan, *Children Without Homes*, p. 119.

38. Kadushin, "Children in Foster Families and Institutions," p. 119.

39. Theodore J. Stein, Eileen Gambrill, and Kermit Wiltse, *Children in Foster Homes: Achieving Continuity of Care* (New York: Praeger Publishers, 1978), p. 91.

40. Shapiro, *Agencies and Foster Children.*

41. Fanshel and Shinn, *Children in Foster Care,* p. 119.

42. Kadushin, "Children in Foster Families and Institutions," p. 117.

43. Ibid.

44. Ibid., p. 116.

45. Edward Sherman, Renee Neuman, and Ann Shyne, *Children Adrift in Foster Care* (New York: Child Welfare League of America, 1973).

46. Stein, Gambrill, and Wiltse, *Children in Foster Homes.*

47. Vasaly, *Foster Care in Five States,* pp. 17ff.

48. Kadushin, "Children in Foster Families and Institutions," p. 117.

49. Shapiro, *Agencies and Foster Children,* p. 94.

50. Shirley Jenkins and Elaine Norman, *Beyond Placement: Mothers View Foster Care* (New York: Columbia University Press, 1975), p. 136.

51. Fanshel and Shinn, *Children in Foster Care,* p. 75.

52. Fanshel, *Computerized Information . . . The Availability and Capacities,* pp. 20ff.

53. Ibid., p. 66.

54. Knitzer, Allen, and McGowan, *Children Without Homes,* p. 23.

55. Jenkins and Norman, *Beyond Placement,* p. 135.

56. Fanshel, *Computerized Information . . . The Availability and Capacities,* p. 30.

57. Fanshel and Shinn, *Children in Foster Care,* p. 147.

58. Ibid., p. 159; Sherman, Neuman, and Shyne, *Children Adrift in Foster Care,* p. 84.

59. Fanshel and Shinn, *Children in Foster Care,* p. 161.

60. Knitzer, Allen, and McGowan, *Children Without Homes,* p. 26.

61. Mary Ann Jones, Renee Neuman, and Ann Shyne, *A Second Chance for Families, Evaluation of a Program to Reduce Foster Care* (New York: Child Welfare League of America, 1976), pp. 59ff.

62. Ibid., p. 62; Sherman, Neuman, and Shyne, *Children Adrift in Foster Care,* p. 85.

63. Jenkins and Norman, *Beyond Placement,* p. 82.

64. Jones, Neuman, and Shyne, *A Second Chance for Families,* p. 56.

65. Ibid., p. 96.

66. Jenkins and Norman, *Beyond Placement.*

67. Dorothy Murphy, "A Program for Parents of Children in Foster Family Care," *Children Today* 5 (November/December 1976): 38 –39.

68. Lahti et al., *A Follow Up of the Oregon Project,* pp. 5.13–5.15.

69. Pike, Downs, Emlen, Downs, and Case, *Permanent Planning for Children in Foster Care,* p. 14.

70. W. Eugene Claburn, Stephen Magura, and Susan Chiseck, "Case Reopening: An Emerging Issue in Child Welfare Services," *Child Welfare* 56 (December 1977): 659.

71. Fanshel and Shinn, *Children in Foster Care,* p. 159.

72. Sherman, Neuman, and Shyne, *Children Adrift in Foster Care,* p. 82.

73. Stein, Gambrill, and Wiltse, *Children in Foster Homes,* p. 95.

74. Lahti et al., *A Follow Up of the Oregon Project,* p. 5.5.

75. Ibid., pp. 5.13–5.14.

76. Fanshel and Shinn, *Children in Foster Care,* p. 148.

77. Robert Hill, *Informal Adoption Among Black Families* (Washington, D.C.: National Urban League, Research Department, 1977).

78. Stein, Gambrill, and Wiltse, *Children in Foster Homes,* p. 80.

79. Alfred Kadushin, *Adopting Older Children* (New York: Columbia University Press, 1970), p. 228.

80. William Meezan, *Adoption Services in the States* (Washington, D.C.: U.S. Department of Health and Human Services, 1980), p. 5.

81. Ibid., p. 6.

82. Pike, Downs, Emlen, Downs, and Case, *Permanent Planning for Children in Foster Care,* p. 16.

83. Kadushin, "Children in Foster Families and Institutions," p. 118.

84. Vivian Hargrave, Joan Shireman, and Peter Connor, *Where Love and Need Are One* (Chicago: Illinois Department of Children and Family Services, 1975), p. 28.

85. Christopher Unger, Gladys Dwarshuis, and Elizabeth Johnson, *Chaos, Madness and Unpredictability . . . Placing the Child with*

Ears Like Uncle Harry's (Chelsea, Mich.: Spaulding for Children, 1977), p. 66.

86. Pike, Downs, Emlen, Downs, and Case, *Permanent Planning for Children in Foster Care,* p. 64.

87. Arthur Emlen, *Barriers to Planning for Children in Foster Care* (Portland, Ore.: Regional Research Institute for Human Services, Portland State University, 1976), p. 81.

88. Knitzer, Allen, and McGowan, *Children Without Homes;* Persico, *Who Knows? Who Cares?*

89. Emlen, *Barriers to Planning for Children in Foster Care;* Emlen et al., *Overcoming Barriers to Planning for Children in Foster Care.*

90. Eugene Weinstein, *Self Image of the Foster Child* (New York: Russell Sage Foundation, 1960).

91. Fanshel and Shinn, *Children in Foster Care,* p. 404.

92. Ner Littner, "The Importance of the Natural Parents to the Child in Placement," *Child Welfare* 54 (March 1975): 178.

93. Fanshel and Shinn, *Children in Foster Care,* p. 412.

94. Ibid., p. 411.

95. Weinstein, *Self Image of the Foster Child,* p. 8.

96. Littner, "The Importance of the Natural Parents."

97. Unger, Dwarshuis, and Johnson, *Chaos, Madness and Unpredictability,* p. 84.

98. For example, see ibid.; Hargrave, Shireman, and Connor, *Where Love and Need Are One;* Emlen et al., *Overcoming Barriers to Planning for Children in Foster Care.*

99. Alfred Kadushin, "Children in Adoptive Homes," in *Social Service Research: Reviews of Studies,* ed. Henry S. Maas (Washington, D.C.: National Association of Social Workers, 1978), p. 51.

100. Meezan, *Adoption Services in the States,* p. 9.

101. Joan Shireman and Kenneth Watson, "Adoption of Real Children," *Social Work* 17 (July 1972): 29–38.

102. Unger, Dwarshuis, and Johnson, *Chaos, Madness and Unpredictability.*

103. Ibid., pp. 83ff.

104. Ibid., pp. 144–45.

105. Linda Katz, "Older Child Adoptive Placements: A Time of Family Crisis," *Child Welfare* 56 (March 1977): 169–70.

106. Lilian Ripple, "A Followup Study of Adopted Children," *Social Service Review* 42 (December 1968): 479–97.

107. Unger, Dwarshuis, and Johnson, *Chaos, Madness and Unpredictability*, pp. 153ff.

108. Ibid., pp. 158ff.

109. Celia Bass, "Matchmaker—Matchmaker: Older-Child Adoption Failures," *Child Welfare* 54 (July 1975): 79.

110. Reprinted with permission of Macmillan Publishing Co., Inc. from *Child Welfare Services*, Third Edition by Alfred Kadushin. Copyright © 1980 by Alfred Kadushin.

111. Elaine Schwartz, "Adopting Older Children: A Comment," *Children Today* 8 (July/August 1979): 9.

112. Unger, Dwarshuis, and Johnson, *Chaos, Madness and Unpredictability*, p. 218.

113. Kadushin, *Child Welfare Services*, p. 545.

114. Kadushin, *Adopting Older Children*.

115. Lahti et al., *A Follow Up of the Oregon Project*, p. 6.11.

116. Meezan, *Adoption Services in the States*, p. 6.

117. Kadushin, "Children in Adoptive Homes," p. 51.

118. Ibid., p. 50; Unger, Dwarshuis, and Johnson, *Chaos, Madness and Unpredictability*, pp. 64ff.

119. Goldstein, Freud, and Solnit, *Beyond the Best Interests of the Child*, pp. 17ff.

120. Margaret Gill, "The Foster Care/Adoptive Family: Adoption of Children Not Legally Free," *Child Welfare* 59 (December 1975): 712ff.

121. Ibid.

122. Fanshel, *Computerized Information . . . Foster Children*, pp. 54ff.

123. Hargrave, Shireman, and Connor, *Where Love and Need Are One*, p. 24.

124. Goldstein, Freud, and Solnit, *Beyond the Best Interests of the Child*, p. 174.

125. Pike, Downs, Emlen, Downs, and Case, *Permanent Planning for Children in Foster Care*, p. i.

126. Margaret Ward, "Parental Bonding in Older Child Adoptions," *Child Welfare* 60 (January 1981): 25ff.

127. Kathleen Proch, "Adoption by Foster Parents" (D.S.W. dissertation, University of Illinois, Urbana-Champaign, 1980), pp. 84ff.

128. Lois Raynor, *The Adopted Child Comes of Age* (London: George Allen and Unwin, 1980).

129. Hargrave, Shireman, and Connor, *Where Love and Need Are One*, pp. 65ff.

130. Fanshel and Shinn, *Children in Foster Care*, p. 400.

131. Ibid.

132. Fanshel, *Computerized Information . . . Foster Children*, pp. 49ff.

133. Gill, "The Foster Care/Adoptive Family."

134. Raynor, *The Adopted Child Comes of Age.*

135. Kadushin, *Child Welfare Services*, pp. 373–74.

136. Hargrave, Shireman, and Connor, *Where Love and Need Are One*, p. 65.

137. Stein, Gambrill, and Wiltse, *Children in Foster Homes*, pp. 86–87.

138. Ann M. Rothchild, "An Agency Evaluates Its Foster Home Services," *Child Welfare* 52 (January 1974): 48.

139. Pike, Downs, Emlen, Downs, and Case, *Permanent Planning for Children in Foster Care*, p. 77.

140. See, for example, Ner Littner, *Some Traumatic Effects of Separation and Placement* (New York: Child Welfare League of America, 1956).

141. Fanshel and Shinn, *Children in Foster Care*, pp. 464ff.

142. Elinore Jacobson and Joanne Cockerum "As Foster Children See It," *Children Today* 5 (November/December 1976): 34.

143. Ellen Rest, "Foster Children as Adults" (unpublished data, Chicago Child Care Association, Chicago, Ill., 1981).

144. Jacobson and Cockerum, "As Foster Children See It."

145. Fanshel and Shinn, *Children in Foster Care*, pp. 455ff.

146. Weinstein, *Self Image of the Foster Child.*

147. Ibid., pp. 35–36.

148. Jacobson and Cockerum, "As Foster Children See It."

149. Martin Wolins, *Selecting Foster Parents* (New York: Columbia University Press, 1963).

150. Proch, "Adoption by Foster Parents," p. 85.

151. Kadushin, *Child Welfare Services*, p. 379.

152. Bernice Madison and Michael Shapiro, "Long Term Foster Family Care: What Is Its Potential for Minority Group Children?" *Public Welfare* 27 (April 1969): 167–94.

153. Elizabeth G. Meier, "Current Circumstances of Former Foster Children," *Child Welfare* 44 (April 1965): 206.

154. Persico, *Who Knows? Who Cares?*, p. 18.

155. Ann W. Shyne and Anita G. Schroeder, *National Study of Social Services to Children and Their Families: Overview* (Washington, D.C.: U.S. Government Printing Office, 1978), p. 26.

156. Persico, *Who Knows? Who Cares?*, p. 18.

157. Stein, Gambrill, and Wiltse, *Children in Foster Homes,* pp. 19–20.

158. Theodore J. Stein and Eileen D. Gambrill, *Decision Making in Foster Care: A Training Manual* (Berkeley, Calif.: University of California, University Extensions Publications, 1976).

159. Pike, Downs, Emlen, Downs, and Case, *Permanent Planning for Children in Foster Care.*

David needs lots of attention, affection

David, 6, has beautiful black hair, big black expressive eyes, a dark complexion and a Puerto Rican ancestry.

David is a loving little boy who likes a lot of attention and affection. He is a satisfying child to parent because adults easily can see the growth and change in him. David takes pride in his accomplishments and is eager to please.

Nothing fazes David. He swims in Lake Michigan, plays soccer, rides his bike and goes to camp. He loves the outdoors and all kinds of sports.

DAVID MAKES HIS bed, sets the table and picks up his toys. He is very helpful. If his foster mother asks him to dust or sweep the floor, he w' quickly complete the chore.

David has a large collection of h wheel cars that he plays with quently. He also enjoys watch derman" and "Batman"

His favorite movie*
Lost Ark" and "The Empire Strikes

Although David will be in sm he will be in a regular fir' day. David loves sch can spell his nam' draw realis'

Dav'

level. However, when David came into his foster home from a home in which he was neglected, he had no speech at all.

DAVID'S CASEWORKER SAID: "David is a special-needs child who needs a two-parent family. However, a single parent would be considered. He needs someone who has had parenting experience.

"*here needs to be a firm structure in his home. Although ~~mas have left scars, he has developed a good --hment.

-hildren. He needs a '-ter and

>pts

Tim is a talkative, affectionate child

Tim, who just turned 15, has blue eyes, a fair complexion and red hair.

Tim needs to have people around him. He talks a lot and will talk to any adult who will listen. If Tim is quiet, it's because he wants attention. Tim is well-liked by the adults who work with him. He is an affectionate child who will adapt easily to a new family.

Tim is developmentally delayed and is in a special-education program. Tim likes school, and he received all As and Bs. His favorite subjects are math and science.

This summer Tim attended overnight camp for a few weeks and also had the opportunity to attend day camp. He liked each camp equally well and especially enjoyed the arts and craft projects.

ONE OF TIM'S favorite pastimes is drawing with a pencil or chalk. He sketches sport scenes, individual cars or hot rods. When Tim is not sketching, he likes to go swimming, ride his bike or watch the "Dukes of Hazzard."

Tim has participated in the Special Olympics every year. His specialty is the foot races. Each year Tim also participates in the music programs at school. He always has enjoyed music and finds these programs exciting.

Tim has been in foster care since birth and has never h family of his own.

TIM'S CASEWORKER SAID: "Tim needs either r parent family or a single father or mother. Tim needs that has a loving and nurturing parent who will with him.

"Tim was a premature baby. He has a mi'

These 5 kids need a home together

Since spring, three sisters and two brothers have been orphans, and their relatives are unable to provide a home for them.

Stephanie, 13, is the oldest, with dark shoulder-length hair and brown eyes. Stephanie has an outgoing personality. So far, she is not interested in either makeup or boys but she is strongly home oriented. She will en' eighth grade in Septer With proper motiv Stephanie will achie in school than she past.

Stephanie enjoys ga ing, riding her bike or pla' ing with other children. She likes playing Uno, stitching and drawing or eating pizza.

HELENE, 11, is quiet and shy. She looks people over before she extends her friendship. Helene needs affection and loves to be cuddled.

This fall, Helene will be in fifth grade. She likes school and has been heard to ask, "Can I do my homework right now?"

Helene, with her long straight blond hair and brown eyes, is a pretty girl. Although she is developmentally delayed, it is only obvi-

Blu-
Jon is *
will be in
though Jon '

CHAPTER 11
TOWARD AN EXPANDED ROLE FOR ADOPTION SERVICES*

William Meezan

Adoption is a legal process through which a family unit is created by severing the ties between a child and his or her biological parents and legally establishing a new parent/child relationship between persons not related by blood. It thus involves the creation of a family *by the state* rather than through procreation. Through such state action the adopted child becomes a permanent member of a new family and is entitled to all of the benefits accorded a biological child.

Until quite recently adoption was not seen as an alternative for all children needing homes. Traditionally, adoption served to meet the needs of parents by guaranteeing the continuation of family lines through the creation of an heir. Thus, it was seen primarily as a service to the family and only secondarily as a service to the child (see Chapter 2). Children placed were viewed as "biological expressions"[1] of the adopting couples. Close matches between parent and child in physical characteristics, intellectual potential, ethnicity, and religion were attempted. Agencies created family units that approximated, as closely as possible, those which would have been created had the adopting couple not been infertile. Since the great majority of adoption agency clients were white, middle-income couples, the children placed for adoption were primarily healthy, white infants. As one commentator has noted, "Black children were unplaceable for adoption. Black single mothers approaching adoption agencies were told that the agency could not help them."[2] The same was true for many other groups. Older children, chil-

*This chapter is based, in part, on William Meezan, *Adoption Services in the States* (Washington, D.C.: U.S. Department of Health and Human Services, 1980).

dren with physical, developmental, intellectual, or emotional handicaps, or children who were part of sibling groups were excluded from this service and characterized as "unadoptable." Such children could not be considered "biological expressions" of the typical adopting parents. One could not expect adoptive parents to accept a "damaged" child.

Recently, however, the adoption field has begun to shift its emphasis from the healthy, white infant to groups of "special needs" children. Children excluded from adoption as little as ten years ago are now being placed in permanent families, and people who would not have been approved as adoptive parents at that time are currently adopting.

There are a number of reasons why this shift has occurred. First, there has been a dramatic decrease in the number of healthy white infants available for adoption.[3] A greater tolerance of birth out-of-wedlock and of single parenthood is making it possible for many young women to keep their babies rather than to surrender them for adoption, and the availability of contraceptive devices and legal abortions may be reducing the number of unwanted pregnancies within the cohort of young women most likely to surrender babies for adoption. With the decrease in infant relinquishments, potential adoptive parents have begun to consider special needs children as a way of completing their families. Likewise, agencies have begun to consider special needs adoption as a way of justifying continuation of their adoption services when few infants are available.

The emphasis on permanency planning for children who have spent long periods in foster care has also increased the interest in the adoption of special needs children. Theoretical works[4] have argued for the child's need for a permanent, stable home life. Research studies[5] have documented that children, after a number of years in foster care, are unlikely to return home. Since many of these children experience multiple placements, thought to be damaging to their healthy functioning, adoption is seen as a way of providing with stable home environments.

Adoption is also seen as a way of decreasing the cost of foster care services. Even when subsidized, adoption is a less costly service than foster care. Legislators thus find the prospect of special needs adoption appealing, as adoption is not only "better" for the child, but less expensive as well.

Also forcing the rethinking of adoption policy have been vocal, organized constituency groups who have placed pressure on adoption agencies to rethink their policies regarding the adoptability of special needs children. Groups such as the Committee on Adoptable Children and others have focused attention on the unmet needs of "waiting children" in foster care and have demonstrated that adoptive homes are available for them.

Finally, the movement toward adoption of special needs children has been influenced by research demonstrating that such adoptions *can work*. For example, a 1970 study reported a success rate of over 80 percent for children placed for adoption between the ages of five and twelve, despite the fact that most had experienced multiple foster care placements. The author concludes that "children have varying capacities to deal with potentially traumatic conditions and that these strengths enable them, when provided with a healthier environment, to surmount the damaging influences of earlier developmental insults."[6] Similarly a 1969 report of a study of the adoption of children with medical conditions found 77 percent of these children to be adjusting well to the adoptive situation. The authors believed that their findings validated the possibility of a broader definition for "adoptability" and that the "emphasis on children of normal growth and development provided unreasonable protection of adoptive families from risk taking and denied the families and many children the opportunity of adoption."[7]

The fact that special needs adoptions have become a primary concern of the field can be demonstrated in a number of ways. First, federal attention has been focused on this type of adoption. The Model State Adoption Law, developed by the Department of Health and Human Services, clearly focuses on the adoptive needs of this group of children. The Adoption Assistance and Child Welfare Act of 1980 includes provisions for the first federal financial aid for the adoption of special needs children and requires all states to establish an adoption assistance program.[8] (See Chapter 3.)

Research has also shown that greater effort is being expended on finding adoptive homes for this group of children. A recent study of the national adoption exchange indicates that compared to 1971, current children registered with the exchange are more likely to be older, black, and have physical, emotional, and intellectual impairments. The median age of children registered has risen from five to eleven; the proportion of black children has risen from two-fifths to more than half; and the proportion of children with physical, intellectual, or emotional impairments has more than doubled in the last ten years.[9]

Yet more needs to be done, and it will take time to consolidate the gains that have been made. Recent findings from the *National Survey of Social Services for Children and Their Families*[10] estimate that there are currently 102,000 children legally free for adoption, many of whom are not receiving adoptive planning services. Of the 97,000 children for whom data are available, 62 percent are white, 29 percent are black, 3 percent are Hispanic, and 7 percent belong to other ethnic groups including Native American and Asian. The median age of these children is over seven years. Fully 40 percent are over the age of eleven. These data also show that younger children are more likely than older children to receive adoption services. While children under the age of four represent 24 percent of the children free for adoption, they represent 34 percent of children receiving adoption services. At the other end of the age continuum, children over eleven represent over 40 percent of the children freed for adoption, but only 21 percent of those receiving adoption services.

The fact that waiting children are underserved in the current system becomes more evident when one looks at the data from this study concerning children actually placed in adoptive homes. There was a direct relationship between the age and ethnicity of the child and whether an adoptive home had been found. Over 80 percent of the children under age three who were freed for adoption had been placed in an adoptive home, compared to about 40 percent of the children between the ages of eleven and fourteen, and fewer than 20 percent of the children over fourteen. Of the children freed, homes had been found for 54 percent of the white children and 83 percent of the Asian/Pacific children, but for only 47 percent of the Hispanic, 37 percent of the black, and 27 percent of the Native American children.

There was also a relationship between the presence of emotional, developmental, or physical problems and whether or not an adoptive home had been found. Homes had been found for fewer than one-fourth of the children who were receiving services due to their delinquency or status offense, drug addiction, emotional problem, home behavior, mental retardation, physical handicap, or school behavior. On the other hand, homes had been found for about half of the children who were receiving service because of abandonment, abuse, or neglect; their parents' emotional, financial, or medical problems; their parents' unwillingness or inability to care for them; or their parents' arrest.

The need for increased adoption services for these children is also highlighted by other data from this study:

—Foster care was seen as a permanent arrangement for 22 percent of the children currently in care

—110,000 children had been in foster care over six years

—55,000 children (44 percent over age eleven) had agency decisions regarding the possibility of termination of parental rights pending

—51,000 children (35 percent of them over age eleven) had court actions to terminate parental rights pending

—18,000 children (36 percent of them over age eleven) had voluntary surrenders for adoption pending

This chapter will focus on the adoption of special needs children and will suggest ways that these services can be improved. If the needs of these children are to be met, a number of strategies must be pursued *simultaneously* including:

—Active, continuous recruitment of adoptive homes

—Elimination of agency eligibility requirements that are not predictive of the ability to parent special needs children

—Expansion of adoption opportunities to groups not traditionally considered appropriate for adoptive parenthood

—Elimination of barriers to the adoption of special needs children in the service delivery system

—Provision of meaningful services to the various parties involved in adoption

FINDING ADOPTIVE FAMILIES

Agencies concerned only with the adoption of healthy white infants have little need to recruit adoptive parents. The number of applicants for these children far exceeds the number available for adoption. Unfortunately, this is not the case for special needs children; concerted efforts must be made if homes are to be found for them.[11]

One approach to recruiting families is educating the broad community to the fact that homes are needed. These community education efforts can take place through a variety of media. Some agencies have used television and radio programs successfully. Others have used written media including newspapers, brochures, and posters to inform the public. Still others have sponsored special events to attract media attention to the problem of finding families.

No matter which method is used, agencies must exercise caution when planning public information campaigns. They can be expensive and, if done incorrectly, can result in a large number of inappropriate inquiries. Individuals not truly interested in, or capable of, parenting a special needs child may be drawn to the agency if recruitment campaigns do not accurately and clearly depict the children actually available.

While general community education programs can be helpful in recruiting adoptive parents, some feel that such methods are too broad in scope and advocate for "targeted" community education. Such campaigns can attract attention from the specific groups most needed for waiting youngsters—especially minority populations. Ethnic media such as radio stations, magazines, and community newspapers can be used to attract attention. Personal appearances at service clubs, PTA's, church groups, and festivals can put the need for adoptive homes before the targeted population.

Even more intensity in recruitment can be gained by establishing offices in targeted neighborhoods and sending workers into these areas. Outreach in the neighborhoods makes the agency more visible and gives community residents a contact place or person close to home. It allows for better access to community groups and leaders, and may give the agency greater credibility with community residents.[12]

In approaching special target populations, agencies should stress the positives these groups possess for adoption and should dispel fears and anxieties they may have concerning adoption and/or the agency. For example, one black agency stresses that the black community has always adopted at higher rates than other groups although these adoptions were "informal."[13] They give a realistic picture of the children, while insuring potential applicants that they need not meet any specific requirements regarding income, religion, or home ownership. Other projects have included information regarding subsidy and have done door-to-door recruitment in an effort to get their message across.[14]

In addition, through targeted community education, social agencies can dispel their negative images—the contradictory yet common beliefs that adoption agencies are "welfare" mechanisms but serve only middle-class and white clientele; that agencies are inaccessible and unresponsive; that they are rigid and inflexible in their requirements; that they conduct excessive psychological and social probes into the lives of applicants; and that high fees are charged. Further, these campaigns can give potential adoptive applicants factual information about the step-by-step procedures which must be taken in order to complete an adoption, thus preparing the potential applicants for agency contact.

A third potential approach to the recruitment of adoptive parents for special needs children is the use of persons known to the agency. These include staff members, foster parents, and former adoptive parents. All of these groups have been shown to be effective agents in recruitment efforts,[15] demonstrating that recruitment is not the sole responsibility of professional personnel.

Finally, a number of agencies have recruited adoptive homes through "individual family finding" rather than through public information campaigns. Such methods are geared to finding a home for a *specific* child, not a group of waiting children. Thus, they successfully control applicant response. Agencies opting for "individual" family finding believe that "individualized publicity has been the most effective means of attracting sufficient potential adoptive parents and of reducing the number of applicants looking for the kinds of children who are either not placed by the agency or not currently available for adoption."[16] Such efforts are accomplished through radio, television, and newspaper columns that focus on a single waiting child. Effective campaigns of this type present an accurate description of the child's abilities as well as information about his or her handicaps; information about the child's level of functioning, avoiding labels that might scare off potential parents; and information that personalizes the child.

There has been some resistance in the field toward the use of these personalized approaches. Some feel that the "hard" sell of children and the "advertising" of their availability are wrong. Others fear that such publicity may be seen by members of the biological family who may object to this approach, renew their interest in the child, and attempt to interfere with the placement. Still others believe that such publicity can negatively affect children and cause them embarrassment and conflict.

Proponents of such methods counter each of these arguments. They claim that publicity is very different from advertising or selling, and that the publicity usually leads to the prompt location of an appropriate family for the child. Such publicity, they feel, facilitates adoption by bringing attention to the positive characteristics of the child. They counter the arguments of possible reinvolvement of the biological parents by noting that this rarely occurs and that biological parents are often more concerned that the child will never be placed. Regarding the final argument, agencies involved in individual home finding often insist that the child be involved in the decision to publicize. Most children understand the need for this effort and support it. If, however, the child objects, plans to publicize are abandoned.[17]

If any recruitment effort is to be successful, agencies must not only publicize their needs but insure that their practices are responsive to potential applicants. Families must be assured of an immediate response, with interviews taking place quickly and in a location convenient to the family, including their own home. Such interviews must be scheduled at the families' convenience, not at the agencies'. Weekend and night hours should be available. Paperwork must be kept to a minimum and application forms, if necessary, should be easily understood. The workers should approach the applicants not as investigators but as a partner to the parents and a facilitator for the child's placement, with the full understanding that external circumstances should not be the major criteria in determining a family's suitability for a given child.[18]

It has been suggested that one way of helping to insure that agencies are responsive to the families it recruits is through the employment of minority staff. By employing minority workers, agencies demonstrate their commitment to minority children and may reduce the social distance between themselves and the adoptive applicant. The presence of minority workers in an agency may reduce the hesitation some minority applicants have about approaching an agency. Further, minority co-workers can act as interpreters of minority culture to white social workers and can point to strengths in a given family that a white worker might not see. They can provide valuable ideas about reaching the minority community and can encourage the agency in its attempt to find homes for minority children.[19]

ELIGIBILITY AND MATCHING REQUIREMENTS

Over the years adoption agencies have developed criteria to determine the acceptability of an applicant. A number of these, such as the parent's emotional stability, commitment to parenthood, or ability to parent, were based on judgments of the workers. A number of others were based on socioeconomic characteristics such as age, income, family composition, infertility, length of marriage, working status of the adoptive mother and housing. Such requirements were seen as protections for the child—to help insure that the home was suitable and that the adoption would be successful.

These requirements, however, had an additional effect. When enforced, numerous prospective parents became ineligible to adopt through agencies. In this way agencies were able to "screen out" prospective couples and thus maintain manageable intake case loads. Such practices were beneficial to the agency in times when "acceptable" children were in short supply and there was an abundance of possible adoptive homes.

In the last ten years these socioeconomic criteria have come under attack for a number of reasons: a growing realization that they are not predictive of parenting ability; a greater acceptance of differing life-styles in society and a recognition that different life-styles are not necessarily harmful to children; and a growing need for adoptive homes as the definition of who is "adoptable" has broadened to include children with special needs.

However, a survey of ninety-two agencies conducted in 1976 found that many agencies continue to hold these requirements.[20] Other studies have shown that approval rates of adoptive couples are higher for married couples than for single parents; for applicants who own their own homes; and for households in which the child will have a separate room and the wife is not working.[21] This has led some commentators to feel that "Adoption agencies have designed policies whereby home ownership, money, prestige and education have been given far more weight in determining whether a family can adopt a child as opposed to a family's ability to nourish, love or rear a child."[22]

Age

Agencies with maximum age requirements usually set the upper limit at forty. The rationale for this requirement is to insure, in so far as possible, that the parents will be alive until the child reaches majority. It is further justified on the assumption that young parents are likely to demonstrate more stamina, patience, and flexibility in their child rearing.

Age requirements have come under criticism for a number of reasons. First, life expectancy for adults is currently over seventy. Thus, even if parents adopted an infant at age fifty, most would be alive through the child's minority. Age requirements for couples adopting special needs children are even less defensible, since these children are usually older and will remain dependent on adoptive parents for fewer than eighteen years. It has also been argued that while stamina and flexibility may decrease with age, older adoptive parents may be able to provide for children in ways younger parents cannot. For example, they are less likely to be struggling financially, may be more relaxed, and may have more time for the child.[23]

While not all older persons have the capacity to provide for a special needs child, many do. Rigid requirements which screen out applicants based on age do not serve the special needs child well. They eliminate a large pool of potential adoptive parents from consideration and have been challenged successfully in the courts.[24]

Religion

The majority of states have "religious protection" statutes as part of their adoption laws. These statutes usually direct that children be placed, whenever practicable, with adoptive parents of the same religious faith as they or their biological parents. Such statutes are the result of early sectarian involvement in the foster care and adoption field and are being questioned in current adoption practice.

One major problem with religious protection statutes is the wide range of interpretation given to the "whenever practicable" provision. Sometimes such clauses are "given a mandatory interpretation and treated as the most important factor in an adoption,"[25] and take precedence over all other considerations. In such cases, adoptions meeting all other criteria may not be approved by the court. At other times much greater flexibility is used. Some courts have ruled that it is not practicable to meet religious matching requirements when such requirements would delay adoptive placement for more than a month or two. Recent reforms in these statutes have begun to require religious matching only when expressly requested by the biological mother or only when the child has experienced sufficient religious training to be truly a member of a faith. Some states, however, have continued to enforce such requirements, and a few have made them more strict in recent years.[26]

Proponents of religious requirements usually cite three reasons for their continuation: the right of parents to control the child's religion; the insurance that the adoptive couple are persons of high moral and ethical standards; and the fact that religion is only one part of the general matching procedures used to select children and adoptive parents best suited for each other. Each of these arguments is countered by opponents of these statutes. They argue that, with these statutes, ·religion becomes "the only area [in] which a natural parent retains a right subsequent to relinquishment";[27] that religious affiliation is not an indicator of high moral and ethical standards; and that such statutes reduce the number of possible adoptive parents available to the child and introduces the risk of unnecessary delay into the adoption process.

Perhaps the most cogent argument against religious matching is that it may discourage potential adoptive parents from becoming involved with agencies. People without religious affiliation or who are members of minority religions may be subjected to closer scrutiny by the agency and may withdraw from the adoptive process. As one writer states, "unfortunately, white workers, put off by religious behavior they do not understand, sometimes discourage good potential black applicants simply because they are active in non-traditional churches."[28]

There have also been constitutional arguments raised about religious matching. Such arguments are based on church-state entanglements, the denial of religious freedom for those who choose not to belong to a church, and the assigning of a religious affiliation to a child.[29]

Infertility and the Presence of Other Children

For many years agencies required that couples applying for adoption supply them with proof that they were highly unlikely to achieve parenthood through biological means. One consideration in approving a home for adoption was the couple's perceived adjustment to their infertility. It was believed that a positive adjustment in this area was essential to successful adoptive parenthood.

Agencies also limited the number of children they would place in a home and often refused to place infants in homes with biological children. This was done to serve as many infertile couples as possible by placing children where the "need" of the couple applying for a child was greatest.

While such considerations might still be important in deciding to place infants, infertility requirements appear to have little place in the adoption of special needs children. It is not possible to argue that fertile couples make poorer parents than infertile couples. In fact, there is some evidence that special needs children do better in homes with other children present.[30] Larger families, with their previous child-rearing experience, may be less anxious about raising children and may be more tolerant of nonnormative behaviors. Expectations and aspirations may be more flexible in larger families that have had to deal with individualizing their children prior to their adopting.

Income and the Adoption Subsidy

For many years agencies imposed income requirements on potential adoptive parents. While usually not stated in dollar amounts, couples were expected to have a sufficient and steady income, as well as the ability to manage their income. This was done to insure that the family would be able to provide for the child. Often this meant that working-class or poor families were denied consideration for adoption.

Income considerations also deterred families from considering adoption. Children with special needs, especially those with physical, psychological, or developmental handicaps, or who are part of large sibling groups, may require an extraordinary expenditure of funds. Even middle-class families might resist such adoptions because of financial considerations.

In recognition of such concerns voluntary agencies began, in the late 1960s, to offer adoption subsidies to families considering the adoption of children who otherwise might remain in the foster care system. With the success of these voluntary agency programs, states began to follow suit. Currently, all but a very few states have adoption subsidy programs, and new federal legislation will, if implemented, make federal monies available for adoption subsidies for the first time.

Subsidies are payments to the adoptive family that continue after the adoption is completed. Medical subsidies provide for the child's medical expenses. Continuing board subsidies are similar to foster care payments and help with the expenses of raising a child. Such board subsidies are, in most cases, means-tested and are usually linked to the foster care reimbursement rate. Subsidies can also be available for single expenditures (such as legal fees) to help the adopting parents with the costs of the adoption. The amount of the subsidy payment, how long it will continue, and what conditions can be covered currently vary from state to state.

Subsidy legislation initially met with some opposition in the adoption field:

> To generalize broadly, social workers were concerned about the effects of subsidy on the adoptive family and its possible stigmatic effects on the child; the general public asked why people should be allowed to adopt children for money rather than love, and the legislators wondered where they'd get the money for subsidies.[31]

Additionally, some feared that subsidy would diminish the family's ability to feel like the child's "true" parents while others, including some adoptive parents, felt that such a program had "welfare" connotations and would affect their independence as parents. Some were also concerned about the children's reaction to learning that their parents were receiving money for their support.

In response to these issues, it was argued that agency interference would not occur in the family's life and subsidy would not be linked to the receipt of agency services. It was also argued that children are aware of the financial involvement in foster care.

Because subsidy is usually considered after the child has been in foster care and the state has taken financial responsibility, cost factors were easier to address. Children adopted with subsidy no longer need the supervision of the agency; subsidy payments do not exceed foster care board payments; and demonstration projects have now shown that subsidies can result in substantial financial savings to the state.[32]

A number of problems in the subsidy programs need to be addressed if their potential for countering foster care "drift" is to be maximized. Some of these problems stem from the fact that adoption subsidy, as all adoption legislation, is state-determined. Until the federal program for adoption subsidy is implemented, the following concerns will continue to exist:[33]

—Not all states have subsidy legislation. There is added difficulty in placing special needs children in those states without subsidies.

—Adoption subsidy relies on authorizations of state legislatures. Some adoptive parents fear that continuity of the program is not guaranteed and that the program may be discontinued despite their continued need.

—Levels of subsidy are inconsistent across states, and subsidy payments may not keep up with the cost of living.

—Subsidy legislation often requires a search for nonsubsidized placements prior to placement in a subsidized home. This may cause unnecessary delays.

—Most states require that adoptive parents meet financial eligibility requirements in order to qualify for subsidy even if the child's handicapping condition establishes the need for subsidy. Thus, eligibility is determined by the family's needs, not the child's.

—Subsidy payments may be included in determining a family's eligibility for Medicaid or public assistance. Thus, other benefits may be lost if the adoption is completed.

—Medical subsidies are usually limited to a predetermined condition diagnosed before adoption. They may not cover subsequent medical conditions which can be devastating for family finances.

—Benefits available to foster children may not be extended to children adopted with subsidy. These include Medicaid eligibility and educational benefits.

—Procedures for establishing subsidy eligibility vary not only between states but within social service districts in the same state. In some states unreasonable documentation of need is required, and the determination of eligibility may be arbitrary and subjective.

Despite these problems, and even without the savings in cost to the state, a program of subsidies would be justified if they helped to provide permanent homes for children in the foster care system. A number of projects have demonstrated that the use of subsidy can expand the number of adoptive homes available to waiting children.[34] By eliminating financial barriers, families who could not afford to adopt a child in the past can now consider adoption.

Race and Transracial Adoptions

In keeping with the idea that adopted children should be "biological expressions" of their adoptive families, matching children with their adoptive parents on the basis of race was long the practice of child welfare agencies. If children do not look like their adoptive family, how can they be incorporated into it? In reality this meant that few minority children were placed for adoption, since the vast majority of adoptive applicants were white.

With the end of World War II and the beginnings of the civil rights movement, attention began to be focused on minority group children who waited for adoption (see Chapter 2). Spurred in part by adoptive parent groups, agencies were forced to focus attention on adoptive resources for these children. One resource championed by these groups were white homes for minority youngsters.

During the early and middle 1960s the number of transracial adoptions was small and went relatively unnoticed. However, toward the end of the decade there was a rapid increase, and the number of completed transracial adoptions tripled between 1968 and 1971. By 1971, 35 percent of all black children placed for adoption through agencies were placed in white homes.[35]

This trend of placing minority children in white homes rapidly expanded during a time when minority groups were becoming more dissatisfied with their gains through the civil rights movement and began to turn inward to solve their problems. Demands for autonomy, cultural pluralism, and "power" to control their own destiny replaced the ideas of integration and mainstreaming posited during the early 1960s. One demand for control was the right to care for minority children in minority homes.[36]

The strongest early statement of this demand was made in 1972 by the National Association of Black Social Workers. In part it read:

> The National Association of Black Social Workers has taken a vehement stand against the placement of Black children in white homes for any reason. We affirm the inviolable position of Black children in Black families where they belong physically, psychologically and culturally in order that they receive the total sense of themselves and develop a sound projection of their future.
>
> Black children in white homes are cut off from the healthy development of themselves as Black people, which development is the normal expectation and only true humanistic goal.[37]

Similar positions were taken by other minority groups during this period of time. A 1976 report on Native Americans stated:

> The placement of Indian children in non-Indian homes has come under broad attack in recent years. Numerous tribes have passed resolutions

condemning the practice. . . .
Many tribes have taken formal legal action to forbid off-reservation placement as a way of expressing their opposition to the high number of placements with non-Indian families.[38]

In response to such protests, the 1978 Indian Child Welfare Act (P.L.
95–608) requires that preference in an adoption situation be given first
to the child's extended family, then to other members of the child's
tribe, and then to other Indian families. Only after these possibilities
have been exhausted may an Indian child be placed in a non-Indian
home. Many adoption agencies have taken the same position in regard
to other minority children.

There are numerous reasons cited for the opposition to transracial
adoption. It is believed that transracial adoptions threaten the development of ethnic pride and the identification with ethnic culture and that
children raised in such homes are being made "white." The possibility
has been raised that minority children raised in white homes might identify with the white culture, present themselves as better than others within their minority group, and possibly further racism.[39]

Concern has also been raised regarding the ability of white families to
equip minority children with the necessary tools to deal with a racist
society. It has been stated that blacks must function in two cultures, one
of which is hostile, and that mechanisms must be developed to cope
with this hostility—"psychosurvival" mechanisms.[40] It is questioned
whether white parents, who have never developed these mechanisms,
can teach them. As one author asks: "Can white parents equip a black
child for the inevitable assaults on his personality from a society that
considers his color to be enough reason to reject him . . . How can the
black child learn the necessary maneuvering, seduction, self-enhance-
ment through redefinition and many other tactics taught by black parents, by word and deed, directly and indirectly?"[41]

The question of the ability of white parents to impart a sense of black
identity to the child has also been raised as an objection to transracial
adoptions. Some fear that minority children raised in white homes will
experience identity crises throughout life; they will be confused about
which culture they belong to and may be accepted by neither.[42] Since
development of a positive cultural identity is taken from a broad range of
experiences and involves everyday living within the culture, it is feared
that white families cannot impart this, especially if they continue to live
in all-white neighborhoods as most do.[43] The question is asked: What
happens to these children during adolescence—a turbulent time for any
child—when they must break away from their parents? Will they be
prepared with a strong cultural identity and the tools with which to face
the racist world?

Questions have also been raised about the motives of white parents wishing to adopt black children. Some wonder if adoptive parents are aware of what they are getting themselves into—the possibility of rejection by friends and extended family and the incursion of insults, racial slurs, stares, and ostracism by the public.[44] Research has shown that the extended families of these parents do not respond positively to the idea of a transracial adoption and many remain opposed.[45] Along these same lines, others question whether white families confront and cope with the idea that they were a "second choice" family for the child or that they might have preferred a white child if one had been available.[46] Furthermore, the question of whether these parents are playing out "rescue fantasies" or compensating for the guilt they feel regarding society's treatment of minority peoples has been raised.[47]

Finally, some have argued that transracial adoptions are simply a way for white agencies to continue their adoption business as usual—avoiding the black community. Agencies, it is claimed, perpetuated the myth that "blacks don't adopt"—an argument refuted by research and black leaders. In fact, the amount of informal adoption within black families is quite high,[48] and when one controls for economic status, the rate of formal adoptions is at least equal to that of white families.[49] By perpetuating the myth that blacks do not adopt, agencies can continue to ignore the black community and the higher attrition rate of blacks who do apply. It is believed that the need for transracial adoption would significantly diminish, if not disappear, if agencies would be responsive to the needs of the black community, eliminate racist attitudes, and recruit black families.[50]

Proponents of transracial adoptions generally agree that changes in current practices that deter minority families from adopting and increased services to minority families are needed. However, they also offer a number of arguments in defense of this practice.

Many of the arguments are objected to as abstract, theoretical, and political rather than motivated by concern for the children. They are seen as insensitive to the needs of children, particularly when long-term foster care is advocated as preferable to transracial adoptions.[51]

Some supporters of transracial adoptions point to the fact that a majority in the black community are not opposed to transracial adoptions. One study reports that a majority of black respondents felt that white parents would be qualified to raise black children if they gave up some of their "white" culture; that a white adoptive home is preferable to keeping a child in foster care; and that a white home might be beneficial for a child if a black home was not available. Very few respondents felt that black children could not adjust to living in a white home.[52]

Those who defend transracial adoptions also state that motivation is an individual and personal matter, and that while a few transracial adopters view their actions in a political way—as a commitment to an integrated society—most do not.[53] As one author noted "There is a strong quality of 'ordinariness' about them [transracial adopters] that defies many of the images presented by their foes."[54]

While most transracial families live in white neighborhoods and are not directly involved in the black community, research also indicates that these families are able to impart to their children a sense of racial identity and awareness. While the children studied were still quite young, and none had yet reached adolescence, at least two studies have now concluded that transracially adopted children have at least as good, and in some cases a better, ability to identify themselves correctly and tend to perceive being black less negatively than other black children.[55] One study concluded:

> The data strongly suggest that something is happening in these multiracial families that is eroding the superior, or favored, or more attractive status that white seems to enjoy so pervasively among other American children. The erosion seems to be taking place without any noticeable confusion in the children's awareness of race or in their ability to label and identify themselves accurately.
>
> . . . black children who are reared in the special setting of multiracial families do not acquire the ambivalence toward their own race that has been reported among all other groups of young black children.[56]

Other research is also cited to support the continuation of transracial adoptions. Outcome studies show results similar to those for other types of adoptions, with success rates between 70 and 80 percent.[57] However, whether children will learn "psychosurvival" mechanisms in these homes and whether the sense of identity apparent in early childhood will continue is not yet known.

The effect of this highly volatile controversy was a precipitous decline in the number of children adopted transracially during the mid-1970s. While this has begun to dissipate, transracial adoptions continue to represent a smaller percentage of black children adopted than was true in the early 1970s.[58] Many in the field believe that even if every effort is made to find minority homes, there will still be children who cannot be placed in the minority community and that transracial adoptions still represent an important alternative to foster care. However, such adoptions will never be done as naively as was the case in the early 1970s. A number of authors[59] have developed guidelines for this practice. Taken together, the following appear to be the principles for guiding such placements:

—Children whenever possible should be placed with parents of the same race.

—Permanent care in an adoptive home is preferable to long-term foster care or institutionalization of minority children.

—Placing a child in a home of another race should be based on the needs of the child, not the desire of parents for a child or an expedience for an agency.

—Motivating factors for transracial adoption must be explored thoroughly with adoptive parents to insure that their expectations are realistic.

—Any parent adopting transracially must be able to accept racial and cultural differences between themselves and their child on more than an intellectual level. Such couples must be sensitive to their own prejudice and racism and the way it affects the child.

—Adoptive couples must be committed to imparting a sense of racial or ethnic identification to their child. This means that they must demonstrate ability and desire for sustained contact with members of the child's ethnic/racial group. They must relate to the cultural milieu with which the child will need to identify.

—Transracial adopting parents must be able to confront the racist nature of society and be committed on all levels to combatting this situation. They must prepare their child to face discrimination when it occurs and help diffuse its impact.

Other Requirements

A number of other agency requirements have been challenged as barriers to the placement of "waiting" children. One is housing requirements that stipulate that the children must have rooms of their own. Critics of this practice point to the fact that such external indicators are not predictive of the care the child will receive and place importance on externals rather than the ability to parent.[60] They further point out that such requirements usually bar any but the middle class from adopting and point to the number of working-class children successfully reared in homes in which they shared rooms.

It has also been stated that the requirements that the adoptive mother not be employed outside the home deters many working-class and minority parents from adopting. It is argued that for waiting children (many of whom are older and away for most of the day) such demands serve no purpose. In addition, opponents of these requirements note that in this society over half of the women with school-aged children and well over one-third of those with preschool children are currently working. This trend is likely to accelerate as women continue to enter the labor force and make a significant contribution to family income. Many families now make alternative plans for children (see Chapter 4). It is argued that requiring women to remain at home after adoption is contrary to current societal expectations, hurts families financially, and diminishes the possibility of women achieving self-fulfillment.

EXPANDING THE POOL OF ADOPTIVE PARENTS

In addition to removing agency requirements in order to facilitate the adoption of special needs children, some agencies have begun to place children for adoption in homes that only a few years ago would not have been considered appropriate. The consequence of this action is the expansion of the pool of potential adoptive homes. Among the groups gaining acceptance as potential families for children are single parents, foster parents, and working-class parents.

Single Parents

Adoption of children by single parents (never married, divorced, or widowed) is a relatively new practice. The first such placements occurred in Los Angeles in 1965, and the practice has expanded since that time. While some states continue to have prohibitions against such placements, single-parent adoptions are less conspicuous and cause less concern than in the past because of the growing number of single parents raising children in the general population. It is estimated that as of 1977 approximately 2000 single parent adoptions had been completed.[61]

There are a number of factors that cause concern about single parent adoptions.[62] First, the motivation for single parents wanting to adopt can be suspect; some fear that they are motivated by loneliness, and that children are sought primarily to fill a void in their lives. Second, concerns have been expressed about the consequences to the child of having only one parent in the home. These include the probability that the parent will work, requiring substitute child care arrangements; the possibility that the parent will die, requiring provision for the child's future care; the absence in the home of a figure of the opposite sex for the child to identify with; and the lack of a model of a two-parent family. A third set of concerns about single parent adoption focuses on the single parent's ability to cope with the responsibility of child rearing. Some point to the fact that the parent is without the emotional support of a spouse and must cope alone with domestic responsibilities. With the probability that the single parent will work and have to be a full-time parent, there is a fear that there will be less physical and psychic energy for the child.

On the other hand, a number of arguments have been made in favor of a single-parent adoptive homes. First, by utilizing single parents, a substantial number of homes become available for waiting children. Second, it is generally believed that stability and permanence in a one-parent home is more beneficial to the child than the uncertainty of foster care, or than a two-parent home in which there is marital disharmony or conflict. Finally, supporters of single-parent adoptions also point to research findings that do not support the idea that being raised in one-parent families leads to pathology.

Research tends to show that the majority of children in single-parent homes do well; that it is the instability of broken homes rather than parental absence itself that might cause difficulty for the child; and that adjustments of adolescents in unhappy, unbroken homes is poorer than that of adolescents in single-parent homes. In reviewing the literature, one author concludes: "Available research on development in single parent families does not tend to lend strong support to our presuppositions that this is a highly hazardous context for child rearing. The association between single parent familyhood and psychosocial pathology is neither strong nor invariable."[63]

The limited research on single-parent adoptions tends to support this conclusion. Single-parent adopters report substantially the same experiences as adoptive couples in the area of child's health, growth, and development. In one study, overall adjustment of the children, when reported by the parent, was rated at least "good" in more than 90 percent of the cases.[64] Another study reported that there were no indications that the children of single-parent adopters had any problem in the area of sexual identification—a major concern for this population of children.[65]

However, both of these studies on single-parent adoptions report greater emotional adjustment problems for these children than children in two-parent adoptive homes. Both studies point out, however, that children placed in single-parent homes are more likely to be older and to have experienced multiple placements and greater deprivation before adoptive placement than children placed in two-parent homes.[66]

Strength is added to the argument in favor of single-parent adoptions when one looks at the single people pursuing this course. Research indicates that they have a high level of emotional maturity and a high capacity to tolerate frustration. They tend to be self-aware and to have strong connections with relatives and friends of both sexes. Many have had child-rearing experience prior to the adoption, and some live as part of larger extended families where they find support and help. They are generally child-oriented and appear to have little need for institutional supports.[67] They are reported to be older than other adoptive parents and to have made a conscious decision about wanting a child. Many had good incomes and were better educated than other adoptive parents, although this was not true universally. Most seemed prepared for the adjustments in their personal lives that a child would necessitate.[68]

It has also been posited that single parents may be a placement of choice for some children. It has been noted that the special needs child manifesting emotional problems may be better placed in a one-parent home where there is a high caliber of parenting potential, a simplified environment with fewer complex relationships among adults, fewer demands placed on the child, and sharply focused nurturing, since single parents tend to have fewer outside involvements than married couples and seem to concentrate extraordinary efforts on the parent/child relationship.[69]

Despite these arguments and the relatively good adjustment the children appear to be making, single parents remain a "second choice" for agencies.[70] Single parents report a longer wait for a child and a more negative agency experience than couples. Furthermore, the children who are placed with them often have more handicapping conditions than children placed with couples and are more likely to be of mixed racial backgrounds.[71] Thus, the ironic situation persists that "those who are felt to possess the least resources to parent have been assigned the children who would seem to require the most demanding kinds of care."[72] This "discrimination" seems to work against finding homes for waiting children—only when two-parent families are not available are single parents usually considered.

Foster Parents

For many years agencies did not consider foster parents as possible adoptive resources. Foster care was seen as a temporary arrangement for children who would eventually return home, and foster parents were encouraged to keep emotional distance between themselves and the children in their care. Foster parents were viewed as "clients" of the agency or paraprofessionals who were expected to accept the removal of a child from their home with very little notice.[73]

Even with the realization that many children remain in foster care until their majority, foster parent adoption was not viewed as an alternative. An experience survey of persons in the field in 1971 revealed that while many of the respondents saw the need for expanding the pool of adoptive parents, only one-third mentioned the idea of foster parent adoption.[74] As late as 1974 almost two-thirds of the states had a cautionary note or a prohibition of adoption in their placement agreements with foster parents.[75]

A number of objections have been raised regarding the adoption of children by their foster parents. First, foster parents may not be as carefully selected or screened as adoptive parents and may not meet the same criteria. Second, it is feared that such adoptions "drain off" a valuable agency resource[76]—the agencies' best foster homes may be lost to them. Third, foster parent adoptions may be disruptive to other children in foster care. Adoption of only one child from a group of foster children in a home may create emotional upheaval for the other children and may lead to their replacement.[77] Fourth, such adoptions may not permit the traditional provision of confidentiality. Biological and foster parents may have been involved with each other, and siblings and other relatives may continue to have contact with the child.[78] Fifth, since children are often placed in foster care under crisis conditions, the matching of children with parents, long a tenet of adoption practice, may not take place. Finally, if adoption by foster parents is anticipated, some fear that less work will be done with the biological family in order to restore the child to them.

With the growing awareness that many children now in foster care may never return to their biological parents, agencies have begun, despite these fears, to reevaluate the role of the foster parent in the life of the child. Many of the barriers to foster parent adoptions have been removed by legislation or agency policy. Most states now grant foster parents preference in the adoption of children who have been in their homes, either by law, policy, or practice.[79] It is clear that subsidy legislation also encourages this practice—the first subsidy legislation provided for subsidies only to foster parents.

Research studies have indicated that many foster parents react positively to the idea of adoption. One study reports that over 70 percent of the foster parents who were approached reacted in this fashion.[80] Furthermore, every project concerned with moving children out of foster care and into adoptive placement has found that foster homes are a primary resource, often constituting a majority of adoptive homes found for children.[81]

The advantages of these adoptions are described in the previous chapter. Some agencies have found the benefits of foster parent adoption so attractive that, in order to maximize this possibility, they have created the "three-option" or "legal risk" foster home.[82] These homes serve as the child's initial foster placement. However, if it appears that the child cannot be returned home within a reasonable length of time, these families are willing to become the child's legal guardians (if the child cannot be freed for adoption) or to become adoptive parents if parental rights can be terminated.

The limited follow-up studies of foster parent adoptions seem to conclude that children adopted by their foster parents generally do well. They report that in some cases the child's behavior improves after the adoption is completed.[83] One study concluded "on all our scales, . . . foster parent adoption has done as well as other permanent placements including new parent adoptions."[84]

Given the positive indication from the limited research and the availability of subsidy, the question becomes: Why do some foster parents adopt and others decline? Available research shows that foster parents are reluctant to adopt for a number of reasons. Their age or health might deter them, as might the degree of the child's handicaps. The foster parents' fears about the child's behavior upon entering adolescence, a lack of "bonding" between foster parent and child, and a fear that the family will lose agency supports have also been identified as possible deterrents.[85] On the other hand, there is some indication that the more enjoyment the foster parents get from the child, the greater their sensitivity to the needs of the child and their capacity to meet those needs, and the more enjoyment the foster parents get from nurturing, guiding, and interacting with the child, the more likely they are to adopt.[86] This augurs well for positive outcomes.

However, a word of caution is needed. There is some indication that, in the push to find adoptive homes for children, practices thought to be important to help assure that the adoption will "work" are not being followed with foster parents. Two studies report that some foster parents felt pressured or blackmailed to adopt their foster children. Some were threatened with the removal of the child if the adoption was not completed. Some have reported that there was little preparation in anticipation of the adoption.[87]

While many would agree that a full home study is not necessary when the family has been known to the agency, there are issues in adoption that are different from those in foster care. In order to help assure that these adoptions are successful, good practice dictates that these issues be discussed and resolved with the foster parents and the child.

Working-Class Families

The presence of subsidies and the elimination of income requirements by some agencies has meant that working-class adults can now be considered as adoptive parents. While this group represents a large pool of potential adoptive parents, there is some indication that they are unlikely to approach agencies for fear of rejection. It seems that recruitment efforts, discussed previously, need to be directed specifically at this group. Just as with single parents, it has been argued that working-class families represent a "placement of choice" for some children. In describing its philosophy, one very successful agency that deals only with the most difficult-to-place children, has stated:

> . . . the traditional adoption agency policy of choosing adoptive parents who meet ideal white middle class standards as parents for hard to place children is a practice which is detrimental to the placement of such children, . . . Most older and handicapped children are more readily assimilated into working class homes.[88]

This report points out that children experience the least amount of difficulty if they are placed with parents like those they have known in the past. Since most foster parents are not middle class and most of the children's biological parents are poor, the social gap between the child and adoptive parents is diminished if the child is placed in a working-class home.

It is further noted that middle-class parents are more likely to hold higher expectations for their children than working-class parents. Since many waiting children have experienced deprivation and may be handicapped, they may be unable to meet these expectations. This creates emotional stress for both the parents and the child and may impede the formation of a relationship. Working-class families, it is felt, are more likely to allow children to progress at their own rates and to accept their limitations.

These impressions have been confirmed in a demonstration project concerned with special needs adoption.[89] It has been noted that disruptions of special needs adoptions are most likely to occur in middle-class, well-educated, achievement-oriented families, where the primary motivation for adoption is either to act out of "social consciousness" or the

desire to "fill out" their families. Such families have difficulty in relating to special needs children and addressing their needs once they are placed.

ELIMINATING SYSTEMS BARRIERS

In order to provide optimally for children awaiting adoptive placements, it is necessary to look at the service delivery system, identify the dysfunctional elements present, and eliminate them. Dysfunctions can occur on two levels—within a single agency itself and among agencies delivering similar services.

Intra-Agency Barriers

The process of placing special needs children in adoptive homes can be impeded by the way a single agency organizes its services and delivers them. Some of these problems stem from the way services are structured. Others, however, arise because of the limited financial base for adoption services and the inadequate preparation and training of workers.

It has been noted that foster care and adoption workers are often in conflict with each other around planning for children. Each may view the other as obstructive. Foster care workers can be perceived as too cautious and reluctant to move toward termination of parental rights and adoption. Adoption workers, on the other hand, may be viewed as "child snatchers," more interested in the child than the biological family. There is often conflict between these two units in a single agency. Furthermore:

> Another significant . . . problem . . . lies in confusion and competition among local public agency foster care and adoption units, which usually share responsibility for planning to provide a permanent home for the legally free child. Specific problems identified include (1) poor and unsystematic communications between foster care and adoption units; (2) lack of clearly defined responsibility for children legally free for adoption between foster care and adoption units; and (3) inadequate coordination between these units in planning for these children.[91]

Still another problem identified in this area is the way responsibilities are divided between these two types of units. Different units, housed in different places, are often responsible for work with the different parties to the adoption. Workers freeing children for adoption may have no contact with workers doing home studies. Workers who know the children best may have no contact with workers who know the families waiting for a child.

A number of suggestions have been made to rectify these problems. First, workers need to be informed of what others in their agency are doing and must work from a common set of assumptions and values. The establishment of clear decision-making standards and criteria (discussed earlier in this volume) will help eliminate friction. In addition, the institution of goal-directed casework methods and case contracting can alleviate some of this conflict. For example, foster care workers, upon seeing that goals are not met or contracts are not fulfilled, might be less hesitant to move toward termination of parental rights.

Another approach that might help insure that delays in moving toward adoption are eliminated is the establishment of monitoring units within the agency. These units would internally monitor whether case goals have been set, whether these goals are appropriate, and whether progress is being made toward these goals. Monitoring units would insure that all divisions of the agency are working toward similar goals. To be effective, these units ". . . would require sufficient authority, or be attached to a principal with sufficient authority, to intervene in situations where case plans are not being carried out or where the wrong case plan has been designated."[92]

Another suggestion that has been made is the creation, within an agency, of permanency planning teams composed of foster care and adoption workers. One part of this team would focus on children in placement and work with biological parents for the child's return home. If this is not possible, this team would be responsible for legally freeing the child for adoption. When free, the adoption worker attached to the team would be called into play to recruit and study homes, prepare the child and family for placement, place the child, and serve the family after the placement has been made.[93] There is growing support for such teams, as it is felt that generalist workers have neither the time, the incentives, nor the training to concentrate on all of these tasks.

Another model that has been proposed is the creation of special agencies to deal only with the placement of special needs children. These agencies take referrals from regular adoption units when they are unable to make a placement. Such agencies have been created in a number of states. While effective in their work, these agencies operate on a purchase-of-service basis—that is, the referring agency pays for the cost of the service for the child. Such purchase-of-service arrangements are certainly less costly than continuing a child in foster care; yet, many states do not provide for them.[94]

No matter which model is used, there is, and will continue to be, a clear need for well-trained adoption workers. This has presented a consistent problem in many agencies. In the public sector increasing case loads resulting from funding and hiring freezes have compounded the problem of staff turnover. Those workers who stay are often overwhelmed with crisis situations and are often unable to devote the necessary time to free children and refer them for adoption, especially if the foster care placement is stable. Similar problems have been noted in the voluntary sector.

As the field moves toward the placement of special needs children, numerous training needs arise. There is the need to sensitize workers in all aspects of adoption and to provide them with the knowledge and skills necessary to complete these adoptions. Specifically, some of the areas that training should address include:

—The philosophy of permanency planning and the importance of goal-directed, time-limited service

—Legal issues in termination and adoption including laws of evidence and testimony so that workers can be more effective in court

—Worker attitudes regarding the "adoptability" of children in the foster care system

—Knowledge about the needs of children awaiting placement

—Information regarding specific medical/developmental handicaps that children have

—Recruitment of adoptive homes

—Preparation of children for adoption

—Screening of adoptive applicants on meaningful criteria and the elimination of institutional racism and other forms of discrimination that block families from adopting

—Preparation of families for adoption

—Work with families and children after placement

—Feelings about and acceptance of a higher rate of adoption disruption since this is more likely to occur in special needs adoption[95]

Interagency Barriers

Within any location there may be a number of adoption agencies all attempting to accomplish the same goals. Often, however, each operates independently of the others, and little effort is made to work together toward mutual goals. The results are that adoption services within a community may be:[96]

—Duplicative—agencies compete for scarce resources while attempting to provide the same services. Often no agency is able to do a fully adequate job in all areas of adoption services.

—Unstandardized—each agency sets its own policies and practices. Both clients and the public may get conflicting messages from the agencies.

—Provincial—each agency may look out for its own needs, ignoring those of other agencies in the community. Thus, gaps in services may develop.

—Isolated—adoption workers may not come together to discuss mutual concerns and may feel a lack of support and stimulation for their work.

The lack of cooperation between agencies may mean that scarce resources are not being used in an effective or efficient manner, thus delaying the placement of special needs children. Two examples make this point clearly.

First, as mentioned previously, recruitment is an essential part of any adoption program for special needs children. Yet, if an agency does not have special needs children waiting for placement, often no attempt is made to recruit families despite the fact that many children may be waiting in other agencies for an adoptive home.

Second, in the area of home studies, a lack of uniformity of standards often leads to a mistrust by one agency of another agency's work. Since licensure sets only minimum standards of practice, one agency may feel that other agencies do not practice at a comparable level. Thus, home studies done by one agency may not be accepted by another.

With scarce resources, it appears that agencies within the same community and/or state need to coordinate their efforts on behalf of waiting children better. A number of suggestions have been made.

First, licensing standards need to be tightened, so that agencies can begin to trust the judgments and decisions of other agencies. In this way efforts will not have to be duplicated. Second, cooperative efforts between agencies can be expanded so that duplication is reduced and resources conserved. Furthermore, agencies can pool resources and undertake joint efforts when no single agency can afford a given service. For example, legal services related to adoption can be expensive, and many small agencies cannot afford a full-time counsel. It would be less expensive for a number of agencies to employ a full-time attorney jointly to represent them than for each to pay an attorney at an hourly rate.[97]

The scarcity of adoption resources is often felt most acutely in rural, low-population areas. Often, there is only one adoption worker or unit for a county and a very limited budget for these services. In such situations, a number of counties could pool resources and thus better serve the waiting children in their area. These "regional models" have been demonstrated to be effective; the centralization of adoption services has led to a greater number of placements for special needs children. The main advantages of these regional approaches are: (1) consolidation and centralization of professional staff, (2) wider availability of potential adoptive families, (3) opportunities for general staff development, and (4) expansion of coordination among individual agencies.[98] However, these advantages can be realized only if certain ". . . conditions exist in a region and . . . organizational concerns are addressed before the model is implemented."[99]

Another mechanism that has been implemented to encourage interagency cooperation is the adoption exchange. These exchanges are designed to facilitate the placement of special needs children by making available a larger pool of applicants than would be available through a single agency. Children awaiting adoptive placement are listed with the exchange, which may encompass a city, state, region, or the entire nation. Approved adoptive families who are waiting for children are also registered. The exchange then attempts to match children available through one agency with families available through another.

A similar mechanism is the adoption listing service, with which children are registered. The descriptions (and often pictures) of the children are then available to agencies to share with potential adoptive applicants.

While many states and regions have created adoption exchanges and listing services in order to facilitate the placement of children with special needs, there are problems that impede their effectiveness. One evaluation of a state program found that:[100]

> —Agencies were given great discretion in determining which children to list with the exchange. While the intent of the state's law was to insure the listing of all children freed for adoption for more than three months, 80 percent of the legally freed children were not listed.

> —There was no way to monitor the statutory requirement that children be listed, and no sanctions were available if agencies did not comply with the listing requirement.

—The presentation of children in exchange books was disorganized and often confusing.

—Potential adoptive parents had access to the exchange books only through their caseworker, who may not feel that adoption is the best plan for many special needs children.

—Agency personnel exhibited reluctance to pursue matches of children and families made by the exchange.

—Staff for the exchange was insufficient.

—Families listed with the exchange were not prepared to adopt the kinds of children listed.

These identified problems demonstrate that an exchange cannot be fully successful unless: (1) workers believe that all children freed for adoption are "adoptable" and list these children; (2) exchange books are made available to waiting families, and the children are presented in a realistic and orderly way; (3) social workers in different agencies have confidence in each others' competence and trust the judgment of exchange workers; and (4) mechanisms for purchasing the services of the placement agency are available.

In order to insure that exchanges and listing services operate in the most beneficial manner for the children awaiting adoptive placement, some have advocated that they move from their "passive" role (simply making agencies aware of the children available or matching children and families) to a more active, dynamic role. They believe that these services should assume leadership in the area of special needs adoptions by directly recruiting adoptive families; making listings available to any interested party, not just agencies; serving as clearing houses for information about specific handicapping conditions that waiting children have; and providing consultation, technical assistance, and training for agencies and their staffs in the placement of special needs children.[101] In this way the possibility of the exchanges being more successful is enhanced and agencies are helped to place more children directly.

The problems of interagency cooperation are compounded when agencies in different states are involved in an adoption. This situation arises when an adoptive home in one state is located for a child living in another state. Such placements, when they involve special needs children, are usually arranged by a regional or the national adoption exchange. However, they may also occur if a family moves from one state to another after the child's placement but before the adoption has been finalized. Interstate placements may also occur when a home in one state is recruited directly by an agency in a neighboring state.[102]

In order to overcome some of the problems of interstate placement, the Interstate Compact on the Placement of Children was developed. This compact provides guidelines for the placement of children across state lines, including:[103]

—Prior to making a placement across state lines, the sending agency must furnish the appropriate public agency in the receiving state written notice of its intention; the name, date, place of birth of the child; the name and address of the legal guardian; the name and address of the receiving family; and a full statement of the reasons for the proposed placement.

—The receiving state may request any additional information on the placement.

—The child cannot be sent until the receiving state notifies the sending state, in writing, that the placement does not appear contrary to the best interest of the child.

—The sending agency retains jurisdiction over the child until the child is adopted, reaches majority, or becomes self-supporting. The sending agency also maintains financial responsibility for the child but may contract for services.

There are problems in the implementation of the compact, which hinder its effectiveness. First, not all states belong to the compact. Second, while the financial responsibility for the child is fixed with the sending state once the child is placed, there is no agreement as to who pays the cost of transporting the child, the accompanying worker, or the adoptive parents for preplacement visits and so forth. Third, because of the complexity of coordinating activities in two states and two local agencies, as well as among numerous attorneys, courts, and workers, there are often large amounts of paperwork and unnecessary delays in placements. Finally, the judgment of workers in one state is often not respected by workers in another state—the problem of provincialism mentioned previously.[104] In addition, the fact that adoption laws vary from state to state can present barriers to the interstate placement of children.

A number of suggestions have been made to overcome these barriers: (1) full participation in the Interstate Compact and acceptance of its provisions by all state governments; (2) greater uniformity in state adoption laws (especially regarding termination of parental rights) as contained in the Model State Adoption Statute proposed by the Children's Bureau in 1980; (3) agreement on the financing of not only the child's placement but costs involved in effecting that placement; and (4) the strengthening of licensing standards, so that mutual trust can be developed between agencies in different states.[105] Until these policy matters are addressed, there will continue to be obstacles to the interstate placement of special needs children and unnecessary delays in finding permanent homes for them.

PROVIDING MEANINGFUL SERVICES

No matter what the recruitment methods used or how many agency and interagency barriers are removed, the successful placement of special needs children depends on meaningful services delivered in a skillful way to the parties involved in the adoption. These include choosing adoptive parents and preparing them for the child's placement, preparing the child to become a permanent member of a family, working with the newly constituted family before the finalization of the adoption, and being available for postadoptive services if any member of the family perceives the need for them. Without these services, the probability of a successful placement is significantly diminished.

Choosing and Preparing Adoptive Parents

Earlier in this chapter some of the criteria currently in use for screening and matching adoptive applicants with children were discussed. Many were shown to be barriers to the adoption of special needs children. These criteria, as well as deep psychological probing with applicants, served to screen parents out of the adoption process. In many ways, adoption agency practice has been investigatory and overly intrusive.

As the field moves toward greater concern with the adoption of special needs children, new methods are being developed for working with prospective parents to help them evaluate their capacity to rear a child who may be older or handicapped. As one report noted, "To achieve stable family ties, it is often necessary to sacrifice the optimal and somewhat irrelevant standards of former years."[106] This is especially important, since research has shown that even using these "high" standards, workers often disagreed with each other as to the acceptability of applicants for adoption.[107]

Rather than screening applicants, a number of authors have written of the need to create a "partnership" with them,[108] so that applicants can *decide for themselves* whether this type of adoption is a good plan for them. Creating such a partnership requires that agencies change some basic assumptions about the adoptive applicants.

The first assumption that must be changed is that adoptive parents are somewhat "damaged" and the extent of this damage must be evaluated. Rather, it should be assumed that most applicants do not have serious pathological problems that must be resolved. Workers must be trained to see the strengths in adoptive families and realize that with proper supports, most applicants have the capacity to become adoptive parents.[109]

A second assumption that must be reevaluated is that the "worker knows best." If one assumes that most applicants have strengths, then one must respect their ability to select, *for themselves,* the child they would feel most comfortable in adopting.[110] This assumes that agencies are willing to share full (other than identifying) information about the child, so that applicants understand the child's history, the reasons the child is free for adoption, the child's current behavior patterns and feelings, and future needs.[111] If applicants do not have this information, they cannot properly judge for themselves whether a child can be incorporated into the family. With this information they also become aware of problems to expect in the placement and have a good sense of the child's life before the placement is made.

If this approach is adopted, the social worker's role shifts from "evaluator" to "educator." The worker informs the family as to the child's history, the nature of the child's condition, the child's behavior, and prognosis. Further, the worker can teach the applicants appropriate skills for dealing with the child and can make them aware of resources in the community, such as special schools or clinics, which can help them meet the child's needs.[112]

This partnership also implies that parents will be encouraged to discuss with their worker the kinds of children for whom they have positive feelings and the types of behaviors and handicapping conditions that intimidate them or they cannot accept.[113] In this way the worker and parents can focus on children available in the agency who might be "right" for this prospective family. Thus, the "distance" between the worker and prospective family is reduced, and trust can be established quickly.

Agencies have used a number of techniques to carry out this new method of choosing and preparing adoptive parents. While individual work with families is often used and families have expressed satisfaction about their decision-making responsibility,[114] group methods can also accomplish these goals. Education groups can help explain the meaning of separation and adoption and the types of adjustment problems families and children have. They can inform prospective parents about handicapping conditions and teach parenting skills. They can also provide the family with a legal framework for adoption.[115] Group methods can be used as vehicles for the actual selection of children, for clarification of personal interactions within the family, and for parent effectiveness training.[116]

The use of groups is not limited to prospective adoptive adults alone. Sibs-to-be groups have been formed by some agencies. Such groups can help children who are already part of a family adjust to a new sibling.[117] Other groups have incorporated parents who have previously adopted through the agency. This has been found to be an effective way of introducing prospective adoptive parents to the hazards posed and satisfactions available from special needs adoption. It is also a way for people with "hands-on" experience to impart their knowledge and the meaning of adoption to families considering this option.[118]

No matter which method is used, there are some underlying principles that guide this new practice in adoptive parent screening and preparation. These include:

—Most applicants are assumed to be capable parents.
—Clients make the primary decision regarding their interests, strengths, and limitations.
—Children are presented realistically with their strengths and limitations.
—All information is shared about the children under consideration.
—The role of the worker is educative, and the worker is present for exploration, clarification, and information.

Preparing the Child

The worker's first step in preparing a child for adoption is assuring that the child is legally free or that legal termination of parental rights will occur in the near future. This process is often difficult. The reasons for this difficulty have been explained in previous chapters and will only be summarized here. First, children are often not identified as needing adoptive services and therefore steps are not taken to free them. They continue to drift in the foster care system. Mandatory review and the institution of information systems, mandated by the 1980 child welfare amendments, should help with this problem.

Second, caseworkers are often reluctant to pursue this course. Some fear that disruption of the foster home would be damaging for the child. Others are fearful that the court will not terminate parental rights because work with the biological parents while the child was in placement has not taken place. In some cases, the work with biological parents has taken place but is so poorly documented that it is inadmissible in court. Training workers in the areas of case effort, case documentation, testifying in court, and the importance of permanency for children can help overcome these barriers.[119]

Third, termination procedures can be complex, expensive, and time consuming. Not only must the biological mother's rights be terminated but, by court decision,[120] the biological father's rights must, in some cases, be terminated even if he was never married to the mother. While involvement of both parents and the provision of services to them can be beneficial in helping them resolve their conflicts about the child (and such procedures clearly protect their legal rights), this requirement can cause delays in freeing the child for adoption. Publication of notice to the putative father is required, and at times, a "diligent search" is carried out in order to guarantee his rights. Each of these steps takes time, agency energy, and funds, all of which may be scarce.[121] It seems that clear guidelines must be developed to help agencies conform to legal requirements and at the same time expedite the termination of parental rights when this is indicated.

Finally, there are problems in the termination statutes themselves. They vary from state to state, have vague wording which is left to the interpretation of judges, and are premised on vague standards. Clearer and consistent decision-making guidelines, the training of judges in permanency planning principles, and the adoption of more precise standards would all help to free children for adoption expeditiously.

Once this legal process is underway children must be helped to resolve feelings about their past. In order to do this, they must be given the truth about their parents' situation in a realistic way and at a level that they can understand. One tool that has been helpful in preparing children for adoption is the "life book." In this book the child places pictures, drawings, documents, and stories in time sequence. The preparation of such a book can help children understand what has happened to them and why. It can help clarify their self-concept.[122]

It is essential that the child's foster parents be positively involved in the preparation process and be committed to the idea of permanency. Despite probable ambivalent feelings about the child leaving the home, they must be committed to the plan. If they are not, they can sabotage the adoption preparation.

The worker can engage the foster parents in this process by encouraging them to help children work through their feelings about their relationship with them and their biological parents. Furthermore, since they know the child most intimately, the worker should encourage them to share critical information about the child.[123]

Children are ready for adoption when they are able to adjust to the loss of old parental ties and accept new ties to an adoptive family. This is manifested, at times, by an ability to express an explicit desire for adoption and the motivation to adjust to the adoptive situation. The ability to talk about anxiety and ambivalence in relation to the changes that are about to occur and a willingness to approach the new situation with some amount of acceptance is a good indicator that the child is ready to proceed to an adoptive home.[124]

At this point preplacement visits with the adoptive family can begin. The family and child are brought together, and work with both continues around their fears, anxieties, and ambivalences. Children should take from these visits something concrete (often a family life book similar to the child's book just described), so that the idea of adoption begins to become a reality.

Services After Placement

When one considers the added difficulties and stresses that the adoption of a special needs child might place on the family, it is not surprising that the provision of postplacement services is seen as a crucial investment to insure that the placement can be maintained. The need for these services may continue long after the adoption is finalized in court. Yet, some workers fail to comprehend the need for postplacement services, and many lack the time, training, and institutional supports necessary to provide them.[125]

There are numerous problematic situations that can occur after a child's adoptive placement, each of which can be helped by intervention. Some of these situations are transient and are settled relatively quickly. Others, however, are complex and may repeat throughout the child's history with the family.[126]

One transient but difficult problem is the "unbalancing" of the family because of the child's entrance. The mere fact that there is a new child present means that roles and relationships within the family change. The family must be helped to recognize that this is normal and would occur with any child. They must be helped to establish a new homeostasis in the family.[127]

Another transient problem is learning to cope with the child's behavior and learning what is "normal" for this child and what is not. No matter how much preparation the family has had and how much they have accepted the child's behavior in the abstract, actual confrontation with disturbing behavior can be difficult for a family.

Parents may also need help in dealing with their feelings about the child's attachment to them and loyalty to the family. Bonding between the older child and new parents will take time. There will probably be a "testing" period for the parents before the child incorporates into the new family. Through this period the parents may question their decision and begin to doubt their capacity to deal with the new child. They must be helped to understand that incorporation takes time, loyalties form slowly, and new patterns emerge only after careful work has been done.[128]

In order to incorporate a new child in the home, there need to be opportunities for the members of the new family to "claim" each other. This can start before the child is placed by giving each a sense of entitlement to the others and getting validation from the outside community for the formation of a new family. Once the family is together, the agency can encourage sharing of important times, information, and emotions, and the use of ritual behaviors ("adoption" day, "my" daughter, family "codes") to enhance this process.[129] The slow but consistent introduction of routine, rules, and discipline can also be important in allowing this family formation to occur and trust to build. Families may need help to accomplish this.[130]

While these problems are transient, the family may also face long-range problems for which services may be needed on an ongoing basis. These ongoing problems are often due to the family's and child's previous history and their ways of adapting. After numerous years in foster care, the child may have difficulty in trusting a new relationship, may continue to have identity problems, or may have loyalty conflicts between previous and current "parents." Defenses that have developed may take a long time to be unlearned.

Families may also need to make changes in their life-style. The child may have continuing needs that will tax the family over time. The mere presence of another person in the family means that the family life-style will change, and may have to change continually, depending on the child's needs and condition. Marital conflicts, conflicts between the parents and other children in the family, and conflicts between children may crop up periodically as new family "unbalances" arise over the course of time.[131]

Given these circumstances, some agencies have begun to develop postplacement services, which incorporate a number of programs to support adoptive families and children. Individual and family counseling services after placement and finalization have proved helpful. Groups of adoptive parents have been formed by both agencies and parents. Adoption agencies must also develop strong linkages to other community resources in order to help families provide for the individual needs of their children.[132]

The need for such supports is great. In response to a lack of agency services, groups of adoptive parents have come together without formal agency support. Some have formed support groups or a "buddy" system, much like self-help groups in other areas. Such efforts appear successful, not only in terms of supporting each other but also in advocating for the adoption of special needs children and the removal of agency barriers that impede the placement process. While becoming better organized and more cohesive in the last few years, these groups, which serve an important function for waiting children, have had little money on which to operate.

Disruption

It is clear that as the field of adoption moves toward placing greater numbers of special needs children in adoptive homes, the possibility that adoptive placements will not work out increases. Research has shown that the rate of adoption disruption increases with the age of the child, the number of moves the child has experienced while in foster care, and the presence of other siblings in the home.[133] While disruption rates for infant adoptions is usually under 3 percent, those for special needs children are reported to be about 15 percent.[134]

There has been some speculation as to why adoptions disrupt. In some cases, the reason is unforeseen or situational circumstances such as financial stress, illness, or a death. However, in the majority of cases the disruption is caused by a problem in the parent/child interaction. It may be that the family cannot cope with the child's behavior or that the child's effect on the family homeostasis is too disruptive. It may be that the family's expectations of the child are too high, and the child cannot meet them, or that the family had trouble accepting the "real" child.[135] Whatever the reason, the "match" between parent and child was not right.

The reason that adoptions disrupt can often be traced, in retrospect, to the assessment process. There may have been unrecognized preexisting problems in either the family or the child. There may have been problems that were known but left unexplored by the worker. There may have been a misjudgment about the capacity or readiness of either the family or the child to make an attachment.[136] Whatever the specific reason, writers seem to feel that strengthening the assessment process will lower the disruption rate. Services during the placement can help to head off emerging problems before they get out of hand.[137]

It is important to let the parties to the adoption know, prior to the placement, that disruption is a possibility. In this way the agency can assume a nonjudgmental stand if problems do emerge. Hopefully, this also gives parents "permission" to ask for help early, so that feelings do not intensify to the point that nothing can be done to avoid the disruption.

Workers should also watch for signs during placement that may signal a possible disruption. These include the intensification of discomfort with the placement after the initial "adjustment" period and the personalizing of events rather than attempting to understand why behaviors are occurring.[138]

Disruption is painful for all concerned. However, there is no evidence that a disruption signals the end of either the family's or the child's ability to form another relationship. In many cases, children have been replaced after a disruption and have had successful subsequent experiences in their new families. Likewise, families have been able to incorporate new children after an initial placement has been unsuccessful.[139]

The Search

While there is strong agreement in the field that agencies should provide supportive services to the adoptive family which enable them to "bond" and, if necessary, to continue these services even after the adoption is finalized, the same consensus does not exist in relation to other postadoptive services. This is especially true when the adopted child returns to the agency seeking information about or the identity of his or her biological parent.

It should be remembered that adoption has traditionally been seen as severing the ties between the biological family and the child and creating new ties between the child and the adoptive family. The decision to relinquish or terminate parental rights was seen as a matter between the agency and the biological mother; the decision to place a child for adoption was between the agency and the adoptive parents.

In order to protect the adoption and the various parties to it, most adoption statutes provide for the "sealing" of court records and original birth certificate. This provision was intended to guarantee confidentiality to the parties in the adoption. It protected the new adoptive family from intrusion by the biological mother. The biological mother was protected from "her past" and from an intrusion at some future point by a child who might be an embarrassment. Children were "protected" from information about their birth circumstances or the reason for their relinquishment.

With the greater emphasis on special needs adoption, many of these tenets of adoption are no longer possible. Children often have known their biological parents and remember them; adoptive parents are being given greater information about their children; and, in the case of foster parents and "open" adoptions, biological parents and adoptive parents may have met. Yet court adoption records remain sealed in most states, and adopted children, even as adults, are often denied information about their background by agencies. Most states continue to require "good cause" to be shown in order to open court records, and judicial rulings appear to recognize few grounds for this purpose.[140] While the vast majority of agency records are *not* sealed by law, many agencies believe they are, and will not share identifying and other information with the returnee.[141]

Why do some adoptees, or for that matter, some biological parents, return to the agency for additional background information or information regarding the other parties' identity? For the adopted adult, this need appears to stem from unresolved identity questions. Adopted children have some unique developmental tasks including the incorporation of two sets of parents into their identity. Insufficient information about their biological heritage and background compounds the difficulty of fulfilling these tasks. Adoptees can feel cut off from their past. Not knowing the circumstances of their birth, who their biological parents were, why they were relinquished or why their parents' rights were terminated may cause anxiety, feelings of isolation, or alienation.[142]

Reality factors may also lead to the need for information on the part of the adult adoptees. For example, a family medical history, which adopted children may not know, may be crucial to their physical health. A predisposition to a hereditary illness may remain untreated until symptoms appear. And, a lack of medical background information can hamper any medical diagnostic process.[143]

It appears that adoptees who seek further information from agencies were often not provided with enough background information by their adoptive parents. While some of these parents were not given enough information by agencies (especially about the biological father), others withhold it from their children in order to make them "their own." Adoptees may be fearful of approaching this subject with their parents for fear of hurting them or because they sense their parents' insecurity in this area.[144]

It appears that adoptees who do return to agencies for information or who search for biological parents have often been told about their adoption late in their childhoods and often in an unsatisfactory or hostile way. Discussion about the adoption often did not take place. Thus, they were not able to work through their feelings about being adopted. Some adult adoptees who return to agencies perceive their relationship in the adoptive family negatively.[145] Interestingly, the need for information or to search for biological parents often coincides with important changes in the adoptee's life.[146]

No matter what the reason for the need for information, many adopted adults feel that they have the right to information and to search. Some have organized to assist each other in these efforts. Others have filed suits on a number of constitutional grounds.[147] Still others have organized to change current law and agency practice.

Biological parents have also begun to speak out about the issue of being contacted by their surrendered children. Those opposed appear to have put this child "behind" them. Some have married and had families without revealing that this child exists; others have painful memories, which they do not want to stir up.[148]

Yet, many biological parents appear to be supportive of those adoptees who want information about them or contact with them. Many biological parents believe that the agency did not give them adequate information about the care the child would receive. They were disillusioned or upset with the way the adoption was handled. It appears that many biological parents would be willing to provide agencies with information about themselves for the child's use. Many would also like information about the child.[149]

Adoptive parents appear much more mixed in their reaction to the child's need for information. While some are supportive of their children and recognize this need, others resent any encroachment upon the sanctity of the sealed record. Some feel strongly that agencies have no right to provide even background information to the adult adoptee. They have also expressed concern for the well-being of the biological parents or the child, especially if the information received is perceived as negative or overtures to meet are rejected.[150]

Some authors have expressed the opinion that adoptive parents are threatened by the possibility of the child receiving information or having a reunion with the biological parent. Such parents may view the need for information or reunion as a rejection and an indicator that they have failed as parents.[151]

Given the strong opposition of many adoptive parents, the former promises made by agencies to biological parents, agency anxiety about parents whose rights have been terminated and the positions taken by adoptees and many biological parents, it is not surprising that the field is strongly divided on this issue. Many believe that commitments must be maintained and records must remain sealed. While they believe that agencies should gather more information about social and medical backgrounds, that this information should be made available to adoptees, and that biological parents should be encouraged to update information in the agency record, they stop short of allowing the adoptee identifying information.[152]

This appears to be the current sentiment in most agencies. One survey of agencies found that 47 percent felt that confidentiality was broken if the *agency* attempted to contact a biological mother at the request of an adult adoptee; 57 percent felt that the biological mother's right to privacy and anonymity was paramount over the child's right to know (27 percent said the child's right was paramount); 34 percent stated that they never reveal identifying information; and 40 percent said they would do so only sometimes, even if they were not restricted by law.[153] Another agency survey found that 52 percent of the agencies continue to assure confidentiality to biological and adoptive parents, and two-thirds had a general policy not to release identifying information to adoptees.[154]

Others have suggested that agencies act as intermediaries between adoptees and their biological parents. In such instances the agency, at the request of the adoptee, would attempt to locate the biological parent. If located, and the biological parent agreed, identifying information would be provided to the adoptee. This concept is gaining acceptance both in practice and in law.[155]

Still others have suggested that all information be available, as a matter of right, to any adult adoptee wishing it. This is currently the law in a number of countries including Scotland, England, Finland, and Israel.

For this author, the question becomes: Who is the primary client of the agency? If adoption is truly a child-centered service, then the rights of the child are paramount, even after the child becomes an adult. If information or reunion is needed to resolve conflicts or "complete" a picture for the adult adoptee, then it should be provided.

This position is supported by the fact that reports about completed reunions indicate that, no matter what the climate of the reunion or the reality that was found, almost all adoptees reported satisfaction that they had searched and believed that they had benefited from the reunion. Most felt personally fulfilled and believed they were now able to resolve their genealogical concerns. They found that their biological parents were usually open to this contact. After the contact they felt closer and more intimately connected to their adoptive parents.[156]

CONCLUSION

Because this chapter has addressed issues concerned with the adoption of children who have spent time in the foster care system, a number of important areas of adoption practice have not been addressed. These include independent adoptions, international adoptions, and the adoption of infants relinquished at birth.[157] While these areas are important and deserve attention, the adoption field is now clearly moving toward addressing the needs of children already in the child welfare system and in need of adoption services. It is within this area that future directions lie.

Much of the knowledge needed to accomplish these adoptions successfully is already present. Clearly, the field needs to do more in the five areas that have been addressed.

But perhaps most importantly, if adoption services are to meet the needs of these children, attitudes about adoption must change. Adoption must continue to move toward becoming a more child-centered service with an emphasis on the needs of the child for continuity of relationships. Children needing permanent homes, no matter what their age, race or handicapping condition, must be defined as "adoptable," and agencies must further commit themselves to providing services to these children. Unless this is done, children who need, want, and can benefit from stable home environments will continue to be underserved. They will continue in a foster care system that, at times, is unresponsive to their needs. They will be the "children who wait."

NOTES

1. Graeme Gregory, "No Child Is Unadoptable," in *No Child Is Unadoptable,* ed. Sallie R. Churchill, Bonnie Carlson, and Lynn Nybell (Beverly Hills, Calif.: Sage Publications, 1979), p. 15.

2. Ibid., p. 14.

3. William Meezan, Sanford Katz, and Eva Russo, *Adoptions Without Agencies* (New York: Child Welfare League of America, 1978), pp. 9–11, 25–26.

4. See especially Joseph Goldstein, Anna Freud, and Albert Solnit, *Beyond the Best Interests of the Child* (New York: The Free Press, 1973).

5. For example, David Fanshel and Eugene Shinn, *Children in Foster Care: A Longitudinal Investigation* (New York: Columbia University Press, 1978); Alan Gruber, *Children in Foster Care: Destitute,*

Neglected, ... Betrayed (New York: Human Sciences Press, 1978); Henry Maas and Richard Engler, *Children in Need of Parents* (New York: Columbia University Press, 1959).

6. Alfred Kadushin, *Adopting Older Children* (New York: Columbia University Press, 1970), pp. 218–19.

7. David Franklin and Fred Massarik, "The Adoption of Children with Medical Conditions—Part II: The Families Today," *Child Welfare* 48 (November 1969): 537; David Franklin and Fred Massarik, "The Adoption of Children with Medical Conditions—Part I: Process and Outcome," *Child Welfare* 48 (October 1969): 460.

8. John Calhoun, "The 1980 Child Welfare Act," *Children Today* 9 (September/October 1980): 2.

9. William Meezan, *The Adoption Resource Exchange of North America: A Final Evaluation* (New York: National Adoption Information Exchange System, Child Welfare League of America, 1980, mimeographed).

10. Ann Shyne and Anita Schroeder, *National Study of Social Services to Children and Their Families* (Washington, D.C.: U.S. Department of Health, Education and Welfare, 1978), pp. 124–35 and unpublished materials from this study.

11. These techniques are mentioned in a number of publications. See Dawn Day, *The Adoption of Black Children: Counteracting Institutional Discrimination* (Lexington, Mass.: Lexington Books, 1979), pp. 122–29, 141–46; Vivian Hargrave, Joan Shireman, and Peter Connor, *Where Love and Need Are One* (Chicago: Department of Children and Family Services, 1975), pp. 52ff; Elizabeth Herzog, Celia Sudia, and Jane Harwood, "Some Opinions on Finding Families for Black Children," *Children* 18 (July/August 1971): 147–48; Jacqueline Neilson, "Tayari: Black Homes for Children," *Child Welfare* 55 (January 1976): 45; *Adoption Project For Handicapped Children, Ohio District 11* (Washington, D.C.: U.S. Department of Health and Human Services, 1980), pp. 9–12.

12. Day, *The Adoption of Black Children*, p. 27.

13. Clarence Fischer, "Homes for Black Children," *Child Welfare* 50 (February 1971): 108–11.

14. Hargrave, Shireman, and Connor, *Where Love and Need Are One*, p. 57.

15. Charlotte Bytner et al., "A Positive Approach in Evaluating Potential Adoptive Families and Children," *Child Welfare* 51 (June

1972): 387; Hargrave, Shireman, and Connor, *Where Love and Need Are One,* p. 61; Herzog, Sudia, and Harwood, "Some Opinions on Finding Families," p. 149.

16. Christopher Unger, Gladys Dwarshuis, and Elizabeth Johnson, *Chaos, Madness and Unpredictability . . . Placing the Child With Ears Like Uncle Harry's* (Chelsea, Mich.: Spaulding for Children, 1977), p. 114.

17. Ibid., pp. 121–24.

18. Delores Aldridge, "Problems and Approaches to Black Adoptions," in *No Child Is Unadoptable,* ed. Sallie R. Churchill, Bonnie Carlson, and Lynn Nybell (Beverly Hills, Calif.: Sage Publications, 1979), p. 36; Fischer, "Homes for Black Children"; Herzog, Sudia, and Harwood, "Some Opinions on Finding Families," p. 145; Neilson, "Tayari," pp. 46–48; *Adoption Project for Handicapped Children,* p. 12.

19. Aldridge, "Problems and Approaches," p. 34; Day, *The Adoption of Black Children,* p. 32; Fischer, "Homes for Black Children."

20. Meezan, Katz, and Russo, *Adoptions Without Agencies,* pp. 37–38.

21. Aldridge, "Problems and Approaches," p. 33.

22. Day, *The Adoption of Black Children,* p. 45.

23. Irving Fellner, "Recruiting Adoptive Parents," *Social Work* 13 (January 1968): 93.

24. *In re Haun* (31 Ohio Misc, 9, 277 NE, 2nd 258).

25. Sylvia Gollub, "A Critical Look at Religious Requirements in Adoption," *Public Welfare* 32 (Spring 1974): 23.

26. Ibid.

27. Fellner, "Recruiting Adoptive Parents," p. 93.

28. Day, *The Adoption of Black Children,* p. 63.

29. Gollub, "A Critical Look at Religious Requirements," pp. 24–25.

30. Lucille Grow and Deborah Shapiro, *Black Children—White Families* (New York: Child Welfare League of America, 1974), p. 227.

31. Kenneth Watson, "Subsidized Adoption: A Crucial Investment," *Child Welfare* 51 (April 1972): 224.

32. Hargrave, Shireman, and Connor, *Where Love and Need Are One,* p. 78.

33. Ibid., pp. 76–78; Rita Simon and Howard Alstein, *Transracial Adoption* (New York: John Wiley and Sons, 1977), pp. 76–78; *The Children of the State: Incentives to Adoptive Placements* (Al-

bany, N.Y.: Temporary State Commission on Child Welfare, February 1977), pp. 85–104.

34. For example see Hargrave, Shireman, and Connor, *Where Love and Need Are One*, pp. 64–80.

35. Joyce Ladner, *Mixed Families: Adopting Across Racial Boundaries* (Garden City, N.Y.: Anchor/Doubleday, 1977), pp. 56–71.

36. Ibid., pp. 72–75.

37. National Association of Black Social Workers, "Position Statement on Transracial Adoption," 1972.

38. *Indian Child Welfare: A State of the Field Study* (Washington, D.C.: U.S. Government Printing Office, 1976), pp. 245, 253.

39. References to this argument are made by a number of authors. See Leon Chestang, "The Dilemma of Biracial Adoption," *Social Work* 17 (May 1972): 103; Amuzie Chimezie, "Transracial Adoption of Black Children," *Social Work* 20 (July 1975): 299; *Indian Child Welfare*, pp. 249–52; Ladner, *Mixed Families*, p. 87.

40. Chimezie, "Transracial Adoption," p. 229.

41. Chestang, "The Dilemma of Biracial Adoption," p. 103.

42. Ibid.; Edmund Jones, "On Transracial Adoption of Black Children," *Child Welfare* 51 (March 1972): 159; *Indian Child Welfare*, p. 252.

43. Most studies show this figure to be between 80 and 90 percent. See Day, *The Adoption of Black Children*, p. 104.

44. Chestang, "The Dilemma of Biracial Adoption," p. 104.

45. Grow and Shapiro, *Black Children—White Parents*, p. 223; Ladner, *Mixed Families*, p. 31; Simon and Alstein, *Transracial Adoption*, p. 95.

46. Ladner, *Mixed Families*, p. 54.

47. As reported in ibid., p. 68.

48. Robert Hill, *Informal Adoption Among Black Families* (Washington, D.C.: National Urban League, 1977).

49. As cited in Ladner, *Mixed Families*, p. 68.

50. Chimezie, "Transracial Adoption," pp. 196–97.

51. Jones, "On Transracial Adoption," p. 164.

52. Alicia Howard, David Royse, and John Skerl, "Transracial Adoption: The Black Community Perspective," *Social Work* 22 (May 1977): 185–86.

53. C. Lincoln Johnson, "Transracial Adoption: Victim of Ideology," *Social Work* 21 (May 1976): 241; Ladner, *Mixed Families*, p. 241.

54. Ladner, *Mixed Families,* p. 55.

55. Joan Shireman and Penny Johnson, *Adoption: Three Alternatives —Part II* (Chicago: Chicago Child Care Society, 1980), pp. 44– 45; Rita Simon, "An Assessment of Racial Awareness, Preference and Self Identity Among White and Adopted Non-White Children," *Social Problems* 22 (October 1974): 43–57; Simon and Alstein, *Transracial Adoption,* pp. 126ff.

56. Simon, "An Assessment of Racial Awareness," pp. 50, 55.

57. David Fanshel, *Far From the Reservation: The Transracial Adoption of American Indian Children* (Metuchen, N.J.: Scarecrow Press, 1972), Chapters 9–11; Grow and Shapiro, *Black Children —White Parents,* pp. 89–114; Shireman and Johnson, *Adoptions: Three Alternatives—Part II,* p. 25.

58. Charles Jones and John Else, "Racial and Cultural Issues in Adoption," *Child Welfare* 58 (June 1979): 374.

59. Jones, "On Transracial Adoption," p. 163; Jones and Else, "Racial and Cultural Issues," pp. 379–80; Linda Katz, "Transracial Adoptions—Some Guidelines," *Child Welfare* 53 (March 1974): 183; Ladner, *Mixed Families,* p. 125.

60. Elizabeth Herzog, et al., *Families for Black Children—The Search for Adoptive Parents: An Experience Survey* (Washington, D.C.: U.S. Government Printing Office, 1971), pp. 8–10.

61. William Feigelman and Arnold Silverman, "Single Parent Adoptions," *Social Casework* 58 (July 1977): 418.

62. Alfred Kadushin, "Single Parent Adoptions: An Overview and Some Relevant Research," *Social Service Review* 44 (December 1970): 265–67.

63. Ibid., p. 271.

64. Feigelman and Silverman, "Single Parent Adoptions," p. 423.

65. Shireman and Johnson, *Adoption: Three Alternatives—Part II,* p. 26.

66. Ibid., p. 33; Feigelman and Silverman, "Single Parent Adoptions," p. 33.

67. Ethel Brahm, "One Parent Adoptions," *Children* 17 (May/June 1970); Joan Shireman and Penny Johnson, "Single Parents as Adoptive Parents," *Social Service Review* 50 (March 1976).

68. Sharon Dougherty, "Single Adoptive Mothers and Their Children," *Social Work* 23 (July 1978): 311–12; Feigelman and Silverman, "Single Parent Adoptions," p. 421.

69. Kathryn Donley, "Single Parents as 'Placement of Choice,'" in

No Child Is Unadoptable, ed. Sallie Churchill, Bonnie Carlson, and Lynn Nybel (Beverly Hills, Calif.: Sage Publications, 1979). p. 47.

70. Ibid., p. 46; Feigelman and Silverman, "Single Parent Adoptions," p. 419.

71. Dougherty, "Single Adoptive Mothers," pp. 313–14; Feigelman and Silverman, "Single Parent Adoptions," p. 422.

72. Feigelman and Silverman, "Single Parent Adoptions," p. 419.

73. Trudy Festinger, "Placement Agreements with Boarding Homes: A Survey," *Child Welfare* 53 (December 1974): 647.

74. Herzog, Sudia, and Harwood, "Some Opinions on Finding Families," p. 147.

75. Festinger, "Placement Agreements with Boarding Homes," p. 646.

76. Elizabeth Cole, "Adoption Services Today and Tomorrow," in *Child Welfare Strategies in the Coming Years* (Washington, D.C.: U.S. Department of Health, Education and Welfare, 1978), p. 143; Janet Lahti et al., *A Follow Up Study of the Oregon Project* (Portland, Ore.: Regional Research Institute for Human Services, Portland State University, 1978), p. 2.8; Kathleen Proch, "Adoption by Foster Parents," (D.S.W. dissertation, University of Illinois, Urbana-Champaign, 1980), p. 9.

77. Herzog et al., *Families for Black Children,* p. 47.

78. Margaret Gill, "The Foster Care/Adoptive Family: Adoption of Children Not Legally Free," *Child Welfare* 54 (December 1975): 715.

79. Proch, "Adoption by Foster Parents," p. 13.

80. David Fanshel, *Computerized Information for Child Welfare: Foster Children and Their Foster Parents* (New York: Columbia University School of Social Work, 1979), p. 38.

81. Hargrave, Shireman, and Connor, *Where Love and Need Are One,* p. 45; *The Children of the State,* p. 61; George Strauss, *The Children Are Waiting* (New York: New York City Comptroller's Office, 1978), p. 25.

82. Gill, "The Foster Care/Adoptive Family"; Cornelius Hegarty, "The Family Resource Program: One Coin, Two Sides of Adoption and Foster Family Care," *Child Welfare* 52 (February 1973): 92.

83. Lahti et al., *Follow Up Study of the Oregon Project,* pp. 7.2–7.9; Lois Raynor, *The Adopted Child Comes of Age* (London: George Allen and Unwin, 1980), pp. 144–45.

84. Lahti et al., *Follow Up Study of the Oregon Project,* p. 7.12.

85. Fanshel, *Computerized Information: Foster Children,* pp. 38ff; Claudia Jewitt, *Adopting the Older Child* (Cambridge, Mass.: Harvard Common Press, 1978), p. 67.

86. Hargrave, Shireman, and Connor, *Where Love and Need Are One,* pp. 65ff.

87. Ibid., p. 39; Proch, "Adoption by Foster Parents," p. 109–110.

88. Unger, Dwarshuis, and Johnson, *Chaos, Madness and Unpredictability,* p. 187.

89. *Adoption Project for Handicapped Children,* p. 25.

90. Cole, "Adoption Services Today and Tomorrow," p. 149.

91. *The Children of the State,* p. 19.

92. Cole, "Adoption Services Today and Tomorrow," p. 151.

93. Ibid.

94. Ibid., p. 153.

95. Ibid., p. 150

96. Ibid., p. 152.

97. Ibid.

98. *Adoption Project for Handicapped Children,* p. 2.

99. Ibid.

100. Hannah Grossman et al., *An Evaluation of the New York State Adoption Exchange* (Albany, N.Y.: Welfare Research, Inc., 1976).

101. Cole, "Adoption Services Today and Tomorrow," p. 154; Meezan, *Adoption Resource Exchange of North America,* pp. 60–66.

102. Roberta Hunt, *Obstacles to Interstate Adoption* (New York: Child Welfare League of America, 1972), p. 6.

103. *Interstate Compact on the Placement of Children* (Chicago: Council of State Government, 1960), Article III.

104. Hunt, *Obstacles to Interstate Adoption,* pp. 19–24.

105. Ibid., pp. 24–32.

106. *The Child and the State,* p. 64.

107. Trudy Bradley, *An Exploration of Caseworker Perceptions of Adoptive Applicants* (New York: Child Welfare League of America, 1967), pp. 186–94; Edwin Brown and Donald Brieland,

"Adoptive Screening: New Data, New Dilemmas," *Social Work* 20 (July 1975): 293–95.

108. Unger, Dwarshuis, and Johnson, *Chaos, Madness and Unpredictability*, p. 133.

109. Joan Shireman and Kenneth Watson, "Adoption of Real Children," *Social Work* 17 (July 1972): 30; Barbara Tremitiere, "Adoption of Children with Special Needs—The Client Centered Approach," *Child Welfare* 58 (December 1979): 682.

110. Shireman and Watson, "Adoption of Real Children," p. 30; Tremitiere, "Adoption of Children with Special Needs," p. 682.

111. Leon Chestang and Irmgard Heymann, "Preparing Older Children for Adoption," *Public Welfare* 34 (Winter 1976): 39; Shireman and Watson, "Adoption of Real Children," p. 31; Tremitiere, "Adoption of Children with Special Needs," p. 683.

112. Unger, Dwarshuis, and Johnson, *Chaos, Madness and Unpredictablity*, pp. 142ff.

113. Jewitt, *Adopting the Older Child*, pp. 45–46.

114. Shireman and Watson, "Adoption of Real Children," p. 31.

115. *Adoption Project for Handicapped Children*, p. 12.

116. Tremitiere, "Adoption of Children with Special Needs," p. 683.

117. *Adoption Project for Handicapped Children*, p. 13.

118. Unger, Dwarshuis, and Johnson, *Chaos, Madness and Unpredictability*, p. 162; Tremitiere, "Adoption of Children with Special Needs," p. 683.

119. Theodore Stein, Eileen Gambrill, and Kermit Wiltse, *Children in Foster Homes: Achieving Continuity of Care* (New York: Praeger Publishers, 1978), pp. 119–28.

120. *Stanley* v. *Illinois* (405 US 645, 31 L ED 2nd 551, 92 Sup Ct 1208 (1972)); *Rothman* v. *Lutheran Social Services of Wisconsin and Upper Michigan* (47 Wisc 2d 220, 173 NW 2nd 56, vacated 4/17/72, 40 USlW 3198).

121. Rita Durkette and Nicholas Stevenson, "The Legal Rights of Unmarried Fathers: The Impact of Recent Court Decisions," *Social Service Review* 43 (March 1973): 6–11.

122. Jewitt, *Adopting the Older Child*, pp. 70ff; *Adoption Project for Handicapped Children*, p. 7; Martha Jones, "Preparing School Aged Children for Adoption," *Child Welfare* 58 (January 1979): 29.

123. Chestang and Heymann, "Preparing Older Children for Adop-

tion," p. 37; Hargrave, Shireman, and Connor, *Where Love and Need Are One*, p. 39; Jewitt, *Adopting the Older Child*, pp. 64–65; *Adoption Project for Handicapped Children*, p. 9.

124. Jewitt, *Adopting the Older Child*, pp. 82, 113.

125. *The Child and the State*, p. 73.

126. Unger, Dwarshuis, and Johnson, *Chaos, Madness and Unpredictability*, pp. 155–62.

127. Linda Katz, "Older Child Adoptive Placement: A Time of Family Crisis," *Child Welfare* 56 (March 1977): 157–58.

128. Margaret Gill, "Adoption of Older Children: The Problems Faced," *Social Casework* 59 (May 1978): 276–77.

129. Margaret Ward, "Parental Bonding in Older Child Adoptions," *Child Welfare* 60 (January 1981): 25–32.

130. Gill, "Adoption of Older Children," p. 277.

131. Unger, Dwarshuis, and Johnson, *Chaos, Madness and Unpredictability*, pp. 155–62.

132. Ibid., pp. 162–63; *Adoption Project for Handicapped Children*, p. 16; *The Children and the State*, p. 74.

133. Alfred Kadushin and Frederick Seidl, "Adoption Failure: A Social Work Postmortem," *Social Work* 16 (July 1971): 34–36.

134. Day, *The Adoption of Black Children*, p. 78; Ibid., p. 33; *Adoption Project for Handicapped Children*, p. 26; Unger, Dwarshuis, and Johnson, *Chaos, Madness and Unpredictability*, p. 218.

135. Celia Bass, "Matchmaker—Matchmaker: Older Child Adoption Failure," *Child Welfare* 54 (July 1975): 507; Robert Borgman, "Antecedents and Consequences of Parental Rights Termination for Abused and Neglected Children," *Child Welfare* 60 (June 1981): 398–99; Kadushin and Seidl, "Adoption Failure," p. 37.

136. Sallie Churchill, "Disruption: A Risk in Adoption II," in *No Child Is Unadoptable*, ed. Sallie Churchill, Bonnie Carlson, and Lynn Nybell (Beverly Hills, Calif.: Sage Publications, 1979), p. 121; Unger, Dwarshuis, and Johnson, *Chaos, Madness and Unpredictability*, p. 196.

137. Bass, "Matchmaker—Matchmaker," pp. 508–09.

138. Churchill, "Disruption," p. 122; *Adoption Project for Handicapped Children*, p. 26; Unger, Dwarshuis, and Johnson, *Chaos, Madness and Unpredictability*, p. 196.

139. Unger, Dwarshuis, and Johnson, *Chaos, Madness and Unpredictability*, pp. 196, 218.

140. Donald Brieland, "Social Work and Law: Responses to the Identity Crisis," (speech given at the Loyola University School of Social Work, 1980), p. 8.

141. Mary Ann Jones, *The Sealed Adoption Record Controversy: Report of a Survey of Agency Policy, Practice and Opinion* (New York: Child Welfare League of America, 1976), pp. 13–14; C. J. Bell, "Accessibility to Adoption Records: Influence on Agency Policy" (D.S.W. dissertation, University of Illinois, Urbana-Champaign, 1978) as cited in Brieland, "Social Work and Law," p. 16.

142. C. Wilson Anderson, "The Sealed Record in Adoption Controversy," *Social Service Review* 51 (March 1977): p. 144; Ruben Pannor et al., "Opening the Sealed Record in Adoption: The Need for Continuity," *Journal of Jewish Communal Services* 51 (December 1974): 200; Arthur Sorosky et al., "Identity Conflicts in Adoptees," *American Journal of Orthopsychiatry* 45 (January 1975): 21; Arthur Sorosky et al., *The Adoption Triangle* (Garden City, N.Y.: Anchor Books, 1979), pp. 86–106; John Triseliotis, *In Search of Origins* (Boston: Beacon Press, 1973), p. 18.

143. Anderson, "The Sealed Record," p. 144; Annette Baran et al., "The Dilemma of Our Adoptees," *Psychology Today* 8 (December 1975): 176; Reuben Pannor et al., "Birth Parents Who Relinquished Babies for Adoption Revisited," *Family Process* 17 (September 1978): 330.

144. Sorosky et al., *The Adoption Triangle,* p. 66.

145. Ibid., p. 198; Raynor, *The Adopted Child Comes of Age,* p. 148; Triseliotis, *In Search of Origins.*

146. Baran et al., "The Dilemma of Our Adoptees," p. 39; Sorosky et al., *The Adoption Triangle,* p. 198.

147. Anderson, "The Sealed Record," p. 148; Brieland, "Responses to the Identity Crisis," pp. 12–15.

148. Sorosky et al., *The Adoption Triangle,* p. 58.

149. Pannor et al., "Opening the Sealed Record," pp. 4–5; Sorosky et al., *The Adoption Triangle,* pp. 39–58.

150. Annette Baran et al., "Adoptive Parents and the Sealed Record Controversy," *Social Casework* 55 (November 1974): 534–36; Sorosky et al., *The Adoption Triangle,* pp. 70–73.

151. Baran et al., "The Adoptive Parents," p. 535; Sorosky et al., *The Adoption Triangle,* pp. 62–67.

152. Rita Durkette, "Perspectives for Agency Response to the Adoption Record Controversy," *Child Welfare* 54 (September/October 1975): 553–54.

153. Jones, *The Sealed Adoption Record Controversy.*

154. C. J. Bell, "Accessibility to Adoption Records," p. 16.

155. Ruth Weidell, "Unsealing Sealed Birth Certificates in Minnesota," *Child Welfare* 59 (February 1980): 114.

156. Ibid., p. 118; Baran et al., "The Dilemma of Our Adoptees," p. 96; Jones, *The Sealed Adoption Record Controversy,* p. 18–20; Pannor et al., "Opening the Sealed Record," p. 6; Sorosky et al., *The Adoption Triangle,* p. 199.

157. See, for example, Meezan, Katz, and Russo, *Adoptions Without Agencies;* American Public Welfare Association, *Draft Report on Intercountry Adoptions—Survey of Federal and State Laws and Private Sector Policies and Practices* (Washington, D.C.: American Public Welfare Association, April 1978); Barbara Joe, "In Defense of Intercountry Adoptions," *Social Service Review,* 52 (March 1978): 1–14; Cole, "Adoption Services Today and Tomorrow," pp. 158–59; *Standards for Adoption Services* (New York: Child Welfare League of America, 1978.

CHAPTER 12
STAFFING ISSUES IN CHILD WELFARE

Carol H. Meyer

Staffing in child welfare is best understood in the context of all that has gone before in this book. For staffing patterns to be functional, they have to reflect the purposes, policies, and practices of the field at large and of the particular agency employing the staff to do its work. Staffing is so integral a part of child welfare that even the history of the field itself can help to explain current staffing practices. After all, whatever it is that the field and its agencies seek to do, the essential activities have to be carried out by staff. Policies and legislative frameworks are but pieces of paper until they are enacted by staff; practices are only theory unless they are carried out by staff; administrative actions are hollow unless there is a staff in place to do the work. One of the most serious problems in fields that are "labor intensive," as is child welfare, is to treat staffing as an appendage rather than as a central concern in the management of child welfare services.

In this chapter we shall try to present and analyze staffing issues in the context of child welfare programming in order to formulate an integrative approach to the selection, utilization, training, and development of child welfare staff. It is particularly important to do so at this time because in recent years it has become increasingly difficult for the field to attract, recruit, and keep staff. Child welfare work is the one social institution that is governed by social work itself; yet, it is a field that is held in low esteem by many professional social workers. Naturally, many explanations can be put forth for this problem: low salaries, overwhelming jobs, large case loads, criticism of the field and resultant low status, and so on. Yet, these factors occur in other fields in social work as well, although in different weighting, form, and intensity. One cannot, without research, be certain of the sources of dissatisfaction, but one can draw implications for building morale by exploring those aspects of the field that have bearing upon social work staff involvement.

A field like child welfare that is not completely professionalized tends to have ambiguous job definitions and to lack fit between work to be done and capacity of the worker to do it. Furthermore, child welfare is a field that is exposed to the public's view and subject to its pressures; thus, administrators of agencies are especially sensitive about social worker autonomy, often tending to restrict professional judgments and actions. These two factors—lack of fit between capacity and job, and lack of autonomy—may be the most important reasons for social workers' apparent avoidance of the field of child welfare.

DIFFERENTIALS AMONG CHILD WELFARE STAFF

No matter how narrowly one defines the boundaries of the field of child welfare, a broad range of activities comprises the field. Despite the fact that a single agency might provide only one or two of the "basic" child welfare services, rapidly shifting public demand, changing populations, and funding vagaries always stand poised to challenge the way services are arranged. Thus, a foster care program may offer adoption services, family services, and homemaker services at various times, and a child-caring institution may extend itself to provide small group home services and community-based in-home services as well. In such a wide-ranging field that is so much a part of the changing society it is not possible to plan for staffing once and for all time to carry out a narrowly defined service program. (See Chapters 1, 2, 4, and 6 for a further discussion of boundary issues). That is both the hazard and the challenge offered to the field and to the imaginations of agency administrators.

In view of this range of activity, it is fortuitous that there is a wide array of differentially prepared personnel potentially able to be recruited to carry out child welfare services. In the professional social work group there are graduates on the bachelor's (B.S.W.), master's (M.S.W.), and doctoral (D.S.W./Ph.D.) level. (We shall say more about the differential use of these graduates later.) Depending upon the program in question, staffing resources also rest in lay adults who are potential "professional" foster parents, house parents, and cottage parents. There are almost limitless numbers of people in the employment market who could be engaged as trained homemakers, home helpers, and home visitors. In another arena of child welfare there are young people who could be utilized as big brothers and sisters, tutors, child care aides, and family helpers. In the community at large, there are self-help groups developing for the purpose of mutual aid for innumerable special human problems, and there are community members who have the potential of being engaged as neighbors in the professionally based child welfare enterprise.

Child welfare as a social institution is capable of utilizing human resources on a broad scale. The chief principle governing the selection of staff *type* has to be appropriateness—differential personnel for different purposes. A field that seeks to carry out such a wide range of purposes, from child care to psychotherapy, must use a wide range of staff. But staff must be used for appropriate purposes at the appropriate time, in the appropriate manner. Disappointments on the part of both agencies and staff occur when staff are underutilized in relationship to the skills and aptitudes they have, or when job descriptions are unclear and ambiguous. The less training a staff member has, the clearer and less ambiguous must be the job description.

We cannot exclude from our discussion professional personnel from allied fields that continually move in and out of the child welfare enterprise, for while they maintain their own disciplines in practice, they are governed by child welfare programs and policies while they practice in the field. Here we refer to psychiatrists, pediatricians, psychologists, and nurses. Also, in view of the boundaries of child welfare that intersect with other *fields,* we need to consider judges, attorneys, police personnel, hospital personnel, and school personnel as sometime professional colleagues in the delivery of child welfare services.

How does a field cope with such a conglomerate? Who is to do what, and how? What principles determine the type and educational level of staff that is to do direct line work with children and their families? Who is to supervise the work, and how does one build in accountability? Is agency-based, specialized staff training sufficient for some or all of these personnel, or is professional education necessary for some? What is the difference in capacity to carry out tasks between professional social workers and experienced career bureaucrats? How does one match worker skill with the work to be done? How is staff morale supported, and how is worker burnout prevented? These and other questions about staffing in child welfare baffle administrators because there has been insufficient serious research done in the area of staffing issues, and in fact, there is little clarity about the issues themselves.

Child welfare as a field of social work practice has developed unevenly as both a professional and voluntary endeavor. In the United States in the 1980s, allocation of staff has no recognizable pattern, perhaps because the field is so open an institution that in different geographical and political areas it is governed by different interests and public demand. Thus we note that in some urban areas, board members of voluntary agencies work directly with children, and in other areas, rural agents or visiting nurses have the most significant contact with families. Public child welfare agencies in some states seek professionally educated M.S.W. social workers, while other public agencies lean toward social workers with a B.S.W. or toward B.A.'s with a liberal arts background. Voluntary agencies are most identified with M.S.W. staff utilization, but they also use psychologists interchangeably. This lack of patterned use of staff is one of the most serious professional issues in the field, for one cannot easily describe "what is" in order to propose newer models of staffing.

Further compounding this confusion in patterns of differential staff utilization are the pressures of selective shortages, lack of funding, conflicting community interests, and ambiguous purposes that contribute to hit-or-miss staffing arrangements. Yet, it is not possible to begin again and reinvent the field in order to rationalize staffing policies. Whatever is to be said about staffing models, it has to be kept in mind that changes will be incremental. Once entrenched, staffs do not turn over readily to make way for innovation. Factors like seniority, civil service, labor unions, and other organizations function to protect existing staff patterns. Bureaucracies and boards can find professionalized staff threatening, and in view of the fact that child welfare is not a totally professionalized field, professional staff often have difficulty finding a clear role in which to function.

In summary, staffing issues in the field of child welfare have grown out of the unevenness of the field itself. The lack of a coherent pattern in staffing has been generated by the inherent dilemmas of the field. The boundaries in child welfare are so flexible as to be uncertain in many quarters, so there is need for a wide range of professional and nonprofessional staff to carry out the uncountable and wide-ranging tasks. Furthermore, the parallel public and voluntary organizational and funding systems have created a competitive staffing situation within the field itself. Also, the child welfare "culture" differs in rural and urban areas and in various parts of the country, and staffing requirements are thus defined differently. Finally, because there is no superior, unilateral force or system with the authority to define the child welfare enterprise, professionals of all disciplines and lay participants can often determine individually the tasks they choose to do.

Because of the nonpatterned staffing arrangements that appear nationally, research on staff in child welfare has necessarily been confined to individual programs and agencies. The few national studies that exist are descriptive of educational levels of staff and job descriptions. There has been little work done to analyze staffing issues or to propose new staffing models.[1] In this chapter programmatic and staffing issues will be reviewed, always in the context of the child welfare "culture," so as to propose alternative staffing models in the form of a repertoire for selective use. This approach is in keeping with the view that the field is continually evolving in unplanned ways.

PROFESSIONAL SOCIAL WORK STAFF

We begin with a look to the future. While the doctoral-level practitioner has not yet entered into the staffing debate, the advanced social work degree (D.S.W./Ph.D.) prepares social workers for clinical, administrative, policy development, teaching, and research work in the field. In all of these areas there is opportunity to enlist these most qualified of graduate social workers in the field of child welfare. More often than is as yet the case with M.S.W.'s, doctoral social workers specialize in a specific field of practice such as child welfare and are thereby prepared to enter the field with direct M.S.W. practice experience and a high degree of expertise in child welfare. Although the utilization of these top-level professionals has the potential of improving the quality of service and staffing in the quickest, most parsimonious way, the field has been slow to recognize and use this cadre of staff in other than research and teaching roles. In recent years, the general downgrading of educational and training requirements for front-line staff and the frequent denigration of traditional social work leadership within child welfare has been accompanied by a widespread search for clinical administrators, management experts, and legislative analysts from other professions who could help to "straighten out" the child welfare morass. This search testifies to the need for greater clinical, legal, policy, and management expertise than has been available previously in many areas of child welfare practice. Yet, there has been little effort to recruit doctoral-level personnel with specialized knowledge of child welfare as a field of practice who could be used appropriately to design and implement innovative programs, lead specialized clinical teams, direct staff development programs, provide consultation to supervisory staff, analyze legislative changes, develop new policies, conduct needed research, and administer direct service programs. The particular knowledge and skills of individual D.S.W.'s varies depending on their experience and area of specialization, but as a group they constitute a relatively untapped body of experts who could provide significant leadership for the child welfare field at large.

In the last decade, the profession of social work created a new degree level of professional education for entering staff, the B.S.W. degree. The decision to do so derived from internal professional pressures and from governmental concern that the public agencies, mainly the public child welfare agencies, were insufficiently staffed by graduate (M.S.W.) social workers and inadequately staffed by B.A. graduates. The rush to develop the B.S.W. professional level of social worker occurred without clarification of the difference in functions and tasks that would occur between the M.S.W. graduate and B.S.W. undergraduate social worker. In 1978 there were 36 independent M.S.W. graduate programs, 178 independent B.S.W. undergraduate programs, and 50 joint B.S.W. and M.S.W. programs in the United States.[2] While neither the public nor the voluntary sector employs a full complement of professional (B.S.W. and/or M.S.W.) staff, the public sector persists in employing the least qualified staff.[3]

However, the fact that B.S.W. social workers have begun to meet the staffing requirements of those agencies does not mean that a rational differentiation of professional functions, tasks, and roles has been made between the M.S.W. and B.S.W. staff. This differentiation has to be made if both levels of staff are to be used in the way most appropriate to their training aptitudes. From a qualitative standpoint, it would be detrimental to child welfare services to assume that B.S.W. social workers could do the same level of work as M.S.W. social workers, even though quantitative criteria were met.

Selective staff shortages and lack of staff planning, particularly in public child welfare, have contributed to the perpetuation of B.A. liberal arts–educated staff in many agencies. This may be due to the unavailability of B.S.W. personnel or to a leaning of some public welfare commissioners away from professionally educated social workers. We mention B.A. workers here because although they are not professional staff, being undergraduate level, non–social work and nondifferentiated in their preparation, they serve in some of the same professional *roles* as do some B.S.W. and M.S.W. personnel. Naturally, without educational preparation, B.A.-level staff must be totally dependent upon the agency's training program. While this may be a burden upon the agency's resources, it may also suggest—falsely, we believe—that the agency can imprint its own philosophy upon this staff and free itself of the challenges that accompany professionally educated staff.

In view of the B.S.W. complement of graduates entering the field, we expect that there will be a diminishing need for B.A. workers functioning as social workers. The nonprofessional jobs that are discussed later in this chapter do not require staff with a particular level of education, but rather people with the personal or technical qualifications necessary to carry out specific tasks. B.A. graduates might qualify for any number of nonprofessional jobs, but they do not bring any preparation for social work practice to the public or voluntary child welfare agency.

This lack of differentiation of professional staff occurs in the voluntary sector as well, although not to the same degree. For a period of time in the 1970s, when there was an actual shortage of M.S.W. staff in child welfare, B.S.W. workers were introduced into voluntary agencies. There have been mixed reports about their comparison with M.S.W. social workers. Some agencies believed that B.S.W. workers had a greater commitment to the way the agencies worked than did the M.S.W. workers, while other agencies reported that M.S.W. workers could work with greater autonomy than B.S.W. workers. There has been limited research in this area, and research would be difficult due to the great differences among the voluntary agencies in the purposes they seek to carry out. In any case, we do not know of any program, public or voluntary, that has *planned* staffing arrangements to fit differentially prepared professional staff to differentially defined functions, tasks, or roles. Staff assignments in general have been arranged for expedient reasons.

In order to allocate this range of staff in a rational way, programmatic issues have to be thought through. For example, there are several ways to think about "hard" and "easy" cases, although it is understood that there are no really easy cases; there are only limited *perceptions* of some cases—they may look easy to the untrained eye. Following is a repertoire of possible ways to allocate professional staff in keeping with the principle of appropriateness of training and aptitude to the job at hand. There may be no "best way" because our knowledge and experience are so limited in this unplanned field of child welfare. Yet, there are adequate knowledge and experience in professional social work practice for us to determine, more or less, appropriate planning and differential allocation of professional social work staff.

Assessment: The Crucial Function

The appropriateness of fit between client need and the child welfare service offered is central to effective practice. An accurate estimate of the client's problem at the outset in the career of a case is the best guarantee of successful outcome. The need for staff that is the most competent, best trained, and at the highest level of professional education in direct practice to enact the central decision-making role at the point of access to services cannot be exaggerated. This gate-keeping, diagnostic function is a thread that runs through each and every service, surely at intake, and periodically throughout the contact with the child and family so as to ascertain the appropriateness of the service being given. Assuming as we do that this assessment function is crucial in child welfare, then it follows that the most qualified professional social work staff should be located in those areas where assessments are to take place. The M.S.W. graduate is most likely to be the best qualified by education, although the B.S.W. social worker can also undertake this function. Knowing the case problem and the resources that would best suit the case is, after all, central in the professional education of social workers. In the child welfare agencies in America, it is not uncommon for nonprofessional staff including receptionists and board members to carry out the gate-keeping function. This is an example of the need to think through the purposes and activities of child welfare programs before determining how and where differential staff is to be best allocated.

Programs: Everything Is Not Equal

What programs or parts of programs require the greatest staff skill? The personnel involved in every program undoubtedly would claim that its work was the most demanding, or funding specifications might influence administrators to assess particular programs or parts of programs as especially difficult. It may indeed be an imponderable question to which one can offer only theoretical answers. By what criteria do we determine the difficulty of a particular job?

Given a finite staffing situation to which all social service programs are subject, choices must be made as to program priorities: Where does the most staff belong? What tasks require the most skilled staff? How can the work be divided so that professional and nonprofessional personnel each do its most natural or most educated best? Are some professional tasks capable of being carried out by natural helpers? Are some tasks better served by professionals than by nonprofessionals? Are personnel being overutilized or underutilized? There is so little research or shared experience available that we can offer precious few guidelines, but perhaps a principle or two.

Client vulnerability is a long-established criterion for differential utilization of social work staff.[4] Yet, even this idea of vulnerability would not find general agreement in its definition. One might think that a homeless child, a waif on the streets of a city, would be the most vulnerable, and yet the most skillful staff in that same city might be allocated to a psychotherapeutic program, which would not include homeless children. Abused children surely would be deemed vulnerable if they were to remain in the same abusing situation, and yet in public child protection services throughout the country, one can find the least, not the best trained staff dealing with these vulnerable children. In the AFDC case load where public assistance allowances are meager and the misery associated with poverty is all too common, it is evident that children are vulnerable to starvation, disease, and neglect, and yet AFDC families with children are ordinarily not counted in child welfare case loads and programs. The number of children in juvenile detention centers and even adult prisons is rapidly increasing in the United States. Their physical, psychological, and social vulnerability cannot be questioned, and yet there is a dearth of highly skilled professional social work staff to work in juvenile detention centers and prisons. The concept of vulnerability, clear though it may be, requires value consensus in the field of child welfare before it can be applied as a useful criterion for differential utilization of staff.

However, within the established boundaries of the existing field of child welfare, in the identified programs of in-home service, foster care, group care, residential treatment and adoption we can identify *degrees* of client vulnerability, even though once children enter the child welfare system they gain the basic protection that is not always available for the street urchin, the imprisoned child, or the AFDC child.

Services for Families—Prevention of Placement

Notwithstanding the current efforts to enlist biological families in the child welfare enterprise to a degree not attempted before, prevention of placement through family work will not just happen without recognition of the knowledge and skill required to provide effective family services. The fact that child welfare as a field does not include "family" as part of its title indicates that a century of avoidance of direct family work will have to be overcome—and rapidly. The Adoption Assistance and Child Welfare Reform Act of 1980 and the current pressure to insure permanency for children with their biological families if possible suggest that a maximum effort will have to be made to introduce family practice into the field of child welfare.

There are but two ways to prepare staff for practice with families: through careful selection of social work graduates and through intensive staff development. Recent experience has shown that child welfare workers do not pay adequate attention to families unless they have agency supports and training; it is a direction to practice that is not traditional in a field so long characterized as child placement. (See chapters 1, 2, and 6 for a full discussion of this problem.) Family services go quite a bit beyond "involving the family" in order to expedite placement plans. Family services mean attention to the family as a family, and not merely as a resource for the child. To focus on *the family* as the unit of attention requires a conceptual and attitudinal shift for child welfare staff, a shift that will not occur without attention paid to making it work.

Beyond training of staff to learn how to understand and work with dynamic family relationships and to provide psycho-physical-social services as they are needed to support the family, family work must also be viewed as close to community work. In the area of prevention there is opportunity to utilize the array of young and adult lay or community people referred to earlier. Services to families ideally would include help from personnel who are close to families in their culture and life-style, as well as the most expert, skillful social work professionals. The investment of staff in careful and planned ways will be the clearest barometer of agency investment in preventive work with families.

Substitute Care

Foster care, group care, residential treatment, and adoption are all different forms of substitute family care. They each have unique program purposes as well, but in the life of a case in the field of child welfare most of the time is spent by the child living life, growing up and developing. Because these professional/bureaucratic programs have entered the lives of families and children in an artificial way—that is, a way that is not endemic to child and family life—it would seem that the child's ordinary, daily life should mirror as closely as possible a normal family life. The staffing principle that derives from this assumption is that the daily caretaking functions in child welfare are best carried out by caretakers, not professional social workers, in order to maintain for the child the least artificial (professional/bureaucratic) milieu. (We shall say more later about caretakers; here we are only discussing the utilization of professional social work staff.) Nevertheless, exactly because child-caring programs are not identical with ordinary family life, there are gatekeeping, assessment, and decision points in the career of every child welfare case. These generate professional tasks that can only be effectively carried out by skilled social workers.

Foster Care. The assessment having been made and the decision to place a child in foster care having been established, the professional functions are: to engage the biological family in the work of repair in order to receive the placed child home as quickly as possible; to engage the foster parents in the work of the ongoing responsibility for the child and to be particularly active at points of change in the foster family's and child's circumstances; and to help the child cope with problems of identity and change. Child welfare agencies all have unique ways of organizing social workers' roles in these areas of work; sometimes a worker is assigned the biological family, or the foster family and child; less often does a social worker's job include responsibility for all three of the actors in the case, although this organization of staffing would be more apt to fulfill the family-centered mission of child welfare. In foster care there are tasks enough for a host of differentially qualified staff—professional social workers, "professional" caretakers or foster parents, case aides to attend to medical visits and so on, tutors, psychologists, psychiatrists, and other personnel from allied fields that are brought in as necessary. Foster care is a mini-system of life for a child, a system that complicates all of the ordinary events, transitions, and stresses experienced by every growing child. The professional is most capable of orchestrating the various forces impinging on a foster child's life but need not carry out all of specific developmental and caretaking tasks.

Staff morale suffers most when the differential tasks just noted are not carried out by appropriate types of staff. For example, it is not a professional task to count blankets or to check up on the foster mother's hygiene training of the foster child, and it is not a foster parent's role to explain the conditions of placement to a biological parent. In foster care, as in all other child welfare programs, purposes have to be thought through in order for a coherent and rational staffing plan to be in place.

Group Homes. In some ways group homes provide care that is closer to the normal social and community life of the older child, despite the fact that it is not family care. The child in group care does not have to deal with identity issues in the same way as does the foster child cohort. Children in group care are not faced with confusion about their own names while living with a family of a different name; they do not have to make choices between their own family and the foster family upon whom they depend; children in small group care, by definition, because group homes are located within urban communities, are less likely to be placed outside their own family's community, so that ties to friends, school, and relatives can be maintained. What has this to do with staffing? Children in group homes can pursue their developmental tasks with less professional intervention just because their living situations are closer to the natural life circumstances of children than in other areas of child welfare. The role of the professional in those locations where decisions and crises occur remains the same as in other programs in child welfare, but the essential developmental tasks are usually most propitiously supported by role models found in caretaking staff. Whether these be married or single individuals, young or old "houseparents," or a series of young adult mentors, the house staff in group homes play life roles for group home residents—theoretically at least, these children have their own ongoing family and community ties that the professional social worker can promote or help to maintain. The course of child development is unerring, and professional and nonprofessional personnel have different skills to do different tasks in support of this development.

Institutional Care. As in foster family and group home care, the way in which an agency deploys its staff in a rational manner depends upon the way it views its programmatic requirements and priorities. Nowhere is the necessity to think through program purposes more sharply highlighted than in the arena of institutional care. The primary question the institution has to ask itself is whether it is to provide real residential *treatment* or be a setting in which children can *develop* normally. Each type will generate different types of staffing arrangements. The therapeutically oriented institution should, of course, have as residents more disturbed children than will the developmentally oriented setting. This will mean that both professional and caretaking staff must have specialized and extensive knowledge and skills regarding work with disturbed children, and probably disturbed families. The professional role remains differentiated from the caretaker role, but this uniqueness in itself requires that professional staff have the capacity to coordinate both the therapeutic and living programs of the institution and of the families of the children. The ability to maintain objectivity among the contesting forces of children, house staff, and families, all of whom are entwined in problematic human relationships, demands the services of the most highly qualified professional staff available.

In a developmental type of institution, the staffing themes are similar, but the level of psychological disturbance should demand less intensive therapeutic attention. The issue of whether or not developmental institutions require the same kind of therapeutic milieu as do residential treatment institutions is beyond the scope of this discussion.[9] But the staffing issue remains crucial in both types of settings. The confusion of professional and caretaking roles in institutions is similar to the confusion often present in foster care. Professional social workers are not appropriately used to supervise a child's habit training, and caretaking staff is not appropriately used to intervene with a child's family. The appropriate utilization of professional social work personnel takes place when the institution is clear about the real nature and purposes of its program.

Adoption. Assessment and decision making in adoption programs are central to succesful staff work. The organizational power over children and families in this area of child welfare requires sensitive, delicate skills and extensive knowledge. The decision to place for adoption, the preparation of children, the selection of adoptive parents, the handling of "failed placements," the termination of biological parent rights, and the engagement with courts and other agencies are among the most serious tasks social workers can do, partly because of their life-long implications. The choice points involved in the adoption process rest in highly complex psychosocial dynamics; thus it would be almost self-evident that professional staff with the greatest preparation in the development of knowledge and skills would be located at those decision-making sites.

When it is necessary to sort out differential tasks in the adoption process, due to lack of available M.S.W. social work personnel for example, or because an agency is seeking newer models of staff allocation, the ongoing adoption process holds promise for many innovations. Indigenous groups of potential or experienced adoptive parents have a great deal to share with each other, since the experience of adoption is something *felt* as well as *known*. People with like experiences can offer something to the articulation of feelings that goes beyond the information, clarification, and emotional supports that even the most skillful professional social worker can offer. In addition, in the early part of the adoption process there are countless technicalities, legal and familial, that may not require the technical skills of the most qualified staff but nonetheless may require simple information. Nonprofessional, technical personnel can be trained to provide this information; every question that arises does not reflect a problem, conflict, or ambivalence. As one considers the parts of the adoption process that demand differential types of services and staff, one thinks through adoption itself as well as the nature of social work practice.

Children who have begun living with adoptive parents, no matter what their age, are going to have to cope with the fact of adoption itself. Many variables come into play, of course, but clearly all children in adoption do not necessarily require professional attention. As in foster care, the problems children must deal with in their developing lives ought to be handled by their caretakers if at all possible. Good adoptive work with adoptive parents and sound preparatory work with adoptive children should diminish the necessity for continuing professional intervention. In the case of older adopted children, self-help groups of adopted children might serve some of the need. Of course, in the case of adoptions that are not working out for children or parents, highly skilled professional social work, psychiatric, or psychological personnel may be required as they are in any family where there are problems.

In the adoption process, the biological parent in the 1980s is likely to be a teenage unmarried mother, who herself is in need of social services and would qualify for entrance into the child welfare system. As emphasized earlier in this discussion, professional staff is most needed at the assessment phase, when decisions have to be made in the life career of the adolescent mother. The medical and social needs of the unmarried mother are so varied as to offer the unmarried mother as a model for staff planning. The professional social worker might assume the central case planning role in such a case, and enter the case directly at crucial times where there are turning points and issues to be worked out. Beyond these tasks, unmarried mothers always have need for medical care, housing, education, recreation, and child-caring arrangements. The array of nonprofessional personnel and allied professionals then becomes the requisite child welfare staff. In keeping with our favored guideline, appropriate use of staff occurs when the aptitude and skill of a staff person is suited to the needs and tasks generated by the case itself. That is why a range of differentially prepared staff can be utilized planfully and parsimoniously.

NONPROFESSIONAL STAFF: CARETAKERS, FOSTER PARENTS, HOME HELPERS

As presented in this book, the field of child welfare is primarily concerned with family supports for children at risk and substitute care of children. Consequently, the preponderance of program effort is involved with parenting. The ordinary conception of staffing has to do with professional social work staff, but as we have indicated, professional tasks constitute but a part, albeit a vital part, of the child welfare enterprise.

The matter of substitute versus biological parenting is a permanent and unresolved dilemma in child placement, a dilemma that has to be tolerated and mitigated where possible, but one that will never go away because of the basic structure of child placement itself. Love and caring aside, children who are brought up or cared for temporarily by parents or caretakers who are substitutes for their own parents always have the burdensome developmental task of coping with who they are. Questions about the child's identity are inevitable, no matter how improved the placement situation is over the original family situation. Furthermore, in the case of foster care and institutional or group care, placement is intended to be temporary, so that the foster parent's or caretaker's affections are inevitably tempered by the reality of the time-limited placement. These two factors, the identity of the child and the tentativeness of the caretaker's ties, have to be confronted, so that adaptation can take place. So the task of foster parents and caretakers is to love children and care for them—but within bounds. This demand in child placement is the central task to be dealt with, and coping with it takes more than "natural parenting;" it takes the conception of *staff* to provide for really competent foster parents and caretakers who can do the required job.

It is not possible to discuss staffing issues outside of a programmatic context. For example, to the extent that foster care is utilized as the modal child welfare service, the field is continually faced with the problem of supply and demand. Considering the flow of children into the foster care system, many agencies struggle to keep up the supply of foster parents by adjusting their criteria for selection.[5] With the limitations upon selection imposed by the demand for care, it is almost impossible to take hold of the situation of imbalanced supply and demand. Selective recruiting is the essential first step in the process of developing effective foster parent *staff.* When viewed as staff and not just as substitute parents, haphazardly chosen, the field can begin to consider criteria for performance as well as for selection. The ideal model would be an agency cadre of carefully selected and trained foster parents who were adequately compensated for the "professional" job of foster parenting. A permanent cadre like this would be more likely to tolerate the vicissitudes of foster parenting—the difficult growing child, the tensions injected by the child's own family, and the standards imposed by the agency itself. "Professional" foster parents, viewing themselves in a particular role, serving on call for successive children in placement, and gaining monetary rewards, would be more apt to experience less emotional heartbreak at the inevitable loss of the child in placement, and thus the parent-child relationship could be less ambivalent and more straightforward. This would be a *staff* view of foster parent, requiring that we confront the reality that neither the child nor the foster parent can long be fooled into believing that the foster home is the same as the biological home. It would also follow that where foster parents are more competent to do the job required, there would be decidedly less need for professional social work staff to intrude into the daily lives of the child and the foster parents. In this fashion can we begin to create child welfare jobs that are appropriate to the capacities, aptitudes, and training of the staff involved.

When it comes to caretakers such as those used in institutions and group homes, or homemakers and other kinds of home helpers, it is easier to consider these personnel as staff, with the selective recruitment, clear job definition, and training that is implicit in such a classification. Such caretakers are not generally viewed in the same way as are foster parents, probably because in extra-familial care it is not as possible to delude oneself that the child's substitute care is "like" ordinary family care. The sharp differences that characterize institutional and group care actually make for a much clearer differentiation of caretakers from parents, and staffing issues become self-evident. This is also true of homemakers, who are not viewed as parents either but are understood to have quite specific tasks for which staff can be recruited and trained.

In summary, the differential use of professional and nonprofessional staff in child welfare is largely dependent upon one's philosophy of child placement. The need for intrusion of professional and bureaucratic assessment and decision making into the ongoing lives of families and children in itself sets child placement apart from natural living. Once this fact is faced, the field can be less sentimental and self-deluding about the use of nonprofessional personnel as *staff*. The professionalizing of child welfare throughout the century has led to an objective and planned field of practice that is a far cry from the early "saving of children" and erasing of their identity in order to suit them to "new lives." In all child placement except adoption, child welfare seeks but an "interim life" for children, and the most thoughtful, planned, and professional staff to care for children while work is done to help biological families resume care. This view of staff, as opposed to that of well-meaning (substitute) parents, invites us to recruit, train, and allocate staff professionally and imaginatively in accordance with the program's needs and the unique skills and capacities of many kinds of personnel. As we have noted throughout this chapter, the key to effective practice is the differential and purposeful utilization of staff.

MODELS OF PROFESSIONAL STAFFING

Designing staff models is useful to deal with shortages of personnel and to adapt available personnel to the particular requirements of a child welfare program. Again, the choice of staff organization relies heavily upon the agency's view of the purposes of social work practice and of the child welfare tasks to be carried out. The single approach to a staffing design that is not a design at all but is probably the most prevalent model in use across the country is to use whatever personnel are available to do what is necessary. Thus, we find highly trained M.S.W. social workers carrying out jobs that are best done by caretakers and agency-trained college graduates performing the demanding assessment function. This approach has only expedience to justify it; it ultimately leads to inappropriate services and staff turnover, so that in the long run it would seem to be more expedient to think through a planned organization of staff in keeping with some model or other that can be rationalized.

The term *staff shortage* is too nonspecific to be of significant value. What *kind* of staff is lacking? Does using a higher or lower level of staff than is needed become a permanent or a substitute accommodation? Should the program itself be modified to accommodate to the staff levels available? Can work-study arrangements be made with neighboring schools of social work in order to develop a resource for trained staff? Can the programs involved be divided in some way, so that a greater range of personnel can be brought in to carry out partialized tasks? We are not suggesting that staff shortages do not occur; we are only raising questions whose answers could deal more analytically with the staffing problems that are ordinarily unique to each agency program.

The traditional staff model in child welfare, which still maintains an aura because of its great historical prestige, is the *rural child welfare worker.* Beyond its rural connotations, it has metaphorical overtones, much as does the urban settlement house worker. These people did social work jobs in the pre–World War II era, when life as far as bureaucratic organizations were concerned appeared to be simpler. Like the settlement house worker, the rural child welfare worker usually was not professionally educated, as indeed were few practicing social workers of that era. Their most significant characteristic was that they "did what had to be done." They were in one person what in the 1980s might be the differentially trained and utilized staff to which we have been referring in this chapter. Nostalgic recollection reminds us that they asked no quarter, they worked seven days a week from early morning to nightfall; they managed, treated, helped, cared for, placed, rehabilitated, and stood up for their clients; they were autonomous because they traveled so far from their home base; they were often publicly supported and sometimes were college graduates. Where is the agency director today who would not yearn for such a staff member? But, apart from the fact that their effectiveness might have been romanticized, life has become more complex today, and there is no more physical, psychological, organizational, or professional space left for these self-made, individualistic, one-person armies of social work. As a model for child welfare staffing, there is still rural countryside, but no more are child welfare agencies separated from federal and state legislative policy and demands for accountability. Child welfare has become so fragmented into programs, each with its specialized policies, that it is hard to imagine that the single child welfare worker could reemerge as a *model* for staffing, despite the fact that there are probably some still "out there," and that some agencies still seek the person who can do the same job as the pre–World War II rural child welfare worker. It is a model, of course, but the evidence suggests that its time is over.

At the other end of the spectrum of child welfare philosophy is the *social worker as therapist* model for staffing. Similar to cohorts in family service agencies and child guidance clinics, a psychotherapeutic role suggests a totally different kind of child welfare work. Since in this kind of design it would be assumed that the child's one-to-one ongoing, therapeutic relationship has to be with one therapeutically-oriented social worker, the obvious requirement would be that professional social workers be abundant in the agency. Purpose apart, one could not operate a child welfare program with psychotherapy as its primary purpose without a full complement of highly trained clinical staff. This is not to say that clinical M.S.W. staff in a developmentally oriented child welfare program would not undertake psychotherapeutic functions with children and families, but rather that the latter role would not serve as the *primary* model for child welfare work. Child and family development as purpose is different from psychotherapy as purpose, and the difference in use of professional staff is profound.

Most experimentation and research into models of staffing has been done with *social work teams*.[6] This model is designed to deal specifically with certain kinds of staff shortages and with the issue of differential utilization of personnel. The program's purposes should determine the composition of the team, but a typical child welfare team in a preventive service program might ideally be comprised of a graduate social worker, a B.S.W. social worker, a case aide, a housing specialist, and a home helper or family day-care worker. Of course, modifications of this model should be made to accommodate particular agency requirements. Numbers can change, proportions of professional to nonprofessional staff can shift, and roles can be made flexible or rigid, but the important principle guiding the use of teams governs—to provide for differential and more appropriate use of varied personnel. For example, because of expanded requirements for different types of external review procedures in various states, increasing numbers of agencies are employing lawyers as regular staff members, a relatively rare phenomenon only a few years ago. The challenge this development poses is to construct models of legal–social work collaboration and team functioning that do not fall into the attorney as expert/primary decision-maker trap.

Teams in work with families are both practical and efficient. The needs of families and children are so varied and multilayered that one might almost say that the team is the model for staff allocation in this area of child welfare practice. Teams of differential personnel not only are capable of carrying out the requisite differential tasks in family situations, but can also provide for selective, differential utilization of staff. Teams can allow professionals and nonprofessionals the opportunity to do what they are best qualified to do. This then means a saving of expensive staff time and effort and a practical use of less expensive staff.

(See case examples in Chapter 6 to illustrate potential use of teams in the provision of preventive/protective services.) Teams are therefore of significant use for service and staffing. They provide a structure for personnel to work together on separate tasks, purposefully, toward agreed-upon goals in a nonfragmented fashion.

Teams are useful in foster care, particularly during times of emergency because it can be arranged that all team members are not away at once. Teams are adaptive to a contextual or ecological view of cases, because they may be multidisciplinary and are always capable of multiple levels of task performance. Teams are less costly in the long run because they make it possible to use costly staff more sparingly and appropriately. Teams engender higher staff morale, because they can autonomously perform as a "clinical conference," determining within the team itself what is needed in a case and which team member is most suitable for the tasks involved.

The model of staffing employed depends upon the agency's program purposes. Both the traditional "rural child welfare" and "therapist" models of staffing suggest that child welfare practice can be carried out by using one social worker as the primary helper. These models then presume a narrow view of child welfare, when in fact child welfare in the 1980s has many aspects to it—not only child and family and caretaking family, but also a variety of programs each funded from different streams, and a new, ecological perspective in social work practice that directs attention to many spheres of life in a typical child welfare case. For this kind of practice, a team model has much to say for it.

An analogous model for child welfare as a *field* is a general hospital that employs a wide range of personnel, not all highly qualified doctors. In a metaphorical sense, the hospital staff operates as does a large and complex team, all of the members, professional and nonprofessional, addressing the complex needs of patients. The team notion, like the hospital construct, reflects the interdisciplinary and fluid boundaries of knowledge and skill that mark the professional practice of modern times.

TRAINING CHILD WELFARE STAFF

Recognizing that the work of child welfare agencies is ideally a planned, professional endeavor, there is only very limited room among personnel for indigenous, self-trained people. The major exceptions are self-help groups, community people, and those people who are engaged to "be themselves," such as big brothers and sisters, foster grandparents, and neighborhood helpers. Beyond these groups, whether the staff is professionally trained social workers or agency-trained foster parents, caretakers, or homemakers, agencies have responsibility to provide or account for the worker's training for the tasks being carried out.

In the case of D.S.W./Ph.D., M.S.W., and B.S.W. social workers who enter child welfare jobs with professional education, the agency should be able to rely upon at least a minimum standard of generalist training and increasingly upon specialized child welfare expertise. Yet, schools of social work cannot prepare graduates for the specific work and philosophy of each agency, and the agency itself has to provide for in-service orientation and information giving. Beyond this early phase of training, staff development has to be a career-long endeavor. For professional social work staff this might entail agency training programs conducted by professional leaders from within the agency or from the profession at large or related disciplines. Staff development also takes place when staff are encouraged to attend conferences outside the agency, when agency libraries are used, when seminars are held, and when staff is enabled to participate in many forms of continuing education. We shall discuss staff development further in the context of worker morale and burnout.

Where nonprofessional staff members are involved, such as foster parents and other caretakers, homemakers, aides, and so on, there can be no expectation of prior professional education, because these personnel are nonprofessional in their preparation. While recruitment of professional staff is a serious matter, the burden is mitigated by the fact that professional schools ordinarily screen out people with severe disturbances. This task of screening in and out nonprofessional staff rests with the employing agency. We have noted earlier that the child welfare job demands more than that the staff member be a nice person, or even a loving person. Staff training, usually by the agency itself, is a necessity in the case of nonprofessional staff. Although the content of staff development programs would be different for professional and nonprofessional staff, the commitment to ongoing, career-long staff development needs to be as firm with both levels of staff, if the agency recognizes the extent to which its philosophy and policies rely upon nonprofessional staff to be carried out.

Staff development programs differ considerably among agencies, depending upon the kinds of staff employed, the size of the staff complement, the bureaucratization of the work, the presence of labor unions or civil service requirements, the distance of the agency from local schools of social work and conference centers, the time, effort, and money provided by the agency, and the attitude of the agency toward a staff that is learned, independent, and effective. Although we view staff development as an essential part of agency administration,[7] it is impossible to offer a single model because of the presence of the multiple variables just mentioned. There is not a large literature on staff development from which principles can be highlighted.

In a large bureaucratic agency such as a public child welfare agency in an urban center, for example, it is likely that most of the staff carrying out professional tasks are not professionally trained at all. Typically, one might find a mix of M.S.W., B.S.W., and B.A. (nonprofessional) staff working side by side without differential job assignments. The staff development process is always more complicated when, as is often the case, experienced, nonprofessional staff supervise newly graduated M.S.W. or B.S.W. social workers. The more recent alternative model of hiring new M.S.W.'s to supervise very seasoned nonprofessional staff can be equally dysfunctional. What has to be kept in mind is that orientation to the agency and its programs and policies is always best done by experienced staff, and in the example just cited, if that staff is less prepared educationally than the staff to be trained, they are nevertheless best prepared to train for the agency's work. Certainly they are better qualified to do this than is a policy or practice professor in a neighboring school of social work. When it comes to general theory and innovative practices that are not indigenous to the agency, calling upon other professionals from schools or from settings where the innovations are going on is useful. Clarity about what is to be taught where, and what personnel inside or outside the agency are most appropriate to do the teaching, is the best governor of effective staff development.

In smaller voluntary agencies staff levels and specified tasks may not be as complex, but the principle of clarity holds nonetheless. In both kinds of agencies there are risks involved at any point where staff development is offered by a person outside of the agency structure, even if the teacher is from another discipline like psychiatry. The risks are that staff will get new ideas, perhaps to challenge their own agency's ideas. That is often the outcome of good staff development, and the administration of the agency has to be prepared to deal with such challenges. Usually, a systemic balance between new ideas and the way the agency does things can be affected by agency administrators involving themselves in a careful planning process with a potential staff teacher, but the best preparation takes place through the readiness of the agency to allow its staff to become expert—even more expert than the agency itself is about certain policies, practices, and program ideas. Staff development is not a process that can be relegated to a trainer of low rank in the agency; it has to be viewed as one of the most vital and sensitive administrative functions in any agency.

STAFF MORALE AND BURNOUT

It has been said that staff turnover is like burnout, except that turnover occurs in times of high employment and burnout in times of low employment. Both phenomena reflect staff dissatisfaction. The economic and professional loss to any agency that suffers staff turnover or burnout of staff is immeasurable and can only be counteracted by the administration and staff of the agency analyzing its organizational problems. The burgeoning literature on burnout—which may lead to staff turnover, work slowdown, and uncommitted practice—suggests that while there are multiple causes for burnout, among the most significant is the constraint that results from lack of autonomy in one's job. Autonomy in the work place is not unlike the experience of freedom in one's individual life. People become really engaged in their personal and work lives only when they see meaning and purpose in their actions. Rewards help, and concrete rewards at work include salary and fringe benefits, decent office space, clear job definitions, fair administrative treatment—and for professionals, the opportunity to practice one's profession with the freedom to exercise judgments and make decisions appropriate to one's capacity. Autonomy is the consequence of such a milieu, and autonomy is the motor that generates active, productive, responsible professional practice.

Now we can once again reconsider the notion of staff development as an aid to staff morale. Staff development is not just job training; it is an all-encompassing administrative/educative process that helps to keep the professional person curious, learning, and effective. It is a support for autonomy. It reinforces professional identity and it offers respect to the staff member. Burnout on a professional job takes place when the worker loses interest, feels unrewarded, and acts bored and sometimes depressed.

The concept of team models of staff organization also deserves reconsideration in the context of problems related to worker morale. A recent small study of 129 participants in a workshop on occupational tedium indicated that the variables of work relationships, work sharing, supervisory support, time out, and social feedback were all significantly associated with workers' experience of occupational tedium or the general sense of physical, emotional, and attitudinal exhaustion.[8] Certainly team models of organization, unlike many other staffing patterns, offer agencies a means to build in opportunities for workers to experience the work sharing, positive work relationships, support, feedback, and time out that can help to combat occupational tedium. The demands placed upon staff in child welfare are heavy indeed. Some workers find it overwhelming to separate children continually from their parents or to confront child abuse day after day. Yet, some workers react quite differently and seem to fail at other kinds of child welfare tasks. Suiting the task to the worker, rotating jobs, and building in special supports are some of the ways in which staff can be helped to go on year after year doing the demanding work of child welfare.

Throughout our discussion of staffing in this chapter, we have commented upon the relationship between program and staffing; the relationship between administrative attention to job demands and staff morale is no less compelling. Holding staff responsible for its work is appropriate, but holding staff responsible for failures that are generated within the agency or the larger social welfare sector is truly "blaming the victim." In the labor intensive field of child welfare, the key to excellent service is the child welfare staff itself.

NOTES

1. Willard C. Richan, "Personal Issues in Child Welfare," in *Child Welfare Strategy in the Coming Years* (Washington, D.C.: U.S. Department of Health, Education and Welfare, 1978), pp. 227–81; Ann W. Shyne and Anita G. Schroeder, *National Study of Social Services to Children and Their Families* (Washington, D.C.: U.S. Department of Health, Education and Welfare, 1978). Both of these publications note the lack of systematic methods for obtaining staff data, mostly due to lack of uniform delivery systems and definitions and utilization of staff in chiild welfare.

2. *Statistics on Social Work Education, 1978* (New York: Council on Social Work Education, 1979).

3. *The Annual Salary Study and Survey of Selected Personnel Issues* (New York: Child Welfare League of America), p. 22. Of the 177 CWLA member voluntary agencies reporting, 61 percent of the 3604 full-time practitioners had graduate social work degrees, Shyne and Schroeder, *National Study*, p. 25. Of a representative sample of 315 public social service departments in the U.S., 46 percent of practitioners had a college degree in a field other than social work, 16 percent had a bachelor's degree in social work, and 9 percent had a master's or doctorate in social work.

4. Willard C. Richan, "A Theoretical Scheme for Determining Roles of Professional and Non-professional Personnel," *Social Work* 6 (October 1961): 22–28.

5. Martin Wolins, *Selecting Foster Parents* (New York: Columbia University Press, 1962).

6. Donald Brieland, Thomas L. Briggs, and Paul Leuenberger, *The Team Model of Social Work Practice* (Syracuse, N.Y.: Syracuse University School of Social Work, Manpower Monograph No. 5, 1973).

7. Carol H. Meyer, *Staff Development in Public Welfare Agencies* (New York: Columbia University Press, 1965); *Child Welfare Grants Program and Regional Training Centers* (Washington, D.C.: Children's Bureau, 1981).

8. Alaya Pines and Kafry Ditso, "Occupational Tedium in the Social Services," *Social Work* 23 (November 1978): 499–506.

9. Some would argue that no child who does not require very specialized services should be placed in an institutional setting. (See Chapter 9 for further discussion.)

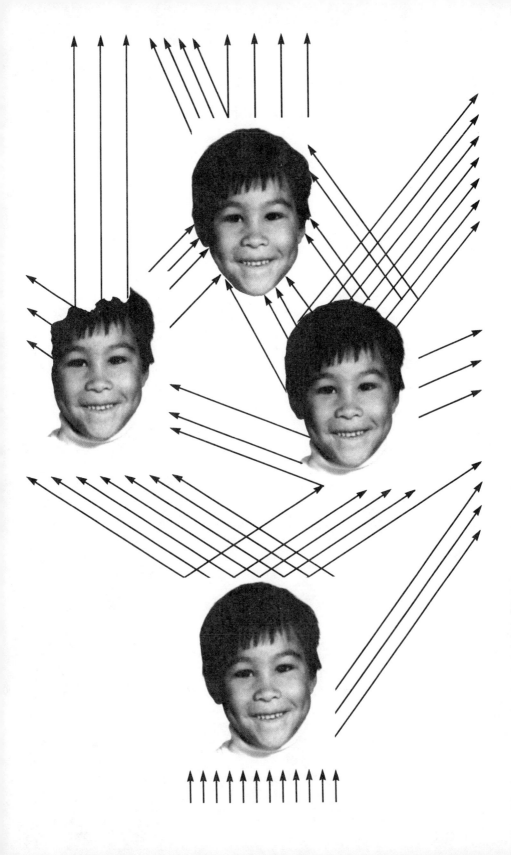

EPILOGUE

This book was translated from a casual conversation about the need for a new child welfare text to a published manuscript in a little over three years. Yet, during this relatively brief period we have all witnessed massive changes in the social context, structure, and objectives of service provision for families and children in this country. These changes have not only heightened the usual writers' anxiety about the need to update and revise just one more time, but have also caused us and our authors to undergo some real soul-searching about whether what we have to say is still valid. Yes, we are all "child welfare experts" in one way or another, but what does that term really mean when the very premises underlying the field of child welfare are under attack, when it is no longer possible to assume an even begrudging social consensus about what constitutes family well-being and the welfare of children, when public debate no longer focuses on how best to insure optimal developmental opportunities for all children, but rather on whether the state has any minimal obligations in this regard, and when professional child welfare expertise is commonly viewed as almost *a priori* grounds for suspicion and disdain rather than as a valued commodity?

Such shifts in public perceptions of social need and responsibility and of the role of the social work profession in enhancing family and child welfare are humbling indeed. Yet, as we review the chapters prepared for this volume, we find ourselves even more firmly convinced of three premises that have guided our earlier work in this field. First, there are now and probably will always be large numbers of troubled families and children who require external social supports and services in order to achieve a satisfactory level of functioning. Second, the concept of social entitlement undergirding the child welfare field's many efforts—no matter how limited or misdirected—to insure adequate developmental opportunities for all children remains as valid now as at any earlier time in our history. And third, because of the current pace of social and technological change, the need for professional knowledge, expertise, and leadership in the provision of child welfare service is increasing rather than decreasing.

Given these assumptions, we believe that the contributors to this book have brought together as much professional knowledge and practice wisdom as is currently available about how best to meet the needs of children at risk. And we hope that the policy recommendations, programming suggestions, and practice principles outlined here will be viewed not as quixotic ideas of people far removed from the realities of current practice or blind to the threats imposed by current efforts to undermine the concept of social entitlement, but as a challenge to maintain the goal of enhancing family and child welfare and to discover more innovative and effective means of achieving this end.

Before concluding, several caveats seem in order regarding the policy and service directions suggested in this volume.

■ Our focus on needed directions for change led inevitably to our highlighting the problems and failings of the child welfare system. Therefore, we must again underscore the fact repeated research has demonstrated: the vast majority of children are served well by this system. Moreover, children are incredibly resilient and tend to thrive both because of—and in spite of—the institutionalized services they may receive.

■ The service directions proposed by our authors are, we believe, as valid as current knowledge permits. However, there is a clear need for further research regarding the impact and unanticipated consequences of implementing these "new" solutions, especially in relation to the feasibility and desirability of achieving the goal of permanency planning for all children.

■ Recent change efforts in the child welfare field have tended to highlight legislative and administrative reform. But the quality of any type of human service is ultimately dependent on the knowledge, skills, and resources of the individual practioners providing the service. Therefore, although the implementation of external review procedures and other efforts to broaden the community support base for child welfare services should help to enhance the quality of service provision, we believe that the current trend toward de-professionalization can only lead to further problems within the child welfare system. Instead we would urge increased effort to upgrade the qualifications for social workers and to provide ongoing training for all levels of professional staff in child welfare agencies.

■ The preceding chapters naturally tend to emphasize solutions based on "scientific" research knowledge and applicable to the majority of families and children. However, decisions about the lives of specific families and children can never be totally systematized and rationalized. Effective individualized intervention always reflects in part the *art* of professional practice. Hence, there will be a continued need for professional wisdom, judgment, and creativity within the child welfare field.

■ The current emphasis on permanency planning will inevitably move the field toward decreased rather than increased intervention in the lives of families. This trend, of course, fits neatly with current efforts to reduce the costs of service provision. Moreover, child welfare agencies in the past have clearly tended to err in the direction of overintervention in family life. But underintervention, no matter how well intentioned the goal of preserving family unity, may pose a different, yet equally as serious a threat to child welfare as overintervention. Therefore, we hope that readers will continually seek to strike an appropriate balance between efforts to preserve parental rights and to meet children's needs.

■ The preceding chapters have emphasized the need to implement policies and programs designed to enhance permanency planning. But the individualized long-term care and commitment children need in order to reach their full developmental potential cannot be fully legislated, regulated, or planned; as Gaylin has documented so beautifully, such nurturance ultimately requires love, which must be given.[1] Therefore, although it is a professional responsibility to develop policies and programs and to provide direct services that are consonant with the best available knowledge about the service needs of children at risk, the child welfare field must guard against the danger of erecting closed administrative and professional boundaries. Planned efforts to enhance child welfare must always leave room for the idiosyncratic, freely given, critical contributions that may be made by relatives, friends, neighbors, or other concerned community residents.

■ As discussed in the Introduction, we believe it has been unrealistic to expect the child welfare field to expand its boundaries to the point where it could assume the responsibility of providing for the welfare of all children, and we would urge a renewed emphasis on its original function of providing service to children whose developmental needs cannot be fully met by their own families, even with the assistance of the community support services available to all families and children. In other words, we view child welfare as essentially a residual service system. But by the same token, improvements in child welfare services cannot be contemplated in isolation from changes in the larger social sector. The child welfare field can meet its service goals only when it functions as a subsector of a larger personal social service system that is closely linked to adequate income maintenance, health, education, and housing programs. Current efforts to dismantle social guarantees for all families and children could well result in an increased number of children requiring child welfare services, thereby reversing the recent trend toward reducing the size of the pool entering care. Therefore, it is now more important than ever for child welfare workers to advocate strenuously for adequate income maintenance programs, universal family support services, and expanded community resources for families and children with special needs.

In conclusion, we would like to note that the policy and programming directions suggested here reflect our understanding of the sources of the many strengths and deficiencies in the child welfare system, and we believe that they represent the best currently available knowledge about how to meet the developmental needs of children at risk. We recognize that many of the proposals for specific solutions to current dilemmas can and should be modified over time as knowledge advances and social needs and conditions change. But we hope that the ultimate mission of the child welfare system and the goal implicit in all of the specific recommendations presented in the preceding chapters—to insure that all children at risk receive adequate care and nurturance and the opportunity to achieve their full developmental potention—will never be compromised. We trust our readers will agree.

NOTE

1. Willard Gaylin, et al., *Doing Good: Limits of Benevolence* (New York: Pantheon Books, 1978).

NAME INDEX

SUBJECT INDEX

BOOK MANUFACTURE
CHILD WELFARE: CURRENT DILEMMAS-FUTURE DIRECTIONS
was typeset at Auto-Graphics, Inc., Monterey Park, California.
Printing and binding was at Edwards Brothers, Ann Arbor, Michigan.
Cover design was by Jane Rae Brown, Chicago. Internal design was
by F. E. Peacock Publishers art department. The typeface is Optima.